Central
Asia

Central Asia Book Series

Central Asia

130 Years of Russian Dominance, A Historical Overview

Third Edition

Edited by
Edward Allworth

Duke University Press
Durham and London   1994

Third printing, 2002
© 1994 Duke University Press
All rights reserved
Printed in the United States of America
on acid-free paper ∞
Central Asia: 130 Years of Russian Dominance, A Historical Overview was first
published as *Central Asia: A Century of Russian Rule* by Columbia University
Press in 1967. An updated edition, *Central Asia: 120 Years of Russian Rule* was
published by Duke University Press in 1989.

Library of Congress Cataloging-in-Publication Data
Central Asia, 130 years of Russian dominance : a historical overview / edited by
  Edward Allworth. — 3rd ed.
    p. cm. — (Central Asian book series)
    Rev. ed. of: Central Asia, 120 years of Russian rule. New ed. 1989.
    Includes bibliographical references and index.
    ISBN 0-8223-1554-8 (cloth). — ISBN 0-8223-1521-1 (pbk.)
    1. Asia, Central.   I. Allworth, Edward.   II. Central Asia, 120 years of
  Russian rule.   III. Title: Central Asia.   IV. Series.
  DK851.C46 1994
  958—dc20   94-18395 CIP

Contents

Central Asia Book Series   vii

FIGURES   xi

TABLES   xv

PREFACE   xvii

PART I   CONFRONTATION BETWEEN TWO CIVILIZATIONS

1   Encounter   1
    Edward Allworth

2   People, Languages, and Migrations   60
    Karl H. Menges

3   The Population and the Land   92
    Ian Murray Matley

*PART II   FROM THE RUSSIAN CAPTURE OF TASHKENT
TO FULL SOVIETIZATION, 1865–1966*

4   Systematic Conquest, 1865 to 1884   131
    Hélène Carrère d'Encausse

5   Organizing and Colonizing the Conquered Territories   151
    Hélène Carrère d'Encausse

6   The Stirring of National Feeling   172
    Hélène Carrère d'Encausse

7   Social and Political Reform   189
    Hélène Carrère d'Encausse

8   The Fall of the Czarist Empire   207
    Hélène Carrère d'Encausse

9   Civil War and New Governments   224
     Hélène Carrère d'Encausse

10   The National Republics Lose Their Independence   254
     Hélène Carrère d'Encausse

11   Agricultural Development (1865–1963)   266
     Ian Murray Matley

12   Industrialization (1865–1964)   309
     Ian Murray Matley

13   The Changing Intellectual and Literary Community   349
     Edward Allworth

14   The Focus of Literature   397
     Edward Allworth

15   Musical Tradition and Innovation   434
     Johanna Spector

16   Modernizing Architecture, Art, and Town Plans   485
     Arthur Sprague

     PART III   *FOLLOWERS AND LEADERS, 1967–1993*

17   The New Central Asians   527
     Edward Allworth

18   The Hunger for Modern Leadership   573
     Edward Allworth

     BIBLIOGRAPHY   609
     GLOSSARY   619
     INDEX   625
     CONTRIBUTORS   649
     ACKNOWLEDGMENTS   651

Central Asia Book Series

By the last two decades of the nineteenth century, the road to the growth of outside knowledge about Central Asia abruptly branched out in several directions. And, within a decade came the insistent modern rise in self-knowledge among Central Asian reformists. It began notably from around the outbreak of World War I and grew until the partition by the Soviet Government of the Central Asian region into monoethnic administrative units in the mid-1920s.

These developments remind everyone that knowledge about areas of the world advances unevenly, often sporadically. That seems equally true for the internal awareness reached by inhabitants of a region such as Central Asia. As this new edition of *Central Asia* comes out, readers and observers again have started paying great attention to the region. These stages in the expansion of information and inquiry long ago ended the possibility that any single individual or volume could systematically master, even with the instrument of the computer, all learning about the region.

For the study of Central Asia, a few extraordinary orientalists, such as the Russian Professors Vasiliy V. Bartol'd (1869–1930) and Vasiliy V. Radlov (1889–1914), stand as the last exemplars of the virtually all-knowing savant. But even as they lived, research into Central Asian arts, culture, economy, geography, history, languages, and other fields far exceeded the control of any one person. That inexorable evolution toward scholarly specialization enforced a salutary division of labor in the field that has ramified further during succeeding decades.

Central Asia: 130 Years of Russian Dominance offers a concrete example of that necessary diversification. The dispersion of the six scholars who wrote this book—then in East Lansing, New York, Paris, Vienna, and Waynesburg, Pennsylvania—mirrors both the expansion that already broadened the field and the widespread attention given to the subject. Short of a multi-volume encyclopedic undertaking, probably no single work can provide a comprehensive treatment of Central Asia. This one offers readers a starting point and overview.

The new subtitle for this volume reflects the reality that pertains even after the formal dissolution of the Union of Soviet Socialist Republics. Political "Rule" of Central Asia's people and territory by Russia formally ceased in 1991. Most scholars recognize that the thirteen decades of extremely strong Russian impact still shape nearly everything modern in Central Asia, whether form or substance. That situation promises to persist far into the future. Consequently, the editor believes that the word "dominance" in the subtitle does not exaggerate the extent of Russian influence prevailing so far in Central Asian life, thinking, or development. Questions about how and with what effect that Russian dominance continues to function in the region late in the twentieth century receive tentative answers in Chapters 17 and 18 of this new edition of *Central Asia: 130 Years of Russian Dominance.*

A positive result of the need to share in preparing a volume such as this reveals itself in the great wealth of languages and materials brought together in research. The authors of the previous edition, as of this one, all employ primary sources and several of them use Central Asian language in addition to Russian in this work. That fact, added to their abundant experience and lists of publications, provides respectable authority in this presentation.

Medieval and early modern poets have beautifully reflected the emotion of parting from family members, lovers, and friends, the most painful feeling known to Central Asian readers and listeners. So it happens that the contributors to this volume deeply regret their separation from two of the book's original authors: Arthur R. Sprague, who lost his life early in a promising career, and Ian Murray Matley, who recently passed away before he could complete all his mature research.

The Central Asia Book Series emphasizes the publishing of inquiries into the modern life of Central Asians based on research that employs indigenous language sources to a substantial degree. The Series intends to issue learned studies, documents, eyewitness accounts, and reference materials that will make a lasting addition to knowledge about the region.

Edward A. Allworth, General Editor of the Series
Columbia University

Andras J. E. Bodrogligeti, Advisory Editor
University of California, Los Angeles

Richard N. Frye, Advisory Editor
Harvard University

Figures

1.1	Central Asian frontiers, 1801, 1864	12
1.2	Tribal chieftain Iset Kutebar-uli	17
1.3	Tashkent, 1865	46
2.1	Ethnic and linguistic distribution	61
2.2	Uzbek dialects, 1929	71
2.3	The Latinized Turkic alphabet	80
3.1	Urban and rural population in 1910	99
3.2	Urban and rural population in 1959	100
3.3	The landforms	114
4.1	Bukharan Emir Muzaffar al-Din	134
4.2	Khivan Khan Sayyid Muhammad Rahim Bahadur	135
4.3	Khokand's ruler Khudayar Khan	136
4.4	Khudayar Khan's palace at Khokand	144
5.1	Old Tashkent, c. 1890	158
6.1	Jadid leader Aqmet Baytursin-uli	176
7.1	Jadid leader Munawwar Qari	190
7.2	First issue of *Ay qap*	202
7.3	First issue of *Ayina*	203
8.1	Tashkent, c. 1913	209
9.1	Political subdivisions, c. 1922	240
10.1	Boundaries as established in 1936	258
10.2	National Communist Turar Riskul-uulu	261
10.3	National Communist Faizullah Khoja-oghli	262
11.1	Irrigation, mining, and industry, 1910	268
11.2	Irrigation, mining, and industry, 1962	269
11.3	Flocks along the banks of the Sir Darya	286
11.4	Canal irrigating orchards of an oasis	287
12.1	Traditional methods of silk weaving	311
12.2	Modern silk weaving in a Samarkand factory	313

12.3	Land and water transportation, 1910	325
12.4	Land and water transportation, 1962	326
12.5	The Merv railroad station, c.1900	346
12.6	Dushanbe's modern airport	347
13.1	Dormitory at Barak Khan, Central Asia's only active madrasah	352
13.2	Tashkent's worshipers, 1964	352
13.3	Sketches (1922) by Central Asians contrast the new schooling with the old	353
13.4	Mir Jaqib Duwlat-uli and Ahmed Vali Ibrahim-oghli (Menger)	364
13.5	Izzat Sultanov, Abdullah Qahhar, and Wahid Zahidov	391
14.1	Cover design of *Layli and Majnun*	422
14.2	Kirgiz novelist Chingiz Aytmatov	423
15.1	Display of musical instruments: strings	441
15.2	Display of musical instruments: winds and percussion	442
15.3a	Musical instruments: nay, surnay, dutar, tanbur, ghij-jak, and setar	452
15.3b	Musical instruments: rabab and chang	453
15.4	Buzruk and rast maqamat transcribed into Western notation	468
15.5	Khwarazm notation for the tanbur	471
16.1	The Islam Khoja minaret	489
16.2	Entrance to a twentieth-century madrasah building	492
16.3	Room in a Bukharan palace	495
16.4	*Äywan* (veranda) of a Khivan home	496
16.5	Carved wooden column from Khiva	498
16.6	Decorated ceiling of a mosque	499
16.7	Decorative wall hanging, Tashkent	500
16.8	Detail from decorative wall hanging, Chimkent	501
16.9	*Äywan* of a mansion in Tashkent	502
16.10	Sketch for the Tashkent duma building	503
16.11	Interior wall decoration in a mosque	505
16.12	Alma Ata telegraph office building	509
16.13	Perspective of a plan for Przheval'sk	510
16.14	Plan for a Kirgiz museum	512
16.15	Ali Shir Nawaiy State Opera and Ballet Theater	514
16.16	Floor plan of the Ali Shir Nawaiy Theater	514

16.17   Bukhara Hall in the Ali Shir Nawaiy Theater   517
16.18   Room in a kolkhoz "rest home"   518
16.19   Apartment house in Krasnovodsk   519
16.20   Tomb of Jambil Jabay-uli   520
16.21   Tashkent, 1958   522
16.22   Painting, "Portrait of an Uzbek"   523
16.23   Ornamental plate with head of Stalin   524
17.1   Mahmudov's *The Immortal Cliffs*   533
17.2   Prominent Central Asian politicians   549
17.3   Teachers and girls in Central Asian kindergarten   569
17.4   Schoolchildren waiting for bus in Alma Ata   570
18.1   Dr. Abdurahim Pulatov, Chair, Uzbekistan's Birlik
        Popular Movement   579
18.2   Muhammad Solih, Chair, Uzbekistan's "Erk" Demo-
        cratic Party   581
18.3a   Independent Press in Uzbekistan, 1989–93   582
18.3b   Independent Press in Kazakhstan, 1990–93   583
18.4   Khasen Kärimzhanulï Qozha-Akhmet (Kozhakhmetov),
        Leader of Kazakhstan's Zheltoqsan Committee   585
18.5   Five Central Asian presidents   596
18.6   Qozi Akbar Turajonzoda Hajji, Tajikistan's Main Spiri-
        tual Leader   606

Tables

1.1	Russia's Trade with Central Asia in Rubles, 1840–1867	28
3.1	Population of Central Asian Republics within Boundaries of September 17, 1939	96
3.2	Percent of Urban Population to Total Population, 1926–1959	97
3.3	Population of Key Cities in Southern Central Asia	98
3.4	Nationalities of Central Asia	104
3.5a	Central Asians Residing Throughout the Soviet Union	106
3.5b	Aliens Residing in Central Asia	106
3.6	Cities of Kazakhstan	107
11.1	Irrigated Areas of Southern Central Asia	272
11.2	Number of Livestock in Kazakhstan, 1916–1929	302
11.3	Number of Livestock in Kazakhstan, 1934–1962	302
11.4	Grain Production in Kazakhstan, 1953–1963	306
12.1	Raw Materials, Fuel, and Ferrous Metals in Kazakhstan, 1940–1963	344
13.1	Population and Literacy, 1915	369
13.2	Literacy in Central Asia in the Soviet Period	376
13.3a	Distribution of the "Intelligentsia" by Profession, Institutionally (State) Employed, 1926	378
13.3b	Distribution of the "Intelligentsia" by Profession, Non-institutionally (Privately) Employed, 1926	379
13.4	Distribution of the "Intelligentsia" by Profession, 1959	394
15.1	Musical Structure and Range	445
15.2	Musical Form, Rhythm, and Meter	446
15.3	Musical Instruments	450
15.4	Microtonal Scales of Central Asian Musical Instruments	458
15.5	Intervals of Central Asian Musical Instruments Compared to Intervals of the Azerbaijan Tar and the Pythagoran Chromatic Scale	460

15.6	Microtones of Central Asian Musical Instruments Compared to Microtones of the Ancient Arabic Lute and Western Equal Temperament	461
15.7	Modes	466
15.8	Music Examples	474
17.1	Publishing in Central Asian Sublanguages, 1958–1986	545
18.1	Central Asian Nationalities in Central Asia, 1989	588
18.2	Traits of an Effective Leader	598
18.3	Distribution of Slavs, Germans, and Kazakhs in Kazakhstan in 1989	600

Preface

The sudden breakup of the Union of Soviet Socialist Republics in 1991 has stimulated fresh thinking about newly liberated Central Asia. Yet, the brevity of this period of unearned independence among the former Union republics does not yet offer enough depth or perspective to provide balance for the longer view. Chapter 18, "The Hunger for Modern Leadership" treats certain dilemmas faced by the five newborn Central Asian states and helps give an understanding of the tremendous problems facing those societies at present. That new, final chapter, written especially for this latest edition, considers the crucial problems stemming from a deprivation of sovereign indigenous leadership over the past 130 years (calculated from the attacks and final Russian conquest of Tashkent, 1864–65, though Czarist troops earlier had invaded much of northern Kazakhstan).

The chapter focuses mainly upon the eventful period, 1989–93, since the appearance of the previous edition of the book. But only some grasp of the previous history can prepare readers for interpreting the astonishing developments of the most recent years.

Central Asia holds special meaning for informed persons everywhere, owing to its extraordinary human and cultural qualities. For centuries before the present one, Central Asia stood out as a leading civilization, an Islamic heartland, a nexus for trade routes. Its centrality defines the great importance that this region also possesses for international affairs connecting West and East, situated as it is between Russia, the People's Republic of China (PRC), countries of the Middle East, and of Southern Asia. Yet it remains politically divided into three major segments—Eastern (Chinese) Turkistan, the region of the former Russian Turkistan, including Kazakhstan, and Afghanistan.

The present inquiry into the situation in Western Turkistan—the sector with the largest Central Asian population—after 130 years of Russian dominance responds to these three significant questions, among others:

1. To what extent and how lastingly have the presence and influence of outsiders most modified Central Asian life?
2. As a result, how much have Central Asians relinquished or altered their
   sense of regional identity?
3. Why does it matter whether Central Asia keeps or loses its special character?

To find the basis for answers, the authors of this book analyze changes
in several Central Asian arts and in culture, demography, economics,
history, language, politics, and related fields. They endeavor to distinguish between normal growth and compulsory change. They also wish
to convey a sense of the region's underlying community, notwithstanding the great heterogeneity of human resources and the divisive policies
that affected it so long.

This approach stresses similarities still apparent throughout Central
Asia, rather than differences between subregions. The book intentionally focuses upon the accomplishments of the region's people as much
as possible. Less attention goes to the manipulation of affairs in Western Turkistan by Russian or Soviet administrators. The authors make a
conscious effort to present the outlook and actual voice of the Central
Asians in this coordinated examination of life in the area. While presenting these arguments, the volume means to serve well as a substantial
source of useful information about the territory and its population.

For an understanding of what led up to the twentieth-century configuration of Central Asia, this book provides a broad background. Central Asian affairs insistently find their way more than ever onto the pages
of the world's press. Travel into Western and Eastern Turkistan (Central
Asia) has become common. The end in 1989–90 of Russia's invasion and
decade-long war in Afghanistan not only coincided with the dramatic
events unfolding in Russian Central Asia, but also that war had a strong
and destabilizing impact upon the neighboring territories, especially
Tajikistan.

In response to the new interest in Central Asian cultural and political
affairs, colleges and universities in Europe, North America, and some
parts of the Middle East have added programs, institutes, and courses
devoted to the study of Central Asia. That has created a hearty appetite
for textbooks and other instructional materials that shape curriculum,
especially at the advanced secondary school, the undergraduate, and
the initial graduate levels of education. Copies of the first two editions
of this book, now out of print, rarely show up in bookstores.

This new, augmented edition, *Central Asia: 130 Years of Russian Dominance*, preserves the previous 17 chapters intact. They offer careful analysis and abundant background data. They give basic coverage and the breadth needed for independent study or for classroom discussion in general and comparative courses of instruction devoted to the study of Central Asia and related areas. Besides writing a new final chapter, the editor has also revised the preface and notes about contributors, and has enlarged and brought up to date the bibliography of English-language sources and readings at the end of the book.

The encouragement and good ideas of Valerie Millholland at Duke University Press, deserve great credit for bringing this publishing effort to fruition. For their special courtesy in offering advice and sources important for this work, I want to thank in particular Robert Austerlitz, Arthur Bonner, Cassandra Cavanaugh, Hilda Eitzen, Leslie Kaufman, Robert A. Lewis, Martha Merrill, Munevver Olgun, Eleonora Omerova, Peter Sinnott, Shahrbanou Tadjbakhsh, Maliheh Tyrrell, Elizabeth Valkenier, and Ibrahim Yüksel. Recently, numbers of intellectuals and professionals of Karakalpakistan, Kazakhstan, Kirgizstan, Tajikistan, Turkmenistan, and Uzbekistan both in Central Asia and during visits to New York have contributed insights and information beneficial to this research. I wish to express my gratitude to them and to other colleagues.

In addition, I owe more than general acknowledgment to the most excellent librarians serving or helping out in the Reference Divisions of Columbia University, notably, Walter Barnard, Elizabeth Brennan, Michael Stoller, Robert Scott, and Sarah H. Spurgin; to those in the Slavic Division of the New York Public Library, Robert Davis and Chief of the Division, Edward Kasinec; as well as to colleagues in the Near East Section, Library of Congress, Ibrahim Pourhadi, Christopher Murphy, and Chief of the Section, George Atiyeh.

My project with Richard Bulliet, Barnett Rubin, and four estimable graduate students of Columbia University, has aided some of this research into Central Asian leadership. Staff members at The U.S. Institute of Peace deserve commendation for that support.

And, most of all, thanks to my wife, Janet Lovett Allworth, for much sound counsel and encouragement in this effort.

E. A.

1 Encounter

When Russian troops stormed Muslim Tashkent near daybreak June 15, 1865, chaplain Andrei Y. Malov of the Fourth Orenburg Line Battalion was first through the battered Kämalan gate. The Russian Orthodox priest, who won a military cross from army authorities for valor, headed a leading assault column with Russian battle cries of "*ura!*" and, holding his ecclesiastical cross high before him,[1] urged on the attack as though in the name of Christianity. The fall of Islamic Tashkent, the first large town in Central Asia[2] seized by czarist soldiers, marked a new, domestic period in affairs between Central Asia and Russia. Simultaneously, the capture signaled an imminent end to the latest stage in their independent religious, economic, military, cultural, and diplomatic relations, some of which had begun a thousand years before.

This confrontation at the gates of Tashkent was by no means the first spiritual encounter involving Central Asia and Russia, for religion had apparently brought about formal relations linking the two as early as A.D. 986. Kievan princes then reputedly sought instruction concerning Islam from Khwarazm,[3] whose shah pre-

---

[1] *Turkestanskii krai: Sbornik materialov dlia istorii ego zavoevaniia* (Tashkent, Izdanie Shtaba Turkestanskago Voennago Okruga, 1914), vol. XIX, part 1, p. 210; Mikhail A. Terent'ev, *Istoriia zavoevaniia Srednei Azii* (St. Petersburg, Tipo-Litografiia V. V. Komarova, 1906), I, 315.

[2] "Central Asia" applies to territory approximately coextensive with the old "Western Turkistan" or the area currently designated by the Russians as "Soviet Central Asia and Kazakhstan."

[3] Sharaf al-Zaman Tahir al-Marvazi, *Sharaf al-Zaman Tahir al-Marvazi on China, the Turks, and India* . . . trans. by V. Minorsky (London, Royal Asiatic Society, 1942), pp. 36, 118–20; cited by S. P. Tolstov, *Drevnii Khorezm* (Moscow, Izdanie Moskovskogo Gosudarstvennogo Universiteta, 1948), p. 15; S. Radzhabov, *Rol' velikogo russkogo naroda v istoricheskikh sud'bakh narodov Srednei Azii* (Tashkent, Gosizdat Uzbekskoi SSR, 1955), p. 21.

maturely expressed his gladness "about their [the Russians'] desire to accept Islam, and welcomed them with rich gifts and sent one of his imams to teach them Islam's rules." These Russians, said Islamic historians with unwitting irony, became Muslims because of "a desire to receive the right to conduct war for the faith." [4] But Vladimir of Kiev, according to an old Slavic version of the story, in A.D. 986 rejected the teachings of Muslim missionaries, saying, as a Russian leader might today, that "undergoing circumcision and neither eating pork nor drinking wine were disagreeable to him." [5] If, as both Islamic and Russian Orthodox traditions agree, the Central Asians had that chance to spread Islam, they failed to convert the Russians at this critical juncture and thus lost a great opportunity to employ religion for tying this largest Slavic group to the East rather than the West.

Although the question of faith nearly always colored relations between Russian Christians and Central Asian Muslims, at least until the fall of Tashkent religion never became a primary issue between the regions, never sent crusades on the offensive solely to convert populations inhabiting one of those competing areas. This was probably because, in the time after Russia had accepted Christianity, the Central Asians dominated Russian territory only as accessories to Mongol rule in the third quarter of the thirteenth century, and the Mongols at that time did not favor Islam in Russia.[6] Soon after the Golden Horde's collapse in the fifteenth century allowed the czars to push forward their frontiers in the direction of Siberia, Russia ran headlong into a recently formed khanate allied to Bukhara. Although Christian-Muslim antipathy had not brought them there, this deliberate engagement became for both sides a

[4] Muhammad al-Aufi, "Jami al-hikayat wa lami' al-riwayat," A.D. 1236, trans. by V. V. Bartol'd, *Sochineniia* (Moscow, Izdatel'stvo "Nauka," 1963), vol. II, part 1, p. 807.

[5] *Polnoe sobranie russkikh letopisei, "Lavrent'evskaia letopis'"* (2d ed.; Leningrad, Izdavaemoe Postoiannoiu Istoriko-Arkheograficheskoi Komissieiu AN SSSR, 1926), I, 85.

[6] George Vernadsky, *The Mongols and Russia* (New Haven, Yale University Press, 1953), pp. 165–66; N. I. Veselovskii, "Neskol'ko poiasnenii kasatel'no iarlykov, dannykh khanami Zolotoi Ordy russkomu dukhovenstvu," *Zapiski Imperatorskago Russkago Geograficheskago Obshchestva po Otdieleniiu Etnografii*, XXXIV (1909), 531–32.

religious contest as well as the first real test of political strength
matching a Central Asian khanate against Moscow.

Abdullah Khan (r.1557–1598) of Bukhara in 1572 had sent a
religious mission to bolster Islam in Siberia, and in 1598 in a message to his protégé, Kuchum Khan (r.1563–1598) of Siberia, re-
emphasized the religious importance of Siberia's defense against
the Russians:

The enemies of our faith at the present time are the kafirs [Russians]
. . . you must conclude peace [with local Asian chieftains] and think
about taking your lands out of the kafirs' hands again. If you carry on
the present practices without coming to an understanding . . . you
will remain powerless before the kafirs.[7]

Kuchum and Abdullah died not long after this message was composed, and Russia went on to absorb Siberia, but though this clash
strained diplomatic ties between Bukhara and Moscow, it raised
no permanent religious barriers to their later intercourse.

Aside from this isolated collision of "believers" and "unbelievers,"
as members of both religious groups saw each other, religion became an important matter of state for Central Asian–Russian affairs
early in connection with pilgrimage and marriage, two kinds of
special situations which repeated themselves sporadically between
the time Astrakhan lost its independence to Russia in the sixteenth
century and the Russian occupation of Central Asia three hundred
years later. The most direct pilgrimage routes from Central Asia
to Mecca lay directly across Persia, but were blocked by the hostile
Shiite Muslims, and now the Central Asian Sunnites' chief alternate
road through Astrakhan Tatar territory to Mecca was also cut off.
Consequently, the Central Asians had to sue for permission to cross
land held by Russia to go the long way via the Black Sea to Istanbul
and thence to Mecca. Diplomatic correspondence to Russia from
Bukhara and Khiva, particularly in the seventeenth and eighteenth
centuries, often pleaded for unobstructed passage of Muslims to
their Holy City or between their countries, permission which the
Russians were usually reluctant to grant. Until Catherine II's ukase

[7] H. Ziyayev, *Ortä Asiya wä Sibir'* (*XVI–XIX äsrlär*) (Tashkent, Ozbekistan
SSR Fänlär Äkädemiyäsi Näshriyati, 1962), p. 41.

of May 9, 1780, the czarist attitude regarding communication between Muslim countries remained negative: "One of the rules of
policy had been . . . to block communication both to Muslims
living in the bounds of the present empire with co-religionists, as
well as equally to Muslims not subject [to Russia] inhabiting
Greater Tatary, via this territory, with the Crimea, the Kuban, and
the Ottoman Porte." [8]

Further evidence for this Russian change of heart regarding religion came later in the decade. The Empress set in motion a program
to convert the Kazakhs to Islam by employing Tatars from Kazan
as missionaries to the plains. Their activity was meant to reduce the
influence of Bukharan mullahs in that area. Regardless of persistant
Kazakh resistance to the idea, such Tatar proselyting continued
fairly successfully with support from Russian officialdom.

Despite a seeming turn in Russian foreign policy at that time,
provoked by the request submitted in 1780 from the Bukharan
ruler Abul Ghazi (r.1758–1785) through his envoy to St. Petersburg, Mullah Ir Nazar Bek Maqsud-oghli, no certain answer to requests for free passage across Russia by Central Asian religious
pilgrims subsequently came from the Russian government. It persisted in dealing cautiously with each separate appeal. Russian
foreign minister Count Karl V. Nessel'rod as late as 1842 could only
temporize in answering Shir Ali (r.1842–1845), the khan of Khokand, regarding the same matter:

I feel it necessary to declare to you that the passage of pilgrims can
relate not alone to subjects of Khokand but also to inhabitants of the
other Central Asian domains. Therefore, it is deemed necessary, pre-
liminarily, to make a general consideration of this subject and when
means are found for satisfying this petition, without breaking police
regulations existing in Russia, the Khokand government will be informed. . . . However, out of regard for your personal request in the
past year permission was given to Muhammad Sharif Khoja Qasim Khoja-
oghli to proceed to Mecca via Russia.[9]

[8] P. P. Shubinskii, "Bukharskiia posol'stva pri dvorie Ekateriny II," *Istoricheskii viestnik*, LXVIII (1897), 532.
[9] Graf Nessel'rod, "Vitse-kantsler poslanniku vladietelia kokanskago; 25
fevralia 1842 g. No. 512," *Sbornik materialov dlia istorii zavoevaniia turkestanskago kraia* (Tashkent, Tipografiia Shtaba Turkestanskago Voennago Okruga,
1914), IV, 12.

The other religious problem often raised in diplomatic exchanges, intermarriage between Central Asian and Russian subjects, developed out of long sojourns by Central Asian merchants who commonly married Tatar or Bashkir women while in Russia. Obduracy on the part of czarist authorities, who were unwilling to allow the Central Asians to take such Muslim wives and their children back to Khiva or Bukhara, stimulated formal petitions to permit these families to emigrate. Often they were turned down, less on religious grounds, it seemed, than upon the morbid fear then, as now, of allowing a human soul to escape from Russian state control.

In some respects, comparable to this situation stood the permanent problem of Russians, many of whom lived their entire adult lives as slaves in Bukhara or Khiva, who not uncommonly converted to Islam and married local girls. Apostasy, a capital crime under Islam, had also been particularly repugnant to the Russian Orthodox, to whom turning Muslim seemed worse than reverting to paganism. Especially distressing to Russian churchmen strong in government councils was this loss, in the relations with Central Asia, of any Russian who became Muslim (*obusurmanilsia*) to the extent of identifying his interests permanently with the Islamic community. Such persons made Russian efforts to liberate their countrymen from captivity very hazardous. The fact that Russian apostates at times served as double agents against Russian diplomats who attempted to recruit them for intelligence work while in Bukhara or Khiva was confirmed by Peter the Great's ambassador, Florio Beneveni. He reported that a Russian-turned-Muslim who knew of the envoy's activities at Bukhara once revealed the identity of Beneveni's undercover courier to Khivan authorities.[10]

After 1800, probably no other cause involving Central Asia stirred popular resentment in Russia more than the imagined plight of these Christians under "heathen" oppression and the feeling that it was a sacred duty to free them. Although religious reasons for such a crusade were frequently spoken of, very likely national pride as much as piety motivated officials in focusing attention upon the

---

[10] A. N. Popov, "Snosheniia Rossii s Khivoiu i Bukharoiu pri Petrie Velikom," *Zapiski Imperatorskago Russkago Geograficheskago Obshchestva*, IX (1853), 297.

Russian captives in Khiva. The religious fanaticism which Russia, rightly or wrongly, always feared it would arouse in Bukhara, the old Muslim religious center of Central Asia, erupted only momentarily there during the czarist conquest, but even before, sectarian zeal exploded in its most dangerous form in the Khokand khanate southeast of Khiva and Bukhara.

Khokand's ruthless Alim Khan (r.1800–1809), after subjugating most of the lands adjacent to his domain and coming to terms with his remaining Asian neighbors, deduced who his real enemy was. At the end of his career, recognizing the czarist threat to Khokand's ascendance as well as to Islamic Central Asia's separate existence, Alim Khan declared:

No enmity toward us persists in these regions except that of *urus-i bidin* [the Russian infidel]. Now it behooves us to conduct campaigns in defense or furtherance of Islam (*ghāzat*) as well as *jihad* against that worthless herd and gird our loins in hostility toward them.[11]

Following this injunction his successors strengthened Khokand's frontiers to the north while Russian and Khokandian armies rapidly approached one another. The religious warfare proclaimed by Alim Khan was delayed about two decades, however, until the adversaries found common borders and developed their mutual antipathy further.

One step in this direction resulted from a diplomatic rebuff foolishly administered by the Russian foreign ministry to Khokand's ambassador Khoja Mirqurban at Petropavlovsk in 1831. A direct consequence of czarist refusal to admit the ambassador to inner Russia was the strong agitation created by the Tashkent Qushbegi's revival of the call to Kazakhs of the Middle Horde (*Orta Jüz*) and to Khokand generally to conduct a war for the Faith against Russian "infidels."[12] Holy War had also been incited in Central Asia by Muslim Turkey in connection with that country's conflict with Russia in 1828,[13] and in the tension of the early 1860s, especially

[11] Mullah Niyaz Muhammad b. Mullah 'Ashur Muhammad Khokandiy, *Ta'-rikh-i shahrokhi* (Kazan, Nikola Pantusif, 1885), pp. 75–76.
[12] *Sbornik materialov dlia istorii zavoevaniia turkestanskago kraia* (Tashkent, Tipografiia Shtaba Turkestanskago Voennago Okruga, 1912) III, 91–92.
[13] Terent'ev, I, 233.

after Russia's capture of Tokmak, this clash of religions was seldom ignored. *Jihad* was widely heralded again by General Mullah Alim Qul, who, on being notified in 1864 that a body of his troops had surrounded a sizable Russian force at Aq Bulaq in the area northeast of Tashkent, ordered his subordinates, in the accepted Muslim way:

> to enter into negotiations with them [the Russians]. . . . If they accept the faith of Islam and repent their actions then render kindness to them, and they will be alive and well. In the opposite case, I shall come myself . . . with all my troops and all artillery and blast them to dust and ashes through the power of my sword.[14]

At least a fifth of the Russian unit was killed or wounded before it could extricate itself from this encirclement.

MILITARY INROADS

Thus, near the end of the contest between Khokand and Russia before the capture of Tashkent, the strife took on the identity of Holy War, but the broader Central Asian conflict had been preceded by centuries of skirmishes and some large-scale battles between the adversaries in which, though they usually aligned Muslims against Christians, religious considerations remained of secondary importance. Direct clashes which occurred in the ninth century A.D., even before Muslim and Christian religions could have constituted a serious factor for the Central Asian Turkic or Russian combatants, broke out as the result of repeated plundering raids launched from the Russian area by Slavs or Scandinavians upon the eastern shore of the Caspian Sea.[15] Often fighting alongside stronger powers, from the tenth to twelfth centuries, Central Asians met Russians in battles involving mainly the Khazars, Bulgars, or Polovetsians (Cumans).[16]

[14] *Turkestanskii krai: Sbornik materialov* . . . , vol. XVII, part 1 (1914), pp. 236, 235.

[15] Muhammad ibn al-Hasan ibn Isfandiyar, *History of Tabaristan*, "E. J. W. Gibb Memorial Series" (Leiden, E. J. Brill; London, Bernard Quaritch, 1905), II, 177, 187, 199; cited by D. M. Dunlop, *The History of the Jewish Khazars* (Princeton, Princeton University Press, 1954), p. 238.

[16] *Polnoe sobranie russkikh lietopisei* "Ipatievskaia lietopis'" (St. Petersburg, Izdannoe po Vysochaishemu Povelieniiu Arkheograficheskoiu Kommissieiu, 1843), II, 128, 319; A. Iakubovskii, "Feodal'noe obshchestvo Srednei Azii i

In a similar manner, Central Asian warriors, particularly the Turkic nomads of the plains, made up considerable strength in Batu Khan's armies invading Russia between 1237 and 1240,[17] and during the late fourteenth century, Russians found themselves once again embroiled in such wars when Timur (Tamerlane) (r.1370–1405) and his Central Asians smashed the Golden Horde, with its Slavic contingents, in battles fought over northern Khwarazm and southern Russia. Thereafter, because of the breakdown of the Golden Horde and rise of separate khanates, military contact between Russia and Central Asia lessened, though it continued in an indirect fashion on a smaller scale until such relations took another twist when the Russian southern frontier, which had contracted under nomadic pressure in the eleventh and twelfth centuries, pushed down far beyond its earlier limits.

Forerunners of that southern expansion were Cossack settlements which prepared the Russian base for direct military action against Central Asia from their Yaik (Ural) River outposts. During the collapse in Russian central government around the turn of the seventeenth century, these Russian frontiersmen struck the first of a number of unrewarding, bloody thrusts into settled Central Asian territory. Ataman Nechai Starenskoi and his Yaik band penetrated with the surprise overland campaign of 1603 all the way into the heart of the Khivan khanate where the Cossacks first occupied, plundered, and devastated Urganch, the capital,[18] but were then surrounded, besieged by Arab Muhammad Khan I (r.1602–1621), and slaughtered before they could escape with the women and booty they had captured.[19] Twice more in the same century Cossacks were reportedly cut down while attempting to succeed in the same exploit.[20]

---

ego torgovlia s Vostochnoi Evropoi v X–XV vv.," *Materialy po istorii uzbekskoi, tadzhikskoi i turkmenskoi SSR* (Leningrad, Izdatel'stvo Akademii Nauk SSSR, 1932), pp. 12–13, 29.

[17] Vernadsky, p. 49.

[18] S. V. Zhukovskii, *Snosheniia Rossii s Bukharoi i Khivoi za posliednee trekhsotlietie* (Petrograd, Trudy Obshchestva Russkikh Orientalistov, 1915, No. 2), p. 19.

[19] "Stateinyi spisok posol'stva v Bukhariiu dvorianina Ivana Khokhlova," *Sbornik Kniazia Khilkova* (St. Petersburg, 1879), p. 396.

[20] J. A. MacGahan, *Campaigning on the Oxus and the Fall of Khiva* (New York, Harper, 1874), p. 238.

Russian pacification at home contrasted with increasing strife among the Central Asians themselves, and created, during most of the seventeenth and eighteenth centuries, a climate in which true military adventures could not have been expected to emanate from the khanates upon Russia. But the opposite was not true. As empire builders like Peter the Great began to take an interest in expansion to the southeast, the Russian government planned an elaborate expedition in force—described as a diplomatic mission—against Khiva.

In 1717, a 3,500-man Russian command overcame great logistical problems, sharp resistance, and the desert, and reached Khiva only to be destroyed as a military unit, with all but a very few survivors taken into lifelong captivity. This fatal Russian campaign, led by the Circassian officer Alexander Bekovich-Cherkassky, had been preceded in 1716 by attempts to establish the first Russian fortress upon the eastern shore of the Caspian Sea at Tub Qaragan bay and farther south at what is now Krasnovodsk. The Russian debacle at Khiva soon forced the abandonment of these outposts, and Peter's approach to Central Asia from the west was ended.[21]

More effective, in the long run, was the Russian advance from the north in a campaign led in 1715 by Colonel Ivan Bukhgol'ts with nearly 3,000 men down along the Irtish River from Tobolsk to Yamish lake, where they built a fort. Besieged there by Kalmyks under Cherin Donduk, this Russian force abandoned the fort, and only 700 survivors were able to retreat to the mouth of the Om River. There, in 1716, the depleted detachment established a fort which became the town of Omsk. Bukhgol'ts, like Bekovich-Cherkassky at Khiva, lost his life in the effort.[22]

Only two years later came the erection of the Semipalatinsk fort, and in 1720 a similar stronghold appeared at Ust-Kamenogorsk. The new frontier post of Orenburg was established in 1735 where Orsk now stands, at the mouth of the Or, by 1743 shifting west to

---

[21] *Narrative of the Russian Military Expedition to Khiva Conducted by Prince Alexander Bekovitch Cherkasski in 1717* (London, India Office, 1873), pp. 21–39.

[22] Stepan V. Russov, "Puteshestvie iz Orenburga v Khivu samarskago kuptsa Rukavkina v 1753 godu, s priobshcheniem raznykh izviestii o Khivie s otdalennykh vremen donynie," *Zhurnal Ministerstva Vnutrennikh Diel*, vol. XXXIV, No. 10 (1839), p. 368.

its present site at the confluence of the Ural and Sakmara rivers. Troitsk was founded in the same year Orenburg took its second location, and a decade later, Petropavlovsk (1752) was established.

A great arc now marked the Russian–Central Asian frontier. Pivoting in the West on the old city of Astrakhan, Yaitski Gorodok (Uralsk), built 1620, and Guryev, built 1645, the edge cut down through the old line drawn along Ufa-Tobolsk-Siberia to clip the fringes of Central Asia all the way from the north Caspian littoral to the Chinese frontier. Henceforth, combining military pressure with diplomatic activity, the Russians carried on an offensive designed to upset the delicate equilibrium between the closely synchronized but not centrally regulated parts of Central Asia's defensive mechanism. The nomadic Kazakhs, the Kirgiz, and Turkmens formed an outer ring of fluid defenses for the vital nuclei provided by the khanates at the heart of the great complex. These settled centers thus constituted a fixed foundation upon which the nomads in certain situations could base themselves or fall back. Kazakh and Turkmen perimeter defenders shared their antipathy to the attackers with Khiva, Bukhara, and Khokand, which, separately in many cases, supplied forces to bolster the entire defensive organism in its military functions.

The Russian task in attacking this unwillingly interdependent device was to strip away essential parts and throw the machine out of balance. They began both to understand and to be in a position to act upon this necessity when their new forward posts placed them in constant contact with the Central Asians for the first time. Throughout the eighteenth century czarist soldiers toiled to build a whole series of fortified strips, the Yaik (Ural), Orenburg, Ishim, and Irtysh lines, which hardened Russia's defenses against penetration by unwanted Kazakh horsemen and facilitated preparations for a further forward advance. Forty-six forts and ninety-six redoubts went into the system of these lines constructed throughout a period in which Russian troops actually found themselves in a defensive attitude before the Kazakhs.[23]

Although the czarist forces suffered a brief setback when many Kazakh warriors joined Emel'ian Pugachev to strike the authorities

---

[23] Zhukovskii, p. 95.

in 1773–1774, seizing Guryev, Petropavlovsk, and Troitsk, and besieging Orenburg, thereafter, from the new bases, Russian units shoved southward nearly everywhere along the line. They dealt brutally with the Kazakh resistance their advance triggered in the first half of the nineteenth century, and replaced with hatred much of the good will which earlier diplomatic efforts had gained.

Sultan Kenisari Qasim-uli (Kasimov) (1802–1847), onetime friend of the Russians, became their most effective opponent in the Kazakh plains from about 1836 to 1846. The grievances harbored by the Kazakhs against the Russians were numberless in this period, and, as an effective military leader, Kenisari Qasim-uli not only served to focus Kazakh resistance to Russia, but openly recited the wrongs suffered by his people at czarist hands. In a complaint written to the chairman of the Orenburg Border Commission in June, 1841, Kenisari Qasim-uli summarized the reasons he fought:

Following the example of our ancestors, of Ablay Khan, who took the oath of allegiance to the emperor, we wandered on the Isel Nur trusting in God and not worrying about anything except the tranquility of our people, but suddenly a thunderclap struck us. . . . In 1825 . . . Sultan Yamantay Bokey-uli . . . slandered us to the chief of the Qarqarali jurisdiction (*prikaz*), Ivan Semenovich Karnachev, who, moving out with 300 Russians and 100 Kazakhs . . . sacked the village (*aul*) of Sultan Sarjan Qasim-uli . . . plundered an untold quantity of cattle and property, and slaughtered 64 people; the remainder saved themselves by flight. In 1827 . . . 200 men under Major Mingriav destroyed the villages of the Alike and Shuburtpaly divisions, slaughtered 58 people, and plundered untold property. In 1830 . . . a command . . . slaughtered 190 persons . . . In 1831 . . . 500 men under . . . Lt. Col. Aleksei Maksimovich . . . slaughtered 450 persons and kidnapped a child of Sarjan [Qasim-uli]. . . . In 1832 . . . 250 men under . . . Petr Nikolaevich Kulakov . . . killed 60 persons. . . . In 1836 . . . 400 men under . . . Major Tin'tiak . . . slaughtered 250 persons. . . . In 1837 . . . 400 men under . . . Ivan Semenovich Karpachev sacked the Alikins, Kalkaman-uli's, Turtul-uli's, and slaughtered 350 persons.[24]

In addition to these depredations, Kensari Qasim-uli reported that in 1838 four more such punitive raids led by Russian or Kazakh czarist officers heading 1,600 troops in various detachments pil-

[24] *Sbornik materialov . . . turkestanskago kraia,* "Sultan Kenisara Kasymov Predsiedateliu Orenb. pogran. Komissii; 7 iiunia 1841 g.," III (1912), 70–71.

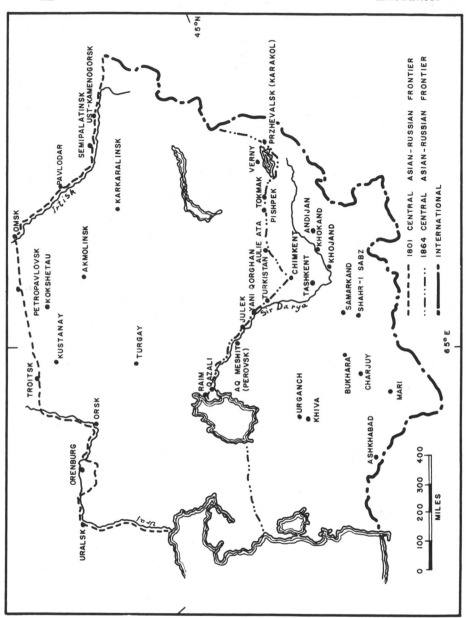

FIGURE 1.1   Central Asian frontiers, 1801, 1864.

laged and harassed several thousand Kazakh villages, killed 854 persons, and abducted more than 180. In 1840 troops ravaged the villages of Sultan Sarjan Qasim-uli, killed 70 persons, took 20 women into captivity, and drove off 2,300 horses, 300 camels, 3,000 sheep, and 100 head of cattle. In the same year two other Russian raids employed 900 men in pillaging six different Kazakh groups, killing 111 persons, capturing 20, and stealing thousands of sheep, cows, and camels.[25]

While Kenisari Qasim-uli and the Russians prolonged their hit-and-run warfare in the northern plains, czarist commanders at Orenburg, irritated by Khiva's open sympathy for the Kazakh struggle and forgetful of the old lesson taught to the Cossacks in the seventeenth and to Bekovich-Cherkassky in the eighteenth century, once again planned an assault upon the khanate of Khiva. Like all governments bent on aggression, the Russian leaders summoned up convenient injuries to justify their action and launched a full-scale attack in 1839–1840 upon these Central Asians.

Although the fiasco in which this ended is customarily excused by citing the snowstorms encountered by the army, that campaign, led by a man familiar with the area, General V. A. Perovskii, had been deliberately planned for winter conditions in order to avoid extreme summer heat. It might well have reached its destination, where the outcome of a battle could not have been considered a foregone conclusion, if the Khivans and their few Turkmen and Kazakh allies had not so effectively detected and exploited Russian weaknesses in transport and supply. A series of guerrilla actions skilfully carried out by light forces which burned Russian supply ships from Astrakhan, as well as fishing boats anchored off Fort Novo-Alexandrovsk on the Caspian, drove off sheep needed as food and, capturing the czarist remount officer and his train, drastically curtailed the roundup of camels, taken from Kazakh nomads, which were required for carrying provisions to the advancing Russian columns.[26] These losses, plus casualties inflicted by severe weather,

---

[25] *Ibid.*, pp. 71–72.

[26] *A Narrative of the Russian Military Expedition to Khiva under General Perofski in 1839* (Calcutta, Office of the Superintendent, 1867), pp. 150, 156–57, 163.

forced the Russians to begin their retreat on February 1, 1840, before covering half the distance to the objective.

Provoked by the failure, Russia later sent more punitive detachments to attack supposedly friendly Kazakhs who had refused to
aid the czarist campaign against Khiva. As Kenisari himself was
being hunted to earth and killed by his Kirgiz rivals, Russia, no
longer deterred by large-scale Kazakh military opposition, built up
a new line of fortifications across the middle of the plains starting in
the west with Fort Novo-Alexandrovsk erected in 1834 on the Caspian shore and shifted to another coastal point in 1846. They quickly
constructed new forts at Irgiz (1845), Turgay (1845), Ulu Tau
(1846), Raim (Aral) (1847), and Kopal (1847).

While the Kazakhs suffered their ordeal and this new front line
between occupied and unoccupied Central Asia was being roughed
out by the czarist army, a fresh force was rising from the south to
meet and challenge the Russian advance. From approximately the
beginning of the nineteenth century, as the influence of Khiva faded
in the Kazakh plains and elsewhere, and as the Kazakh disorders
increased, Khokand systematically pushed its lines northward until
at the height of the khanate's power in the century a chain of
Khokandian forts extended beyond Aq Meshit (Masjid), which was
built in 1817, and included Chim Qorghan, Kumish Qorghan, Kosh
Qorghan, Julak, and Yangi (Yani) Qorghan, which were constructed
after Khokand conquered that part of southern Central Asia in
1814.[27] New Khokandian strongholds appeared also north of the
Hungry Steppe on the Sari Su River at Qara Jar village and seventy-
nine miles below on the river at Jurt Qulaq. Although the Russians
attacked and destroyed both of these small forts in 1832, the Tashkent qushbegi persevered to build another, stronger, advance fort
in the Ulu Tau mountains two years later from which to harass the
Russians and stir up their Kazakh subjects.[28]

At mid-century the principal antagonists faced one another
squarely, and exactly in 1850 the Khokandians began to press
local Kazakhs who cooperated with the Russians, driving off their

[27] Chokan Chingisovich Valikhanov, *The Russians in Central Asia* (London,
Edward Stanford, 1865), pp. 314–15.
[28] *Sbornik materialov . . . turkestanskago kraia*, III (1912), 91–92.

herds from near Fort Raim and adjacent areas. The center for Khokand's action at this stage became Aq Meshit, from which patrols in strength pushed out regularly. Early in March, 1852, Yaqub Bek, future ruler of Kashgar, leading 1,700 men down the Sir Darya to harass "Russian" Kazakhs, clashed violently with a Russian punitive detachment, inflicting some casualties before the Khokandians melted away to return to their small, unguarded forts in the desert. Another skirmish on the Sir Darya with the Khokandians turned back an eighty-man czarist reconnaisance detachment in April, 1852. Reacting to Yaqub Bek's tough opposition, General Perovskii ordered a reinforced unit sent from Fort Raim to execute a surprise attack on Aq Meshit, Khokand's strongest advance post, and destroy it. In Yaqub Bek's absence, the commandant at Aq Meshit, Batir Basi, led a furious fight against the Russian attackers on July 20, 1852, and repulsed them with heavy losses. In this battle, and in many subsequent engagements between the Russian and Khokand armies, the czarist forces tremendously outnumbered and outgunned the Central Asians. At Aq Meshit, for example, the garrison of defenders totaled only 50 soldiers and about 100 merchants.[29]

The ratio of attackers to defenders by chance coincided with the relative size of populations in the two areas. Russia around the early nineteenth century was estimated to have a population of 60 million people, as opposed to one of 5 or 6 million in Central Asia.[30] It is one of the striking ironies in the conflict that Khiva, which Russia habitually regarded as its archenemy in Central Asia, was the smallest of the three khanates and, by all accounts, the poorest. Near the end of the eighteenth century Khiva's population was considered by one Russian diplomat to be not over 400,000 people, counting four to a household, and in 1842, shortly after the unsuccessful Russian invasion attempt, another czarist ambassador who carefully canvassed the khanate's settled population, reported fewer than 300,000 persons all told.[31] The number of people inhabiting the town of

[29] Valikhanov, pp. 318, 330–36.

[30] Michael T. Florinsky, *Russia: A History and an Interpretation* (New York, MacMillan, 1953), II, 784; Lawrence Krader, *Peoples of Central Asia* (Bloomington, Indiana University; The Hague, Mouton, 1963), p. 178.

[31] [Blankennagl'], "Putevye zamietki maiora Blankennagelia o Khivie v

Khiva and its environs, according to a parish census conducted around 1858, the year of Russia's final, formal, diplomatic mission to the khanates, came to fewer than 18,000 (4,493 households).[32]

Khokand was far more populous than Khiva, but the question of size of populations or opposing armies in the battle for Central Asia was not the direct key to victory. Decisive, rather, was the position and availability to the Central Asians of defenses which sufficiently counteracted the effects of the up-to-date heavy weapons which the Russians alone regularly employed. In open encounters when the Central Asians stood against the concentrated firepower, particularly grapeshot, of Russian units, the local forces absorbed terrible casualties, losses which the extended Russian offensive columns could not have withstood, and it is therefore misleading to picture, as observers sometimes had, a cowardly Muslim rabble fleeing everywhere before heroic Russian exploits. Courage, when it showed itself on a large scale, was characteristic of Central Asians against frightening odds, as at Aq Meshit, in both cannon and riflemen. Russian troops actually had little to fear from opposing armament. Nevertheless, Russian commanders, backed by considerable experience in wars with Poland, Hungary, England, France, Turkey, Persia, and the Caucasus mountaineers, time and again failed to profit from their many military advantages.

Despite the fighting spirit of the Khivans and Khokandians, however, superior arms, modern organization, and probably greater physical fitness won the war step by step for the czar. On their second attempt, for example, against Aq Meshit a year after the defensive victory of Batir Basi, Russian troops, again enjoying nearly ten-to-one numerical odds, took the fortress on July 28, 1853, only after killing the new commandant, Muhammad Wali, and 230 out of the 300 defenders in four weeks of brutal fighting. The Russians under the leadership of General Perovskii himself in this return engagement had mustered seventeen cannon and were supported

1793–94 gg.," *Viestnik Imperatorskago Russkago Geograficheskago Obshchestva*, vol. XXII, part 2 (1858), p. 94; G. I. Danilevskii, "Opisanie khivinskago khanstva," *Zapiski Imperatorskago Russkago Geograficheskago Obshchestva*, V (1851), 99–100.

[32] P. P. Ivanov, *Arkhiv khivinskikh khanov XIX v.* (Leningrad, Izdanie Gosudarstvennoi Publichnoi Biblioteki, 1940), pp. 32–49.

by the steam launch *Perovskii* anchored in the river, but their losses reached 164 men and officers killed or wounded.[33]

Khokand continued to fight each Russian advance after Aq Meshit, while in the plains, with Kenisari Qasim-uli gone, the Little Horde Kazakhs were led by Iset Kutebar-uli and those on the lower

FIGURE 1.2 Tribal chieftain Iset Kutebar-uli, who led Little Horde (*Kishshi Jüz*) Kazakhs against the Russians, 1855–1857.

Sir Darya by Jan Qoja Nurmuhammad-uli (d. 1860), who, having barred the Kazakhs from supplying camels for the Russian campaign against Aq Meshit in 1853, came into open conflict with czarist units and their tame Kazakhs again.[34] Iset Kutebar-uli reestablished liaison with Khiva in the west, and Russian troops again took the initiative on the eastern front against fortified Khokandian places,

[33] Terent'ev, I, 221–27.
[34] *Ibid.,* pp. 234–40.

capturing Tokmak in late August, 1860, and Pishpek, after heavy bombardment, on September 3, 1860. Losing both towns, czarist units took them again in 1862. Among the Central Asian prisoners of war captured at Pishpek, as at Din Qorghan in 1862, were a few Russian deserters. Yangi Qorghan fell to Russia September, 1861, Aulie Ata, June 4, 1864, and the town of Turkistan, June 12, 1864, as the Russians once more moved to establish and close a new frontier between occupied Central Asia and independent territory.

By mid-1864 Khokand had managed, too late, to alter slightly the complexion of the fighting with Russian troops by obtaining some better cannon and particularly by mastering the use of high explosive shells. A Russian unit on its way to Chimkent was surrounded by a large detachment of Khokandians at Aq Bulaq, July, 1864, and the retreating Russian commander, who extricated his troops by falsely promising to give up the town of Turkistan to Khokand,[35] reported: "After noon the Khokandians emplaced three weapons on the high ground, and the first shell which flew through our camp produced a shocking effect on morale—it exploded, and everyone saw that we had business with an enemy the like of which the Sir Darya army had not met before." [36] This was the same encounter that evoked a demand by Mullah Alim Qul, quoted earlier, that the Russian troops embrace Islam or die.

Shortly after this, the future general M. G. Cherniaev, moving from the eastern sector of the Russian front, attempted to seize Chimkent, but he too was beaten off by stout resistance and strong reinforcements led by the tough Mullah Alim Qul.[37] Finally, on the third try, Chimkent fell to Russian pounding September 22, 1864.

Encouraged by this important conquest, Cherniaev pushed on rapidly to Tashkent, in Russian eyes the prize of Central Asia. As in the case of Aq Meshit and Chimkent, the first attempt aborted on October 4, 1864, when Cherniaev's troops were thrown back with heavy losses, and he retreated to Chimkent. But in spring,

[35] *Ibid.*, p. 288.

[36] *Turkestanskii krai: Sbornik materialov* . . . , vol. XVII, part 1 (1914), p. 233.

[37] *Istoriia uzbekskoi SSR* (Tashkent, Izdatel'stvo Akademii Nauk Uzbekskoi SSR, 1956) vol. I, part 2, p. 88; Terent'ev, I, 291.

1865, an event occurred which may have determined the ultimate course of the struggle. On May 9, Mullah Alim Qul, still commanding Khokand's armies and serving as regent to the Khokand throne, was killed during a pitched battle before Tashkent, and although a subsequent Russian attack on Tashkent, June 7, 1865, was also beaten off, without his inspired leadership the Khokandians seemed to lose much of their formidable fighting ability.

Popular local legend concerning the battle for Tashkent attributed Mullah Alim Qul's death not to enemy action but to the treachery of certain Central Asians themselves (see chapter 14). This view gains credibility not only because vicious rivalry among Khokandian, Bukharan, and pacifist factions in Tashkent was known to be rampant at the time, but also because of evidence that prominent Tashkent figures opposed to Khokand rule betrayed that city of 60,000 to 80,000 to the enemy.[38] Abdurrahman Bek, governor of the eastern borough of Tashkent, an important defector, and Muhammad Saatbay, a wealthy, Muslim trade magnate, provided information in 1864 and 1865 to General Cherniaev regarding conditions and defenses in the city, and, at the crucial moment:

Partisans of the Russian orientation played a certain role in the comparatively quick attainment of victory [over Tashkent]. Particularly during the period of the assault when czarist troops held the city wall, Muhammad Saatbay and his followers called on the Tashkent people to stop their resistance . . . and facilitated the surrender of the city.[39]

TRADE OFFENSIVES

Shocking as this treachery seems, it was inevitable that merchants and trade exerted great influence upon relations, military or otherwise, between Central Asia and Russia, for then, as a thousand years before, economic ties constituted the most persistent, positive links between the two areas. In many respects the pattern of trade, methods of transport, location of trading centers, and identity of goods exchanged remained essentially the same in 1865 as they had in the ninth and tenth centuries. Furthermore, up to the last,

---

[38] *Istoriia uzbekskoi SSR*, vol. I, part 2, pp. 21–23, 25, 26; Terent'ev, I, 312.
[39] N. A. Khalfin, *Politika Rossii v Srednei Azii, 1857–1868* (Moscow, Izdatel'stvo Vostochnoi Literatury, 1960), p. 201.

centers like Bukhara, Khwarazm (Khiva), Khokand, and to a lesser extent Tashként, served as transit points for goods moving mainly to the east and west but also north and south.

Because Russia had, for Central Asian trade, no centers of great importance at first, Bulgar on the mid-Volga and Kama rivers, and Itil near the mouth of the Volga, served as intermediaries for commercial operations between Russia and Central Asia. In those markets resident Bulgars, Bukharans, Khazars, Khwarazmians by the thousands, and other Muslim businessmen met Scandinavians, Russians, and additional East Europeans to exchange goods. To Bulgar and Itil in the tenth century, Central Asians exported textiles, including cotton broadcloth, wool, and silk, as well as rice, dried fruit, metal utensils, and the like. From there, Khwarazm and Bukhara especially drew Slavic slaves, furs, hides, tree bark, hunting falcons, honey, walrus tusks, nuts, candles, and similar commodities. Much of this the Central Asians purchased for cash, paying silver Samanid dirhems to the Russians, who, because of their primitive condition as yet had no adequate coinage of their own.[40]

To reach Itil and Bulgar, tenth-century Central Asian merchants crossed the plains and desert northwest of the Aral Sea by caravans ranging in size from a few dozen camels and horses to unusually large groups such as a religious and trade mission in A.D. 922 to Bulgar from Bukhara in which 3,000 pack animals and 5,000 men traveled together.[41] Another important route connected Itil with Khwarazm by boat across the Caspian Sea and by caravan from the shore to Jurjan (Urganch).[42] For the Russians, Bulgar in the tenth century was not only a trading post but the main depot handling the commerce of north East Europe.[43] Regardless of political vicissitudes, the importance of that location, earlier outside Russia proper, as a trade point for Central Asian–Russian commerce, was primary even in the mid-nineteenth century, long after Kazan,

---

[40] Iakubovskii, pp. 11–14; Bolat Saliyef, *Orta Asiya tarikhi, 11–15nchi 'äsrlär* (Samarkand-Tashkent, Ozbekistan Däwlät Näshriyati,, 1926), pp. 20f.

[41] [Ibn Fadlan] *Puteshestvie Ibn Fadlana na Volgu,* ed. by I. Iu. Krachkovskii (Moscow-Leningrad, Izdatel'stvo Akademii Nauk SSSR, 1939), pp. 55–78 passim.

[42] *Istoriia uzbekskoi SSR,* vol. I, part 1 (1955), pp. 200–1.

[43] Iakubovskii, p. 11.

though an internal market place, had assumed Bulgar's old function as a focus for trade.[44]

The temporary setback to trade relations occasioned by the Mongol invasion was quickly recouped because of Mongol interest in taking over the development of the profitable caravan trade. At this time the economy of Mawaraunnahr (Transoxiana), the heart of Central Asia, became linked temporarily to that of Russia in yet another manner, first under the common rule of Batu Khan (r.1251–1255), and then under the Muslim, Berke Khan (r.1256–1266), both descendants of Chingis Khan (r.1206–1227). Particularly in Berke Khan's reign, Russian taxpayers, like the people of Central Asia's main population centers, felt the exactions of experienced Khwarazmian and Bukharan tax farmers (*basqaq* or *darugha*) employed by the government throughout this newly unified domain. That they resented these Central Asian agents violently was demonstrated in a number of Russian towns which rebelled against the revenue collectors, killing or driving them off in 1262 and at other times.[45] After the Mongol assault, Urganch, Khwarazm's capital, rapidly recovered its role as a great, populous, commercial city, and by the time of Ibn Battuta's visit there in 1333 was "the largest and most beautiful town of the Turkic people." [46] Berke's Saray, located near present-day Volgograd, then the capital of Uzbek Khan (1313–1341), ruler of the Golden Horde, served also as a busy market for traders from Central Asia and Russia, and it was remarkable that in those years caravans moved safely between Uzbek Khan's principal city and Khwarazm, the northern part of which he also controlled, without escort.[47]

But this orderly conduct of business was short-lived because of changes in the lives of two men. When Uzbek Khan died he deprived the Golden Horde and thus Russia of a firm hand able to control all political and trade affairs. With the Golden Horde's gov-

[44] M. K. Rozhkova, *Ekonomicheskie sviazi Rossii so Srednei Aziei, 40–60–e gody XIX veka* (Moscow, Izdatel'stvo Akademii Nauk SSSR, 1963), p. 77.

[45] *Polnoe sobranie russkikh lietopisei,* "Sofiiskaia pervaia lietopis'," V (1851), 190.

[46] Ibn Battuta, *Voyages d'Ibn Batoutah* (Paris, Société Asiatique, 1877), III, 3.

[47] Vernadsky, p. 198.

ernment in chaos in the mid-fourteenth century, Russian bandits by
the thousands, who had previously been held somewhat in check
by their princes and the punitive action of Mongol detachments,
terrorized outlying Russian settlements and the ports along water
routes to the Caspian Sea from Russia. In their raids against Nizhegorod (Nizhni Novgorod, Gorky) and other towns between 1366
and 1375, the Russians caught large numbers of Central Asian merchants by surprise, slaughtered them, and plundered their boats,
carrying off many Slavs to the slave markets at Bulgar and Hajjitar-
khan (Astrakhan).[48]

While the Russian pirates from Novgorod were scourging the
Volga and paralyzing trade there as well as throughout the Bulgar
principality, in Central Asia Timur rose to become the second strong
figure since the thirteenth century to affect the entire range of relations, including trade, between the two areas. His main contribution in the economic field was to conquer Bulgar and destroy, between 1388 and 1395, the main trading centers of the Golden Horde,
including Urganch, Berke's Saray, Astrakhan, Kaffa in the Crimea,
and Azov, plus the northern Caucasus, and thus, in seven years,
to knock out all important intermediate market places between
Russia and Central Asia.[49] Timur's second major influence upon
Central Asian–Russian relations came with his armed invasion of
Russia to smash Tokhtamish in 1395. There he reduced even further the Golden Horde's already weak political control over the
Russians, thus in effect granting, as a Central Asian, the gift of
greater political independence to Russia.

Timur's Central Asian domain disintegrated under the Timurids
who followed him into component parts under increasing pressure
from the nomadic Uzbeks of the plains north of the Sir Darya, and,
after the Uzbek conquest of the area late in the fifteenth century,
soon split into separate Uzbek khanates. Meanwhile Russia's warring princes had gradually come under Moscow's sway. In the practice of political centralization or regional autonomy, the two regions
had virtually exchanged places with one another in the late sixteenth
century.

[48] *Polnoe sobranie russkikh lietopisei,* "Simeonovskaia lietopis'," XVIII
(1913), 104; "Novgorodskaia tret'ia lietopis'," *Ibid.,* III (1841), 231.
[49] *Istoriia uzbekskoi SSR* vol. I, part 1 (1955), p. 322.

Governmental contacts were then established to promote trade between Central Asia and Russia. Instigated by the London Muscovy Company, the mission of Anthony Jenkinson to Central Asia in 1558–1559 performed commercial functions for the English while carrying out diplomatic duties assigned it by Russia's Ivan IV (the Terrible) (1533–1584). Jenkinson found Astrakhan under the Russians engaged in petty trade, and, having caravanned from the Caspian beaches to Urganch and Bukhara on 1,000 camels (he returned that way with 600 of the pack animals), he reported Urganch ruined by civil wars which had driven most traders to other markets. Bukhara, though queen of the Central Asian commercial centers, by then offered little to an experienced European:

There is yerely great resort of Marchants to this citie of Boghar, which travaills in great Caravans from the countries thereabout adjoining, as India, Persia, Balgh, Russia, with divers others, and in times past from Cathay . . . but these Marchants are so beggerly and poore, and bring so little quantity of wares, lying two or 3 yeares to sell the same, that there is no hope of any good trade there to be had worthy of the following.[50]

As they had five centuries before, Russian traders were then bringing hides, cloth, wooden vessels, sheepskins, and the like to Central Asia, and Jenkinson saw them taking back, as of old, cotton cloth, silk, and dyestuffs, goods generally brought to Bukhara from India or Persia. For Russia, much more important than Jenkinson's trade information was probably the assistance he gave to Central Asian–Russian relations by escorting Khivan, Bukharan, and Balkh representatives to Moscow, and by redeeming and returning to the czar twenty-five Russians enslaved in Central Asia. Both these acts, no doubt matters of secondary concern to Jenkinson the businessman, had a lasting effect upon contacts in other spheres between the governments of Central Asia and that of Russia.

The principal alteration in economic links occurred in the sixteenth century as a result of Russia's acquiring the main intermedi-

[50] [Anthony Jenkinson], "The voyage of Master Anthony Jenkinson, made from the citie of Mosco in Russia, to the citie of Boghar in Bactria, in the yeere 1558: written by himselfe to the Merchants of London of the Muscovie companie," E. D. Morgan, ed., *Early Voyages and Travels to Russia and Persia* (London, Hakluyt Society, 1886), p. 87.

ary centers between the two areas serving mutual trade: Kazan, Astrakhan, and Siberia. Soon after these places came under Russian management, the merchants from Central Asia were again busy plying their trade in the bazaars there. But in the first part of the seventeenth century, as in the thirteenth, an incursion of Mongolian invaders from the East, this time the Kalmyks, drove a wedge between Russia and Central Asia which, especially in the 1620s and 1630s, disrupted traffic on the overland and water routes used by caravans.

Although the khans attempted to secure Russian cooperation in protecting trade against the Kalmyks, the Russian government remained essentially passive. Not only was it indifferent to this trade disability, but the Central Asians complained passionately that the Russians themselves were then responsible for putting additional difficulties before Khivan merchants. Czarist ship captains denied passage to Astrakhan via the Caspian Sea once caravans had traversed the desert from Urganch to the landing at Qaraghan.

Such harassments comprised the sole subject of one official Chaghatay-language dispatch from Asfandiyar Khan (r.1623–1642) of Khiva, addressed to the czar. In it the khan complained that while Russian merchants were trading and traveling comfortably in groups of forty or fifty in his domain, Khivan businessmen by contrast were not only being harassed by Russian sea captains to sell their goods at less than cost or be turned away from passage, but officials in Astrakhan were levying burdensome illegal duties upon them. The czar responded by ordering a stop to such discriminatory practices.[51]

These events in commercial life and on the nomads' battlefields were not the only bars to Central Asian–Russian trade in the seventeenth century, for the Russian government then seemingly first employed sanctions against Central Asian merchants within the empire in order to influence diplomatic relations. Disgruntled over the extremely impolite reception given a Russian envoy, the czar in 1623 detained three ambassador-merchants from Khiva and Bukhara, confiscated their goods, and curtailed the customary sub-

[51] *Materialy po istorii uzbekskoi, tadzhikskoi i turkmenskoi SSR* (Leningrad, Izdatel'stvo Akademii Nauk SSSR, 1932), part 1, pp. 178n., 429–31.

sistence allowance paid to such foreign envoys while in Russia.[52] This fiasco damaged trade for nearly two decades, but it was not the last time that Russia used the device, more out of anger than wisdom.

After Peter the Great's fruitless military adventures against Khiva in 1714–1717, trade was again halted by the czar, but Florio Beneveni, Russia's envoy to Bukhara, discovered in 1721 that the prohibitions damaged Russia more than Khiva, since the Nogays and Tatars continued a contraband trade in Russian products. Without payment of duty, they smuggled goods from Saratov and Astrakhan to Khiva.[53] Large numbers of clandestine caravans even transported Russian commodities forbidden for export, such as pewter and rifle barrels.

Czarist retaliation against Khivan envoy-traders was attempted also in 1754 when Russia arrested all Khivan merchants at Orenburg in order to force Khiva to release Russian merchant-envoys Ia. Guliaev and Danila Rukavkin.[54] Again in 1836, over 570 Khivan merchants were detained and 1.4 million rubles worth of their goods impounded in Russia to protest trade disadvantages and other grievances,[55] but the procedure by itself in the Russian view produced no lasting improvement of relations.

Efforts by Russian authorities to regulate their trade with Central Asia shortly after the founding of Orenburg (1735) took the form of licensing a czarist commercial organization to trade through Bukhara with India,[56] and in 1762 at Astrakhan another company with exclusive purvey over Russian business with Persia, Khiva, and Bukhara gained official approval. Although this move was backed by a specific ukase from Catherine the Great,[57] it exercised little

---

[52] Zhukovskii, pp. 21–22.

[53] Popov, p. 303.

[54] *Sbornik materialov . . . turkestanskago kraia,* III (1912), 14.

[55] "Review of the Causes that Led to the War with Khiva," *A Narrative of the Russian Military Expedition to Khiva, under General Perofski in 1839* (Calcutta, Office of the Superintendent, 1867), pp. 62–63.

[56] Ia. V. Khanykov, "Poiasnitel'naia zapiska k karte aral'skago moria i khivinskago khanstva s ikh okrestnostiami," *Zapiski Imperatorskago Russkago Geograficheskago Obshchestva,* V (1851), 285.

[57] *Polnoe sobranie zakonov rossiiskoi imperii s 1649 goda,* "O raznykh postanovleniiakh kasatel'no torgovli" (St. Petersburg, Pechatano v Tipografii II otdieleniia Sobstvennoi Ego Imperatorskago Velichestva Kantseliarii, 1830), XVI, 35.

influence over such trade. The initiative remained with the Central Asians who, from as early as 1675–1678, when they tried without success to persuade Russia to build itself a trading town on Mangishlak peninsula,[58] had begun to reach the understanding that by excluding Russian traders from Central Asia, the Khivans, Bukharans, and other local merchants could dominate trade between Russia and Central Asia at their end of the caravan routes. As if by agreement, then, the Kazakh, Turkmen, and khanate businessmen concerted to discourage traveling Russian salesmen from operating within Central Asia while the Asians proceeded to gain control of the import and export market within Russia, as well, for Central Asian trade. Though the Russians attempted also in 1823 and 1837 to meet this competition by proposing to found special trading monopolies to handle Central Asian business, their measures remained ineffective for lack of vitality and because of apparent greater acumen of Bukharans and Khivans in this field.

Before the end of the eighteenth century, under pressure from plundering and physical threats, as well as discriminatory customs levies sometimes four times as high as those paid by Muslim merchants, most Russian traders had been literally ejected from the profitable caravan business in the khanates. Shipments destined for Central Asia which were not in the control of Central Asians frequently became the responsibility of the czar's Tatar subjects. They, often capitalized by Russian houses, quietly worked to their own advantage against their creditors or employers, and sometimes absconded with the goods they carried to market to set up shop for themselves permanently in Tashkent or Bukhara.

Why Russian merchants should have persisted in trying to sell their goods in Central Asian bazaars under these manifold difficulties is hard to determine. The regularity of their reports regarding commercial disasters suffered almost suggests that they were not really losing so much as they claimed, but advertised such hazards in order to frighten away competition, reduce czarist taxation, and ultimately secure government sympathy in the form of subsidies to save them from assuming the financial risks of their

---

[58] *Materialy po istorii uzbekskoi, tadzhikskoi i turkmenskoi SSR*, part 1, pp. 224–40.

business ventures. Skepticism regarding the merchants' laments
could have been engendered by the revelation that through Orenburg, for example, from 1787 to 1796 Russia was said to have gained
a trade advantage over Khiva and Bukhara because she received
goods valued at more rubles than she sent there.[59] Most evidence
belies the interpretation that Russia gained more than it paid out,
but barter trade across certain frontier points like Orenburg appeared to favor the Russians when considered without reference to
transactions concluded through similar points such as Troitsk or
Astrakhan and those managed elsewhere between the same two
parties, or disregarding the nationality of the merchants actually
engaged in such trade, ignoring the parallel flow of gold and silver
between the two areas, and underestimating indirect imports, exports, and other factors relevant to a determination of the balance
of trade involving specified countries. Although commerce with
the Central Asian khanates at the middle of the nineteenth century
totaled but 6 percent of imports and 4.2 percent of exports out of
Russian trade with all her Asian neighbors, business with the
Kazakhs constituted 13 percent of imports and 16.8 percent of exports Russia handled with her Eastern neighbors.[60] Central Asian
trade was admittedly very important to that part of Russia east of
the Volga.[61]

For the Central Asians, however, the share of their business
exclusively with Russia has been judged to be much more substantial. Khiva, for example, not depending upon Russian markets,[62]
traded with Bukhara, Khokand, Persia, and Afghanistan, but the
khanate's commerce with Russia in the 1800s was called the easiest
and most profitable of all.[63] Khivan perseverance in dealing with
Russia would seem to substantiate the view that Russian commerce
was vital to it. From counting their profits the Central Asians realized, and the Russians also learned when they began to analyze

[59] E. V. Bunakov, "K istorii snoshenii Rossii s sredneaziatskimi khanstvami,"
Sovetskoe Vostokovedenie, II (1941), 8–9.

[60] *Ibid.*, p. 22.

[61] Khanykov, p. 289.

[62] Bunakov, p. 14.

[63] A. R. Muhammadjanov and T. Ne"matov, *Bukhara wä Khewäning Rossiyä
bilän munasäbätläri tärikhigä dair bä"zi mänbälär* (Tashkent, Ozbekistan
SSR Fänlär Äkädemiyäsi Näshriyati, 1957), p. 139.

statistics drawn more broadly from customs records of all their southeastern trading posts, that in the late eighteenth century, and probably earlier, Central Asia enjoyed an important trade advantage with relation to Russia. Around 1794, Bukharans and Khivans, who dominated Central Asian commercial activity, were selling roughly 2 million rubles worth of goods annually to the czar's empire, which sent back only half that much,[64] and the pattern continued in the first decades of the nineteenth century.[65] As Table 1.1 shows, through the middle of the century, the trade balance continued to favor the Central Asian khanates.

TABLE 1.1

Russia's Trade with Central Asia (Excluding Kazakhstan)
in Rubles, 1840–1867

	From Central Asia		To Central Asia	
	All trade	*Trade in raw and processed cotton*	*All trade*	*Trade in processed cotton*
1840	1,655,000	1,302,000	1,164,000	519,000
1845	1,304,000	926,000	873,000	314,000
1850	1,263,000	1,025,000	812,000	423,000
1855	1,885,000	1,184,000	757,000	351,000
1860	2,324,000	1,349,000	1,920,000	1,015,000
1864	7,699,000	6,931,000	4,740,000	2,395,000
1865	4,704,000	3,897,000	3,775,000	2,380,000
1867	8,504,000	6,030,000	10,275,000	6,952,000

Source: M. K. Rozhkova, *Ekonomicheskie sviazi Rossii so Srednei Aziei, 40–60–e gody XIX veka* (Moscow, Izdatel'stvo Akademii Nauk SSSR, 1963), pp. 50–69.

The extent of Kazakhstan's trading with the khanates as well as its exports to Russia up to 1867 has apparently not been precisely ascertained, partly because the Russian army occupied many positions throughout the Kazakh domain during the first half of the nineteenth century. In effect, this made sections of the Kazakh plains an interior trade zone of the empire, though the czar's Orenburg-Siberia customs frontier was not officially moved southward

[64] [Blankennagl'], p. 102.
[65] Khanykov, p. 287.

to the Sir Darya line until 1868.[66] That administrative action removed duty from goods going out of the Turkistan guberniia to Russia in order to protect Russian trade with Central Asia. It also prohibited importation of English and other West European goods
through the Central Asian khanates and the Turkistan guberniia to
Russian territory.

The transport of commodities between Central Asia and Russia
in modern times moved by camel caravan over the same old routes
which had served it in the tenth century, later variations arising
from the shift southward of the frontier posts serving Russia from
Bulgar and Tobolsk to Orenburg and Troitsk. Khiva continued to
send and receive some traders by sea from and to Mangishlak, but
most went overland across the Ural and Emba rivers to and from
Astrakhan or northward to the other border towns.

The goods these merchants dealt in had scarcely altered from
early days, with Bukhara, probably the great all-time center for this
commerce, exporting to Russia in 1840 chiefly cotton, muslin, raw
and dyed silk, silk robes, shawls, dried fruit, rice, indigo, tur-
quoises, and skull caps.[67] In return, Russian suppliers at that time
exported to Bukhara, chiefly via Bukharan merchants, chintz, calico,
muslin, broadcloth, silk cloth, brocade, hides, some iron, and cast
iron articles.[68]

Cotton (see Table 1.1), both raw and processed, cloth and thread,
grew in importance mainly as a result of the American Civil War,
which cut off Russian sources of supply. In 1865, cotton represented,
in value, 74 percent of all commerce registered, with *raw* cotton
exports from Central Asia to Russia having risen by that date to
74.1 percent of the total Central Asian exports of cotton, and fabricated cotton having dropped to 8.7 percent of that export total
from 55.1 percent in 1840.[69]

Central Asian traders had altered the method of their trade from
barter to cash sale, and the resulting flight of gold and silver from
Russia to Central Asia grew rapidly, especially in the 1830s and

[66] M. K. Rozhkova, p. 207.
[67] Khanikoff, *Bokhara: Its Amir and Its People* (London, James Madden,
1845), p. 217.
[68] *Ibid.*, p. 218.
[69] Rozhkova, p. 56.

1840s, reaching almost 4 million rubles in 1863. Czarist authorities, who had been coveting Central Asia's natural gold since Peter the Great's time, felt strong pressure from Russian merchants to ban these exports of money, for the traders believed that such outflows to Bukhara and Khiva represented the single greatest obstacle to the development of Russian trade in that area.[70] These czarist businessmen felt that the greater liquidity acquired with Russian metallic rubles permitted Central Asians to deal actively with Russia's most feared competition—Iranian and Indian merchants selling English manufactures who demanded cash payments for their wares. In sum, Russian merchants seemed unable to succeed in Central Asia's open market, whereas the Bukharans, Khivans, and to a lesser extent Khokandians, so long as Central Asia remained independent, thrived on the rivalry they met in Nizhni Novgorod and other Russian cities.

SLAVES AND CAPTIVES

Frustrated beyond endurance by failures in trade competition and related diplomacy, the Russian leadership focused unhappy attention more and more upon one aspect in Central Asian commerce which, quite apart from its profitability, now humiliated czarist sensibilities for other reasons. This was the slave trade, the selection of which for censure by czarist officials gave a curious twist to affairs, for Russia itself, quite aside from serfdom and the institution of free peasants (*smerdy*), had had an ancient and persistent tradition of domestic slavery and foreign slave trading which lasted into the nineteenth century.

The princes of Russia's greatest early city, Kiev, had regarded traffic in human beings as "one of the prime sources of their wealth," and sold slaves to Byzantine and eastern buyers as well as Europeans at least as early as the ninth century. Slaves were valuable to the princes not only as commodities for export, but were of critical importance in supplying manpower for Russia's internal economy,[71] and they were procured by the Kievan rulers mainly

[70] *Ibid.*, pp. 46–47.
[71] Jerome Blum, *Lord and Peasant in Russia from the Ninth to the Nineteenth Century* (Princeton, Princeton University Press, 1961), pp. 49, 50.

from wars with other Russians or with nomadic Asians. Bulgar and Itil in that early time were true slave markets, and much later Kazan and Astrakhan inherited their function. In 1559, when Anthony Jenkinson ransomed and brought back to Ivan IV some Russians who had long been in Central Asian slavery, he forced the government of the czar to face publicly the well-known fact of foreign, Muslim enslavement of Russian nationals. The slave trade of sixteenth-century Russia had been made a state industry next in importance to the monopoly over export of silver and gold. Great numbers of slaves were auctioned in the cities of Qasimov, Pereiaslavl'-Riazansk, Nizhni Novgorod, and Sviiazhsk. One explicit limitation provided that ethnic Russians not be sold into foreign slavery and foreign Christians not be bought.[72]

By the seventeenth century Tobolsk and Astrakhan had become Russia's principal slave markets.[73] The czar, in exercising his monopoly over the export of slaves, then often granted licenses to Central Asian merchants permitting the purchase of slaves in Russia for the Khivan court.[74] At the same time, numbers of persons from other parts of Asia and probably Central Asia worked as bondsmen in Russia, whose slave population increased sharply in the seventeenth century, labor being particularly needed in the Russian steppes.[75] Although Russian traders ambushed Asians and sold them in Russia, suppliers of many of these slaves in Russia were Kazakhs or Bukharans themselves who brought captives such as Kalmyks and Siberian tribesmen to the Russian markets for sale.[76] A man's religious affiliation often remained the key to whether he could be sold into slavery abroad, either from north or south.

Peter the Great was reprimanded in 1706 for permitting the sale

---

[72] A. Chuloshnikov, "Torgovlia moskovskogo gosudarstva s Srednei Aziei v XVI–XVII vekakh," *Materialy po istorii uzbekskoi, tadzhikskoi i turkmenskoi SSR* (Leningrad, Izdatel'stvo Akademii Nauk SSSR, 1932), part 1, p. 69.

[73] *Ibid.,* pp. 86–87.

[74] "Chelobitnaia bukharskogo i khivinskogo gontsa Sheikh-Baby ts. Mikhailu Fedorovichu o razreshenii emu kupit' neskol'ko chelovek iasyria dlia khivinskikh sultanov," *Materialy po istorii uzbekskoi, tadzhikskoi i turkmenskoi SSR,* part 1, p. 196.

[75] Blum, pp. 271–73.

[76] *Materialy po istorii uzbekskoi, tadzhikskoi i turkmenskoi SSR,* part 1, pp. 380–85.

of Swedish prisoners to the Turks.[77] This suggests that a Bukharan ambassador's 1717 request for "nine Swedish girls" for his khan may not have gone unanswered.[78] Just as the Russian Orthodox found it possible to sell Christians of other sects to Muslim "infidels" for slaves, the Central Asian Sunnites were willing to enslave the Persian Muslims captured in Turkmen forays.

Though they may have been callous toward slavery's injustices, Central Asian rulers did not remain entirely indifferent to the fact that Russia's expanding frontiers were absorbing great numbers of Muslim Tatars, Bashkirs, and Nogays. But the realization that their co-religionists were falling under Christian control did not usually arouse Khiva and Bukhara to active protest in solidarity with those Muslims. Through diplomatic channels, however, the khans more than once countered Russia's repeated demands for release of Russians enslaved in Central Asia by raising the question of liberating the Muslim people under Russian hegemony, as this forceful note from Bukharan Khan Nadir Muhammad (r.1642–1645) to the czar shows.

You wrote us that we should set free and send to Russia the Russian people, prisoners, who are in Bukhara and our other cities, whether they have served out their work or not and who live in captivity, and we are informed about the fact that in your state by God's will there are many people of Nogay Mirzas and of their tribal areas (*ulus*) of the Muslim law; we are Muslims and the Nogays are Muslims too, and the Nogay Mirzas roamed alongside our ancestors and there was friendship and love between them, and we now ask you that you likewise order the seeking out and setting free into our state of the Nogay captives who are in your state, and when you . . . cause that beneficial act, we also shall have all the Russian prisoners in our state sought out and will free them.[79]

Moscow flatly rejected this proposed exchange, but Bukharans and Khivans at different times nevertheless endeavored with some success to secure the freedom of their subjects who, especially in the

---

[77] Florinsky, I, 375.

[78] Popov, p. 270.

[79] "Iarlik bukharskogo khana Nadir Mukhammeda ts. Mikhailu Fedorovichu o vstuplenii svoem na prestol i o zhelanii podderzhivat' po prezhnemu druzhestvennye snosheniia s moskovskim gosudarstvom," *Materialy po istorii uzbekskoi, tadzhikskoi i turkmenskoi SSR,* part. 1, p. 179.

eighteenth century, had been imprisoned or otherwise detained in Russia for long periods of time.

One such effort by the Bukharan Yadigar Mahlar Mugly Alim-oghli in 1730 brought a request from his sovereign that Russia free two Muslim nobles who had been incarcerated, according to the petition, for fifteen years.[80] The Russian government, moreover, by a ukase of January 28, 1767, specifically authorized the seizing of travelers from Central Asia to serve as hostages for Russian prisoners held there.[81] These methods may have given Russia its greatest single preconquest success in attempting to liberate Russians held in Khiva. In 1840, using a combination of diplomacy, economic sanctions, and military threats, the czarist government, represented by Muhammad Sharif Ait-oghli, a czarist Tatar military officer, persuaded the Khivan khan to release over 400 Russian captives and to issue a ban on trafficking in Russian prisoners. Tashkent, too, had disposed of all its Russian slaves by 1865, for none were found there when the czarist army finally took the city.[82]

At the very time when nineteenth-century Russian spokesmen expressed their public outrage over the enslavement of Russians in Central Asia, slavery was quietly continuing to be practiced in Siberia (until 1825)[83] and along the Russian-Kazakh frontier. There, the purchase of young Kazakh girls by Russian soldiers was sanctioned by an 1808 Russian law and such transactions occurred in Orenburg at least as late as 1818.[84] One of the many complications in this situation, especially between 1750 and 1850, grew out of an intensification of kidnapping and slave trading by the Kazakhs, Turkmens, Khivans, and Bukharans caused by declining economic health in general. As czarist officials applied tougher sanctions

---

[80] Zhukovskii, p. 68.

[81] "Review of the Causes that Led to the War with Khiva," p. 47.

[82] *Sbornik materialov . . . turkestanskago kraia*, IV (1914), 53–54; F. Azadaev, *Tashkent vo vtoroi polovine XIX veka* (Tashkent, Izdatel'stvo Akademii Nauk SSSR, 1959), p. 24.

[83] Blum, p. 274.

[84] *Kazakhsko-russkie otnosheniia v XVIII–XIX vekakh: Sbornik dokumentov i materialov* (Alma Ata, Izdatel'stvo "Nauka," 1964), p. 179, 183–84; "O rasprostranenii pravil o vodvorenii Kirgiztsev, i o pokupkie rossiiskim poddanym kirgizskikh dietei po vsei sibirskoi linii," *Polnoe sobranie zakonov Rossiiskoi Imperii s 1649 goda*, XXX (1830), 277–78; "O vodvorenie kochuiushchikh po blizosti orenburgskoi linii kirgiztsev," *ibid.*, pp. 276–77.

against Central Asia through confiscation of merchandise and arrest of traders found in Russia, this loss, coupled with an already difficult agriculture problem, drove the Central Asians even more urgently into slave trade and especially to the seizing of Russians along the frontiers, for they brought better prices than Persians and often could be ransomed.

Given this background for the tradition and practice of slavery and slave trading in both Central Asia and Russia, and remembering that serfdom continued in Russia until 1861, it is necessary to look beyond the question itself to understand why Russian officialdom at various times, beginning, it seems, late in the sixteenth or early in the seventeenth century, became so outraged when Russian subjects fell into bondage in Bukhara and especially in Khiva. Religious differences have already been suggested as one significant element in this Russian attitude. Humanitarian reasons have sometimes been cited. There is also no doubt that the loss of considerable manpower from Russia, besides being an affront to the feeling that a Russian ruler's subjects may never lawfully escape his control, constituted a definite economic loss which the empire could ill afford.

Finally, although those Russians sold through Central Asia's markets to India and beyond were nearly forgotten, the presence of Russians living in Central Asian slavery under what Russians considered to be a backward, perhaps inferior, people, hurt Russian self-confidence and damaged the esteem and status in the European community to which Russia aspired. This wounded vanity later reflected itself repeatedly in the words of Russian leaders who demanded that the Khivans and Bukharans be "taught a lesson," or be made to "come to their senses" through aggressive military action justified by the need to "punish" them for the enslavement of what was actually a relatively small number of Russians.[85]

The captives were peasants, in most cases, who were ordinarily not brutally treated unless they attempted to escape,[86] and who lived under conditions hardly worse and in some instances evidently far better than those experienced by the average Russian

[85] "Review of the Causes that Led to the War with Khiva," pp. 51–52.
[86] Muhammadjanov, and Ne"matov, p. 150.

in his home village. Regardless of the real motives, the subject of these slaves, first treated by both sides as an economic question, moved into the realm of religious significance and, almost simultaneously, diplomatic concein, finally furnishing, when diplomacy faltered, the provocation for war and conquest.

CULTURAL AND INTELLECTUAL EXCHANGES

As a corollary to economic or diplomatic initiatives, occasionally a khan would exhibit his curiosity about Western civilization or techniques. Moscow's ambassadors learned this when faced with questions about the religious practices, governmental procedures, social behavior, and even personal habits of Russian or European rulers.

Certainly through the sixteenth century and possibly even later, Central Asian achievements in literature, art, architecture, music, philosophy, theology, astronomy, medicine, mathematics, and education stood on levels as high or higher than those of Russia so that in these fields the capitals of the south had little to learn from Moscow. The Russians, nonetheless, limited themselves to sporadically collecting military intelligence and impressions, topographic or ethnographic observations of that extraordinary land, to whose genuine values they seemingly remained quite immune. Thus, beyond exchanging certain types of wearing apparel, for example, which became fashionable at one time or another in the two areas, or the momentary transmission of a taste for special food or drinks to a few wealthy men, no appreciable influence was exerted perhaps up to 1700, upon the general way of life of either country by the other. The Russians succeeded temporarily in making the Central Asians follow czarist diplomatic protocol (which they themselves had largely borrowed from the Golden Horde) in ceremonies and written communication, but this minor achievement was transitory. Until the actual physical confrontation around the early eighteenth century, neither society showed great interest in the literature or language of the other, and neither made much effort to learn about the other's way of life.

But when Russian ambassadors Boris and Semen Pazukhin enjoyed an audience with Khiva's Anusha Khan (r.1663–1687) in January,

1671, the potentate discussed at some length the amusements engaged in by the czar as well as the favorite royal sport in Khiva, hawks and hawking. The Pazukhins were later also exposed to Khivan indoor diversions when they banqueted at the khan's table out of golden dishes before watching and listening to nine entertainers who performed and sang songs using a book, very unusual for this time.[87]

In 1675 the Bukharan ruler attempted to acquaint himself with Western music, sending his ambassador Hajji Fariq to request an organ and organist from Moscow.[88] Bukhara, in return, a hundred years later exported Central Asian music to Russia, but encountered a very negative response when the citizens whose homes adjoined the house assigned to the Bukharan ambassador were outraged by the "noise" made in the Bukharans' often repeated practice sessions. The Muscovites insisted that these nine musical envoys along with the ambassador move out of that part of Moscow.[89]

In the sharing of ideas, the khans and czars long depended to an extraordinary extent upon the acquisition of views and information from chance visitors. As late as the nineteenth century when Russian envoy, Captain Nikiforov, was presented to Allah Quli (r.1825–1842), khan of Khiva, the khan spent a long time asking probing questions about Russian domestic affairs and made pointed queries regarding international relations between Turkey, Russia, England, China and other powers. Besides such general answers as Nikiforov was able to supply, Allah Quli received during the following exchange, in 1841, specific advice in connection with Khiva's contacts with England:

Khan. The rumor is that the English are prepared to occupy Balkh?
Nikiforov. I have not heard, but if they intend to do this, they will do it. . . .
Khan. You advise me to be at peace with them, but my friends Abbott

[87] Khanykov, pp. 310–11.

[88] Vladimir Antonovich Ulianitskii, "Snosheniia Rossii s Sredneiu Azieiu i Indieiu v XVI–XVII vv. Po dokumentam Moskovskago Glavnago Arkhiva Ministerstva Inostrannykh Diel," *Chteniia v Imperatorskom Obshchestvie Istorii i Drevnostei Rossiiskikh pri Moskovskom Universitetie*, book 3 for 1888 (1889), pp. 45–46.

[89] Shubinskii, pp. 523–25.

and Shakespear [English officers] told me not to make peace with the Russians.

Nikiforov. I repeat to you once more that both friendship and enmity with Englishmen are dangerous for you. These people seek to collect countries. In the last seventy-five years they have subdued up to 150,-000,000 people in India; . . . they took possession of Kabul and have come within almost 500 miles of Herat. These people are dangerous for Khiva.

Khan. But I shall defend Balkh.

Nikiforov. You will not succeed, but had better defend yourself and your people from English power by concluding a firm alliance with Russia.

Khan. Will the czar send troops to defend me?

Nikiforov. One word is sufficient for this, and in the message of His Highness the fact that you are an ally of Russia will be declared.[90]

Not only city Khivans but the Kazakh plainsmen stood to gain most of their knowledge of the new European life from such Russian reports about it. This information mainly concerned the techniques, innovations, and discoveries of the industrializing West. Thinking about this kind of modern communication to the undeveloped nomadic areas south of Russia, Friedrich Engels wrote a letter to Karl Marx in 1851 which is often quoted to justify past and present Russian measures in all Central Asia, including the settled south. Engels said: "For all its baseness and Slavonic dirt, Russian domination is a civilizing element . . . in Central Asia." Though its renown preceded it, the direct influence of such "civilization" had scarcely begun in the great centers of southern Central Asia by the time of Tashkent's fall.

DIPLOMATIC RELATIONS: THE KHANATES

If the written record of agreements and negotiations beginning around the turn of the eighteenth century, when politics again began to find a serious place in Central Asian-Russian diplomacy, did not correspond to the actual situation upon the ground or to the wishes of both attesting parties, the explanation lies to some degree in the discrepancy between Central Asian and Russian

[90] "Kratkii otchet o peregovorakh Kap. Nikiforova s khanom Alla Kulom, vedennykh v 1841 godu; 15 avgusta 1841 g.," *Sbornik materialov . . . turkestanskago kraia,* III (1912), 96–97.

recognition given to the validity of written documents, including treaties between governments or people. From this misunderstanding arose much of Russia's frustration over her diplomatic contacts with all Central Asians.

Earlier, setting aside the religious missions exchanged between Kiev and Bulgar, and Kiev and Khwarazm, the record of independent diplomatic relations began after the Mongols ceased to dominate either territory and when viable self-government functioned in both. In these initial stages of formal foreign relations, the very existence of diplomatic activity was largely a testimony to the personality of the rulers who sent envoys, for most kings and princes by necessity remained preoccupied with internal affairs.

Only a few outstanding Timurid figures like Abu Sa'id Khan (r.1451–1469) and Sultan Husayn Bayqara (r.1473–1506), or the Shaybanid Abdullah Khan, and their Russian counterparts, Ivan III (1462–1505) or Ivan IV, persistently advanced their countries' foreign service activity. Not accidentally, each of these strongmen excelled also either as the builder of stable government, a great patron of the arts, or the consolidator of empire. Ivan III sent an embassy which reached the court of Abu Sa'id Khan at Herat in 1464–65, and in 1490 a Timurid mission came to Moscow.[91] Around the 1480s Kazakh khans also apparently first entered into relations with Moscow.[92]

These inconclusive beginnings in the fifteenth century receded to insignificance in comparison with the genuine achievements in diplomatic activity from 1550 to 1599, when at least twenty-five embassies from Central Asia visited Russia, and the czar sent no fewer than six envoys, counting Anthony Jenkinson, to the khanates and Kazakhs.[93] Though sheer numbers of contacts did not tell the entire diplomatic story even then, the Central Asians, in particular

---

[91] V. Tizengauzen, "Pervoe russkoe posol'stvo v Kheratie," *Zapiski Vostochnago Otdieleniia Imperatorskago Russkago Arkheologicheskago Obshchestva,* I (1886), 30–31; *Istoriia uzbekskoi SSR,* vol. I, part 1 (1955), p. 434.

[92] Chuloshnikov, p. 62.

[93] *Polnoe sobranie russkikh lietopisei,* "Dopolneniia k nikonovskoi lietopisi," vol. XIII, part 2, pp. 313, 318, 385; Radzhabov, p. 23; *Istoriia kazakhskoi SSR* (Alma Ata, Izdatel'stvo Akademii Nauk Kazakhskoi SSR, 1957), I, 225; *Materialy po istorii uzbekskoi, tadzhikskoi i turkmenskoi SSR,* part 1, pp. 66, 400, 404–7.

Abdullah Khan, were undertaking against Russia no less than what would today be called a diplomatic-economic offensive, with the initiative clearly on the Central Asian side.

Russia first faced Central Asia over a real political issue arising from the czarist conflict with a Bukharan ally, the Siberian khanate, in the late sixteenth century. By then, Kuchum Khan had come under acute military and diplomatic pressure applied by both Russia and his Kazakh enemies, Haqq Nazar (r.1538–1580) and Tevekkel (r.1586–1598). Out of this early conflict of interests grew a rivalry for influence over the Kazakh nomads which almost continuously exacerbated the uneasy relations between southern Central Asia and Russia until the conquest, but the issue was never to be resolved through diplomacy. Because of internal dissensions among the Kazakhs, as well as strained ties between the khanates and the Kazakhs, leaders of the nomadic groups were unable to withstand the temptation, readily offered by Russia, to invite intervention by the northern power.

In 1594 the tension between Russia, the Siberian khanate, the Kazakhs, and Bukhara was again reaching a climax, when Tevekkel sent his envoy, Qul Muhammad, to Russia to request troops equipped with firearms with which to oppose the Nogays and Bukharans, and to gain the protection of the czar. The following year Moscow's emissary, Vel'iamin Stepanov, answered Tevekkel's inquiry when he delivered an official message (*gramota*) to the Kazakh leader which announced that the czar was not only sending troops with firearms to Samara so that the Kazakhs would fight Kuchum Khan and Abdullah Khan, but that Russia was taking Tevekkel and his people under its aegis. He added repeated warnings to them not to withdraw from that protection.[94]

Although Stepanov survived the grueling horseback trip to the Kazakh camp and back (Russia's first envoy to the Kazakhs in 1573 had been captured and killed by a relative of Kuchum Khan before reaching his goal), this diplomatic exchange accomplished little more than setting a precedent. Affairs at the end of the six-

[94] *Kazakhsko-russkie otnosheniia v XVI–XVIII vekakh: Sbornik dokumentov i materialov* (Alma Ata, Izdatel'stvo Akademii Nauk Kazakhskoi SSR, 1961), pp. 3–9.

teenth century in Russia, especially during the interregnum, soon
became so troubled, and the situation in Central Asia simultaneously
changed so dramatically, that official international relations between
the two for the time being became extremely difficult. That uncertainty may partly explain Boris Godunov's message of July,
1589, to Abdullah Khan peevishly insisting that communications
from Bukhara to Russia thereafter be prefaced with the czar's full
name and entire, lengthy, title, and that similar "respect" be shown
to Godunov himself.[95]

Another manifestation of the strained relations between Bukhara
and Russia at that time was the seemingly arbitrary detention by
Russia of two Central Asian envoys, Qutluq Adam and Isen Gildey,
together with their suites, for several years beginning in 1595.[96]

Except for a lone visit to Moscow from an unsuspecting Bukharan
ambassador, Adnash, in the first year of the new century, no formal
diplomatic contacts occurred between Central Asia and Russia
until the end of the interregnum. With Boris Godunov and Abdullah
Khan gone, relations appear to have begun anew around 1613 on
the old, commercial, basis, but very soon came an embassy whose
impact appears to have marked the path of all future relations of
both Bukhara and Khiva with Russia.

Bukhara's envoy, Adam Biy, delivered a dispatch from his ruler,
Imam Quli Khan (r.1611–1642), to the czar in which, among other
matters, he mentioned that Crimeans and Nogays had captured
a great many Russian prisoners and transported them to Bukhara,
where Imam Quli offered to turn the captives over to any reliable
Russian envoy whom the czar would send to receive them.[97] The
Russian government reacted promptly by returning a new ambassador to Bukhara with Adam Biy, although it had known since
Jenkinson's mission sixty years earlier that numbers of Russians
lived as slaves in the khanates. The quick response at this time was
no doubt caused by the fact that Imam Quli Khan had taken the
unusual course of raising the question of repatriation himself. In so
doing, regardless of Bukhara's later dubious performance on the

---

[95] *Sbornik Kniazia Khilkova* (St. Petersburg, 1879), pp. 487–88.
[96] *Materialy po istorii uzbekskoi, tadzhikskoi i turkmenskoi SSR* part 1, pp.
406–7.
[97] Zhukovskii, pp. 14–15.

matter, he earned Russia's lasting good will, and in Russian minds put the onus of slave trading permanently if not quite exclusively or accurately upon Khiva.

Beginning with the embassy of the long-time Russian foreign service officer, Ivan D. Khokhlov, to Bukhara in 1620, the freeing of enslaved Russians became, from the Russian side, one of the major, persistent themes of diplomacy, and the khans, who quickly recognized the usefulness of this new lever for collecting ransom, and especially for achieving their diplomatic aims with Moscow, used it mainly to extract trade advantages. In fact, for the Russians, too, trade then retained precedence over the question of prisoners, as the priority assigned to subjects in the government's instructions to Khokhlov shows.[98]

Ambassador Khokhlov experienced great difficulty in bringing back in 1622 only thirty-one Russians after trying all possible persuasion and resorting finally to cash purchase when diplomacy remained impotent. Painful harassments undergone by Khokhlov at Bukhara and Khiva, both in respect to the Russian prisoners and the daily problems of living in a foreign country, so offended the Russian government that after Khokhlov's return the czar ordered that Adam Biy and a Khivan envoy, Mahtumbay, also accompanying Khokhlov, along with another Khivan, be detained. This caused relations to be broken off for a decade after 1623.

This negative result of Khokhlov's trip was slightly redeemed when the ambassador agreed with the khan of Khiva to be employed as a safe conduct out of Central Asia for a Khivan prince. The prince, Awgan Mirza (d. 1648), son of Arab Muhammad I, served at the Muscovite court and there initiated to the czar a request that Russia provide troops in order to unseat a rival faction which had deposed his father. The prince offered, if successful against his brothers, to make himself subject to the czar.[99] This first Khivan appeal to the czar for help to intercede for one local political faction against another deep in Central Asia received no tangible, active support, but it has never been forgotten when the subject of Russia's "legal right" to rule Khiva arises.

[98] "Nakaz poslanniku Ivanu Khokhlovu, pri otpravlenii ego v Bukhariiu," *Sbornik Kniazia Khilkova*, pp. 426–27.
[99] Zhukovskii, p. 19.

Most of the seven Russian missions which preceded or followed Khokhlov in the seventeenth century gave attention to the freeing of Russian captives in the khanates, and all dealt with matters of trade as well as the formalities of protocol, delivering gifts of gerfalcons and other prized items to the khans, and transmitting or receiving official messages between the rulers. While the pace of Russian diplomatic efforts continued at less than their deliberate speed of the previous century, the khans in the seventeenth century were sending on the average more than one emissary every two years, between 1600 and 1699 posting over forty to the Russian domain.[100]

As the Russian ambassadors came back one by one throughout the century, their consistent failure to succeed as anything more than agents for disbursing funds to ransom a very limited number of enslaved Russians probably restricted the Russian activity and gradually forced a change upon the emphasis of the already small number of missions dispatched from Moscow. Especially with ambassador Ivan Fedot'ev in 1669–1670, primary importance began to be given to the collection of information valuable for military, economic (routes to India), and political purposes. Traders, travelers, and earlier diplomats had all provided their share of observations concerning the areas they visited. Diplomatic agents were not, of course, the only spies sent by Russia into that territory, but rarely were they Russians. Usually the Muslims living in the czar's empire were employed for this work, but they did not always prove to be such reliable operatives as could have been hoped. In the eighteenth century a Russian agent who visited Central Asia in the role of an eye doctor said, on this point, that:

the Tatars whom we send to Khiva and Bukhara for intelligence activity represent themselves just like those who trade there. They are received very hospitably, are given gifts, and duty [on imports] is remitted, so that when they return to Russia they depict and describe Khiva and Bukhara as the strongest states, although in reality they actually are insignificant.[101]

---

[100] *Materialy po istorii uzbekskoi, tadzhikskoi i turkmenskoi SSR* part 1, pp. 400–1, 406–11.

[101] [Blankennagl'], pp. 101–2.

As Russian spying intensified, overt official Russian approaches to and into Central Asia also multiplied dramatically to at least one a year and added an active military dimension in the eighteenth century, while the khans slowed down their initiatives in communication with the czarist government to about half the Russian frequency. In both the diplomatic and military arenas, czarist moves became much more aggressive, with Russian officials for the first time seeking opportunities to intervene directly in Central Asian affairs and to increase dissension there by arranging selective alliances which might aggravate tensions between local factions and thus weaken further the entire area's defensive equilibrium. Aside from standing on a strong position created by the planting of fortified detachments directly upon Central Asian soil, the changed diplomatic situation had come about mainly as a result of the economic decline in Central Asia itself, coupled with painful, deteriorating relations among the various local rulers.

The door to Russian intervention opened at the very beginning of the century, when the Khivan khan, Ishaq Agha Shah Niyaz (r.1694–1701), authorized his envoy, Dostek Bek Bahadur, to convey a message dated January 21, 1700, to Prince Boris A. Golitsyn, Peter the Great's close confidant, suggesting a treaty with Moscow. In this document the emissary raised the possibility of the Khivan potentate's becoming a subject of the czar and of entering into a mutual defense alliance, but he stressed mainly the khan's interest in trade arrangements, especially Russia's lifting of embargoes on the export of steel and lead and the import there of certain semiprecious stones, raw silk, and the like.[102]

The emphasis upon commercial matters should have warned Russian foreign officers that the clauses in the message concerning subjection and alliance had been inserted mainly as bait to encourage acceptance of the trade provisions and were therefore not to be taken at face value, but the czar, apprised of Khiva's internal problems and eager for greater empire, responded hastily to the khan's approach in his message of June 30, 1700. To Khan Ishaq Agha Shah Niyaz, ignoring any reference to trade, he wrote:

[102] *Materialy po istorii uzbekskoi, tadzhikskoi i turkmenskoi SSR,* part 1, p. 269.

"We the great sovereign, our czarist majesty . . . command you to be subject to us."[103] By the time Khiva, in 1703, responded to this royal pronouncement, a new khan sat upon the throne and all talk of governmental ties and alliance with Russia, except for remarks about peace and friendship, were forgotten, with the substance of the official Khivan dispatch predictably concentrating upon trade policy.[104]

Russia's diplomatic relations with the khanates traversed this tortuous path for the next 170 years. Czarist officials attempted unsuccessfully until the mid-nineteenth century to arrange formal treaties under which Russia would increase its influence, if not acquire control, over all or part of southern Central Asia.

In this traditional pattern of diplomacy, relations between Khokand and Russia were exceptional because they began with this youngest (founded c.1710) Central Asian khanate only toward the end of the eighteenth century with approaches in 1784 from and in 1796 to Tashkent, then a town of some 10,000 population,[105] which became incorporated in the khanate in 1815. Despite the fact that a Russian soldier murdered the Khokand envoy visiting Petropavlovsk in 1812,[106] until rivalry between the two countries for dominance of the Middle Horde Kazakhs became bitter, relations were not characterized by the rancor which had repeatedly soured the long experience of the older khanates with Russia.

Making up for lost time, however, the Khokandians by the 1830s became incensed over Russia's rebuff to their diplomats. Combining this with grievances concerning the plundering of Tashkent's caravans by Kazakhs supposedly subject to Russia, the building of Russian fortresses in the Besh Kazliq (Qarqarali) mountains and at Qaratal, and the Russian refusal to aid Khokand's fight against the Chinese in eastern Bukhara, Khokand cooled to the possibilities of diplomatic relations with Russia, though the Tashkent officials and Khokand too, occasionally, as in 1836 and 1841, attempted to

[103] *Ibid.*, p. 272.
[104] *Ibid.*, pp. 273–74.
[105] Iu. A. Sokolov, "Pervoe russkoe posol'stvo v Tashkente," *Voprosy istorii,* No. 3 (1959), pp. 166–77.
[106] Zhukovskii, p. 156.

harmonize the discord by communicating with border authorities.[107] From 1850, Khokand remained almost constantly at war with Russia in defense of southern Central Asia until after Tashkent fell, and the need for diplomatic relations then was soon obviated by the dissolution of the khanate.

The earliest formal treaties ratified between Russia and Central Asian governments finally came near the end of the khanates' independent life. The first was negotiated by Colonel G. I. Danilevskii with Khiva and the second arranged by Major Nikolai P. Ignat'ev with Bukhara. In the earlier treaty Rahim Quli Khan (r.1842–1845) of Khiva on December 27, 1842, approved an undertaking to cease overt or covert hostile acts against Russia, to avoid causing or conniving in plundering or brigandage of Russian subjects in the Kazakh or Turkmen plains or on the Caspian Sea, to outlaw holding Russian captives, to provide no asylum for rebels (mainly Kazakhs from Russian territory), and to grant improved trade conditions and security for merchants from Russia. In return Russia agreed to forgive only what it termed past insults, indignities, and caravan losses, and to continue previous trade arrangements for Central Asians.[108]

When Major Ignat'ev came to Khiva sixteen years later the Khivans had made no apparent effort to abide by the Danilevskii treaty, claiming that they had no copy of it, and refused to enter into a new agreement with Russia. Moving to Bukhara the Russian envoy succeeded in persuading the emir to endorse without modification an act of agreement, dated October 11, 1858, calling for Bukhara to free all Russian prisoners, to allow ready access of Russian boats to the Amu Darya, to permit a temporary Russian trade agent in Bukhara, and to improve trade conditions for Russian merchants.[109] Not worth the paper it was written on, this treaty, too, was completely ignored by the Central Asian signatory, and the diplomatic results of either mission had to be assessed by the Russians at zero. The large suites escorting Danilevskii and especially Ignat'ev excited Khivan suspicion, but collected a con-

---

[107] *Sbornik materialov . . . turkestanskago kraia*, III (1912), 81–82, 89–92.
[108] *Ibid.*, IV (1914), 82–84.
[109] Zhukovskii, pp. 153–54.

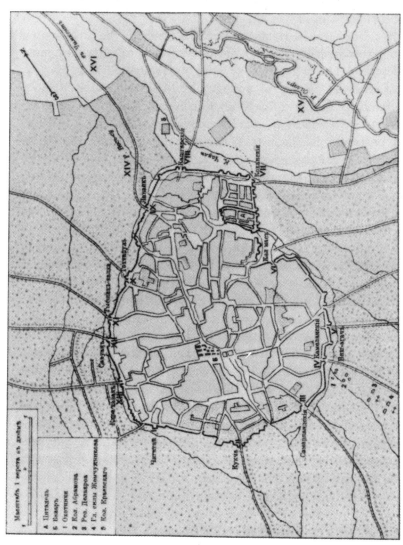

FIGURE 1.3   Tashkent, 1865. A: citadel; B: bazaar. 1, 2, 3, 4, 5: Russian assault forces. Gates: I. Chighatay; II. Kokcha; III. Samarkand; IV. Kámalan; V. Besh Aghach; VI. Kalmas; VII. Khokand; VIII. Kashgar; IX. Labzak; X. Takhtapul; XI. Tiship Kapka; XII. Sauwan; XIII. Qara Saray (Qara Qazaq). Watercourses: XIV. Bos Su; XV. Salar. XVI. Road to Chimkent. Scale 2/3 mile.

siderable quantity of intelligence useful to the czarist army. Also, several informative descriptive studies regarding Central Asia came from the military leaders of these missions as well as specialists who accompanied them such as V. V. Grigor'ev, Th. Basiner, P. I. Lerkh, E. Kilevein, and K. V. Struve.[110]

The Central Asian governments, on the other hand, up to this point presumably were satisfied that their diplomats invariably came out on top, as indeed they had in blocking the attainment of Russian diplomatic aims and in trade matters, Central Asia's only area of genuine interest. Czarist diplomacy with Central Asia fared no worse, however, than similar relations between the three khanates, which could not as late as the crucial 1860s accomplish even a mutual assistance pact against their common Russian enemy, though Khokand desperately sought in 1864 to engage Khiva's and Turkey's help to save Tashkent and the khanate.[111]

DIPLOMATIC RELATIONS: THE NOMADS

Contacts with Russia in political matters signified, throughout Karakalpakiia, Kazakhstan, Kirgiziia, and Turkmeniia, much more than they did in the khanates. Onslaughts from the Dzungarians flooding in from the east created the principal force driving Central Asia's nomads to secure ties with Russia in the first half of the eighteenth century. Already feeling the military pressure applied by new Russian advance posts like Omsk, Zhelezinsk, Iamyshevsk, and Semipalatinsk, and divided by their own internecine struggles, parts of the Kazakh "hordes" (*jüz*) appealed to Russia as early as 1716–19 for protection or acceptance as subjects,[112] and especially for military aid against the Dzungarian invaders.[113] Because of Russian preoccupation with events in Khiva and Persia, they received no appreciable diplomatic or military response to these requests at that time. Nor did the overtures of Karakalpak Khan Ebdul

[110] *Obzor russkikh puteshestvii i ekspeditsii v Sredniuiu Aziiu* (Tashkent, Izdatel'stvo SAGU, 1956), part 2, pp. 32–36.

[111] Muhammad Riza Agahiy, *Shakhid-i iqbal* (manuscript of the Aziatskii Muzei #590 od [S572], leaves 18a–19a), cited by V. V. Bartol'd, *Sochineniia,* vol. II, part 2, p. 403.

[112] L. Kostenko, *Sredniaia Aziia i vodvorenie v nei russkoi grazhdanstvennosti* (St. Petersburg, Izdatel'stvo Bazunova, 1870), p. 106.

[113] *Istoriia kazakhskoi SSR,* I (1957), 229, 235, 599.

Muzafar Devlet Saadet Ishim Muhammad in 1722 regarding peace, friendship, and protection, receive more definite answer.[114]

These approaches, together with contacts made by the Kazakhs in 1726 and 1730 eventually produced an affirmative reply from Russia when, on October 10, 1731, an oath of allegiance was administered to Abulkhayr Khan (r.1716–1748), acting for his Little Horde (*Kishshi Jüz*), in which the Kazakh khan promised to protect Kazakh-Russian borders, defend trade caravans in the plains, provide troops when needed, and pay tribute in wild animal skins. In return, Russia undertook to confirm in his tribe a perpetual line of khans and to build a fort at the confluence of the Or and Yaik (Ural) rivers for his defense.[115]

Also at the end of 1731 much of Semeke Khan's Middle Horde took such an oath to the czar. This was repeated by other Middle Horde sultans in 1734, and in 1740 by Abulmambet Khan and by Ablay Khan, who also, from 1757 to 1781, became subject simultaneously to the Ts'ing (Manchu) empire.[116] The Great Horde (*Ulu Jüz*) under Jolbaris Khan followed suit in 1734 and 1738 by asking Russia to accept them as subjects, but only a small portion of that "horde" actually took the oath through their representatives at Orenburg in 1742. Like the Kazakhs, some Karakalpaks swore allegiance in 1731 and 1734 and later sent an embassy to Russia, where in 1743 St. Petersburg again accepted the Karakalpaks as subjects.[117]

Stimulated by this flurry of diplomatic interaction in the plains, Russian personnel were moved to use the Kazakh vassals to involve themselves actively in the internal affairs of Khiva as well, where domestic strife terminating with the conquest by Persian ruler Nadir Shah (r.1736–1745) had temporarily left the throne

[114] "Gramota karakalpakskogo khana Ishim Mukhammeda k Petru Pervomu. Stat'i, ot karakalpakskikh poslantsev Dzhanbek Bogadyria s tovarishchi predlozhennye," *Materialy po istorii Karakalpakov* (Moscow-Leningrad, Izdatel'stvo Akademii Nauk SSSR, 1935), pp. 170–171.

[115] Kostenko, p. 107; I. Kraft, "Priniatie kirgizami russkago poddanstva," *Izviestiia Orenburgskago Otdiela Imperatorskago Russkago Geograficheskago Obshchestva* No. 12 (1897), pp. 1–59.

[116] N. G. Appollova, *Ekonomicheskie i politicheskie sviazi Kazakhstana s Rossiei v XVII–XIX v.* (Moscow, Izdatel'stvo Akademii Nauk SSSR, 1960), pp. 80–94.

[117] *Istoriia uzbekskoi SSR*, vol. I, part 2, p. 62.

vacant. To it in 1740 the Russians tried to elevate their nominal subject, Kazakh Khan Abulkhayr. Accompanying Abulkhayr Khan when he entered Khiva were the Russians Dmitri Gladyshev, Muravin, and Nazimov.

Muravin proceeded on to Nadir Shah's camp to inform the shah that he "should surrender to Abulkhayr the town of Khiva in the name of His Imperial Majesty, the khan elected [Abulkhayr] being a faithful subject of the Russian Empire." [118] The Khivans themselves removed the problem from the hands of the Kazakh puppet and both Russian and Persian interventionists by frightening Abulkhayr Khan and his son Nurali away, murdering Nadir Shah's candidate, Tahir, and selecting a series of very short-term rulers between 1741 and 1747, when another Kazakh, Kaip (r.1747–1757), took power with the support of dominant local factions. Russia once more tried to meddle in Kazakh-Khivan affairs in 1753 when envoy Ia. Guliaev attempted unsuccessfully to conciliate Nurali Khan (r.1748–1786) of the Kazakh Little Horde, with Kaip in Khiva.

The apparent harmony in St. Petersburg's relations with the westernmost Kazakhs was disturbed in the 1770s when Emel'ian Pugachev easily found allies in the Kazakh "hordes" for his revolt against Catherine the Great. Kazakh sultans Dosali and Nurali, confused by the events in Russia and uncommitted in their own minds to earlier allegiances, notified Pugachev before the end of 1773, in response to his "ukase," of their support for him. Dosali, in addition, permitted his son Said Ali Sultan to join Pugachev's headquarters, and promised additional military aid to the rebels.[119]

To bring the unruly Kazakhs under control of Russia after the Pugachev trauma the czarist government temporarily departed somewhat from further attempts at such alliances and entertained a scheme for buying influence in the Kazakh plains by paying salaries to sultans loyal to Russia. Moreover, czarist officials gained authority over the office of the khan by allowing a sizable stipend to the incumbent in return for his willingness to reside in Orenburg, where the election of such khans was easy for the Russians

[118] "Review of the Causes that Led to the War with Khiva," p. 38.
[119] *Kazakhsko-russkie otnosheniia v XVIII–XIX vekakh* (1964), pp. 18–19.

to manage. Khans from each "Horde" accepted these conditions in the 1780s.[120]

Russian influence among the Kazakhs became greater yet when an entirely new Kazakh "horde" was brought into being with the help of the Russians at the beginning of the nineteenth century. In 1801 Sultan Bokey Nuraliqan-uli (d. 1815), one of Nurali Khan's sons, took action to split off some of the contending Little Horde tribes and establish himself in another area. The sultan's petition to Emperor Paul I for permission to migrate northward onto the land between the Volga and Ural rivers vacated by the recent Kalmyk flight gained quick consent.

The government was convinced, quite rightly, that placing this *Bokey Jüz,* or Inner Horde, as the Russians called it, in such close proximity to the czarist lines surrounding it on several sides, would make the nomads easy to keep under surveillance. The separation of this group also would weaken the parent Little Horde and make it more vulnerable to Russian approaches. Thus, by 1812 the czarist government had named Sultan Bokey khan of his "horde," but the office of khan lasted only until 1845, when the Russians abolished the title, as they had earlier for the Middle Horde in 1822 and the Little Horde in 1824.

Taming the Kazakh khans and some sultans by bribery did not settle their relations with Russia to the czar's satisfaction, however, and diplomacy gave way to the combination of tough negotiation and military force, already described, prevalent throughout the first half of the nineteenth century. Under this physical pressure, in 1819, 1823, and again in 1846, dozens of sultans, biiys, and other dignitaries representing the last free Kazakhs, the Great Horde, affixed their seals on oaths of allegiance to Russia, the czar's acceptance of which making them, in Russian eyes, subjects of the empire.[121]

[120] "Arkhiv Grafa Igel'stroma," *Russkii arkhiv,* XI (1886), 356; Alan W. Fisher, "The Turkic Peoples of the Russian Empire and the Administration of Catherine II," (New York, Columbia University master's thesis, Faculty of Political Science, 1964), pp. 87–91.

[121] *Kazakhsko-russkie otnosheniia v XVIII–XIX vekakh* (1964), pp. 207, 214, 319–22.

Two major consequences of this view followed quickly after one another. First, the new "subjects" like Kenesari Qasim-uli, who now refused to bow to Russian authority, became known as "rebels." Persistent rebellion of course had to be put down, and government officials with the help of the army responded accordingly. But the Kazakhs' attitude differed radically from the Russian. Many nomads showed in practice that pacts made by ancestors or associates were not felt to be binding on their successors or colleagues. Even those Kazakhs who honored the previous agreements with Moscow or St. Petersburg, agreements which they understood to guarantee their integrity, believed with reason that the Russians had breached the treaties by continued territorial encroachments and increased interference in Kazakh life.

The second result of the divergence in Russian and Kazakh comprehension of the agreements, then, was outright resistance by heretofore more or less friendly Central Asians. In this tense situation Russia's leaders and diplomatic corps stubbornly clung to the idea that their eighteenth-century links still bound the Kazakhs to the czar, though this resolve nearly collapsed when caravans continued to be harassed and raided, Russians taken captive, and whole groups of tribes demonstrated their independence by moving from assigned pastures. The denouement of the impending tragedy came on the Kazakh battlefield rather than in the embassies, as has been seen.

In the czarist bureaucracy, administratively, in 1821, affairs of the Middle Horde Kazakhs had passed from the jurisdiction of the Russian Ministry of Foreign Affairs into control of the West Siberian Omsk oblast. The Inner Horde, in turn was transferred in 1838 to control of the Ministry of State Property. A large part of the Middle Horde was subordinated in 1854 to general government control, then in 1859 the Little Horde entered the concern of the Ministry of the Interior, and in 1863 the Great Horde Kazakhs were shifted from the Ministry of Foreign Affairs to the responsibility of the Western Siberian Military Command, with the Kazakhs of the Sir Darya line going over to the jurisdiction of the

Ministry of War finally in 1864.[122] Thus, on the eve of the last Russian drive to Tashkent, with the Kazakhs still protesting, their problem had in the main been transformed by the Russians from an external to a domestic concern.

Some Kirgiz tribes, too, with the approach of Russian armies toward the Issik Kol region in the 1840s, began to ask for czarist protection, which in several instances was promised in return for subjection to Russian rule. This procedure continued with various exposed groups while Russian lines moved forward in the 1850s and 1860s. By 1864 a Russian fort stood on the shores of Issik Kol, and the northern Kirgiz of the Issik Kol and Tien Shan regions had ratified written oaths of allegiance to the czar.[123]

Unlike the Kazakhs and Kirgiz, the nomadic Turkmens had not suffered much pressure from Slavic invaders because Turkmen lands were mainly unattractive desert and because the Turkmens before 1865 had seldom found themselves in unavoidable confrontation with Russian troops. Foreign relations between small groups of Turkmens and the Russians began to touch on trade and protection in the seventeenth century, but one portion, the Mangishlak tribes, disturbed by some of the main Russian thrusts toward the khanates and simultaneously under heavy demands from Khivan and Bukharan allies or masters, in 1745 sent a deputation to St. Petersburg to request Russia's patronage.[124] This happened when the Kazakh khans strengthened their influence at Khiva in the mid-eighteenth century and also extended control over the Mangishlak Turkmens by appointing Pirali, another son of the Kazakh Russian vassal Nurali Khan, the Mangishlak ruler. These Turkmen tribes then served Russia by launching punitive actions in pursuit of the Kalmyks fleeing toward Dzungaria in 1771 and against Pugachev's bands in 1773–1774, as Pirali acknowledged in a letter to Catherine the Great.[125]

[122] *Ocherk istorii Ministerstva Inostrannykh Diel, 1802–1902* (St. Petersburg, Ministerstvo Inostrannykh Diel, 1902), pp. 92, 160–61.

[123] *Istoriia Kirgizii* (Frunze, Kirgizskoe Gosudarstvennoe Izdatel'stvo, 1963), I, 334–49; T. R. Ryskulov, *Kirgizstan* (Moscow, Gosudarstvennoe Sotsial'no-Ekonomicheskoe Izdatel'stvo, 1935), pp. 27–30.

[124] *Istoriia turkmenskoi SSR* (Ashkhabad, Izdatel'stvo Akademii Nauk Turkmenskoi SSR, 1957) vol. I, part 1, pp. 495–96.

[125] "Proshenie turkmenskogo khana Pirali Ekaterine II, 9 maia 1775 g.," *Krasnyi arkhiv,* II (1939), 251–52.

Although the Turkmens reportedly again took an oath of allegiance to Russia in 1791, the pact had no visible effect upon later relations between the parties involved.[126] Diplomatic representatives from this same section of Turkmeniia appeared in the Russian capital again in 1802, 1811–12, 1813–14, and 1824, and likewise asked local Russian frontier officials in 1798 and 1835 for protection from the czar against assorted Central Asian or Persian enemies.[127] Paradoxically, while Turkmens were petitioning the czar for protection, Russian traders were issuing repeated public demands for stern measures against the Turkmens, who harassed Russian caravans and fishermen. No permanent agreements were reached between the Turkmens and the Russians on any important diplomatic question until the peace treaties imposed by Russian arms, two decades after 1865.

GOVERNMENT POLICIES

In general, the policies of Central Asian governments toward Russia since Timur in the late fourteenth century seem to have remained essentially passive except in connection with trade. Because of the great expanses separating settled areas, and owing to the extremes of climate and the forbidding deserts in Central Asia, Muslim leaders had always been able to put great trust in their natural stronghold. Furthermore, a kind of apathy resulting from low physical vitality attributable to disease, drug addiction, malnutrition, and other causes accorded with an inclination to accept the unmanageable international situation as something preordained by God's will. Therefore, though religious zeal and fierce attachment to political independence occasionally stimulated the khans to act against the Christian invader, their position remained, almost to the end, mainly defensive and continuative. Outside of commerce, to which they devoted energy and skill, if their fragmentary and sporadic official actions can be collectively spoken of as a policy, it must be labeled as an intention to react rather than initiate.

Nor does the reverse of this attitude precisely define Russia's

[126] "Review of the Causes that Led to the War with Khiva," p. 58.

[127] *Istoriia turkmenskoi SSR*, vol. I, part 2 (1957), pp. 497–98; "Review of the Causes that Led to the War with Khiva," p. 57.

Central Asian position. It too, betrayed some defensive traits which were seen particularly in the repeated reliance upon the idea of employing buffer states as at Qasimov or Tashkent to shield Russia from Central Asian adversaries. One of the overriding aims of government policy when Russia's frontier had reached Kazakh territory became the securing of a borderline between the empire and Central Asia, and the annoying necessity to defend that new frontier constantly against the Kazakhs throughout the eighteenth century seemed only to intensify czarist emphasis upon a policy to fix southern boundary lines.

Russia's push to the southeast, however, not only required new decisions, but was also a product of previous policy. The cause of this earlier aggressive movement has been explained as a kind of blind inevitability, an irrepressible urge to expand, primarily to the east, rooted in the predatory Cossack spirit, Russian merchant-adventurism, and messianism connected with Moscow's Orthodox heritage from Byzantium.[128]

Possibly the reasons were simpler. Russia had grown strong as her Central Asian neighbors became enfeebled. Exploiting this accident, the czars, like European empire builders of the time, were sucked into a power vacuum where justification for expansion, if any was needed, seemed to be provided by alleged provocations from the Central Asians or supposed superiority of Russian civilization.

It is striking that the parallel American invasion of western Indian and Mexican territory, which occurred exactly when Russia moved into Central Asia in force, also was spoken of as inevitable, as an expression of "manifest destiny." This familiar rhetoric claimed that the United States, by expanding into the sparsely populated, undeveloped areas of the Southwest and driving out tyrannical, inefficient, and corrupt Mexican governors or ignorant chieftains—replacing them with good (European-American) leaders—would obviate the threat of British intervention there, acquire economic advantages, protect American traders wandering in the area, and even solve some problems of slavery. In both the Russian and

[128] Geoffrey Wheeler, *The Modern History of Soviet Central Asia* (London, Weidenfeld and Nicolson, 1964), pp. 49, 59, 64.

American expansion, although there were differences, it would have been too honest to state that in those imperialistic days the strong stole openly from the weak. No casuistry relying upon presumed or real advantages to the robbed and conquered could alter the facts.

The purpose attributed to nineteenth-century czarist policy was, besides countering British competition, not so much to snatch away advantages from Central Asian merchants, as to achieve, as the primary aim of their efforts, "trade equality." [129] To this end, felt the government, peace and order were required in the plains and deserts surrounding the khanates to provide free access to Khiva and Bukhara. To attain that goal the Turkmens, Kazakhs, and Kirgiz had to be subjugated, and the Khivans, in particular, had to be chastised.[130] Such a policy of conquest, aimed above all at Khiva, had been urged by Russian diplomats from Peter the Great's time. One Russian observer visiting the khanate had already confidently estimated that 5,000 troops could and should "take possession of Khiva." [131]

The Russian government began to build mechanisms to deal specifically with Central Asian affairs when, in 1782, it created the Orenburgskaia Pogranichnaia Ekspeditsiia, later called the Orenburg Border Commission. Next, a royal committee of ministers met in 1819 to discuss the intentions of the khan of Khiva and the Kazakh plundering of caravans. Born of these conferences, a new Asiatic Committee (Aziatskii Komitet) formed by the czar's ukase in January, 1820, included the ministers of foreign affairs, finance, and interior, and the military chief of staff. Later, M. M. Speranskii, former governor general of Siberia, was seated, and the director of the Asiatic Department (Asiatskii Departament), founded in 1819 within the Ministry of Foreign Affairs, became the committee's chairman. This group of influential officials convened frequently between 1820 and 1824, devoting its main attention not

[129] V. V. Grigori'ev, "Russkaia politika v otnoshenii k Srednei Azii. Istoricheskii ocherk," *Sbornik gosudarstvennykh znanii* (St. Petersburg, 1874), I, 233–61.
[130] "Review of the Causes that Led to the War with Khiva," pp. 37, 51, 79.
[131] [Blankennagl'], pp. 102–4.

so much to the question of whether or why the Kazakh hordes should be subjugated, but of how they could promptly be put under Russian authority. In later years, as the Kazakhs succumbed to military force, the Asiatic Committee became less and less active until, in 1847, the year Kazakh "rebel" Kenisari Qasim-uli was killed, the committee ceased to function, its main problems solved.[132]

The Asiatic Department, in contrast, grew stronger and enlarged its scope of external affairs steadily. Starting in 1819 with a mandate to focus primarily upon the Asians subject to Russia or with whom the empire was conducting relations, the department at first lacked authority for dealing with essentially political matters. Then in 1846 all correspondence concerning Asian affairs was concentrated in its hands, though in 1856 the agency was relieved of jurisdiction over Kazakh relations.[133] A series of formal proposals originating from within the Orenburg Border Commission, the Asiatic Department, and the Asiatic Committee, or delivered to them from specialists in Central Asian affairs, usually military officers, contained projects for solving Russia's "Central Asian problem." By 1846 this was a question mainly touching upon relations with the khanates, but even at the beginning of the century the plans almost invariably concluded with a call for the use of force against southern Central Asia.

One of the most characteristic "position papers" came from Major General Aleksander I. Verigin, prepared for Alexander I and submitted officially to Nicholas I in 1826. Entitled "A Brief Elucidation of the Ideas of Major General Verigin about the Necessity to Occupy Khiva as the Sole Means for Widening and Conducting Our Trade Safely in Central Asia," the document drew from General Ivan Dibich, then chief of staff, an added endorsement advocating further measures "in order to curb the insolent deeds of the Khivans." So, while Verigin was admitting that Russian industry and trade could not, because of low standards and inefficiency, compete successfuly either at home or in Europe against European competition and therefore required for its survival a captive

---

[132] *Ocherk istorii Ministerstva Inostrannykh Diel, 1802–1902,* pp. 90–91.
[133] *Ibid.,* pp. 90, 127, 160.

market—specifically Central Asia under Russian mastery—Dibich was supplying a revealing, irrational note which typified Russian behavior toward the khanates. Verigin, too, had spoken anxiously of Russia's declining reputation abroad and the need "to support the prestige of Russia" which had suffered from the plundering of Russian caravans in the Kazakh plains.[134]

To improve Russia's international image, then, a renewed decision to strike Khiva was taken by the czar and his advisers in March, 1839. Described secretly as an expedition "for the purpose of compelling the khan by force of arms to deliver up all the Russians and to establish complete security for the Russian caravan trade," [135] preparations were at first awkwardly disguised as the sending of a scientific expedition to the Aral Sea, and then on November 24, 1839, as czarist troopers tramped forward, the Orenburg Corp Commander announced: "By order of His Majesty the Emperor, I am going to march with a portion of the troops under my command against Khiva. Khiva has for many years tried the long-suffering patience of a strong and magnanimous Power, and has at length brought down upon herself the wrath which her hostile conduct has provoked." [136]

Mobilization to punish Khiva's sins was intended to culminate in the replacement of the khan by a "trustworthy Kazakh sultan," [137] but when this campaign, too, ended in disaster, the debacle added military relations to the czarist list of unsatisfactory connections between Central Asia and Russia. Stunned by this setback to their strongest efforts to gain the upper hand in Central Asia, Russian policy makers in the foreign ministry momentarily lost confidence in the ability of their army to solve international problems between Khiva and Russia. Displaying some confusion concerning the country's immediate and long-range objectives in Central Asia, Russia's minister of foreign affairs in 1841 personally

[134] [Aleksandr I. Verigin], "Kratkoe izlozhenie myslei gen.-maiora Verigina o neobkhodimosti zaniat' Khivu, kak edinstvennoe sredstvo dlia rasprostraneniia i privedeniia v bezopasnost' nashei torgovli v Srednei Azii," *Sbornik materialov . . . turkestanskago kraia,* II (1912), 6–7.

[135] "Review of the Causes that Led to the War with Khiva," p. 67.

[136] *A Narrative of the Russian Military Expedition to Khiva, under General Perofski in 1839,* p. 126.

[137] "Review of the Causes that Led to the War with Khiva," p. 69.

ordered the czarist ambassador leaving for Khiva, as the chief aim
of the mission, to warn the khanate against renewing hostile acts
and caution the Central Asians to guarantee the security and wel-
fare of Russian subjects. No sooner had these aims received highest priority than the minister changed his emphasis by writing to
the same diplomat: "the chief aim of your errand is not so much
the gaining of material benefits for Russia as the strengthening of
trust in her by Khiva . . . you must be guided by this aim in all
your acts as the most important condition for the future political
influence of Russia on the khanates of Central Asia neighboring
her." [138]

Here, although talk about the righteousness of Russia's cause
against the khanates continued to be heard in public and private,
the minister struck a conciliatory note which suggested that czarist
officials had gained from events of the 1840s more respect for the
difficulties of reaching and overturning the government there. This
somewhat more reasonable tone, downgrading the primacy of
commerce in external affairs, and probably more moderate because
trade had been momentarily discarded as the aim of such policy,
continued to characterize the thinking of the foreign ministry up
to 1865, and perhaps later.

That the views of the foreign minister did not prevail in Russian
government councils on this question was amply demonstrated by
the record of czarist military actions in Central Asia from 1846
up to 1865 and the reasons, connected with improving trade, given
for those campaigns. Colonels and generals, with sufficient backing
from someone in the czar's groups of advisers, took the managing
of Central Asian policy into their own hands by converting each
additional reconnaisance patrol and campaign into the necessity for
another, and in this manner blocked out a functioning, piecemeal
policy for the area. This method was based on the doctrine of the
physically possible.

Contemporary observers remarked that the Central Asian campaigns had at least provided idle Russian generals with something

[138] Graf Nessel'rod, "Vitse-Kantsler Kapitan Nikiforovu; 19 fevralia 1841 g.
No. 446. (Sekretno; instruktsiia)," *Sbornik materialov . . . turkestanskago
kraia*, III (1912), 13, 24.

to do, or that militaristic Russia, in Central Asia as elsewhere, carried on a policy of aggrandizement. Although foreign commentators at the time remained uncertain whether this particular Russian conquest had come about through an opportunistic seizure of available territory or a long, traditional policy of aggression, the result, they admitted, was the same.[139]

For Central Asians the succession of battlefield defeats leading up to Russia's final drive on Tashkent imposed a humiliation which they had never before suffered at the hands of a European power. Moreover, the military realization of Russian aims in Central Asia was inflicting scars upon the relationships between the invaders and invaded which would probably never disappear. Though Tashkent was to be famed neither as the first prize in Central Asia nor the last, the Russians themselves believed that the entire area's destiny rested upon the fate of Tashkent. The town acquired from this attitude an importance disproportionate to its real significance for the region as a cultural, economic, or political center. The idea of the capture or control of the town as a keystone for Russian policy became lodged so firmly in czarist thinking, however, that had Russian armies been stopped short of Tashkent a century ago the whole of southern Central Asia might have remained free of direct Russian rule to this day.

E. A.

[139] MacGahan, p. 425.

2

People, Languages, and Migrations

Turkistan is appropriately named because the Soviet part (which is called Central Asia today), along with the Chinese portion, comprise one of the most compact and unified major Turkic language areas in the world. Ethnologically and linguistically, the entire area east of the Caspian Sea as far as the Altay mountains and the Lob desert separating the Taqlamaqan from the Gobi (roughly between latitude 35° and 50°N), may well be called Turkistan. The term, nevertheless, generally designates the central two-thirds of this vast area.

In historical sources, however, the name appears at first more or less with reference to the outer prairie areas northwest of the sedentary regions of the upper Sir and Amu Darya systems, to those near the great mountains of Central Asia plus other regions nearby, and to the large oasis region of Khwarazm (Khiva) immediately south of the Amu Darya delta. With the growing number of Turkic tribes who continued to arrive from the northeast and east, the Turkification of Central Asia also increased, and naturally the term "Turkistan" assumed an ever larger connotation. But the word was never clearly defined, and its usage did not always accord with the extent of the territory actually inhabited by Turkic-speaking people. Thus, when the term "Turkistan" was employed by Emperor Babur (1483–1530), what he generally had in mind were the prairies or plains of Central Asia extending northwest, north, and northeast beyond the settled, irrigated areas and the big cities. He had in view regions which today form a considerable section of Kazakhstan, the largest Turkic republic of the Soviet Union.

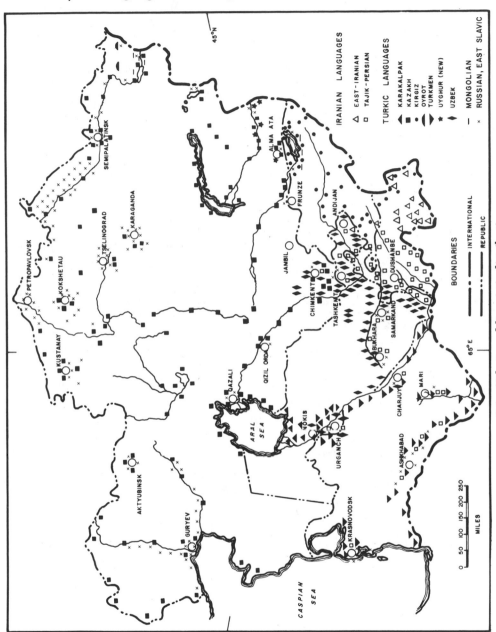

FIGURE 2.1 Ethnic and linguistic distribution.

GEOGRAPHICAL DISTRIBUTION OF TURKIC LANGUAGES

The Turkic languages of Central Asia are, proceeding from west to east, Turkmen, Uzbek, Kirgiz, and New Uyghur, and, north of these, Kazakh and Karakalpak.

Turkmen is found in the area bounded by the Caspian in the west, the Kopet Dagh in the south, the Amu Darya in the east and northeast, and the Amu Darya's ancient river bed to the Caspian, the Uzboi, in the north. This is also the territory of Soviet Turkmenistan. As nine-tenths of this is desert—the famous Qara Qum—the majority of the Turkmens live in the south, along the northern slopes of the Kopet Dagh, where there is one small oasis after another interspersed with ruined sites, some of them of considerable size. Turkmens also live scattered in the adjacent parts of Persia, in Anatolia north of the Caucasus near Stavropol, in Syria, and in Egypt.

Their northeastern and eastern neighbors are the Uzbeks, the most compact groups of whom live in the cities of Uzbekistan, in the Farghana Valley on the upper Sir Darya between the towering ranges of the Tien Shan and the Alay, and all along the western ends of the Tien Shan beyond the oasis of Tashkent, the capital of the Uzbek SSR, further in the central and lower Zarafshan valleys down to the Amu Darya. Here is Samarkand, the old capital of the realm of Chaghatay and the Timurids, and of Uzbekistan in the first period of Soviet rule. Farther down, no longer reached by the water of the Zarafshan, is Bukhara.

Uzbeks live also on the lower Amu Darya, on the left side of its delta, and in and around the cities of Urganch and Khiva, and south of the Zarafshan Valley and the Hisar range, in the valleys watered by tributaries of the Amu, as well as west of the Kafirnihan Valley which belongs to Tajikistan. South of the Amu Darya, in the adjacent part of Afghanistan, Uzbeks constitute a not insignificant fraction of the local population, so that the plains between the Hindu Kush and the Amu Darya are correctly called Afghan Turkistan. The boundaries of the Uzbeks in the Farghana Valley show a great many indentations, as there are many valleys with Uzbek populations bordering closely on Tajik- and Kirgiz-speaking people, often in one and the same valley, usually in neighboring ones. This can always be observed with languages and dialects in high mountain regions, the classical example being the Caucasus, although the Himalayas and the Alps do not lack these features either.

East and northeast of the Uzbek language area follows that of the Kirgiz, which is a language of a typical retreat area, that of the high mountains and deep valleys of the eastern Alay and the greatest part of the western Tien Shan. Kirgiz is spoken from the Chatqal range of the western Tien Shan and the central Talas Valley in the west to the source valleys of the Tekes and Khuyilju, immediately west of the Khan Tengri and Mount Pobeda, the highest of the entire Tien Shan system in this eastern part of the Kirgiz speech area, which comprises the uppermost reaches of the Sir Darya, called here by its Mongolian name Narin, and the basin of the Issik Kol.

North of this, the Kirgiz language boundary runs west along the crestline of the Küngöy Ala Tau, and west of the Chu, along that of the Alexander range, often also called by the local name of Ala Tau. In the diaspora Kirgiz are found in northwest Eastern Turkistan (Sinkiang province), along the Yarkant Darya and Kashgar Darya, between the cities of Yarkant and Kashgar and Maral Beshi, but also far beyond their present habitat, in some of the eastern Pamir valleys and south of them, in valleys of the western K'un-Lun and Karakorum ranges.

In the high mountain ranges between Tien Shan and Karakorum, Kirgiz separates Uzbek from New Uyghur, the Turkic language of Eastern or Chinese Turkistan. Like Turkmenistan, this huge territory, containing the largest and most compact desert area of Central Asia, or even of all Asia, is inhabited only on its fringes at the foot of the majestic ranges of Tien Shan in the north, Pamir in the west, and K'un-Lun in the south. The more populous settlements of New Uyghur are located only along the upper course of the Tarim's western source rivers—in towns such as Kashgar, Yangi Hisar, Yarkant, and Qarghalyq—and on the upper course of its northern tributaries along the southern slopes of the Tien Shan. Similarly, a New Uyghur population lives along the northern slopes

of the K'un-Lun south of the great desert, and along the slopes of
the central and eastern Tien Shan. Naturally, the age-old caravan
routes, the "Silk Roads," connecting China with Iran and the
Roman empire followed these rows of settlements along the high
mountains. South of the Tien Shan, east of the famous oases of
Qarashahr and Turfan, New Uyghur is spoken as far as the oasis
of Qomul or Hami (Igu in Mongolian times). In this area the language borders on Mongolian, but in New Uyghur territory Chinese
is spoken in all the larger towns of this province of the Chinese
empire.

North along this entire area between the Caspian Sea and the
Altay mountains extends the vast territory of the Kazakh SSR. As
the political frontiers of the national republics were drawn to a
great extent in accordance with the linguistic boundaries, in view
of the coincidence of language and nationality or nation, the area
of the Kazakh language extends from the Lower Volga to the foot
of the Altay and the Ektagh, and the source rivers of the Irtish,
the main constituent of the Ob River system.

This entire area is rather uniform geographically and linguistically, the eastern dialects differing somewhat from the western
ones. Only in the east of Khwarazm does the Karakalpak dialect
show some more specific features, partly because of the influence
of Uzbek and Turkmen, so that it was given the status of a literary
language and its land the rights of an autonomous region.

While the southern boundary of this huge language area is
relatively simple, more or less following latitude 41°N between
Qaraboghaz and the Sir Darya, with an indentation in Khwarazm
and the Tien Shan where Uzbek and, farther east, Kirgiz are
spoken, it reaches beyond the Soviet frontier into Chinese territory
in western and northern Dzungaria (Jungaria). In the north, however, this entire stretch between the Volga and the Irtish is dis-
sected by a great many indentations and enclaves, mostly those of
the Russian language. Nowhere along the 1,250-mile length of this
boundary line does Kazakh have any immediate contact with one
of the neighboring Turkic languages to the north, the Kazan Tatar,
Bashkir, or the West Siberian Tatar (Turkic) languages. Only in
the extreme west, in the Volga delta, does Kazakh have any con-

tact with Kazan Tatar diaspora groups, while in the extreme northeast, at the foot of the Altay, it touches on Oyrot. Only in the south does Kazakh have any permanent contact with Uzbek, Kirgiz, and New Uyghur. Contacts with Turkmen take place in the Karakalpak region; otherwise they are insignificant, as the border area south of the Ustyurt consists of desert.

The largest Turkic group in Central Asia which is not provided with a separate republic in that area is made up of the Tatars. They are scattered throughout the six republics and number nearly as many as the Kirgiz inhabitants of Central Asia. The Tatar population reached its level in part because of artificial and drastic changes that took place in the distribution of many nationalities of the USSR during the 1930s and World War II. One such shift was Stalin's deportation of the entire Turkic population of the Crimea, some 200,000 persons, from their homeland to Central Asia in 1944.

DISTRIBUTION OF IRANIAN AND MINORITY LANGUAGES

Besides the Turkic languages of Central Asia, which constitute the overwhelming majority in that area, there are a number of Iranian languages represented. Together with the Indo-European Indian languages, they constitute the easternmost of the living Indo-European languages and are most closely related with Balto-Slavic, Iranian particularly being closer to Slavic.

Today, the most numerous Iranian-speaking population of Central Asia is the Tajik, who live mainly in the Tajik SSR, but also in the diaspora on the territory of neighboring countries such as Uzbekistan, Kirgizistan, Afghanistan, and Eastern Turkistan. Tajik is a term which probably goes back to a rather old Persian designation of the Arabs, *Tazi.* Later, this term was used throughout Central Asia in a much broader sense, meaning all people of Muslim faith, regardless of nationality. Thus it also came to be known as *Da-shy* (*Ta-shih*) in China, where it is used in the same vague sense, sometimes meaning Turkistan, at other times the realm of the caliphate.

Tajik is a modern Persian dialect, digressing from the literary language only in insignificant features. There are New Persian dialects in Iran proper which exhibit much stronger differences from standard Persian than Tajik. Therefore, it is quite easy to exchange the names and call New Persian "Tajik" as has been done in the USSR. Apart from a few features of phonology, for example, the preservation of Middle-Persian (Pahlavi) $\bar{e}$ and $\bar{o}$ in certain positions, or morphology, it is the syntax and the vocabulary where Tajik diverges more from Persian. This is because of numerous and quite strong influences of both Turkic, especially Chaghatay and Uzbek, and Russian. As the influences exerted by Russian are of a more recent date than the Turkic, they are mostly limited to the vocabulary, but those from Turkic have irrupted also into the syntax, so that the typically Altayic coordinative features, participial and gerundial constructions, have been adopted by Tajik. This is the consequence of a reaction following the all-pervasive influence of Iranian upon the Turkic languages of Central Asia which has probably lasted an entire millennium or even more.

The origins of Tajik are not at all clear. It is spoken on ancient Iranian ground in Outer Iran (Western Turkistan), but in an area where from the eighth to eleventh centuries East-(earlier, North-)-Iranian languages were spoken, here particularly and chiefly Soghdian, a language which expanded enormously in a narrow latitudinal strip along the "Silk Road" all across the Asiatic continent right into northern China, for the silk trade between China, Iran, and the Roman empire was in Soghdian hands. Soghdian was more closely related to Saka, the Pamir languages, Afghan, Baluchi and Osset (in the Caucasus) than to the West-Iranian languages such as Persian, Kurd, Tat, and Talish, and it was the language and the culture upon which the ancient Uyghur language and culture developed in Eastern Turkistan from the eighth and ninth centuries on. The earlier Uyghur translations of Christian and Manichaean texts drew considerably from Soghdian, among the other languages of Central Asia.

Only with the growing expansion of Buddhism and Chinese power did Soghdian begin to lose to Chinese. In Eastern Turkistan, the Soghdians were gradually absorbed by the Turks, mainly the Uyghurs, while in Western Turkistan they could not, in the long run, resist Arabic pressure from the southwest and Turkic infiltration from the northeast. Thus, the Soghdian nation and its language disappeared.

Although the Arabs remained in Western Turkistan only in insignificant numbers, it is to be assumed that together with or soon after the Arab armies conquered the area (from A.D. 711), Persian-speaking Muslims from Iran had come to ancient Soghdiana and superimposed upon the local Soghdian-speaking population their West-Iranian language. Otherwise, the vanishing of Soghdian and the appearance of Persian there remains inexplicable, especially in view of the fact that the Turks, although they usurped political power, did not become sedentary for a long time and did not replace or absorb the city population, repeating their earlier behavior in Eastern Turkistan. The Islamization of western Central Asia starting with the Arabic military conquest seemed to have been effected by Muslims of Persian nationality and language.

Some close relatives of the ancient Soghdians and the other East-Iranians have survived because they had moved to the high mountain valleys; the Ossets in the Caucasus and the "Mountain Tajiks"—the Ghalcha or Pamir people—were such groups. The latter are the immediate neighbors of the Tajiks in the west, the Kirgiz in the north, northeast, east, and southeast, and the Dardistan or Piśācha people in the south. The language of the Ossets belongs to the East-Iranian group, and is thus in a closer relationship to the Pamir languages, Pashtu (Afghan), Baluchi, and certain other Iranian languages of Central Asia such as Soghdian, than to Tajik and Kurd.

The exploration of the Pamir languages is not yet complete; much still remains to be done in those spoken outside of the USSR. Somewhat apart from the relatively well-known Pamir languages is Yaghnobi, spoken in some isolation from the other Pamir languages in the valley of the Yaghnob, a left tributary of the Zarafshan above Varzaminar. Those on the Pamir proper are, from north to south, Shughni or Shighni in the valley of the Shughnan (Shighnan); Vakhi south of it in the valley of the Vakhan; and Ishkashimi southwest of this, for the most part on Afghan territory, in and around the little town of Ishkashim on the upper Amu Darya, called here Panj. Sarykoli is spoken in southeastern Pamir in the

Taghdumbash and Sarykol valleys, separated from the western valleys opening into that of the Panj by the icy, barren central plateaus of the Pamir. In recent years, Bartangi and Khufi, spoken in the valley of the Murghab, also called Bartang, Sarez, and Aq Su, in the Rushan countryside of the northwestern Pamir, have become known through the efforts of Russian scholars. But those spoken in the high valleys of the main range of the Hindu Kush, such as Sanglichi in and around the village of Sanglich, and Munjani (Minjani or Mungi) along the upper course of the Ab-i Jarm, in the district of Minjan, famous for its lapis lazuli mines, still are insufficiently known. The southernmost Pamir people are, as far as is known, the Yidghah (Yüdghā or Leotkuh-i Wār), speaking Yidakh, the only Pamir language south of the Hindu Kush, south of the Dorah Pass, in the district of Chitral, the northwesternmost part of Pakistan where they are found in the Dardic speech area.

The distinction in the Pamir languages between dialect and language is often not clear; for example, Sanglichi, Zebaki, and Yazgulami are occasionally mentioned as languages, while more recent research[1] gives evidence for considering all three of them as dialects of Ishkashimi. The relative inaccessibility of those geographically difficult frontier territories prevents systematic fruitful research such as that conducted on the Soviet side of the Pamir region.

Other than Turkic and Iranian language groups, minorities such as Armenians and other Caucasians, Ukrainians, Germans, or Jews, are settled in most cities and towns of the USSR, and in the cities of Central Asia, particularly Persians, Afghans, Indians, and Chinese can be found. Two additional groups, the Arabs and the Mongolians, have remained in Central Asia. They once had a major historical significance, the Arabic speakers now being found in the neighborhood of the Uzbek town of Ziyaddin between Samarkand

---

[1] T. N. Pakhalina, *Ishkashimskiy iazyk* (Moscow-Leningrad, Izdatel'stvo Akademii Nauk SSSR, 1959); Wilhelm Geiger, *Grundriss der Iranischen Philologie* (Strassburg, K. J. Trübner, 1895–1904), I, 287ff.; Wolfgang Lentz, *Die Pamir-Dialekte* (Göttingen, Vandenhoeck and Ruprecht, 1933); G. A. Grierson, *Linguistic Survey of India* (Calcutta, Office of the Superintendent of Government Printing, 1903–1928), vol. X, part 3, pp. 455ff., 480ff.; cf. also *Ibid.*, vol. VIII, part 2, p. 4ff.

and Bukhara, and the Mongols seem to have remained in the Issik Kol area after one of the major Mongolian campaigns.

OUTSIDE INFLUENCES AND THEIR EFFECTS

The languages which surround those of Western Turkistan (Central Asia) are, starting again in the west, New Persian, which borders on Turkmen in the south and also on the territory of Afghanistan where Pashtu (Afghan) also touches Turkmen slightly. Turkmen also has permanent contacts with Persian in all the major towns of Turkmenistan. Uzbek in the east and northeast, Karakalpak and Kazakh in the northeast and north are also its neighbors. The contacts with Kazakh are the least intensive of these. In the diaspora Turkmen is exposed to Nogay, Kalmyk, Osman (Ottoman) Turkish, and Arabic. As is true for all the languages of the Soviet Union, Turkmen is subject to the pervasive influence of Russian, not only as the cultural vehicle of the USSR but also as an omnipresent, everyday contact language through Russians living in most of the larger towns of the land. This is valid in varying degrees for all the languages of Central Asia.

Apart from its marginal contacts with Turkmen, Karakalpak, and Kazakh, Uzbek, like Chaghatay, its predecessor in the same part of Central Asia, has been exposed to long-lasting, intensive influences from Iranian, almost exclusively from Tajik. This permanent contact with Persian gave rise to those particular Uzbek dialects spoken by the settled rural and urban populations which have thus been called the Iranized dialects of Uzbek.[2] They constitute the basis for the modern Uzbek literary language. The present standard Uzbek is based on the Uzbek dialect of Tashkent, although attempts were made in the late 1920s by national Uzbek leaders to select the north Uzbek dialects of towns such as Turkistan, Mankent, and Qarabulaq as the official literary language. There, the Iranization is felt less than in the large Uzbek cities, and, in fact, the Uzbek dialects of the nomadic population, which is constantly decreasing in numbers, are almost free of Iranian influences,

[2] E. D. Polivanov, "Obraztsy ne-iranizovannykh (singarmonisticheskikh) govorov uzbekskogo iazyka," *Izvestiia Akademii Nauk SSSR* (Otdelenie Gumanitarnykh Nauk), VII (1929), 511–37; I (1931), 93–112.

which means that they have not undergone the same strong, pervasive penetration by Persian as the language of the sedentary population, and therefore are essentially different from it.

In Chaghatay, as well as in the Uzbek dialects of the settled population, the Iranian influence, especially that of Persian, has been profound, so that the phonological and to an important extent also the syntactical type (sometimes called structure) of the Chaghatay and Uzbek languages has assumed a great many distinctive non-Turkic and non-Altayic features. Outstanding are mainly the loss of sound harmony in the phonology, and the use of grammatical subordination in the syntax. No other Turkic language, with perhaps the sole exception of the literary language of the Qarayim, strongly influenced by Hebrew and Slavic, has undergone a comparably powerful extraneous penetration.

Kirgiz, in its alpine isolation, is a relatively pure Turkic language, but its literary form experienced quite a strong influence from its northern Kazakh neighbor during its formative years in the very recent past when the Kazakhs took an active part in the development of the Kirgiz literary language. The popular language shows a few Mongolian influences, mostly in its vocabulary. The southern dialects of the Alay-Pamir region, or those of the diaspora, are still quite unknown.

Kazakh borders throughout the west and north on Russian, by which it has been separated from its Turkic relatives there. Individual Kazan Tatar influences penetrated the plains of Kazakhstan during the last seventy-five to a hundred years of Russian imperial rule, since a number of the officials at that time were Kazan Tatars. An earlier layer of influences is that of Mongolian, as the Kazakhs for a long time had been either the subjects or the opponents and enemies of the Mongolians, mostly the Kalmyks of the post-Chingisid Dzungarian realm, which was finally subjugated (1757–1759) by the Chinese under the Manchu dynasty. With Kazakh, too, the strong Russian influence is due not to the long border with that language, but to the fact that in Kazakhstan, as elsewhere in Central Asia, Russians are present in all of the larger towns.

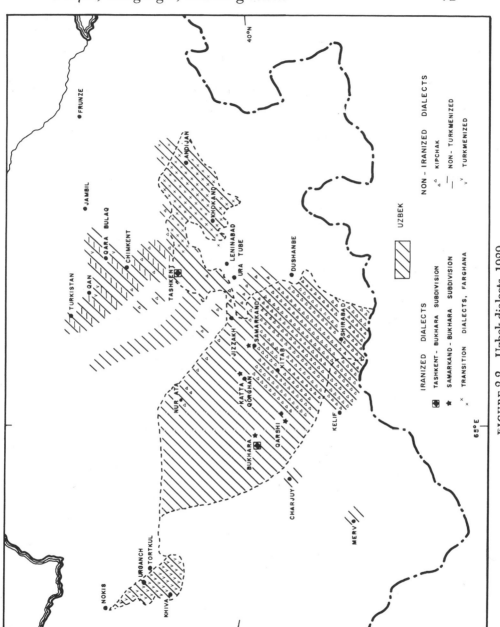

FIGURE 2.2   Uzbek dialects, 1929.

CLASSIFICATION AND CHARACTERISTICS OF TURKIC LANGUAGES

The following classification of the Turkic languages again proceeds from west to east.[3]

Turkmen is the only language of Central Asia which belongs to the southwest or Oghuz group of the Turkic languages and thus has close ties with languages such as Azeri and Osman Turkish, but also has some features typical of the Central Asian ("Turki") group proper. It has preserved a few archaisms such as the distinction of long and nonlong vowels, lost in Turkic languages other than Yakut and traces in Chuvash, so that it has particular value for the solution of problems in the history of the Turkic languages. Its dialects have not yet been explored to a satisfactory degree, a fact equally true for all the Turkic languages.

Uzbek alone had undergone dialectological research which has led to the cognition of its actual nature and its position within the Turkic languages. The Iranized Uzbek dialects previously mentioned in connection with the city populations of modern Uzbekistan exist also in some linguistic enclaves in cities of southern Kazakhstan and in Tajikistan. Uzbek is a language which can be considered the direct descendant or a later form of Chaghatay, the language of the great Turkic Central Asian literary development in the realm of Chaghatay Khan, Timur (Tamerlane), and the Timurids.

The Uzbek dialects of the dwindling nomadic population are, or were, at least until the 1930s, a part of the Northwest or Kipchak group of the Turkic languages, and are therefore, as a linguistic unit, called Kipchak-Uzbek. Their closest relatives are Kazakh and Karakalpak, with which they share some essential classificatory features. This Kipchak-Uzbek language has a certain restricted influence upon the literary Uzbek language, so that the latter is essentially a Central Asian language of Turkic. Kipchak-Uzbek, along with Kazakh-Karakalpak and Nogay, in the Ponto-Caspian

---

[3] Johannes Benzing and Karl H. Menges, "Classification of the Turkic Languages," *Philologiae Turcicae Fundamenta* (Wiesbaden, Aquis Mattiacis: Apud Franciscum Steiner, 1959), I, 1–10.

plains (north of the Caspian and to the Black Sea), belongs to the eastern or Aralo-Caspian branch of the Kipchak group.

Kipchak-Uzbek dialects also were spoken at least as late as the 1930s in southern Kazakhstan, in the areas of the town of Turkistan, and in and near Chimkent. The dialects of the semisedentary rural population, in Farghana, for instance, exhibit all the features of a transition from true, that is, Kipchak-Uzbek, to the Iranized type of Uzbek. The sedentary city population of Central Asia also used to be called Sart, a term commonly found in works of the period prior to 1917. It was done away with after that, since it was used by the nomadic population—Uzbek and Kazakh as well—as a pejorative nickname for the city dwellers, whether Turkic or Iranian (Uzbek, New Uyghur or Tajik).

Kirgiz, like literary Uzbek and its eastern neighbor New Uyghur, originally belonged to the Central Asian group which once also comprised ancient Uyghur and the oldest Turkic known to be recorded, Orkhon. Modern literary Kirgiz, however, occupies an intermediary position, as it has been influenced by Kazakh, so that it often is classed with the Kipchak languages.[4] But the language of the epic songs, an abundant preliterary source for all the Turkic languages of Central Asia and Siberia, exhibits closer ties with Uyghur, New Uyghur, and Chaghatay, the Central Asian group of Turkic. This does not exclude features shared by the Kipchak languages which Kirgiz also has in common with the Oyrot group in the Altay.

While the final determination of the position of Kirgiz within the Turkic languages must be postponed until more is known about its dialects, that of New Uyghur in the Central Asian group is certain. It is the direct descendant of ancient Uyghur, which was spoken in the same country, and might very well be considered a later form of ancient Uyghur if the final irruption of Islam into Eastern Turkistan had not brought about fundamental changes in the vocabulary, supplying all abstract terms pertaining to religion, philosophy, social life, and politics, among others, from Arabic and Persian. This latter feature also constitutes the principal difference between ancient Uyghur and the "Islamized" forms of the

[4] Karl H. Menges, "Die aralo-kaspische Gruppe," *ibid.*, pp. 434–88.

language in Central Asia, resulting finally in Chaghatay, and, to a lesser degree, literary Uzbek.

Foreign influences are stronger in Karakalpak than in Kazakh, since by its very location Karakalpak is more exposed to outside effects caused by both Uzbek and Turkmen. This is particularly true of the southwestern Karakalpak dialects. Except for Karakalpak, the dialectological differentiation of Kazakh goes in an east-west direction, so that the dialects found farthest to the east in the Great Horde (*Ulu Jüz*) and to the west in the Little Horde (*Kishshi Jüz*) and the dialects of the Inner Horde (*Ish* [or *Bokey*] *Jüz*) now the farthest west between the Volga and Ural rivers, and the Middle Horde (*Orta Jüz*) exhibit the sharpest contrast. Dialectological research has been considerably encouraged only within the last fifteen years, a period during which scholarly work on Kazakh language and literature has greatly increased.

The Turkic languages of Central Asia discussed here may be grouped, along with certain others in the Turkic family, in the following three categories according to their basic classificatory features. The Central Asian languages are italicized.

Group I. "Turki": *Orkhon,* ancient *Uyghur, Middle Turkic, Chaghatay, Kirgiz* (vernacular), *New Uyghur, Uzbek* (sedentary).

Group II. Oghuz: Osman Turkish, Azeri Turkish, *Turkmen,* Gagauz, Crimean Turkish.

Group III. Kipchak: *Kazakh, Karakalpak,* Nogay, *Kirgiz* (literary), *Uzbek* (nomadic), Tatar.

The classifications, including the Central Asian Turkic languages, can be illustrated by the following sketch of the most significant distinctive characteristics.

GROUP I. "TURKI"

Phonology. Vocalism: all eight vocalic phonemes exist, and presumably did so in ancient times. A tendency toward labial harmony exists, with labial attraction a regular feature of Kirgiz only; there are also such tendencies in New Uyghur.

Consonantism: -*gh*/-*g*, -*q*/-*k* in Orkhon Turkic separated; later, in ancient Uyghur this was not distinguished in the script. There was a coalescense into *-q/-k* in Chaghatay, New Uyghur, and Iranized Uzbek: *qurugh* (dry) > *quruq*. Suffix-initial *gh-, g-* exist in *-gha* (dative), *-ghan* (past participle), *-ghaly* (gerund). No voiced stops occur in initial position. The voiced interdental fricative of Orkhon, ancient Uyghur "*d*", Kashghariy, Rabghuziy, and others, changed to *y* in Chaghatay, New Uyghur, Uzbek, and Kirgiz.[5]

Morphology. Nouns: a somewhat greater number of declension cases are found in the ancient than in the modern languages, which have, for example, no instrumental *-ïn*, equative *-cha*, or comparative *-däg;* there was no ablative in Orkhon, but directive cases not found in the modern languages existed in Orkhon: *-ra, -qa-ru.* Orkhon had genitive in *-ïng* and accusative in *-ïgh*, but ancient Uyghur and Kashghariy employed genitive *-nïng*, accusative *-ïgh/ -nï.* Chaghatay, New Uyghur, Uzbek, and Kirgiz have genitive *-ïng*, accusative *-nï.* The ancient Uyghur ablative in *-dïn* has been preserved through Chaghatay and New Uyghur. Uzbek vacillates, but now has *-dan* like Kirgiz. Plural, mostly unmarked in Orkhon, is regular in ancient Uyghur and later. Relics of other ancient plural suffixes also exist.

Pronouns: exert influences upon the nominal declension from ancient Turkic on, especially in Uyghur, Chaghatay, New Uyghur, and Uzbek, as in the accusative *-nï.* Pronominal declension was abandoned in New Uyghur and Uzbek: the first person singular pronoun in dative is *men-gä*, second person singular pronoun in dative is *sen-gä;* likewise, there was abandonment of the pronominal *-n-* in the possessive third person suffix in Chaghatay, New Uyghur, and Iranized Uzbek: Uzbek *atäsigä* (to his father), Kipchak-Uzbek, Kazakh *atasïna.*

Verbs: perfect has *-t* and *-mïsh*, the latter being replaced beginning with Chaghatay by *-ghan.* The future-optative is *-ghay.* Pres-

---

[5] Mahmud Kashghariy, *Dewanu lughatit turk* (3 vols.; Tashkent, Ozbekistan SSR Fanlar Akademiyasi Nashriyati, 1960–1963); Rabghuzi, "Narrationes de Prophetis," *Monumenta Linguarum Asiae Maioris* K. Grönbech, ed. (Copenhagen, Levin and Munksgaard, 1948), vol. IV; C. Brockelmann, "Mitteltürkische Wortschatz," *Bibl. Orientalis Hungarica,* (Budapest, Leipzig, 1928), vol. I. In the transliteration system employed here for Turkic linguistics, yodh is represented with a *y* and velar i is represented by *ï.*

ent-future in -*a* appears from the Chaghatay period on. Aspect-forming verbal composition increases.

Syntax. Non-Altayic influences in ancient Uyghur came from Indo-European and Semitic languages; in Chaghatay, New Uyghur, and Uzbek from Arabic and New Persian. The rise of subordination came from Indo-European.

Vocabulary. Non-Altayic influences came to Orkhon from Chinese and Iranian; into ancient Uyghur from Indo-European, Semitic, and Chinese; into Chaghatay, New Uyghur, Uzbek, and Kirgiz from Arabic and New Persian; and recent ones from Russian.

GROUP II. OGHUZ

Phonology. Archaic features are contained in Turkmen.

Vocalism: this group also exhibits the eight vocalic phonemes and has strict labial harmony. Proto-Turkic vowel length is preserved in Turkmen.

Consonantism: -*gh*>-*O* except after *a* as in Turkmen *dāgh* (mountain); -*g*>-*O* or -*y*. No gutturals exist in the suffix anlaut: -*a* (dative), -*an* (past verbal noun), -*ali* (gerund). Initial voiced stops are regular: *dil* (tongue), *gör-* (to see) in each language of this group, but, as in all Turkic languages, there is no initial *gh*-. Turkmen has the change *q*->*ġ* (voiced velar stop) as in *qal-:ġāl-* (to remain). The voiced inderdental fricative>*y; s, z*>unvoiced interdental fricative and voiced interdental fricative, respectively, in Turkmen.

Morphology. Nouns: the declension is archaic, with genitive in -*ing*, accusative -*i* (<-*igh*); ablative -*dan*. The pronominal declension is preserved.

Verbs: perfect in -*t* and -*mish* have been retained, the latter implying "unwitnessed action." The compound durative present is in Turkmen in *iyōr, -yōr*, as is the future in -(*a*)*jaq*. There is no verbal noun in -*a, -ghay*, but there is the verbal noun future optativ in -*asi*. The comparative degree in Turkmen is conveyed by -*raq/-rak*.

Syntax. Non-Altayic influences from New Persian show in the subordination with *ki*, noticeable also in Turkmen.

Vocabulary. Non-Altayic influences came from Arabic and New Persian, later, also from Russian, into Turkmen.

GROUP III. KIPCHAK

Phonology. Vocalism: all eight vocalic phonemes are present. The vacillations *o/u* and *ö/ü* occur. The vowel sequence in *Codex Cumanicus* is not always regular.[6] There is labial harmony. Labial attraction exists in Kazakh and Karakalpak, and traces occur also in Kipchak-Uzbek.

Consonantism: postvocalic *-gh>-u, -g>-y;* intermediary *gh/g>v.* Suffix-initial gutturals exist, as in *-gha, -ghan* (past verbal noun), *-ghach* (gerund). The voiced interdental fricative*>y.* The modern languages have assimilations and dissimilations in dental, nasal, and liquid combinations. In Kazakh-Karakalpak: *ch>sh, sh>s, y->j-;* in Kipchak-Uzbek: *y->j-.*

Morphology. Nouns: declension has genitive *-nïng,* accusative *-nï,* ablative *-dan.* The pronominal declension is preserved. The comparative degree is conveyed by *-raq.*

Verbs: perfect has *-t* (first person suffix *ïm*), *-ghan* (first person suffix *-man*); *-mïsh* for all languages has been lost or is found only in relics. This group has the present-future in *-a,* optative-future in *-ghay,* and future respectant necessitative in *-asï.* They also have personal pronouns as enclitics or suffixes after verbal nouns in predicative function.

Syntax. Non-Altayic features are weak.

Vocabulary. Non-Altayic influences came from Arabic, New Persian, and modern Russian into Central Asian Kipchak languages.

WRITING SYSTEMS

"Diplōma gegramménon Skythikoîs grámmasin" (a document written in Scythian letters) is mentioned in connection with one of the earliest known facts in Turkic history—the report on Zemarchos' mission to the Türküt qaghan Istämi in 568–569. At that time the Türküt already had a script which was the same as the rune-

---

[6] K. Grönbech, ed., "Codex Cumanicus," *Monumenta Linguarum Asiae Maioris,* vol. I (1936).

like script of the Orkhon, or perhaps an earlier, western form of it. As this script is based on Aramaic, and, like it, written with unconnected letters, the Türküt must have become acquainted with it somewhere in the western portion of their domain in the "Land of the Seven Streams" south of Lake Balkhash in southern Kazakhstan, still called Jeti Su, and, in Russian, Semirechie, where Soghdian Nestorians once lived. Or perhaps the script came from even more distant Soghdian, Khwarazmian, or other regions inhabited by Iranian kinsmen.

The earliest known Iranian alphabet was a cuneiform dating from the sixth century B.C., in the reign of Ariyaramna, grandfather of Cyrus. The change from this and its successors (Pahlevi, Syriac, Hebrew, and other scripts used quite early in different parts of the Iranian world) to Arabic took place after the Arab conquest of Persia during the seventh century A.D., although the oldest manuscript extant of Persian in Arabic writing belongs to the eleventh century A.D.

With the development of Turkic cultural and literary centers in Eastern Turkistan, the Soghdian script, a later form of Syriac, was adopted by the ancient Uyghurs, and thus Soghdian developed into a slightly variant form called the Uyghur script. This was used preponderantly by the Turkistan Turks of all religions, and it was only under Islamic pressure that Arabic gradually replaced Uyghur. Rather late Middle Turkic texts dating up to the fifteenth century and sporadically even later were written not in Arabic but in Uyghur script both south and north of the Tien Shan. One of the Uyghur books is the famous *Qutadhghu Bilig* (eleventh century), a didactic poem of Muslim faith.[7] Chaghatay texts in Uyghur script are not at all extraordinary. With the transition from Uyghur to Arabic script, orthographic features typical of Uyghur were transferred into Arabic, so that the Arabic writing of Chaghatay or pre-Chaghatay texts was simply an Arabic transliteration of Uyghur.

[7] Reşid Rahmeti Arat, ed., *Kutadgu Bilig* (Istanbul, Türk Dil Kurumu, 1947), vol. I; Yusuf Has Hacib, *Kutadgu Biliğ*, 3 vols. (Istanbul, Türk Dil Kurumu, 1942–1943); Jusuf Chass-Hadschib aus Bälasagun, *Kudatku Bilik*, 2 vols., ed. by W. Radloff (St. Petersburg, Buchdruckerei der Kaiserlichen Akademie der Wissenschaften, 1891).

While in the long run the Soghdian Uyghur script lost out to Arabic, it lives on in the eastern part of Central Asia, because after the conquest of Eastern Turkistan in 1218 the Mongols employed Uyghurs as secretaries and scribes and in this way introduced the Uyghur script into Mongolian, where it was given preference over Tibetan P'ags-pa and Chinese. Major modifications of Uyghur were made by adding a few special forms and diacritical dots for Kalmyk and Manchu. The latter being one of the two imperial languages of the Manchu (Ts'ing) dynasty, this alphabet acquired extraordinary significance for 300 years. Uyghur script, as used by the Mongolians, is still alive, whereas the great majority of the Altayic people today use the Cyrillic alphabet as the instrument for their writing and literature.

Voices advocating discarding the use of Arabic script for languages other than Arabic were heard not only after the Russian revolution, but a number of decades before. Mirza Fath Ali Akhundzada and his circle began actively working for alphabet reform in Azerbaijan in the middle of the nineteenth century. While literacy was quite limited at the time of the Russian revolution among all the Turkic people, Arabic script rightfully bearing part of the blame for this backwardness, the Central Asian nationalities still used Arabic writing in the first years after 1917, although in a reformed system.

At the beginning of the 1920s, some simplifications had been introduced into writing Arabic script; for instance, the letters which exhibited quite a variety of forms in different positions within a word, such as Arabic *q*, *s*, and *h*, were reduced to one form each. And, more important, a regular and systematic representation of the vowels was introduced to better previous attempts at simplification like that of the Osman Turks earlier in the twentieth century. Thus, in the reformed Arabic script all the vowels (palatal or velar) had to be clearly expressed, notwithstanding the fact that in Iranized as well as literary Uzbek, for example, their sound-harmonic distinction had no significance because sound harmony was lost.

The first to replace Arabic script with a Latin alphabet was Soviet Azerbaijan, in 1922. It was followed several years later by other Iranian and Turkic nationalities and also by Kemalist Turkey in 1928. Kirgiz, Uzbek, and Turkmen began to use the Latin script in 1927, Kazakh and Karakalpak in 1928, and New Uyghur in 1930. Tajik, which had also been in Arabic script, began to appear

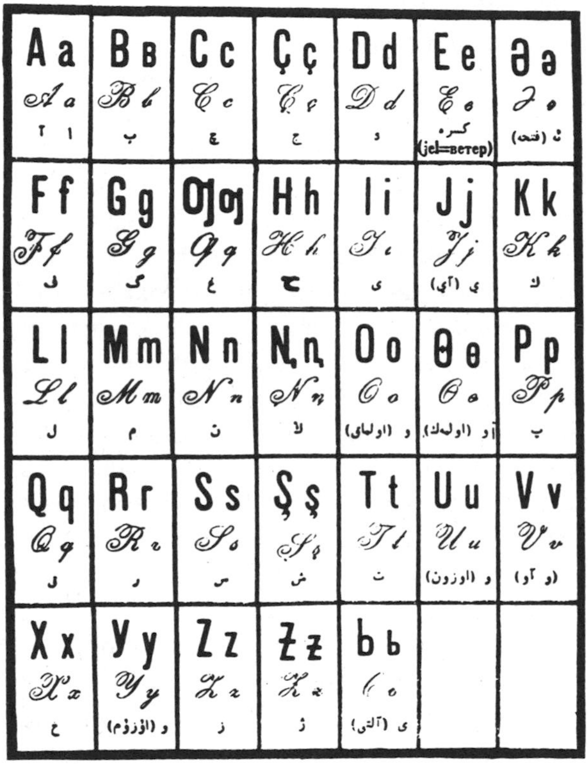

FIGURE 2.3   The Latinized Turkic alphabet.

in Latin script in 1928, about the same time as Kazakh and Karakalpak.

After Soviet Azerbaijan converted to a Latin alphabet, a similar adoption by all the languages of the USSR using Arabic script was only a matter of time. The years 1927–1930 became a period of transition in Central Asia during which a number of journals and newspapers were still being printed in both reformed Arabic and the new Latin script. By 1930 the Latinization (*latinlashuirish*) was completed, and the new alphabet (*yangalif*) had been established. In Eastern Turkistan, on the other hand, a reformed Arabic was introduced for New Uyghur as late as 1947 and a new Latinized alphabet was announced in 1965.

Summing up for Central Asia: the reformed Arabic alphabet was used from 1923 to 1928, the Latinized from 1928 to 1940 with a few alterations between 1935 and 1940, and finally, Cyrillic was adapted to local alphabets there from 1940 onward, with further slight reforms around 1952 or 1953. Specific data concerning the alphabet changes in Central Asia are presented in numerous Soviet sources.[8]

The first draft of the Cyrillic orthography for Karakalpak was really a step backward in orthographic precision compared with the Latin or even the reformed Arabic spelling, for three vocalic-phoneme pairs *a/ä, o/ö,* and *u/ü* were rendered by one letter each: *a, o, y.* Karakalpak may well serve as an example for the other Central Asian languages, because they, too, had to undergo not one but several changes in orthography.

By 1940, apparently, all Latinized alphabets of Central Asia, except New Uyghur in Kazakhstan and Uzbekistan, had been replaced by Cyrillic, with strange variations introduced for purposes unrelated to linguistics. Some quite divergent orthographic devices were adopted there, while a unified Cyrillic transcription like that already refined for some great scholarly works around a hundred years ago,[9] as well as for all the linguistic publications of the Russian Academy of Sciences, was carefully avoided. There was or is no need to render the sound *j* three different ways in three alphabets, or *q* with two letters, or *ö* with two letters, or *ü* in various manners among these languages. The advantage of spelling in Cyrillic lies mainly in its greater versatility, derived from the fact

[8] N. A. Baskakov, *Karakalpakskii iazyk,* 2 vols. (Moscow, Izdatel'stvo Akademii Nauk SSSR, 1951–1952), II, 127f.

[9] Otto Böhtlingk, *Über die Sprache der Jakuten* (St. Petersburg, Buchdruckerei der Kaiserlichen Akademie der Wissenschaften, 1851); V. V. Radlov, *Opyt slovaria tiurkskikh nariechii,* (4 vols.; St. Petersburg, Imperatorskaia Akademiia Nauk, 1893–1911).

that its alphabet has more letters than Latin, and that diacritical marks are therefore required less than in Latin transcriptions or transliterations.

MIGRATIONS

At present the Turkic and Iranian people of Central Asia are disposed almost as they were after the completion of the great migrations in and across Central Asia which ceased at the end of the fifteenth century. At that time the Uzbeks infiltrated with ever-increasing power out of the northwest from their former habitat south of the Urals and in the Aral region into the sedentary and highly civilized areas of the upper Sir Darya, the former nucleus of the realm of Chaghatay (d. 1242) and his successors, Timur, and the Timurids. Babur, the last Timurid to rule over what was Chagatay's realm, yielded to pressure and withdrew to Afghanistan and India, leaving the Uzbeks in control.

Western Turkistan was at first occupied and in the course of time Turkified by Turkic people whose languages later showed the features of the Oghuz or southwestern group; the leading tribal confederacy of those Turks was the Oghuz, from whom the Osmans and the Seljuqs descended. "Turki" Turkic groups arriving from the east *after* the Arab invasions differed slightly in language from the Oghuz, since they were more closely connected with historical ancient Turkic, the language of the Orkhon and Uyghur confederations. They pushed the Oghuz tribal groups to the southwest, while they themselves occupied the entire area as far as the Amu Darya, the age-old boundary between Iran and Turan (Outer Iran).

Even today the Amu Darya line is a visible anthropological boundary. Irano-Caucasian features are found to the west of it and, with the exception of the cities of Turkistan, a preponderance of Altayic features are found to the east of it. North of the latitude of Khwarazm, a rather uniform linguistic as well as ethnic blanket covered Kazakhstan, where even before the consolidation of the Turkic tribal groups into the Kazakh people, and after the elimination of the Iranians, it must be assumed that there was a preponderance of northwest Turks far beyond the river Volga and northward into the Volga-Kama region.

The Kirgiz in considerable numbers seem to have come to their present home in the high valleys of the Tien Shan, Pamir, Alay, and Qara Qorum no earlier than the sixteenth to seventeenth centuries, although the Orkhon realm after 840 reached as far as the eastern Tien Shan. Since the Kirgiz had no written literature of their own and did not yet play a major political role, their whereabouts on the way from the Orkhon to the Alay are not always discernible or even known. Their rule over the Orkhon realm was broken by the Mongolian Qytan (Liao) in 924. From 1254 to 1270 they played a major role among the seditious tribes on the northern fringe of the Mongolian empire, and time and again were slaughtered and forced to move their location, as in 1293 under Qublay Khan, when they were forced to go to northern Manchuria. Those who could escape moved westward toward Uriangkhay, and finally the Altay, the Tarbaghatay, and the Tien Shan. As a result of their unhappy wars with the Dzungarians in the seventeenth century, the Kirgiz were forced to move toward and into the Tien Shan.

Notwithstanding the fate suffered by the Kirgiz people in the course of their history, their language has preserved a remarkably pure state of Turkic, along with certain rather archaic features such as the Proto-Turkic vocalic length, typical of the northern dialects. In the southern dialects this length is partly replaced by a diphthong. With both latter features Kirgiz is a connecting link between Turkmen and Yakut.

Since the Kirgiz occupation of their present habitat and the consolidation of the Kazakh tribes at about the same time (end of sixteenth century), the Turkic and Iranian ethno-linguistic map of Central Asia has undergone no major changes.

Earlier, the Turkic people had been located far from where they were in the sixteenth century. Their immigration into the territories they now occupy can be quite specifically determined throughout history. Only the original home from which they started on their historical wanderings is less clearly definable. The Turkic migrations from some region north of China were a part of all the Altayic migrations. They are no less spectacular than the Mongolian campaigns under Chingis Khan, but in contradistinction to his movements, they were migrations and not merely campaigns.

The first Altayic migrations, by the Huns, became known historically because they not only shook the Chinese and, later, Roman empires to their foundations, but were also the ultimate cause of the great European migrations. Despite the fact that some scholars, preponderantly in Hungary, consider the Huns to have been Turks, this can only be stated as a hypothesis until further proof is found. It is probably feasible to say that the language of the Huns occupied an intermediate position between Turkic and Mongolian, of which some remnants are still extant in the Chuvash language on the Volga west of Kazan. It may be assumed, in consequence of the Hunnic invasions of Europe, that with or shortly after Attila's defeat on the Catalaunian fields in 451, Turkic tribes in small numbers appeared in eastern Europe, where some of them, such as the Bulgars, roamed the steppes of the Volga region and the Ponto-Caspian lowlands.

Turkic tribes in greater numbers seem to have come westward to the Aral and Ponto-Caspian plains about a century later with the Avar invasions of Europe. The Avars, like their Zhuan Zhuan predecessors and ancestors, were definitely Mongolians. If later Avar waves—designated pseudo-Avars—were not entirely Turkic as some have assumed, they must have comprised a good many early Kipchak-speaking groups who were probably the earliest Turkic invaders of western Asia and eastern Europe.

Until the destruction of the Avar realm in eastern and southeastern Europe by Charlemagne in the last decade of the eighth century, Turkic groups of some size roamed about the plains between the Irtish and the Volga, practically on the territory of present-day Kazakhstan, while no earlier than the tenth century some groups started to move westward across the Don and finally toward the Dnieper and Danube rivers. Some of those movements of entire populations, including the two major ones, the Huns (or at least part of them) and the Avars, passed through Central Asia. Notwithstanding the fact that they were eventually expelled from there by the local population, often with the military assistance of the great Sassanian and Chinese powers, some groups must have remained in the prairies remote from the sedentary population of Central Asia. This is not only natural, but can be assumed in view of the disappearance from those regions of other people known to have inhabited the area previously.

The northeast fringes of the *orbis terrarum* of Western classical antiquity were inhabited by mythical wild nomadic people. In Herodotus' account the Scythians first emerged from prehistorical obscurity. They were of uncertain linguistic and ethnic affiliation, with a strong Iranian admixture. Their ruling clans may even have been of Iranian origin. Toward the beginning of the first century B.C., they began to disappear eastward, and in their place appeared the Sarmatians and Sauromatae, who had previously been mentioned as living northeast of the Scythians, evidently near or on the central Volga.

They seem to have been relatives of tribal confederacies known under the names of Alans and Aorses, living and roaming mostly in the great spaces between the lower Don and the Irtish. However, the name of the Scythians remained with Roman and Byzantine writers a general designation for all tribal groups north and east of the Black Sea and the Caspian. Even as late as the fifteenth century Turkic people were still now and then called Scythians.

A certain proportion, probably large, of the Alans took part in the great migrations into and across Europe caused by the general westward migratory movements which originally had gained momentum with the Hunnic invasions. Along with numerous Germanic tribes, such as the Vandals, Suebes, and Visigoths, Alanic groups in the early fifth century crossed the Rhine and drove as far as Spain and North Africa. Other Alanic tribes remained in the Ponto-Caspian plains, but were forced out under Altayic pressure exerted by Mongolian and Turkic people in the twelfth and thirteenth centuries, so that they took refuge in the Caucasus. There they survived and are now known as the Ossets, a name by which they are designated in Old Russian, *Iasi,* and in Islamic sources *As* (Astrakhan< *As-tarkhan*).

Soghdiana, the northeasternmost province of the old Persian, and then of Alexander's short-lived empire, became known to the West through Alexander's conquests. In those remote lands of the Macedonian empire and beyond its northeastern frontiers, many nomadic tribes left no trace, but others, like the Parthians, the Chorasmii (in Khwarazm), the Sakai, and the Soghdians, became quite well known through remnants of their language and literature.

The Soghdians seem to have been one of the most numerous and important linguistic groups in Western Turkistan, but with their extensive commercial activities they also probably formed a considerable proportion of the population in a number of cities in Eastern Turkistan and beyond. This was true as early as the fourth century A.D. along the eastern end of the "Silk Road" in Ch'ang-An, the later capital of China during the T'ang dynasty (618–907). While traces of Soghdian literature were found in both Eastern and Western Turkistan, the more important texts are still those which were unearthed in the eastern part. The language of the Sakai is known from Eastern Turkistan only, where it was first found in and near the city of Khotan, and is therefore often called Khotanese.

All this provided quite an important background for the formation, almost a thousand years after Alexander the Great, of the Turkic culture in Eastern, and somewhat later in Western Turkistan. The Iranian tribes (Massagetae and others) east and northeast of the Persian empire, who disappeared without leaving a trace, were nomadic, as were originally most, if not all, of the Iranian people as well as those known as Soghdians, Khwarazmians, and Sakai. They were generally called, in the Persian national tradition, "Turan," as opposed to Iran, and were always considered enemies of the sedentary Persians. After the arrival of the Turks in those areas, the term Turan was ascribed by the Persians to them also, as the Turks played the same dangerous, often disastrous, historical role as had the Iranian nomadic tribes.

In closer proximity to the Chinese empire, where Turkic groups were exposed to intensive influences and at times even domination and oppression by that empire, Turkic groups began to unite into political units of varying sizes which had the form of tribal confederacies. In some circumstances Chinese pressure led to dissipation of Turkic tribes, in others it brought about their consolidation, and this resulted in resistance and military action. Turkic nomadic cattle breeders were able to organize cavalry that at some points was extremely dangerous to the Chinese empire. Not only did those Turkic units break through the Great Chinese Wall more than once and penetrate deeply into Chinese territory, but they even interfered in Chinese domestic affairs and were instrumental in setting up the T'ang dynasty.

The habitat of this early Turkic confederation, the Türküt (Chinese: *T'ut-g'uät*), in the sixth to eighth centuries was in present-day northern Mongolia and along the southern and southwestern slopes of the Altay mountains. From this base, campaigns were undertaken in all directions except north. The Türküt were unified from 558 to 582 under one qaghan, after which a split of their confederacy into an eastern and a western branch took place, and the two confederacies fought each other with generous Chinese aid for one or the other side. For short periods the Türküt empire extended as far west as the Ural River or even the Volga, with the Aral region, excluding Khwarazm, generally their westernmost possession. In a similar way, the eastern Türküt domain occasionally stretched as far as Manchuria and northeastern China.

Turkic tribes belonging to the Türküt empire, as well as those seceding from it, moved far west to the Ural and Volga, and in a southwesterly direction into neighborhoods closer to the sedentary Iranian population of Western Turkistan. The huge plains and fresh pasture lands of these areas immediately adjacent to the vulnerable East-Iranian principalities offered these cattle-breeding nomads enormous opportunities. Chinese pressure upon the Türküt gave a forceful incentive for many groups to move to the west, so that the plains of Outer Iran (Western Turkistan) and beyond were peopled more and more by Turkic tribes. As a result, at the beginning of the eighth century, the Iranian principalities were engulfed by an ever-increasing number of Turkic nomads from the northeast, and by the conquering Arabs from the southwest, who began their conquest of the East-Iranian lands, *Mā-warā-'n-nahr*, as they called Transoxanian Outer Iran. There, it was the Turkic nomadic groups, whose stronghold was the vast plains, which offered the Arabs fierce and tenacious resistance.

Under these forceful Turkic and Arabic waves, the Iranian principalities in Western Turkistan finally had to break down. The Arabs
occupied the cities and with great difficulty converted the inhabitants to Islam. The Turks in the plains increased in numbers and
were the last to become converted. In 740 the western Türküt
qaghanate came under the rule of the Turkic Türgäsh in the area
of south central Kazakhstan, and in 751 the Arab and Chinese
armies clashed on the Talas River, after which the Arabs, although
they were victorious, retired to Mawaraunnahr.

The qaghanate of the eastern Türküt had in the meantime (745)
been overrun and defeated by the Uyghurs, speaking the same or a
very closely related language, who invaded the territory in the
Orkhon River system from the east. This again caused a certain
amount of migration westward and southwestward into the area
of the Tarim basin, which soon after was to become Eastern Turkistan.

It is not improbable that Turkic language had already infiltrated
into the Tarim basin, at least its northern oasis region, before that,
but the more numerous Turkic tribes to move into that part of the
Tarim basin were probably the Uyghurs themselves, since their rule
over the eastern Türküt realm in the Orkhon area lasted not quite
one hundred years, and they themselves were overthrown and dis-
placed in 840 by the Kirgiz, who attacked from the northwest, the
upper Yenisey valley, the region which is now the Minusinsk basin,
and the autonomous region of Tannu Tuva, the former Uriangkhay,
and finally occupied the Uyghur realm.

Those Kirgiz, the forebears of the present-day Kirgiz, were originally not Turks at all, but either Yeniseyans, the relatives of the
present-day Kets, or else South Samoyeds. It seems probable that
the Kirgiz had been exposed, during the time immediately preceding their intrusion into the Orkhon realm, to a certain "organizational" Turkification, as might be guessed from the few Kirgiz
words and titles quoted in the Chinese Annals of the T'ang dynasty.[10] But it was probably during their stay in the Orkhon area
that they finally acquired the Turkic language. The Chinese were

[10] "Hsin T'ang shu," *Erh shih wu shih* (Shanghai, Kai Ming, 1934) ch. 217B,
pp. 4141–43.

very explicit about the striking anthropological features of the Kirgiz, as they differed essentially from all the other people of Central and northern Asia known to the Chinese at that time, being fair-skinned, green-eyed, and red-haired, with Europoid features which fit in well with the fresco paintings of Tokharian or Aryan donors in the grottoes of Eastern Turkistan. They had Uralic affiliations through Samoyed, or, if they were Yeniseyic, those with the Daghestanian languages, not at all with "Paleo-Asiatic" of Siberia.

The bulk of the Uyghurs, and undoubtedly with them a number of Türküt, migrated to the southwest into the Tarim basin; fewer groups went southward into the immediate neighborhood of ambivalent China to the provinces of Kan-Su and Ts'ing-Hai (Kökö-Nōr), where their descendants still live on as the Sary Yōgur (Yellow Uyghurs) and Salar. But after the fateful year 840 when the Kirgiz overran the ancient Uyghurs, the Turkic-speaking population in the Tarim basin and all around the central and eastern Tien Shan increased, and finally, after having acculturated to as remarkable a degree as must have occurred in an area so rich in languages, literature, and religions, in turn Turkified most of the region, apparently without bloodshed or even oppression, so that this country could now be called Eastern Turkistan. These Turks had Uyghur as their literary language, into which a great number of Manichaean, Nestorian Christian, and Buddhist texts were translated from Pahlavi, Soghdian, Syriac, the two Tokharian languages of Agni and Kucha, Sanskrit, Pali, Khotanese (Saka), and Chinese. Thus, in the history of Turkic languages and culture Uyghur occupies a very special place.

This florescence in Eastern Turkistan came to an end under Islamic pressure in the twelfth century as a consequence of the final expansion of the realm of the Qarakhanids ("Ilig-khans"), who in the middle of the tenth century had begun to form an Islamic Turkic empire there. The conquest of Eastern Turkistan by the Mongols under Chingis Khan in 1218 did the rest. The great majority of today's population is New Uyghur.

In tracing the Turkic people through historical sources it can be seen that they all emerged from Central Asia, and according to the older sources (only the Chinese records) containing information on the Turks they go back to eastern, or rather northeastern, Central Asia, an area which would be identified in modern terms as all of Mongolia and the northern part of Manchuria. Two thousand years ago, when the first Altayic groups, the Huns, began to move, this area was far less arid than it is today, or has been for the last millennium; instead, it abounded in the richest pasture lands and could thus easily sustain a relatively large number of people and herds, a great many more than now. All historical sources lead back to this area, and thus it is certainly right to assume that Mongolia and Manchuria are the original home not only of the Turks, but of all Altayians as well.[11]

However, this does not seem to hold true for earlier times. The assumption of a still earlier habitat during the epoch of the first half of the second and the third millennium B.C. for the Turkic as well as all Altayic languages and people in the area of present-day Western and Eastern Turkistan is based on purely linguistic considerations. The language group most closely related to Altayic is Uralic, a relationship so close that both Uralic and Altayic may be considered to form one larger unit, much as Hamito-Semitic, for example. This again is related to Indo-European and Dravidian, the relationship of Uralic with Indo-European being closer than that of Altayic, while the ties connecting Ural-Altayic with Dravidian are far closer and more numerous than those which connect Ural-Altayic with Indo-European.

This means that during a remote period in the history of these early great language families (Semitic, Indo-European, Ural-Altayic, and Dravidian), the habitats of the speakers of those languages must have been contained within one large area, where, for a long period, they lived as neighbors without being separated by stronger external groups. This area would have been eastern Europe, starting at the Carpathians, north of the Black Sea and south of latitude 50°N, western Asia, that is, Turkistan as previously delimited, and probably also the eastern part of the plateaus of Iran or present-day Afghanistan and Baluchistan. The approximate location of the three families would have been, in rough outline, Indo-

[11] G. J. Ramstedt, "Einführung in die altaische Sprachwissenschaft," *Mémoires de la Société Finno-Ougrienne* (Helsinki), No. 104 (1952, 1957).

European in the west, Uralic in the north, Dravidian in the south, and Altayic in the east, without too definite boundary lines between them, since the great number of highly mobile nomadic tribes did not permit clear-cut or permanent boundaries.

Toward the end of the third and the beginning of the second millennia B.C., gigantic movements began—probably caused by growth in population as well as severe changes in climate—during which the Indo-Europeans forcefully pushed out in all directions, their Aryan branches migrating southeastward and eastward. This drove a wedge between Uralic and Altayic groups, who now were on the move too, and caused them to migrate to other places—the Uralians northward and northwestward, the Altayians due eastward. At the time the Indo-Europeans were beginning to move eastward and southeastward, the Dravidians seem to have been moving to the southeast and taking possession of a great part of India. Only after the Altayians had pushed eastward and the Dravidians had moved into India were the plains of western Asia and the plateaus of Iran gradually occupied by the Aryans, the southeasternmost branch of the Indo-Europeans. It was probably only at this period—the middle of the second millennium B.C.—that the Altayians took Mongolia and Manchuria as their habitat for the next 1,500 years.

K. II. M.

3

The Population and the Land

Prior to the Russian conquest of Central Asia, little was known about the number of people living in the region. Because few accurate assessments of the total population were published at this time, it is necessary to rely on estimates made by foreign travelers and residents, including Russian military observers. Such reports concerning the population throughout various regions of Central Asia in 1885 have been compared with other statistics from Russian sources and some from visitors to Central Asia in 1888 and 1889.[1]

The total population in the Russian-controlled guberniia (a province under the czarist governor) of Turkistan, plus the vassal states of Bukhara and Khiva, was put at 6 million in 1889. A contemporary observer found a figure of 5,490,538 inhabitants for the same region in 1885 too low, and criticized the inclusion of 642,000 inhabitants living on "Afghan territory," that is, in the small Afghan khanates, such as Maymene, Andjuy, Akche, and Shiborgan, which were, in fact, not under Russian control.[2] The total population of the Russian guberniia of Turkistan (excluding Bukhara and Khiva) was estimated at 2,448,538 in 1885, while one of the first American observers of the Central Asian scene in 1876 placed it at the low figure of 1.6 million.[3]

The variation poses the problem of attempting to assess the accuracy of these estimates in the light of later and presumably more

---

[1] G. N. Curzon, *Russia in Central Asia* (London, Longmans, Green, 1889), pp. 252–53.

[2] *Ibid.*, L. Kostenko, *Sredniaia Aziia i vodvorenie v nei russkoi grazhdanstvennosti* (St. Petersburg, Izdatel'stvo Bazunova, 1870), pp. 19–21.

[3] Eugene Schuyler, *Turkistan: Notes of a Journey in Russian Turkistan, Khokand, Bukhara, and Kuldja* (New York, Scribner, 1877), I, 109.

accurate statistics. This is because of the division of the whole Central Asian region at this period into three major areas: the guberniia of the Steppe, the guberniia of Turkistan, and the vassal khanates. In the case of the guberniia of Turkistan, several changes in territorial organization took place between the period of the population estimates made between 1885 and the first census of the region in 1897. In 1882 Semirechie oblast was included in the territory of the Steppe guberniia, only to be united with the Turkistan guberniia in 1899. Thus the estimate of population established in 1885 did not include Semirechie oblast, although a figure for Transcaspia is shown. The actual delineation of some of the territories given is also uncertain at this period.

Not until the czarist census of 1897 did accurate population statistics for the guberniia of Turkistan first appear. At this date the total population for the region (including Semirechie) was 5,281,-000. An estimate of the population of the same area in 1911 was 6,493,000, giving an increase of 23 percent during the period, or an annual rate of over 1.5 percent.[4] Assuming a rate of increase of 1 percent per annum for the period 1885–1897, this would give a total population in 1885 for the guberniia of Turkistan (in terms of the 1911 boundaries) of some 4.7 million, which makes the estimate for that date look very low, even allowing a very generous addition of one million inhabitants of Semirechie and other territories possibly excluded from this estimate.

The census of 1897 did not include the vassal khanates of Bukhara and Khiva, and, until their incorporation in the Soviet state, figures for their population were recorded locally on the basis of family units. In 1885 the population of Bukhara was calculated by the Russians to comprise 2 million and that of Khiva 400,000 inhabitants.[5] In 1913 the Bukharan population was put at 2.5 million, or not less than 2.25 million and probably not as high as 3 million. The population of Khiva then was said to be 550,000. Adding these estimates to a 1909 figure for the guberniia of Turkistan of 6.48 million produced a total population of the guberniia and the

[4] *Aziatskaia Rossiia, Atlas* (St. Petersburg, Pereselencheskoe Upravlienie Glavnago Upravlieniia Zemleustroistva i Zemledieliia, 1914), plates 34 and 25.
[5] Curzon, p. 252.

khanates at that date of 9.53 million.[6] Another estimate of the
Bukharan population in 1913–14 was 3.6 million, and for Khiva
800,000. Adding these to a total population of the guberniia of
Turkistan of 6,761,000 gives a total population in 1913–14 for the
guberniia and the khanates of 11,161,000.[7]

If the 1897 census total for the guberniia of Turkistan of 5,281,000
inhabitants is accepted as the only reliable report for the prerevolutionary period, the figure of 6,761,000 for the same area in 1913–
14 represents an annual increase of about 1.6 percent, which seems
reasonable for the period under consideration. The high totals for
Bukhara and Khiva are probably more reliable than the lower, as
underestimation of the population of less-developed countries was
as common at that time as it is today. Whatever the accuracy of
these various estimates may be, there is little more to go on in attempts to arrive at an accurate picture of the prerevolutionary population of Central Asia.

Direct comparison of the population of Central Asia during the
Soviet period with that of the prerevolutionary period is impossible
because of the boundary changes which took place in the region in
1924 and 1925. The area described in Soviet publications as "Central Asia" (Uzbekistan, Tajikistan, Turkmenistan, and Kirgizistan),
and so designated in the population censuses from 1926 on, is
smaller than the total area of the old guberniia of Turkistan plus
the states of Bukhara and Khiva by the removal from it of parts of
Semirechie and Sir Darya oblasts and their addition to the republic
of Kazakhstan. Between the censuses of 1926 and 1939 several
changes took place in the areas of the republics, which make direct
comparison of the population figures given in the two censuses
difficult. Apart from losing some minor areas between 1926 and
1929, Kazakhstan lost Karakalpakistan to Uzbekistan in 1936, while
the Tajik ASSR was promoted to a Union republic in 1929 and de-

[6] V. P. Semenov-Tian-Shanskii, ed., *Rossiia: polnoe geograficheskoe opisanie
nashego otechestva*: vol. XIX, *Turkestanskii krai* (St. Petersburg, A. F. Devrien,
1913), pp. 346, 347, 348.

[7] V. Suvorov, *Istoriko-ekonomicheskii ocherk razvitiia Turkestana* (Tashkent,
Gosizdat UzSSR, 1962), p. 68. The estimate of the population of Russian
Turkistan given by Suvorov is very close to a 1915 estimate of 6,779,783,
given by A. M. Aminov, *Ekonomicheskoe razvitie Srednei Azii* (*kolonial'nyi
period*) (Tashkent, Gosizdat UzSSR, 1959), p. 141.

tached from Uzbekistan, receiving at the same time part of the Farghana Valley. Kirgizistan and Turkmenistan remained virtually unchanged in area from 1925 to the present. However, Soviet statisticians have made allowances for these boundary changes, as well as for minor changes occurring between 1939 and 1959, and it is possible to compare directly the population totals for Central Asia given in Table 3.1.

These figures show the rapid growth of population experienced in the Central Asian republics at all times, when compared with average rate of growth of the Soviet Union as a whole. World War II caused a marked drop in the rate of growth of the population of all regions of the Soviet Union, but the Central Asian republics still maintained an average rate of growth well above the national average. This was caused by the great influx of people from the western regions of the Soviet Union to the cities of Central Asia, in particular to Tashkent, Dushanbe (Stalinabad), Frunze (Pishpek), and others. In the 1939–1940 period the population of Tashkent increased by 5 percent, with more than one-third of this increase consisting of immigrants from the RSFSR.[8] This movement of an estimated 2 million people to Central Asia was, of course, a deliberate policy on the part of the Soviet government, and was linked to the transfer of industrial plants from areas threatened with enemy occupation. In 1941 and early 1942 over 250 enterprises of various sizes were evacuated from the west and relocated in southern Central Asia and Kazakhstan.[9] The expansion of other branches of industry also called for an increase in the Central Asian labor force, which was met largely by the resettlement of workers from other regions.

URBANIZATION

With the movement of industrial rather than rural workers into the region it is not surprising to find that the rate of urbanization

[8] E. Tashbekov, "Migratsionnye sviazi naseleniia Tashkenta," *Izvestiia uzbekistanskogo filiala geograficheskogo obshchestva SSSR,* No. 6 (1962), pp. 91–102.
[9] N. A. Voznesensky, *The Economy of the USSR during World War II* (Washington, D. C., Public Affairs Press, 1948), p. 30. This is a translation of *Voennaia ekonomika SSSR v period otechestvennoi voiny* (Moscow, 1947).

TABLE 3.1

Population of Central Asian Republics within Boundaries of September 17, 1939

	1926 census	1939 census	Average annual increase, 1926–39 (percent)	1959 census	Average annual increase, 1939–59 (percent)	1962 estimate	Average annual increase, 1959–62 (percent)
Kazakh SSR	6,074,000	6,094,000	—	9,310,000	2.7	10,934,000	5.8
Kazakhs	3,713,000	2,640,000	−2.2	2,755,000	0.2	—	—
Kirgiz SSR	1,002,000	1,458,000	3.5	2,066,000	2.1	2,318,000	4.1
Kirgiz	661,000	760,000	1.2	837,000	0.5	—	—
Tajik SSR	1,032,000	1,484,000	3.4	1,980,000	1.7	2,188,000	3.5
Tajiks	619,000	890,000	3.4	1,051,000	0.9	—	—
Turkmen SSR	998,000	1,252,000	2.0	1,516,000	1.1	1,683,000	3.8
Turkmens	720,000	740,000	0.2	924,000	1.3	—	—
Uzbek SSR	4,565,000	6,336,000	2.9	8,106,000	1.4	8,986,000	3.6
Uzbeks	3,299,000	4,080,000	1.8	5,026,000	1.2	—	—
Central Asia	13,671,000	16,624,000	2.2	22,978,000	1.9	26,109,000	4.6
(Soviet Union)	(147,000,000)	(190,678,000)	(1.2)	(208,827,000)	(0.5)	(219,745,000)	(1.8)

increased rapidly during World War II. This can be seen in Table 3.2.

TABLE 3.2

Percent of Urban Population to Total Population, 1926–1959

	1926	1939	1959
Kazakh SSR	9	28	44
Kirgiz SSR	12	19	34
Tajik SSR	10	17	33
Turkmen SSR	14	33	46
Uzbek SSR	22	23	34
(Soviet Union)	(18)	(32)	(48)

Source: Population statistics from 1926 on are from various statistical yearbooks as well as from I. Iu. Pisarev, *Narodnonaselenie SSSR* (Moscow, Sotsekgiz, 1962), and P. G. Pod"iachikh, *Naselenie SSSR* (Moscow, Gosizdatpolitlit, 1961).

This compares with an urban population in the guberniia of Turkistan of 13.8 percent of total population in 1897 and 16.3 percent in 1911.[10]

Table 3.3 gives some idea of the different rates of growth and decline experienced by some of the major cities and towns of southern Central Asia since the beginning of the period of Russian control.

Many Central Asian cities of some importance during the pre-revolutionary period either stagnated during the. Soviet period or actually lost population. Such were Bukhara (shown in Table 3.3) and Qarshi (Behbudiy), the second city of the emirate, with an estimated 70,000 inhabitants in 1911 and only 19,000 in 1959. Osh, with about 52,000 inhabitants in 1914, had only 65,000 by 1959, and Shahr-i Sabz dropped from an estimated 33,000 in 1910 to 16,000 in 1959. The ancient city of Khiva dropped from its 1910 population of 20,000 to 17,000 in 1959, being eclipsed by Urganch, which had 44,000 inhabitants in 1959. Mari (Merv) on the other hand has shown a steady, if not spectacular growth, from an estimated 2,000 inhabitants in 1870 to 16,000 in 1910 and 48,000 in 1959.

One of the reasons for the loss of population in some of the cities, and the relatively slow growth of others between 1914 and 1926,

[10] Semenov-Tian-Shanskii, p. 349; Suvorov, p. 349.

TABLE 3.3

Population of Key Cities in Southern Central Asia

	1877 Schuyler	1897 census	1910 Russian estimate	1914 Russian estimate	1926 census	1939 census	1959 census
Tashkent	120,000	156,000	234,000	271,000	324,000	550,000	911,000
Alma Ata	12,000	23,000	36,000	43,000	45,000	222,000	455,000
Dushanbe	—	—	20,000	—	5,000	83,000	224,000
Frunze	—	7,000	14,000	14,000	37,000	93,000	217,000
Samarkand	30,000	55,000	90,000	98,000	105,000	136,000	195,000
Ashkhabad	—	19,000	44,000	—	52,000	127,000	170,000
Chimkent	—	11,000	16,000	20,000	21,000	74,000	153,000
Andijan	20,000	47,000	76,000	87,000	73,000	85,000	129,000
Namangan	—	62,000	74,000	81,000	74,000	80,000	122,000
Jambil	—	12,000	19,000	20,000	25,000	63,000	113,000
Khokand	75,000	82,000	114,000	120,000	69,000	85,000	105,000
Bukhara	—	75–100,000*	100,000	—	47,000	50,000	69,000

* estimate

Source: Estimates for 1877 from Eugene Schuyler, *Turkistan* (New York, Scribner, 1877), vols. I and II, passim. Estimates for 1910 from V. P. Semenov-Tien-Shanskii, ed., *Rossiia: polnoe geograficheskoe opisanie nashego otechestva* (St. Petersburg, Devrien, 1913), XIX, 348, and *Aziatskaia Rossiia: Atlas* (St. Petersburg, Pereselencheskoe Upravlienie Glavnago Upravlieniia Zemleustroistva i Zemledieliia, 1914), plate 61. Estimates for 1914 from V. V. Zaorskaia and K. A. Aleksandr, *Promyshlenniia zavedeniia turkestanskago kraia* (Petrograd, M. Z. Otdiel Zemel'nykh Uluchshenii, 1915). Wide variations occur in Soviet statistical yearbooks for the populations of cities in 1926, 1939, and 1959. These differences are mainly caused by attempts to make city populations comparable for at least two of the dates by calculating them within a fixed city boundary. Figures for 1939 and 1959 are from *Narodnoe khoziaistvo SSSR v 1958 godu* (Moscow, Gosstatizdat, 1959), which contains data based on the 1959 census, and are directly comparable. The unrealistic total given for Jambil has been replaced by one from P. G. Pod"iachikh, *Naselenie SSSR* (Moscow, Gosizdatpolitlit, 1961), p. 183.

was the disastrous famine of 1919. It is not possible to deduce these losses from the census figures because of the considerable changes in administrative areas which occurred between the two dates, but local nationalist leaders quote an official figure of 1,114,000 dead in southern Central Asia, and state that probably about one-third of the population, or three million people, died during the famine.[11] However, the larger figure seems high and in any comparison of the census figures it is difficult to account for such a great loss of life.

[11] M. Chokayev, "Turkestan and the Soviet Regime," *Journal of the Royal Central Asian Society*, XVIII (1931), 410.

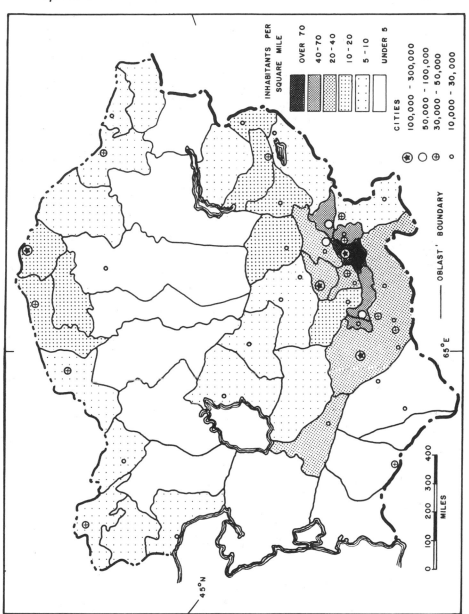

FIGURE 3.1 Urban and rural population in 1910.

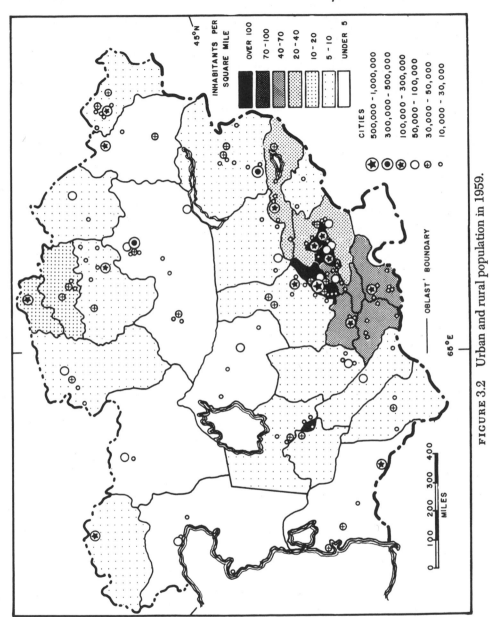

FIGURE 3.2 Urban and rural population in 1959.

Most of the cities with a striking rate of growth during the Soviet period have been centers of industry and administration, often with no significant economic function during the pre-Russian period. Some of these cities were established during the czarist period, such as Farghana (Skobelev, Novyi Margelan), Krasnovodsk, Frunze, Alma Ata (Vernyi), Termez, and Kagan (Novaia Bukhara). Frunze, originally a Khokand fort, Alma Ata, and Termez achieved some importance at an early time as Russian military posts, the first two later developing into important administrative and industrial centers. Krasnovodsk was primarily a port and railroad town, while Kagan and Farghana were small industrial centers. When the railroad was extended to Bukhara in 1907 Kagan lost its reason for existence, but Farghana has continued to grow from an estimated 13,000 people in 1914 to 80,000 in 1959, reflecting its importance as a petroleum-refining and cotton-ginning center and sharing the growth of its three important industrial neighbors, Andijan, Namangan, and Khokand.

Chimkent, once a trade center between the nomads of the plains and the sedentary farmers, owes its increased population (see Table 3.3) in the Soviet period to its importance as a processing center for the metallic ores from the nearby Qaratau, and is the largest producer of lead in the Soviet Union. Jambil (Auliye Ata) (see Table 3.3), once considered in the 1870s as a possible capital for the guberniia of Turkistan, has also become an important industrial center during the Soviet period, and has a large superphosphate plant, sugar refinery, and footwear factory.

Of all the cities of Central Asia Tashkent has shown the most remarkable growth. Although the exact date of the city's founding is not known it is probable that a settlement existed on the site of present-day Tashkent in the first or second century B.C. The location of this settlement in the valley of the Chirchiq River was favorable for the development of a prosperous oasis and for the development of trade links between the inhabitants of the mountains and the plains as well as between the sedentary farmers and the nomads. These factors account for the rise of Tashkent as a trade and handicraft center of some significance before 1865, but a center of only secondary importance when compared with Bukhara, Samarkand, or

Khokand. The rapid growth of Tashkent during the czarist period was due to its selection as the administrative center of the guberniia of Turkistan, and the development of the Trans-Caspian and Oren-burg-Tashkent railroads was also instrumental in ensuring the further economic growth of the city. Tashkent became, during this period, the largest city of Central Asia and its main administrative, trade, and industrial center.

During the Soviet period the expansion of Tashkent, now the capital of Uzbekistan, has continued at an even greater rate than before. Added to its administrative and economic functions are those of a major center of education with the foundation of a large university and other educational establishments. Industrialization has proceeded speedily, and at present about half the labor force of the city is employed in industry with about a quarter employed in government and educational establishments. Tashkent is also the major center of Russian concentration in Central Asia, more than half its present population of over a million being made up of Russians and Ukrainians. Its convenient location in regard to the capitals of the other Central Asian republics, whether by design or accident, enables this center of Russian domination to exercise a strong economic influence over the whole of the Central Asian region.

In contrast to Bukhara, Samarkand has maintained its importance as a trade center throughout both the czarist and Soviet periods. Once the railroad reached Samarkand in 1888, having bypassed Bukhara, the former developed more rapidly and during the Soviet period became one of the largest industrial centers in Uzbekistan, apart from Tashkent and the industrial cities of the Farghana Valley.

It should be noted that the cities of Andijan and Khokand, apart from their present industrial significance, also owed their growth in the prerevolutionary period to their importance as trade and administrative centers for the Farghana Valley. Andijan became one of the terminal points of the Trans-Caspian Railroad in 1898, while Khokand had been the capital of the khanate and the administrative center of an uezd in czarist times, which accounts for its rapid growth during the prerevolutionary period. Khokand lost its place as an administrative center after the revolution to the rising industrial center of Farghana, and suffered a drop in population. The growth of its cotton-ginning industry and the addition of metal-working and chemical fertilizer industries have helped to revitalize the city, and in recent years its population has again been on the increase.

The growth of many of these urban centers has been closely linked with the movement of Russians into the region since the 1860s, and before the effects of this movement on urban growth can be understood, it is necessary to take into account the changes which have occurred in the ethnic composition of the population of Central Asia through the years. As it is difficult to distinguish between the Kazakh population of the southern part of the guberniia of Turkistan and of the plains oblasts after the Kazakhs in these areas were united in the one republic, it will be proper to consider the whole of Central Asia and not merely the southern area alone. However, as the influx of Russians into Kazakhstan has created special problems, Kazakhstan will also be treated later as a special case.

CHANGES IN NATIONAL COMPOSITION

Table 3.4 shows the growth of the main nationalities in Central Asia between 1897 and 1911.

Perhaps the most striking fact emerging from the figures given in Table 3.4 is the rapid growth of the Russian population between 1897 and 1911. Most of this increase took place in the Steppe guberniia, where the Russian population rose from 493,000 in 1897 or 20 percent of the total population, to 1,544,000 in 1911 or 40 percent of the total. Much of the growth occurred in the rural areas when Russian settlers moved into the plains in large numbers after the settlement law of 1904 removed the necessity for the settlers to obtain special permission from the government. In the Turkistan guberniia the Russian population was proportionately much smaller than in the Steppe guberniia because of restrictions placed on Russian settlement in the rural areas until 1910. Apart from the strict limits placed on the influx of Russian peasants into the guberniia of Turkistan, the necessity of operating and maintaining an irrigation system as well as the cultivation of cotton did

TABLE 3.4

Nationalities of Central Asia (Excluding Bukhara and Khiva)

	1897 census	1911 survey
*Kazakhs	3,787,000	4,692,000
"Sarts"	1,458,000	1,847,000
Uzbeks	535,000	592,000
Tajiks	338,000	397,000
Turkmens	249,000	290,000
*Kirgiz	202,000	not shown
Karakalpaks	112,000	134,000
Tatars	60,000	87,000
*Taranchis	30,000	83,000
*Kashgaris	41,000	55,000
*"Turks"	440,000	not shown
(Russians and Ukrainians)	(690,000)	(1,950,000)
Total (excluding Russians and Ukrainians)	7,252,000	8,177,000

* In the 1897 census the Kazakhs were called "Kirgiz" and the Kirgiz "Kara-Kirgiz." However, the Kirgiz as such were not shown in the 1911 survey and were presumably included in the number of Kazakhs. The "Turks" seem to have been included among the Uzbeks in the 1911 survey. These "Turks," of whom more than half (261,000) were living in Farghana oblast in 1897, probably were the groups of nomadic peoples of the Farghana Valley and Tajikistan, who referred to themselves variously as Turks, Kipchaks, or Qarluqs. Some Azerbaijanians, or other Turkic-speaking people from outside the Central Asian region, also may have been included in their numbers. The Taranchis and Kashgaris belonged to groups which are today included with the Uyghurs. In the 1926 census, however, they were still listed separately.

Source: Based on figures given in *Aziatskaia Rossiia* (St. Petersburg, Pereselencheskoe Upravlienie Glavnago Upravleniia Zemleustroistva i Zemledieliia, 1914), I, 79, and on census returns quoted in various publications.

not appeal to the Russians, who preferred areas suitable for dry farming where wheat or other grain could be grown—hence, Russian preference for the northern plains lands. The subject of Russian rural settlement has been dealt with in detail by scholars who have shown that this settlement was at all stages clearly detrimental to the interests of the local population both in Kazakhstan and southern Central Asia.[12]

The 1897 census showed 197,420 Russians in the guberniia of Turkistan (including Transcaspia) of which 95,465 were in Semirechie oblast. By 1910 the number had risen to 382,688, of which

[12] Aminov, pp. 120–40; R. A. Pierce, *Russian Central Asia 1867–1917* (Berkeley and Los Angeles, University of Californa Press, 1960); pp. 107–38.

188,016 were in Semirechie, reflecting the attraction of this area of dry farming for the Russian peasant. There were large numbers of Russian Cossacks as well as peasants in the region and, around 1910, Cossacks were farming 1.6 million acres (610,000 *desiatin*) in Semirechie, while in 1908 the Russian settlers had occupied about 624,000 acres (231,000 *desiatin*). The only other oblast with a large Russian population was Sir Darya, which had 101,289 settlers in 1910, while the more densely populated oblasts of Farghana and Samarkand, with their predominantly irrigated agriculture, had only attracted 29,000 and 23,000 Russians, respectively, by 1910.[13]

By no means all of this Russian population of the Turkistan guberniia lived in rural areas, and the growth of the cities was to a considerable extent due to Russian immigration. Tashkent by 1914 had a large Russian section, built along European lines, with a population of 84,500 or 31 percent of the total population of 271,-000, while Samarkand in 1908 had 11,650 Russians out of a total population of 80,700. Farghana, which was established as an industrial center by the Russians, had a predominantly Russian population, with about 70 percent of the 1911 population of 11,000 being Russian. In the same year the 36,000 inhabitants of Vernyi included 26,000 Russians, while Frunze had a Russian population of 8,000 out of a total of 14,000.[14]

The vassal states of Bukhara and Khiva began to attract a small core of Russian population. The 1897 census shows 12,150 Russians in Bukhara and 3,951 in Khiva. By 1911 there were 27,000 Russians in Bukhara state, including troops, of which 8,000 were in Charjuy, 6,000 in Termez, and 5,000 in Karki. Kagan had 3,000 Russians, while the city of Bukhara itself had only about 2,000.[15]

By the 1917 revolution a solid core of Russian population had developed in the whole area of Central Asia, and by 1911 about 40 percent of the total population of the Steppe oblasts were Russians, compared to only 6.3 percent of the total population of the guberniia of Turkistan. However small these beginnings may seem,

[13] Semenov-Tian-Shanskii, pp. 362, 419.
[14] V. V. Bartol'd, *Istoriia kul'turnoi zhizni Turkestana* (Leningrad, Izdatel'-stvo Akademii Nauk SSSR 1927), pp. 161–63, 168.
[15] D. N. Logofet, *Bukharskoe khanstvo pod russkim protektoratom* (St. Petersburg, V. Berezovskii, 1911), I, 186.

they represented a trend which was to accelerate rapidly during the Soviet period, as can be seen from Table 3.5b.

TABLE 3.5a

Central Asians Residing Throughout the Soviet Union

	1926 census	1939 census	1959 census
Kazakhs	3,968,000	3,099,000	3,581,000
Uzbeks	3,905,000	4,844,000	6,004,000
Tajiks	979,000	1,229,000	1,397,000
Turkmens	764,000	812,000	1,004,000
Kirgiz	763,000	884,000	974,000
Karakalpaks	146,000	186,000	173,000
Taranchis	53,000	—	—
Kashgaris (Uyghurs)	13,000	—	—
Uyghurs	43,000	—	95,000

TABLE 3.5b

Aliens Residing in Central Asia

	1926 census	1939 census	1959 census
Russians and Ukrainians	2,726,000	—	7,300,000
Tatars	119,000	—	786,000
Germans	61,000	—	791,000
Koreans	—	73,000	213,000

In the 1926 census the "Sarts" were divided into Uzbeks and Tajiks, but there were no doubt some people who had been classified in 1897 as Uyghurs, Taranchis, and Kashgaris, and who had been reclassified in 1926 as Uzbeks or were included with other groups. It is therefore difficult to compare all figures in Tables 3.5a and 3.5b with those for 1897 or 1911. Reports from the 1939 Soviet census gave no detailed breakdown of ethnic groups by republics. This means that accurate figures are not available for the number of Russians, Ukrainians, or other foreign groups in the Central Asian republics between 1926 and 1959.

In spite of this lack of specific data, revealing analyses have been made of the drop in Kazakh population between 1926 and 1939 because of loss of life during the collectivization campaign in Kazakhstan, and of the number of Russians in the republic in 1939. The figures quoted in Table 3.5a show that the total Kazakh population of the Soviet Union (a few thousands live outside the boundaries of that Central Asian republic) decreased between 1926 and 1939

by 869,000 or by 21.9 percent. Applying this percentage decrease
to the Kazakh population of Kazakhstan in 1926 produces a 1939
figure for this population of 2,833,000. Taking the number of other
non-Russians at the same date and adding it to the estimate of the
Kazakh population, and subtracting this figure from the total population of Kazakhstan in 1939 gives a Russian population of 2,877,000
compared with 2,165,000 in 1926, an increase of 33 percent. In 1939
about 47 percent of the population was thus Russian, compared
with 35 percent in 1926. The Kazakh population formed only 46
percent of the total population of its own republic in 1939 as compared with 59 percent in 1926. The influx of Russians during the
period of the early Five Year plans was directed mainly to the
cities of Kazakhstan, the rural population of Russian origin remaining stable at that time.[16]

This movement of Russians to Kazakhstan is reflected in the
rapid increase in the size of cities shown in Table 3.6. The rapid
growth of these cities after 1926 in particular is accounted for by
the increasing numbers of Russians moving into the region.

TABLE 3.6

Cities of Kazakhstan

	1897	1911	1926	1939	1959
Karaganda	—	—	—	156,000	398,000
Semipalatinsk	26,000	34,000	57,000	110,000	155,000
Ust-Kamenogorsk	9,000	13,000	14,000	20,000	149,000
Petropavlovsk	20,000	43,000	47,000	92,000	131,000
Uralsk	37,000	46,000	36,000	67,000	105,000
Tselinograd (Akmolinsk)	10,000	14,000	13,000	32,000	101,000
Aktyubinsk	3,000	11,000	21,000	49,000	97,000
Pavlodar	8,000	10,000	18,000	29,000	90,000
Kustanay	14,000	25,000	25,000	34,000	86,000

Note: For Alma Ata and Jambil, see Table 3.3.

The recent growth of several of these cities is explained by the
expansion of mining and ore processing in the plains during and
since World War II. Karaganda is a coal-mining and more recently
an iron-and-steel center, while Ust-Kamenogorsk has a large zinc-
smelting plant and a titanium-magnesium plant, processing ores

[16] O. Caroe, *Soviet Empire* (London, MacMillan, 1953), pp. 166–69.

from the Altay region. Pavlodar has an alumina plant, processing bauxite from the Kustanay region, while Kustanay itself has recently become the center of an iron-mining region. Aktyubinsk is an important center for the production of chromium and ferroalloys. Smaller mining centers such as Leninogorsk (Ridder) and Ziryanovsk in the Altay have also shown rapid growth, and in 1959 had populations of 67,000 and 54,000 respectively, compared with 50,000 and 16,000 in 1939. Many of the other large cities have become important as service centers for the farming areas of the Virgin Lands. Tselinograd (Akmolinsk), as capital of the Tselinnyi Krai, has not only become an important administrative and transportation center, but has the largest farm machinery plant in Kazakhstan (the "Kazakhsel'mash"), while Petropavlovsk also manufactures farm machinery and processes foodstuffs. Semipalatinsk has, like Petropavlovsk, a large meat-packing plant and processes wool, while Kokshetau (40,000 inhabitants in 1959) and Kustanay both process agricultural products. The population of all these cities is predominantly Russian and Ukrainian. Table 3.6 shows also that a period of stagnation or even of decreasing population occurred in such cities as Ust–Kamenogorsk, Petropavlovsk, Uralsk, and Tselinograd during World War I and the civil war. This low period was due to a decrease in Russian immigration, and to famine and loss of life. In fact, until the 1930s, most of the cities of northern Kazakhstan contained little industry or other significant economic activities. Because of their lack of population the city of Orenburg was chosen as the capital of the Kirgiz (Kazakh) ASSR from 1920 to 1925.

The details given in the 1959 census show quite clearly the large numbers of Russians now in the Central Asian region. In Kazakhstan the census reported 4,014,000 Russians and 762,000 Ukrainians, who together made up 51 percent of the total population of the republic, as compared with the 2,755,000 Kazakhs comprising about 30 percent of the total population. If to the figure for Russians and Ukrainians are added the totals given for other nationalities in Kazakhstan who have come from outside the Central Asian area, it is clear that no less than 64 percent of the population is alien to the region. This predominance of foreigners is even more marked in the Tselinnyi Krai, where out of a total population of 2,753,100 in 1959, 46.2 percent were Russians, 14 percent were Ukrainians, 12.1 percent Germans, and only 19 percent were Kazakhs.[17]

To a lesser extent, the same trend can be seen in the other Central Asian republics. In Kirgizistan in 1959 there were 624,000 Russians and 137,000 Ukrainians, together forming about 37 percent of the total population, while there were 837,000 Kirgiz living within the boundaries of their own republic, making up only 40 percent of the total population, compared to 52 percent in 1939 and 66 percent in 1926. Most of the remaining population of the republic consisted of other Central Asian ethnic groups as well as some Tatars. Uzbekistan had 1,101,000 Russians and 88,000 Ukrainians at the same date, but these formed only 15 percent of the population, the 5,026,000 Uzbeks making up 62 percent of the total, compared with 65 percent in 1939 and 74 percent in 1926. In Tajikistan 15 percent of the total population were Russians and Ukrainians, and only 53 percent were Tajiks, compared to 60 percent in 1939 and 75 percent in 1926. However, there were 454,000 Uzbeks in Tajikistan in 1959, who made up about 23 percent of the population.

Turkmenistan is the only area where a slight gain over the Russian increase has been registered by the local population in recent years. The number of Turkmen living in their own republic rose slightly from 720,000 in 1926, or 72 percent of the total population, to 740,000 in 1939, or only 59 percent, as Russians and others moved into the area in greater numbers. However, by 1959 the number of Turkmen in the republic reached 924,000 and formed 61 percent of the total population, a greater proportion than before the war. The number of Russians in the Turkmen republic did not increase significantly during this period, being about 226,000 or 18 percent of the population in 1939, and 263,000 or 17 percent in 1959.

The trends in Russian immigration illustrated by the above figures were already beginning to be established during the czarist

[17] Ia. R. Vinnikov, "Formation of the Population of Tselinnyi Kray of the Kazakh SSR," *Soviet Geography*, vol. III, No. 4 (April, 1962), p. 37.

period. The Kirgiz republic was formed in 1926 mainly from the southern part of what was Semirechie oblast, one of the areas of original Russian settlement in southern Central Asia. The Chu Valley and the Issik Kol basin are areas of Russian agriculture, based on wheat and sugar beet, while the urban population of the republic is predominantly Russian, with the Kirgiz population still located mainly in the mountain regions. In Uzbekistan the main influx of Russian population took place during the prewar Five Year plans and the World War II period, and thus most of the Russian population is located in the major urban and industrial areas, such as Tashkent, Samarkand, and the cities of the Farghana Valley, the rural areas being predominantly Uzbek, a pattern already apparent in czarist times. The same pattern exists in Tajikistan. Turkmenistan had not attracted many Russians during the czarist period, and even after the revolution the lack of industry in the republic did not encourage the influx of a large number of Russian workers.

In the face of this increasing number of Russian immigrants about the only consolation for the local people is their relatively high rate of increase. Between 1939 and 1959 the number of Uzbeks increased by 25 percent, the number of Turkmen by 23 percent, of Kazakhs by 17 percent, of Tajiks by 14 percent, and of Kirgiz by 10 percent. This compares with an increase in the Russian population in the Soviet Union of about 8 percent during the same period, and an increase of 9.5 percent for the whole population of the Soviet Union. At the present rate of Russian immigration into the Central Asian region, however, even these high rates of natural increase of population will not be sufficient to stabilize the ethnic balance of population in the region within the foreseeable future.

Apart from the large numbers of Slavs who have appeared in the Central Asian region over the last hundred years, there are some smaller groups which are worthy of comment because of their unique character. Perhaps the most unusual of these groups has been the Korean. The 1959 census listed 139,000 Koreans in Uzbekistan, 74,000 in Kazakhstan, and 2,400 in Tajikistan. Many of these Koreans were moved to Central Asia from the Far East

in the 1930s, probably because of their resistance to collectivization and also possibly because of fears that they might prove to
be an unreliable element in case of war with Japan. They were
employed mainly in scattered areas where rice was grown.

The German population has grown in size considerably since
1926. In 1959 there were about 700,000 Germans in Kazakhstan,
40,000 in Kirgizistan, and 33,000 in Tajikistan.[18] About half the
Germans in Kazakhstan live in the area of the Tselinnyi Krai,
many of them being Volga Germans, deported to the area like
the Crimean Tatars during World War II when their republic on
the Volga was abolished. Some are also no doubt prisoners-of-war
who were never returned to Germany after the war. Many of the
Germans in Tajikistan seem to live in Dushanbe.

Although they cannot be classified as one of the indigenous nationalities of Central Asia, the Tatars as a group have increased
greatly in size and importance during the last hundred years.
Many Tatars arrived during the czarist period as political or commercial agents of the Russians, who assumed, not always correctly, that the Tatars, being Muslims, would be acceptable to
the Turkic-speaking Muslim people of Central Asia. Between
1897 and 1911 the number of Tatars in the guberniias of the
Steppe and of Turkistan rose from 60,074 to 87,015, of which
about two-thirds lived in the guberniia of the Steppe. By 1926
the number of Tatars in Central Asia had reached 119,000.

In the census of 1959 no fewer than 786,017 Tatars were recorded in Central Asia, of which 450,987 resided in Uzbekistan
and 191,925 in Kazakhstan. This great increase in the Tatar population is without doubt accounted for not only by the traditional
emigration of numbers of Tatars from the Volga region to other
parts of the Soviet Union and Central Asia in particular, but also
by the deportation of the Crimean Tatars to Central Asia in punishment for alleged collaboration with the Germans during World
War II. Unlike such groups as the Kalmyks and Chechen-Ingush,
the Crimean Tatars have never been restored to their homeland,
probably in view of the strategic and somewhat sensitive nature

[18] "The Size of the German Population in Kazakhstan and Central Asia,"
Central Asian Review, X (1959), 372–73.

of the Crimean location, and continue to live among their Turkic-speaking fellows in Central Asia.

Figures 3.1 and 3.2 illustrate the changes which have taken place in Central Asian population densities between 1910 and 1959. Alterations in administrative boundaries between those two dates make an exact comparison impossible, but the maps show the great concentration of population in the Farghana region. At present, the population density on the alluvial fans of the Farghana Valley averages over 1,000 per square mile, while around Andijan at the eastern end of the valley it rises to over 2,000 persons per square mile. This great concentration of population in a small area is in strong contrast with the large desert and semidesert still virtually uninhabited.

THE LAND AND ITS USES

Few regions of the world offer such a dramatic background to man's activities as does Central Asia. It is a land of great contrasts with vast lowlands scorched by the heat in summer and swept by icy winds in winter, crossed by great rivers. Beyond these grasslands and deserts rise the huge mountain ranges of the heart of Asia, capped with eternal snow and ice.

A glance at the map of Asia does not convey the immense size of the Central Asian region, small as it may seem in relation to the whole Eurasian continent. The total area of Central Asia is some 1.5 million square miles, or just less than half the area of the continental United States, excluding Alaska. Kazakhstan alone covers over 1 million square miles, and is four times the size of Texas. Uzbekistan, with its 158,000 square miles, has the same area as California, while the smallest of the Central Asian republics, Tajikistan (54,000 square miles), is comparable in area to Wisconsin. By far the largest part of Central Asia consists of plains and low uplands, rising to mountain ranges on the east and south.

The western area of Kazakhstan includes part of the Caspian lowland, a region of desert and salt marshes, lying below sea level. Moving eastward, however, the land gradually rises, and north of the Aral Sea the Mugojar hills, a spur of the southern Urals, reach a height of some 2,000 feet. East of this the land becomes flat again, forming the Turgay lowlands. These lowlands in fact form a wide gap between the southern end of the Urals and the Kazakh uplands to the east. The Kazakh uplands are the eroded remnants of a formerly large mountain region, and contain many deposits of varied minerals. They average about 1,200 feet in height, with occasional elevations of 3 to 4,000 feet and cover most of central and eastern Kazakhstan. The northern edge of the Kazakh uplands is bordered by the southern part of the great West Siberian plain. This plain forms one of the major regions of settlement and agricultural activity in northern Central Asia. Between the southern edge of the Kazakh uplands and the Chu River lies the Betpak Dala (Plain of Misfortune) generally referred to as the "Hungry Steppe." (This region is not to be confused with the Mirzachol Sahra, to the southwest of Tashkent, also known as the "Hungry Steppe.") The Betpak Dala is a plateau covered with a clay and salt-marsh desert, with no running water in any form.

East of the Kazakh uplands rise the Altay mountains to a height of over 14,000 feet in west Siberia. A hundred miles to the south of the Altay the outlying ranges of the main massif of the Central Asian mountains begin. The northern mass of mountains, known as the Tien Shan, stretch over a thousand miles from east to west and reach over 15,000 feet in many areas, and up to 24,000 feet in Kirgizistan. These mountains contain two basins, one filled by the Issik Kol and the other forming the Farghana Valley, about 180 miles in length and 90 miles across at its widest point. The southern part of the Central Asian massif is known as the Pamirs, a solid mass of east-west ranges, rising to over 24,000 feet, and capped with eternal snow and ice. In contrast to the valleys of the Tien Shan, the Pamir valleys lie at a high altitude and support only a sparse population. To the west and north of the Tien Shan stretch the vast Turanian lowlands, consisting of desert and semi-desert country. These lowlands are bisected by the Amu Darya, which also marks the boundary between the two largest areas of sand desert in Central Asia, the Qizil Qum to the north and the Qara Qum to the south. Although the translation of "Qizil Qum" as "red sand" and "Qara Qum" as "black sand" is generally accepted,

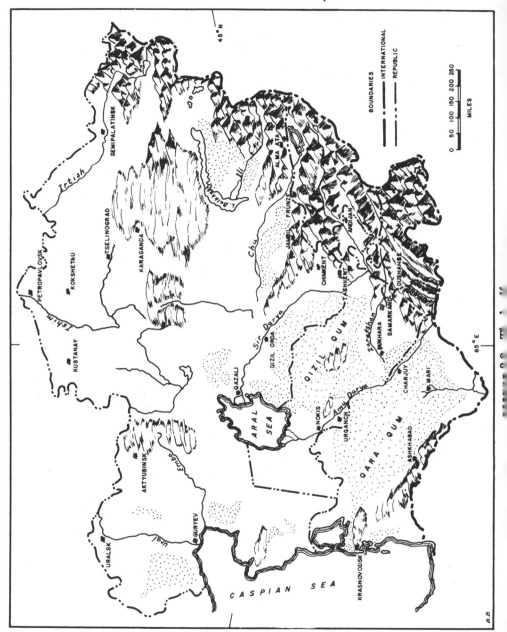

a Soviet geographer claims that *qara* in this context should be translated as "land" rather than "black." Thus "Qara Qum" would mean "land sand," that is, immovable, fixed sand. This interpretation seems unlikely in view of the color contrast offered by "Qizil Qum." [19] Along the southern edge of the Qara Qum lies the range of the Kopet Dagh, a spur of the northern Iranian mountains, and to the northwest of the Qara Qum rises the plateau of the Ustyurt, a clay and gypsum desert containing many depressions which is virtually uninhabited. The plateau of the Mangishlak peninsula also contains many depressions and hollows, but supports a small population.

In a region of such recent mountain-building activity it is not surprising to find that earthquakes are common. In 1948 the city of Ashkhabad was practically destroyed by a severe earthquake, while in 1964 an earthquake on the upper reaches of the Zarafshan caused a major landslide which dammed the river and threatened the Zarafshan valley and the city of Samarkand with serious flooding. The northern ranges of the Tien Shan have also experienced earthquakes of various intensities, as have the northern parts of the Pamirs. The people of Bukhara experienced so many earth tremors and shocks during the course of the year that it is reported that they believed that the new year must always begin with an earthquake. The wise men of the city stuck a knife in the ground and when a tremor toppled it this was taken as a sign that the new year had begun.[20]

WATER

The whole Central Asian region has the form of a large basin, fringed by uplands and mountain ranges. Consequently, the drainage of this basin is toward its center, and, with the exception of some of the northward flowing rivers of northern Kazakhstan, none of the rivers of Central Asia reach the ocean. The two largest rivers, the Amu Darya and the Sir Darya, flow into the Aral Sea, while the Ural, Emba, and Atrek rivers flow into the landlocked

[19] A. M. Kononov, quoted in *Sovetskaia geografia* (Moscow, Gosizdatgeolit, 1960), p. 410.
[20] Kostenko, p. 27.

Caspian Sea. Many of the smaller rivers simply disappear into the desert, their volume greatly reduced by evaporation.

The Sir Darya, known to the Greeks as the Jaxartes, is the longest river in Central Asia, and is named the Narin in its upper reaches. Much of the water of the river is drawn off for irrigation purposes during its passage of the Farghana Valley, while its tributaries, such as the Chirchiq, also supply large quantities of irrigation water. Consequently, little water is available for irrigation purposes in the lower stretches of the river, and Soviet geographers foresee the day when demands for water in the upper parts of the river will be so great that virtually no water from the Sir Darya will reach the Aral Sea.[21] The Sir Darya carries much silt in suspension, and, in contrast to the Amu Darya, which carries much sand, the Sir Darya's bed and shoals are firm and stable. In spite of this, the river is not navigable due to the braiding of its channels and their lack of depth, especially in the lower course of the river. The river freezes only near its mouth for any long period, while at Leninabad (Khojand), in some years it often does not freeze at all. Flooding is quite common in the middle and lower reaches, and inhibits the development of settlements along the banks in these areas.

The Amu Darya, the Oxus of the ancients and the Jayhun of medieval Arab writers, supports life throughout almost its entire length. It has its source in a glacier in the Hindu Kush in Afghanistan and is known in its upper reaches as the Panj. Because of its volume of water and its considerable drop, the river carries enormous quantities of material in suspension. Among this material are large quantities of fertile silt (layqa), which adds greatly to the river's value for agricultural purposes. The bulk of this silt is deposited along its course and forms an excellent basis for the development of fertile soils.

Unfortunately for navigation on the Amu Darya, the large quantities of sand carried in suspension cause shifting sandbanks, which appear and disappear with amazing speed. Erosion of the river banks by the swift current is also a serious problem, the current often being deflected against the soft banks by the formation of

---

[21] Z. Murzaev, *Sredniaia Aziia* (Moscow, Gosizdatgeolit, 1957), p. 148.

a new sandbank, which causes the river to form a completely new bed for itself. In 1925 the city of Tortkul stood five miles from the river, while in 1950 the river had reached its streets. The city of Urganch on the lower Amu Darya was left waterless by a change in the course of the river in 1578.

The Sir and Amu Darya and most other rivers rising in the Tien Shan and Pamirs have two main periods of flooding, the first being when the snow on the lower mountain slopes melts in April and May, the second when the snow and ice of the upper slopes melt under the hot sun of June and July. Flooding in the case of the Amu Darya generally occurs in the flat plains near its mouth.

The Amu Darya does not freeze for long in winter so that the ice is never thick and it supports irrigation throughout its entire length, with the greatest area of actual and potential irrigated land occurring in the lower stretches, from south of Tortkul to the Aral Sea. Part of the river's waters once flowed through a channel which left it near its mouth, passed westwards through a lake, and reached the Caspian Sea south of the Cheleken peninsula. Traces remain of this dried-up river bed, known as the Uzboi, as well as swamps marking the site of Lake Sariqamish. Traces of an old irrigation system and accounts of travelers suggest that the Uzboi and the lake contained water up to the beginning of the sixteenth century. Another dead river, the Kelif Uzboi, stretches parallel to the Amu Darya, just north of the Afghan frontier, and has been used as a route for part of the Qara Qum canal.

Among the smaller rivers of Central Asia which have significance as suppliers of irrigation water must be noted the Zarafshan, the Qashqa Darya and Qarasu, the Murghab, the Tejen, and the three tributaries of the Amu Darya, the Vakhsh, the Kafirnihan, and the Surkhan Darya. Most of these rivers have a markedly seasonal flow; for example, the Zarafshan has 80 percent of its annual flow in the five months from May through September. Most of them also carry large quantities of silt in suspension.

In Kirgizistan and southern Kazakhstan the Chu and Ili rivers support considerable areas of irrigated agriculture. The Ili flows into Lake Balkhash and is navigable by small vessels in its upper reaches. The region watered by the Ili and the smaller parallel rivers to the north is known to the Kazakhs as Jeti Su, the Russian Semirechie. The main river of Kazakhstan is the Irtish, the principal tributary of the Ob. In spite of being frozen over for about four months in northern Kazakhstan, it is an important transporation route and is navigable northward from Lake Zaisan, although sandbanks are a hindrance in some stretches. A wide area on the right bank of the river has some potential importance for irrigated agriculture. The Ishim, a tributary of the Irtish, has little economic importance.

The inland seas and lakes of Central Asia are unique. The water level of the Caspian Sea has been dropping markedly in the last forty years and is now more than ninety feet below ocean level. Between 1929 and 1961 the water level fell 8 feet and 3 inches, affecting both transportation and fishing, especially in the Volga delta region. On the Central Asian shore the port of Krasnovodsk has had some difficulty in maintaining its facilities, and navigation is only possible by constant and expensive dredging of channels. This drop in the water level seems to be caused by a combination of diminishing precipitation in the Volga basin, and the increasing use of Volga water for irrigation, plus a high rate of evaporation from the surface of the reservoirs recently formed on the lower reaches of the river.

Several plans have been suggested for the solution of the problem, but none so far has been implemented. These involve such varied solutions as damming the north part of the Caspian to raise the water level in that section, diverting the waters of some of the north-flowing rivers into the Volga or into the channel of the Uzboi, or building a canal from the Amu Darya.[22] The latter scheme was a favored project of Stalin and went by the name of the Main Turkmen Canal. The plan, dropped around 1953, called for water from the Amu Darya to be diverted south of Nokis and led along the channel of the Uzboi to the Caspian near

[22] S. N. Bobrov, "The Transformation of the Caspian Sea," *Soviet Geography*, vol. II, No. 7 (September 1961), pp. 47–59; S. Iu. Geller, "On the Question of Regulating the Level of the Caspian Sea," *Soviet Geography*, vol. III, No. 1 (January 1962), pp. 59–66.

Krasnovodsk. This project was, however, not primarily aimed at raising the water level of the Caspian, but rather at irrigating the desert between it and the Amu Darya. It was actually the revival of a czarist scheme first considered by Peter the Great and then again in the 1870s and 1880s by Russian engineers. A German scientist of the time described the scheme as the "great Central Asian sea-serpent," a name which caused resentment in Russia.[23]

In contrast to the Caspian, which carries no less than 40 percent of Soviet coastal trade by volume, the Aral Sea has little economic value because of its size and location in desert country away from main routes. Fishing has some local importance. Lake Balkhash likewise has no economic significance. The Issik Kol, a lake which never freezes because of its salinity and the strong winds which generally keep its surface in motion, and hence is known to the Kirgiz as the "hot lake," provides an important transportation route for eastern Kirgizistan, being linked by a railroad to the rest of Western Turkistan.

CLIMATE AND VEGETATION

Central Asia, far removed from any large bodies of water, is reached by only residual amounts of rainfall from air masses of oceanic origin. Thus, the major factor controlling the climate is the region's location deep in the interior of the Eurasian continent. Precipitation is highest in the northern part, where about ten to twelve inches of average annual precipitation reach the northern borders of Kazakhstan, representing the southern edge of a diminishing wedge of moisture brought by westerly winds from the Atlantic. As we move southward, annual average precipitation decreases to about eight inches in the center of the republic, marking the southern limit of the climatic zone generally referred to as mid-latitude plain. To the south the land lies in the rain shadow of the great mountain mass of the Central Asian region which acts as a barrier to the moisture-laden air masses which originate over the oceans of southern Asia. This complete blocking of moist, warm air from the south and the increasing distance from the Atlantic cause semidesert and desert

[23] Curzon, p. 404n.

conditions to exist over most of the central and southern areas. Precipitation varies from four to eight inches per annum in the semidesert areas to less than four inches in the deserts. The mountain and foothill regions receive a higher rainfall on the average, and even the lower slopes of the mountains receive amounts of annual precipitation which vary from eight up to twelve inches.

In a dry, sunny climate evaporation of moisture out of the soil proceeds at a rapid rate, and, as might be expected, this rate increases as one moves from north to south into regions of higher summer temperatures. Unfortunately, the periods of maximum summer temperatures and maximum rainfall coincide to a great extent throughout Central Asia and result in very high rates of evaporation in areas such as central Turkmenistan. Average temperatures in July range from 75°F along the northern Kazakhstan border to over 90°F in south and central Turkmenistan, while winter temperatures are low, reflecting the extreme continentality of the region and the lack of any barrier to the cold, dry air masses originating in northeastern Siberia during the winter months. Northern Kazakhstan experiences January temperatures ranging on the average from 14°F in the west to 4°F in the east, and only the western and southeastern areas of Turkmenistan have temperatures on the average just above freezing in January. These temperatures are, of course, only averages, and temperatures of below zero are quite common throughout the whole of Central Asia. Snow cover is light and ranges from an average of eight to twelve inches in Kazakhstan to less than four inches over most of southern Central Asia.

The mountain regions form an exception to most of the above statements about climate, and in common with mountain regions the world over, climate changes with vertical movement. Because of the strong heating and drying of the air over the deserts, the snow line on the Tien Shan and Pamirs starts at a level higher than on such mountains as the Alps or the Caucasus, but in spite of this the summits of the Central Asian mountains carry a year-round snow cover, and considerable numbers of glaciers exist.

Both are important sources of perennial water supply to the rivers. The plains are subject to periodic storms, such as blizzards in winter and hot, dry winds in summer. Southern Central Asia also experiences hot, dry winds in summer, such as the *gärmsil,* a type of foehn, blowing from the mountains along the Turkmenistan-Iranian border.

The vegetation patterns reflect the climate, and the transition which takes place from north to south in types of vegetation reflects the diminishing amounts of moisture available for plant life. There are in effect four main zones of vegetation, beginning with grasslands in the north, followed by a zone of semidesert vegetation, then a zone of desert vegetation, and finally the areas of mountain vegetation. The plains of northern Kazakhstan contain a variety of grasses as the natural cover, with feathergrass as the dominant type. Mixed with the grasses are such plants as wormwood (*artemisia*), thistles, and camel thorn. Southward, the grass becomes shorter and sparser, and there is a transitional zone of semidesert vegetation, characterized by such plants as wormwood and saltwort, until the desert is finally reached.

Contrary to popular belief, most deserts are covered by sparse vegetation, even in areas where sand predominates. However, it must be remembered that these Central Asian deserts are mid-latitude and not tropical deserts and contain few of the plants popularly associated with deserts in the southwestern United States and Mexico. Characteristic of the Central Asian deserts are ephemera plants, such as tulips, irises, and varieties of grass and sedge, which blossom for a short time after the period of maximum rainfall in the spring. A more permanent cover is given by bushes and small trees such as the desert acacia, saltwort, kandym, and juzgun (varieties of Calligonum), which along with aristida grass are found even in the sand deserts. It is only in areas where the wind has piled up mobile crescent-shaped sand dunes (*barkhan;* Uzbek: *bärkhan* or *qumtepä*) that plant life can obtain no foothold. In many parts of the desert the saksaul tree (Uzbek: *säksawul*) grows to a height of twenty-five feet on occasion and taps the available soil moisture with long root systems. This remarkable tree, which is found generally in small scattered groves, is the main source of fuel in spite of the hardness of its wood. Because of its twisted branches, it is of little use for building purposes.

Along the southern edge of the desert where it meets the mountains are extensive grasslands, mainly on the foothills and lower slopes of the mountains where the rainfall is higher than in the desert. With increased height come zones of deciduous and coniferous forest, the former containing a variety of fruit trees, such as apple, pear, and apricot, as well as walnut, pistachio, and almond trees. On the upper slopes and valleys are found alpine meadows, which have considerable value for the grazing of livestock. An exceptional type of vegetation growing along the course of the Sir Darya, the Amu Darya, the Ili, the Chu, and the Sarisu is the toqäy, a dense jungle of reeds, poplars, oleasters, willows, tamarisks, and other plants, notably in areas of frequent flooding. Those along the Amu Darya are the most widespread and dense, and contain such wild animals as the boar, the reed cat, and the pheasant. In the toqäy areas of the Amu Darya and the lower Panj and Vakhsh rivers tigers can be found.

Vegetation and soil patterns are closely linked, with soil zones corresponding in general to the major vegetation zones. The soils of northern Kazakhstan are transitional from chernozems (black soils) along the northern border to chestnut soils in the center. These soils contain a rich layer of humus and have a good structure for moisture retention and are thus excellent for agricultural purposes. It is not the soils but the lack of regular precipitation which has made agriculture a gamble in this region. Not only does lack of rainfall affect the yield of the crops, but a long dry spell can dessicate the topsoil and lead to subsequent soil erosion by the characteristic high winds. Most of the surface of the Turanian lowlands south of the grassy plains is covered by brown and grey-brown desert soils and sand, neither of which offer much inducement to agriculture, especially when combined with the lack of water. However, at the edge of the mountains the picture changes. Here are serozems (grey soils) developed from an underlying layer of loess. This zone of grey soils concides with the grasslands along the foothills and lower slopes of the mountains, where the soil contains a little humus which has been developed from the sparse grass cover. Serozems are rich in calcium and form good soils for agricultural purposes.

Although these soils will produce a good crop they can be quickly exhausted if fertilizer is not applied constantly, and before the advent of chemical fertilizer, mud and silt from canals and broken pieces of loess walls of buildings were added to the soil, animal manure being mixed with straw and used only as fuel (Uzbek: *chälmä*). The farmer has to be very careful in irrigating these soils rich in alkali salts, as too much water and insufficient drainage can cause the salts to rise from a lower horizon of the soil to the surface of the ground, where they form a white layer of salt. Under extreme conditions this can result in the formation of a salt marsh (*solonchak;* Uzbek: *shor tupraq* or *shorkhaq*). On such a salt marsh nothing but saltwort will grow. These salt marshes also develop under natural conditions in other areas of Central Asia.

Although the only effective prevention of salt-marsh formation is a good drainage system, these salinized soils can be reclaimed by heavy and repeated applications of water which leach the alkali away in drainage ditches. If this water is not carried away an intermediate stage of salinization may occur and a *solonets* soil be formed, where the lower layers of the soil harden into columnar units which are impervious to water. Such soils are unfit for the growth of plants except wormwood and some grasses, mainly because of the accumulation of sodium salts. *Solonets* soils have developed from natural causes over wide areas of the Kazakh plains. In areas of salt-marsh formation a type of soil formation between salt marsh and *solonets* develops, known as a takyr or shor, similar to the playa of the American southwest. The takyrs have the appearance of dried lakes and are free of vegetation, the layer of salts lying just under the surface of the ground. In the spring, the takyrs are often inundated with rain water and the inhabitants drain it off into wells before the surface of the takyr dries. Takyrs occur mainly in the Turkmen desert and east of the Aral Sea. The soils of the mountain regions have little significance for agriculture, except where serozems have developed in valleys, such as the Farghana, part of the Narin, the Frunze region, and the slopes of the mountains south of Dushanbe.

FORAGE, FOOD, AND INDUSTRIAL CROPS

In the Central Asian region certain environmental factors are of great importance to the lives of the inhabitants and the manner in which they feed, clothe, and house themselves. Most important of these conditions are the general lack of water, the complementary lack of wood for fuel and building material, and the sharp division between the plains and desert lowlands on the one hand and the mountain region on the other. A combination of these factors has played a part in shaping the division of economic activities into two major branches: sedentary agriculture and nomadic pastoralism. Looking at these economic activities from the point of view of the physical environment, it can be observed that Uzbekistan contains most of the major areas of sedentary agriculture in southern Central Asia. To the Uzbek the largest part of his country is of no immediate use for agricultural purposes. This area is the chol or waterless plain and desert. Within the area of the chol the only distinctive area is the toqäyzar along the rivers, which apart from toqäy vegetation also includes some oases. The chol is thus no area of sedentary agricultural activity, except in the scattered locations where water does occur. However, it provides sufficient vegetation in many areas for year-round pastoral activities, and the herding of qarakol (karakul) sheep is of considerable economic importance. The chol is also the area from which saksaul wood is obtained.

Toward the mountains is the *ädir*, a hilly area or a mountain slope such as the Uzbek foothills of the Tien Shan from about 2,000 feet of elevation up to 5,000 feet. This is part of the area of serozems with grass cover, which has already been described. It forms the only region of dry farming in Uzbekistan. This type of agriculture is called *lälmikarlik* or *bäharikarlik* (from *bähar:* spring season), and is known to the Russians as *bogara*. Dry agriculture remains possible in this region because of the slightly larger quantities of rainfall on the higher ground compared with the plains, but even then only grain crops, mainly wheat and barley, can be grown successfully in the dry conditions. The *ädir* is in fact more suitable for pastoral activities and is a potential source of good quality hay, especially hay cut in the spring. The higher slopes of the mountains are known to the Uzbeks as the *tagh* (mountain). This region has little importance in Uzbek life, except as a source of wood from the mountain forests and for such plants as *kiyik ot* (literally "antelope grass"), a source of volatile oil with medicinal qualities. More important are the mountain meadows above the tree line, the *yäylawlär* or summer pastures, although they have less economic significance in Uzbekistan than the corresponding *jailoolor* in Kirgizistan, which are the scene of an annual transhumance of considerable proportions.

None of the above areas is suitable for sedentary agriculture on any scale. Such places must be locations with a combination of a constant and reliable water supply and fertile soils. This occurs in the areas of serozems adjacent to streams fed by mountain snows. It is under these conditions that the irrigated (Tajik: *ābikārī;* Uzbek: *suwli*) or autumnal (Tajik: *tiramāhī*) agriculture of the densely populated oases or *wahälär* of the Farghana Valley and Tashkent region, and those along the Zarafshan and Qashqa Darya, and in the area south of Dushanbe, have developed. Another group of significant oases are those in the areas of Khiva, Urganch, and to the north of Nokis, along the upper stretches of the Amu Darya, where large quantities of fertile silt from the river are constantly being added to the top soil. Finally, there are the important oases of southern Turkmenistan, Mari on the Murgab, and Tejen on the river of the same name, and the scattered oases along the edges of the Kopet Dagh, fed by waters in the alluvial fans at the foot of the mountains. The soils of the Mari and Tejen oases are fertile, and this fact, combined with the clear atmosphere and constant sunshine, make them important areas for the production of high quality cotton.

In the varied conditions offered by the environment a considerable range of local domestic crops also can be grown. In the oases the main grain crops are wheat (*bughday*), barley (*ärpä*), and sorghum (*jokhari*), which gives a high return per acre and serves for fodder as well as for human consumption. The stalks can be burned for fuel. Unfortunately, sorghum exhausts the top soil rapidly and requires much water, but it is tolerant of salt soils. Alfalfa (*yonghichqä, bedä*) is the most important of the fodder crops grown in the irrigated areas, and is fed to the animals in a green state, several cuts a year being possible. Although it re- turns nitrogen to the soil, alfalfa requires much water and tends to dry out the soil. However, it forms a valuable rotation crop with cotton as it improves soil structure and raises its permeability to water, as a consequence of which the quantity of water required for cotton plants is reduced after alfalfa has been grown.

Rice (*shali*) is grown wherever surplus water is available, particularly along the banks of rivers where swamps or frequent flooding occur. Rice has a high yield per acre, never fails to give a crop under normal conditions of irrigation, and is the main ingredient of the popular dish pilaf (*pilaw*). The standing water required for rice growing often acted in the past as breeding grounds for the malarial mosquito. Maize (*mäkkä jokhari*) is not a common crop, but millet (*täriq* or *qonqaq*) occurs in two varieties and is grown often on unirrigated land as it requires little water. It is popular with the Kazakhs who make *boza*, an alcoholic drink, from it. Central Asians raise various vegetables, of which the most important are carrots (*säbzi*), required as an ingredient of pilaf and other dishes. Potatoes and sugar beets are not indigenous, but were introduced by the Russians.

Melons (*qawun*) are very popular with the Central Asians and grow well in conditions of constant sunshine and irrigation. They are tolerant of a high degree of salinity in the soil and fit well into the local crop pattern. Over one hundred different varieties of melon are found in the region, but the watermelon (*tärwuz*) is not so popular with the local population and is grown mainly by the Russians. Fruit is grown mainly in orchards (*mewäzar bagh*), generally surrounded by adobe walls attached to the houses. The fruit trees are irrigated, and often the garden will contain a pond (*hawuz*). Apricots (*orik*) and peaches (*shäftali*) are the most popular fruit. The apricots used to be dried and sent to Russia. Apples (*almä*) have little importance as fruit in spite of the fame of Alma

Ata (the "father of apples"). The growing of apples has in fact been encouraged by the Russians.

The mulberry tree (*tut däräkhti*) is also common in Central Asian gardens, and occurs in several varieties, forming the basis for the local silk industry. The leaves are used to feed the silkworms, while the berries can be used for human consumption in various forms. Grapes (*uzum*) are also grown in the gardens, and occur in many varieties. Before the Russians arrived in the area, the grapes were mainly eaten, the making of wine being in the hands of foreigners only. Small seedless grapes (*kishmish*) were used for the production of sultana raisins, which were exported to Russia. In the 1870s the Russians introduced varieties of commercial grapes for wine making. The local citizens prepared a nonalcoholic drink (*musalla*) from grapes, as well as a syrup called *shinni*.

Apart from food, several industrial crops are grown in the irrigated areas of Central Asia. Of these by far the most important is cotton (Uzbek, Tajik: *päkhtä;* Turkmen: *pamïk;* Kazakh: *maqta*), which occupies the greatest acreage of any single crop in the irrigated areas. The local cotton is grey in color, with a short, thick fiber. It proved to be too poor in quality to compete on the world market, so that the Russians introduced American "upland" cotton after their arrival. "Sea Island" cotton of the Egyptian type was also introduced, but under local conditions gave too coarse a fiber. Cotton grows well under conditions of irrigation and bright sunshine and the yield per acre in this case is higher than in areas with natural rainfall. The cotton seed (*chigit*) also yields edible oil (*päkhtä mayi*), and the stems of the plant make excellent fuel.

Sesame (*kunjut*) is another important source of vegetable oil. *Hälwa* is prepared from sesame pressings. Hemp (*kendir*) was grown in the past not for its fiber, but for its seed and as a source of hashish (*bäng* or *näshä*), prepared by pulverizing the hemp flower and mixing it with hemp oil. Poppies (*koknar*) were grown in Eastern Turkistan by the Dungans and Uyghurs with an eye on the Chinese opium market. Smoking tobacco (*aq tämäki*) and chewing tobacco (*kok tämäki*) are grown. The latter is low quality tobacco, similar to Russian *makhorka,* and is widely grown, being the basis for *nas* or *nasway,* prepared by powdering the tobacco leaf and mixing it with ash and lime or cement to form pellets, which are placed under the tongue or in the cheek. Recent Soviet studies suggest that *nas* chewing may be the cause of the high incidence of mouth cancer in Central Asia.[24]

To the north, in Kazakhstan, there is little irrigation and the major crop is durum wheat, known to the Russians as *tverdaia pshenitsa,* which thrives in a warm, dry climate, and can tolerate a little alkalinity in the soil. This type of wheat was introduced by the first Russian settlers in the region, and still forms the major grain crop on the state farms of Kazakhstan. Because of the severe winters and inadequate snow cover, wheat is sown in northern Kazakhstan only in the spring, and is harvested about mid-August. Millet is grown in the western part of the republic and also along the Irtish, where spring barley and oats are also grown as fodder crops. Corn (maize) has recently been sown in considerable quantities, but does not mature well, and is cut green for silage. Sunflowers are also cultivated for vegetable oil.

LIVESTOCK AND GRAZING

Before the arrival of the Russians, the plains of Kazakhstan were utilized almost exclusively as grazing grounds by the nomadic Kazakhs. To the Kazakhs horses were more important than cattle. The Kazakh horse (*at* or *jïlqï*) was small and wild, and able to live in the open all the year round. It was capable of getting grass from under a greater depth of snow than could cattle or sheep and in general fared best of all livestock in the local environment. Not only did it serve as transportation, but supplied leather, meat, and milk, the latter forming the basis for kumiss (Kazakh: *qïmïz*).

Sheep (*qoy*) were more numerous than horses and made up about two-thirds to three-quarters of the average Kazakh herd. They provided meat, milk, and cheese, and wool for clothing, felt, and carpets. The northern Kazakhs did not keep many qarakol sheep, the herds consisting mainly of fat-tailed sheep (Russian:

[24] A. V. Chaklin, "The Geographical Distribution of Cancer in the Soviet Union," *Soviet Geography,* vol. III, No. 8 (October 1962), p. 62.

kurdiuk; Kazakh: *qazaqi qoy;* Uzbek: *dumbä* or *quyruq*). These sturdy animals have a long thick tail containing fat, and a thick coat of coarse wool, a testimony to the rugged conditions of the open plain. The Kazakhs provided little shelter and no winter fodder, and the only relief for the animals was the annual winter movement of the herds to the fringe of the desert in the south where slightly higher temperatures and a thinner snow cover made life a little easier. For the sheep, the sparser vegetation of the southern areas is in many ways preferable to the feather grass of the northern steppes, which is more suitable as fodder for horses.

Some goats (Kazakh: *yeshkï;* Uzbek: *echki, täkä*) were kept, but in much smaller numbers than sheep. They were generally herded with the latter as they had a steadying influence on the flocks.

Cattle did not thrive in the plains environment, and although they were kept in substantial numbers, they often had great difficulty in finding winter feed. During the winter a thaw followed by freezing weather would cover the ground with a thick crust of ice, so that even the horses could not break through to the grass beneath and livestock perished wholesale. This refreezing was named in Kazakh *jüt* or *kökmüz.* One observer reported that "by spring the cattle are scarcely on their feet; they have to be dragged to the spring pastures and even helped to their feet." [25]

Camels of the two-humped Bactrian variety, known to the Kazakhs as *ayïr tüye* were better adapted to the severe winters of the plains than were the one-humped dromedary or *nar,* which was more sensitive to the cold and was found only in southern Central Asia. The camel formed virtually the only means of transportation over long distances before the advent of the railroad, and was thus of great economic importance.

Groups other than the Kazakhs herded livestock, and sheep were kept by the Kirgiz, the Turkmens, and the Uzbeks. The Turkmens specialized in horse breeding, and, in contrast to the Kazakhs, pampered their horses, feeding them on fodder in winter and protecting them with warm covers. This *argamak* breed of horses was specially trained for military purposes, their speed and reliability being essential to the Turkmen during a raid or attack. The donkey (*eshäk*)

[25] M. A. Tsvetkov, in *Aziatskaia Rossiia,* II, 310.

was a popular form of transportation for the oases dwellers in both urban and rural areas, but was not used by the nomads, except to accompany caravans of camels. In the mountain areas of Kirgizistan, yaks supplied both transportation and milk from which cheese was made.

During the Soviet period the livestock picture has changed little. Fat-tailed sheep are still herded, although other breeds with finer wool have also been introduced. Cattle are more important than in the earlier period, mainly because of the increased use of winter fodder. Now that the Kazakh is no longer completely nomadic, horses have become less important, although camels are still used in desert areas. Herds continue to be moved south in the winter to the fringes of the desert, but only a limited number of herdsmen take part in this migration; the length of the drives has been reduced, and shelter and stocks of emergency forage are supplied at the winter pastures. The mountain Kirgiz still move their flocks of sheep every spring to the mountain meadow, returning to the lower foothills and plains in August.

With careful and intelligent use of its natural resources Central Asia can achieve considerable potential for the support of its rapidly expanding population. Correct irrigation procedures, selection of crops, and controlled grazing of livestock could make the region a broader new frontier of settlement for the people of the Soviet Union and an example for the economic development of neighboring countries.

I. M. M.

4

Systematic Conquest,
1865 to 1884

The Crimean War at first had the effect of arresting Russian progress in Central Asia, but led, after its disastrous conclusion, to a renewal of interest in this region. For a while, at least, the czar had to give up the great foreign engagements which had involved him in the Balkans and the Near East, and he found it necessary to reinforce his position in Central Asia. For Russia, set on a course of capitalist development, the control of this region, with its unrivaled market and suspected rich raw materials, was of considerable importance.

Around 1860–1862, interest in Central Asia increased, as all Europe was feeling the effects of the American Civil War which was depriving it of cotton. At this time, fifteen Muscovite merchants asked the minister of finance for government aid to seek in Central Asia, especially Bukhara, the raw materials which the American crisis was denying them. The interest which England, already solidly established throughout India, was taking in this region added urgency to the czarist initiatives. The Russian defeat of Imam Shamil in the Caucasus had freed the armies engaged there and allowed them to envision a great effort in Western Turkistan.

Military operations in the summer of 1864, which had won Russia the city of Turkistan, then Chimkent, also put an end to the sovereignty of the Khokand khanate over southern Kazakhstan. The khan, still in no wise resigned to this defeat, was contemplating a reconquest of the north, while the emir of Bukhara was particularly eager to take advantage of Khokand's difficulties to realize his old dream of expansion. Thus, the fundamental questions were raised. First, what was Russia's policy in Western Turkistan to be?

Systematic pursuit of conquests, or stabilization and reinforcement of the possessions acquired? Second, around what geographic point and upon what political strengths should the Russian presence be based? Last, what forms should this Russian presence take? The first question would become crystallized for the advocates of the two theses around one particular geographic center—Tashkent—the fate of which would be for nearly two years the subject of the most contradictory debates between the central administration and the Russian representatives on the Western Turkistan periphery.

TASHKENT

Early in 1865, the Tashkent problem had been clearly set forth by General M. G. Cherniaev, who emphasized that it was impossible for Russia, after his ill-starred attempt in the autumn of 1864, to maintain her positions in Central Asia and especially the existing frontier with Khokand, if Tashkent were not conquered.[1] To justify a new expedition he argued that, for one thing, the city was under the covetous eye of the emir of Bukhara, Muzaffar al-Din (r.1860–1885), and that, for another, its internal situation was dangerously unstable, the populace being divided between the pressures of the Muslim dignitaries who were demanding the protection of the emir, and the commercial middle class which was hoping to see contacts develop with Russia which would be more favorable to its interests. Cherniaev suggested that in spite of Mullah Alim Qul's recapture of control in Tashkent, one might shortly expect a turnabout in which Russia would have to defend her supporters there against the "Bukharan clan."[2]

The Russian rulers, while considering the development of the czarist position in Central Asia particularly important, were not all in favor of an extension of the conquest. At the Ministry of Foreign Affairs, the director of the Asiatic Department, Petr N. Stremoukhov, entertained considerable distrust for Cherniaev's military plans

[1] *Turkestanskii krai: Sbornik materialov dlia istorii ego zavoevaniia* (Tashkent, Tipografiia Turkestanskago Voennago Okruga, 1912–1916), vol. XIX, part 1, pp. 48–49.
[2] *Ibid.*, pp. 4, 30.

and was in favor of leaving Tashkent outside the orbit of Russian conquest. The city, he said, should throw off the Khokand yoke by itself, rather than by the action of Russian troops. It was in remaining independent that Tashkent would allow Russia to profit best from its central location.

The minister himself, Prince A. M. Gorchakov, unreservedly upheld this thesis. He demanded an end to military operations in order to prepare the conquered territories and to assure in them the uncontested authority of Russia instead of plunging into ventures which were bound to create external difficulties with England as well as internal problems by involving Russia in a series of campaigns which might even run the risk of stirring up people already conquered. The important thing, he thought, was to weaken Khokand from within by progressively provoking the secession of Tashkent, which Russia would then take under her protection. On January 25, 1865, a special commission, after debate, decided that the direction of policy and trade with Central Asia had to be centered at Orenburg and that the Khokand and the Sir Darya lines of conquest from the western end of the Issik Kol to the Aral Sea had to be linked into one single region, which would fall under the guberniia of Orenburg. The first military governor of the new region, provided with special powers by virtue of the area's remoteness and the particularly complex situation, was General Cherniaev.

These decisions had, on the one hand, the effect of giving Cherniaev extended powers sufficient to assure his success in rapidly winning acceptance for his thesis of resumption of conquest, and, on the other hand, of putting settlement of the Central Asian question under the control of men far removed from St. Petersburg's authority—first and foremost, into the jurisdiction of the governor general of Orenburg. Cherniaev could assert, more loudly than in the past, that it was not a question of settling the frontiers of the Russian empire amicably, as the government was suggesting, because, he said, Western Turkistan had no natural frontiers. In his opinion the whole region had to be dominated and dominated militarily. And this domination had to begin in Tashkent, whose possession was essential for Russia.

Events favored Cherniaev. While the Russian government was

debating its intentions, the emir of Bukhara was taking advantage of the lull to throw his troops against Farghana. Early in 1865 he had concentrated troops in Samarkand from whence he marched against Ura Tube, opening the way to Farghana. Turning to his own account the conflict setting the armies of Bukhara and Khokand against each other, Cherniaev, on April 28, 1865, rushed to the assault of Niyaz Bek, a fortress located on the Chirchiq, which controlled the Tashkent water supply. He then advanced toward Tashkent where on May 9 he encountered Alim Qul's army. Despite the disparity of the forces present (Cherniaev had 1,300 men and 12 cannon; Alim Qul about 6,000 men and 40 cannon),[3] the fighting was murderous, particularly for the Khokand army, which lost 300 men, including its leader, while the Russian troops suffered only a score of casualties.

Cherniaev then turned to his government, asking instructions about the future of a leaderless Khokand and inquiring how to deal with the emir of Bukhara's greedy ambitions, which were only further whetted by Alim Qul's disappearance. The government's reply further reveals the uncertainty of its position. Gorchakov affirmed on the one hand the necessity of strictly opposing all of Emir Muzaffar al-Din's claims to Khokand, but at the same time he urged moderation upon Cherniaev, reminding him that above all, Russia wanted peace in Central Asia so as to be free to develop her commercial aims there—aims which a state of war and perturbation would only prejudice.

At the same time that the government launched its representatives on a bargaining course with Bukhara to obtain for Russian merchants terms similar to those that Russia was granting the Bukharan merchants, Gorchakov sent to General N. A. Kryzhanovskii, the governor general of Orenburg, a shrewd plan for the civil and military authorities in the Khokand khanate, making clear to them the aims of Russian policy. But Gorchakov indicated with what precaution this shrewdness was to be turned to account, for "the text could be fallaciously interpreted as an appeal to insubordination against the legal authorities, that is why this document

[3] *Ibid.*, pp. 146–49, 152–55.

must be used only with utmost prudence and in those situations alone where its success can not be questioned." [4]

In Tashkent, meanwhile, famine and drought had brought about a test of strength between the people and the authorities.[5] Khokand's Sultan Sayyid Khan had fled the city on June 10 to ask Bukhara for help. Cherniaev thereupon decided to settle the matter once and for all and, dispatching troops under the command of A. K. Abramov to neutralize the Bukhara road, he encircled Tashkent and late at night on June 14 launched an attack. The city surrendered June 17, 1865. As soon as he had entered the city, Cherniaev issued a proclamation designed to soothe the populace, promising respect for the Islamic faith and local customs, and promising as well that Muslims would not be inducted into the Russian army. These promises and a one-year exemption from all taxes quieted the population.

No sooner had Cherniaev captured Tashkent than he opposed the idea of making an independent khanate of it; he felt that the security of the accomplished conquests required an extension of the frontier to the headwaters of the Sir Darya.[6] General N. A. Kryzhanovskii was opposed to the shifting of frontiers and supported a khanate because "a sovereign is easy to control," and favored the creation of a fortified line through Niyaz Bek, Chinaz, and beyond. He especially urged a respite in the expansion so that administrative work might bring about a consolidation of the Russian position in the conquered territories. In the capital, while Stremoukhov at the Ministry of Foreign Affairs remained apprehensive in view of the difficulties which "a unilateral decision concerning the destiny of Central Asia as far as Bukhara" might entail,[7] D. A. Miliutin, the minister of war, was moving toward a position halfway between the expansionism of Cherniaev and the desire of the minister of foreign affairs to establish Tashkent as a separate khanate. In a practical manner, he suggested that Tashkent should

[4] *Ibid.*, p. 199.
[5] N. I. Veselovskii, *Kirgizskii razskaz o russkikh zavoevaniiakh v turkestanskom kraie* (St. Petersburg, Parovaia Skoropechatnia P. O. Iablonskago, 1894), pp. 54–56.
[6] *Turkestanskii krai: Sbornik materialov*, vol. XX, part 2, p. 37.
[7] *Ibid.*, pp. 69–70.

FIGURE 4.1   Bukharan Emir Muzaffar al-Din.

FIGURE 4.2   Khivan Khan Sayyid Muhammad Rahim Bahadur.

FIGURE 4.3   Khokand's ruler Khudayar Khan.

retain a certain autonomy, under the form of a municipal authority "protected against Bukhara by Russia." [8]

The Foreign Ministry's plan seemed to be winning out at first, since in September, 1865, Kryzhanovskii went to Tashkent with the idea of assembling its influential citizens to designate a sovereign and to proclaim the independence of the city outside of the territories extending to the Sir Darya.[9] But the prominent figures, mainly the religious authorities, presented him with a document in Uzbek claiming that the control of the religious life of the city must be in the hands of the Qazi Kalan.[10] Kryzhanovskii refused to consider this request, for it ran counter to his plan of weakening the clergy by favoring the merchant middle class which, to his way of thinking, was to play a predominant role in the selection of the sovereign. He argued the matter strongly with Cherniaev so that he might carry out his program. Cherniaev quietly forgot about the proclamation of Tashkent's independence, advancing as justification

[8] *Ibid.*, p. 63.
[9] *Ibid.*, pp. 162–65.
[10] D. I. Romanovskii, *Zamietki po sredneaziatskomu voprosu* (St. Petersburg, Vtoroe Otdielenie Sobstvennaia Ego Imperatorskaia Velichestvo-Kantseliariia, 1868), pp. 177–79.

the disorders that it would unleash and the danger of intervention
by the emir. The question was to be settled finally in line with his
recommendations, for the economic forces of the empire were
going to tip the balance in his favor.

Beyond these contradictory positions, everyone in Central Asia,
just as in the capital, clearly felt the basic facts of the problem as
it was raised after the capture of Tashkent. The city was to become
the vital center of all Central Asia, and thus the prestige of Bukhara would gradually diminish. Even in the event of a conquest, a
man like Cherniaev, who had lived in Central Asia, knew that
Bukhara, with its immense historical and religious prestige, would
always be an element dangerous to Russian domination. On the
other hand, if Tashkent became the real economic center of Central
Asia, if the benefits of its new situation were reflected on the local
population as well, then the Russian empire might hope to counterbalance and destroy the prestige of Bukhara-i Sharif (Holy Bukhara). From this time forth, it was clear to the Russian rulers that
success through the imperial enterprise in Tashkent would be the
most reliable way for the empire to undermine progressively the
elements of spiritual resistance that they already sensed.

That is why Kryzhanovskii pressed Miliutin to direct all his
current effort to the transformation of Tashkent into the true commercial hub of Central Asia. Under Miliutin's stimulus, several of
the most important Russian commercial enterprises, Sava Morozov
& Sons, Ivan Khludov & Sons, and Baranov Bros., joined together
in January, 1866, in "an association for trade with Tashkent and
Central Asia." Through Colonel D. I. Romanovskii, who was to play
the role of an instigator and a veritable representative of the government, they asked from the government certain guarantees (protection of the convoys and insurance of the goods) and important
concessions (lands in Western Turkistan, posts, and the right to buy
raw materials from the government at wholesale prices) in return
for a systematic orientation of business toward Central Asia. In its
discussions with the Association about the dispatch of scientific
missions to make an inventory of Western Turkistanian resources,
the government clearly showed the importance it attached to the
problem.

Yet, since such an effort was being made to give Tashkent a central role in Russia's eastern trade, it was hardly possible to put off any longer the settlement of its status. The problem of the security of the Russian merchants and their goods was in the forefront. Since the emir of Bukhara had regained a new prestige among the conquered people thanks to some military successes, without wavering the czarist government sided with Cherniaev. The population of Tashkent had to be thoroughly and permanently shielded from Bukharan yearnings. Annexation was the only solution. In August, 1866, an imperial decree proclaimed the annexation of Tashkent to the empire.

BUKHARA

The Bukharan question now came to the foreground in Russian preoccupations. For some time the government temporized with regard to the emirate and sought negotiated solutions, in spite of the emir's military threats against Farghana. Various factors explain this hesitation.

In the first place, the government avoided attacking the emirate because it believed Bukhara to be militarily strong and at the same time it feared explosions of religious fanaticism that a Russian penetration in this territory might set off. Actually, the government was inclined to exaggerate the strength of the Bukharan army as well as the popular attachment to the sovereign. On the other hand, as time would prove, it was not mistaken in anticipating the influence that the Islamic clerics would exercise upon their faithful. But on the eve of the conquest, the Bukharans were so overwhelmed by material difficulties stemming from the social and economic transformations of the nineteenth century that they were ready to rise up spontaneously against their own authorities rather than defend the establishment or defy a foreign conqueror, even if he were an infidel (*kafir*).[11]

Moreover, the government was urged toward moderation by the representatives of mercantile groups, who, for economic imperatives, insisted on the necessity of preserving normal relations between Russia and Bukhara. Establishment of such relations quickly

[11] H. Carrère d'Encausse, *Réforme et Révolution chez les musulmans de russie l'Empire: Bukhara, 1867–1924* (Paris, Armand Colin, 1966), pp. 29–68.

proved impossible. Diplomatic missions charged with smoothing over the difficulties on both sides generally ended up by being more or less incarcerated, and all the parleys ended in failure.[12]

The government's position had to be clarified. Vis-à-vis Bukhara the government would not and above all could not make any political concessions. In the Russian capital people shared Cherniaev's belief that the most dangerous policy in Central Asia was to enhance the emir of Bukhara's prestige. That is why, when Kryzhanovskii demanded Cherniaev's dismissal over the political attitude to be adopted toward Bukhara, Miliutin let Cherniaev continue for a while and recalled him only after the failure of his attack on Jizzakh in January, 1866.[13] Miliutin replaced him with D. I. Romanovskii, who carried out the line advocated by Cherniaev in the ultimate conquest.

The policy of continued expansion triumphed from that moment. In May, 1866, General Romanovskii conquered successively Irjar, Khojand, and Nau, then presented the conditions of Russian peace to the emir, conditions which were without question unacceptable. They included recognition of all the Russian conquests, recognition of the frontier running through the Hungry Steppe and Qizil Qum, granting the same rights to Russians in Bukhara as those accorded Bukharan subjects in Russia, guarantees for Russians traveling to Bukhara, and lastly the payment of a sizable tribute within ten days. It was this last point in particular that Russia was counting on to halt the parleys and give her an excuse for launching a final attack against the emirate, while still shifting the responsibility for her action on the emir.[14] As had been foreseen, the Bukharan plenipotentiaries demanded the removal of the last clause, and on September 23, Kryzhanovskii, who had already announced to Miliutin his intention of attacking,[15] occupied Jizzakh on October 18, and Ura Tube on October 20, 1866. In May, 1867, General Abramov, in turn, took possession of Yangi Qorghan.

[12] *Turkestanskii krai: Sbornik materialov*, vol. XXI, part 1, p. 20.

[13] A. I. Maksheev, *Istoricheskii obzor Turkestana i nastupateľnago dvizheniia v nego russkikh* (St. Petersburg, Voennaia Tipografiia, 1890), pp. 239–40.

[14] *Ibid.*, p. 246.

[15] *Ibid.*, p. 248.

In the early months of 1867, the government began to consider the organization of the conquered territories. Under the chairmanship of Miliutin met a commission in which all those who had participated in the conquest, as well as Count Ilarion I. Vorontsov-Dashkov, and others, collaborated with Stremoukhov and Count Fedor L. Heiden, the chief of staff. Returning again to the proposition advanced two years earlier by Cherniaev, the commission removed the southern part of Western Turkistan from the authority of the Orenburg governor general and created a new governor generalship. The first governor general was General K. P. von Kaufman, who was granted almost unlimited powers.

Just as the governor generalship (guberniia) of Turkistan was being established, the great industrial and commercial middle class of Russia, which since the 1860s had been evincing a growing interest in the Central Asian problems, intervened more actively to win acceptance for its view that total conquest was imperative. The attitude of this class is readily understandable if one considers how much it had profited in the development of the conquest. Not long after the Crimean War various authors had noted that trade with Central Asia was almost entirely in the hands of the local population.[16] With the capture of Tashkent, the rapid penetration of Russian trade into Central Asia began, and the merchants increased their *démarches* so as to pressure the government into pursuing the work of conquest. Newspapers, such as *Moskva* and *Birzhevye viedomosti*, supported their position and insisted on the necessity of conquering Bukhara, the vital commercial center of Central Asia. Thus, von Kaufman, arriving in Western Turkistan in 1868, proceeded first to settle this question which had been widely raised by public opinion. Before grappling with Bukhara, whose forces he also thought were formidable, von Kaufman, in January, 1868, signed a commercial accord with Khudayar Khan (r.1845–58, 1862–63, 1865–75) which, in point of fact, placed Khokand under complete economic dependence to the empire.

In Bukhara, the emir's situation was unstable, and the clerics

[16] P. Nebol'sin, "Ocherki torgovli Rossii so stranami Srednei Azii, Khivoi, Bukharoi, i Kokandom (so storony orenburgskoi linii)," *Zapiski Imperatorskago Russkago Geograficheskago Obshchestva,* X (1856), 18–20.

who reproached him for his dilatory policy threatened him with forced abdication in favor of his eldest son. In April, 1868, the clergy proclaimed holy war (*ghazawat*), and the emir had to march on the Zarafshan. Encouraged by the czarist government, von Kaufman, who had enjoined the emir to leave the banks of the Zarafshan and had met with a refusal, rushed to an attack May 1, 1868, and the emir's armies having fallen back, he conquered Samarkand almost without firing a shot. Dashing off in pursuit of the Bukharan troops, von Kaufman's army conquered Katta Qorghan on May 16. On June 2, the Zirabulaq defeat opened the Bukhara road to the Russians. But General von Kaufman could go no farther, for a popular rebellion recalled him to Samarkand in relief of the garrison. In any event, the emir, plagued by the internal difficulties, poorly propped up by a weak army,[17] capitulated to save his throne.

The peace treaty, signed on June 30, 1868, gave Russia all the conquered territories: Khojand, Ura Tube, Jizzakh, Katta Qorghan, and especially Samarkand, which controlled the headwaters of the Zarafshan (all Bukhara's water), and finally, all the commercial advantages which the Russian leaders had previously been unable to obtain. Bukhara became a state under Russian suzerainty. The organization of the conquered territories provoked the same debates as had the Tashkent problem three years earlier. The okrug of Zarafshan was formed from these territories and in 1872 it was finally annexed to the empire.[18]

In the dependent emirate, fighting broke out again, not long after the signing of the treaty, in the mountainous regions of eastern Bukhara, which were constantly in rebellion. In the beginning, the fighting was directed as much against the emir's authority as against the foreign conqueror.[19] The emir asked for Russian assistance against the rebels, who were led by Abdul Malik Khan, Jorabek,

[17] Abdalrauf [Fitrat], *Razskazy indiiskago puteshestvennika* (Samarkand, Izdanie Makhmuda Khodzhy Bekhbudi, Tipo-litografiia T-va Gazarov i Sliianov, 1913), p. 35.

[18] V. N. Troitskii, ed., *Materialy dlia opisaniia khivinskago pokhoda 1873 goda* (Tashkent, 1881), V, 32.

[19] V. V. Bartol'd, *Istoriia kul'turnoi zhizni Turkestana* (Leningrad, Akademiia Nauk: Kom. po Izucheniiu Estest. Proizv. Sil., 1927), pp. 230, 231.

and Bababek,[20] while apparently promising independence at the same time to the chiefs of the unsubjugated tribes if they would chase the infidels out of the emirate.[21] Then the emir stood by submissively while General Abramov's troops attacked them and was rewarded for his calculations when the treaty of 1873 placed under his control the very eastern Bukhara that had always contested this authority.[22]

KHIVA AND KHOKAND

Having now subjugated Bukhara and Khokand, the Russian government could not allow the last of the Central Asian khanates, Khiva, to survive. The situation was all the more intolerable, as the khan of Khiva was also trying to play a leading role in Central Asia, both through his contacts with India and through the support that he lent the uprisings which broke out among the Kazakhs in the 1870s.[23]

As early as 1868, General von Kaufman had tried peaceful negotiations with the khan of Khiva, but it was soon clear that only the Russian annexation of the khanate would permit Russia to give a real solidity to her Central Asian conquest.

In 1869, troops from the Caucasus under the command of Colonel N. G. Stoletov had gone from Port Petrovsk (Makhach Kala) via the Caspian Sea into the Gulf of Krasnovodsk, where they founded the city of the same name. At the time that they were establishing themselves on the southern fringe of the Caspian, Russian troops carried out reconnaissance in Turkmen territory. Thus, Khiva was progressively encircled on three sides contiguous to the military okrugs of the Caucasus, Orenburg, and Turkistan.

Prepared by General von Kaufman, the Khivan campaign assembled multiple forces, involving the armies of the three surrounding regions, in all some 13,000 men and about 50 cannon. During

[20] *Ibid.*, p. 231.

[21] A. A. Semenov, *Ocherk ustroistva tsentral'nogo administrativnogo upravleniia bukharskogo khanstva pozdneishego vremeni* (Stalinabad, Izdatel'stvo Akademii Nauk Tadzhikskoi SSR, 1954), p. 22.

[22] B. G. Gafurov, *Istoriia tadzhikskogo naroda* (Moscow, Gospolitizdat, 1955), I, 431.

[23] Bartol'd, p. 234.

FIGURE 4.4   Khudayar Khan's palace at Khokand.

their advance on Khiva, the imperial troops encountered scarcely any resistance, and on May 29, 1873, the capital, already thrown into confusion by a coup d'état which had occurred a few days earlier, was taken. On August 12, 1873, the khan signed a peace treaty without arguing the conditions imposed by Russia.

Everything about the Khivan expedition contributed to an enhancement of Bukhara's privileged position and increased the foreign prestige of its sovereign. Indeed, the Russian troops had avoided entering Bukhara-i Sharif, whereas Khiva had been besieged. Its khan, Muhammad Rahim Bahadur II, had fled and had been replaced by his brother Ata Jan; General von Kaufman had then recalled the fallen sovereign and had put him back on his throne. The emir of Bukhara had signed a treaty of friendship with Russia and could communicate directly with the Russian government,[24] whereas the khan of Khiva, who had acknowledged himself "the docile servant of the emperor of all the Russias," had to proceed through the medium of the Russian administrative hierarchy. Finally, the Khan, whose territory had been circumscribed, had seen a real limitation of his powers imposed by a semblance of a constitution.[25] These differences in the hour of humiliation were to play a considerable role in the internal evolution of the two countries.

Although humbled by the fall of Tashkent and the settlements of 1868, Khokand continued nonetheless to survive, and its tumultuous existence furnished Russia with the needed pretext for suppressing the khanate once and for all. Increased taxation provoked intense unrest throughout the khanate during 1873–74, and the khan's armies engaged in cruel repression. This did not put an end to the disturbances entirely, and in 1874, deserters from the khanate were seeking asylum in the guberniia of Turkistan, while the population of Ozgan (Uzgen) was asking General von Kaufman for help against their sovereign, Khudayar Khan.

After several months of relative calm, the rebellion broke out anew in the neighborhood of Ozgan in July, 1875, under the leader-

[24] S. V. Zhukovskii, *Snosheniia Rossii s Bukharoi i Khivoi za posliednee trekhsotlietie* (Petrograd, Trudy Obshchestva Russkikh Orientalistov, No. 2, 1915), p. 192.
[25] Bartol'd, p. 235.

ship of Ishaq Hasan Oghlu, who took the name of Polat Khan. Against the rebels the Khokand khan sent a column under the command of one of the highly placed officials of the khanate, Abdurrahman Awtobashi, who ran across Polat Khan's troops at Andijan July 17 and threw in his lot with them. This was the beginning of the disintegration of authority; everywhere the troops, the aristocracy, and the local leaders joined the rebellion. Nasriddin Bek, eldest son of the khan and governor of Andijan went over to the rebels July 19, the governor of Marghilan joined them the following day, and part of the khan's own troops, led by his youngest son, Muhammed Amin Bek, deserted him on the night of July 21.

The rallying of all military and civilian authorities to the rebellion rapidly changed the very character of the movement, however. From a popular revolt directed against a cruel and tyrannical sovereign, it became, officered and shepherded by the ruling figures of the country, a local Muslim resistance against the Russians, the clear manifestation of a will to preserve the state of Khokand with its structure and its customs. Born of the ordinary people, the movement had within a few weeks transcended its origins and turned into a holy war.

While Khudayar Khan, abandoned on all sides, was in flight to Tashkent to put himself under Russian protection, his son, Nasriddin Bek, was swept to power. He immediately established relations with Russia and was recognized sovereign by General von Kaufman on April 6. Yet, in spite of this agreement, the war went on. The Khokand troops laid siege to Khokand August 9 and attempted to cut the route to Tashkent. The Russians felt that an end had to be made of it, and without delay General von Kaufman launched his troops on the attack against Khokand, occupied it August 29,[26] and on September 20 imposed upon Nasriddin Bek a settlement which put an end to the khanate's independence.

Abdurrahman Awtobashi, backed by numerous troops, continued the resistance, however, and on October 9 took possession of Khokand; on the vacant throne—for Nasriddin Bek had fled to the Russians like his father before him—he placed Polat Khan. The

[26] M. A. Terent'ev, *Istoriia zavoevaniia Srednei Azii* (St. Petersburg, Tipolitografiia V. V. Komarova, 1906), I, 357–58.

rebels then seized Marghilan and threatened Namangan.[27] But on November 11, a decisive battle matched General M. D. Skobelev's troops with the rebels in Baliqchi, and the rout began. A few days later Skobelev bombarded Andijan, putting his enemies to flight. The rebels surrendered after the fall of Andijan on January 9, 1876, and Polat Khan fled to Uch Qorghan where Skobelev's soldiers captured him January 28. He was executed at Marghilan shortly thereafter. On February 19, 1876, the khanate of Khokand was abolished, to be replaced by the region of Farghana, under the rule of a military governor, initially General Skobelev.[28]

TURKMENISTAN INVASION OPENS ALL CENTRAL ASIA

While the Khokand operations were unfolding, imperial troops had begun another conquest, that of Turkmenistan. On the day after the treaty with Khiva was signed, the English press expressed great agitation, declaring that this new Russian conquest was a threat to Afghan independence and demanding that Russia give assurances on both this point and the Turkmenistan question. The Russian government willingly renewed the assurances given in the declaration of January 19, 1873, about the Afghan question: "Russia repeats that Afghanistan is outside of her sphere of influence," but it was more reserved about the Turkmenistan matter since, said Gorchakov, this depended on the attitude of the Turkmens, who were "very aggressive." [29]

In 1873, an expedition under General N. N. Golovachev had attacked the Yomud Turkmens and had occupied the Turkmen villages of the Khwarazm oasis. After the end of Khiva's independence a Transcaspian military zone (*otdiel*) had been formed with two centers—Mangishlak and Krasnovodsk—which came under the command of the army of the Caucasus. From there various expeditions set out into Turkmen territory. In 1877, they occupied Qizil Arvat, and in 1879, attacked Gok Tepe, where the troops of General Lazarev were soundly defeated by the Tekke Turkmens.[30] The ef-

[27] *Ibid.*, p. 376.
[28] Maksheev, p. 344.
[29] *Ibid.*, p. 225.
[30] *Ibid.*, p. 355.

fect of this defeat was disastrous to czarist prestige outside of the Russian empire as well as in Central Asia. Consequently, the following year, the expedition under General Skobelev, whose mission was to settle the Turkmen affair, received rigorous instructions from the czar:

Under no circumstances may the fixed plan be departed from, nor the least backward step be taken, for this would be for Europe and Asia a sign of our weakness, would inspire still greater boldness on the part of our adversaries, and might cost Russia infinitely more than the whole expedition.[31]

General Skobelev's army totaled more than 11,000 men and some 100 cannon. The decisive moment of the campaign was the capture of the fortress of Gok Tepe January 12, 1881, after a long and bloody siege which destroyed any possibility of lasting Turkmen resistance.[32] Three days later, a detachment commanded by Colonel A. N. Kuropatkin took possession of Ashkhabad. In a few weeks, the chief of the Turkmen tribes in the conquered regions surrendered to Skobelev.

For three years, Russia checked her expansionist movement in Turkmenistan at the oases of the Akhal Tekke which, united with the Transcaspian military zone, formed the Transcaspian oblast centered on Ashkhahad which was tied to the Caucasus command. The Russian government had given strictest instructions to Skobelev to allow no troop movements outside of the oasis to the east or no threat to the Persian frontier, so great was its fear of English and Persian reactions. Until 1884, the situation was continually upset by the incursions of the Mari Turkmens into the Russian zone.[33] In 1883, Colonel Alikhanov was sent to Mari where he labored to convince the tribal chiefs and the prominent citizens of the necessity of submitting to Russian authority of their own accord.[34] This

[31] *Istoriia uzbekskoi SSR* (Tashkent, Izdatel'stvo Akademii Nauk Uzbekskoi SSR, 1956), vol. I, book 2, p. 96; N. I. Grodekov, *Voina v Turkmenii: Pokhod Skobeleva v 1880–1881 godakh* (St. Petersburg, Balashev, 1883–84).

[32] Terent'ev, III, 220.

[33] *Afganskoe razgranichenie: Peregovory mezhdu Rossiei i Velikobritaniei 1872–1885* (St. Petersburg, Ministerstvo Inostrannykh Del, 1886), part 2, p. 136.

[34] Arminius Vambery, *La lutte future pour la possession de l'Inde* (Paris, Cassell, 1886), pp. 63–70.

campaign bore fruit, for on January 1, 1884, an assembly of the leading Turkmen figures in Mari called for its linking up with Russia. The oasis was organized into the okrug of Mari.

England's reaction to this extension of the empire was immediate. On February 29, 1884, the British government protested the annexation of Mari. Russia, to avoid a seemingly inevitable conflict, replied by proposing a joint delimitation of the Afghan frontier, and the two parties agreed on this score.[35] The frontier was fixed for the northern part—from the Amu Darya to Persian Khorasan—in 1887. However the accord had fixed the frontier only as far as Lake Zarkol; beyond, toward China, nothing had been specified, and England retained access to the Pamirs. The delimitation of the Pamir frontier in 1895, which gave Russia Rushan, Shughnan, and part of Vakhan, which were all linked with the Bukhara protectorate, put an end to Russian expansion in Central Asia and marked the acquisition of a vast new empire.

Despite initial anxieties as to the supposed strength of existing Muslim states and English opposition, the conquest of Central Asia had been, in the final analysis, rapid, and, on the whole, not very bloody,[36] at least for Russia, who, save for a few failures, easily put her adversaries to flight. It is true that the khanates had sapped their own strength with domestic struggles, and weakened by these quarrels, having neither sufficient troops nor modern war matériel, and handicapped by the latent popular discontent stemming from a backward economy and the worsening of conditions, had been rather lame adversaries for their conquerors. Thus it appeared that making the Pax Slavica and Russian order hold sway over such thoroughly vanquished people would be easy. Similarly, problems seemed permanently settled in the apparently "pacified" Kazakh plains after the bloody rebellions which marked the years 1825 to 1865.

The conquest of Central Asia appears at first to have had an essentially economic significance. The truth probably is more complex. As early as 1858, Ignat'ev, the Russian military attaché in Lon-

[35] *Afganskoe razgranichenie*, part 2, pp. 63–65, 243–381.
[36] A. L. Popov, "Iz istorii zavoevaniia Srednei Azii," *Istoricheskie zapiski*, No. 9 (1940), p. 202.

don, was writing: "In the case of a conflict with England, it is only in Asia that we shall be able to struggle with her with any chances for success and to weaken her." [37]

H. C. d'E.

[37] *Ibid.*, p. 202.

5

Organizing and Colonizing the Conquered Territories

As soon as Tashkent fell to Russian troops, the problem of organizing the conquered territories arose. From 1866 to 1898, the status of Central Asia underwent many modifications, some of which were of great importance. The hesitations and turnabouts of the Russian government over the question of organizing Central Asia stemmed above all from a profound ignorance of the region. Just as the Russian government had believed the military power of the local sovereigns to be greater than it was, so it often assigned an incorrect value to the influence of certain individuals upon the whole of the local population. It misunderstood the aspirations of the conquered people, and constantly had to try to readjust its policies to realities as it was progressively made aware of them.

One of the factors that explained these oscillations and adjustments of Russian policy was the very nature of the conquest. In Central Asia, the Russian troops had not been preceded, as they were in Siberia, for example, by a movement of poor Russian peasants coming to seize the lands. Ever since the abortive attempt of Cossack Ataman Nechai Starenskoi early in the seventeenth century, Central Asia had remained relatively sheltered from incursions of Russian peasants. When the Russian government conquered the region, it could at first dispose of the area's future freely without having to deal with any Russian settlers.

The first stage in the organization of southern Central Asia became the discussion, in 1865, by the Steppe Commission, presided over by Privy Councilor F. K. Giers, of two possible statutes, one for the region of the plains, the other for southern Central Asia. A provisional statute remained in effect from 1865 to 1867 providing for the concentration of all power in the hands of the military authorities. This power was to be reduced to a minimum so as to cause the least possible interference in the life of the indigenous population—a policy applying equally to local customs and to agrarian, judicial, and social relations.[1]

It was not until 1867 that a real administrative and territorial organization of the conquered territories was worked out. The discussions of the Steppe Commission were continued by a new commission, termed "special committee," presided over by the minister of war, which took up again and spelled out in detail the recommendations of 1865. From the territorial point of view, the committee proposed creation of a guberniia of Turkistan,[2] detached from the tutelage of Orenburg, and called for adding the southern part of the Semipalatinsk area to its two original regions, Semirechie and Sir Darya.

From the political standpoint, the commission made two recommendations: the concentration of civil and military power in the hands of the military authorities, who alone would be responsible for this region, and the relinquishment of all local affairs not of a political nature to the traditional hierarchies who would continue to apply the customary procedures. Lastly, considerable power was entrusted to the governor general on account of the exceptional circumstances of the conquest and remoteness of the area. He had full latitude to deal with neighboring states,[3] to establish and dispose of the regional budget, to fix taxes, and to grant privileges to the Russian citizenry; he even had the right to confirm death sentences on local citizens or to pardon them.

On July 11, 1867, the czar signed the decree creating the guberniia of Turkistan,[4] and on July 14, the military chiefs summoned to

---

[1] M. A. Terent'ev, *Istoriia zavoevaniia Srednei Azii* (St. Petersburg, Tipolitografiia V. V. Komarova, 1906), I, 328.

[2] K. K. Palen, *Otchet po revizii turkestanskago kraia, proizvedennyi po velichaishemu poveleniiu Senatorom Gofmeisterom Grafom K. K. Palenom: Kraevoe Upravlenie* (St. Petersburg, Senatskaia Tipografiia, 1910–1911), p. 7.

[3] *Ibid.*, pp. 11–12.

[4] *Polnoi svod zakonov rossiiskoi imperii*, vol. 42, Uk. 44.844 (1867), p. 1156.

administer the region were announced.[5] General Kryzhanovskii, then governor general of Orenburg, had opposed the directives of the commission of which he himself was a member, arguing that it was perilous to allow full administrative autonomy to a region so far removed from the center of the empire and so separated from it by deserts. He felt, moreover, that it was particularly unfortunate to destroy the unity of command over the Kazakh plains.[6]

The plains region was organized the following year in accordance with the recommendations of the Steppe Commission. On October 21, 1868, three new entities were created: Uralsk, Turgay, and Akmolinsk. While the new arrangements were accepted without incident in Akmolinsk, as they had been in the regions attached to Turkistan guberniia, this was not true for Uralsk and Turgay, and the 1868 arrangements were the occasion for the last, great, anti-Russian revolts in the period of conquest in the Kazakh plains. These arrangements put an end to an order maintained since 1822, and ruined forever the authority and privileges of the local aristocracy.[7] Rapidly, the tribal uprisings assumed the proportions of a holy war, and it took the intervention of an army to put them down.[8] A few months later, the rebellion broke out anew among the Kazakh tribes of the Mangishlak region, where more than ten thousand insurgents attacked Russian villages. The organization of Turkistan guberniia likewise underwent territorial modifications as the conquest wore on. In 1868, the lands taken from Bukhara were to form the okrug of Zarafshan, while those taken from Khiva five years later would form the military district (*otdel*) of Amu Darya.

STRUCTURES OF THE GUBERNIIAS

The structures employed at this time were characterized by the system of territorial organization in effect throughout Russia—oblast, uezd, and uchastok—*but* all the power in Central Asia was held by

[5] *K otkrytiiu pamiatnika: General ad"iutant K. P. fon-Kaufman kak ustroitel' turkestanskago kraia, 1867–1882 gg.* (Tashkent, 1915).

[6] Eugene Schuyler, *Turkistan: Notes of a Journey in Russian Turkistan, Khokand, Bukhara, and Kuldja* (New York, Scribner, 1877), II, 204.

[7] V. V. Bartol'd, *Istoriia kul'turnoi zhizni Turkestana* (Leningrad, Akademiia Nauk. Kom. po Izucheniiu Estest. Proizv. Sil., 1927), p. 118.

[8] Terent'ev, II, 69–70.

the military. On a parallel with this Russian hierarchy and organization, the authorities allowed the former local judicial institutions, as
well as the political institutions of the villages, to continue. The
Russian command interposed to confirm the elections or designations of judges, who were chosen for three years by their electors,
and placed judges under the control of low-ranking czarist officials.
But for any affair involving neither Russian subjects nor interests,
and not falling within politics that might interest the Russian administration, judgments were rendered according to traditional
standards, and, except when the accused sought recourse to the
arbitration of a Russian tribunal,[9] Russian officials did not intervene. On the political level, Russian authorities supported the traditional village leaders. Villages were supposed to elect a salaried
elder (*aqsaqal*) for three years; in practice, though, he would almost always, as in the past, be appointed as a result of his belonging
to the ruling group. The gathering of several villages (*qishlaqs*) in
an administrative unit called a volost represented by an assembly of
electors, one for every five households, permitted the election of a
volost leader and the judges mentioned previously. The same
principles governed the organization of the nomad villages.

In actual fact, Russian intervention in local institutions was then
very limited. For a long time the local and the Russian hierarchies
coexisted with very loose ties. When the Russian government took
a hand in supervising local appointments, the system deteriorated.
Men were chosen by virtue of their links with the Russian authorities and their alleged influence with them. Compromise and corruption quickly developed. The shortcomings of this organization were
not slow in appearing, however, and in 1873 General von Kaufman
was the first to anticipate the need for reform. In his view, it was
important to strengthen Russian authority in Turkistan guberniia,
and he drew up a plan to this end. It came to nothing, however,
when various scandals which had broken out the guberniia im-
plicated his closest associates, like General Golovachev.[10] His suc-

---

[9] V. P. Nalivkin, *Tuzemtsy ran'she i teper'* (Tashkent, Tipografiia Lakhtin,
1913), p. 126.

[10] *Kaufmanskii sbornik v pamiat' 25 let so dnia smerti pokoritelia turkestanskago kraia* (Moscow, Kushnerev, 1910), p. LXXXIII.

cessor, General Cherniaev, asked the government to send a commission of inquiry to Turkistan guberniia.

The investigators, who arrived in Tashkent at the end of 1882, were led by F. K. Giers, whose mission it was first to examine the regional administration and then to propose a reform plan. The Giers Commission found that at all levels of the Russian administration, and in fact on all sides, flagrant and spreading abuses were prevalent.[11] But it also attacked the extraordinarily multiform nature of the organization of Turkistan guberniia, noting the simultaneous existence of four separate statutes: Sir Darya was governed according to the statute of 1867; Zarafshan in terms of the provisional statute drawn up by von Kaufman in 1868; Amu Darya with provisional texts of the guberniia of 1874; and finally, in Farghana measures proposed in the von Kaufman plan of 1873 were applied. The Giers Commission suggested, in conclusion, that a special commission establish a thorough reform of the structures, moving to decentralize power.

Turkistan guberniia, from a territorial point of view, at this time was no longer the same Turkistan guberniia which General von Kaufman had administered, and here, too, readjustments were necessary. The governor of Semirechie, General Kolpakovskii, had more seniority than Cherniaev, and it was not easy to place him under Cherniaev's orders. And so a guberniia of the Steppe was set up for General Kolpakovskii in which Semirechie, taken from Turkistan guberniia, and both Akmolinsk and Semipalatinsk, taken from eastern Siberia, were included, whereas Turkistan guberniia was limited to the Sir Darya and Farghana regions and the Zarafshan district.

The question of reform progressed after General Cherniaev, who had provoked several incidents through his authoritarian attitude and maneuvers as clumsy as those of his predecessor, was replaced by General N. O. Rosenbach. While General Rosenbach was taking over his post, in St. Petersburg the Ignatiev Commission was working on the directives of the Giers Commission and produced the statute of 1886, which was to continue hardly modified until the

[11] Schuyler, II, 210.

Russian revolution of 1917. The prime aim of the new statute was to attempt a progressive integration of Turkistan guberniia within the empire, on the one hand by settling the political and economic life of the local population, on the other by limiting the exceptional aspects of Russian authority.

The governor general, who was subordinate to the minister of war, from 1886 on would no longer be sole master, for a council of civil and military officials was to assist him. The executive organ of power would be the chancellery of the governor general, divided into three departments: the first devoted to administrative problems, the second to agrarian, educational questions, and so forth, the third to all the financial problems, the statistics, and the administration of the local philanthropies (*waqf*). Finally, one of the main jurisdictions of this chancellery would be diplomacy, a jurisdiction it held until 1899, when it lost this function to a representative of the Ministry of Foreign Affairs specially charged with the relations of the dependent emirate and khanate.

One of the great innovations of this reform was the assurance of the judicial hierarchy's independence in relation to the military. The reaction of the members of the Russian administration in Turkistan guberniia to the 1886 statute was extremely hostile. The governor general and his entourage protested the weakening of Russian authority, predicting that the consequence would be a loss of Russian prestige. Actually, the power of the governor general was hardly restrained by the council, for the latter's role was only advisory.

Any lowering of authority and decline of Russian prestige from this time forth in local opinion stemmed not, it would appear, from political or judicial limitations, but quite simply from the scandals which marked the von Kaufman period,[12] and especially from the personality of his successors, who did not know how to assert themselves among their associates or over their subordinates. In the remote colony of Turkistan guberniia each local Russian leader tended to behave as a petty king whose power was not limited by any authority; this provoked frequent clashes with the Muslim population. In the following years, several reform projects were

[12] Bartol'd, p. 204.

again proposed,[13] but the only political modifications of any importance would be those which Baron A. V. Vrevskii, who governed from 1889 to 1898, provided for the Tashkent statute after the cholera riots in 1892. Actually, Vrevskii dreamed of restoring, by exploiting the uprising, the authority of the governor general to its 1867 status; but in practice, his plan was limited to abolishing the function of the chief elder of Tashkent, in his capacity as head of the local police, and replacing him with a Russian. After the revolt of 1898, the principle that all the indigenous administrative cadres would no longer be elected but appointed by the governor general was reestablished,[14] because Turkistan guberniia was declared a region in a state of unrest.

TERRITORIAL ORGANIZATION

During this entire period, the real modifications brought to the organization of Turkistan guberniia were territorial. The Transcaspian region, conquered between 1869 and 1885, which had at first been placed under the jurisdiction of the governor general was taken from him in 1890 and put under the direct supervision of the minister of war. In 1898 the organization of Turkistan guberniia was thoroughly redrawn, partially no doubt in consequence of General Kuropatkin's ambition to see himself at the head of a virtual Central Asian viceroyalty; in fact, the post he coveted was entrusted to General S. M. Dukhovskii, and not until some years later did Kuropatkin finally reach the governor generalship of Turkistan guberniia. The result of the new organization was the creation of a greater Turkistan guberniia composed of five regions: Sir Darya, Farghana, Samarkand, Semirechie, and Transcaspia; Tashkent became the capital of both the guberniia and Sir Darya.

The guberniia of the Steppe was reduced once again to the regions of Akmolinsk and Semipalatinsk, while Turgay and Uralsk were to be governed separately and subject to the minister of the interior. Finally, Bukhara and Khiva retained the status of protectorates. This territorial organization continued until the 1917

[13] Terent'ev, II, 369.
[14] Nalivkin, p. 137.

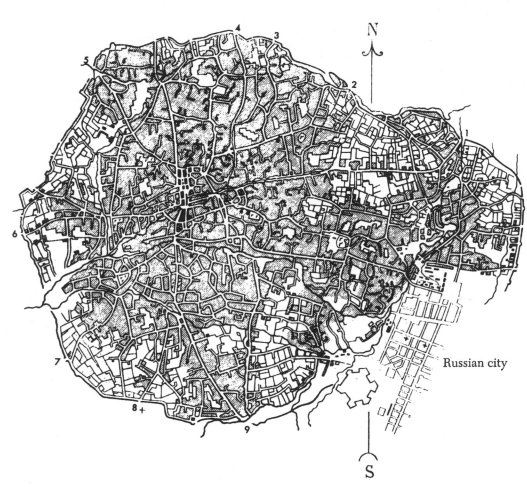

Russian city

LEGEND

		Gates:				
Heavily built up			1. Labzak		6. Kokcha
Walled plots			2. Takhtapul		7. Samarkand
Canals			3. Tiship Kapka		8. Kämalan
Monument mosque			4. Qara Saray		9. Besh Aghach
Cemetery or tomb			5. Chighatay		
Bazaar					

FIGURE 5.1　Old Tashkent, c.1890.

revolution, but was always threatened by the plan to annex Bukhara, which, however, was not put into effect.

During the period between the conquest and the revolution of 1905, Russian policy toward Central Asia might appear to have been uncertain and confused. Nevertheless, rather definite principles guided it, and certain constants can be found. In the first place, in southern Central Asia as in the Kazakh plain, Russia did not seek to integrate the conquered people, but simply to keep them in hand. They were not Russian subjects, and as aliens (*inorodtsy*) they were exempt from military service; in other words, mixing them with the Russian population was not attempted, even temporarily.

Legislation and administration, at least on the local level, remained in local hands and for all practical purposes in the control of traditional authorities. In Turkistan guberniia especially, the Russian government was at first wedded to the political line, advocated by von Kaufman, which ignored Islam and the Muslim society. The political organization of Central Asia was based on one definite principle: Manage the population without interfering in its affairs; above all render the machinery of colonial domination progressively lighter and less costly.

Yet, one very clear difference in attitude toward southern Central Asia and most of the Kazakh plain becomes evident. In this difference can be seen the main explanation for the constant modifications changing the political map of Central Asia. Whereas in Turkistan guberniia, conscious of the strength of Islam, the Russian government simply ignored it; in the Kazakh plain, still only barely converted to Islam, czarist officials sought to destroy the structures of the traditional society and break the prestige of the local authorities. By constantly recarving the Kazakh region and dispersing the tribes in several districts, the Russian authorities hoped to break up the existing units.[15]

However, this policy did not seem to bear fruit, and events after 1905 confirmed this. As early as 1886, in materials collected at the request of V. P. Nalivkin, General N. I. Grodekov stated that Russia had already failed in her Kazakh policy.[16] Islam, he wrote, was

---

[15] Terent'ev, III, 343.

[16] N. I. Grodekov, *Kirgizy i Kara-Kirgizy sir darynskoi oblasti* (Tashkent, Tipografiia Lakhtin, 1889).

gaining rapidly among the nomads. One of the signs of this new trend—which amounted to another Russian failure—was the nomads' frequently expressed desire to give up customary law and adopt Muslim law (*Shariat*). Finally, Grodekov felt, the authority of the traditional leaders had hardly suffered from the Russian efforts.

If, during the early years of Russian presence in Central Asia, the government had been especially busy settling problems relating to its own administration, it would very quickly have realized that to dispose finally of the local population's destiny was hardly possible. After a period of expectation in which the people awaited an improvement and rapid transformation of their condition thanks to the Russian presence, they gradually reacted to colonial conditions and to the social and economic changes that it brought about. Thus, about 1880, Central Asia, which until then seemed removed from the great awakening of consciousness that was beginning to throw the rest of the Muslim world into confusion, also began to become aware of its national and even its social problems. From that time forth, it became impossible for Russia to ignore Islam.

PREPARATION FOR CONFLICT

Just as local resistance to Russian penetration into Central Asia had been on the whole rather passive, so the reaction to the Russian presence was at first rather slight. For a few years, a certain peace reigned throughout all of Central Asia, creating the impression that the conquered people had accepted their fate or that the might displayed by Russia was enough to pacify them. In the Kazakh plain, the old nobility had exhausted all its strength in the bloody succession of attacks upon the conquerors between 1783 and 1870, the most important of which was that of Sultan Kenesari Qasim-uli. Local leaders could no longer make any serious effort to unite the tribes again and oppose the Russians.

But starting in the 1890s, the Russian rural colonization upset this relative tranquility. In 1891-1892, a first massive wave of Russian and Ukrainian settlers broke upon the plain, drawn there by the virgin lands. Between 1896 and 1916, more than a million peasants coming from Russia settled in the regions of Turgay, Akmolinsk, Semipalatinsk, and the Kirgiz lands, causing a brutal constriction of the nomadic territories, a reduction of livestock, and a lowering of the nomads' standard of living, which, though already very low, sank to a wretched level. Consequently, conflict between Russian settlers and local nomads became a daily occurrence on the plain and the inevitable crisis burst forth in 1916.

Southern Central Asia, a thickly populated oasis land possessed of an ancient civilization, hardly lent itself to Russian rural colonization as did the Kazakh plain and the Kirgiz mountains,[17] and so was relatively protected. The settlers did not arrive there until the beginning of the twentieth century; they were then few in number, but the arable lands were so scarce that even this light influx was enough to cause clashes between Russians and local citizens.

What profoundly altered the economic, social, and cultural life of Turkistan guberniia was the construction of a railway system which changed the country (see Figure 12.3), allowed the development of a textile industry, and led to the arrival of many Russian workers who gave a new character to the urban life of Central Asia. Purely Russian towns sprang up along the railway line. Above all, the old cities of the south rapidly took on the personality of "colonial" cities through the juxtaposition of a modern European quarter peopled exclusively with Russians with the old city (see Figure 8.1 and chapter 16). Here again, causes for conflict were not lacking. The social and political agitations which developed in the twentieth century among the Russians of these cities spread to the local populaces who reinterpreted them from their own perspective.

Russia's attitude regarding the local population was dominated by a twofold concern: limiting the influence of the Tatars and weakening Islam. This line was conceived and passed on by General von Kaufman, who had truly sought to understand the spirit of the community he was in charge of administering. He knew that the Tatars were, before the conquest, the real "colonizers" of Central Asia. After the Russian occupation, he was aware of the need to eliminate the Tatars to keep them from extending their influence and that of Islam to the nomads of the still protected

[17] Bartol'd, p. 119.

plains. This would have been a simple matter at the time when the plains were tied to the guberniia. Also, he wanted to screen from Turkistan guberniia the influence of the dangerous innovations developed by the Tatars since the beginning of the nineteenth century.

Thus, it was necessary, on the one hand, to oppose the Central Asians' contact with their co-religionists from the Volga and reject the Tatars' claims of extending the jurisdiction of the ecclesiastical administration of Orenburg to Central Asia. On the other hand, no support could be lent to Islam, and the best means of seeing to this, according to von Kaufman, was not to attack it—which would only push the Muslims closer to their faith—but on the contrary, to act as if there were no Muslim problem, no Islam. This was the rule to which von Kaufman remained faithful all his life; he ignored Islam. He had a clear presentiment that Islam was the force around which the conquered people might unite, and he knew that the peace of the region was but relative.[18]

Only against his successors, however, did the first signs of local resistance begin to mount. Ever since their installation in Central Asia, Russian authorities had been obsessed with the fear of revolts by a population whom cunning religious leaders might stir to fanaticism. The very status of the conquered people revealed this fear. By not turning Central Asian Muslims into Russian subjects, by sparing them military service, the imperial government hoped to avoid the formation of a local army and to prevent the populace's learning how to handle modern arms. The Russian desire was clearly to maintain the inequality in this domain which had favored the conquest so greatly. In 1882, the Giers Commission cited the precedent of the Sepoy mutiny (1857–58) and the impossibility of maintaining more than 30,000 Russian troops in Central Asia, a force which would be feeble when confronted with a nucleus of local troops organized, equipped, and qualified to use modern weapons.[19]

---

[18] N. P. Ostroumov, "K istorii narodnago obrazovaniia v turkestanskom kraie," *Konstantin Petrovich fon Kaufman, ustroitel' turkestanskago kraia: Lichnye vospominaniia, 1877–1881* (Tashkent, 1899), pp. 7, 12, 43f.

[19] F. K. Girs, *Otchet revizuiushchago po Vysochaishemu Poveleniiu turkestanskii krai tainago sovietnika Girsa* (n.p., n.d.), p. 414.

General von Kaufman's replacement moreover, coincided with a moment when the empire and Central Asia were undergoing great changes. The assassination of Alexander II heralded an era of political reaction which spread to Central Asia. Cherniaev's successor, General Rosenbach, violently criticized von Kaufman's policy, declaring it thoroughly bankrupt. What seemed dangerous to him was the advancement of Islam among the Kazakhs and the withdrawal of the Muslims into their own culture, whereas von Kaufman had dreamed of both Russifying the local elite and extending Russian culture and Christian civilization even to the common people of the area. Finally, von Kaufman had been upset by the growth of an increasingly obvious "disrespect" toward the Russian authorities.

REVOLT

Beginning in 1885, at a time when no conscious idealogical movement was behind the local opposition to Russia, the populace gave vent to its hostility through sporadic revolts. All these revolts followed the same pattern; they ended up as movements of a religious nature, assuming in certain instances the form of veritable holy wars, sometimes with a view to the restoration of the Khokand khanate. They were generally led by religious leaders, frequently of the Sufi orders, and their troops were formed of farmers and artisans from the towns, whose living conditions had worsened considerably with the increase of capitalist dealings in Central Asia. Russian industrial competition, the chaos existing in the agrarian relations, the dispossession of the peasants, and finally the excesses of the administration and the whole of the Russian population contributed greatly to the unrest.

Passing judgment on the colonial morality and events at the close of the nineteenth century, Nalivkin, a Russian ethnographer distinguished for his knowledge of Central Asian languages and customs, who later played a cultural and political role there in 1913, observed:

The scandals involving certain officials which burst out in 1902 raised a small corner of the curtain that was concealing a vast and disgraceful mire, and yet it seems to me that nowhere did these administrative excesses reach such towering proportions as they did in the Andijan uezd toward the end of the 90s and about the year 1900.[20]

Provoked by indignation, bitterness, and extreme poverty, all the revolts which shook Central Asia at the end of the nineteenth century had in common their popular, anarchistic, and spontaneous character; they were enhanced by no outside support and were easily suppressed because the rebels had only antiquated arms to fight with—mainly sticks and scythes—and their faith.

The first revolt, chronologically, was that led by Darwis Khan Tore, which broke out in 1885 in the Farghana Valley. Darwis Khan Tore was an important landowner who had served the fallen khan. He roused the districts of Andijan, Osh, and Marghilan, and seems to have been proclaimed khan of Khokand. The Russian troops rapidly put down the rebellion and arrested a great number of rebels, some of whom were executed, but were never able to find their leader.[21]

In the following years, the peasants rose up sporadically to attack the local Russian authorities, generally to protest the fact that "no solution had been provided to the land problem," particularly so far as colonization was concerned.[22] The administration first reckoned by tens, then by hundreds, this kind of clash, which sometimes, as in Namangan in 1891, bordered on full-scale rebellion.

However, the most important revolt in the early 1890s turned out to be an urban one, the cholera riots which shook Tashkent in 1892.[23] The crisis was brought on by a cholera epidemic which, on account of the poverty among the Muslim population, struck the old part of Tashkent with infinitely more severity than the European part.

To stem the epidemic the Russian authorities took measures which deeply shocked local feelings because they ran counter to the traditional customs, whether these were bound up with Islam or not. The sanitary inspections that the Russians imposed provoked an intense reaction, for the local men would not allow the women to be examined. But it was over the burials in particular that the

---

[20] Nalivkin, p. 138.

[21] Terent'ev, III, 325–27.

[22] *Istoriia uzbekskoi SSR* (Tashkent, Izdatel'stvo Akademii Nauk Uzbekskoi SSR, 1956), vol. I, book 2, p. 131.

[23] Terent'ev, III, 372–78.

conflict crystallized. As a security measure, the authorities had forbidden the dead to be buried in the old cemetery, insisting that the funerals be held with dispatch in a new cemetery far from the city without all the ritual so dangerous in time of epidemic. Stricken families proceeded to hold clandestine funerals, and the arrest of those who had taken such initiative caused a widespread outburst. In fact, these grounds for discontent had done nothing but deepen hostility toward the Russians, a hostility which increased among the artisans of the old city. Proof of this can be seen in the information that among the fifty-one persons apprehended by the troops which General Grodekov had led into the old city were a number of craftsmen. After the rioters had laid violent hands on Colonel S. R. Putintsev, the commander of the city, and had sacked his headquarters and the house of the head of the old city, Muhammad Yaqub Karimberdi-oghli, twenty-two artisans, some merchants, and even a few religious dignitaries who had played a very important role in the outbreak were arrested.[24]

General Vrevskii, then governor of Turkistan guberniia, concluded from this that the reason the populace had lost all respect for their conquerors was that the latter had relaxed their hold and limited the authority of their local representatives.[25] Yet, the problem was not simply one of authority, it went back to the basis of Russian-Muslim relations, to the very incompatibility of the ideas which directed their actions. After the years of general apathy which followed the conquest, the Russian presence was being challenged throughout all Central Asia, for it ran counter to the whole foundation of beliefs and customs upon which the local life was built and which the Russian authorities, with the exception of a few curious minds, like von Kaufman, or of scholars, like N. P. Ostroumov and Nalivkin, thoroughly ignored. As a result of this, even the most promising efforts seemed diabolic to the local people if they came from the Russians.

In Bukhara, where the Russians were present only in a very indirect fashion, this is particularly evident. After the protectorate was set up, Russia had offered her cooperation to the sovereign,

---

[24] *Istoriia uzbekskoi SSR,* vol. I, book 2, p. 131.
[25] Bartol'd, p. 206.

Abd al-Ahad (r.1885–1910) in order to help him overcome the great scourges which were forever menacing his subjects: locusts, the unregulated waters of certain rivers, and epidemics.

Locusts, a permanent nightmare for the peasant of the emirate, could destroy all his efforts within a few moments, condemning him to famine. The authorities proposed effective methods of combatting this plague,[26] but these methods were never systematically applied, partly because the peasants were unwilling to take a hand in the collective labor they entailed, but mainly because these methods offended them, went against their age-old acceptance of the plague. In the long run, they dreaded "offending God by destroying His creatures" even more than they dreaded the calamity that their acceptance would lead to.[27] Consequently, all efforts to take preventive measures against locusts brought about explosions of peasant fury, and under the last two sovereigns a direct cause-and-effect relationship can be found between these salutary campaigns and the popular revolts.[28]

In like manner, the Central Asians reacted violently to Russian plans for the construction of dikes to control rivers, like the Kafirnihan or the Vakhsh, whose sudden floods menaced not only the farmers' crops but their lives as well. Again they refused to take part without pay in these tasks, even though such efforts would obviously benefit the community. But there were deeper and more obscure motives—preoccupations of a magic nature, and a fear of offending the water spirits. To this peril the peasants far and away preferred the danger of periodic flooding, or the danger of reprisals that the refusal to take part in the work or even the revolts against the operations entailed.[29]

Lastly, the efforts of Russian authorities, who were appalled by the extent and frequency of the epidemic diseases, to intervene in

[26] R. Y. Rozevitsa, "Poiezdka v iuzhnuiu i sredniuiu Bukharu v 1906 g.," *Izviestiia Imperatorskago Russkago Geograficheskago Obshchestva*, XIX (1908), 70–73.

[27] A. A. Semenov, *Ocherk ustroistva tsentral'nogo administrativnogo upravleniia bukharskogo khanstva pozdneishego vremeni* (Stalinabad, Izdatel'stvo Akademii Nauk Tadzhikskoi SSR, 1954), p. 16.

[28] *Ibid.*, p. 15.

[29] D. N. Logofet, *V gorakh i na ravninakh Bukhary (ocherki Srednei Azii)* (St. Petersburg, Berezovskii, 1913), p. 270.

sanitation problems sometimes created misunderstandings.[30] More often they set off real outbursts among a population that was thoroughly under the influence of shamans and fortune tellers (*falbins*) who,[31] feeling that they were menaced by the Russian doctors, increased their pressure on the ordinary people and denounced Russian solicitude as a subterfuge destined to further subjugate the Muslims.

These unending clashes and systematic opposition to every Russian proposal were looked upon in the guberniia as alarming symptoms of an evolution in the local mentality. And yet the policy of ignoring Islam advocated by von Kaufman still continued, for the Russians could not quite distinguish, as far as the attitude of the Muslim populace was concerned, what was connected with Islam and the influence of the religious leaders, what was direct popular discontent, and finally, what was pure disorder. To these questions, which would become more clear from revolt to revolt, the Andijan rebellion provided a definite answer and put an end to this Russian bewilderment.

HOLY WAR IN ANDIJAN

Of all the popular uprisings in prerevolutionary Central Asia, disregarding the great 1916 revolt which really belongs to the history of the 1917 revolution, the most serious and most significant was that of 1898. As early as 1895, disturbing reports foreshadowed a mass movement considerably more important than the unorganized and anarchic explosions that were occurring elsewhere. In 1895, a Naqshbandi ishan from Andijan, Ismail Khan Tore, was arrested in Aulie Ata, where he was collecting funds to finance the holy war (*ghazawat*) of his disciples (*murids*). For lack of sufficient evidence (his exact role was then not quite clear), he was released and disappeared.

Three years later, May 18, 1898, it was again in Andijan that a revolt broke out which spread immediately to the districts of Osh,

[30] Iskandarov, *O nekotorykh izmeneniiakh v ekonomike vostochnoi Bukhary na rubezhe XIX–XX v.v.* (Stalinabad, Izdatel'stvo Akademii Nauk Tadzhikskoi SSR, 1958), pp. 22, 23.

[31] D. N. Logofet, *Strana bespraviia: Bukharskoe khanstvo i ego sovremennoe sostoianie* (St. Petersburg, Berezovskii, 1909), p. 32.

Namangan, and Marghilan. Leading it once again was an ishan of the Sufi brotherhood of the Naqshbandi, Muhammad Ali (Madali, or Dukchi Ishan). He was an astonishing figure, this religious leader.[32] Born not far from Marghilan, he had a reputation for wisdom, holiness, and charity, which at the age of forty-two, on the eve of the outbreak, had spread throughout all Farghana. With the help of disciples attracted to him, he had erected a madrasah, two mosques, and a library, and his power was substantial.

Around him gradually gathered Muslims who, for the most part, had been prominent figures before the conquest, and who had been deprived of their functions and often ruined by the Russians. Most important, the movement which the ishan would take over was very amply organized and financed by the Naqshbandi brotherhood. For the first time since 1865, it was no longer a matter of a spontaneous uprising, nor an uprising still looking for its ideology, but of a prepared holy war, beginning according to a plan and not haphazardly on some pretext.[33]

At the head of 2,000 men, Madali, who had proclaimed the holy war May 17, 1898, marched on Andijan. His lieutenants, at the head of other troops, were to besiege Osh and Marghilan at the same time. Through his military successes he hoped to rouse the population of Tashkent and Samarkand, reestablish the khanate, and from there, perhaps, rush on to the reconquest of Dar-ul Islam.

But the Russian retaliation was prompt; after a few initial triumphs on his march to Andijan, Madali encountered before the city the Russian 20th Line Battalion, which routed the rebels. The repression was particularly severe; 546 men were brought to trial. Madali and five of his lieutenants were hanged July 18 in Andijan; most of his faithful were imprisoned or sentenced to various jail terms.

In the course of the trial, an attempt was made to show that the rebellion was above all else due to the intrigues of the sultan of Turkey; evidence centered about a letter from the sultan found on Madali.[34] The true picture seems more complex. It cannot be de-

[32] Terent'ev, III, 473, 477–79.
[33] *Ibid.*, pp. 440f.
[34] *Turkestanskie viedomosti*, No. 48 (1898), cited in *Istoriia uzbekskoi SSR*, vol. I, book 2, p. 100.

nied that the ishan did ask the sultan, according to a tradition that the khans of Central Asia had followed from the days of the Abassid caliphs,[35] to recognize subsequently the investiture of the sovereign whom he hoped to place on the Khokand throne, and who was none other than his nephew Abdulaziz.[36] Such could be the contents of the document that Madali showed, it was said, to his followers as proof of the support found in Turkey. But that is uncertain.

What is clear, and the commission of inquiry noted it,[37] is that the Andijan revolt challenged Russian policy in Central Asia. This was a religious revolt in which not only the elite of the former khanate, but also the poor people, exasperated by the Russian presence, had gathered round a Naqshbandi ishan. Even the Soviet historians, who criticized an interpretation of the rising as a "popular movement," [38] admitted that "the organizers . . . succeeded in gaining the support of a part of the working population."

The consequences of the uprising were manifold. To the reprisals against the guilty were added "economic" disabilities upon certain villages accused of having lent too much support to the rebels. In the Marghilan district, several villages or hamlets were destroyed, their inhabitants expelled for having taken part in the revolt, and the population replaced by Russians who were allotted a great amount of well-irrigated land, where they began growing cotton. The Central Asians were transplanted to barren lands and founded a new village, Marhamat.[39]

In spite of premonitions about the revolt, the incident had not been foreseen by the Russian administration. The prevailing criticism of this astonishing blindness was epitomized thus: "In Farghana, we have carried a policy of blindness (*doignorirovalis*) right up to the Andijan incident." [40]

The czar immediately recalled Governor General Vrevskii, and

[35] T. M. Arnold, "Khalifa," *Encyclopedie de l'Islam* (1st ed.; Leiden, E. J. Brill; London, Luzac, 1913–   ), II, 933–38.
[36] Terent'ev, III, 440.
[37] *Istoriia uzbekskoi SSR*, vol. I, book 2, p. 99.
[38] *Istoriia narodov Uzbekistana* (Tashkent, Izd. Akademii Nauk Uzbekskoi SSR, 1947), vol. II.
[39] Bartol'd, p. 157.
[40] Nalivkin, pp. 137–38.

named General S. M. Dukhovskii in his place. For its part, the commission of inquiry decided on two sorts of causes: the pan-Islamic propaganda encouraged by the policy of noninterference in effect since the conquest, and the administrative lack of interest. The reforms effected during the governorship of General Dukhovskii all were aimed at strengthening Russian military authority.[41] The military administration's powers over the local hierarchies were increased. During the whole time that the region was in a state of unrest, the military had the power to replace the elections of local authorities by nominations at its own discretion; it also had the right to dismiss the people's judges if the Russian authorities deemed it necessary. Russian police forces were increased and lastly, Russian settlers were armed. This did not prevent the judicial structures introduced in Russia by the reforms of Alexander II from being put into effect in Central Asia on May 14, 1399—thirty years overdue—although with certain limitations.

Moreover, the Russian authorities decided to make a real stand against the growing influence of the Islamic authorities. They then found out how fatal their own ignorance of Islam and of Central Asian standards had been, and they established a plan to save themselves from this dilemma. Governor General Dukhovskii sought to bring humane solutions to the various problems raised by the revolt. He did not want to close the door to an entente between Russians and Muslims, but found himself trying to cope with two tendencies among the Russians who had been working in the area for years, and whose advice he sought. For everyone, the origin of the drama lay in the Muslim "fanaticism" exacerbated by the intellectual backwardness of the Central Asian population to whom the Russians had brought nothing. "People speak of our civilizing role in Central Asia. At this juncture our cultural influence is remarkable for its nonexistence." [42] Yet, while on one hand the Russian educators and scholars gathered round Nalivkin in the Samarkand group preached the final abandonment of the von Kauf-

[41] *Ibid.*
[42] *Turkestanskie viedomosti*, No. 101 (1899), cited by K. E. Bendrikov, *Ocherki po istorii narodnogo obrazovaniia v Turkestane* (Moscow, Izdatel'stvo Akademii Pedagogicheskikh Nauk RSFSR, 1960), p. 82.

man policy, others like F. M. Kerenskii continued to defend the policy of noninterference.

Between the two positions, which he considered equally dangerous, Dukhovskii decided in favor of an intermediate doctrine which consisted of an essentially political control of the Muslim madrasah and maktab and a refusal to create an ecclesiastical administration for the Central Asian Muslims, who were in addition cut off from their coreligionists of the Volga. Above all, Dukhovskii tried to improve relationships between the two communities by initiating the Russian military and administrative cadres into the languages and the religious problems of the Central Asians and by introducing at least a small elite of the local people to the Russian tongue and culture. Dukhovskii was counting on this elite later to wean the whole populace away from their religious leaders and orient it toward the modern world, represented by Russia. But this effort came at a moment in history when the reconciliation of the communities was particularly difficult to effect.

H. C. d'E.

6

The Stirring of National Feeling

Up to the end of the nineteenth century, Central Asia seemed protected from the influence of Jadid (reformist) ideas; nevertheless, it was in the madrasahs of Bukhara that the great debate began which would shake the spiritual, intellectual, and political life of Muslims there until the 1905 revolution. As early as the beginning of the nineteenth century, the need for a religious revival had been advocated by the Tatar Abu Nasr al-Khursavi (1783–1814), whose attacks on Muslim scholasticism and the degradation of mystical theology provided the basis for all the Muslim reformist thought formulated after him, especially by his compatriot Shihabeddin al-Marjani (1818–1889).[1] This challenging of all forms of religious life profoundly stirred people's minds, and the next step was an anguished quest to find the causes of the decline of Islamic society.

People's difficulties and the consciousness that the Central Asian elite felt a basic, irreconcilable conflict between Islamic society and the West were expressed by Ahmad Mahdum Kalla (Dānish) (1827–1897), one of the greatest nineteenth-century thinkers of Central Asia and theoretical precursor of the local reformists. Although the lofty figure of Ahmad Mahdum and his thought are still not widely known,[2] few men have shaken the traditional attitudes as deeply as he. In a poem addressed to the emir, Ahmad Mahdum wrote that a state gloried in seven individuals: the philosopher, the doctor, the astrologer, the singer, the calligrapher, the poet, and

[1] A. Arsharuni and Kh. Gabidullin, *Ocherki panislamizma i pantiurkizma v Rossii* (Moscow, Bezbozhnik, 1931), pp. 9, 10–11.

[2] Sadriddin Aini, *Vospominaniia* (Moscow-Leningrad, Izdatel'stvo Akademii Nauk SSSR, 1960), parts 3 and 4.

the painter—and that he himself was all these at once! [3] The encyclopedic learning gathered by this prodigious figure prompted Sadriddin Ayniy (1878–1954) to characterize him as "the most dazzling star in Bukhara's murky sky." [4]

Ahmad Mahdum, who had very early given thought to problems of a basic internal reform of Islam, was quickly to go beyond the purely religious perspective of his predecessors to a secular, social, and political approach to life. He was particularly impressed by what he saw in trips he took to Russia at the very time when the empire was extending its power over Central Asia and the khanates were floundering in insoluble difficulties. He became acquainted with diverse representatives of liberal thought in Russia such as the utopian socialists Petr I. Pashino and Petr B. Struve.[5] He was also in Russia at the time of N. G. Chernyshevskii's trial, and he followed attentively the ideas brought to light during the proceedings, just as he took a great interest later on in circumstances surrounding the assassination of Alexander II.[6] Ahmad Mahdum was particularly impressed by the opposition existing between a conquering and powerful Russia, where liberal ideas abounded even though prohibited, and his own declining, humiliated, land where any thought straying the least bit from fixed limits was branded "disloyal." [7]

At first Ahmad Mahdum extended his analysis to the Bukharan interior, denouncing the degradation of power and its abuses:

The Mangit [dynasty's] leaders have seized everything which their wickedness has inspired them to take. From the widow they have snatched away her hearth, from charitable institutions their resources. . . . Amongst the rulers and the propertied classes reign drunkenness and games of chance, revelry, and debauchery, while the poor people are at their wits' end. Whether the poor wretches are from the country

[3] Sadriddin Ayniy, *Bukhara inqilabi ta'rikhi uchun materiyallar* (Moscow, 1926), p. 25.

[4] Sadriddin Ayni, *Namuna-yi adabiyat-i Tajik* (Moscow, Tsentrizdat, 1926), p. 295.

[5] Kamol Aini, "Vstrechi Akhmada Donisha s P. I. Pashino," *Narody Azii i Afriki*, VI (1963), 144–47.

[6] I. Muminov, *Ozbekistanda ijtimaiy falsafiy tafakkurning tarikhidan (XIX asrning akhirlari wa XX asrning bashlari)* (Tashkent, Ozbekistan SSR Fänlär Äkädemiyasi Näshriyati, 1960), pp. 120–30.

[7] *Ibid.*, pp. 130–31.

or the city, they cannot utter a single word nor escape the constant levies.[8]

This historian of Central Asia's grandeur, addressing himself to the problem of its collapse in words as beautiful and as inspired as those of Jamal ed-din al-Afghani, adds to the explanations of his Indian and Arab predecessors a new, social dimension which, for the end of the nineteenth century, expresses a somewhat revolutionary note. The social order and the immoderate accumulation of wealth seem to him responsible for the corruption of traditional power, as well as the rupture with the order of early Islam. Like Jamal ed-din al-Afghani, a contemporary whom he apparently never met, Ahmad Mahdum attributed a considerable role to human initiative, and sought, while still reconciling such a force with divine will, to make of it a fundamental element in man's destiny.

Reflecting on human nature, Ahmad Mahdum at times seems to be tempted by a materialistic explanation of the universe, and while he does not yield completely to this temptation, the influence of rationalist and democratic thought is no less evident. He openly preaches that Central Asia should base its modern evolution on Russian support by studying the language and techniques of the Russians which, for Ahmad Mahdum who spoke Persian (Tajik), were the means of gaining access to the material achievements of Europe. Finally he is practically the only person of his time to examine, with regard to his community, the universal problem of man's lot in certain economic and social settings.

Unlike the city pattern, the evolution of the educated Kazakh circles was soon affected by Russian intervention in the cultural life of the plain. Very early, the Russian authorities grew uneasy about the influence pan-Turkic and pan-Islamic ideas brought to Kazakh lands by the Tatars of the Volga, ideas which helped precipitate the formation of an awareness of nationality. Kazakh groups, toward the middle of the nineteenth century, were beginning to feel that they were part of a larger nationality and no longer merely clans or tribes. That is why, about 1850, the Russians devised a policy aimed at eliminating the Tatars from the plain. As a result, Tatar teachers were barred from Kazakh educational institu-

---

[8] Ahmad Mahdum Dānish, *Navadir-ul vaqaye,* cited by Muminov, p. 126.

tions, and Russo-Kazakh schools were opened in order to substitute Russian influence for that of the Tatars. Thus could be seen the rapid development of educated Kazakhs turning toward the West and convinced that the way to progress and modernity was to be found in collaboration with the Russians.

The chief representatives of this group were three Kazakh enlighteners: Shoqan Shingis-uli Valiqan-uli (Valikhanov) (1835–1865), Ibray Altynsarin (1841–1889), and Abay Qunanbay-uli (1845–1904). The first accumulated all the titles which destined him to such a reconciliation with the invaders: he was a descendant of the khans of the Middle Horde, an officer of the Russian army, a prominent Orientalist, and an ardent admirer of Russia.[9] He carried on a close correspondence with Dostoevskii,[10] and was greatly impressed by Chernyshevskii.[11] Altynsarin, an ethnographer and educationist, worked under the tutelage of V. I. Il'minskii on the development of a new Kazakh literary language and was one of the first to express himself in this language, into which he also translated certain works from Russian literature.[12] Abay Qunanbay-uli, the son of a clan chief, considered then and now as a Kazakh national poet, was also a bold thinker already won over to modern ideas.

Other intellectuals, usually descended from the old nobility and formed in the Russian schools, were Aliqan Bokeyqan-uli (1869–1932), a descendant of the khans of the Inner Horde, Aqmet Baytursin-uli (1873–1937), and Mir Jaqib Duwlat-uli (1885–1937). They carried on the work begun by the three earlier activists of the Kazakh awakening into the twentieth century.

IMMIGRANTS AND EXILES AGITATE THE MUSLIMS

But in 1890–1892, the virgin lands of the plains attracted countless Russian and Ukrainian settlers who continued, up until 1916,

[9] Chokan Chingisovich Valikhanov, "Sochineniia," *Zhurnal Rossiiskago Imperatorskago Geografcheskago Obshchestva,* Otdiel Etnografii (1904), pp. i–xxxif.

[10] Ch. Valikhanov, *Stat'i-perepiska* (Alma Ata, 1947), pp. 107–15.

[11] *Letopis' zhizni i deiatel'nosti N. G. Chernishevskogo* (Moscow, Akademiia Nauk SSSR, 1953), p. 232.

[12] V. I. Il'minskii, *Vospominaniia ob I. A. Altynsarine* (Kazan, Tipografiia Kliuchevskago, 1891).

to spread into the regions of Turgay, Akmolinsk, and Semipalatinsk, upsetting the already precarious economic equilibrium, aggravating bad local living conditions, and setting the nomads against the newcomers. At the first vague signs of this movement, it became clear that the dream of a fruitful cooperation with the Russians in order to uproot the Kazakhs from their intellectual and material backwardness was impracticable. Kazakh nationalism, forged in

FIGURE 6.1   Jadid leader Aqmet Baytursin-uli.

part with the aid of the Russians against the Tatars, began to turn against Russia. A few years later this change became clear; in 1916 it would be complete.

The discussions in the madrasahs of Central Asia and in the works of reformist writers about the way to salvation for the Islamic community or for the Muslim people conquered by Russia, achieved their vigor in the years preceding the revolution of 1905, thanks to various initiatives of the reformists that were destined to bring theoretical discussions down to concrete terms very early. Under the influence of Ismail Bey Gaspirali (1851–1914), the Crimean Tatar who had opened a reformed maktab in Bakhchisaray, reformed schools were opened in the closing years of the nineteenth century. All these were at first Tatar schools located in Andijan 1897, Samarkand and Tokmak 1898.[13] Then in 1901 Munawwar Qari Abdurrashid Khan-oghli (1880–1933) opened in Tashkent the first Uzbek reformed maktab.[14] Even in Bukhara, where the religious life was dominated by the conservative clergy, Mullah Jorabay in 1900 opened a school of this type in the Pustinduzan qishlaq near the capital. For want of pupils he soon had to close the doors.[15]

In the Kazakh plain, the Tatars also endeavored to open a few reformed institutions, but the important event in the schools of the Turgay region was Altynsarin's introduction of Kazakh as the language of instruction in place of Tatar and the development of Russo-Kazakh instruction which, in contrast to the situation in southern Central Asia, attracted the local people and permitted the Russian language to make headway.

The accent placed by the Tatar and Central Asian reformists and by the Kazakh enlighteners on instruction became politically significant, for it raised questions bearing on the entire future of the Muslim people. For everyone, even for the educators, instruction was not an end but a means of answering the question that at least part of the Muslim community was asking itself with a growing anxiety: how can we transcend the current humiliation and regain the grandeur of bygone days?

In the following years the reformists often violently opposed the conservatives over the matter of education. This was because the conservatives, too, wanted an answer to the same question, and because their answer was diametrically opposed. For them, every step made toward Europe, even if it were to acquire the techniques which had brought about Europe's triumph, kept Islam still further away from the state it had reached at its greatest splendor. Further-

---

[13] I. I. Umniakov, "K istorii novometodnoi shkoly v Bukhare," *Biulleten' I-go Sredne-aziatskogo Gosudarstvennogo Universiteta*, book 16 (1927), p. 84.
[14] Jarcek, "Türkistan cadidçiliginin atasi (Münavvar Qarinin bolşeviklar tamanidan öldüruluvini)," *Millij Turkistan*, No. 77A (March 1952), pp. 1–6.
[15] Umniakov, p. 85.

more, the Tatars did not limit their action in Central Asia to educational reform. Through their efforts, the idea of pan-Turkism rapidly gained ground in Central Asia. Not long after the Young Turk revolution in 1876, Gaspirali published his famous pamphlet about the Muslims of Russia which was widely distributed in Tashkent, Samarkand, and Bukhara.[16] Two other works concerning Islam and modernization captured a very broad audience among educated Central Asians.[17] The authors of these writings asserted that the teaching of Muhammad, far from being inert and paralyzing, was dynamic and would lead in the direction of progress. Gaspirali's newspaper, *Terjuman,* and periodicals like al-Afghani's *Qanun* shook the framework of thought in Central Asia. In a report to the police department, the military governor of Sir Darya noted how far Gaspirali's newspaper had penetrated, making clear that its circulation was assured by the Tatars settled in Central Asia and by Gaspirali's travels. Similar reports can be found for other regions of Central Asia. All stressed the success of the ideas, especially pan-Turkism, stated by *Terjuman,* among the people under their jurisdiction.[18]

While the first years of the twentieth century saw far-reaching changes among the Central Asian leaders they were also years of exceptional gravity for the Russian empire. In 1904, the empire, to all appearances so strong, was defeated by Japan and this setback had world-wide significance. For the first time in a long while a conquering power of the Christian West collapsed before a nonwhite people, and this event was regarded as vengeance by all colonized people.[19] For the Muslims of Central Asia, this defeat was even more deeply felt since it involved their own conqueror, and it appears to have dealt a rather serious blow to the attempts at cultural cooperation. Ostroumov had pointed out that the whole effect

[16] I. Gasprinski, *Russkoe Musul'manstvo: Mysli, zamietki i nabliudeniia Musulmanina* (Simferopol', 1881).

[17] Devlet Kil-deev, *Magomet kak prorok* (St. Petersburg, Tipografiia Suvorin, 1881); Baiazitov, *Otnoshenie Islama k nauke i k inovertsam* (St. Petersburg, 1887).

[18] A. V. Piaskovskii, *Revoliutsiia 1905–1907 godov v Turkestane* (Moscow, Izdatel'stvo Akademii Nauk SSSR, 1958), p. 102.

[19] B. Vernier, *Qedar, Carnets d'un mehariste Syrien* (Paris, Plon, 1938), p. 202.

produced upon the Central Asian schoolboys who had visited Russia in 1904 was swept away by the announcement of the Russian military disasters.[20] From this time forth, the Muslims envisaged the possibility of an end to colonial domination, and the new weakness of Russia gave support to the anxious dreams of the reformists and supplied them with a definite direction. The revolution of 1905 would further accelerate and extend this awakening of the national consciousness. The liberal ideas conveyed by the revolution encouraged both the development of bitterness among the populace over their material condition, and the aspirations of educated men toward political and social reform; the very conditions of the revolution in Central Asia, which was not a simple local variant of the revolution in Russia proper, contributed to a widening of the breach that had been created between the Russians and the Muslims ever since the Andijan rising in 1898, and which would go on widening until the revolution of 1917.

The revolution of 1905 had in this typically colonial environment one specific characteristic: it was a Russian revolution followed, for the local people, by a state of perturbation whose gravity and even existence at first escaped official notice. This can be explained by two factors: the class differentiation of the proletariat, and the weakness of political organizations.

The problem of the proletariat involved Turkistan guberniia particularly, but existed similarly any place in Central Asia where there was a proletariat, on the plains and in Transcaspia, mainly along the railroad system. In the guberniia of Turkistan the workers and peasants were clearly differentiated into two groups whose aspirations and social situation were fundamentally distinct. In 1906, there were in Turkistan guberniia 5,378,000 Central Asians and 322,000 Russians.[21] The bulk of the indigenous population was comprised of peasant farmers, nomads and seminomads who had been arriving on their lands since the final decades of the nineteenth

[20] K. E. Bendrikov, *Ocherki po istorii narodnogo obrazovaniia v Turkestane* (Moscow, Izdatel'stvo Akademii Pedagogicheskikh Nauk RSFSR, 1960), p. 221.

[21] K. K. Palen, *Otchet po revizii turkestanskago kraia proizvedennyi po vysochaishemu poveleniiu Senatorum Gofmeisterom Grafom K. K. Palenom: Pereselencheskoe dielo* (St. Petersburg, Senatskaia Tipografiia, 1910), p. 19.

century. The settlers, who had many a time resolved their land problem by simply expelling the local people, with the support of Russian administrators, continually grew in numbers. The tension created by these dealings, which had led to the 1898 explosion, was not allayed, and at the beginning of the twentieth century, the local administration reported that "the Russian colonization, which has already led to tragic outbreaks, runs the risk henceforth of bringing about a general uprising." [22] Haunted by this threat, the authorities had armed the Russian settlers. Early in 1905, the Russian government, eager to avoid the spread of unrest to the countryside, finally decided to organize the immigration by limiting it. But it could not prevent the massive entry of immigrants driven out of Russia by the crop failure of 1905. These clandestine immigrants, unable to appropriate land because of new regulations, vegetated in the cities in exceedingly wretched conditions, and contributed powerfully to the agitation there.

The situation of the industrial workers was even more distinct. The industrialization of Central Asia, which was just beginning, was of a colonial sort. The working people were few in number there,[23] only 14,500 workers labored in the twenty-nine mining industries; 15,000 railway employees and workers maintained the rail system; in all, this made some 32,000. Yet, although weak, this proletariat grouped itself in a handful of cities, generally the important railway junctions of Tashkent, Samarkand, Ashkhabad, Qizil Arvat, and Vernyi. Seventy-seven percent of the workers were indigenous.[24] Russian workers alone were skilled and the local men mere laborers. Moreover, while the Russians were permanently employed, most of the others were peasants who had been dispossessed of their lands or unable to live on the produce of the land alone, persons who worked seasonally for lower wages than the Russians.

[22] G. P. Galuzo, *Turkestan koloniia* (Moscow, Izdanie Komm. Un-ta Trudiashchikhsia Vostoka imeni I. V. Stalina, 1929), p. 130; A. A. Kaufman, *K voprosu o russkoi kolonizatsii turkestanskago kraia* (St. Petersburg, Kirshbaum, 1903).

[23] Palen, *Otchet po revizii turkestanskago kraia . . . Gornoe dielo*, p. 132.

[24] Palen, *Otchet po revizii turkestanskago kraia . . . Promyshlennoe dielo*, pp. 36–38.

For practical purposes, the only permanent proletariat was Russian. In the mining industries where the Central Asians worked all year, 45.6 percent of the personnel were Russian, 34.4 percent Muslim from outside the country (Persian, Afghan, or Tatar), and only 18.9 percent were local laborers.[25] Here again, the Muslims held the most menial jobs at trifling wages. Among the railway employees, who alone represented nearly half the labor pool, for security reasons there were mainly Russians. Finally, certain military railway battalions in charge of guarding the rail lines lived with the employees and not in barracks.[26] These battalions were now filled with Russian students guilty of having liberal views, suspects, and soldiers deemed undesirable in Russia because of their "poor spirit." It is not surprising that the revolution of 1905 developed mainly around the railway lines.

The proletariat of Turkistan guberniia was thus, in 1905, essentially Russian. In order to prevent the penetration of revolutionary ideas among the Central Asians, the government had systematically restrained the development of local proletarians, favoring at the same time the Russian proletariat, who, in local eyes, looked like a privileged class.

RUSSIAN POLITICAL ACTIVITIES

For a long time Russian political parties showed hardly any interest in the Central Asian periphery. Socialist ideas penetrated the area from the end of the nineteenth century onward thanks to the czarist political deportees whose numbers kept on swelling, and via the suspects entering the rail brigades. In the beginning, these deportees, who were only awaiting the moment to return to Russia, engaged in very limited action among small groups of Russian workers. Beginning in 1903, under the influence of events in Russia and the Caucasus, the need to organize the agitation became clear to the politically minded. Small opposition groups arose eager to reach the workers as well as young people and students.

[25] Palen, *Otchet po revizii turkestanskago kraia . . . Gornoe dielo*, pp. 31–149.
[26] E. S. Markov, *Rossiia v Srednei Azii: Ocherki puteshestviia po Zakavkazii, Turkmenii, Bukhare, i tak dalee* (St. Petersburg, Tipografiia Statsulevich, 1901), I, 72.

One of the first and the most important of these groups was the Pushkin Society (Pushkinskoe Obshchestvo) whose avowed aim was to conduct schools on Sunday for workers, open public reading rooms, and give lectures. Until 1904–1905 all the opposition groups flocked around this society without worrying about the divergences expressed then in Russia between the parties. The activities of the society very quickly disturbed the local authorities, and the military commander of Tashkent pointed out in 1905 that "the Pushkin Society for cultural dissemination has long since been transformed into a social-democratic and revolutionary society." [27] The same kind of confusion could be found in other groups of a more openly political denomination, such as the Tashkent General Revolutionary Group (Obshche-revoliutsionnaia Gruppa), directed by Ilia Shendrikov, the Morkovin brothers, and two Socialist Revolutionaries, Vedeniapin (who later became a member of the Socialist Revolutionary Central Committee) and Khvorostov.[28]

A similar organization was created in Samarkand in 1904 by a Bolshevik Social Democrat, M. V. Morozov, who came there after deportation to Irkutsk, where he took part in the activities of the Bolshevik group. The group he founded in Samarkand would be, until 1905, like the others, an assemblage not only of Bolsheviks, Mensheviks, and Socialist Revolutionaries, but would even welcome anarchists, Zionists, and Dashnaks. Morozov had at his disposal a legal Russian newspaper, *Samarkand,* in which to express the chaotic ideas of this agglomeration. It was not until 1905 that the tendencies became clear.[29] The revolutionary groups of Tashkent and Samarkand then underwent serious crises because of internal conflicts among sympathizers of the various parties and police surveillance.

In Ashkhabad, which during this period was one of the most restless centers in Central Asia, a certain unity was preserved during the whole period 1905–1907 between the two great groups, the Social Democratic group of Ashkhabad and the Socialist Revolution-

[27] V. V. Ershov, "Revoliutsiia 1905–1907 gg. v Uzbekistane," *Revoliutsiia 1905–1907 gg. v Uzbekistane: Sbornik statei i vospominanii* (Tashkent, Izdatel'stvo Akademii Nauk Uzbekskoi SSR, 1955), p. 32.

[28] Piaskovskii, p. 88.

[29] *Krasnaia letopis' Turkestana,* Nos. 1/2 (1923), p. 24.

ary committee of Ashkhabad.[30] Only after the revolution had broken out, in February, 1906, did the revolutionary movements attempt to organize themselves in a broader manner. The first regional conference of the Social Democratic organizations of Turkistan guberniia met in Tashkent and decided that all the organizations and Social Democrat groups of Turkistan guberniia would be joined together in the Union of Turkistanian Organizations of the Russian Social Democratic Workers' Party (Soiuz Turkestanskikh Organizatsii RSDRP).[31] The texts concerning these first opposition groups, mainly the Social Democratic organizations, reveal only Russian names, and the indication is that these groups acted only in Russian surroundings; the Social Democrats were aware of it, for the Tashkent conference concluded citing the need for agitation among the local inhabitants.

Even before the revolution of 1905 had broken out in Russia, social ferment was developing in Central Asia. It is characteristic that these spontaneous movements, particularly important in the Transcaspian region, were at the basis of the expression of the indigenous workers' discontent.[32] There were longshoremen's strikes in Krasnovodsk in 1900, the strikes of the Uspenskii copper miners and of the Karaganda miners in 1902, and the strikes of the Mughozar railway employees, of the workers in the Omsk repair shops, of the Kala-i Mor railway workers near Kushka, and others. In December 1902, the governor general of the Steppe guberniia noted the importance of the clandestine agitation among the indigenous railway workers, especially at Omsk, Petropavlovsk, and in the neighboring cities.[33] In 1903, the governor general of Turkistan guberniia received reports cautioning him about the role played by railroad workers in various conflicts, and the use made of this by professional agitators. Within business concerns, the number of petitions increased, and the indigenous workers referred from 1903 on to successful demands made at Baku for an eight-hour day and

[30] Piaskovskii, pp. 95–96.
[31] Ershov, pp. 37–38.
[32] Piaskovskii, p. 63.
[33] A. F. Iakunin, "Revoliutsiia 1905–1907 gg. v Kazakhstane," *Revoliutsiia 1905–1907 gg. v natsional'nykh raionakh Rossii: Sbornik statei* (Moscow, Gosudarstvennoe Izdatel'stvo Politicheskoi Literatury, 1955), p. 680.

wages equivalent to those paid Russian workers. May 1, 1904, saw
for the first time a demonstration by the Russian rail workers of
Tashkent, and the authorities of the Transcaspian region were
fearful that disorders would erupt that same day at Qizil Arvat.[34]

THE REVOLUTION OF 1905 AND ITS AFTERMATH

When revolution burst forth in Russia, the Social Democrats in
Central Asia took the cue. Beginning on January 10, 1905, they
spread the news among the workers, and organized collections,
workers' demands, and even banquets in all the large cities. From
this time on, only the Russian workers took part, and the revolution
of 1905–1907 in Central Asia was purely a Russian phenomenon.

When, in 1906, the Social Democrats affirmed the need for agitation among the Muslim inhabitants, they were drawing a lesson
from past events. What they had been able to observe was that, in
the first place, the revolutionary centers in Central Asia in 1905 had
been primarily Russian. The revolution had in fact followed the
rail lines and the cities that lay along them, and had been concentrated mainly around stations, railway depots, and repair shops. The
military uprisings at the end of 1905 and in the summer of 1906 had
swelled this movement, the bulk of which was made up of railway
employees, almost all of whom were Russian.[35] Agitation in industry was much more limited and was chiefly on a material level,
all the more easily satisfied in that it only concerned the permanent
(Russian) proletariat. At no time was there any sign that sweeping
demands would turn to the equalization of conditions between the
two groups, Russian and Central Asian. At no time was the precarious and inferior situation of the indigenous proletariat considered. Moreover, whether it was a cause of the foregoing or an
effect, the Muslim workers seem to have taken part so seldom in the
revolutionary events and in such small numbers, that history has not
revealed even their names.

This apparent indifference of the Central Asians toward the revolution greatly impressed the Russian authorities,[36] who concluded

[34] Piaskovskii, pp. 66, 68.
[35] *Revoliutsiia 1905–1907 gg. v Uzbekistane: Sbornik statei i vospominanii*
(Tashkent, Izdatel'stvo Akademii Nauk Uzbekskoi SSR, 1955), pp. 127–28.
[36] A. Kuropatkin, "Dnevnik," *Krasnyi arkhiv,* II (1922–1927), 73.

that ordinary Muslims as well as the educated owed their lack of interest in events that had shaken the empire and their own land to the feeble development of the reform spirit and to the influence of the maktabs and the old-fashioned madrasahs.[37]

The revolution of 1905 spread to the countryside, however, and outside the cities the situation was completely different. There were two distinct revolutions. Until 1906–1907, the countryside remained calm, a calm to which the reports of the local administration bore witness. There was calm among the settlers who were fearful that agitation on their part would spread to the Central Asians and preferred to make sure of the authorities' support; there was calm among those who were, in Turkistan guberniia, under the complete influence of a Muslim hierarchy hostile to both the revolutionary spirit and to a common movement with the kafirs. The only peasant unrest came among the "voluntary" Russian settlers who, languishing in the new cities of Central Asia, plunged eagerly into the revolution to which they gave its substance. But they also brought to it their bitterness toward the Central Asians who, they felt, had been maintained on lands at the settlers' expense, and the disgruntled Russians focused an equal hostility on the czarist hierarchy and the indigenous peasants.

The authorities, watchful of the evolution of the local people, noted all through the revolutionary period that local peasants as well as local workers had not participated. But their optimism was short-lived, for just as the Russian revolution was subsiding, a second revolution was developing in Central Asia, deriving from the Russian revolution, but this time, arising from the indigenous population alone and reaching both the countryside and the educated city groups.

Order in the countryside was disrupted by bands of brigands made up mainly of dispossessed local peasants. Toward 1905–1906, this organized plundering changed its character rather abruptly and tended to turn into a wide resistance movement against the Russian administration. During the period 1906–1910 these bands developed to an extraordinary degree, and their ties with the local population, who considered them not a menace but a safeguard against the administration and the Russian settlers, were strong.[38] The most famous was the legendary Namaz Premkulov, who became a sort of hero in Central Asia and whose image was at once that of a liberator and a knight-errant.[39]

The movement was clearly anti-Russian. Whereas in 1905 the brigands contented themselves with robbing travelers and convoys, after 1905 they frequently clashed with the authorities, attacked them without any motive of plunder, and, with the Muslim people, organized demonstrations against the settlers and the payment of taxes.[40] Whenever such bands appeared in these later years, the rural population rose quite openly in rebellion against the authorities, systematically refused to give them any overt sign of respect, and blamed everything on the settlers. Nowhere, on the other hand, did this poverty-striken population attack their own propertied countrymen. It is clear that the unsettled state of Russian authority, and the revolutionary demonstrations extended to the countryside by the indigenous seasonal workers, made a deep impression on the local population and stimulated this parallel movement.

In the revolutionary years, the political life of the Muslims in the Russian empire was expressed through two new manifestations, an attempted Islamic unification, and their participation in the Duma. In each case, the role of the Central Asian representatives remained very limited.

In the three Muslim congresses, called on the initiative of Kazan's (Tatar) Galimjan Ibragim-oghli (1887–1938) in 1905 and 1906,[41] the Tatars and the Azerbaijanians (Azeris) played a decisive role. The representatives of Central Asia did not appear until the third Congress, at which a Kazakh, Shahmardan Koshshegul-uli, descended from the Inner Horde,[42] was elected to the presidium

---

[38] Galuzo, p. 136.

[39] D. Sharipov, S. Bakbaev, and S. Khudaibergenov, "O Namaze Premkulove," *Revoliutsiia 1905–1907 gg. v Uzbekistane,* pp. 137–39.

[40] Galuzo, pp. 134–37.

[41] Arsharuni and Gabidullin, pp. 23–31, 114, 122, 123.

[42] F. N. Kizeev, *Revoliutsiia 1905–1907 gg. v Kazakhstane: Sbornik* (Alma Ata, Akademiia Nauk Kazakhskoi SSR, 1949), p. 45.

along with Eminjan Ilhamjan-oghli who, although coming from Central Asia, was actually a Tatar.

The parliamentary experience of the Central Asians, while real, was short-lived. Still, the possibility of having Central Asian demands heard in this assembly had aroused great hope. At the first Duma, delegates from Turkistan guberniia were absent because the electoral laws for the area had been adopted too late for a vote. The Kazakh plain, on the other hand, sent nine representatives, including four Kazakhs: Alpispay Kalmen-uli (Uralsk), Aqmet Qorghanbek-uli Beremjan-uli (Turgay), Mullah Kulman-uli (Akmolinsk), and Aliqan Bokeyqan-uli (Semipalatinsk).[43]

The first Duma having been abruptly dissolved on July 9, 1906, because of its overly liberal leanings, the second Duma convened on March 5, 1907, with thirty-one Muslim delegates, of whom four came from the plains and six from the guberniia of Turkistan:[44] Vakhitjan Besali Karatay-oghli, Aqmet Qorghanbek-uli Beremjan-uli, Shahmardan Koshshegul-uli, Hajji Temir Ghali Tute-oghli Narokon-oghli, Muhamedjan Tanishbay-uli, Abdul Vakhit Qari-oghli, Veli Allah Allabergen-oghli, Salihjan Muhamedjan-oghli, Mahdum Quli Khan Nurberdikhan-oghli, and Tashpulat Abdul Khalil-oghli. Although some representatives from Central Asia played an eminent role in the nationality movements, and this was especially true of Tanishbay-uli, certain others were quite retiring and sometimes even unable to express themselves in Russian, which severely curtailed their effectiveness. Delegations from Central Asia generally supported the Muslim majority that had come from the Muslim Union (Ittifaq) and was allied with the Constitutional Democrats.[45] Representatives from the Russian community of Central Asia were distinctly more radical than the local delegates and identified themselves with the parties of Russia. Thus, the Russian representation

[43] Arsharuni and Gabidullin, p. 120.

[44] *Chleny Gosudarstvennoi Dumy, Portrety i litografi—Pervyi sozyv* (Moscow, Izdatel'stvo T-va Sytin, 1906), pp. 491–96; *Chleny vtoroi Gosudarstvennoi Dumy* (St. Petersburg, Pushkinskaia Skoropechatnia, 1907); *Chleny Gosudarstvennoi Dumy, tretii sozyv, 1907–1912* (6th ed.; Moscow, Tipografiia T-va Sytin, 1910).

[45] *Programma musul'manskoi parlamentarskoi fraktsii v Gosudarstvennoi Dume* (St. Petersburg, Tipografiia Balianskii, 1907).

of Turkistan guberniia numbered seven, including three Social Democrats, one Socialist Revolutionary, two Trudoviks, and one not affiliated with a party.

After the dissolution of the second Duma, on June 16, 1907, a new electoral law restricted the number of Muslim representatives to ten and simultaneously deprived Central Asia of all parliamentary representation, because, it was specified, there was unrest in the region. To this brief parliamentary experience for the Central Asians was added a first attempt at an organized indigenous effort which marked their initial independent steps on the political scene. After the imperial message of October 17, 1905, representatives from among the dignitaries of Islam, intellectuals, and important citizens decided to bring action to obtain equal rights among Russians and Muslims. In March, 1906, at a meeting in Tashkent, they demanded guarantees of religious freedom, that real estate be untaxed, the restitution of pasture land expropriated from nomads, and the creation of a Muslim Ecclesiastical Administration (Musulman Diniy Idaräsi) in Tashkent. These demands remained a dead issue, but the movement which had led to them had contributed both to the Central Asian political experience and to the awakening of a consciousness of nationality.

H. C. d'E.

7

Social and
Political Reform

After the revolution of 1905, leaders of the Tatar movement gave
their help to Central Asian partisans of reform, who attentively read
Tatar and Azeri newspapers published in Russia: *Terjuman,* of
course, and also *Ul'fet, Yulduz, Vaqit,* and *Irshad.*[1] But above all,
taking advantage of the brief relaxation of government control during the years 1905–1907, the Tatars and Uzbeks published newspapers in Central Asia itself.

One of the first of these papers was *Taraqqiy,* founded in 1906
in Tashkent by a Tatar Socialist Revolutionary, Ismail Abidiy. With
the collaboration of the Russian Orientalists Vasiliy L. Viat'kin and
Nalivkin, Abidiy produced a paper very critical of the czarist administration that demanded answers and defended the idea of unity
for Central Asia. *Taraqqiy* expressed the reformist positions and
certain Socialist Revolutionary ideas at the same time.[2] It seemed
"seditious" to the authorities, and disappeared after seventeen issues.

Stimulated by this example, however, Uzbeks began to publish
other papers: *Khurshid, Shohrat,* and *Tujjar. Khurshid* was founded
in 1906 by Munawwar Qari Abdurrashid Khan-oghli, who earned
recognition from that time forth as one of the chief leaders of the
Central Asian movement.[3] His paper was presented as "the organ
of the Muslims, published two or three times weekly in the Turki
language; a literary, scientific, and socio-political organ." Actually,

[1] A. V. Piaskovskii, *Revoliutsiia 1905–1907 godov v Turkestane* (Moscow,
Izdatel'stvo Akademii Nauk SSSR, 1958), p. 544.
[2] A. Zeki Velidi Togan, *Bugünkü Türkili (Türkistan) ve yakin tarihi* (Istanbul, Arkadaş, Ibrahim Horoz ve Güven Basimevi, 1942–1947), p. 353.
[3] Jarcek, "Türkistan cadidçiliginin atasi (Münavvar Qarinin bolşeviklar
tamanidan ölduruluvini)," *Millij Turkistan,* No. 77A (March 1952), pp. 1–6.

its publication was very irregular, and it disappeared in November, 1906. Munawwar Qari replaced it with *Shohrat*, which appeared from the end of 1907 to the following spring, and when that was prohibited he substituted *Asiya* for it. *Asiya* was simply a new name for *Shohrat* and ran for only five numbers. *Tujjar* was founded by one of the richest men in Tashkent, Said Azimbay Muhammadbay-

FIGURE 7.1   Jadid leader Munawwar Qari.

oghli, who,[4] while still a youth, had been sent to school in Nizhni-Novgorod where he had learned Russian. He always believed in the transformation of Central Asia by opening it up to the outside world and Westernization. His paper, expressing his own ideas and, as the masthead indicated, "appearing two to three times weekly

[4] H. Carrère d'Encausse, "La politique culturelle du pouvoir Tzariste au Turkestan, 1867–1917," *Cahiers du Monde russe et sovietique*, No. III (July–September 1962), pp. 383, 387.

in a Muslim language—a national, political, and social organ," soon vanished for lack of readers.

The ideas presented by these papers were nearly identical, and their evolution and decline between 1905 and 1908 reflected very accurately the worsening of the liberal climate in Russia in the years that followed the revolution. *Taraqqiy* enjoyed enough liberty to oppose both czarist authority and the conservatism of the Muslim religious leaders.

Khurshid, founded later, was distinctly more level-headed on this last point, for the Russian authorities, analyzing the revolution of 1905 in Turkistan guberniia, had thought that the neutral attitude of the Central Asians was attributable to the ascendancy of traditional, conservative Islam. Therefore the Russian doctrine of noninterference and then of control was gradually replaced by one calling for the protection of Islam in its most rigid, hardened forms, as a barrier to social movements. In its issue No. 6 of October 11, 1906, *Khurshid* published, under the signature of Mullah Mahmud Khoja Behbudiy (1874–1919),[5] a genuine program for the Jadids of Central Asia, and preached adherence to the Muslim Union (Ittifaq ul-muslimin), the eventual mainstay of the Constitutional Democratic Party. It attacked Russia, her autocracy, and her colonial policy. But the conservative backwash after the revolution brought about a constant curtailment in freedom of expression. Consequently the Jadid publications clung desperately to the only hope for political existence, representation in the Duma. After *Khurshid* had been banned, Munawwar Qari wrote to the governor general:

The aim of our newspaper was simply to make the local population understand the activity of the Duma and its significance; also to prepare this population adequately for the next elections . . . My intention was not to propagate antigovernment ideas, but to devote my efforts to calming passions, to preparing tranquil and useful elections.[6]

Shohrat followed a similar line, as far as the representation of Turkistan guberniia in the Duma was concerned. But emphasis was also often placed on the problem of spiritual reform for Islam, and here all compromise with the West was banished. In it Munawwar

[5] Piaskovskii, p. 551.
[6] *Ibid.*, p. 552.

Qari stressed the necessity of forming the Muslim elite in Islamic areas such as Bukhara, Istanbul, Cairo, and Alexandria, whose independence in these matters was relatively protected.

Tujjar took a very different line from the other papers, preaching total collaboration with Russia.[7] Its failure, astonishing considering that it effectively represented the interests of local wealthy merchants, followed, nevertheless, the logic of the evolution in Turkistan guberniia. *Tujjar* became disturbing to the Russian authorities disconcerted by the zeal of Said Azimbay, who was always suspected of wanting to advance some personal ambitions.[8] The paper did not interest the Uzbeks nor even the merchants because it did not offer guidance to the nationalistic aspirations asserting themselves more and more clearly.

Through their negative attitude to spiritual reform, which received considerable coverage in the press of Central Asia, the Russian authorities contributed greatly to widening the breach that separated reformists from conservatives. Munawwar Qari brought this clearly to light in *Khurshid* when he reported how, in permitting him to start his newspaper, the guberniia authorities had said through the editor of *Turkestanskaia tuzemnaia gazeta*, into whose presence he was summoned: "Under no circumstances are you to print any articles directed against the personality or the activity of the religious hierarchy without having talked it over with us." [9] Actually, such interference was not absolutely necessary in Turkistan guberniia. While *Taraqqiy*, a Tatar paper, indulged in extremely violent attacks against Muslim dignitaries, Munawwar Qari affirmed in 1906 that the Jadid critics were not taking aim at the religious hierarchy, nor its orientation, but only at individual failings.[10]

This difference in tone between the Tatar press and the Central Asians' papers can be explained somewhat by the events of 1906,

[7] Carrère d'Encausse, p. 383.
[8] K. E. Bendrikov, *Ocherki po istorii narodnogo obrazovaniia v Turkestane* (Moscow, Izdatel'stvo Akademii Pedagogicheskikh Nauk RSFSR, 1960), p. 423.
[9] Piaskovskii, p. 562.
[10] I. I. Umniakov, "K istorii novometodnoi shkoly v Bukhare," *Biulleten' I-go Sredne-aziatskogo Gosudarstvennogo Universiteta*, book 16 (1927), p. 84.

but mainly by the fact that the social foundation of the southern Central Asian Jadid movement differed somewhat from that of the Tatars. Reformist thought had been born in Bukhara and Turkistan guberniia in the madrasahs, and one of its chief leaders, Mahmud Khoja Behbudiy, was a mullah. In any case, the reformists tried to win over the whole of the Muslim clergy to their cause, for their movement was perhaps first of all an indigenous regrouping. The cautious position of the Russian authorities and their defense of the old-fashioned Muslim clergy against the Jadids lent the criticisms made by the reformists considerable weight. This helped to set the conservative hierarchy against them.

In 1908, all the southern Central Asian Jadid newspapers ceased publishing. The denial of Central Asian representation in the Duma gave the Russian authorities an excellent excuse for proscribing publications which justified their existence on the grounds of reporting the participation of Turkistan guberniia in parliamentary proceedings. At any rate, these papers could not survive in 1908, for they had been born in the glow of the revolution, and three years later the imperial power rescinded all the liberal concessions obtained in 1905.

If the life span of this press was ephemeral, its role was nevertheless considerable, because it brought to Central Asia the echoes of the revolution and of the liberal ideas that were exciting Russia. Above all it brought together men who felt united by the same as yet confused aspirations around a concrete enterprise compelling them to set forth, clarify, and coordinate their ideas. It removed them from the dominant Tatar influence which they had been experiencing until then and gave their effort a proper direction: the struggle for a transformation of Central Asia and the rallying of a Turkistan nationality. What until then had been only dreary meditations on bygone grandeur opened onto a newly discovered local consciousness. When the activity of the Central Asian Jadids is considered, one cannot accept the harsh judgment that "the press of Turkistan existed for only two years, 1906 to 1908, and it was entirely in the hands of the Volga Tatars." [11]

[11] V. V. Bartol'd, *Istoriia kul'turnoi zhizni Turkestana* (Leningrad, Akademiia Nauk. Kom. po Izucheniiu Estest. Proizv. Sil., 1927), p. 138.

The retreat of liberalism which paralyzed the expression of reformist thought in Turkistan guberniia had the effect of turning Jadid efforts toward Bukhara and Khiva. Here the aspirations of nationality and reform of Turkistan guberniia rather quickly found support from an organization, and, in particular, a master thinker who was to transform the still confused currents of ideas into a mobilizing ideology.

THE NEW EDUCATION IN BUKHARA

Reformist thought penetrated Bukhara rather late. Despite the hostility of the Bukharan religious hierarchy, the Tatars insisted upon the need for reformed schools, and after several fruitless attempts,[12] Gaspirali himself came to solicit the support of Emir Abd al-Ahad for these efforts, and helped to open a reformed school there for Uzbeks as well as one for Tatars. The Tatar promoters of this project, Mullah Niyaz Sabir-oghli and Burnash-oghli, had devoted themselves to the reformed instruction for several years. In spite of an unfavorable ruling (*riwayät*) from the theologians, which had initially caused the project to be condemned,[13] the emir finally relented and in October, 1908, authorized the creation of a reformed school for his subjects where instruction would be given in Persian (Tajik). This about-face was of great importance in the political history of Central Asia, for it marked the beginning of an open Bukharan reformist movement.

Emir Abd al-Ahad had been brought to this concession by diverse considerations and pressures. In the first place, the original ruling revealed a deep division in the ranks of the ulema, who had been able to command only a slight majority against the reformed school. Second, Bukharan merchants, reading the Jadid papers from Turkistan guberniia, had come to believe in a need for change. The businessmen exerted all their influence on the emir's decision. Finally, Russian representatives had played an extremely complex role in the affair.

In Turkistan guberniia, the Russian authorities had belatedly dis-

[12] A. Mashitskii, "Materialy po istorii bukharskoi revoliutsii," *Vestnik Narodnogo Komissariata Inostrannykh Del,* No. 4/5 (April–May 1922), p. 122.
[13] Umniakov, pp. 85–86.

covered the extent of the educational reform movement,[14] and had opposed it forcefully because they saw in it the germ of liberal and pan-Turkic ideas hostile to Russia, and because they believed in the political value of Muslim conservatism. In Bukhara, on the contrary, Russia considered that the greatest danger came from the conservative Muslim hierarchy whose "fanaticism" and influence on the populace she feared. Just as it had seemed desirable to develop a high quality of Russian instruction in Turkistan guberniia to compete with the lure of Bukhara, in Bukhara the Russian authorities wanted to weaken the clergy by making use of the reformed schools. The place accorded the Russian language in certain reformed establishments also seemed to be a means of reducing the local "fanaticism," a label which the Russian political agent applied to any anti-Russian demonstration.

Although it has often been said that the Jadids developed with Russia's assistance, this was not so in Turkistan guberniia, and was true in Bukhara only for a brief time. As soon as the Russian authorities saw how Bukhara's Jadidism evolved, quickly taking off from the educational platform to become a movement of indigenous emancipation and social reform, they withdrew their support.

Reformist leaders soon noted that transforming the schools of Bukhara in no way promptly resolved the emirate's problems, for the real obstacle to any genuine evolution of the community lay in the very structure of the state. Altering the social substructure seemed to them an indispensable preliminary to any reform.

Outside of this basic consideration, the problem of textbooks helped considerably to orient the Bukharan Jadids toward political action. In the reformed maktabs of Russia, Tatar texts were used, or again, as Munawwar Qari had done, texts prepared by Gramenitskii for the "Russo-native" schools were used.[15] In Bukhara it was unthinkable to use such texts, both for linguistic reasons and because of their content.

To find the books necessary for the reformed instruction, some

[14] K. K. Palen, *Otchet po revizii turkestanskago kraia, proizvedennyi po velichaishemu poveleniiu Senatorom Gofmeisterom Grafom K. K. Palenom: Uchebnoe dielo* (St. Petersburg, Senatskaia Tipografiia, 1910–1911), p. 134.

[15] Bendrikov, p. 270.

local intellectuals formed an association called the Union of Holy Bukhara (Shirkat-i Bukhara-i Sharif), which was a hint of the Jadid organizations to come. By meeting in this group with limited objectives, men like Usman Khoja-oghli, Ahmadjan Mahdum, Mirza Abdul Wahid Munzim (1877–1934), Hajji Rafik, and Sadriddin Murad Khoja Zada Ayniy (1878–1954), with the millionaires Mirza Muhitdin Mansur-oghli and Fazliddin Mazum, laid the foundations of the future Young Bukharan party. Originally, they were engaged in organizing the printing of texts in Orenburg on the presses of *Vaqit*, and in sending some of their members to Bakhchisaray and to Turkistan guberniia to find out about the methods of reformed instruction and the progress of the reformist movement in Tatarstan.

Jadidism in Bukhara was fortunate that, as in Kazan and Tashkent, it was supported by a wealthy middle class eager for change, but especially that it took its first steps at a time when Muslim Turkey seemed to be fulfilling the dream of rejuvenation by which the Bukharan Jadids were sustained. Although the "cultured" language of Bukhara at this time was Persian (Tajik), it was toward the model of Turkey that all the Jadids of southern Central Asia turned in 1909, and this choice of a model gave direction to their activity.

Conscious of the need to extend their action to the entire social structure, the Jadids found their opportunity at a tragic moment in Bukhara's history, when there was a clash between the two great religious communities of the emirate, the Sunnites and the Shiites. In January, 1910, some derisive students disrupted a Shiite religious celebration in Kagan, and the Shiites reacted by killing one of the demonstrators and wounding a few others. This triggered a general massacre of Shiites in the capital and in all the regions where the Sunnite population was in the majority.[16] The new conflict between communities which had recently lived in peaceful proximity brought out many of the scandalous aspects of the Bukharan regime such as the negligence of the authorities, the doubtful practices of the administration, and the cruelty of the repression.

[16] O. A. Sukhareva, *K istorii gorodov bukharskogo khanstva: Istoriko-etnograficheskii ocherk* (Tashkent, Akademiia Nauk, 1959), p. 85.

Moreover, Jadids were found among the victims of this repression, for the new qushbegi, Mirza Nasrullah, who succeeded Astanqul-biy when he fell into disgrace, relied on the conservative hierarchy. Fortified by this position, and having settled accounts with its Shiite enemies, the hierarchy undertook to destroy the Jadids, its other enemy. Jadids were denounced as being among those responsible, even though indirectly, for the religious disturbances and had no choice but to go under cover or to flee to Turkey, as Abdalrauf Fitrat (1886–1938) did.[17] But the danger and need for secrecy united those who stayed behind.

The religious massacres of 1910 also influenced the evolution of domestic power. Russian authorities again considered the annexation of Bukhara;[18] P. A. Stolypin, president of the czarist Council of Ministers, very much favored this idea. While matters of international policy were briefly diverting Russia from the project, Emir Alim Khan, who ascended a very tottery throne, tried to preserve his power and his country's independence by the promise of reforms. He proclaimed that the old order was finished and attacked one of the basic problems of Bukhara, the administration, the financing of which he would put in order, he said, to end corruption and exactions from the citizenry. Responding to appeals by students, Alim Khan even considered a reform of the madrasahs. He entrusted the fulfillment of the project to the Qazi Kalan,[19] an arch-conservative, who passed it on to the traditional authorities where it was buried in oblivion. Then, under the influence of the mullahs, peasants were threatening the countryside, and the emir, seeing the menace of Russian annexation diminish, considered that the essential problem now was the need to appease the clergy.

To combat any reform, he found examples in the Russian policy for Turkistan guberniia, where since the end of 1910, measures to limit the reformed instruction were being prepared. In 1911, Governor General A. V. Samsonov declared that teachers were obliged

[17] A. N. Samoilovich, "Pervoe tainoe obshchestvo mladobukhartsev," *Novyi Vostok*, No. I (1922), p. 98.

[18] D. N. Logofet, *Strana bezpraviia: Bukharskoe khanstvo i ego sovremennoe sostoianie*, (St. Petersburg, Berezovskii, 1909), p. 12.

[19] Umniakov, p. 90.

to be of the same ethnic groups as their pupils. Considering the number of Tatar teachers in the reformed institutions of Central Asia, this could only paralyze numerous institutions.[20]

In Bukhara, the qushbegi used these conditions to argue for a transfer of the Tatar school from the capital to the confines of the Russian city,[21] and later for a request that the governor general of Turkistan guberniia prohibit any sort of reformed instruction by the Tatars, who were Russian subjects settled in the emirate. Barely a few months after Alim Khan's promises of liberalization, reaction again triumphed, administrative reforms were abandoned, the madrasahs were condemned to ultraconservatism, and the sole reformed school that had enjoyed a legal existence was closed.

SECRET SOCIETIES

On December 2, 1910, the Society for the Education of Youth (Jamiyat-i Tarbiya-i Atfal) was founded surreptitiously in Bukhara,[22] headed by the chief of the Union of Holy Bukhara, which merged in fact with the new clandestine organization. Hardly created, the Society for the Education of Youth assembled under its authority all the existing little groups, giving a new strength to their scattered activity. The men who had emigrated to Istanbul, like Abdalrauf Fitrat, had a year earlier founded a Society for Spreading Knowledge among the Populace, the object of which was to send students to Turkey. It also merged with the secret organization,[23] which later on created two offshoots.

One, Ma'rifat, came under the direction of Abdalrauf Fitrat and Usman Khoja-oghli. It undertook to spread the spirit of reform among the common people by distributing books and newspapers and organizing political discussion groups.[24] Barakat, the second society, hidden under the innocent cloak of an importing company, sent abroad to secure the popular educational and propaganda ma-

[20] Bendrikov, pp. 280f.
[21] Umniakov, p. 90.
[22] Togan, p. 354.
[23] A. Arsharuni and Kh. Gabidullin, *Ocherki panislamizma i pantiurkizma v Rossii* (Moscow, Bezbozhnik, 1931), pp. 135–38.
[24] Togan, p. 354.

terial required for work begun by the Jadids.[25] The financing of all this organization was assured by a few rich merchants of the emirate,[26] especially Mansur-oghli, who was sometimes accused of displaying such great zeal for the reformist cause not only out of conviction, but because his chief commercial competitor was supported by the conservatives.

Bukhara's secret organizations had to adopt very strict security rules. Candidates were subjected to a rigorous, complicated check. The candidate had to throw open his past, his whole existence, his way of life, to the scrutiny of several tribunals, and to make firm pledges. Only at the end of a long investigation and multiple interviews was he permitted to enter the society, of which he became a "brother" in the course of an initiation ceremony with a very complex ritual thought, probably wrongly, to derive from French Masonry.

Not a mass organization, before World War I, the society's followers must have numbered from a few dozen to around twenty.[27] The society flourished in the provinces and was said in 1915 to number ten clandestine organizations outside of the capital.[28] Its activities rapidly spread to wide layers of the population and extended to renovating political, administrative, and financial structures and bringing about the unity of the population by putting an end to religious and, indeed, ethnic partitioning.[29]

This secret society had a precise social foundation. According to Faizullah Khoja-oghli (Khojaev) (1896–1938):

It was recruited mainly in an urban setting. Most of its members had come out of the lower middle class of the cities, moderately well off on a material level, but often very badly off. But on an intellectual level, this middle class was the richest part of the emirate's population, students from the religious schools, little merchants desirous of a better knowledge of the world in which they made their way, and petty officials.[30]

---

[25] Umniakov, p. 88.
[26] F. Khodzhaev, "O mlado Bukhartsakh," *Istorik marksist*, I (1928), 128.
[27] Samoilovich, p. 98.
[28] Khodzhaev, p. 129.
[29] Sadriddin Ayniy, *Bukhara inqilabi ta'rikhi uchun materiyallar* (Moscow, 1926), pp. 87–88, 92f.
[30] Khodzhaev, p. 128.

As a matter of fact, it was the creation of a few men urged on by a tide of requirements, disappointments, and hopes born, too, of the evolution in a society which new economic tendencies were endlessly shaping. Until the Russian revolution, there was no reformist organizational structure except in Bukhara and in Khiva, but the Khivan one was infinitely less important and less effective.[31]

Not until July, 1914, did Bukhara's merchants, exasperated by the reaction which, under conservative pressure, closed all reformed maktabs and outlawed their teachers, turn to the resident Russian political agent with an appeal to the sovereign for liberalization.[32] The Jadids also put forth great efforts to send students from Bukhara to Turkey, fifteen in 1911, thirty in 1913, and only World War I put a stop to this advance.[33] While these figures seem insignificant in themselves, the young students in Turkey were living in an exciting atmosphere of pan-Turkism and hostility toward Russia. These sojourns resulted in the development, among a small group of intellectuals who later played an important role in the history of their country, of an intense, patriotic consciousness of nationality and a deep feeling of humiliation with respect to Russia.

THE TAJIK, UZBEK, AND KAZAKH PRESS, 1911 TO 1916

Early in 1912, with the help of a domestic *détente*, the Jadids believed that the moment had come to attempt a more open action. They founded the first newspapers that the emirate had known. They resolved the considerable political and technical difficulties by asking the Russian political agent for his cooperation in publishing a paper that, they said, would show local readers what Russia proper really was like. In this way they got permission to use the presses of the Levin printshop in New Bukhara, and produced a paper which was quite different from its alleged initial design.[34] Thus was born *Bukhara-i sharif*, a Persian-language newspaper, on March 11, 1912, with Mirza Jelal Yussuf Zade, who had come for this purpose from Baku, as editor. For its first four months, the paper came out daily; then, starting July 14, *Turan*, a Turkic-language pe-

[31] Samoilovich, p. 98.
[32] Umniakov, p. 93.
[33] Arsharuni and Gabidullin, p. 139.
[34] Samoilovich, p. 99.

riodical appearing twice weekly, was merged with it, while *Bu-khara-i sharif* was reduced to four issues weekly in order to preserve the fiction of a single paper. The publication interval of the two papers was further reduced in the fall, for financial reasons, and on January 2, 1913, they were totally suppressed. *Bukhara-i sharif* had come out 153 times and *Turan* 49.

When these papers were prohibited, the Jadids again had to bring in from neighboring Turkistan guberniia papers and magazines which appeared in the years preceding the war: *Ayina* and *Samarqand*, edited in Samarkand by Mahmud Khoja Behbudiy; *Sada-i Farghana*, 123 issues of which were published in Khokand by Ashur Ali Zahiriy; and *Sada-i Turkistan*, published at Tashkent in 1914–1915 under the direction of Munawwar Qari Abdurrashid Khan-oghli and Usman Khoja-oghli.[35]

Simultaneously, papers were published by Kazakh intellectuals who were also developing a sense of nationality and who were examining the problems caused by the Russian presence, first and foremost, the possession of land. These papers included *Qazaqstan*, which published a score of issues in 1911 and again in 1913 after a long interruption; *Ishim dalasi*, which appeared in 1913 in Petropavlovsk in Kazakh and Tatar; and *Ay qap*, which was published in Troitsk for four years starting in 1911 under the direction of Muhamedjan Seralin. *Qazaq*, possibly the most important, was issued from Orenburg intermittently between 1913 and 1918 by Aliqan Bokeyqan-uli, Aqmet Baytursin-uli, and Mir Jaqib Duwlat-uli.[36] The papers also included some originating from outside Central Asia which brought in extremely explosive ideas: from Turkey, *Sirat-i mustaqim;* from India, *Habl-ul watan;* and above all *Siraj-ul akbar*, from Afghanistan, published by Mahmud Tarzi, proclaiming from the masthead "Asia for Asiatics."

Jadid meetings, open to a limited but growing public, employed the new publications as texts for discussion, and were a common phenomenon throughout all of Central Asia. In Bukhara, they were

[35] Dr. A. Oktay, "Türkistan'da cedid matbuati," *Turkistan*, No. I (5) (Istanbul, August 1953), pp. 19–24; No. I (6) (September 1953), pp. 15–18.
[36] Reiner Olzscha and Georg Cleinow, *Turkestan, die politisch-historischen und wirtschaftlichen Probleme Zentralasiens* (Leipzig, Koelher und Amelang, 1942), pp. 385–86.

FIGURE 7.2   First issue of *Ay qap* (Kazakhstan).

organized by the secret society, in the guberniia of Turkistan by the
Jadids and their societies led by Munawwar Qari and Mahmud
Khoja Behbudiy, and in the Kazakh area by the local intellectuals.
Political circles flourished everywhere, uniting those attracted by

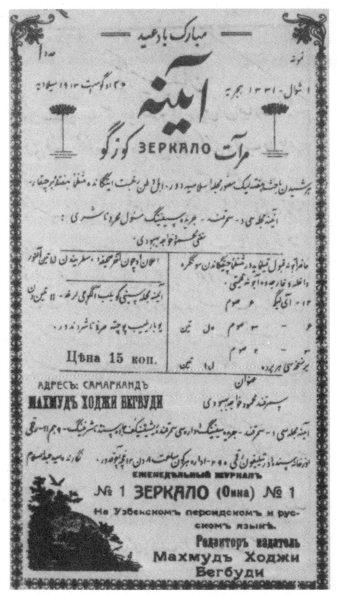

FIGURE 7.3 First issue of *Ayina* (southern Central Asia).

the new ideas. Meetings were held at night in the reformed maktabs, in the homes of the teachers, even in the tea houses, but it was almost always from the reformed schools that the audiences, made up at first of the pupils' parents, were recruited.[37] Russian police, in their numerous reports concerning these activities, recorded that the meetings attracted several social strata and that they benefited from significant material assistance.[38] The various associations that organized this secret political life were financed, in certain cases, by illegal taxes on commerce, property transactions, and the like,[39] destined in theory for charitable works which usually served as a cover for these activities.

Books which circulated under the cloak of secrecy in these circles raised problems which preoccupied many Central Asians. Such were the *Travels of Ibrahim Bek*,[40] a nineteenth-century Persian work which questioned the social and political order of Persia; *Anjuman-i arwah* (The Meeting of the Spirits), portraying a pilgrim from Samarkand conversing in verse with the spirits of the last two emirs of Bukhara; and *Mir'at-i ibrat* (Mirror of a Precept), which directly attacked the structure of the emirate and khanates of southern Central Asia. But above all, the authors most widely read and the most passionately commented upon were, in southern Central Asia, Abdalrauf Fitrat, and, in the plains, Mir Jaqib Duwlat-uli, whose poems were influenced by the events of 1904–1905. The Jadids also used the literature of the theater to spread their political ideas. Local conservatives and Russian authorities opposing this new drama struck mainly at the ideology for which it served as a carrier.

ABDALRAUF FITRAT'S REVIVALISM

One of the early dramatists and teachers, Fitrat was the son of a petty merchant from Bukhara.[41] He wrote his early work, entirely

---

[37] Khodzhaev, p. 129.

[38] P. G. Galuzo, *Turkestan koloniia* (Moscow, Izdanie Komm. Un-ta Trudiashchikhsia Vostoka imeni I. V. Stalina, 1929), p. 142.

[39] Piaskovskii, pp. 548–50.

[40] *Dnevnik puteshestviia Ibragim Beka, ili ego zlokliucheniia po prichine fanaticheskoi liubvi k rodine* (Moscow-Leningrad, Izdatel'stvo Akademii Nauk SSSR, 1963), 266 pp.

[41] Erturk, "Abdur rauf Fitrat," *Millij Turkistan*, No. 80/81 (1952), p. 9.

dedicated to the crisis of Islam in the modern world, in Turkey and Bukhara.[42] Like all the reformists, he took an interest in the glorious past of his country, but recognized the state of degradation ascribable to the general evolution in the countries of Islam.[43] He described the signs of the decline of his country, and then turned to the causes of this decline, which he pinpointed as religious. The clerics had replaced the dynamic faith of the Prophet with a diseased religion, hostile to any progress, and they had killed the Islamic education that created Bukhara's glory. He felt that they were the perfect example of prevarication, vice, and irreligiousness. Fitrat also blamed the clerics for dividing the Muslim community, causing the split which exposed it to the threat of the infidels, not as the strong and united community which bore Islam to the ends of the earth, but as torn asunder by internal quarrels. Not only have the clerics weakened the Islamic community, he thought, they have also betrayed it to the West by prohibiting it, through a hatred of progress, from forging the arms necessary to its defense.

Fitrat not only scourged those in power, but also the wretched and oppressed multitudes, challenging the whole social order of the emirate. He stated clearly in *Bayyanat-i seyyah-i hindi* (Tales of a Hindu Traveler) that although the clerics and the leaders of Bukhara were guilty of having sacrificed Islam to their own interests, the populace was equally guilty for having followed like sheep, even though the Koran opposes such blind submission. Thus Fitrat stressed ideas of the freedom of man, the possibility given man to dominate nature and his destiny, and the notion of equality.[44] If the clerics have distorted the teaching of the Koran on this essential point, wrote Fitrat, it is because they have put Islam at the service of a privileged class.

In *Sayha* (The Shout) he preached a reshaping of political relations of the economic and social foundations of government. *Rah-*

---

[42] Abdalrauf Fitrat, *Munazira* (Istanbul, Matbua-i Islamiyye, 1909); *Spor bukharskago mudarrisa s evropeitsem v Indii o novometodnykh shkolakh* (Tashkent, Elektro-Parovaia Tipografiia-Litografiia, Shtabs Okruga, 1911).

[43] Fitrat, *Munazira*, pp. 23, 40–41; *Razskazy indiiskago puteshestvennika* (Samarkand, Izdanie Makhmuda Khodzhy Bekbudi Tipo-litografiia T-va Gazarov i N. Sliianov, 1913), pp. 64–66.

[43] Fitrat, *Munazira*, pp. 23, 40–41; *Razskazy indiiskago puteshestvennika* pp. 12–16, 22, 24–27, 36–38, 58, 77–78.

bar-i najat (Guide to Salvation) calls for change in the social relations on all echelons, including the family. He preached, in the last analysis, not a compromise between the traditional structures of Islamic society and those of Western society, but a real break with the past, a revolution of human concepts, structures, and relations. Internal reform and renovation was the condition and guarantee of an external renovation, for the final goal was to liberate Dar-ul Islam from the infidels' domination.

H. C. d'E.

8   The Fall
of the Czarist Empire

The Russian empire, which had withstood the pressures of 1904–1905, was sorely challenged by the world-wide conflict that began in 1914. The first fissures in the structure appeared in Central Asia, where an earthquake of excitement shook the area in giddy contrast to the calm which reigned among other Muslims during the war, who were advised to cooperate in the war effort.[1] Later, the Lausanne Conference revealed the strength of the concept of nationality in Central Asia, and the disparity which developed between the demands voiced in this region and those expressed throughout the rest of the Russian empire.

From the beginning of the war, Muslims who had emigrated from Russia to Istanbul had exerted great efforts to influence world opinion regarding their problems. In the Committee for the Defense of the Rights of the Muslim People of Russia,[2] they had appealed to various countries, and in particular they had set up contact with the Union of Nations which, during its third congress held in Lausanne, June 27–29, 1916,[3] offered them a platform from which to state their ideas publicly. At this congress, which was theoretically favorable to the Entente, Russia was arraigned before the oppressed nationalities of the empire who came to defend their position. Their demands were varied, generally prudent, and on the

[1] Ulrich Gehrke, *Persian in der deutsch Orientpolitik: Während des ersten Weltkrieges* (2 vols.; Stuttgart, Kolhammer, n.d.), I, 136f.

[2] A. Zeki Velidi Togan, *Bugünkü Türkili (Türkistan) ve yakin tarihi* (Istanbul, Arkadaş, Ibrahim Horoz v Güven Basimevi, 1942–1947), pp. 475, 477, 542f.

[3] "Comptes rendus analytiques," *l'Union des Nationalites* (Lausanne, Librairie centrale des Nationalites, 1917).

whole scarcely went beyond a wish for autonomy within a federation. Two exceptions were framed by Chaghatay and Finnish representatives, who wanted complete independence for their people. By this radical demand, the Chaghatay representative took a position quite far afield from Ahmad Safar, who spoke in the name of the "Kazakh-Kirgiz" people, and, like Yussuf Akchora-oghlu (1846–1933) in the name of the Tatars, called for equal rights and a certain autonomy. While in all likelihood the delegate of southern Central Asia, Begjan, represented only a limited group of emigrants, his position tallied to a considerable extent with the climate of crisis and sense of deep hostility toward Russia which the events of 1916 would soon reveal.

The great Central Asian revolt which broke out in 1916 caught Russian authorities off guard. Reports from local administrators show that although they distrusted the activity undertaken by educated Central Asians on Turkey's behalf, they were unaware of the peasant and nomad unrest until the very last moment. At the beginning of June, a report stated: "The population of Turkistan [Central Asia] is absolutely peaceful." [4] Until the summer of 1916 no open opposition had been noted locally, but the authorities must have been willfully blind to the mounting tension.

The immediate causes of the revolt were certain measures taken by the Russian government in 1916, but the outbreak cannot be explained without considering the old and deep frictions which rendered the test of strength inevitable. The first of these was the colonization of Central Asia. During the war, of course, it had slowed down, but the situation of the dispossessed nomads was so desperate on the eve of the war that even the very limited colonization of 1915–1916 exceeded the tolerance of the region. "The Kirgiz no longer have anything but the summits of the mountains, where there is no more pasture-land," reads one petition to the governor general.[5] This by itself would have sufficed to trigger the outbreak of 1916, but two other scandals, the excessive exploitation of the

---

[4] P. G. Galuzo, *Turkestan koloniia* (Moscow, Izdanie Komm. Un-ta Trudiashchikhsia Vostoka imeni I. V. Stalina, 1929), p. 156.
[5] *Ibid.*

FIGURE 8.1 Tashkent, c.1913. Russian city with streets in rectangle and radial grid next to original city.

local population through taxes and forced labor,[6] and the unfair price-fixing practiced by Russian merchants had their effect.

The years 1915–1916 thus were marked by a growing discontent among the Central Asians, and their new awareness that the worsening of their situation was indeed linked with the Russian presence. For example, during these years, Central Asia was a vast prisoner-of-war camp, a fact which created still more problems for the region. Then, early in 1916, in the Khivan khanate, Turkmen tribes under Muhammad Qurban Junaïd Khan (c.1860–1938) who had unsuccessfully threatened the Khivan capital three years earlier took advantage of Russia's preoccupations elsewhere to attack again. Russian troops under the command of General Alexander S. Galkin, governor of Sir Darya, came to the aid of the khan, drove the Turk-mens into the desert, and inflicted frightful reprisals upon them, thus adding to the widely felt bitterness.[7]

The powder keg was ignited by a government decree of June 25, 1916, mobilizing the Central Asians, who were not liable to military service, into workers' battalions. General Kuropatkin, analyzing subsequent events, judged that the extremely ambiguous wording of the decree's text had much to do with the angry response to it.[8] People could not understand what its various "categories" meant, and men from nineteen to forty-five felt threatened. Unscrupulous falsifying and manipulating of the lists of draftees aroused further opposition.

The first disturbance broke out in Uzbek country at Khojand on July 4, 1916. Spreading to Jizzakh on July 13, it grew into a real uprising. Some local officials and Russians were killed, others arrested, and communications facilities destroyed. A military expedition smashed the rebels on July 21.[9] Other disorders erupted in most of the cities in Turkistan guberniia, but without reaching the violence that rocked Jizzakh. Still, there were deaths at Marghilan and Namangan and incidents of extreme brutality in Andijan and else-

[6] E. A. Fedorov, *Ocherki natsional'no-osvoboditel'nogo dvizheniia v Srednei Azii* (Tashkent, Gosudarstvennoe Izdatel'stvo Uzbekskoi SSR, 1925), pp. 51–53.

[7] F. L. Shteinberg, *Ocherki istorii turkmenii* (Moscow, Gosudarstvennoe Sotsialisticheskoe Ekonomicheskoe Izdatel'stvo, 1934), p. 62.

[8] A. Kuropatkin, "Dnevnik," *Krasnyi arkhiv*, II (1922–1927), 46.

[9] "Dzhizakskoe vosstanie 1916 g.," *Krasnyi arkhiv*, LX (1933), 63.

where. Farghana had risen against the decree. The rebellion, in spite of efforts to check it, went beyond Uzbek territory on a wide scale and spread to the Kirgiz and Kazakh plains.

The Kirgiz of Semirechie had suffered the most from land expropriations benefiting Russian and Ukrainian settlers. Even before the June 25 decree, the situation in this region was extremely tense, and when the decree was made known, there were rumors that settlers were seizing the last lands left to Kirgiz families. While a large group of Dungans, who had come into Semirechie in the nineteenth century, was fleeing back into China, the Kirgiz rose up in Pishpek (Frunze) August 6, and from there the revolt spread murderously through the whole region.[10] Frightened, the Russian settlers took advantage of the army's support to strip the Central Asians of all their possessions; wherever the army was absent or inadequate, settlers formed armed groups which massacred the local population.[11] The Central Asians struck back, and until the end of August, the region remained an arena of bloody fighting. The settlers took refuge in Przheval'sk, where the local Russian commander organized the defense and repulsed Central Asian attacks. By the time reinforcements put an end to the rebellion, it was estimated that 2,000 settlers perished, but even greater numbers of local people were killed. Entire Kirgiz villages had been put to the torch, and nearly a third of the Kirgiz population had fled to China.[12] In the Kazakh plain, the disorders, generally more localized, reached tragic proportions in the Turgay region. Grouped behind Amangeldi Iman-uli (1873–1919), who later became one of the leaders of Kazakh communism, the Central Asians had started real skirmishes with Russian detachments and then beseiged Turgay.[13] General Lazarev's troops drove them out, but Amangeldi Iman-uli would not lay down his arms until after the general amnesty proclaimed by the Provisional Government.[14]

[10] *Istoriia Kirgizii* (Frunze, Akademiia Nauk Kirgizskoi SSR, 1956), I, 397–404.

[11] M. Belotskii, *Kirgizskaia respublika: Populiarnyi ocherk* (Moscow, Gospolitizdat Sotsial'no-Ekonomicheskoe Izd-vo, 1936), p. 27.

[12] *Istoriia kazakhskoi SSR* (Alma Ata, Izdatel'stvo Akademii Nauk Kazakhskoi SSR, 1943), p. 378.

[13] *Ibid.*, p. 391.

[14] S. D. Asfendiarov, *Istoriia Kazakstana s drevneishikh vremen* (Alma Ata, Kazakstanskoe Kraevoe Izd-vo, 1935), p. 230.

The Transcaspian region was belatedly affected by these disturbances. The Turkmens had accepted mobilization peacefully enough, especially since they were posted on local guard duty in return for the presence of Tekke tribesmen on active service.[15] The Yomud Turkmens alone refused to submit to their new obligations, and after a few clashes with Russian troops at the time draftees were listed, some took refuge beyond the Persian and Afghan frontiers. Others systematically attacked the Russian colonies, took refuge in the fortress of Aq Qal'a, and continued the struggle even after Turkistan guberniia finally seemed pacified. Until the end of 1916, they were a serious menace to communications lines and business concerns, and their subjugation required heavily armed troops led by General Madridov.[16] The repression was accompanied by a thorough plundering of the nomads' possessions. At the end of 1916, except for resistance by Kazakhs Iman-uli and Alibii Jangeldin, the rebellion seemed over.

In Turkistan guberniia alone, more than 3,000 Russians had been killed, and 9,000 rural businesses destroyed. Losses for local people were far heavier, for they had to face clashes with the army, reprisals of the settlers, punitive expeditions, hunger and cold when they fled, and lastly, trial for having participated in the rebellion. Lands were again confiscated, and General Kuropatkin deported the Issik Kol Kirgiz into the harsh Narin region.[17]

The basic problem in 1916 for the Kazakhs and Kirgiz was land, but for the Uzbeks this difficulty was somewhat less; what was important to them was the recognition of equal rights. Investigations into human consequences of the insurrection reveal precisely this difference in basic goals.

In Turkistan guberniia the insurgents killed 55 Central Asian officials and only 24 Russian ones, as well as roughly 3,000 settlers. That more local than Russian officials were killed is explained by the fact that the locals were closer to the population and hence more accessible and less protected. However, regional variants in the apportionment of these figures shed light upon the character of the insurrection. In Farghana, populated mainly with Muslims,

[15] Kuropatkin, pp. 45–51, 71.
[16] Togan, p. 343.
[17] Kuropatkin, pp. 87–88.

the chief victims of the popular though sporadic fury were the local officials, of whom 34 were killed, compared to one Russian. In Semirechie, on the contrary, an area invaded by Russian settlers and where local men were terribly short of land, the revolt assumed a completely different nature. There the two-month outbreak was obviously directed against the Russians; 2,094 settlers were killed, and 14 Russian officials as against 2 local ones perished.

The extreme variables in the revolt raised questions concerning its inspiration and leadership. In these explosions of spontaneous wrath, the political organizations and ideological leaders played only a limited role. Russian political parties who had been active throughout Central Asia in 1905 did not support the rebels, nor did they show any sign of comprehending local protests. The Central Asian groups around Mahmud Khoja Behbudiy and Munawwar Qari in Turkistan guberniia, or around Tanishbay-uli and Baytursin-uli among the Kazakhs, apparently had a most restricted part in the affair, although as early as May, 1916, a meeting had been organized by Behbudiy in Samarkand to consider what policy to follow should the threats of mobilization be carried out. Those present at this meeting, Munawwar Qari, Pahlivan Niyaz, Usman Khoja-oghli, Abidjan Mahmud, and Qari Kamyl, it is said, decided to instigate a general uprising should mobilization occur.[18]

But the clergy, more than these leaders of the nationalistic movement, seem to have played a preponderant role in 1916. The revolt was particularly serious in the backward, colonized regions, far from the large urban centers where the concept of nationality developed, but where the authority of the mullahs was strongest. The rift between the Russian and Central Asian communities, at least in certain regions, was precipitated by this revolt which, in this respect, foreshadowed the direction which the 1917 revolution would take in Central Asia.

THE REVOLUTION OF FEBRUARY 1917

The February 1917 revolution met very favorable response in Central Asia, for the imperial power, challenged there for months,

[18] Baymirza Hayit, *Turkestan im XX. Jahrhundert* (Darmstadt, Leske Verlag, 1956), p. 18.

was sometimes thoroughly rejected, and excitement ran high. The war had exposed all the problems due to the Russian presence and permitted a thorough study of them. The nationalistic demands that had gradually emerged from aspirations for a spiritual reform were, at the dawn of the February revolution, swept to the forefront. What response would the new regime make? What solutions could it provide for the problems of all the nationalities of the empire?

The Provisional Government, erected upon the ruins of the monarchy, was in fact divided and uncertain concerning the nationalities problem and hindered in its choices by a serious prior commitment to continue the war. It rapidly discovered that defending the oppressed nationalities was easier when it was an arm against imperial power than determining their fate in a liberal manner when it itself had attained power. It postponed solution of specific problems until a constituent assembly could decide the matter. On March 19, the government simply offered the different nationalities a declaration of rights limited to the problem of individual equality but avoiding the nationality question. Thus, the inequality which was oppressing individuals was abolished within the different minority groups as well as for the Russians, but the inequality of the nationalities continued implicitly, and sometimes explicitly. As the Provisional Government's difficulties increased, it came to equate too noisily expressed nationalistic aspirations with threats against the revolution, threats which became evident when the Bolsheviks undertook to play off the nationalistic movements against the government.

Considering itself the defender of the revolution, the Provisional Government gradually moved to adopt a rigid policy toward nationalistic aspirations of the non-Russians, until the moment when the failures it was experiencing everywhere outside of Russia, and the growing pressure of the nationalities forced it to make an about-face. September 28, 1917, the government declared: "Recognition of the right to self-determination for all people will be established on foundations which will be laid by a constituent assembly." [19] But it was too late. The hour of the Bolshevik revolution was draw-

[19] S. M. Dimanshtein, ed., *Revoliutsiia i natsional'nyi vopros* (Moscow, Kommunisticheskaia Akademiia, 1930), III, 56.

ing near, and in any case, the different nationalities were henceforth alienated from a Provisional Government which had brought them only disappointment.

The February revolution had been received with mixed sentiments by the Central Asian population, giving the regime empowered there until the October revolution its specific character. For the local people, broken by the repression of 1916, the prevailing feeling was one of relief. They did not participate in the new events, for the scars of coercion still remained, but the downfall of a defeated power filled them with hope. For the Russian prelates, officials, and settlers the response was no less unanimous: what had to be done was to save Russian authority and its position in Central Asia.

As soon as Governor General Kuropatkin learned of events in Petrograd, he declared that he was entering the service of the revolution and proposed to the Tashkent soviet the organization of defense "against a native uprising."[20] The Provisional Government backed him up, since one of its first decrees had been interpreted as ordering "officials and soldiers to stay where they were."[21] This order was especially followed in Turkistan guberniia where the first soviets created in March gave a minimal role to the local population but where were congregated a number of former Russian military chiefs who had taken part in the repression of all the local revolts of the past twenty years.

Not until April, 1917, did the representatives of the old regime give way to new political forces. The Provisional Government replaced the authority of the former governor of Turkistan guberniia by a Provisional Executive Committee, while the guberniia of the Steppe was under the central administration. Kuropatkin was arrested at his home, and on April 7 the Turkistan Committee of the Provisional Government was set up, presided over by Nikolai N. Shchepkin, a former Constitutional Democrat delegate to the Duma. Members included the Russians Pavel I. Preobrazhenskii, Liapovskii, Elpatiev, and Shkapskii, and also four Muslims, not all Central

[20] G. Safarov, *Kolonial'naia revoliutsiia, opyt Turkestana* (Moscow, Gosudarstvennoe Izdatel'stvo, 1921), p. 96.

[21] K. Madarov, "Kontr-revoliutsiia i Vremennoe Pravitel'stvo," *Kommunist*, No. 3 (1935), p. 27.

Asians, General Davletchin, Sadri Maqsud-oghli, Muhamedjan Tanishbay-uli, and Aliqan Bokeyqan-uli.

Many members of the Committee belonged to the Constitutional Democrat Party, and this did not help to establish the authority of the Committee over the soviets being created, particularly in Tashkent. As early as April 22, the Committee was called to account by the Jizzakh soviet which reproached it for being a product of the leaders of the previous regime. In May, the regional soviet elected by the first congress of the soviets of Turkistan (April 7–15, 1917) removed Shchepkin and certain of his associates from power; Nalivkin, who had sat in the second Duma, took over the presidency of the Committee.

Central Asians paid more attention to Muslim organizations in which they thought their destiny was truly being manifested. In March, 1917, the educated Central Asians who had militated for reform met in a Muslim Council (Shora-i Islam),[22] while the conservatives organized a regrouping, headed by Mullah Shir Ali Lapin, in which the clerics were dominant. From April 16 to 23, 1917, these organizations convened the first regional Muslim congress in Tashkent. The 450 delegates, including 93 Russians,[23] were to discuss the future of Central Asia in the new Russian state.

Their conclusions lacked certainty because although they looked to the Provisional Government to erect a new state with a democratic and federal foundation,[24] they did not make clear by what methods Central Asia would choose its course. Would it take part in the formulation of this federation-state or not? Would it be autonomous or quasi-independent? The only point on which the Muslim delegates took a definite stand was that their destiny should not be unilaterally determined by Russia. The congress voted resolutions demanding the cessation of Russian colonization in Central Asia and the return of confiscated lands to the local population. In particular, it decided to create a Turkistan Central Council of

[22] S. Muraveiskii (V. Lopukhov), *Ocherki po istorii revoliutsionnogo dvizheniia v Srednei Azii* (Tashkent, Tipografiia Uzgiza, 1926), pp. 13–14.
[23] Togan, p. 356.
[24] Baymirza Hayit, *Die nationalen Regierungen von Kokand und der Alash Orda* (Muenster, University thesis, 1950), p. 22.

Muslims (Musluman Markaziy-Shorasi), which became known as the National Center (Milliy Markaz).

THE NATIONAL CENTER AND MUSLIM CONFERENCES

For the first time since Central Asia became involved in nationalistic movements, local citizens really took in hand the destiny of the drive. The leadership was assumed by a Kazakh, Mustafa Chokay-oghlu (1890–1941), who lobbied for the territory of the plains in the fourth Duma, and by Mahmud Khoja Behbudiy, Ubaydullah Khoja, Asadullah Khoja-oghli, Abidjan Mahmud, and a few other less-known representatives of the local middle class. Those who headed the Muslim center, as well as those who animated its regional representation, like Nasir Khan Tore in Farghana, Tanishbay-uli in Semirechie, the Turkmen Oraz Sirdar in Ashkhabad, and others, were among the liberals who had already agitated for rejuvenation of their homelands. Up to the October revolution, the National Center tried to win acceptance for the Central Asian cause among local Russian authorities, but it also worked at the congresses which assembled all the Muslims of Russia.

The National Center, and with it Central Asia, participated officially for the first time in these meetings at the Pan Russian Congress of Muslims,[25] which met in Moscow from May 1 to 11, 1917. More than 800 delegates attended,[26] including about 300 members of the clergy. This congress, which reached a number of new decisions, remained divided over the question of relations between the local Muslims and the Russian state.

A "unitarianist" group, formed mainly of Tatars and led by the Lezgin Tsalikhov, defended the idea of a national (extraterritorial) cultural autonomy (Milliy Madaniy Mukhtariyat) in a unitary republic. The supporters of the Tsalikhov motion saw a federative state as a brake on the economic and social progress of the Muslims. Although the "unitarianists" agreed that Central Asia and the Caucasus might enjoy a certain autonomy, even in the framework of the unified state, the Central Asian representatives passionately

[25] Dimanshtein, pp. 292–93.
[26] Hayit, *Die nationalen Regierungen,* p. 25.

upheld the "federalist" motion presented by the Azerbaijanian
Mehmet Emin Resul Zadeh, who proclaimed the necessity for territorial autonomy in a federal state.[27] This position was supported,
460 to 271.[28] To the Central Asians, territorial autonomy seemed
the answer to colonization and the foreign presence on their soil,
and it shaped the idea of a regenerated Central Asia which had
been the dream of local reformists much more than pan-Turkism
or pan-Islamism.

In the National Central Council (Milliy Markaziy Shora), created at the conclusion of the congress "to direct the activity of the
Muslims of Russia until the convocation of the constituent assembly," [29] the Central Asian region provided a third of the total representation. But the first pan-Muslim congress was not followed by
regular congresses, in spite of the decisions reached. The Central
Asians could not even attend the second congress which took place
in Kazan that July, partly because General Kornilov's offensive did
not favor journeys outside the region, but especially because they
were too preoccupied with taking action and imposing their demands locally. Already at the April congress in Tashkent, the Central Asians had come to agree that the Executive Committee of the
Provisional Government should give a wider role to local persons.
They drew from a Russian delegate, Nikora, a comment that was
entirely consistent with the policy then still followed by Russia:
"The revolution has been waged by Russians; that is why the
power is in our hands in Central Asia." [30]

Confronted by diminishing Russian power, indigenous leaders
steered a prudent course for a few months. The reformers of the
National Center did not dare deviate from a conciliatory attitude
toward the Russians if they wished to retain the imagined support
of the "liberal" Russians against Russians who advocated total
seizure of local power and against Muslim conservatives grouped in
the Ulema Jamiyati. Similarly, the conservatives avoided head-on
clashes with the Russians for fear the Russians would support the
reformists. The quarrel which had set conservatives and reformists

---

[27] S. M. Dimanshtein, pp. 293–305.
[28] Togan, p. 359.
[29] Dimanshtein, p. 304.
[30] Hayit, *Die nationalen Regierungen,* p. 31.

against each other before the revolution continued under the Provisional Government, considerably prejudicing Central Asian unity. Elections to the Tashkent Municipal Council in August, 1917, revealed this opposition very clearly. The Ulema allied themselves with Russian right-wing candidates for the occasion and won 60 percent of the votes, leaving the Muslim Council candidates in third place with 10 percent of the votes, behind the Socialist Revolutionaries who had received 25 percent. As mayoral candidate leading the combined tickets of the Ulema and the Russian conservatives stood the former Russian governor, N. S. Lykoshin, the man responsible for the 1916 repression in Farghana.[31] This alliance drove popular support to the Central Asian liberals.

During the summer of 1917, in Samarkand, the Union of Muslim Workers (Ittifaq) Socialist party put up list No. 4 of candidates for the Municipal Council. In election riots, some candidates were killed in Khokand and elsewhere by conservatives,[32] but the group itself became a revolutionary symbol among Muslim workers. The summer of 1917 saw the split between Russians and Muslims become more definite, and the Central Asian confidence in the regime collapsed. Indifference to the revolution, on which the Central Asians had pinned so many hopes, dated from this period, and it was evident that they would not support the regime when it was attacked.

The economic situation became truly disastrous in the summer of 1917. Since the conquest, local agriculture had been pushed toward intensive cotton raising, reducing the acreage reserved for grain and making the region dependent on Russia for food. In 1917, Russia was unable to send cereals into Central Asia, and famine pervaded the countryside. Nor did the cotton buyers function, and the peasants' resources dwindled while their anger continued to mount. Central Asian peasants clashed with Russian settlers, who were hostile to any demands for the land they occupied. Early in the summer, the rumor which spread throughout Semirechie that the Dungans were about to return from China touched off a general uprising of those settlers who had been armed

---

[31] Safarov, p. 157.

[32] P. Alekseenkov, "Natsional'naia politika Vremennogo Pravitel'stva v Turkestane v 1917 g.," *Proletarskaia revoliutsiia,* LXXIX (1928), 122.

against the Kirgiz. *Nasha gazeta* reported the massacre on July 2. Central Asian political organizations then organized a demonstration in Tashkent, August 18, 1917, to draw official attention to what they considered to be genocide. Members of the Governmental Committee, like the Soviets, paid no attention to it.

The second conference of Central Asian Muslims, which met in Tashkent, September 3, 1917, revealed further evidence of the political evolution among local people. For the first time there was created a coalition uniting all local groups and parties, from the ulema to the workers' organizations.[33] The conference also adopted resolutions dealing with Central Asia's future which clearly indicated the wish to move away from Russia.[34]

There was open opposition, to begin with, to the principle of intervention by the Soviets into the internal affairs of Central Asia. What the indigenous leaders sought was the creation of an autonomous republic of Turkistan (Central Asia) which would be federated with Russia, but organized according to its own standards, not basic Russian laws. In this republic the authority was to be founded on the Shariat, and assured by a Mahkame-i Shariat, an assembly of a religious nature presided over by the Shaykh-ul Islam. The conference also urged the union of all existing parties and groups in a coalition organization, Ittifaq-i muslimin. Finally, in a specific and significant recommendation, the conference opposed the intensive cultivation of cotton and called for local production of grain so that Central Asia could supply its own food. The representatives attempted, at the same time, to make one last voice heard in the capital. A delegation from the National Center, made up of Mustafa Chokay-oghlu, Narbutabek-oghli, Shah Ahmed-oghli, and Polat-oghli, managed to work their way through minor officials and get as far as Kerenskii and explain to him how tense the situation was. Kerenskii replied: "I do not believe that there will be an anti-Russian uprising in Central Asia, but were that to happen, I would take the most rigorous measures to crush it." [35]

[33] *Voina v peskakh: Materialy po istorii grazhdanskoi voiny. Grazhdanskaia voina v Srednei Azii* (12 vols.; Leningrad, "Istoriia Grazhdanskoi Voiny," 1935).

[34] Safarov, p. 64.

[35] Togan, p. 357.

Yet it was not the Central Asians who then attacked the Provisional Government, but the Russian Bolsheviks who began their revolution in Central Asia on September 12, 1917. This uprising was the work of the Russians alone, the Central Asians remaining neutral. Nalivkin, the president of the Executive Committee of the Provisional Government, was compelled to recognize the new Committee,[36] while calling on Petrograd for help. On September 16, the rebellion was put down by the moderate Russians and troops who remained loyal or who quickly performed a new about-face. The Soviets, however, remained masters of the situation. On October 26, after Lenin had taken power in Russia, the soviets of Central Asia voted to reject the authority of the Provisional Government and to rally to the Bolsheviks. General Korovnichenko, Kerenskii's special envoy, tried to stem this new movement, and during the night of October 27–28, he arrested the leaders, including A. A. Kazakov, the future president of the Central Executive Committee of Turkistan ASSR (Autonomous Soviet Socialist Republic), and Uspenskii. General Korovnichenko's troops first disarmed certain units of the 2d Siberian Regiment, then ran headlong into the opposition of the majority of troops stationed in Central Asia, and after four days of fighting, were defeated on November 1. General Korovnichenko yielded and Soviet power was proclaimed in Tashkent. On November 2, the Socialist Revolutionaries and Mensheviks of the Tashkent Executive Committee tried to limit the Bolsheviks' share of the power that was being organized by recommending the formation of a coalition committee of nine members which would include two Central Asians. This project did not mature in its original form, and the Revolutionary Coalition Committee that was formed failed to include a single Muslim.

THE FEBRUARY REVOLUTION REACHES THE KAZAKHS

The authority set up on the Kazakh plains in February, 1917, changed very little of the previous organization. The regional governors and the very high czarist officials gradually disappeared, but the administration on the local level, both in the Kazakh and the

[36] Joseph Castagne, "Le Turkestan depuis la revolution russe, 1917–1921," *Revue du Monde Musulman*, No. L (June 1922), pp. 38–39.

Russian villages, remained the same, except that it was placed under the executive committees in which officials from the czarist regime often participated. Two Kazakh leaders took part in government affairs at this time. Tanishbay-uli represented the Provisional Government in Semirechie, and Bokeyqan-uli in the Turgay region. In the plains, the months between the czarist fall from power and the October revolution were less eventful than in Turkistan guberniia, but they were decisive months in the formation of Kazakh nationality. The plains people had, after the February revolution, very special problems distinct from those which were disturbing the Muslim people of southern Central Asia. Before thinking about political organization, they had to resolve the vital land question. Stopping the colonization and stabilizing the indigenous people on arable lands were imperatives which dominated the future of the plainsmen. Two groups emerged among the Kazakhs in these troubled months, the Alash Orda, which was the heir to the Kazakh enlighteners of the nineteenth century, and the politically more radical, nationalistically oriented group of Kazakhs in southern Central Asia.

Alash Orda was organized in March, 1917, by Bokeyqan-uli, Baytursin-uli, Duwlat-uli, and Qalel Dosmaghambet-uli. Its leaders attended the first Pan-Muslim Congress at Moscow in May, and two were elected members of the Council. Yet the Moscow meeting provided no answer to their problems. In many respects it actually discountenanced them. The Pan-Muslim Congress had been urged mainly on the initiative of the Tatars who sought to impose their ideas. Since one of the goals of the Kazakhs of the plains was to rid themselves of the Tatar tutelage, they remained absent from the second Pan-Muslim Congress held at Kazan, and deliberately withdrew into their own organizations.

In April, 1917, a first Pan-Kirgiz (i.e., Kazakh) Congress met in Orenburg, opting in its conclusions for the position of Kazakh leaders supporting the Provisional Government and demands for limited autonomy with local administration. Lastly, these leaders insisted upon the use of Kazakh language in schools, courts, and the administration.[37]

[37] Dimanshtein, pp. 361–63.

Only at the second Pan-Kirgiz Congress held in Orenburg from July 21 to 26, 1917, did the political aspirations of the Kazakh leaders come into focus. Kazakhs and Bashkirs at this congress condemned the Tatars' political aims. For these Kazakhs, the only acceptable future lay in a Russian state based on federation. The Alash Orda leaders knew very well that their social situation did not allow them to move too quickly in pursuit of national aspirations. The prevailing seminomadism with its tribal or clan particularism had to be overcome in order to unify the plains under an autonomous government. To do this, nomadism itself had to be attacked, and clearsighted Alash Orda leaders thought that the nomads could only be prudently and gradually settled. Finally, in order to escape Tatar domination, they wanted to have a religious organization that was independent from the Ufa jurisdiction.[38] Like the intellectuals of the nineteenth century, they were not basically hostile to Russia which, they thought, might help them advance.

The Kazakhs of the empire who were subordinate to the guberniia of Turkistan held a very different position. Even before the revolution, a newspaper appearing in Tashkent, *Ush Jüz,* clearly showed these differences by an unfriendly attitude toward Russia.[39] In the Pan-Kirgiz conferences, representatives of the southern Kazakhs had indicated their opposition to the ideas of Alash Orda and affirmed their will to see the nationality movement take a distinctly anti-Russian tack. This group had no influence in the congresses, for it represented a different population from that of the plains, one which was fixed for the most part, integrated in a framework of areal unity, and deeply stamped with the memory of the 1916 genocide and repression, with the concrete vision of the February revolution and of the Russian settlers armed against them.

H. C. d'E.

[38] *Ibid.,* pp. 363–65.
[39] Z. Mindlin, "Kirgizy i revoliutsiia," *Novyi Vostok,* V (1924), 200.

While the Provisional Government had scorned the nationality
question, the regime born of the October revolution at first seemed
more favorable to autonomist arguments. Bolshevik policy toward
nationalities had been codified in April, 1917, at the seventh Social
Democratic Party congress, which recognized the right of nationalities in the empire to choose their destiny, even if this choice
involved a final separation from Russia. Yet, the Bolshevik assumption of power changed little of the character assumed by the revolution in Central Asia since its beginnings; "it was apparent that
the Revolution in Turkistan [southern Central Asia] followed a colonial direction." [1]

Just as the revolution there had been Russian, the power there
was at first resolutely Russian. Drawn up in opposition to it, indigenous groups, who were definitely disappointed, could choose
either local governments or cooperation with an authority which
habitually rejected them. Also rising up in opposition to the Bolshevik regime were Russians hostile to the revolution who tried
to base their counterrevolutionary activities on the indigenous
movements in rebellion.

Locally, however, the old rivalry between Central Asian liberals
and conservatives had not disappeared in the revolutionary turmoil, and immediately after the Bolshevik revolution, the Ulema
Jamiyati under Shir Ali Lapin initiated an attempt at collaboration
with the new regime. The third regional congress in Tashkent,
November 15, 1917, proclaimed the authority of the soviets over
all southern Central Asia and decided on the creation of a Turk-

[1] G. Safarov, *Kolonial'naia revoliutsiia, opyt Turkestana* (Moscow, Gosudarstvennoe Izdatel'stvo, 1921), p. 67.

istan Council of Peoples' Commissars (Turksovnarkom) for the region. At the same time the third conference of Central Asian Muslims met. It was dominated by the leaders of the Ulema Jamiyati, but was somewhat hostile to the new authority, in spite of pressure from the conservatives. The crisis between Russians and Central Asians flourished from this time on.

The Russian Congress of Soviets had to take a position both on the offers of cooperation from Shir Ali Lapin, who was suggesting the formation of a coalition government in which the conservatives would control half the seats,[2] and on the demands for local autonomy set forth by the representatives of the Muslim Council. The congress expressed strong opposition to autonomy, and, furthermore, opposed Central Asian participation in government. Kolesov's resolution stated:

It is impossible to let the Muslims into the revolutionary government at this time, because the attitude of the local population toward the authority of the Soviets is doubtful, and because the indigenous population has no proletarian organizations which the (Bolshevik) group could welcome into the highest organs of the regional government.[3]

This refusal welded the unity of all the Muslim political groups around the Muslim Central Council, which decided that a fourth conference of southern Central Asian Muslims would be called in Khokand the following month.

The conference opened November 25 in the presence of about 200 delegates,[4] the majority of whom came from Farghana, for, under the troubled conditions of the moment, travel was difficult in Central Asia. Farghana provided 150 delegates, Sir Darya 22, Samarkand 23, Bukhara 4, and Transcaspia 1.[5]

The conference had convened to discuss Central Asia's attitude toward the Bolsheviks and also the creation of a state, proposed by Ataman Dutov, that would include the Cossack regions of the

---

[2] *Ibid.,* p. 64.

[3] *Nasha gazeta* (Tashkent, November 23, 1917), cited by G. Safarov, p. 70.

[4] P. Alekseenkov, "Kokandskaia avtonomiia," *Revoliutsiia v Srednei Azii: Sbornik* (Tashkent, Pravda Vostoka; Ispart Sredazbiuro, Ts.K VKP (b), 1928), I, 31.

[5] Joseph Castagne, "Le Turkestan depuis la revolution russe, 1917–1921," *Revue du Monde Musulman,* No. L (June, 1922), pp. 47–48.

Urals, Orenburg and Siberia, and Central Asia. The gathering also
had to determine what Central Asia's own authority would be.
Although one group insisted upon a definite proclamation of autonomy, the majority were more anxious to deal tactfully with the
established authority in Russia. They rejected Dutov's propositions
and resolved to negotiate with Tashkent for the autonomy of southern Central Asia in the future Russian federal republic on the basis
of the Bolshevik program for nationalities.

Negotiations with Tashkent's Russian leaders, Kolesov, Uspenskii,
and Poltoratskii, were not pushed very far, and at the end of November, the Khokand congress proclaimed the autonomy of southern Central Asia. A council of 36 Muslims and 18 Russians was
elected, and the 12-member government, called the Government of
Autonomous Turkistan, was at first directed by Tanishbay-uli, then
by Mustafa Chokay-oghlu. Thus, the first new indigenous government of southern Central Asia placed two Kazakhs at its head.
Also, there was a workers' council functioning in Khokand.[6]

Tashkent authorities did not react immediately to the setting up
of an independent authority, because at the end of 1917 they did
not have means for military intervention in Khokand. General
Dutov's troops isolated Tashkent from Moscow, and the city soviet
was too weak and vulnerable to run the risk of external ventures.
For nearly two months these two powers coexisted.

Khokand tried to extend its authority to all of southern Central
Asia, and early in December, Muslims demonstrated for autonomy
in Tashkent, but the soviet managed to overcome the local disturbances. Some committees of workers and peasants from Central
Asia threw in their lot with Khokand, and in January, taking advantage of such support, Khokand demanded that the Moscow
government recognize the autonomous government as the sole legal
one in southern Central Asia. The reply drafted by Stalin dismissed
the rival government by reminding it that the soviets were autonomous and that their authority was based upon the popular forces
which supported them.[7]

[6] A. Zeki Velidi Togan, *Bugünkü Türkili (Türkistan) ve yakin tarihi* (Istanbul, Arkadaş, Ibrahim Horoz ve Güven Basimevi, 1942–1947), p. 365.
[7] Baymirza Hayit, *Die nationalen Regierungen von Kokand und der Alash
Orda* (Muenster, University thesis, 1950), p. 69.

The Khokand government, having no military strength which would permit it to win acceptance by armed force, tried to assert itself by resorting to the popular vote. In January, 1918, Khokand announced its intention of convoking a constituent assembly elected by all of southern Central Asia and giving non-Muslims up to a third of the seats. In doing this, the Khokand leaders were more generous than the Russian constituent assembly earlier in the year which had granted no seats to the people of Central Asia. To defend itself, Khokand desperately sought allies and money. Mustafa Chokay-oghlu negotiated with Dutov in December, 1917, but concluded, when preliminary discussions broke off, that Dutov's demands were unacceptable.[8]

Attempts at union with Alash Orda were no more fruitful. The Emir of Bukhara, naturally hostile to a government dominated by liberals and applauded by the Jadids, and anxious to commit no act which might furnish Tashkent with a pretext to take too close an interest in the emirate, refused even to receive the emissaries of the Khokand government who had come to ask for help. Khokand then tried to negotiate purchases of arms, but again failed.

In January, 1918, Khokand decided to float a loan which would permit it to hold out, and this loan provoked a domestic crisis in which Tanishbay-uli resigned and was replaced as president by Mustafa Chokay-oghlu. Although the loan was subscribed within five days, the Khokand government nevertheless failed to find the weapons it needed for defense. In January, 1918, the Orenburg front of the Whites was pierced, and Tashkent asked Moscow for help.

At the fourth regional congress of soviets, Kolesov saw to it that the "counterrevolutionary" character of Khokand was condemned. Returning again to the theses of the III All-Russian Congress of Soviets, which had spelled out the principle of self-determination based on class criterion, he set forth the Tashkent-Khokand conflict not in terms of nationality, but in social ones. To him, it was the conflict of a bourgeois government versus a popular one.[9] Khokand's death knell sounded when, on February 14, 1918, troops from the Orenburg front laid siege to the city and captured it February 18.

[8] *Yash Turkistan*, No. 3/4 (March 1930), p. 31.
[9] *Materialy i dokumenty I-go s"ezda Kompartii Turkestana* (Tashkent, Sredazpartizdat, 1934), pp. 67–68.

Khokand was sacked and practically destroyed, and the inhabitants
were massacred by Red troops,[10] though Mustafa Chokay-oghlu
managed to escape.

The collapse of Khokand autonomy was inevitable, for it had
neither sufficient political forces, nor troops, nor means. While it
represented the heartfelt wishes of southern Central Asians, its
effort could not find support, for it had no real ties with the general
population. Still, this ephemeral government was far more important than its brief duration might indicate. It gave the first manifestation of open opposition to Soviet power in the name of local
autonomy, and it gave birth to the Basmachi movement, which
prolonged Central Asian protest against integration into the Soviet
Union.

INDEPENDENCE MOVEMENTS IN TURKMENIIA, KHIVA, AND BUKHARA

The Khokand government was not, of course, the only manifestation of local aspirations at this time. In Turkmen country, the
situation immediately after the October revolution was similar to
that of Farghana with its two-headed authority. From February 17
on, a movement had been growing among the Turkmen intelligentsia.

After the Provisional Government fell, the Turkmens convoked
a regional congress which elected a National Executive Committee
with Colonel Oraz Sirdar at the head. Soviet authorities called a
congress of Turkmen peasants which sided against the National
Executive Committee and supported the Soviets with Turkmen
participation in regions, cities, and villages. A Turkmen Red Guard
was formed, while the National Executive Committee, which originally asserted that it had only socialist goals, set itself up as a candidate for power, abetted agitation in the countryside, and above all
sought to secure military resources. The squadron of czarist Turkmen cavalry stationed at Ashkhabad provided the basis for a Turkmen army, but this force did not have time to develop further,
because in February, 1918, Kolesov and his troops defeated the

---

[10] *Voina v peskakh: Materialy po istorii grazhdanskoi voiny. Grazhdanskaia
voina v Srednei Azii* (12 vols.; Leningrad, "Istoriia Grazhdanskoi Voiny,"
1935), p. 527.

Turkmens, broke up the movement, and established the authority of the Soviets there.[11]

Two other regions of Central Asia which especially continued to threaten Soviet authority were the Khivan khanate and, even more, Bukhara, whose strategic importance was considerable. After the February revolution, the emir of Bukhara, yielding to liberal pressure and to the very murky political activity of Miller, the Russian resident agent inherited from the previous regime, had proclaimed, in a manifesto of March, 1917, several reforms which seemed as if they might transform the theocratic state into a parliamentary monarchy. But a month later, apprehensive about the development of political agitation within the emirate,[12] and aware that the Soviet government then had too many problems abroad to busy itself with Bukhara, the emir reappointed his conservative advisers, repealed the reforms, and outlawed the liberals.

The latter had taken refuge in the Russian cities of the emirate and even in Turkistan guberniia itself, finding support in the soviets dominated by the Bolsheviks, who were in almost open rebellion against the Provisional Government. The Jadids sought help first from the Khokand government, which scarcely had any means of aiding them, then turned to Kolesov. Faizullah Khoja-oghli (Khojaev) convinced him that a popular uprising, ready to break out in Bukhara, was awaiting only outside assistance to come into being.[13] Kolesov let himself be persuaded and plunged into a Bukharan expedition March 1, 1918. He thought that he could limit himself to a maneuver of intimidation which the internal revolt, heralded by the Jadids, would reinforce.[14]

But the emir, who made him wait forty-eight hours in Kagan under the pretext of negotiating terms of the manifesto that he was going to proclaim, seized the Russian parliamentarians by trickery and put them to death. Then, when he had had time to carry out his preparations for combat, broke the truce by refusing to sign the

---

[11] F. L. Shteinberg, *Ocherki istorii turkmenii* (Moscow, Gosudarstvennoe Sotsialisticheskoe Ekonomicheskoe Izdatel'stvo, 1934), pp. 71–72.

[12] "Bukhara v 1917 godu," *Krasnyi arkhiv*, XX (1927), 78–123.

[13] F. Khodzhaev, *K istorii revoliutsii v Bukhare* (Tashkent, Uzbekskoe Gosudarstvennoe Izdatel'stvo, 1926), p. 45.

[14] *Voina v peskakh*, p. 241.

manifesto, which had been the object of all the dealings. Kolesov rushed to the assault of Bukhara, but he had to face not only the emir's troops but also the local population, whipped into a frenzy by its mullahs, and serving as a shield for the army.

Kolesov had to retreat under dreadful conditions, pursued by the Central Asians over routes where the reservoirs had been destroyed, telegraph poles felled, and rails torn up.[15] Thus, the first Soviet attempt to end Bukhara's independence was repaid sharply by a terrible failure which had the effect of turning the emir, who until then had clung to his neutrality by refusing to support Khokand against the Soviet government, into an implacable enemy. All his efforts polarized around the reinforcement of his army, the purchase of arms, the establishment of external alliances with Persia and Afghanistan, and the reestablishment of a rigorous internal order from which all liberalism was excluded.

Simultaneously came the Basmachi revolt, the Russian counterrevolutionary drives, and foreign intervention. All these gave particular importance to the hostility of Bukhara, which became the real center of opposition to the Soviets. At the same time, these diverse events for two years prevented the Soviet government from settling the fate of the last two independent states of Central Asia. The difficult situation of the Tashkent government worsened at the loss of Orenburg, July 1, 1918, the effect of which was to cut Central Asia off once again from Moscow's government and to leave the local Soviets vulnerable against enemies attacking on three fronts.

The chief danger to Soviet control of Central Asia in 1918–1919 came from support given the counterrevolutionary movements by British troops. British intervention in Central Asia after the October revolution had its origin in British concern over the poltical changes which had occurred in the region. Until this time, Britain had actually denied Turkey and the Central Powers access to the Middle East and India by securing safe positions in the area. The collapse of the Russian empire, causing chaos in the neighborhood of Britain's main sphere of interest, rendered her vulnerable to all attempts at penetration. Replying to this danger, Great Britain

---

[15] *Ibid.*, p. 249.

launched several military missions, including those of General L. C. Dunsterville and General W. Malleson respectively, in the Baku and Transcaspian regions.

There, after the Turkmen outburst of early 1918, the apparent calm was challenged again as a result of unpopular political measures when the Ashkhabad soviet ordered that a population census be taken. This provoked widespread outbursts in June, 1918, in a revolt which began in Ashkhabad, where the insurgents won dismissal of the soviet and the promise of new elections.

Tashkent sent a special commissar, Frolov, to calm things down, to which task he applied himself by instigating bloody repressions which only caused the rebellion to spread.[16] When Frolov arrived at Qizil Arvat, the insurgents killed him. The Ashkhabad rebels seized power, setting up a Government of the Transcaspian Region. They addressed propositions, soon rejected,[17] to the Tashkent government, suggesting the coexistence of the two governments until the gathering of a constituent assembly of southern Central Asia.

To lessen the danger of an attack from Tashkent, the new government turned to General Malleson in Iran, who promised his help.[18] It also negotiated with the movement led by Colonel Oraz Sirdar which had been defeated in February. Sirdar took command over troops of the Transcaspian region.

Here again, the local government was weakened because its power over the population remained inadequately established. The famine, disorders, and Bolshevik propaganda all contributed to the growing anarchy in Transcaspia, and when the Red Army attacked Turkmen troops, no popular uprising supported the Transcaspian forces. In February, 1919, the British government decided to withdraw its soldiers from the region, the Red Army's offensive soon began, and in July 1919, Colonel Sirdar had to abandon Ashkhabad, after which Qizil Arvat fell into the hands of the Reds and by the

[16] Z. I. Mirkin, "Interventsiia v Zakaspii," *K desiatiletiiu interventsii: Sbornik statei* (Moscow-Leningrad, Gosudarstvennoe Izdatel'stvo, 1929), p. 167.

[17] N. Paskuskii, *K istorii grazhdanskoi voiny v Turkestane* (Tashkent, 1922), pp. 9f.

[18] S. I. Filipov, *Boevye deistviia na zakaspiiskom fronte* (Ashkhabad, Tsentral'naia Iubileinaia Kommissiia pri Turkmenskom Ts.I.K.-e. po 10 Letiiu Krasnoi Armii, 1928).

end of 1920 the Transcaspian government's brief existence was terminated.

From 1918 on, while Russian adventures such as the Osipov coup d'état at Tashkent continued, the Moscow government worried about the political deterioration in that area. The Basmachi revolt and the protests of the local populace against Russian excesses prompted Moscow to intervene. In April, 1918, P. A. Kobozev was sent to Tashkent to investigate. The first consequence of his mission was the proclamation, on April 30, of the Turkistan Autonomous Republic and the assembly of a new Executive Council in which ten Central Asians took part.

In June, 1918, the first regional congress of the Russian Communist Party (Bolshevik) met in Tashkent to lay foundations for a local party. Under pressure from Moscow, the meeting sought mainly to work out ways of attracting the indigenous population to the Soviet regime by opening the doors of the government, party, and army to it. Tashkent authorities ignored these blandishments, however, and the hostility between the government and the Central Asians remained. Early in 1919, when the Russian civil war seemed less threatening because the Transcaspian region was at last under control and the threat of intervention averted, the Moscow leadership decided to implement a new Central Asian policy. They wished to integrate the local educated groups within the party rather than to leave them free for any other political adventures. The Bolsheviks also hoped that this elite would bridge gaps between the Soviet government and the local populace.

At the second regional conference of the party, in March, 1919, Kobozev set up a regional bureau of Muslim organizations of the Russian Communist Party. Invited to join on the eve of this conference, local people, led by the Jadids, came en masse. The collapse of successive Central Asian governments had proved to them that it was hardly possible to act effectively against the established power, so they took advantage of these overtures hoping to influence government policy one day by sheer weight of numbers. The regional bureau welcomed leaders of the local liberal tendency like Turar Riskul-uulu (Ryskulov) (1894–1937) and Tursun Khoja-oghli, and once inside the fold these men zealously recruited their compatriots. At the end of May, 1919, at the first conference of Muslim Communists of Central Asia the Muslims openly attacked the Bolshevik attitude toward them saying: "We were obliged to tolerate the hostile attitude of the representatives of the former privileged classes toward the local people. This attitude even exists among those who profess to be Communists and who, being in power, regard the indigenous people as their subjects."[19]

During the following months, the place occupied by the southern Central Asians within the party and in the state structure, which had been intentionally opened up to them by a decision reached in harmony with Moscow on July 12, 1919, continued to grow. The target was soon widely overshot, for the Muslims collaborating with the Communists had brought forward their conception of Central Asia's future, one which turned on the idea of distinctions of nationality above all else. At the fifth regional congress of the party in January, 1920, Central Asian Communists succeeded in securing a majority of seats in the Muslim Bureau, and, in conjunction with the third conference of Turkistan Communists, voted to convert the Turkistan Autonomous Republic into the Autonomous Turkic Republic. Their Communist organization became the Turkic Communist Party.[20] This resolution specified that all the Turkic people of Russia be unified around a Turkic republic in Central Asia, thus offering a center of attraction to the Turkic people who had migrated beyond the frontiers of the czarist empire. And so, through the votes of the Muslim Communists, new life was given to the old dream of a greater Turkistan which they had cherished when they were Jadids.

While Muslims were entering the Communist Party en masse and trying to win acceptance for their ideas of nationality there, on September 13, 1919, the troops of the Soviet First Army finally linked up with the soldiers of the Aktyubinsk front, thus definitely reestablishing Central Asia's liaison with Russia.[21] Immediately a Turkic Commission manned by V. V. Kuibyshev, M. V. Frunze, and others was dispatched to Tashkent to settle once and for all the

[19] G. Safarov, p. 97.
[20] *Ibid.*, p. 110.
[21] *Voina v peskakh*, pp. 504f.

problems born of the hostility between Central Asians and the Russians.

The Moscow government, haunted by Frunze's warnings about the difficulty of defending the revolution when the indigenous people were hostile to it, had not been able to learn in time the consequences of measures advocated by Kobozev. The Turkic Commission acted mainly to purge Russian Communist ranks of deserters from the old regime, and to satisfy the aspirations of the locals.[22] The mission in November, 1919, found itself far outdistanced by the recent changes, and very rapidly after first undertaking to liquidate those Russians who were clearly out-and-out chauvinists and colonialists, realized that the problem at the end of 1919 lay elsewhere, in the aspirations of the Central Asians and in the orientation that they were giving the party.

Local leaders emphasized not so much the destiny of the workers as the development of their whole nation,[23] and they came to the point of asking for a change in the very composition of the Turkic Commission. In the spring of 1920, A. Z. Validov (Togan), who defended Bashkir autonomy, was instructed to ask Lenin to include on the Turkic Commission as many Muslims as Russians.[24] These developments, especially when they followed upon the news from Central Asia and the reports of Frunze, who emphasized that concessions made to the Muslims would encourage the anti-Soviet Basmachi movement,[25] all convinced Lenin that unsupervised cooperation with the local nationalists was impossible.

The military position of Russia and the internal Central Asian situation did not permit any brutal rupture. Lenin temporized until June, 1920, when the cessation of military operations in the Ukraine freed him from that heavy commitment. The Central Committee of the Russian Communist Party declared that there could not be any Muslims in the Turkic Commission and sent new members, in-

[22] Turar Ryskulov, *Revoliutsiia i korennoe naselenie Turkestana: Sbornik statei, dokladov, rechei* (Tashkent, Uzbekskoe Gosudarstvennoe Izdatel'stvo, 1925), p. 77.

[23] G. Safarov, p. 109.

[24] Togan, pp. 370–71, 398–402.

[25] *M. V. Frunze na frontakh grazhdanskoi voiny* (Moscow, Voennoe Izdatel'stvo, 1941), pp. 119–20.

cluding M. V. Kaganovich, Georgi Safarov, and Yakob Peters, to Central Asia to purge the party there. Peters drew up an indictment of the Central Asian Communists, accusing them of having tried to seize power, of having wanted to substitute nationality and pan-Islamic propaganda for Communism, and of having supported the Basmachis.[26]

Immediate sanctions were taken. All the nationalists who had followed Turar Riskul-uulu were eliminated from the party. The regional Muslim Bureau was dissolved and replaced by a less representative organization whose members had been appointed on recommendation of the Turkic Commission. In the same manner, local nationalists lost their government posts.

However, the Soviets did not, in October, 1920, fall into the error committed three years earlier; they gave ample place to Central Asians in both the party and the government. Refusing to cooperate with those from the local middle class, they consistently replaced them with obscure "workers" whose lack of intellectual and political awareness placed them at the mercy of the Russians in both party and government. Moreover, along with the first Turkic Commission, forty ranking Communists had been sent down to southern Central Asia to staff the party.[27] The inexperienced, illiterate Uzbek and Kazakh workers were putty in their hands. By taking this measure Lenin remained faithful to guidance given by the Baku congress.

The Muslims demanded that in a colonial environment where no conscious and organized proletariat existed, priority be granted to the nationality struggle rather than to social liberation, and that the local bourgeoisie be given the opportunity to assume leadership of the liberation movement. The Komintern, through G. E. Zinoviev, Bela Kun, Karl Radek, and M. Pavlovich, replied negatively. The struggle for social liberation had priority and could be coupled if need be with the struggle for liberation of nationalities; the local bourgeoisie could not assume leadership, in these conditions, of a movement which had to be entrusted, in the absence of a proletariat,

---

[26] *Istoriia uzbekskoi SSR* (Tashkent, Izdatel'stvo Akademii Nauk Uzbekskoi SSR, 1956), II, 110–11; *Leninskii sbornik,* XXXII (Moscow, 1938), 320–21.
[27] *Istoriia uzbekskoi SSR,* II (1957), 106.

to the poor peasants.[28] These were the principles that Soviet authorities applied in southern Central Asia at the end of 1920, and their
efforts to organize the Union of Poor Peasants (Qoshchi Ittifaqi)
were, they felt, the start of the class struggle.

THE KAZAKHS AND ALASH ORDA

At the time of the October 1917 revolution, the plains of Central
Asia were in complete chaos. But, although political unity was
nowhere to be found, the existence of multiple military forces
constituted a reality which dominated the evolution of the region
for nearly three years. On one side, there were Cossack forces
whose chiefs wanted to form their own governments. Thus, with
the Orenburg Cossacks, Ataman Dutov tried to organize a government over the Ural-Orenburg territory. Installed with the White
Guard in Omsk, Admiral Kolchak, who tried to save the monarchy,
also needed to extend his dominion over the plains.[29] Finally, the
leaders of Alash Orda thought that the hour of autonomy had come
and that they could insure it by binding their fate to that of Russian
forces hostile to the revolution present in that area.

The leaders of Alash Orda had convened the third Kazakh congress in Orenburg from December 5 to 13, 1917.[30] The congress
proclaimed the autonomy of the Kazakh people and elected an executive committee presided over by Aliqan Bokeyqan-uli,[31] which
also included such figures as Baytursin-uli and Jihanshah Dosmaghambet-uli. The impossibility of a single, centralized administration
for this immense region, populated with tribes often hostile to each
other, under conditions of the Russian civil war caused leaders of
the new government to divide it into two administrative zones.
Alash Orda of the west, which covered the Uralsk provinces and
had the Inner Horde under its authority, was headed by Jihanshah
Dosmaghambet-uli. Eastern Alash Orda, entrusted to Aliqan Bokey-

    [28] H. Carrère d'Encausse and S. Schram, *Le marxisme et l'Asie* (Paris,
Armand Colin, 1965), pp. 48–53.
    [29] G. Mel'nikov, *Oktiabr' v Kazakhstane* (Alma Ata, 1930), p. 20.
    [30] *Istoriia kazakhskoi SSR* (Alma Ata, Izdatel'stvo Akademii Nauk Kazakhskoi
SSR, 1943), p. 427.
    [31] Mel'nikov, p. 21.

qan-uli, covered Semirechie, Semipalatinsk, and Akmolinsk. The Turgay region escaped.[32]

Early in 1918 the Bolsheviks occupied Orenburg and a part of the Orenburg-Tashkent railway line, thus breaking the unity of Alash Orda. Each zone had to organize by itself and turn to its nearby allies. What still unified them during this period of isolation was not so much the program of Álash Orda, on which they held divergent views,[33] but their desire, voiced at the third Kazakh congress and expressed by Bokeyqan-uli, to prevent the spread of Bolshevism throughout the plains.[34] Thus, the West Alash Orda group linked its destiny with that of the Bashkirs and Orenburg Cossacks, whereas the East Alash Orda had to contact Kolchak.

When the Kazakhs turned to the government of Siberia to ask for arms and instructors to form an army to fight beside the Whites, the government replied through General Ivanov, notorious for suppressing the 1916 revolts at Jizzakh, that it would not provide one weapon or one officer for the Kazakhs.[35] What is more, Kolchak demanded that the Kazakhs provide 6 million rubles annually to help support his troops.[36] Unable to obtain any real assistance from the Whites for the realization of its program, Alash Orda tried for a time to join with the Bashkirs of Validov and the southern Central Asians so as to form a union which from the Ural to the Afghan frontier of Central Asia would bring together Turkic people and Cossacks under the military authority of Ataman Dutov. This project quickly proved abortive.[37]

At the end of October, Kolchak, anxious about the anarchy in the plains, decided to withdraw even minor support for Alash Orda and ordered its suppression. His decision flung the Kazakh leaders back toward the Bolsheviks. Their compromise was made

---

[32] Joseph Castagne, "Le bolchevisme et l'Islam," *Revue du Monde musulman*, vol. LI, No. 1 (1922), pp. 173–74.

[33] Baymirza Hayit, *Turkestan im XX. Jahrhundert* (Darmstadt, Leske Verlag, 1956), pp. 162–63.

[34] *Istoriia kazakhskoi SSR, epokha sotsializma* (Alma Ata, Izdatel'stvo Akademii Nauk Kazakhskoi SSR, 1963), p. 50.

[35] Castagne, "Le bolchevisme et l'Islam," p. 175.

[36] Mel'nikov, pp. 20–21.

[37] Togan, p. 371.

easier by those Kazakhs who were already struggling on the Communist side. Since the spring of 1918, the Soviet government had enjoined its plains representatives to attract the local people to them, and some Kazakh groups had already joined the Bolsheviks. The educated nucleus which had militated around the publication *Ush Jüz*, found itself in this awkward position because of its old enmity toward Alash Orda. But other considerations brought Kazakh allies to the Bolsheviks. Amangeldi Iman-uli, the unsubdued warrior of 1916, had naturally come to the Bolsheviks. Another Kazakh, whom Soviet historiography would place in the forefront during this period, was Alibii Jangeldin of the Kipchak tribe whose men followed him willingly, for they had been assured that "Bolshevik" was the Russian translation of *"qipchaq."* [38] Early in March, 1919, Jangeldin, who had been made commissar extraordinary for the plains since May, 1918, succeeded in winning over Baytursin-uli to the Bolsheviks, and then, in November, with the defeat of Admiral Kolchak, the leaders of West Alash Orda.

The heads of Alash Orda had obtained satisfactory assurances about their fate and that of their troops, as well as about the Kazakh political future. After the end of the civil war, the Soviet government seemed to keep its promises, since it granted the Kazakhs and Kirgiz the autonomy for which they had fought, and offered local leaders a place in the state and the party. On July 10, 1919, after having discussed the problems of the plains and its people with a delegation that included not only Jangeldin, but also Baytursin-uli, Lenin signed a decree declaring "the provisional status of the revolutionary committee charged with administering the plains."

The revolutionary committee, nucleus of the future government, was presided over by a Russian, S. Pestkovskii, and included two Kazakhs among its members: Jangeldin and Mindash-uli. In January, 1920, the revolutionary committee was reshaped, and some Alash Orda leaders, including Baytursin-uli, came into it. On March 9, 1920, Kirrevkom (Kirgiz [i.e., Kazakh] Revolutionary Committee) decided to liquidate all the organizations inherited from

[38] Castagne, "Le bolchevisme et l'Islam," p. 176.

Alash Orda.[39] Despite these obstacles, Alash Orda leaders continued to play a considerable role in setting up the political and administrative organization of the plains.

On August 26, 1920, Kazakh territorial autonomy was realized through the creation of a Kazakh Autonomous Socialist Soviet Republic.[40] Baytursin-uli, who had been in the government, was temporarily excluded, but then headed the Ministry of Education. The government included as many Kazakhs as Russians or Europeans.

Opposition between the Bolsheviks and the Kazakh leaders arose in September, when a commission met to draft regulations for the Kazakh constituent assembly. The Communists suggested that the former "privileged classes," the clerics, and all those who had had a hand in the imperial government or in the government of Alash Orda, be deprived of the right to vote. Baytursin-uli fiercely opposed these stipulations and, for a time, prevailed. At the constituent assembly held in Orenburg from October 4 to 12, 1920,[41] in the presence of 700 delegates, nearly half of the members regrouped around Alash Orda leaders Baytursin-uli and Bokeyqan-uli.

For all practical purposes, there were no local forces outside of Alash Orda during the first years of the republic. Amangeldi Iman-uli had died during the civil war, Jangeldin was respected mainly by his fellow tribesmen, and the Kazakh cause continued to be represented by those who had animated Alash Orda. This is why Soviet authority did not break with the nationalist leaders in the troubled years following the civil war.

The constituent assembly of October, 1920, proclaimed an end to colonization. In April, 1921, a decree opened the way to the expropriation of lands held by Russian-Ukrainian settlers, and by Cossacks. Later texts extended the area returned to local control.[42] In 1921, the Kazakh government raised the question of linking the regions of Akmolinsk and Semipalatinsk, which were still dominated

---

[39] *Istoriia kazakhskoi SSR, epokha sotsializma,* p. 175.

[40] *Desiat' let Kazakhstana* (Alma Ata, Izdatel'stvo Gosplana Kazakhskoi ASSR, 1930), p. 16.

[41] "Po sovetskim respublikam, Kirgizy i Bashkiry," *Izvestiia* (October 27, 1920), p. 1.

[42] "Po sovetskim respublikam, Kirgiziia," *Izvestiia* (May 22, 1921), p. 1.

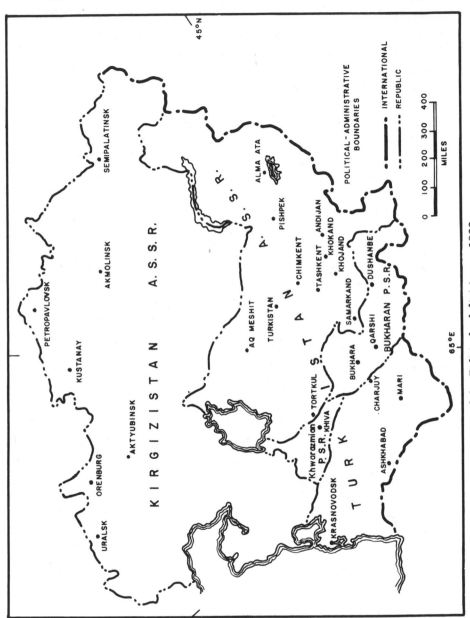

FIGURE 9.1   Political subdivisions, c.1922.

by Siberia to the Autonomous Republic, a merger which was carried out in June, 1921.[43] It also called at this time, unsuccessfully, for the linking to it of the Kirgiz (Kara-Kirgiz) who were under Turkistan ASSR jurisdiction.[44]

Meanwhile, in spite of their participation in the government, from 1920 on the Central Asian nationalists were exposed to growing hostility by the Communists which already foreshadowed their ouster a few years later. While at the first congress of Communist organizations of the Kazakh Republic, July 12–20, 1921, it was agreed that "owing to the deficiency of personnel, educated Kazakhs, whatever their positions had been, would be admitted to the party and the government without discrimination,[45] the II Congress of Soviets, October 4, 1921, openly attacked the members of Alash Orda, shifting upon them the responsibility for the famine then rampant in the plains. The second congress of Communist organizations, February 19–27, 1922, reacted even more violently against Kazakh nationalism, accusing Kazakh Communists of making concessions to nationalism. This provoked an indignant reply from the local Communists.[46] During this period the government's first experiments in rural collectivization were received with indifference by the Kazakhs, so great was their poverty. Although famine was, in 1921, widespread in the Soviet Union, the Russian press made clear that the situation in the Kazakh plains was particularly desperate.[47]

KHIVAN RESISTANCE

Having reestablished a kind of peace in southern Central Asia and in the plains, the Soviet government could at last think about liquidating the last two independent states, the Khivan khanate and Bukharan emirate. Disposing of them was urgent, because both were for various reasons real counterrevolutionary centers where the Basmachis found support and tried to negotiate with foreign countries for the arms they needed.

[43] "Deistviia i rasporiazheniia pravitel'stva," *Izvestiia* (June 26, 1921), p. 2.
[44] "Po sovetskim respublikam," *Izvestiia* (May 17, 1921), p. 2.
[45] Hayit, *Turkestan im XX. Jahrhundert*, p. 165.
[46] *Desiat' let Kazakhstana*, p. 21.
[47] "Bor'ba s golodom. Plenum Ts.K. Pomgol," *Izvestiia* (May 25, 1922), p. 3.

Khiva had been for several years the theater of a persistent struggle between Uzbeks and Turkmens, and this strife had destroyed all the khanate's power even before the revolution of 1920. Exasperated by the cruelty of the Turkmen Muhammad Qurban Junaïd Khan, who set himself up after 1917 as the real master of Khiva, the local Jadids or Young Khivans opposed him from 1918 on, and were led by this opposition to seek help in the Turkistan ASSR. At the end of 1919, a part of Khiva's population was in virtual rebellion against Junaïd Khan, and taking advantage of the disorders, and of the appeals of the liberals,[48] Frunze and Kuibyshev marched the third battalion of the Fifth Turkistan regiment on Tortkul late in November.

On December 22, the order to attack was given, and Soviet troops split into two columns, some advancing upon Khojeyli toward the bulk of Junaïd Khan's troops, while the others approached Yangi Urganch. Then, the two groups were to come together in the capital itself. After a day of fighting, Khojeyli fell on December 29, and despite a few attempts at resistance by Junaïd Khan, on February 1, 1919, the campaign drew to a close with the capture of Khiva. Junaïd Khan took refuge in the Qara Qum, where he continued to struggle against Soviet authority at the side of the Basmachis, while Sayyid Abdullah, khan of Khiva, whose power by then was largely theoretical, abdicated, to be replaced by a revolutionary committee which the same day proclaimed the Khwarazm (Khivan) People's Republic.[49]

The Soviet government, consistent with its desire to pacify rather than to stir up the Central Asians, had to establish an authority dominated by the Young Khivans, in other words by the local middle class. The guiding role they assumed in the struggle against Junaïd Khan and the absence of any other political forces in Khiva made them a logical choice to take power. The first new government of Khiva, presided over by the Jadid Pahlivan Niyaz, was formed only of Central Asians, including Baba Akhund Salim-oghli, prime minister; Mullah Oraz Khoja Muhammad, foreign affairs minister; Juma Niyaz Sultan Murad, interior; Mullah Begjan, education;

[48] *Istoriia uzbekskoi SSR*, II, 149.
[49] Togan, p. 260.

Hassan-oghli, war; Mullah Nur Muhammad Baba, commerce; and Mir Sharaf-oghli, military commander-in-chief. The Turkistan ASSR's representative to Khwarazm was also a Central Asian.[50] On September 13, 1920, the new republic agreed with Soviet Russia on a military and political alliance, and accepted an economic treaty which served as a model for the agreements concluded shortly afterward with the Bukharan People's Republic.[51]

Nevertheless, tribal quarrels quickly gave Soviet leaders an excuse to intervene in Khwarazmian political life and to relieve local leaders of power. From September on, public disturbances broke out and set the new government against Turkmen tribes which had risen up protesting the execution of eight of their chiefs. Through its representatives in Khwarazm, the Soviet government proffered a mission of conciliation which inevitably aggravated the conflict. At the prompting of the Soviet representative, a congress of Turkmens from Khwarazm was convened which, through its demands and Soviet promises, further deepened the internal crisis. The situation exploded in March, 1921, on the eve of the pan-Khwarazmian Congress (qurultay).

The ferment had begun over the question of elective franchises. The Young Khivans' government refused to accept the proposition of the then recently founded Khwarazmian Communist Party, directed by Juma Niyaz Sultan Murad,[52] first chairman of the revolutionary committee established in 1918 at Yangi Urganch, and especially by the Russian envoy Safonov, former head of Farghana's troops. Their intent was to exclude from the electoral lists the "idle" sections of the population along with certain favored social classes. Popular demonstrations organized March 4 by the various opponents resulted in toppling the government and replacing it by a coalition composed of two Uzbeks, one Turkmen, one Kirgiz, and one local member of the Komsomol.[53] Despite the elimination of the most important Central Asian leaders, the new government did not go much farther than its predecessor along the path to socialism. Property remained in private hands, and universal suffrage was not re-

[50] *Ibid.*, p. 424.
[51] Castagne, "Le bolchevisme et l'Islam," pp. 207–15.
[52] Hayit, *Turkestan im XX. Jahrhundert*, p. 149.
[53] G. Skalov, "Khivinskaia revoliutsiia," *Novyi Vostok*, No. 3 (1922), p. 31.

stricted by social criteria. The second pan-Khwarazmian congress met in May, 1921, and seriously tried to smooth over Khwarazm's tribal problems with a broad amnesty.

Nevertheless, Soviet pressure grew more pronounced, in spite of this internal *détente*. Byk, the Russian representative in Khiva, succeeded Safonov, who had been somewhat involved in the downfall there of Pahlivan Niyaz. In November, 1921, Byk, too, intervened very directly in local political life, arranging for the Khwarazmian government itself to be adjudged guilty of counterrevolutionary activities, and for certain of its members to be put to death and others imprisoned.

Thereafter, the heads of the indigenous movement having been removed from political life and in many cases liquidated, the Khwarazm People's Republic had only a flimsy substance. The party, Komsomol, and Qoshchi Ittifaqi, in the absence of the decimated Central Asian leadership, led an existence more theoretical than real, because these organizations were incapable of conscious, effective political action. The newspapers published during this period in the Khwarazm People's Republic, *Inqilab quyashi* and *Qizil Khwarazm*, failed to bolster its shaky independence, and in 1922 and 1923, constant purges slowly prepared the way for its final liquidation.

BUKHARA SUCCUMBS TO RUSSIAN ARMS

Bukhara's destiny greatly resembled Khwarazm's, although the character of the two people's republics was very different in certain respects. In July, 1920, released from military operations in the Ukraine and having subjugated Khiva, the Soviet government had but the Bukharan threat to destroy.[54]

Within the emirate, the situation seemed ripe for Soviet intervention. The emir had forbidden any trade exchange with Russia and the Turkistan ASSR since 1920, and the economic situation was grave. Bukhara's resources were not sufficient to support the population, 70 percent of the nation's herds having been destroyed, the

---

[54] M. V. Frunze, *Izbrannye proizvedeniia* (Moscow, Voennoe Izdatel'stvo, 1950), p. 101.

land no longer irrigated, and popular discontent at a fever pitch.[55] For the Soviets it was essential to take advantage of this discontent if the Bukharans were not again to turn their wrath against the Russians, as they had done many times under the direction of their religious leaders. Such a development, in the context of the Basmachi movement, had been particularly serious.

In the Turkistan ASSR the Soviets had allies for this campaign among the Young Bukharans and the Bukharan Communist Party, these two groups having fled the emirate or developed outside of Bukhara since 1917. The Bukharan Communist Party was founded in 1918 at Tashkent from a minority of the Young Bukharans who supported joining the party.[56] This party developed especially, it seems, between 1918 and 1920 among the Russians of the emirate, while the majority of the Young Bukharans remained outside the party and founded, in February, 1920, a Bureau of the Revolutionaries of Bukhara. For this action they were criticized by the Bukharan Communist Party.[57] A rapprochement between them and the party did not take place until the summer of 1920 when, sensing the imminence of Soviet military operations against the emirate, the two groups united.

To the very end, the Young Bukharans were hostile to intervention by the Red Army, trusting in the possibility of a popular uprising.[58] A telegram from Frunze apprised them that military operations had already begun at the same time the Young Bukharans were still debating the advisability of such a move at the congress of Charjuy.[59] The emir left his bombarded capital, in which resistance seemed hopeless, to try to regroup his troops in eastern Bukhara, and on September 2, the city of Bukhara was captured.[60] Power was assumed by a revolutionary committee formed with a majority of Young Bukharans and presided over by Faizullah Khoja-oghli.

[55] M. N., "Pod znakom Islama," *Novyi Vostok*, No. 4 (1923), p. 81.
[56] A. I. Ishanov, *Pobeda narodnoi sovetskoi revoliutsii v Bukhare* (Tashkent, Izdatel'stvo Akademii Nauk Uzbekskoi SSR, 1957), p. 19.
[57] *Vooruzhennye sily bukharskogo khanstva* (Tashkent, 1920), p. 17.
[58] D. Soloveichik, "Revoliutsionnaia Bukhara," *Novyi Vostok*, II (1922), 272–88.
[59] Frunze, pp. 103–14.
[60] "Bukhara, sovetskaia respublika," *Izvestiia* (September 4, 1920), p. 2.

The committee began by nationalizing all unoccupied land, the water supply, and large private real properties. Next it announced its intention to redistribute confiscated lands to the poor peasants and to place means of cultivating these lands at their disposal.[61] The committee also wanted to establish absolute equality between the various nationalities in the emirate, and this aim received official confirmation at the second pan-Bukharan congress on September 25, 1921.[62] In practice, however, the basic intentions of the revolutionary committee were never realized by the state and were, on the contrary, belied by the actual decrees and statutes.

The constitution of the People's Republic adopted at the Second Congress gave assurances that the new government was responsible to popular sovereignty.[63] This found expression in the existence of a Council of People's Representatives (Khalq Wakillari Shorasi) charged with holding the government in check, but the very composition of this council was far from reflecting the theoretically popular character of the new government. Seventy-two members were moderates unattracted by the revolutionary reforms defended by the Council's left-wing of eight members against a resolutely conservative right-wing numbering five persons.[64]

The constitution guaranteed citizens the respect for private property which this fundamental statute of the Republic in no way defined. The statute insisted upon the basic character of Islamic laws and clearly set forth, in Article 26 that no constitutional provision could be inconsistent with them. Freedom of conscience was guaranteed with the freedom of writing, speech, and assembly in Articles 7, 8, and 9,[65] but Article 26 provided that they could not operate against Islam. The administrative organization also revealed the same concern to reconcile democratic reforms with the traditional structures. At all levels, organizations representing Soviet authority were provided for, but in actual fact they combined with tradi-

---

[61] A. Mashitskii, "Materialy po istorii Bukharskoi revoliutsii," *Vestnik Narodnogo Komissariata Inostrannykh Del,* No. 4/5 (April–May 1922), pp. 127–28.

[62] Dervish, "Bukharskaia Sovetskaia Narodnaia Respublika," *Zhizn' natsional'nostei,* No. 1 (January 1923), pp. 197–98.

[63] N. Arkhipov, "Bukharskaia Narodnaia Respublika," *Sovetskoe pravo,* No. 1 (4) (1923), p. 134.

[64] Castagne, "Le bolchevisme et l'Islam," p. 225.

[65] Arkhipov, pp. 136–37.

tional authorities of elders, so that in the villages, for example, the function of the elder hardly altered. Through certain provisions, however, the constitution introduced notable changes. In the electoral system, for example, Article 58 extended the franchise to young men and women of eighteen. This tended to upset social relations radically. Article 59, particularly, which deprived officials of the fallen regime and certain favored economic categories of the vote, bore the germ of class conflict.

Thus, the Bukharan People's Republic seemed, all things considered, much more complex than the other indigenous states which existed at the time. Its leaders, mainly the Young Bukharans and especially Fitrat, descended from the reformist movement, had the unmistakable desire to introduce socialism to Bukhara and return in this state to principles of social justice and structural transformation preached by the Bolsheviks.

Aware, however, of Bukhara's generally uneducated, frightfully poverty-stricken population and its fierce attachment to Islam, and cognizant of the stark shortage in skilled personnel, the leaders had to face reality in their plans. In order not to clash with the populace, the politicians had to preserve the basic religious principles to which people always referred. To obtain personnel, the new government needed to restore to power the competent men of the fallen regime and so avoid alienating those segments of the population from which they had sprung. This meant, of course, that they could not be dispossessed of their lands, and the promised agrarian reforms were blocked. Despite the electoral arrangements which safeguarded the future, the Young Bukharans, barely a few months after coming to power, thus found themselves seeming to defend the interests of the former rulers rather than those of the general population they wanted to represent.

The population, disillusioned by the lack of agrarian reform in spite of the glowing promises, soon likened the Young Bukharans and Communists to their former masters, saying that the single result of the revolution was to give them "seven emirs instead of only one." [66]

One of the reasons impelling the Young Bukharans to avoid

[66] Castagne, "Le bolchevisme et l'Islam," p. 225.

class conflict was the problem of independence. Soviet Russia had in September, 1920, recognized the absolute independence of the new state,[67] but her pressure was soon making itself felt. Clashes between Bukhara and the Soviet government broke out almost immediately.

Russia had almost ceased her trade exchanges with Bukhara and showed no intention of resuming them in spite of appeals from the local government. This rendered the domestic economic situation tragic.[68] It was aggravated by the presence of Frunze's Soviet troops who had stayed on in Bukhara's territory, moving about at will, imposing requisitions on the population, while the Soviet authorities claimed the right to make the People's Republic provide their maintenance.[69] Arguments between the Bukharan government and Russian representatives became more frequent in 1921, and the chief of state, Usman Khoja-oghli, came to the point of earnestly requesting Afghan intervention against the Russian violations of Bukhara's sovereignty.[70]

Thus, gradually, the Bukharan People's Republic reversed its original direction. The Young Bukharans, initially partisans of radical social reform and standing as allies of the Bolsheviks, little by little had checked the reforms and opposed the Bolsheviks. Furthermore, by officially replacing Persian, which until then was the state's "cultured" language, with a Turkic language, the Young Bukharans took their place in the movement exciting Central Asia for a greater Turkic state. Fitrat, then Bukharan minister of education, undertook to reform madrasah instruction and hastily organized personnel to be trained for the young state[71] and sent them to German universities.

Policies followed by these Jadids-turned-Communist within the Bukharan People's Republic had finally applied the program advanced by Muslims from the Turkistan ASSR (Riskul-uulu and Narbutabek-oghli) at the Baku congress in September, 1920. Com-

[67] "Bukharskii s"ezd sovetov"; "Oktiabr'skie torzhestva v Bukhare," *Izvestiia* (November 27, 1920), p. 3.

[68] D. Soloveichik, p. 20.

[69] Castagne, "Le bolchevisme et l'Islam," p. 224.

[70] Abdullah Receb Baysun, *Turkistan milli hareketleri* (Istanbul, no publisher, 1943, 1945), pp. 63–64.

[71] Hayit, *Turkestan im XX. Jahrhundert*, p. 136.

munism should be adapted to the particular conditions of the East, including the integration of economic, social, intellectual, and, especially, religious structures within the socialist edifice; priority for the "nationality revolution" over the social revolution; leadership in the movement given to the local bourgeoisie in the absence of proletarian leaders; and tolerance for cooperation between levels of society in aspirations of nationality and in socialist plans. Komintern leadership had condemned these goals and brought the colonial revolution back to a more Marxist pattern by substituting hegemony of the poor peasantry for proletarian hegemony when proletarians did not exist.[72] How, having condemned in theory the theses of the Turkistan ASSR in Baku, could the Soviet government tolerate their application in Bukhara?

In 1920 the regime had to accept the Young Bukharans, just as it accepted Alash Orda and the Turkistan ASSR Jadids, to avoid a return to a situation similar to that which existed between 1917 and 1919. In 1920, with the Basmachi danger, the Soviet government could not contemplate a head-on clash with the people of Bukhara and was afraid of setting off an unprecedented popular explosion there.

In 1921–1923, the situation gradually changed. Foreign intervention was repulsed, and the international position of the Soviet government grew stronger. The European revolutions failing one after another, it became clear that socialism had to fall back, for a while at least, on the positions gained and try to develop toward the East. Under these circumstances, as Russian Marxists saw it, the power and unity of the Soviet government were absolute necessities. A strong state had to be built up again, and the centrifugal movements broken. It was also necessary to put an end to socialism "adapted to the particular conditions of the East" if the colonial world outside was not to be offered the example of a distorted, deeply anti-occidental socialism which was destroying the Marxist principle of proletarian unity. A rearrangement had to be effected in all the indigenous governments on the territory of the former Russian empire. Yet, while it was proper to use the Red Army to smash governments which were not basically socialist, it was not

[72] Carrère d'Encausse and Schram, ch. 3.

proper to smash people's republics militarily. That is why the integration of Central Asia came about mainly politically, by an attack on the "deviation" noted as early as 1922, inclining those Eastern lands toward nationalism more than toward socialism and the class struggle.[73]

BASMACHI PARTISANS AND ENVER PASHA

Complicating the Soviet integration of Central Asia was the Basmachi movement born in Farghana,[74] the very region which, some years before the revolution, had seen the development of a protest movement of peasant origin sparked by the dispossession and destitution of the local inhabitants.[75] This protest movement had never fully disappeared, and, as time passed had taken on a distinctly anti-Russian character. After the Khokand government fell, many Muslim leaders, fleeing the repression of the Red Army, joined the peasants, giving their struggle both a nationality and religious meaning.[76] Although the Turkic Commission attempted to rally Central Asians to its cause, Bolshevik moves from 1919 on were generally aimed at subjugating the Basmachi movement. Their efforts did not in the least hurt the Basmachis' popularity among the local people.

After 1920, the revolutions that broke out in Khiva and Bukhara had, above all, the effect of spreading the movement to new regions, and of bringing it new supporters, first Junaïd Khan, Alim Khan, and their partisans, then ever greater numbers of the Central Asian middle class, who were in power in 1920 and who were quickly flung back toward the Basmachis as a result of their clashes with the Russians. Finally, the wretched peasants of the people's republics, deceived by Soviet promises of agrarian reform which would never be carried out, were also attracted to the movement.

Yet, until the end of 1921, the Basmachis, while numerous and

[73] S. M. Dimanshtein, "Metody revoliutsionnoi i kommunisticheskoi propagandy na Vostoke," *Zhizn' natsional'nostei*, No. 14 (April 26, 1922).

[74] Baymirza Hayit, *Die nationalen regierungen von Kokand und der Alash Orda* (Muenster, University thesis, 1950), p. 101.

[75] P. G. Galuzo, *Turkestan koloniia* (Moscow, Izdanie Komm. Un-ta Trudiashchikhsia Vostoka imeni I. V. Stalina, 1929), p. 136.

[76] Joseph Castagne, *Les Basmatchis* (Paris, E. Leroux, 1925).

surrounded with sympathy, remained weak as a result of their internal divisions.[77] The movement contained a conglomeration of separate and often rival bands. In Farghana, several chiefs sought to establish some unity; in the mountains of eastern Bukhara, Mullah Muhammad Ibrahim Bek continued carrying on ancient rivalries with other tribes,[78] which did not simplify the task of Ibrahim Bek, who was named commander in chief of the insurgent troops by Alim Khan, deposed emir of Bukhara.

Early in 1921 Soviet troops seemed to be triumphing. Spectacular recruitment had taken place in 1920 throughout Farghana, where detachments of "Soviet Basmachis" had even been formed.[79] In September, 1920, they suddenly had turned their weapons against the authorities, but for a moment the movement had been weakened. In Bukhara, too, the Red Army achieved a few successes at first, and the press in Moscow was able to write: "The emir's territory is constricted from day to day . . . he now has but a group of some 600 men with him." [80]

But the situation changed quickly in Bukhara itself, where the Basmachis' resistance created a government crisis. Mirza Abdulqadir Muhitdin-oghli, one of the chief leaders of the Young Bukharan Party, and Muhitdin Maqsum-oghli, the republic's minister of police, joined rebel ranks, taking along with them a group of staunch supporters and police, in particular.[81] Young Bukharan unity was broken, and the question of supporting the insurrectional movement or remaining faithful to the revolution was posed. At the end of 1921, despite the rebels' internal quarrels, Basmachiism had spread and grown stronger.

It was shortly to find in Enver Pasha (1881–1922) a leader who would effect its unity for a time. This astonishing Turkish adventurer had had a very full and complex career long before being called by the Soviet authorities to pacify Central Asia. From his

[77] Mustafa Chokaev, "The basmaji movement in Turkestan," *The Asiatic Review* (London, 1928), XXIV, 284–85.

[78] [Emir] Alim Khan, *La voix de la Bukharie opprimee* (Paris, Maisonneuve, 1929), pp. 30, 35–38, 42, 43.

[79] K. Vasilevskii, "Fazy basmacheskogo dvizheniia v Srednei Azii," *Novyi Vostok*, XXIX (1929), 133.

[80] "Likvidatsiia emirskikh band," *Izvestiia* (February 20, 1921), p. 1.

[81] Hayit, *Turkestan im XX. Jahrhundert*, p. 182.

struggle in the Young Turk movement, he had acquired personal ambitions to which the triumph of his rival, Mustapha Kemal Ataturk, put an end. This, and the fact that he had known Radek in Berlin, may partly explain his accepting the Bolshevik invitation. He may also have thought he could impose himself on Turkey by first establishing himself among the Turkic people outside that country. In what way he could unify these Turkic people in a great Central Asian state he probably did not yet know himself when the Soviet leaders asked him to lend his prestige to rally Central Asian rebels to the Soviet government.

Arriving in Bukhara in November, 1921, Enver Pasha saw in the insurrectional movement the possibility of at last fulfilling his dream of revenge upon Mustapha Kemal. Instead of carrying out the mission entrusted to him, he organized an ostensible hunting trip, and used it to join the rebels. He took part of the Bukharan government with him, including Abdul Hamid Afandi, minister of war, and Ali Riza Bek, minister of the interior. His example was followed by Usman Khoja-oghli,[82] president of the republic, who journeyed to Istanbul to found a Committee for the Liberation of Bukhara.

Above all, Enver Pasha endeavored to unite the Basmachi movement by invoking "the struggle of all Muslims" and "the creation of a Central Asian Muslim state." He even gave Russia an ultimatum to abandon Central Asia. After some initial successes, Enver Pasha estranged a number of his allies by his pretentions and blunders. His signing of orders with the pompous title of "commander in chief of all Muslim troops, son-in-law of the Caliph, and representative of the Prophet,"[83] put him on bad terms with the emir, Alim Khan. Gradually, his coalition force fell to pieces, and he came to the point of battling with his former allies. Beaten at Baysun and isolated, Enver Pasha struggled for a few more months before being killed in April, 1922, at the battle of Baljuan.

Soviet troops, led by Simon Budennyi, took advantage of the shock caused by the death of this often hated but still prestigious leader to launch a series of attacks on the Basmachi groups. At the same time, the government, as in 1919, sought to win back the

[82] D. Soloveichik, p. 277.
[83] *Ibid.*, p. 284.

Central Asians by a series of measures rescinding unpopular provisions taken after the revolution. The Turkic Bureau of the Russian Communist Party Central Committee and the Turkic Commission decided that the confiscation of the waqf lands, which had upset Muslim sensitivities, would be repealed, Muslim institutions of learning were reopened, and courts based on the Shariat sat again.[84] Lenin's New Economic Policy permitted a rapid recovery in the Central Asians' material situation. These appeasement measures bore fruit. The people were tired of struggling, and the Basmachi movement, bereft of its popular foundations, gradually grew weaker without completely disappearing. After 1923, though, the problem presented by the rebels was resolved in a manner satisfactory enough to allow the Soviet government to begin the work of integrating Central Asia with the Union.

H. C. d'E.

[84] K. Vasilevskii, p. 135.

10 The National Republics Lose Their Independence

In March, 1923, the first conference of southern Central Asia's republics, the Turkistan ASSR, Bukharan People's Republic, and Khwarazm People's Republic, was held. It laid down a common economic policy for the participating states and organized to this end a Central Asian Economic Council. Currency, public transportation, and telecommunications for the Bukharan and Khwarazm people's republics were to be integrated in the Russian system. Irrigation, commerce, agriculture, and planning became a common domain for all of southern Central Asia. While still preserving the legal character of independent states, Bukhara and Khwarazm were already started irrevocably on the process of unification.[1] Furthermore, the vague outlines of political integration were also developing and 1923 was devoted to preventing any resistance on the part of local personnel.

In the Khwarazm republic after the purges of 1921, those capable of offering resistance to Soviet plans were infinitesimal in number. A few purges in 1922 further decimated the party and administration, and early in 1923, some thirty Russian Communists arrived in Khiva.[2] In October, 1923, the fourth congress modified the republic's constitution, depriving "parasitic" elements of the right to vote, and a year later, the fifth congress decided, under Red Army pressure (later described in a highly colored and perhaps

[1] Turar Ryskulov, "Ekonomicheskoe ob"edinenie sredneaziatskikh respublik," *Izvestiia* (March 28, 1923).
[2] Baymirza Hayit, *Turkestan im XX. Jahrhundert* (Darmstadt, Leske Verlag, 1956), p. 157.

suspect account),[3] to transform the people's republic into a socialist republic which would be integrated in the Soviet federation.

Liquidating the Bukharan People's Republic was more difficult. After a portion of the government had decamped with Enver Pasha, a new government had been formed under Faizullah Khoja-oghli (Khojaev), with Abdalrauf Fitrat as minister of foreign affairs. These two men, who had stayed in Bukhara to preserve what they could of its independence, sought aid on all sides. Informal discussions with Turkey and Afghanistan led to no positive results, and the Central Asian leaders remained all alone for the assault that they soon had to face.

After February 2, 1922, when the Bukharan Communist Party had been linked with the Russian one, purges crippled the Bukharan one just as the purges were striking the Communist organizations of the Turkistan ASSR and the Khwarazm republic. At the fourth "enlarged conference of responsible workers of the republics and nationality regions" in June, 1923, Stalin, attacking Sultan Galiev, denounced the government of Bukhara "which had nothing popular about it," and in July, Ia. E. Rudzutak, chairman of the Turkic Commission, obtained through the Bukharan Communist Party the arrest of all government leaders and a general purge of administrative personnel. The newly purged Bukharan party undertook to socialize the Bukharan regime. All the former officials, clerics, important merchants, and landowners were banned from the political community and deprived of the right to vote. Large business firms and then the personal properties of the well-to-do were confiscated while a start at agrarian reform was attempted.[4]

At last, on September 19, 1924, at the fifth congress, delegates voted unanimously to abolish the people's republic and replace it with a Soviet republic. They expressed the wish that the various nationalities making up the old emirate might henceforth be organized in their own national states. Seven years after the revolution which had seen the Russian empire burst apart, the Bolshevik

[3] G. Agabekov, *OGPU: The Russian Secret Terror* (New York, Brentano, 1931), p. 17.

[4] R. Abdushukurov, *Oktiabr'skaia revoliutsiia: Raztsvet uzbekskoi sotsialisticheskoi natsii i sblizhenie ee s natsiami SSSR* (Tashkent, Gospolit Izdatel'stvo Uzbekskoi SSR, 1962), pp. 32f.

government could think about restoring unity and about reorganizing in the framework of a Soviet federation the nationalities which
had struggled so fiercely for their independence. While the Soviet
government emerged victorious from this painful process leading
to the formation of the USSR, the people of Central Asia were all
the more vanquished in that they submitted to this defeat rather
deliberately.

The creation of an autonomous Turkmen region in 1921, then of
a Kirgiz region in April, 1922, opened the way to reorganizing
Central Asia on the basis of nationality. Yet, while the Soviet authorities, uneasy about attempts at a Muslim unification which were
vaguely discernible between 1920 and 1924,[5] obviously recognized
the necessity of territorial and political reorganization, their projects were far from tallying with local aspirations. Kazakh nationalists defended the idea of a greater Kazakhstan; Kirgiz and Uzbeks
wished similarly for a greater Kirgizia and a greater Uzbekistan.
The young Khivans were struggling for a greater Khwarazm embracing the Uzbeks of the Turkistan ASSR, while the most representative leaders of Bukhara were split in favor of an independent
Bukharan Islamic state and a greater Turkistan bringing together
the Uzbeks of Turkistan ASSR, the Bashkirs, and the Kirgiz.[6]

After the dissolution of the people's republics, the Soviet solution
became apparent from the votes cast in the last congress, following
the line adopted since 1922: replacement of a united Central Asia
with small national republics. In October, 1924, the Central Executive Committee of the USSR voted to establish two socialist republics: Uzbekistan, including the central part of old Bukhara, the
southern part of old Khiva, and the regions of Samarkand, Farghana,
Amu Darya, and Sir Darya formerly included in the guberniia of
Turkistan; and Turkmenistan, which regrouped the Turkmen regions
of western Bukhara, Khwarazm, and the former Transcaspian region.
Voted also were two autonomous republics: Tajikistan, with the
mountainous regions of former Bukhara having an essentially Shiite,

---

[5] E. H. Carr, *History of Soviet Russia* (London, MacMillan, 1954), pp.
286–87.
   [6] S. Radzhabov, "Etapy razvitiia sovetskogo gosudarstvennogo stroia v
Srednei Azii," *Sovetskoe gosudarstvo i pravo*, No. 11 (November 1948), p. 66.

Iranian-speaking population; and Kazakhstan which replaced the republic formed in 1920. Lastly, they called for two autonomous regions: the Qara-Kirgiz, which became, August 25, 1925, the Kirgiz Autonomous Oblast, and May 25, 1926, the Kirgiz Autonomous Republic; and the Karakalpak Autonomous Oblast, linked first to the Kazakh ASSR, then in 1932 becoming the Karakalpak Autonomous Soviet Socialist Republic attached to the Russian SFSR before becoming a part of the Uzbek SSR in 1936.[7] In the following years this structure was completed by the accession of certain autonomous republics and regions to the rank of federated socialist republics. December 5, 1929, Tajikistan became the seventeenth republic of the Soviet Union; December 5, 1936, the same status came to the Kirgiz republic and to Kazakhstan.

Yet these territorial dispositions, in which the very name of Turkistan, the symbol of unification, disappeared, neither immediately shattered all unity nor promptly eliminated the national leaders who had struggled for unity or independence. The ties which continued to exist for a time were political, cultural, and social. Two organizations instrumental in putting an end to the independence of the people's republics and contributing to the regrouping of all southern Central Asia under Soviet authority were the Economic Council of Central Asia and the Central Asian Bureau of the Communist Party of the Soviet Union. Useful before 1924, these organizations later were the means for a unified policy against the Russians. In 1934, both were dissolved, because, it was said, they no longer were appropriate for the stage of evolution then achieved by the national republics of Central Asia.

Unity, however, also continued to exist on the religious level. The elimination of the Arabic alphabet had, in this respect, an essentially political significance. Harsh measures were taken against Islam, a unifying factor, because the problem was particularly grave in most of Central Asia. The people's devotion to Islam was boundless and the new authority had long feared to oppose these popular sentiments directly. Although created in 1924, groups of Allahsizlar or Khudasizlar (Godless) did not appear openly until 1928–1930

[7] I. Khodorov, "Natsional'noe razmezhevanie Srednei Azii," *Novyi Vostok*, No. 8/9 (1925), pp. 68f.

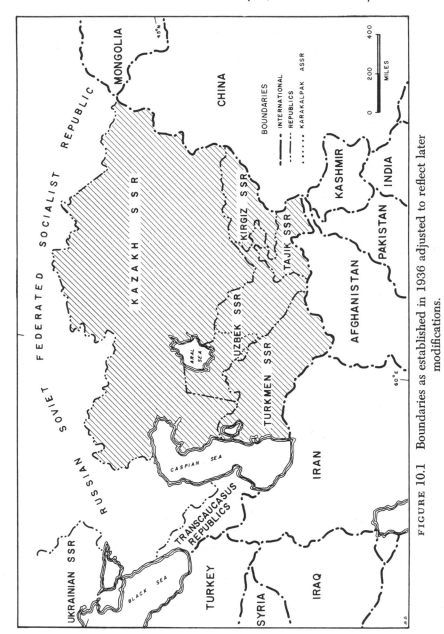

FIGURE 10.1   Boundaries as established in 1936 adjusted to reflect later modifications.

when the government had managed to deal with *waqf* and the Shariat. The problem of *waqf* was tied closely to that of property.[8] It was cleared up by stages, but only in 1930 did *waqfs* disappear.

Putting an end to the canonical jurisdictions and then attracting the populace to Soviet courts was still more difficult.[9] In November, 1920, Stalin had promised Temir Khan Shora not to disturb the Shariat:

We know that the enemies of the Soviet regime are spreading rumors according to which the Soviet regime is getting ready to abolish the Shariat. I must declare here, in the name of the Russian SFSR, that these rumors are untrue. . . . The Soviet government looks upon the Shariat as customary law (?) similar to that in effect among other people of Russia.[10]

Stalin notwithstanding, after 1921, Soviet authorities had undertaken to limit the jurisdiction of the Shariat tribunals, but internal difficulties had led them some months later to reconsider these measures. In October, 1924, at the time of the Central Asian territorial reorganization, new provisions limited the competence of the tribunals again and began to require that their procedure come into line with those of Soviet courts. The year 1925–1926 saw a development of Soviet tribunals in the new republics and a reduction in the number of canonical tribunals. Finally, a decree of September 21, 1927, deprived Shariat courts of the resources and power to enforce their sentences, and refused to recognize such sentences. Soviet law now compelled recognition everywhere.

RECALCITRANCE IN THE PLAINS

This transformation of society, of its way of life and thought, this split with the Islamic community and the past, this dislocation of Central Asia, was not easy to impose upon the indigenous population, however. In the plains, when the former leaders of Alash

[8] L. Shteinberg, *Ocherki istorii turkmenii* (Moscow, Gosudarstvennoe Sotsialisticheskoe Ekonomicheskoe Izdatel'stvo, 1934) pp. 116–17.

[9] Z. Bikkulova, "Bor'ba part-organizatsii Karakalpakii za preodolenie patriarkhal'no-feodal'nykh otnoshenii v bytu," *Nauchnye trudy aspirantov* (Tashkent, Tashkentskii Gosudarstvennyi Universitet imeni V. I. Lenina, 1962), pp. 37–40.

[10] I. Stalin, *Sochineniia* (Moscow, Gosudarstvennoe Izdatel'stvo Politicheskoi Literatury, 1947), IV, 395.

Orda had rallied to Soviet authority, they entered the government and the Communist Party of Kazakhstan in numbers. For a few years they dominated the cultural life of the country, striving to protect the integrity and individuality of Kazakh society.

After 1924, a series of conflicts kept them in constant opposition to the Russian personnel. They were especially dismayed over the settling of the nomads, the brutality and excesses of which process they denounced, and the class struggle which they fiercely opposed: "It is with terror that I hear people speak of the need for a social revolution in Kazakhstan," a Kazakh leader had said, "socialism in our land will only be demagogy. We want social peace in the Kazakh village instead of class struggles!" [11]

Open conflict broke out in 1928, after the Kazakh government, directed by the local Communist Party, had taken, in 1927, very rigorous measures by way of agrarian reform in opposition to the Russian and Ukrainian settlers. The reaction of the Soviet government was instantaneous. At the sixth regional party conference, November, 1927, the activity of the opposition and the platform of the "Trotskyite-Zinoviev bloc," [12] which had been apparent at the fifth conference, were condemned. All the Kazakh leaders were then removed, and the Kazakh Party Secretariat was turned over to a Russian Bolshevik, F. I. Goloshchokin, who applied himself to the work of settling the nomads—without notable success. He was in turn dismissed in 1932 in favor of the Armenian C. I. Mirzoyan, who replaced the Kazakhs in the government with Europeans.

But the local leadership had already been broken before being physically liquidated (beginning in 1935); and it could no longer fight. The population at large, crushed by the famine of 1921 and the economic consequences of the "sedentarization" after 1928, could resist no more. Human losses suffered in this tragic period, plus the almost total disappearance of the national leadership after 1938, and the influx of Russian and Ukrainian peasants and workers after World War II, changed the countenance of the Kazakh people once and for all and insured their integration in the Soviet ensemble.

[11] Hayit, *Turkestan im XX. Jahrhundert*, pp. 256–59.
[12] *Istoriia kazakhskoi SSR, epokha sotsializma* (Alma Ata, Izdatel'stvo Akademii Nauk Kazakhskoi SSR, 1963), p. 298.

The destiny of the Kirgiz after 1924 was hardly different. The role given national leaders had seemed important when the republic was created. The government and party were at first in the hands of Kirgiz, and a Kirgiz, Turar Riskul-uulu, collaborated with Stalin in 1922 at the Moscow Commissariat of Nationalities as assistant commissar, and then became vice-president of the Council of Ministers for the Russian SFSR.

FIGURE 10.2   National Communist Turar Riskul-uulu

As in Kazakhstan, the Russian conflict with the Kirgiz grew up around settling the nomads and collectivization, which here again were reflected by destruction of cattle and resulting famine. After 1928–1930, national leadership had been eliminated, and in 1935, Abdulkerim Sidik-uulu, one of the Kirgiz directors of planning, was accused of having guided an armed counterrevolutionary movement against collectivization. Indicted for the sin of "Sydykovshchina," named after Sidik-uulu, all the leading Kirgiz were liquidated. In

Moscow, Riskul-uulu disappeared in the turmoil of 1937 and another heresy, "Ryskulovshchina" was generated. And so, after 1928, the struggle in the plains and uplands in which Soviet authority opposed the leading local citizens drew to a close with the liquidation of those Central Asians able to head the resistance.

DESTRUCTION OF THE NATIONAL LEADERSHIP IN THE SOUTH

In Uzbekistan, the Jadids had for the most part rallied to the Soviet government in 1924, and the first president of the repub-

FIGURE 10.3   National Communist Faizullah Khoja-oghli.

lic was Faizullah Khoja-oghli, who had sustained the Bukharan People's Republic for four years. Here, opposition to Soviet authority was, as in the plains, economic, social, and cultural at the same time. The first clashes were over the politico-literary aspirations of the Chaghatay group mustered around the old literary language of Western Turkistan, which this group wanted to resuscitate for distinctly nationalistic purposes.

The economic and social conflict had its origin in the raising of cotton, which the Soviet regime sought to emphasize, as the czarist government had done before it.[13] Local personnel who, at the time of the revolution, had seen the perils of economic dependency based on monoculture stirred up the population against orders coming from the central government. Behind the cotton problem, sensed Soviet leaders, was fierce national resistance. What the Uzbeks wanted to save was their integrity in every domain.

From 1930 on, the conflict was in the open. It ended in 1938 in Moscow when Faizullah Khoja-oghli, who had once presided over the Central Executive Committee of the USSR, and Akmal Ikram-oghli (Ikramov) First Secretary of the Uzbek Communist Party, were convicted in a show trial of "the Trotskyite and Rightist bloc" and executed March 13, 1938, along with N. I. Bukharin and A. I. Rykov. In Uzbekistan, too, the elimination of most educated national cadres followed the example of these spectacular executions. Thus ended Russian collaboration with the national figures which for many of these people had begun right after the revolution.

During the collectivization drive between 1930 and 1936 the Tajik SSR saw a rebirth of the Basmachi movement which had been thought to be totally destroyed. Numbers of peasants joined the rebels in the mountains, and it took Soviet forces years to subjugate them. Two waves of purges decimated Tajik ranks suspected of open sympathy for the Basmachis. In 1933, Nasratullah Maqsum, president of the republic, and Abdurrahim Hajjibay-zada, his prime minister, were accused by the Central Committee of the Communist Party of the Soviet Union of having "lacked vigilance" and of bearing responsibility for the agricultural failures. Moreover, they were convicted of harboring national, chauvinistic, and anti-Russian feelings. After their removal, which was accompanied by divers purges, the situation underwent few changes. The Basmachi movement continued, and when it was finally smashed, a number of insurgents fled into neighboring Afghanistan. Also, in 1937, a second purge liquidated what was left of the national leadership. President of the republic Shotemar, and Prime Minister Rahimbay-zada, were ac-

[13] A. Nuritov, "Pervyi s"ezd kolkhoznikov udarnikov Uzbekistana," and "K voprosu o kharaktere i formakh klassovoi bor'by v uzbekskom kishlake," *Nauchnye trudy aspirantov* (Tashkent, 1962), pp. 219–31, 231–45.

cused of "national deviations," of being "Trotskyites" and "Bukharin-ites." Among their most prominent associates, the minister of public education, Hassan-zada, and his assistant, the minister of industry, Qurban-zada, and three secretaries of the Tajik Communist Party disappeared.[14]

Turkmenistan, too, experienced the tragic liquidations. A national opposition apparently had extended its organization quite far, between 1930 and 1935, demanding elaborate political autonomy, and the abandonment of the Turkmen language in favor of either the Turkish spoken in Anatolia, or a language of a more literary character based on ancient traditions.[15] In 1936, the president of the Supreme Soviet of Turkmenistan, Nederbi Aitak-oghli, was denounced for having protected, it was said, the sabotage of collectivization. He was executed, and most Turkmen national leaders were removed from power.

Developments in Central Asia from 1924 to 1934 were thus divided into two periods which overlap everywhere in almost the same way. From 1924 to 1928, the majority of the national leaders tried to salvage what they could of their earlier hopes within the republic governments. In this respect, the interrogation of Faizullah Khoja-oghli at the time of his trial revealed much, between forced confessions and disavowals, about how he had been led from the local struggle to cooperation with the Bolsheviks hoping that the presence of Central Asian personnel would prevent the Russians from seizing the machinery of local power. After 1928 his story is the whole recent history of Central Asia. He had been impelled to oppose collectivization and measures preached by the Soviet authorities concerning the economy and the class struggle, so that the autonomy of his country might be preserved here too. Everywhere the co-operation begun in 1924 led to conflict from about 1928–1930, when it was a question of imposing the Soviet order, and ended with the liquidation of national elites.

Yet, whereas the Kazakh plain seems to have been wracked to the core in this period, southern Central Asia, on emerging from the

[14] *Materialy k istorii tadzhikskogo naroda v sovetskii period* (Stalinabad, Tadzhgosizdat, 1954), pp. 120f.

[15] A. Potseluevskii, "Iazykostroitel'stvo Turkmenii i ego osnovnye problemy," *Revoliutsiia i natsional'nosti*, No. 67 (September 1935), pp. 42–50.

terrible years of purges and even at the present time, offers a somewhat different picture. This region, regardless of the Tajik presence,
appears as the last coherent Turkic bastion of the Soviet Union.
Owing to its geographic configuration, Russian colonization has
been less developed here, and the number of non-Muslims remains
relatively low. Above all, the local elites which survived the purges,
sometimes at the price of spectacular abjurations, have continued to
assure the national traditions and thus have erected a bridge between
the leadership liquidated in 1937–1938 and the younger generation.
After a century of close contacts with Russia, southern Central Asia
seems to be the last and most secure refuge of the active sense of
nationality among the former Muslim people of the USSR.

H. C. d'E.

11

Agricultural Development

The great contrasts represented in the physical environment and the economic development of Central Asia make some nomenclature for division of the area into subregions convenient in the examination of its problems. Czarist authorities employed this device, dividing Central Asia into the guberniia of the Steppe and the guberniia of Turkistan. This distinction has been continued within slightly different boundaries by Soviet authorities, who treat the area as two separate economic regions, Kazakhstan and "Central Asia," the latter for them consisting of Uzbekistan, Tajikistan, Turkmenistan, and Kirgizistan. Central Asia during the czarist period can be divided into two regions, one, the "Kazakh plains" or "northern Central Asia," corresponding to the guberniia of the Steppe including much of Semirechie, and the other, "southern Central Asia," corresponding to the guberniia of Turkistan including Transcaspia. In the Soviet period the term "Kazakhstan" applies to the northern region, and designation "southern Central Asia" specifies the area covered by the four southern republics, whose boundaries do not embrace the foothills of the Central Asian mountains, and the cities of Alma Ata, Chimkent, and Jambil, all included in the czarist guberniia of Turkistan.

In the southern areas, agriculture is possible only with irrigation except on limited sections of hill slopes, but there are substantial quantities of water available for farming, especially along the edge of the mountains and near the major rivers. In the early days of Central Asian agriculture, presumably land subject to natural river flooding or areas watered by springs were used first, and are still cultivated in the water-spring (*bulaq*) agriculture of central Kazakhstan. Zones of flooding along rivers provided the best conditions for agriculture, because the fertile silt carried down from the mountains added to the productivity of river bank soil. Along the lower Amu Darya, farming of naturally flooded areas (*kair*) still continues in some localities; however, the greatest advances have taken place in areas of artificial irrigation. With the development of an organized society capable of undertaking the communal effort required to construct and maintain large-scale irrigation systems, agriculture spread farther and farther from the original cultivated areas at the river banks.

When the Russians arrived in Central Asia they found traces of complex irrigation systems which had been destroyed or had been allowed to deteriorate and eventually abandoned. One was on the right bank of the lower Amu Darya, another in the Mirzachol Sahra west of Tashkent. Around the site of ancient Merv (Mari) there were also indications of vanished agriculture. Much of the irrigation system of Central Asia had in fact been destroyed in the thirteenth century by Chingis Khan and had never been restored or had been neglected and allowed to fall into disrepair because of unsettled conditions. Thus, by no means all the irrigable lands produced crops at the time of the Russian arrival, and may not have been needed, for the population in the settled areas at that date was already apparently being adequately fed from the tracts actually under irrigation.

Extensive canal networks functioned in the Farghana Valley, along the Zarafshan, the lower Amu Darya, the Murghab and the Tejen, and in the oases along the foot of the Kopet Dagh. Smaller irrigated areas flourished on the Qara Darya and the Chirchiq. Many of the main canals (Uzbek: *änhat*) stretched great distances; for example, the Shährikhan Say, one of fifty canals from the Qara Darya, extended over sixty-five miles. Most of these canals bore the title of *say* (stream), *suw* (water), or *ariq* (canal), the last Uzbek term designating all sizes of irrigation canals and ditches. An *ustä* (master) supervised the construction of these canals. He possessed no instruments for leveling, but lay on the ground and used his big toe as a sight lining on the head of a man standing some 400 yards away in order to determine the best route for the canal

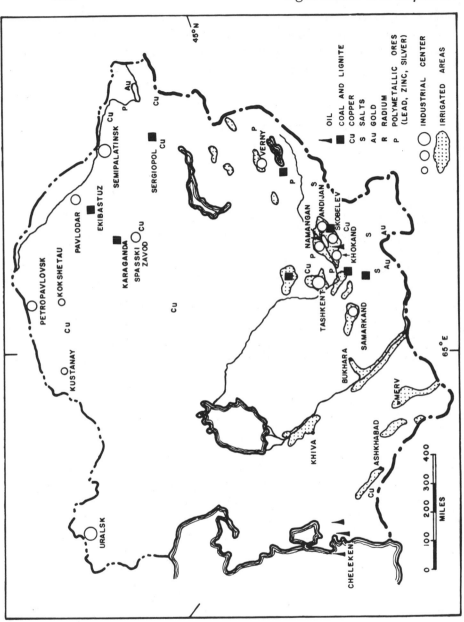

FIGURE 11.1 Irrigation, mining, and industry, 1910. The sizes of circles designating industrial centers are in proportion to the value of production.

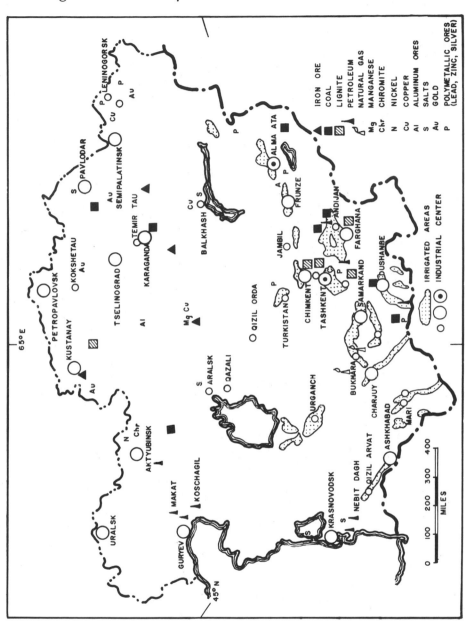

FIGURE 11.2 Irrigation, mining, and industry, 1962. The sizes of circles designating industrial centers are in proportion to the value of production.

to follow and to allow for a slight gradient in its flow.[1] Often canals would meander over the countryside to avoid slight rises in the ground. This irregularity made the canal needlessly long and its undue length led to the evaporation of a large amount of water from the surface. Loss due to ground seepage was also high.

The only large dams (Tajik: *band*) were on the Murghab and Tejen rivers. The Qaziqli Band irrigated the Iolotan oasis, and the Koushut Khan Band served the oasis of Merv, both athwart the lower Murghab. The Karri Band on the lower Tejen completed the number of permanent dams. The Sultan Band or Band-i Merv on the Murghab, built in the twelfth century and destroyed along with the city of Merv in 1784 by the emir of Bukhara, Shah Murad, was not in use when the Russians arrived in the area.

In general, small diversion dikes made of trestles filled with brushwood and stones were used to shunt water into the mouth (*suw bashi*) of the canals. Where water had to be raised to fields from a canal or river whose level lay below the land, a large wheel with a row of pots attached to its rim (*chighir*) was operated. This device could lift water almost the height of its own diameter, and was generally driven by camels, donkeys, or horses. The employment of draft animals meant that in some areas land and water which could have been devoted to raising food for humans had to be used in growing fodder. The *chighir* gave service mainly in the Khiva oasis, along the lower Amu Darya, at Karki and Charjuy farther up the river, and also on the lower Sir Darya.

Maintaining a major canal and its system of distribution canals and irrigation ditches required never-ending attention. When the water entered the canal system its flow diminished and it deposited much of the silt carried in suspension. This silt, which constantly required removal, was used to fertilize the fields, but in some areas it was piled up along the banks of the canals to such a height that further canal cleaning became impossible and a new channel had to be dug. Silt also piled up behind dams and filled reservoirs, especially on rivers such as the Murghab, where it was reported that

[1] L. Golomb, *Die Bodenkultur in Ost-Turkestan* (Posieux, Switzerland. Anthropos Institute, 1959), pp. 60–61.

the reservoir behind the dam built by the Russians in 1910 had become completely silted up by 1932.[2]

Smaller canals and ditches leading into individually owned fields remained the farmer's responsibility, but the cleaning of the main canals was a communal task. Every winter each family had to supply an able-bodied man for a period of two to two and a half months for maintaining and improving the irrigation system. No pay was given and the worker provided his own tools, reeds, and brushwood. Second- and third-stage canals were cleaned at the end of February, and the main canals in March, so that the farmer would have his irrigation ditches in order by the time water was let into the distribution canals. Until then, small dams prevented water from entering the distribution canals and irrigation ditches from the main canal, which was never emptied of its water. When cleaning operations terminated, these dams were torn away.[3]

Along the northern edge of the Kopet Dagh, irrigation water came from the rain which had collected in the alluvial fans along the foothills of the mountains, and it was tapped by a series of underground tunnels (*karizes*). Such tunnels, constructed almost exclusively by professional workers, reached Western Turkistan from eastern Iran. In western Iran the same system is known as *qanat*. The Turkmens brought back Iranian prisoners seized in forays over the border and set them to work to find water, they themselves not being skilled at this kind of work. A settlement would be supplied by a whole series of tunnels, each with a row of shafts or wells to enable the men who built and maintained the tunnel to reach them. At the turn of the century around Ashkhabad there were so many of these shafts that cattle and even camels fell into them.[4] In 1948 an earthquake destroyed the tunnel system of Ashkhabad, but even before that the supply of water to the area had been insufficient. The Soviet decision to extend the Qara Qum Canal

[2] P. Skosyrev, *Soviet Turkmenistan* (Moscow, Foreign Languages Publishing House, 1956), pp. 154, 155.

[3] L. Kostenko, *Sredniaia Aziia i vodvorenie v nei russkoi grazhdanstvennosti* (St. Petersburg, Izdatel'stvo Bazunova, 1870), pp. 168–69.

[4] E. E. Skorniakov, in *Aziatskaia Rossiia* (St. Petersburg, Pereselencheskoe Upravlienie Glavnago Upravlieniia Zemleustroistva i Zemledieliia, 1914), II, 239–40.

from the Amu Darya to Ashkhabad reflected the general lack of water in the area.[5]

Statistics concerning the amount of land irrigated during the period of Russian control before 1917 are inexact, but some districts seem to be represented acceptably in Table 11.1. The major limita-

TABLE 11.1

Irrigated Areas of Southern Central Asia (*in Acres*)

	1903	1913	1913–1914
Guberniia of Turkistan	5,899,500	7,581,600	8,159,400
(Farghana Oblast)	(2,565,000)	(2,468,000)	(2,516,400)
Emirate of Bukhara	1,080,000	4,320,000	4,860,000
Khanate of Khiva	540,000	945,000	810,000
Total	7,519,500	12,846,600	13,829,400

Source: Figures for 1903 from A. I. Dmitriev-Mamonov, *Putevoditel' po Turkestanu i sredne-aziatskoi zheleznoi doroge* (St. Petersburg, Ministerstvo Voennoe: Puti Soobshcheniia, 1903), pp. 67–68. Figures for 1913 from *Aziatskaia Rossiia* (St. Petersburg, Pereselencheskoe Upravlienie Glavnago Upravlieniia Zemleustroistva i Zemledieliia, 1914), II, 244–245, and V. P. Semenov-Tian-Shanskii, ed., *Rossiia: polnoe geograficheskoe opisanie nashego otechestva* (St. Petersburg, Devrien, 1913), XIX, 426–28. Figures for 1913–14 from V. Suvorov, *Istoriko-ekonomicheskii ocherk razvitiia Turkestana* (Tashkent, Gosizdat UzSSR, 1962), p. 68.

tions of the table appear in the estimates for irrigated land in the state of Bukhara, where no accurate surveys seem to have been recorded. Discrepancies evident in the figures for Farghana oblast are not quite so great. It is certain that the irrigated area of Central Asia expanded during the Russian period before 1917, although one source showed an expansion of 815,000 acres of irrigated land in Central Asia between 1870 and 1917, and another Soviet authority cites a total area of 7.4 million acres (2,741,000 *desiatin*) in 1913, both of which look very low when compared with the figures given in Table 11.1.[6] Yet another report about the irrigated area in the Turkistan guberniia indicated increases on the average of one and a half times between 1894 and 1914, the Samarkand, Farghana,

[5] P. Skosyrev, pp. 123–24.

[6] R. A. Lewis, "The Irrigation Potential of Soviet Central Asia," *Annals of the Association of American Geographers,* vol. LII, No. 1 (March, 1962), p. 100.

and Sir Darya oblasts showing a total addition to irrigated land of 1,968,000 acres (729,000 *desiatin*) between 1894 and 1914.[7]

The first major Russian survey of irrigable Central Asian land was conducted in the Mirzachol Sahra where, in 1869, 405,000 acres (150,000 *desiatin*) were declared fit for irrigation. In 1874 local laborers began digging a canal from the Sir Darya, but the project failed in 1879, because the Russians had followed the practice of the khans in using a system known as *häsär* involving masses of unpaid labor. The work seems to have been too heavy, and a certain local recalcitrance also helped bring on the negative outcome of the effort. An attempt to build an irrigation canal from the Sir Darya in 1886 also failed due to serious engineering deficiencies. More successful was the attempt to improve and extend the canal which led off from the left bank of the Sir Darya at present-day Bekabad (Begovat). This permitted the irrigation of about 32,400 acres (12,000 *desiatin*) of the Mirzachol Sahra when the canal, known as the Imperator Nikolai I Canal, was finished in 1898.[8] In 1913 the Romanovskii Canal, which incorporated the Imperator Nikolai I Canal into its system, was completed with the aim of irrigating 121,500 acres (45,000 *desiatin*) in the northeastern part of the Mirzachol Sahra. It was planned eventually to irrigate about 216,000 acres (80,000 *desiatin*) of the Mirzachol Sahra, but three years later only about 75,600 acres (28,000 *desiatin*) were actually being watered by this system.[9] Another try at irrigating the Qizil Qum by diverting water along the dried-up bed of the Janga Darya, one of the arms of the Sir Darya near Qizil Orda (Pcrovsk), resulted only in the formation of new acres of swampland.[10]

Excluding the Mirzachol Sahra irrigation, the most successful czarist scheme was implemented in the Murghab Imperial Domain. This project envisaged restoration of the Sultan Band, key

[7] V. Suvorov, *Istoriko-ekonomicheskii ocherk razvitiia Turkestana* (Tashkent, Gosizdat UzSSR, 1962), p. 68.

[8] *Aziatskaia Rossiia*, II, 247–49.

[9] V. P. Semenov-Tian-Shanskii, ed., *Rossiia: polnoe geograficheskoe opisanie nashego otechestva:* vol. XIX, *Turkestanskii Krai* (St. Petersburg, Devrien, 1913), p. 428; *Aziatskaia Rossiia: Atlas*, plate 45; A. M. Aminov, *Ekonomicheskoe razvitie Srednei Azii (kolonial'nyi period)* (Tashkent, 1959), p. 234.

[10] *Aziatskaia Rossiia*, II, 247–48.

to the canal system of Merv. In 1887, 281,000 acres (104,000 *desiatin*) of irrigable land along the right bank of the Murghab were declared imperial land, and work soon began on reconstructing the dam. It burst, however, shortly after being opened in 1890, and a second dam, the Hindu Kush, was built in 1895 about thirteen miles downstream, creating a reservoir which fed a seventeen-mile-long canal irrigating 38,000 acres (14,000 *desiatin*). Later, the Sultan Band was repaired and the Iolotan Band completed in 1909. In all, about 66,000 acres (25,000 *desiatin*) or 24 percent of the total area of the Imperial Domain were under irrigation by 1913.[11] Large quantities of silt and the irregular flow of the river caused many difficulties met by irrigation engineers in developing this project. Half of the sown area in the Imperial Domain was planted to cotton in 1910, and most of the remainder was under grain and a little alfalfa.[12] Tenant farmers working this land gave 50 percent of their harvest as rent and received water and cotton seed in exchange. The cotton was ginned at plants on the domain in an early attempt to integrate the processing of cotton from ginning to the production of oil, cattle cake, fuel briquettes, and cotton lint;[13] however, the area irrigated was small, and both the Murghab and the Mirzachol Sahra schemes fell far short of their designers' hopes by adding only a small increment to the irrigated land of Central Asia. Still other ambitious plants failed to reach fulfillment.[14]

COTTON AND GRAIN

The Russian desire to increase irrigated acreage was tantamount to a wish to increase cotton production. Supplies of imported cotton began to diminish around the time of the American Civil War, and the Russians decided to concentrate their efforts upon expanding the cotton-growing districts in the Caucasus and Central Asia in order to free themselves from reliance on sources of supply outside the empire. One of the main centers supplying cotton to

[11] V. P. Semenov-Tian-Shanskii, XIX, 430.

[12] *Ibid.*, p. 648.

[13] *Aziatskaia Rossiia*, II, 250.

[14] R. A. Pierce, *Russian Central Asia, 1867–1917* (Berkeley and Los Angeles, University of California Press, 1960), pp. 179–82.

Russia became the Farghana oblast when the area sown to cotton there rose from 14 percent of the land farmed in 1885 to 44 percent in 1915. This extension of the cotton-growing tracts appropriated lands previously used for raising sorghum, alfalfa, and rice rather than grains such as wheat. In the Zarafshan Valley, cotton occupied 25 percent of the total irrigated area in 1909.[15] In the 1913–1914 period, however, despite the concentration of cotton in the Farghana and Zarafshan valleys, only 13 percent of the Turkistan guberniia's irrigated acreage was sown to cotton and 82 percent to grain, and in the emirate of Bukhara grain covered 89 percent of the arable land. In both cases wheat accounted for about half of the area sown to grain.[16] Although a large portion of the irrigated land continued to be used for grain, the area sown to cotton steadily increased from the 1880s until 1917, with some fluctuations notably around the turn of the century when falling world prices caused some diminution in the areas sown to cotton.

The fact that in 1884 about 810 acres (300 *desiatin*) in Central Asia were sown with American cotton, and by 1890 no less than 158,992 acres (58,859 *desiatin*), underscored Russian determination to substitute American for local cotton as rapidly as possible.[17] By 1900–1901, 93.4 percent of the total cotton area of Farghana oblast grew American cotton, and Farghana oblast contained no less than 74 percent of the cotton fields in the Russian-controlled oblasts, if Russian figures are accurate.[18] Between 1902 and 1913 the cotton lands in Farghana oblast increased by 71 percent, and with the introduction of better varieties of cotton the yield increased from 160 lbs. per acre (12 *pud* per *desiatin*) in 1875 to 1,136 lbs. per acre (80 *pud* per *desiatin*) in 1915.[19] This compares with an average yield of about 2,230 lbs. per acre (25 *centner* per hectare) in Soviet Central Asia at present, and over 3,000 lbs. per acre in the irrigated areas of the American Southwest.

[15] *Istoriia uzbekskoi SSR* (Tashkent, Izdatel'stvo Akademii Nauk Uzbekskoi SSR, 1956), vol. I, Book 2, p. 211.

[16] Suvorov, p. 69.

[17] Semenov-Tian-Shanskii, XIX, 458.

[18] A. I. Dmitriev-Mamonov, *Putevoditel' po Turkestanu i sredne-aziatskoi zheleznoi doroge* (St. Petersburg, Ministerstvo Voennoe: Puti Soobshcheniia, 1903), pp. 80, 83.

[19] Suvorov, p. 71.

Along with the increase in cotton acreage, the areas sown to grain also expanded. Rice growing became more important between 1880 and 1917 and provided an income second only to cotton for the local farmer. About 40 percent of the Central Asian rice crop went to Russia. In Semirechie and other dry-farming areas a big increase in grain harvests took place after 1900, and the total grain harvest of southern Central Asia rose from about 2.2 million tons (138.6 million *pud*) in 1900 to 4.3 million tons (264 million *pud*) in 1915, or almost double in fifteen years.[20]

Although the Central Asian farmer knew the basic principles of irrigated agriculture, the lack of tools and equipment limited his effectiveness. Leveling fields was difficult, and in uneven ground, hollows received too much water and hillocks too little. Farmers never undertook the draining of surplus water from the fields, and salinization or the development of swamps often resulted. In 1911, irrigation water covering 270,000 acres on the left bank of the Chirchiq near Tashkent created a swamp, and fertile sections in Semirechie also became salinized.[21] The only digging tool known to the Central Asian laborer was a kind of hoe or spade (*ketman*), consisting of a round iron blade fastened at right angles to the end of a long handle. Other tools were a wooden harrow (*molä*), used for leveling and sealing the soil, and the sickle (*oraq*), used for harvesting grain and alfalfa. A primitive plow with a small iron-tipped plowshare (*amach*) was pulled by a pair of oxen (*qosh*) to prepare the fields for cotton. This type of plow was quite suitable for the arid conditions of Central Asia, because it did not open the soil too much and thus allow excessive evaporation of soil moisture.

After ridges had been made in the soil, water was allowed to flow along the furrows between them in a method of irrigation still used universally for cultivated crops. Alfalfa and rice were grown in specially leveled and diked fields under basin irrigation with the whole tract being flooded to a uniform depth. Rice was often raised in swampy areas along the rivers. Between 1870 and 1899 large amounts of water were diverted for growing rice by

[20] *Ibid.*, pp. 73–74.
[21] *Aziatskaia Rossiia*, II, 236.

farmers situated at the head of many irrigation canals, and flooding became so widespread in the Zarafshan basin that malaria developed and caused many deaths around 1892–1893.[22]

Crop rotation was practiced little in Central Asia at this period. Dry-farming lands were, however, occasionally left fallow to rest the soil and conserve soil moisture after a few consecutive years of grain growing. A distinction was made between fallow land plowed every spring and autumn (*shudgar*) and unworked fallow land (*zayk*). In some places, only one-third to one-half of the land was sown to grain each year, and in the irrigated zones a few large landowners alternated their crops, but generally where sufficient water and fertilizer were available, no rotation occurred.[23] Fertilizer consisted mainly of silt from rivers or canals and the remains of old loess walls. Pigeon droppings were sometimes applied to melon patches, vegetables, and alfalfa, but animal dung was then considered more valuable as a fuel than as a soil additive.

LAND TENURE AND WATER RIGHTS

Land use in Central Asia was not only affected by prevailing agricultural methods, but also by the land tenure system. Although based on certain simple principles, land tenure was in fact complex, varying from region to region, with the confusion magnified by the absence of pertinent legal documents or organization. As in most Muslim countries the Shariat governed land tenure rules, which were to a certain extent modified by local custom (*adat*).

Under Muslim law the head of the state, the khan or the emir, actually owned the land. This state land was known as *ämlak*. Any form of landholding by a private person reflected this fact. The ruler also maintained some territory which was cultivated for his own personal use; moreover, he also directly controlled all land which had never been irrigated and cultivated, and took possession of any land left when the owner died without an heir. Much of the uncultivated state land consisted of desert, plains, and mountain areas. These were in permanent communal use by the no-

[22] Semenov-Tian-Shanskii, XIX, 446.
[23] *Ibid.*, p. 435.

mads, who also could become owners of any of this land which they permanently irrigated or cultivated. This principle applied in general to everyone who irrigated and cultivated any waste land, and a tax on this land was due to the emir or khan.

About 90 percent of all irrigated acreage, the property (*mulk*) land, was held under some form of private ownership. Such tracts were divided into three categories. The first consisted of lands paying no tax (*mulk-i hurr*). The second group was formed by tithe lands (*mulk ushri*) paying a tenth of their harvest to the state. The third consisted of lands paying a tax of from a seventh to a half of the harvest (*mulk-i khiraj*). The difference in taxes paid on *mulk ushri* and *mulk-i khiraj* lands is accounted for historically by the practice of the Arab conquerors in the eighth century, who took over land and divided it among themselves, paying the *ushr* to their ruler, but the original local owners, who may have been allowed to retain their land, having to pay the higher rate of the *khiraj*.

Although in principle all land belonged to the ruler, the owners of *mulk* lands could sell or bequeath them as they wished. The owner of reclaimed state land was in a rather different position because he held his land directly from the emir or khan. He could not transfer title to it without the ruler's consent. He paid his tax directly to the ruler, through the tax collector (*ämlakdar*), whereas the owner of *mulk* land paid taxes to the local bek.

Mulk land then obviously formed the whole basis for agricultural life in Central Asia. The average holding was small, farms of fifteen to twenty acres predominating, but much smaller irrigated plots were cultivated in many localities. In areas such as Khiva, where irrigation presented some problems for the farmer, the average size of the farms was as low as five and a half acres. Large estates were uncommon, and an individual holding rarely reached 500 to 600 *tänabs* (a measure of land that varied in size from two-fifths of an acre to one and a quarter acres depending on the locality; in Khiva, for example, a *tänab* was slightly larger than one acre). Because *mulk* lands were held on a hereditary basis, they were passed on to the next generation according to Muslim law, which provided that a man's property be parceled out among his children. This led to considerable fragmentation, and the emergence of a group of people, especially in the Farghana Valley, who owned little or no land at all.

Landless laborers were forced to move to areas where labor was scarce. The development of cotton growing as a major branch of Central Asian agriculture encouraged the formation of a pool of agricultural laborers, some of whom came from as far as Eastern Turkistan to help with the harvests. Besides this category of landless laborers, there was also a group of farmers who did not own land. These were the sharecroppers (*charäkar*), who farmed a landlord's acreage with tools he supplied in return for a third to half of the cotton harvest.

Another important type of land tenure was the *waqf*, under which lands belonged to a religious or philanthropic institution. These lands either were used entirely for some charitable purpose, remaining completely tax free, or were donated by private persons, often with the intention of avoiding taxation. This second variety of *waqf* was in fact an agreement between the religious institution and the owner of the land which left him in real ownership for the payment of a sum of money. Between these two forms of *waqf* stood other degrees of land ownership enjoyed by religious bodies, including varieties in which the religious establishment received only part of the income from the land, or, alternatively, the *waqf* land reverted to the children of the donor after his death. Furthermore, the owner might build a mosque on his land, declare his descendants trustees, and thus make it possible for them to claim the land for their support. The *waqf* system of land tenure could lead to many abuses, and the power of the clergy did not ease the ruler's problem of controlling it. Among the Turkmens any surplus land, whether belonging to families or villages, could be given as *karanda* land, the revenues from which were devoted to communal needs.[24]

Without access to irrigation water the ownership of farming

[24] Information on land tenure is taken mainly from Semenov-Tian-Shanskii, XIX, 417–19; Dmitriev-Mamonov, *Putevoditel' po Turkestanu i sredne-aziatskoi zheleznoi doroge*, pp. 70–72; and Eugene Schuyler, *Turkistan, Notes of a Journey in Russian Turkistan, Khokand, Bukhara, and Kuldja* (New York, Scribner, 1877), I, 297–303.

land was meaningless, and this reality forged a close link between land tenure and water rights. Water was seen as God's gift which could not be owned or controlled by a private person, so that the distribution of water to the fields was managed at the village level by a water controller (Tajik and Uzbek: *mirab*) who in turn was supervised by the elder (*aqsaqal*) elected from villages using the same main canal. If the extent of the irrigation network required two or more elders to supervise it, one elder was designated senior and put in charge of the whole system. These officials were also responsible for the cleaning and maintenance of the canals.

The farmer's claim to any waste land was limited by the number of ox teams he owned. Oxen were a way of measuring land, because the amount that one team could handle comfortably was generally reckoned at about fifty *tänab* (or about thirty-seven acres) in the Bukhara area, for example.[25] The elders decided which unused land was to be offered for cultivation, and then announced in the villages or towns that all who wished to receive land must assemble with their ox teams at a certain place. The land was divided into as many plots as there were teams, each portion being equal in size. The actual distribution was accomplished by drawing lots, the owners of several teams being awarded adjacent sections. Such portions of land were known as *cheks*.

The elders let water flow to each lot in turn, so that everyone would have his fair share. If the land were maintained under cultivation, or enclosed with a wall, or if a house were built on it, it became the private property of the owner. If the plot lay fallow the owner had to maintain a permanent canal leading to it, and was nevertheless obliged to send an ox team to help in the communal work.[26] Whether watering reclaimed land or private land, the elder relied on his own judgment to determine how much water had actually been permitted to flow into an individual farmer's canal. There was a measure of water called a *qulaq*, but this was gauged only by eye. In theory, water was distributed evenly to all; for example, those owning land at the head of the canal had no right to use more than they were entitled to, so

[25] Schuyler, I, 290.   [26] Kostenko, pp. 168, 170–72.

that those living farther along the canal should not suffer. In practice, a well-placed bribe insured supplementary supplies of water, a situation clearly favoring the well-to-do farmer. In addition, landowners at the heads of the canals often diverted more than their fair share of water for the growing of rice.

After the Russians in Central Asia declared all land to be state property, as indeed it was already according to Central Asian custom, they took further action, ordering that all occupied or cultivated tracts belonged to the persons who actually worked the land.[27] This decree, transforming many tenant farmers and sharecroppers into hereditary owners, has been regarded as "one of the most progressive steps taken by the colonial regime." [28]

LIVESTOCK RAISING GIVES WAY TO FARMING

The private ownership of land did not necessarily govern all important agricultural activities, for cattle and sheep pastures remained unfenced and public. The animals owned by Central Asian farmers and nomads of the south fall into three main categories: those kept by sedentary farmers for transportation or for moving simple machines such as the irrigation wheel and oil presses; those raised by desert and semidesert nomads such as the Turkmens, Karakalpaks, Kipchak Uzbeks, and southern Kazakhs; and animals belonging to Kirgiz and Tajik mountain herders. Under the last two categories belong the 13.3 million sheep reported in 1900 for the Turkistan guberniia. About 11.5 million of these grazed in the semidesert areas of Semirechie, Sir Darya, and Transcaspian oblasts.

Out of 1.7 million cattle, 948,000 tended by Kazakhs and Kirgiz grazed in the Sir Darya and Semirechie oblasts. The surprisingly high number of cattle (422,000) in the Farghana oblast gives evidence not only of the mountain Tajiks' activities, but also of the general use of oxen for plowing in the agricultural areas. The famed Turkmen horse breeders in the Transcaspian oblast accounted for only 124,000 of the 1.7 million horses in the Turkistan

[27] Schuyler, I, 300–3; Pierce, pp. 147–52.
[28] Pierce, p. 148. See his account of land tenure and taxation under the Russians, pp. 147–52.

guberniia. Semirechie alone pastured 714,000 horses. Samarkand and Farghana oblasts supported 63,000 out of the 98,000 donkeys in the guberniia, a figure suggesting that donkeys were used predominantly for personal transportation among the sedentary farmers and urban dwellers of these areas. The 1.9 million goats were distributed throughout Central Asia like the sheep. More than half of the 821,000 camels were in Sir Darya oblast. The only domestic herds of swine were located in Semirechie, where 13,000 pigs belonged to non-Muslims, mainly Russians.[29] These figures may not be accurate because the nomads generally underestimated the size of their flocks and herds to lessen taxation, in addition to which the mobility of nomadic life rendered the counting of animals very haphazard.

Agriculture in the plains regions on the part of the local people was limited to a little millet sowing by the Kazakhs in scattered locations where a group had decided to settle for a short period and where some water was available. Millet can grow in locations where a steady supply of irrigation water is not available. The Kazakhs did not attempt to develop irrigation.

It was the Russian farmer who brought agriculture to the Kazakh plains and who forced the transformation of this vast grazing area into a grain-growing country. Although the first major section of Russian settlement actually began in Semirechie, where Cossack frontier posts (*stanitsas*) founded in the 1860s were supplemented by other Russian migrants, the main agricultural settlement took place in the northern plains beginning in the 1880s and reaching a peak after 1905. By 1913 the total cultivated area in the Kazakh plains amounted to 38.07 million acres (14,101,000 *desiatin*) or about 8.3 percent of the area of the Steppe oblasts. Akmolinsk oblast put 17,588,000 acres (6,514,000 *desiatin*), or 12.5 percent of its expanse, under the plow. This compared very favorably with an irrigated area of 2.6 percent of the Turkistan guberniia around the same date.[30] By 1913, Kazakhstan's fields were sown to wheat, 61 percent; millet, 14 percent (grown mainly by Kazakhs); oats, 13 percent; rye, 5 percent (which covered 16 per-

[29] Dmitriev-Mamonov, p. 108.
[30] *Aziatskaia Rossiia*, II, 245; *Aziatskaia Rossiia: Atlas,* plates 34 and 35.

cent of the Cossack lands in the Ural oblast); with barley, buck-
wheat, potatoes, corn, peas, flax, and hemp completing the roster
of crops. Sunflowers, tobacco, and melons were occasionally
grown.[31]

As Kazakh herders were gradually forced from their grazing
lands by the Russian influx, the government tried to relocate and
encourage some of them to adopt a sedentary life. That this policy
was at all successful was not due to any positive action on the
part of the government, but rather because the Kazakh, with his
best pasture land sequestered and many of his traditional migration
routes blocked by huge new Russian farms, found that he had no
choice but to settle in one spot and start raising crops, although still
maintaining his herds and following more limited routes.

One of the Kazakh's few positive agricultural acquisitions resulting from Russian settlement was his introduction to the scythe.
This enabled him, for the first time, to cut quantities of grass and
hay for winter fodder, and also to keep cattle on a greater scale
than had been possible on the open range where Kazakh cattle,
as already noted, had not been suited physically to finding their
own winter feed.

The nomad's partial adoption of a sedentary life also increased
the areas sown to grain. In fact, by the time of the 1917 revolution, some Kazakhs had already changed from purely nomadic to
sedentary herdsmen who raised herds on fodder. Thus, through
agriculture, the Russians changed the Kazakh's traditional life
more than they did the ways of any other Central Asian people
during the prerevolutionary period, even though many Kazakhs
still remained basically nomadic for decades to come.

The grassland environment and the types of animals herded by
the Kazakhs suggest that animal husbandry was their only real
economic activity before Russian influence altered the pattern of
the local economy. The movement of animals to ensure year-round
grazing on seasonal pastures without recourse to fodder had been
a full-time job. Distances covered in a year might range from 50
or 100 miles up to 450 or 550, and there was a continual struggle
against drought, blizzard, and the refreezing that followed a thaw.

[31] *Aziatskaia Rossiia*, II, 259–60.

To give an idea of the size of the herds, which varied considerably from good years to bad years, the following estimates for 1916 are listed in round numbers covering the area of present-day Kazakhstan: sheep and goats, 18,364,000; cattle, 5,062,000; horses, 4,340,000; and pigs, 278,000.[32] During the period before the 1917 revolution, therefore, the whole trend in the plains turned away from traditional livestock herding to an agrarian economy. The classic battle of the grasslands between the herder and the soil tiller was underway, with victory already assured to the farmer.

The Russians attempted to develop the small commercial fishing carried on by the local people along the rivers and on the Aral and Caspian Seas, but lack of a market and especially of modern methods of preserving the perishable catch kept fisheries from expanding to any great extent.

SOVIET FARM POLICY

Agricultural development during the Soviet period in Central Asia has been to a great extent simply a projection of pre-1917 Russian policy with its emphasis upon cotton growing and upon withdrawal from raising grain and other foodstuffs. The first serious consequence of this procedure for Central Asians was felt during World War I and the subsequent disorders of the revolution, when the southern part of Central Asia relied almost entirely on western Russia for grain supplies. Any break in this lifeline was bound to have disastrous results, because a reversion from cotton growing to grain growing entailed a considerable time lag, during which food supplies could be exhausted.

The volume of grain shipped from Russia had shown signs of dropping as early as 1914, when the supplies were instead dispatched to troops at the Western front, but the real crisis began in December, 1918, when Central Asia found itself completely cut off from Russia. Not only did grain shipments cease, but a serious fuel shortage developed, the railroad locomotives burning saksaul wood, cottonseed oil, and dried fish, while undelivered cotton piled up at the railroad stations. This break in communications was

[32] *Narodnoe khoziaistvo SSSR v 1958 godu* (Moscow, Gosstatizdat, 1959), pp. 451–54, 457.

caused by the destruction of lines and bridges during civil war battles, especially between Orenburg and Aktyubinsk. However, by late 1919 the damage had been repaired and grain and cotton again began to meet along the route between Central Asia and Russia.

Unfortunately for Central Asians no large-scale, organized attempt was made during this emergency to replant any significant acreage with grain or other food crops, but with cotton practically unsalable and likely to be a glut on the market for some time, many farmers ceased to cultivate this crop and began to sow grain. This initiative was soon squelched by Soviet authorities who started forcibly requisitioning grain and foodstuffs from farmers, a practice which caused consternation and gave little encouragement to further grain sowing. In fact, the acreage devoted to all crops decreased rapidly, because anarchy reigned in the Central Asian countryside. Groups of anti-Communist partisans (*basmächi*) added to the chaos by seizing food supplies, killing cattle, and destroying irrigation systems in many places, and shortage of manpower and materials prevented proper repair work. Several major irrigation installations were destroyed, and a large part of the irrigation system, the smaller canals and ditches maintained by the farmers for the irrigation of their own fields, were allowed to silt up and generally fall into disrepair.[33]

This great decline in the amount of irrigated acreage was matched by an equally disastrous drop in the acreage of grain crops grown without irrigation. By 1918 the irrigated portion of the Turkistan ASSR, fitting approximately within the boundaries of the old Turkistan guberniia, was only 37.5 percent of the total area irrigated in 1915, while the dry-farm land made up 36.4 percent of the total for the same year. In 1920 irrigated land had again increased to 3.3 million acres (1.2 million *desiatin*) or 50 percent of the 1915 figure, but the area devoted to dry farming decreased once more in 1919, and by 1920 had only reached the 1915 total of 1.1 million acres (400,000 *desiatin*). Thus, by 1920 the area sown in the Turkistan ASSR was only 45.7 percent of

[33] O. B. Dzhamalov, ed., *Istoriia narodnogo khoziaistva Uzbekistana* (Tashkent, Izdatel'stvo Akademii Nauk Uzbekskoi SSR, 1962), I, 83.

the acreage sown in 1915. The differing rates of recovery for irrigated and dry farming are explained by the greater productivity of irrigated land compared to areas relying on natural precipitation and hence the natural preference of the farmers to restore irrigated plots first. As the food crisis continued, food crops began gradually to supplant cotton despite the requisitioning and looting. A drought in 1917 and a poor cotton harvest had helped to start the relinquishing of cotton culture in the region, and by 1921 cotton cov-

FIGURE 11.3   Flocks along the banks of the Sir Darya in the natural conditions under which much of Central Asian pastoral activity is carried on. *Sovfoto.*

ered only 200,000 acres (80,000 hectares) compared with the 1,-058,000 acres (423,500 hectares) in 1913.[34] In spite of these belated attempts to substitute food crops for cotton, southern Central Asia experienced severe famines from 1919 to 1923, and well over a million people died. Such starvation, along with the general chaos prevailing in the region, reduced the agrarian economy to a state of collapse.

The first step which the Soviet authorities took after the Civil

[34] N. L. Korzhenevskii, ed., *Uzbekskaia SSR* (Moscow, Gosizdatgeolit, 1956), p. 224.

War and the main Basmachi troubles ended was to restore (from 1922 to 1928) the irrigation system. The damage to the major canals and other installations was repaired, and in 1923 a reclamation cooperative was established to advance credit for farmers to aid them in repairing their own local irrigation systems. By 1926–1927, about 78 percent of the land area irrigated in 1914 through-

FIGURE 11.4 Canal flowing through the irrigated orchards of an oasis. The donkey remains one of the principal means of local transportation. *Sovfoto.*

out Uzbekistan had been restored, and by the next year about 82 percent. However, as early as 1927 the area devoted to cotton was slightly larger than in 1914, while the land sown to grain had reached but 64.5 percent of that planted in 1914.[35] In other words, the process of reconverting agriculture back to the almost exclusive growing of cotton was well under way, and the quantity of grain brought from Russia in 1927 already surpassed by about 25

[35] Dzhamalov, I, 153, 157.

percent the imports of 1916. The grain still being grown in southern Central Asia was more and more restricted to areas relying upon natural precipitation in order to release additional land to cotton. To encourage this movement, all taxes on unirrigated crops were lifted in 1926–1927. Study of the revival in agriculture of the settled areas in Central Asia up to 1927 has shown clearly that Soviet authorities in the 1920s pursued exactly the same agricultural policy as had the czarist administration. The southern part of Central Asia became still more firmly tied to Russia as a one-crop colony.[36]

Uzbekistan set the pattern for the development of cotton growing. In 1932 the Uzbeks were raising about 61 percent of all cotton fiber produced in the Soviet Union. By 1928 the area sown to all crops in the republic had reached 4.4 million acres (1,759,000 hectares), of which 3.4 million acres (1,360,700 hectares) were irrigated. Of the irrigated area, 44.7 percent was under grain, 38.9 percent under cotton, and 9.2 percent under alfalfa. Complementary crops consisted mainly of vegetables, melons, and other fruit. By 1932 the area sown had increased to 6.9 million acres (2,786,700 hectares), of which 4.4 million acres (1,776,500 hectares) were irrigated, but by this date the area under cotton had increased to 55.9 percent of the irrigated land, while the area under grain had plunged to only 15.8 percent. Alfalfa occupied 15.6 percent of the irrigated area, one of the few crops, apart from cotton, to register an increase.

The area under dry farming also experienced considerable expansion during this period, becoming two and a half times greater in 1932 than in 1928. However, although the wheat and barley harvest in 1932 weighed 147,600 metric tons compared to 101,800 metric tons in 1928, this was still far from the amount required to feed the population. As early as 1928 just under 61 percent of Uzbekistan's total grain deficit of 617,000 metric tons could be met by imports from Russia, and not until considerably after the completion of the Turkistan-Siberian Railroad in 1931 was sufficient

---

[36] A. G. Park, *Bolshevism in Turkestan, 1917–1927* (New York, Columbia University Press, 1957), pp. 288–320.

grain imported into Uzbekistan to start meeting the full needs of the population.[37]

COLLECTIVIZATION—COTTON VS FOOD PRODUCTION

The beginning of the first Five Year Plan in 1928 thus saw a further extension in the area under cotton and a gradual diminution in other crops. No sooner had the irrigation system been restored and the ravages of the civil war repaired, however, than a further upheaval began as the result of collectivization of all the farm land. The campaign reached its height in Uzbekistan in 1930–1931, but its effects lingered on until 1933–1934.

During the collectivization period the yield per unit area of all crops decreased noticeably, the 1928 average cotton yield in Uzbekistan dropping to 829 lbs. per acre (9.4 *centner* per hectare) compared with the average yield for Central Asia in 1914 of 1,070 lbs. per acre (80 *pud* per *desiatin*). In 1929 the average yield rose to 935 lbs. per acre (10.6 *centner* per hectare), but by 1934 had again dropped to 697 lbs. per acre (7.9 *centner* per hectare).[38] This drop in productivity can be attributed to the disorders and frustrations attending the collectivization campaign in the Central Asian countryside. Although the irrigated portion of Uzbekistan increased steadily during the early part of the collectivization drive, by 1933 and 1934 signs of strain began to appear. In 1933 the area planted to cotton had reached a total of 2.4 million acres (968,000 hectares), compared with 1.06 million acres (425,000 hectares) in 1913 on the territory of present-day Uzbekistan, the total harvest coming to 817,000 metric tons. However, though in 1934 the cotton fields amounted to 2.3 million acres (933,000 hectares), the harvest dropped to 738,000 metric tons in this period of very low yields per hectare.

The drop in cotton production was unwelcome to the Soviet authorities. This was made clear from the planners' vow to free the Soviet Union forever from all cotton importing. In 1927–1928 the Soviet Union was still bringing in about 41 percent of its cot-

[37] Dzhamalov, I, 251–52.
[38] *Ibid.*, I, 251; N. L. Korzhenevskii, p. 226.

ton requirements from abroad, but by 1929–1930 the proportion of such cotton had dropped to 19.3 percent, and by the beginning of the second Five Year Plan in 1933 only 2.6 percent of the country's cotton requirements came from the outside.[39]

To combat the 1934 drop in cotton production, Soviet authorities started a campaign for increasing productivity per acre by applying more chemical fertilizer and planting a better quality of cotton seed. On the area sown to cotton in 1935, 2.3 million acres (932,900 hectares), the cotton harvest rose to 1,082,800 metric tons, the increase thanks to an average yield of 1,032 lbs. per acre (11.7 *centner* per hectare), or about the same as the normal yield in 1914. The turning point had been reached, however, and by 1937 the cotton area of Uzbekistan totaled 2.4 million acres (946,-000 hectares), with an average yield of 1,420 lbs. per acre (16.1 *centner* per hectare), giving a harvest figure of 1,527,900 metric tons. In 1937, 569,000 metric tons of chemical fertilizer were shipped into Uzbekistan, compared with 65,000 tons in 1932, and two large seed selection centers were set up in the Farghana and Khiva regions, with smaller centers throughout the republic.

Although Soviet writers claim that the grain areas in Uzbekistan expanded during the 1930s, there is no doubt that cotton monoculture was given greater emphasis than ever. This led to a substantial reduction in the sowing of many traditional crops such as alfalfa, pulses, and plants grown for their oil content. Not only did these crops suffer, but in many areas orchards and mulberry groves were uprooted and vineyards plowed up to make way for more cotton. Further increases in cotton production were difficult to achieve in spite of the spreading of more fertilizer and better seed selection, because there had been little change in the techniques of Central Asian cotton growing since the prerevolutionary period, and mechanization was practically nonexistent.

Immediately before World War II, the cotton harvest totaled 1,582,200 metric tons, and the yield per acre had grown to 1,517 lbs. per acre (17.2 *centner* per hectare) on the average in 1939. Production rose again in 1941, but after this date a steady decline in production set in. In the face of a diversion of manpower and

[39] Korzhenevskii, p. 225; Dzhamalov, I, 252.

materials to other sectors of the economy, the highly centralized Soviet bureaucracy in time of war could not prevent a decrease in the area sown to cotton from 2.3 million acres (924,000 hectares) in 1940 to 1.8 million acres (720,000 hactares) in 1943, bringing the harvest during the same period down from 1,648,800 metric tons to 826,000 metric tons. Productivity slumped to a low point of only 626 lbs. per acre (7.1 *centner* per hectare). Although this wartime decline in cotton production could be partly attributed to a certain amount of disorganization in the agrarian economy, it was also due to a reversion of land to much-needed food crops. In the Central Asian republics, grain lands increased in area by 20 percent between 1940 and 1942, the increase in winter-sown grain crops being particularly important. Areas that were planted with sugar beet and oleaginous crops also were expanded, and those areas growing vegetables and potatoes then also increased by 32 percent.[40]

The reversion of land to the growing of food crops was only a temporary measure, however, and the first postwar Five Year Plan called for a maximum effort to restore Uzbek cotton production to the prewar level as rapidly as possible. By 1950 the cotton area had passed the 2.5 million acre (1 million hectare) mark, and by 1963 was 4.1 million acres (1,628,000 hectares) with a total production of 3,689,000 metric tons. In 1963 the average yield had reached over 2,000 lbs. per acre (22.7 *centner* per hectare). However, the record cotton harvest in 1963 of 3.7 million metric tons was exceptional, harvests since 1956 hovering around the 3 million metric ton mark, with no sign of any dramatic rise in production predicted for the near future. The 1965 plan called for production of 3.6 million metric tons, or less than the 1963 harvest.

This suggests that Uzbek cotton growing may be facing some serious problems, probably because the Central Asian cotton industry still operates under relatively primitive conditions. A technical study group from the U.S. Department of Agriculture who visited Central Asia recently found that the Soviet cotton belt, with its one-crop economy, compared approximately to the southern United

[40] N. A. Voznesensky, *The Economy of the USSR during World War II* (Washington, D.C., Public Affairs Press, 1948), pp. 56–57.

States of thirty years ago. The Americans noted that alfalfa is the only rotation crop used, apart from small plantings of melons and rice. Most of the cotton picking and weeding is still done by hand, almost entirely by women, and, after picking, the cotton is spread out on the highways to dry for four or five hours before being ginned in equipment resembling U.S. machines of the 1930s. Soviet emphasis seems to be placed now on increasing yields per acre rather than upon the costly enlargement of the cultivated area. In general, cotton yields in Central Asia are well below those of the American Southwest, and expenses seem relatively high, partly because of the outlays for controlling soil salinity, and to some extent from high labor requirements.

The general impression received by the American study group was that the Central Asian cotton economy is suffering, like other branches of agriculture, from lack of investment in machinery and equipment, although adequate fertilizer and animal manure appear to be used. The group reported, however, that mechanical picking might not pay in Central Asia where a large supply of cheap labor is available.[41] This may not be completely true, because the Soviet Union is suffering in general from a manpower shortage, and recent statements by Soviet agronomists have called for increased mechanization of the cotton industry. The particular need is for machines to prepare the soil before planting, to level the land, harvest the crop, and load and unload cotton at the collection point (*khirman*), as well as to clean the irrigation system.

Two operations which require the most manpower are harvesting and weeding. In the United States it has been found that one spindle picker can harvest as much cotton per day as fifty to seventy persons. These machines have an efficiency of over 90 percent and cause little reduction in the grade of the picked cotton. Weeds are controlled in the United States by means of herbicides, cross plowing, and flame cultivation Chemical weed control alone can reduce hand labor by up to 90 percent.

Levelers, cotton planters, cultivators, and cotton picking machines

[41] *Cotton in the Soviet Union, Report of a Technical Study Group* (U.S. Department of Agriculture, Washington, D.C., June, 1959), pp. 1–4; *Soviet Agriculture Today* (U.S. Department of Agriculture, Washington, D.C., 1963), pp. 18, 80.

are all manufactured in the Soviet Union, but their numbers are insufficient and some machines have been defective in design. Furthermore, reports suggest that old prejudices and techniques also hamper the introduction of machinery into some parts of Central Asia, where farmers still believe that a machine picks inefficiently and that it is simpler and cheaper to pick by hand, because it takes extra time to prepare the cotton crop for mechanical picking. The Soviet press confessed, in fact, that the 1963 plan for machine harvesting cotton in Tajikistan had collapsed.[42] Soviet agronomists recognize the shortcomings of their cotton-growing equipment and techniques, and, with greater investment in the agricultural sector of the Central Asian economy, improvements in the mechanization of the cotton industry will probably take place.

Rotation of crops in the cotton-growing areas remains nearly as slight as during the pre-1917 years. The U.S. technical group reported a theoretical crop rotation for southern Central Asia in 1960 scheduling three years of alfalfa, to be followed by six years of cotton, but observed that in fact in some areas cotton was grown continuously or at least for two-thirds of the time, with some modification of the recommended rotation in areas of saline soil.[43] Recent Soviet reports show that agriculturalists understand the value of a suitable rotation scheme, and the sowing of alfalfa as the ideal rotation crop with cotton is now being propagandized. They seem cognizant of the fact that because of alfalfa's slow growth rate in its first year, corn or sorghum should be sown with it, thus making full use of the irrigated land and giving an extra fodder crop. This emphasis on fodder crops is linked with an attempt to increase the amount of livestock kept in cotton-growing areas, not only for the meat, milk, and wool which they produce, but also for the natural manure they supply.[44]

In one aspect of cotton growing, Soviet and U.S. practices seem

[42] "Bogatye vozmozhnosti kolkhozov i sovkhozov Tadzhikistana," *Pravda,* February 12, 1964, p. 4.

[43] *Soil Salinity and Irrigation in the Soviet Union, Report of a Technical Study Group* (U.S. Department of Agriculture, Washington, D.C., September, 1962), p. 22.

[44] A large amount of material on the technical aspects of cotton growing is contained in *Materialy ob"edinennoi nauchnoi sessii po khlopkovodstvu* (Tashkent, Gosizdat UzSSR, 1958).

to coincide; both countries use relatively high amounts of fertilizer per acre. At a time when most other crops in the Soviet Union have been suffering from a lack of fertilizer, cotton has been well provided with the necessary phosphates and nitrogen, and over 25 percent and over 30 percent respectively of the annual Soviet production of phosphate and nitrogen fertilizer goes to Central Asia. Recent problems with grain production in Kazakhstan and other areas of the Soviet Union have demonstrated the lack of fertilizer for normal agricultural requirements, and, in view of the fact that a great increase in fertilizer production has been called for, it will be interesting to see if Central Asian cotton will still retain top priority for fertilizer allotments.

NEW IRRIGATION PROJECTS

If the cultivation of cotton is to be expanded, an ever larger area of land will have to be irrigated. During the first Five Year Plan, work began on extending irrigation of such areas as the Farghana Valley and the Mirzachol Sahra, and land along the Zarafshan, Surkhan Darya, Chirchiq, and Ahangaran rivers. In all, about 500,-000 acres (200,000 hectares) of new land was irrigated between 1929 and 1932. The second Five Year Plan made little progress in extending the irrigated area, and not until 1939 did the first large-scale irrigation projects since the pre-1917 period begin.

The first of these was the construction of the 19-mile-long Lagan Canal in the Farghana Valley, which was said to have been built in seventeen days by 14,000 laborers. In the spring of 1939 forty-five more canals were built, all of them by "people's construction," in other words the traditional Central Asian system of using unpaid laborers. The greatest such feat of this period was the digging of the Great Farghana Canal (Kättä Färghanä Känäli) in the summer of 1939 by 160,000 Uzbeks, 20,000 Tajiks, and about 1,000 supervising engineers and technicians, presumably Russians, who finished the construction of this 168-mile-long canal in forty-five days. The canal brought water from the Sir Darya through the heart of the Farghana Valley, and made possible a further expansion of cotton land throughout the region. In 1940 the smaller North and South Farghana canals were dug by the same methods. The North Canal is about 100 miles long and waters an area north of and parallel to the Sir Darya. The South Canal is about 65 miles long and irrigates the land along the foot of the mountains in the southeastern part of the valley. Other canals were cut to the Tashkent oasis from the Chirchiq, in the Samarkand and Khwarazm oblasts, and in the Karakalpak ASSR.[45]

Apart from these major irrigation projects in Uzbekistan, a canal in the Vakhsh Valley in Tajikistan was completed in 1934, and a canal in the Hisar Valley irrigated 25,000 acres (10,000 hectares) by 1942. In Turkmenistan a canal was constructed between 1927 and 1932 from the Amu Darya along the Kelif Uzboi, extending about sixty-five miles into the desert. This was a forerunner of the later Qara Qum Canal. In Kirgizistan a start was made on the use of the Chu River for large-scale irrigation. Although the building of all these canals no doubt entailed remarkable feats of speed, forced labor construction brought a great deal of suffering and hardship to the local population, who were obliged to turn out in large numbers and work long hours in shifts for no personal return. Even in the days of the khans and the beks it is unlikely that such continuous pressure was ever applied to local labor force.

Although a few canals were completed during World War II, the next extensive irrigation projects did not take shape until after the war. Perhaps the most imaginative of these schemes was the resumption on a large scale of attempts to irrigate the Mirzachol Sahra, which had also been the aim of the czarist authorities between 1870 and 1917. In the 1920s some progress had been made with extending the Mirzachol Sahra irrigation network and by 1925, 109,000 acres (43,500 hectares) of land were irrigated. By 1939 the irrigated area had expanded to 238,000 acres (95,000 hectares), about 45 percent of which was under cotton. On the base provided by the prerevolutionary Romanovskii Canal, in particular its left branch, the Kirov Canal was built across the northern part of the region, expanding the irrigated area to 345,000 acres (138,000 hectares) by 1941.[46]

These considerable efforts before the war notwithstanding, the

[45] Korzhenevskii, pp. 220–21; Dzhamalov, I, 333–34.
[46] "The Hungry Steppe," *Central Asian Review*, Vol. V, No. 1 (1957), p. 43.

greatest emphasis on the development of the Mirzachol Sahra began in 1956, when a concerted drive to irrigate the southern part of the region began, and large numbers of laborers were transferred into the area. Work began on a southern canal and also on a central drainage canal to combat the considerable salinity met in soils throughout the whole area. In fact, much of the soil in the Mirzachol Sahra is of a salt-marsh type, and considerable leaching with water is necessary before it can be cultivated. By 1960 about 470,000 acres (180,000 hectares) of the 2.5 million acres (1 million hectares) of the Mirzachol Sahra had been irrigated, and by 1965 it is expected that between 1.5 to 1.8 million acres (600,000 to 700,000 hectares) will have been reclaimed.

To facilitate and centralize the administration of the Mirzachol Sahra, 425,000 acres (170,000 hectares) of the region which lay within the borders of Kazakhstan were transferred to Uzbekistan in 1956. A much larger transfer of territory, involving some 2.4 million acres (959,000 hectares) was arranged in January, 1963, when the balance of the cotton-growing land in the Mirzachol Sahra was transferred to Uzbekistan, whose borders now encompass the whole area. Part of the transferred expanse consists of range lands, the shift of which was connected with handing over some 6.8 million acres (2.7 million hectares) of grazing land from Chimkent and Qizil Orda oblasts of Kazakhstan. A new Uzbek district, the Sir Darya oblast, has recently been formed, and for all practical purposes can be said to include the entire Mirzachol Sahra. It has an area of 6.2 million acres (2.3 million hectares), in which cotton is being grown on 460,000 acres (184,000 hectares). Much of the population in the new oblast, about 520,000, mainly Uzbeks, along with Tajiks, Kazakhs, Koreans, and Bukharan Jews, are at present concentrated on the land irrigated by the Kirov Canal.[47] Cotton-ginning plants have been erected at the major centers such as Jizzakh, Gulistan, Bayut, Slavyanka, Il'ich, and Bekabad. Yangi Yer, with a population of 25,000 persons, has both a cotton and a silk combine.

In recent years work on other irrigation projects, such as the

[47] "News Notes," *Soviet Geography,* Vol. IV, No. 3 (March, 1963), p. 52; F. V. Koval'chik, "Naselenie Golodnoi stepi," *Sbornik nauchno-issledovatel'noi raboty tashkentskogo tekstil'nogo instituta,* No. 13 (1961), pp. 259–63.

Amu Darya–Bukhara Canal, the Amu Darya–Qaraqol Canal (from near Charjuy to the western end of the Zarafshan), the Chu Canal in Kirgizistan, as well as several reservoirs on the Sir Darya, the Tejen, the Murghab, and branches of the Zarafshan, has begun and in some cases completed. Of the reservoirs, the largest and most widely propagandized has been the Bahr-i Tajik (Tajik Sea) or Qairaq Qum reservoir on the upper Sir Darya at the mouth of the Farghana Valley. This reservoir provides water for irrigating parts of northern Tajikistan, and also supplies electric power for the surrounding region.

Although the ambitious scheme to dig a channel to be known as the Main Turkmen Canal along the bed of the Uzboi was announced in 1950, the plan was dropped in 1953. However, the project for constructing the 500-mile Qara Qum Canal from the Amu Darya at Bosaga to Ashkhabad, which was approved by the Soviet authorities in 1947, has become a reality. Construction began in 1949 on the first stage, which reached Merv and the Murghab oasis in 1959. The second portion pushed on to the Tejen oasis in 1961, and the third section was completed to Ashkhabad in May, 1962, the final 160-mile increment taking eight months to build. The Soviet authorities plan eventually to extend the canal all the way to the Caspian Sea.

American technologists who visited the canal site in 1960 were told that it would irrigate 2.5 million acres (1 million hectares) by 1980. Because the canal lacks a lining, seepage losses were estimated by the Americans at 40 to 45 percent, and serious wind erosion was observed on the land around the canal.[48] In spite of such problems, this canal unquestionably represents one of the most impressive technical feats by Soviet irrigation engineers to date.

Unfortunately for the Soviet planners, however, despite the much-heralded arrival of water at the prime cotton-growing Murghab oasis, the Turkmen farmer has not risen to the occasion. It had been expected that the Qara Qum Canal would facilitate an increase in

[48] *Soil Salinity* (U.S. Dept. Agr.), p. 8. An account of some of the problems encountered in the construction of the first stage of the canal appears in "The Progress of the Kara Kum Canal, 1957–1958," *Central Asian Review,* Vol. VII, No. 1 (1959), pp. 44–46.

cotton production in the Turkmen republic, but this has not been the case. Although the area planted to cotton in the republic increased from 470,000 acres (188,000 hectares) in 1958 to 603,000 acres (241,000 hectares) in 1962, productivity dropped from 1,808 lbs. per acre (20.5 *centner* per hectare) to 1,367 lbs. per acre (15.5 *centner* per hectare) during the same period. This resulted in a drop in production from 584,000 metric tons to 574,000 metric tons. Out of 268 kolkhozes in the republic, only nineteen harvested 2,205 lbs. or more per acre (25 or more *centner* per hectare), not a high figure by American standards, while some sovkhozes picked as little as 847 to 856 lbs. per acre (9.6 or 9.7 *centner* per acre), a very poor performance for farms generally regarded as either models or experimental centers, which should have been obtaining at least thrice this yield.

Although cotton diseases seem to have attacked crops in the Turkmen region, low yields appear to have been caused mostly by poor agricultural techniques, late sowing and harvesting, and the general indifference of all concerned, including cotton specialists, who, on arrival in the Turkmen localities, evidently waste no time in making for the bright lights of Ashkhabad, leaving the cotton farmers without technical advisers.[49] This is one reason why the construction of elaborate and expensive irrigation systems does not automatically increase production in Central Asia. Individuals on the farm do not always have the incentive or the technical ability to till the land to its best advantage, and it is probable that under the present system of collectivized farming the human element is likely to remain the major agricultural problem. Increasing soil salinization, due to inadequate drainage, is also an important factor in explaining low cotton yields.

Although most Central Asian irrigation schemes aim at increasing the area sown to cotton, an exception is the land irrigated in the Chu Valley of Kirgizistan, where sugar beets have become a major crop. Sugar beets grow well under irrigation and bright sunshine, as has also been demonstrated in the piedmont areas of the Rocky Mountains in Colorado, where conditions are very similar

[49] V. Nikolaev, "Ser'eznye nedostatki turkmenskogo khlopkovodstva," *Khlopkovodstvo*, Vol. XIII, No. 6 (June 1963), pp. 1–6.

to those in the Chu Valley. Although the Ukraine and the RSFSR supply most of the sugar beets for Soviet factories, the Chu Valley has the highest yields of beets per acre in the Soviet Union and plays an important part in Central Asian sugar production. With the recent emphasis upon increasing grain harvests in the Soviet Union, it is possible that more grain may again be grown on irrigated land in Central Asia. In February, 1964, winter planting of grain took place for the first time since World War II in Uzbekistan on 300,000 acres (120,000 hectares) of irrigated land, and a plan was formulated to increase sizably the grain harvest in Kazakhstan by sowing 1.4 million acres (556,000 hectares) of irrigated land, presumably in the south of the republic.[50]

THE DECLINE IN ANIMAL HUSBANDRY

The events in the first two decades of the twentieth century which set back Central Asian irrigation, cotton production, and grain growing, also had a drastic effect on animal husbandry. Livestock herded by nomads and seminomads numbered about 8.9 million head in 1900 in the three main oblasts (Sir Darya, Samarkand, and Farghana). In 1917 the livestock in these oblasts was estimated at 8.4 million head, but by 1920 this figure had dropped to 3.4 million. The loss resulted from the droughts of 1917–1918 and the political unrest in the rural areas. In Samarkand oblast, for example, 69.8 percent of the sheep and goats disappeared between 1917 and 1920. Consequently, the amount of wool produced in Turkistan guberniia plummeted from 16,000 tons (1 million *pud*) in 1916 to 3,400 tons (212,000 *pud*) in 1920.[51] This melting away of livestock continued and by 1924 it had dwindled down to its smallest quantity.

At this date in Uzbekistan, livestock numbered about 2.9 million head, of which 1.7 million were sheep and goats. By 1928 this total had reached about 5.6 million, of which 2.9 million were sheep, but collectivization and the slaughter of livestock by the farmers, as well as deaths due to neglect, reduced the size of the herds again.

[50] "Uzbekistan uvelichit proizvodstvo khlopka i zerna;" "Rezervy Kazakhstana—na sluzhbu rodine," *Pravda*, February 12, 1964, p. 3.

[51] Dzhamalov, I, 93–94.

By 1932 the total livestock amounted to only 3.4 million, of which nearly half (1.6 million) were sheep.

The same change could be seen in the other Central Asian republics. In Tajikistan, the number of sheep and goats dropped from 2.2 million in 1929 to 799,000 in 1934, and the number of cattle was halved.

In 1924, Kirgizistan sheep and goats numbered 3.1 million, but only 949,000 in 1932, while cattle in the same period sank from 876,000 head to 315,000. This drop in fact took place during the short period between 1930 and 1932, when the collectivization drive was at its height and a maximum effort was exerted to settle the Kirgiz on the land. The undue haste with which the authorities pressed collectivization led to revolt and the wholesale slaughter of livestock by the Kirgiz, a pattern followed also in the other republics, including Kazakhstan. It has been estimated that in one Kirgizistan raion alone over 5,000 horses, 2,500 cows, 65,600 sheep, and 550 camels were destroyed between January and October, 1931.[52] A long time passed before the herds in all regions recuperated from this catastrophe.

By 1941, Kirgiz sheep and goats had regained the 2.5 million mark, that is, the 1916 total, and only reached 4.5 million in 1951. By 1960, however, they surpassed 6 million. In Uzbekistan sheep increased more rapidly, in 1941 totaling 4.2 million compared to 1.6 million in 1932, and by 1960 approaching 8 million head. Cattle have, however, increased less rapidly (from 1.7 million in 1941 to 2 million in 1959). Two reasons may be cited: the importance of qaraqol wool (two-thirds of Soviet production being supplied by Uzbekistan) and the efforts which have been expended on increasing its production, and second, the mounting difficulty of raising cattle in a region where every available piece of arable land is used to grow cotton, and where the unirrigated land provides a better pasture for sheep.

The recent Soviet drive for more dairy products emphasizes the fact that most of the Uzbek cows in 1956 were not stall-fed and their milk production was very low. At the same time, many sheep and

[52] *Istoriia Kirgizii* (Frunze, Akademiia Nauk Kirgizskoi SSR. Institute Istorii, 1956), II, 195.

goats died from lack of fodder;[53] this accounts for the accent seen in recent years upon growing alfalfa as a rotation crop with cotton. The planners are gradually beginning to see that cotton growing alone is not the best method of utilizing the natural environment of Central Asia, and that a combination of cotton, fodder crops for stock-raising, horticulture, and viticulture in the irrigated areas, along with sheep herding on the arid pastures, may be the best answer to the problem of organizing the region's agricultural economy —in other words, a return to the traditional economy of southern Central Asia.

The influx of Russian settlers into the plains of Kazakhstan, and the displacement of the traditional pastoral economy of the Kazakhs by sedentary wheat-centered agriculture continued after 1917, but at a much slower pace than during the period immediately preceding World War I. The rate of increase of the Russian population in the plains dropped from 14 percent per annum between 1897 and 1911 to only 1 percent a year from 1911 to 1926.[54] This limited immigration is reflected in the lack of growth of the sown area of Kazakhstan between 1913 (present boundaries) and 1928, when the areas totaled 10.4 million acres (4,171,000 hectares) and 10.6 million acres (4,246,000 hectares) respectively.[55] At both dates more than 90 percent of the sown area was devoted to grain. The decreasing numbers of Russians moving to the plains of Kazakhstan is explained by the general chaos which reigned in northern Kazakhstan plus a serious year-long famine which began in the northwestern part in the spring of 1921. Transportation facilities connecting the region to Russia were also disrupted for a considerable time.

During the period of the New Economic Policy before the first Five Year Plan, the Kazakhs experienced little interference from Soviet Russian authorities, and with the slackening of Russian immi-

[53] Korzhenevskii, p. 241.
[54] O. Caroe, *Soviet Empire* (London, Macmillan, 1953), pp. 164–65.
[55] Figures quoted in this section, unless otherwise stated, come from Soviet statistical yearbooks, the *Bol'shaia sovetskaia entsiklopediia* (Moscow, Gosudarstvennoe Nauchnoe Izdatel'stvo "Bol'shaia Sovetskaia Entsiklopediia"), and S. A. Neishtadt, *Ekonomicheskoe razvitie kazakhskoi SSR* (Alma Ata, Gosizdat KazSSR, 1960).

gration the Kazakh economic position remained constant or in many ways improved. Despite a serious refreezing after a thaw in 1920–1921 which killed a large number of cattle, as well as the losses suffered during the civil war and subsequent disorders, Kazakh livestock increased by almost 40 percent between 1916 and 1929, as can be seen from the figures in Table 11.2. Hogs, of course, be-

TABLE 11.2

Number of Livestock in Kazakhstan (Present Borders) 1916–1929

	1916	1924	1929
sheep and goats	18,364,000	11,400,000	27,200,000
cattle	5,062,000	4,750,000	7,400,000
horses	4,340,000	2,500,000	4,200,000
hogs	278,000	300,000	300,000

longed to the Russian settlers, and the absence of growth in their numbers during the period correlates with the lack of new Russian immigration.

In 1927, the first signs of collectivization began to appear in Kazakhstan when the cattle and possessions of a few hundred wealthy Kazakhs (*bay*) were confiscated, the cattle being distributed among the poorer peasants, who were then formed into nuclei for collective farms.[56] The main push to collectivize the nomads in 1933 was accompanied by widespread violence and the destruction of livestock. While the Kazakh population itself dropped by almost a million, the livestock herds were decimated. The number of cattle in Kazakhstan has never managed again to reach the 1929 level,

TABLE 11.3

Number of Livestock in Kazakhstan (Present Borders) 1934–1962

	1934	1941	1946	1951	1962
sheep and goats	2,261,000	8,132,000	10,249,000	18,038,000	30,404,000
cattle	1,591,000	3,356,000	3,519,000	4,455,000	6,139,000
horses	441,000	897,000	851,800	1,453,000	1,110,000
hogs	141,000	451,000	149,200	401,000	2,282,000

as the figures in Table 11.3 show. Recent increases in hogs have followed extension of fodder crops in northern Kazakhstan.

Obviously, collectivization of the Kazakh herds brought economic

[56] *Istoriia kazakhskoi SSR* (Alma Ata, Gosizdat KazSSR, 1943), p. 516.

disaster. Not only did the Kazakhs and the Soviet state throw away a valuable source of meat, hides, and wool, but the wholesale destruction of camels during this period caused serious problems for local and short-distance transportation. The large loss in numbers of livestock, greater proportionately than that in any other part of the Soviet Union, stands as perhaps the most serious economic blunder yet made by the Russians in their entire hundred-year rule of Central Asia.

The period of the prewar Five Year plans again saw an increase of Russian immigration to Kazakhstan, but this time to the industrial and urban centers rather than to the rural areas, even though there had been a rise of about 3 million acres (1.2 million hectares) in the total sown area of Kazakhstan between 1928 and 1932. Collectivization in the region of sedentary agriculture prevented any expansion in the sown area between 1932 and 1937, and in that later year the sown land totaled 14.6 million acres (5,832,000 hectàres), mostly covered with grain crops. Only about 280,000 acres (111,000 hectares) of this was given up to cotton in the southern part. After 1937, although a gradual rise took place in the sown area, the increase was not sufficient to meet the growing demand for grain from Kazakhstan and Siberia. By 1940 the sown area amounted to 17 million acres (6,808,600 hectares), of which 14.5 million acres (5,817,100 hectares) were planted to grain.

The outbreak of war called for an even more rapid expansion of grain production in this area to make up for land lost to the German army in the west. However, despite the deportation of persons from the regions annexed by the USSR from eastern Poland, from the Baltic states, and the Volga German republic, the agricultural territory of Kazakhstan suffered during the war from a lack of manpower and investment. The total area sown dropped to 15 million acres (6,039,900 hectares) in 1945, and the grain area to 12.3 million acres (4,907,100 hectares); however, the land planted with potatoes, sugar beets, and fodder crops increased during the war, although this was scarcely enough to offset the serious (25 percent) drop from 2,516,000 metric tons of grain harvested in 1940 to 1,902,-000 metric tons in 1945. Rising production of fodder crops stimulated the increase of sheep, goats, and cattle, recorded in Table

11.3, which partially helped to alleviate the serious meat shortage experienced in the Soviet Union during the war.

The years between the end of the war and 1953 saw a considerable expansion in the mechanization of agriculture on the plains, particularly in the quantity of tractors and combine harvesters. The number of tractors rose from 25,709 in 1945 to 39,854 in 1953, and combines from 12,579 to 21,668. Although the number was by no means adequate for the size of the territory to be serviced, their use extended the sown area of Kazakhstan to 19.6 million acres (7,854,000 hectares) in 1950 and to 24.3 million acres (9,717,000 hectares) in 1953. This expansion increased the grain harvests, which were, however, still insufficient for the country's requirements. The variation in the grain harvests of northern Kazakhstan soon became evident and should have acted as a warning for the future to Soviet administrators. From a figure of 2.5 million metric tons in 1940 the harvest rose to 4.8 million metric tons in 1950, but dropped back sharply to 2.6 million in 1951. By 1953, however, the total had reached 5.4 million metric tons.

KAZAKHSTAN'S VIRGIN LANDS

One factor which slowed down the increase in area sown to grain after the war was an attempt to extend fodder crops so that livestock could be multiplied. Unfortunately, this effort took the form of sowing large areas with perennial grasses which did not grow well in the arid conditions of the Kazakh plains and resulted in very low harvests of hay.[57] By 1953 the grain situation in the Soviet Union was very serious. The harvest had not reached the 1913 level and there was no sign of any immediate improvement.

Khrushchev then decided to go ahead with a plan for plowing up the idle lands of Kazakhstan and West Siberia on a large scale and sowing them to wheat in an attempt to increase grain production as rapidly as possible with the least investment of capital. The attractions of this scheme were several.

First, northern Kazakhstan was an area where no crops had been grown before and therefore the soil was in prime condition. Moreover, as has been seen, the chernozem and chestnut soils of the

[57] Neishtadt, pp. 113, 112.

region are excellent for the growing of grain crops. The combination of these soil factors meant that fertilizer would not be necessary, at least in the early stages, and in view of the low productivity of the Soviet fertilizer industry this was obviously very important. The effort in Kazakhstan appeared to be preferable to any attempts at increasing productivity per acre in the grain lands of the Ukraine or western Russia, where increased applications of fertilizer would have been required.

The second major argument favoring Khrushchev's plan was that the growing of wheat requires little preparation of the soil except plowing, and minimum cultivation during the growing period. It would, therefore, be possible to dispense with the experienced peasant farmer, with whom the authorities had always had trouble, and bring in young people from the urban areas who would work with greater enthusiasm than the peasant farmers. The stage of collectivization represented by the kolkhoz, not an ideal form of rural organization in Soviet Marxist eyes, could thus be bypassed and here the sovkhoz introduced directly.

The third selling point for the scheme was provided by the flat terrain and the possibility of laying out very large fields which would be suited to mechanized farming. The relatively sparse population and the lack of manpower in the region also made the use of machinery an attractive proposition. The agricultural machinery industry increased the number of tractors in Kazakhstan from 39,845 at the end of 1953 to 94,845 at mid-1956 and 195,700 in 1963. The number of combines climbed during the same period from 21,668 to 75,844 (end of 1956) and 105,000 in 1963. Unfortunately, efficient use has not been made of all this machinery, and the Soviet press has reported instances of machinery being allowed to rust in the fields.

Regardless of mistakes in organization and poor techniques, the sown area in the new lands increased rapidly from 24.3 million acres (9,716,900 hectares) in 1953 to 69.7 million acres (27,883,100 hectares) in 1956 and 71.7 million acres (28,661,500 hectares) in 1958. Of this last figure 58.1 million acres (23,245,000 hectares) were under grain. In all, between 1954 and 1958 over 50 million acres (20 million hectares) of virgin and fallow land had been plowed.

Kustanay and Akmolinsk oblasts led in the total area plowed, followed by Kokshetau and Pavlodar oblasts. The last year of extensive plowing in the Virgin Lands was 1956. Although a slight increase in the total sown area of Kazakhstan had taken place again by 1958, after that date the total sown area and the space sown to grain remained static until 1962, when they rose to 77.8 million acres (31,118,000 hectares) and 62.3 million acres (24,929,000 hectares) respectively. Of the latter figure, 47.5 million acres (18,986,000 hectares), 4.2 times the acreage in 1953, were planted with wheat.

This startling increase in the area sown did not, however, automatically result in constantly increasing harvests. Poor management and variable rainfall caused fluctuations in the annual harvests, sometimes of serious proportions, as is shown in Table 11.4.

TABLE 11.4

Grain Production in Kazakhstan, 1953–1963

	1953	*1954*	*1955*	*1956*	*1957*	*1958*	*1959*	*1960*	*1961*	*1962*	*1963*
Overall production*	5.4	7.7	4.8	23.5	10.6	22.0	19.1	18.7	14.7	15.9	10.6
Average yield per hectare†	0.77	0.91	0.29	1.06	0.46	0.94	0.87	0.85	0.66	0.65	0.44

　* millions of metric tons
　† metric tons

During that eleven-year period really good harvests were gathered only in 1956 and 1958. Khrushchev had asked for two good years, one medium year, and two bad years out of five in order to claim success, but the number of poor years exceeded his specification. He also called for an average grain yield of 1 metric ton per 1.25 acres (2 metric tons per hectare), a challenge which was never met. Only once did the yield reach an average of over a metric ton per hectare.

The fiasco of the 1963 grain harvest in the Soviet Union and the necessity for importing 11 million metric tons of wheat from abroad can be blamed to a great extent on the failure of the Virgin Lands gamble. Bad organization, poor use of machinery, recurrent drought, and soil erosion took their toll, and signs indicate that the Virgin Lands scheme may gradually be replaced by greater emphasis upon wheat growing in the older agricultural lands of European Russia and the Ukraine with the help of more ample supplies of fertilizer and increased irrigation. The combination of environmental and institutional factors which explain the failure of the Virgin Lands scheme brought criticism to the rigid form of planning which the Soviet authorities attempted to apply to the growing of crops in regions where flexibility of action should have been the keynote.[58]

In connection with the expansion of grain growing in the Virgin Lands, the establishment of a special territory (*krai*) in northern Kazakhstan was announced in December, 1960. This unit, administratively between an oblast and a republic, was characteristic of the less developed regions of the Russian SFSR in the prewar period. At present the krais of the Russian SFSR no longer contain oblasts, while the new Tselinnyi Krai (Virgin Lands Krai) of Kazakhstan contains Tselinograd, Kokshetau, Kustanay, Pavlodar, and North Kazakhstan oblasts, with Tselinograd as its administrative center. Behind the creation of this new region lay the hope to improve the administration of economic development in the northern plains and to place the new wheat areas under centralized control. In 1962 the krai contained about three million people, a third of the population of Kazakhstan, over 60 percent being Russians and Ukrainians, 12 percent Germans, and but 19 percent Kazakhs. About 1.2 million of the population came to the region between 1955 and 1962.[59] In May, 1962, a West Kazakhstan Krai was formed from Aktyubinsk, Guryev, and Uralsk oblasts, with its capital at Aktyubinsk, and a South Kazakhstan Krai, including Jambil, Chimkent, and Qizil Orda oblasts, came into being with Chimkent as the capital.

Though the recent effort to increase grain production in Kazakhstan's Virgin Lands appears to revive the possibility of a self-sufficient Central Asia, the two main thrusts in Soviet agricultural planning for the area from the 1920s to the 1960s have remained the effort to save land area for industrial crops by removing staple food

[58] W. A. Douglas Jackson, "The Virgin and Idle Lands of Western Siberia and Northern Kazakhstan," *Geographical Review*, Vol. XLVI, No. 1 (January, 1956), pp. 1–19; W. A. Douglas Jackson, "The Virgin and Idle Lands Program Reappraised," *Annals of the Association of American Geographers*, Vol. LII, No. 1 (March, 1962), pp. 69–79.

[59] A. A. Karsten, "The Virgin Lands Kray and Its Prospects of Development," *Soviet Geography*, Vol. IV, No. 5 (May, 1963), p. 40.

production so far as feasible from territory suitable for cotton growing, and to raise grain and livestock in the Kazakh plains to feed
the USSR at large. Failures in the second drive and success with
cotton—Central Asia produces 92 percent of Soviet cotton—have
unbalanced the agricultural economy of Central Asia and kept the
people there largely dependent upon imports for subsistence while
turning over most of their main commercial crop to Russia.

I. M. M.

12 Industrialization

At mid-nineteenth century the industries of Central Asia were concentrated primarily in the southern part, and in particular in the Uzbek and Tajik areas. The pastoral Kazakhs, Kirgiz, and Turkmens, rarely being in one locality for any length of time, never developed anything more than a rudimentary handicrafts industry, with carpet and rug making as the most advanced branch of their activities. Although the nomads did produce objects of artistic quality, they made few of the everyday articles which entered into the trade of the region, except for animal products, carpets, rugs, and felt. Even in the urbanized areas of southern Central Asia, industry in the modern sense did not exist, most of the activity centered on handicrafts at home or in small workshops. With the advent of Russian trade the small indigenous metal-working industry suffered a decline and most metal articles came from Russia, although some pots, jugs, and other utensils were still manufactured locally from Russian copper. Imported iron was used to make agricultural implements and weapons, and daggers were ground out of old Russian scythes.[1]

The main branch of local industry was the processing of cotton, wool, and silk, and a limited production of materials from these fibers. The textile industry provided the most employment. Domestic cotton had to be picked in the boll, and the bolls had to be laboriously removed by hand—a job mainly performed at home by women. Fiber and seed were then separated by a pair of rough wooden rollers, an inefficient device known as a *chighiriq*. In twelve hours only seventy pounds of cotton could be handled by this

[1] L. Kostenko, *Sredniaia Aziia i vodvorenie v nei russkoi grazhdanstvennosti* (St. Petersburg, Izdatel'stvo Bazunova, 1870), p. 244.

method.[2] The cotton was then cleaned by being placed on the floor and beaten with sticks.

This badly processed raw material was then packed into large sacks, each of which held about 300 pounds, and loaded on the caravans for Russia. By the time the cotton reached its destination the outer layer had been ruined by damp, sand, and dirt, and often some had been stolen by porters. At that time the loss of cotton was said never to be less than 25 percent, often was 50 percent, and averaged about 35 percent.[3]

This picture changed rapidly in the 1880s with the introduction of an American type of cotton and the cotton gin, and in 1899 with the extension of the Trans-Caspian Railroad to the main cotton-growing areas. The Orenburg-Tashkent Railroad, completed in 1906, eased the hauling of cotton to the north even more. These events greatly increased Russia's capacity to avoid bringing cotton from abroad. In 1908–1909, 30.3 percent of all cotton consumed by the Russian textile industry came from Central Asia, and in 1912 this figure had increased to 63.6 percent.[4] In 1915 over 354,000 tons (22,000,000 *pud*) of cotton were sent to Russia, compared with about 8,000 tons (500,000 *pud*) in 1870 and about 11,200 tons in 1877.[5]

The Central Asians retained a small amount of cotton for domestic use and made yarn from the cleaned cotton fiber, using a primitive spinning wheel (*chärkh*). The thread was often colored with one of several varieties of vegetable dye. Various types of cloth were made for the local robes (*khälät*) and turbans (*sällä*), as well as for underwear, blankets, and horse blankets. Cotton and silk materials were woven at home, usually by professional weavers, on a simple loom (*dokandästgah*). Manufacturing of this cotton material had only local significance and was not encouraged by the Russians, who wished no competition for the Russian textile industry. Cotton seed (*chigit*) was squeezed in primitive presses to

[2] *Ibid.*, p. 214.

[3] Eugene Schuyler, *Turkistan* (New York, Scribner, 1877), I, 296. Other information on cotton processing comes from Kostenko, pp. 213–15.

[4] V. Suvorov, *Istoriko-ekonomicheskii ocherk razvitiia Turkestana* (Tashkent, Gosizdat UzSSR, 1962), p. 72.

[5] Kostenko, p. 221; Schuyler, I, 295.

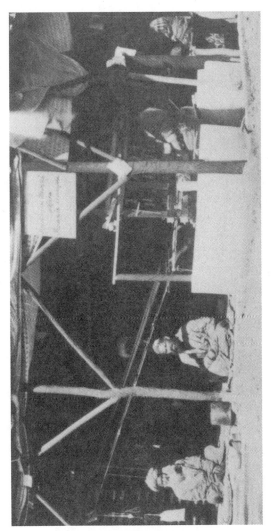

FIGURE 12.1 Traditional methods of silk weaving shown at the exhibition at Tashkent, 1886.

extract the oil, the device often being worked by a horse, ox, or camel in a small workshop (*mayjuwaz*). In Khokand coarse paper was made from cotton fiber and soaked in cottonseed oil to take the place of window glass.[6]

The manufacture of silk (*ipäk*) was carried out in the Persian manner, the silkworms (*ipäk qurti*) being hatched from eggs placed in bags and worn next the body of the brooder (*pillächi*). The worms were fed mulberry leaves on shelves in a room or shed, where they spun their cocoons (*pillä*). The silk was wound off the cocoons by silk winders (*pilläkäsh*) using a spinning reel (*chärkh*). Some of this silk was exported to Russia without further processing. Several types of silken fabric were woven, but because of the Koran's prohibition of luxury, generally only women wore clothes of pure silk material, while material for male clothing was woven from a mixture of cotton and silk.[7]

In contrast with the distribution of local cotton goods, considerable quantities of silk cloth were exported to Russia. Bukharan silk was considered the best, followed by that of Khokand. Around 1873 Central Asia produced about 4 to 5 million pounds of silk annually, of which 3 million pounds came from Bukhara and Khokand.[8] To improve the silk industry the Russians started an institute in 1871, which subsequently closed, but later experimental stations were more successful, and by 1899 the production of silk cocoons in Central Asia reached 7.6 million pounds, of which 6.3 million pounds came from the guberniia of Turkistan.[9]

The manufacture of woolen material was primarily a specialty of the nomads, whose wives loomed sheep, goat, and camel hair. Felt was of particular importance to the nomads, as it formed the basis for the manufacture of tents, bedding, and floor coverings. Carpet and rug manufacturing was, however, the most important branch of the nomad wool industry. The best carpets were made by the Turkmens of the Transcaspian oblast. Women wove them

---

[6] A. I. Dmitiriev-Mamonov, *Putevoditel' po Turkestanu i sredne-aziatskoi zheleznoi doroge* (St. Petersburg, Ministerstvo Voennoe: Puti Soobshcheniia, 1903), p. 117.

[7] Kostenko, p. 230.

[8] Schuyler, I, 193–94.

[9] Based on figures given by A. I. Dmitriev-Mamonov, p. 97.

FIGURE 12.2 Modern silk weaving in a Samarkand factory. Old textile patterns are still used. *Sovfoto.*

on a frame laid flat on the ground, instructions being given by an older woman in charge. White wool of the best quality was selected and treated with vegetable coloring, although by the end of the nineteenth century cheap aniline dyes had begun to appear. The nomads brought their carpets to towns such as Merv (Mari) to sell. In the carpet bazaar (*tim-i giläm*) of Merv which was visited by buyers from Russia and Europe, a carpet without nap was known as a *pälas,* and one with a nap was called a *giläm.* Some *giläms* were also woven in the towns, such as Bukhara. The only other branch of local industry before the Russian conquest worth mentioning was the manufacture of leather, not only for making boots and shoes, but also for making harnesses and liquid containers.

MINING AND OIL EXTRACTION

The region first developed by the Russians industrially was not southern Central Asia but the plains of Kazakhstan. This was due partly to prior penetration of this region by the Russians and somewhat to the early discovery of certain important minerals in the region. In the eighteenth century the Russians had already begun mining for silver, copper, and lead in the Altay mountains, and in 1834 lead and silver mining began in the plains of Akmolinsk oblast, with coal being extracted at Karaganda some twenty years later. Copper mining began at Spasskii Zavod, south of Karaganda, where a smelter using Karaganda coal was built. Mining moved seventy miles south to Uspenskii, where richer ore had been discovered, although the Spasskii smelter still continued operation. Transportation was expensive, the copper having to be brought to Petropavlovsk by oxen in summer and camels in winter, and only the low cost of producing copper from the rich ore made the operation economical.[10] Even the coal was carried from Karaganda by camel, and this reliance on animal transportation raised problems such as the drop in production caused by an outbreak of cattle

[10] P. Alampiev, *Where Economic Inequality Is No More* (Moscow, Foreign Languages Publishing House, 1959), pp. 90–107. Information on early mining operations in the Kazakh area which follows is also drawn from Alampiev and from O. F. Vans-Agnew, "A British Family in the Kazakh Steppe," *Central Asian Review,* vol. X, No. 1 (1962), pp. 5–11.

sickness in 1910. The construction of a light railroad to the coal supplies helped to ease the situation. By 1914 there were 800 workers in the Spasskii plant and 600 in the Karaganda mines, the majority being Russians and Ukrainians. The Kazakhs proved to be unreliable, for they worked in the spring and summer but trekked away in the fall with their herds for the winter pastures.

A copper concentration plant was also built at Sari Su south of Spasskii Zavod to process the Uspenskii ore, and exploitation of the large Jezkazgan copper deposits in the center of Kazakhstan had begun earlier, although the construction of a smelter at Karsakpay was not completed by the time of the 1917 revolution. The outbreak of World War I called for an increase in the production of nonferrous metals, and production was expanded at the Ridder (renamed Leninogorsk in 1940) lead and zinc mines in the Altay. Flooding of these mines in 1916 curtailed production. Coal had been mined since 1900 at nearby Ekibastuz, and plants were built to process lead and zinc from Ridder. In 1916 about 760 workers were employed in the Ekibastuz coal mines. Generally, these metallurgical operations were primitive and the use of the ores wasteful.

Oil was discovered at Dossor in the Emba region on the north shore of the Caspian in 1911, but the operation of the field was hindered by Ural Cossacks who blocked attempts to build a pipeline to Guryev, forcing the oil company to run the pipeline to Rakusha, about forty miles east of Guryev, where the water was too shallow to make an effective port. The Cossacks also prevented the company from using water from the Ural River, compelling the company to draw water from the wells which supplied the Kazakh herds, and thus depriving the Kazakhs of their use. Most of this early development of the mineral wealth of the plains oblasts was in the hands of foreigners. The British ran the Spasskii copper operations, and Americans were active in the Jezkazgan, Ekibastuz, and Ridder areas.[11]

In spite of this energetic mining, the main branch of industry in the plains oblasts involved agricultural processing, such as flour milling. Meat packing, which suffered from a lack of cold storage,

[11] *Istoriia kazakhskoi SSR* (Alma Ata, Izdatel'stvo Akademii Nauk Kazakhskoi SSR, 1957), I, 342–43.

remained a seasonal industry. A number of people were employed washing wool, most of which went to Russia, although a small wool mill was built in 1910 near Alma Ata. An unusual small industry, based at Chimkent, was the manufacture of the drug santonin from wormwood found over wide areas of southern Kazakhstan. This drug, used to treat intestinal worms, was exported to Europe.

Development of industry in southern Central Asia did not take place until after 1865, when the Russians began a systematic survey for the purpose of discovering valuable mineral resources. With an eye on the development of industry and transportation in the region they were particularly interested in locating coal deposits. A mine was opened by the government on the Borolday River, about fifty miles north of Chimkent, and in 1868, 1,250 tons of coal were mined there, about half going to the Aral flotilla.[12] Lack of demand, the poor quality of the coal, and transport problems caused production to cease in the 1870s.

To popularize the use of coal and create a market for it with the Central Asians, the Russian authorities distributed coal free. However, the people reasoned very logically that they would soon be called upon to pay for the coal, while the use of dung as a fuel cost them nothing. Besides, they would have to build proper stoves in which to burn the coal, which would also involve some financial outlay; therefore, they never accepted this new fuel.[13] In the 1870s another coal mine was in operation south of Khojand (Leninabad). It operated only three months of the year and in 1871 produced 625 tons of coal.[14] By 1900 coal had been located in all the oblasts of the Turkistan guberniia and in parts of Bukhara. In addition to four mines near Khojand, there were mines at Chimkent and Uch Qorghan in the Farghana Valley.[15] Production remained insignificant, and the quality of the coal, which was mostly lignite, was unsuitable for most industrial purposes. By 1916 coal production had reached the low figure of 199,820 tons (12.4 million *pud*), which was insufficient to meet the requirements of the region,

---

[12] Schuyler, I, 320.
[13] Kostenko, p. 202.
[14] Schuyler, I, 320.
[15] Dmitriev-Mamonov, p. 10.

which were around 580,000 tons (36 million *pud*) a year at this time.[16]

Before the arrival of the Russians, oil had been located at May Bulaq (Oil Spring) near Namangan in the Farghana Valley, where it was used for manufacturing asphalt. In 1868 a Tashkent merchant obtained the right to work this field from the khan of Khokand in exchange for 10 percent of the proceeds.[17] A second petroleum field was located along the southern edge of the Farghana Valley, about twenty miles southwest of Skobelev (Farghana). A small oil refinery was built in 1907 at Vannovskii (renamed Hamza Hakim Zada in 1963), where small quantities of benzene, kerosene, and oil were produced, total production in 1907 being 51,600 tons (3.2 million *pud*) and in 1913 only 12,700 tons (800,000 *pud*).[18] The reason for this small output was the oil companies' preference to concentrate their efforts on expanding production at Baku and their consequent neglect of the Central Asian operations.

In the 1870s the extraction of oil on a commercial basis began on Cheleken Island, now a peninsula, off the shores of the Caspian Sea near the Kara Bogaz Kol, and operations also began at Nebit Dagh (Turkmen for Oil Mountain) on the mainland, the latter oil-field becoming more important after 1912 because of its greater ease of exploitation. Ozocerite, a mineral wax, was also found in both locations, and at one time was sent to Bukhara as a raw material for the manufacture of candles. The Russians exploited the deposits for industrial and medical purposes.[19]

In spite of the existence of an oil industry in Central Asia, the Trans-Caspian Railroad got most of the oil for its diesel locomotives from Baku. This oil was stored at Ashkhabad and other points along the line.[20] Between 1913 and 1916 the Trans-Caspian and Oren-burg-Tashkent railroads required 685,000 tons (42.5 million *pud*) of

[16] Suvorov, pp. 38–39.

[17] Schuyler, I, 323; Kostenko, p. 210.

[18] *Aziatskaia Rossiia* (St. Petersburg, Pereselencheskoe Upravlienie Glavnago Upravlieniia Zemleustroistva i Zemledieliia, 1914), II, 523.

[19] P. Skosyrev, *Soviet Turkmenistan* (Moscow, Foreign Languages Publishing House, 1956), pp. 45–46.

[20] G. N. Curzon, *Russia in Central Asia* (London, Longmans, Green, 1889), p. 58.

petroleum products, and large quantities had to be imported into the region to meet this demand.[21]

By the time of the 1917 revolutions many deposits of varied minerals had been located in the south. Scattered deposits of iron ore were known, but none was mined and no one endeavored to establish an iron and steel industry. Copper deposits were worked in the Farghana Valley, on the Chirchiq near Tashkent, and in the state of Bukhara, and in 1870 copper which was mined near Namangan in the Farghana Valley was being smelted with local coal.[22] Most of the copper ore was sent to the smelters of Moscow and Riga, however, after being treated in ore-enrichment plants. In 1911, 2,700 tons (170,000 *pud*) of copper were mined in southern Central Asia.[23] One of the few metals mined by the local population was lead, used for the manufacture of musket balls. The khan of Khokand operated lead mines in the Qara Tau mountains north of the town of Turkistan, but only the best grades of ores could be employed because primitive smelting methods were so inefficient. During the Russian military advance into Central Asia these mines were operating at their greatest capacity. A Russian merchant then purchased the mines in order to supply the Russian army with lead, but by the early 1870s this mining operation had ceased.[24] Manganese, zinc, and antimony were all found in southern Central Asia, but none was mined. Small quantities of vanadium and radium were mined in the Farghana Valley and sent to Russia.

One of the major attractions luring Russians to Western and Eastern Turkistan since the time of Peter the Great had been the dream that gold was to be found there in great quantities. This fantasy was sometimes attributed to the boastfulness of the Central Asians, and partly to the fact that numbers of them had come north to Orenburg and Troitsk between 1748 and 1755 carrying large quantities of gold and silver coins and ingots which they had obtained after the assassination of the Avshar ruler of Persia Nadir Shah (r.1736–1747) and the pillaging of his fabled treasure house. Whether these notions formed the basis for Russian expectations

[21] Suvorov, p. 40.
[22] Kostenko, p. 210.
[23] Suvorov, p. 40.
[24] Schuyler, I, 321–22; Kostenko, p. 204.

or not, the Russians found only small, unrewarding deposits of gold.[25]

Among the nonmetallic minerals, salt was the most important to the local economy and was worked in many areas from Kazakhstan to Bukhara. Production of salt employed as many as 2,500 permanent and 5,200 seasonal workers in 1915. Sulphur and saltpeter were also mined, mainly in the khanate of Khokand, first for manufacturing gunpowder, and later to supply a match factory in Tashkent.[26]

PROCESSING AND SHIPPING AGRICULTURAL PRODUCTS

No real beginning was made in these temporary efforts by the Russians to industrialize southern Central Asia before 1917. Mining was in its infancy, coal and oil production elementary, and no iron or steel was manufactured. The emirate of Bukhara was not even properly surveyed to assess its mineral wealth, except by a few gold prospectors in the southern mountains.[27]

As in the case of the plains oblasts, the processing of agricultural products, in particular the processing of cotton, formed the main industrial activity. The first two cotton gins in Central Asia were installed in Khokand by private individuals in 1880 and their number in Farghana oblast had reached 21 by 1890, increasing to 100 by 1901. In 1914 the oblast had 159 ginning plants, which represented the greatest concentration of cotton ginning in pre-1917 Central Asia. In the same year Samarkand oblast ran 33 ginning plants and Sir Darya oblast 28. The Transcaspian oblast employed over 10 plants, including 2 state-owned establishments at the Murghab Imperial Domain, but Semirechie oblast had no cotton-ginning facilities at all.[28] In 1910 the emirate of Bukhara supported about 15 cotton-ginning plants at such places as Novaia Bukhara (Kagan), Charjuy, Karki, and Termez. The Bukharan government required all cotton-ginning plants to be built within two versts (about 1.3 miles) from the railroad, which restricted the development of the

[25] Kostenko, pp. 206–7.
[26] Suvorov, pp. 41, 207.
[27] D. N. Logofet, *Bukharskoie khanstvo pod russkim protektoratom* (St. Petersburg, Berezovskii, 1911), I, 265.
[28] Dmitriev-Mamonov, pp. 85–86; V. V. Zaorskaia and K. A. Aleksandr, *Promyshlenniia zavedeniia turkestanskago kraia* (Petrograd, M. Z. Otdiel Zemel'nykh Uluchshenii, 1915), p. 18.

industry.[29] In 1914, nineteen cottonseed oil plants functioned in the Farghana oblast, the largest being at Khokand and at Katta Qorghan, both with a yearly output of 45,000 tons (2,800,000 *pud*) of cotton seed oil.[30] Cotton processing provided the greatest employment of any industry in the guberniia of Turkistan. From a total of 20,925 workers in industry in 1914, 7,626 or 36.5 percent were employed in cotton ginning and 1,720 or 8.2 percent were employed in the cottonseed oil industry.[31]

Apart from the processing of cotton, prerevolutionary industrial activities like leather tanning, wool washing, and silk spinning virtually completed the inventory. Metal-working establishments served almost exclusively for maintaining the railroads or repairing rolling stock. In Tashkent, for example, the main railroad workshops employed 540 permanent workers out of a total labor force of 2,528 persons in 1914, while the railroad workshops in Qizil Arvat employed around 1,000 workers in the same year, very few of whom came from the Central Asian population. Several workshops were located at other points along the railroad.

In terms of employment, Tashkent led the industrial centers in the Turkistan guberniia in 1914 with 2,528 workers, followed by Khokand with 2,487, Andijan with 2,435, Namangan with 1,779, and Samarkand with 1,421.[32] This information stresses again the importance of the cotton- and silk-processing industries of Farghana oblast in Central Asian industry, because most of the workers were employed in one or another of these industries. In fact, during this period, the Farghana oblast had over three times the number of workers in the Sir Darya oblast and four times the number in the Samarkand oblast.

The importance of the Trans-Caspian Railroad and the later Orenburg-Tashkent line in the development of Central Asian industry was well illustrated by the fact that in 1914 about 81 percent of the industry in southern Central Asia was located within the sphere of attraction of the railway (113 out of 202 cotton-

---

[29] Logofet, I, 279.
[30] Suvorov, p. 43; Zaorskaia and Aleksandr, p. 18.
[31] Zaorskaia and Aleksandr, table IV.
[32] Suvorov, p. 36 and footnote.

ginning plants and 480 out of 697 large industrial establishments were located no more than seven miles from the railroad), and the other 19 percent was mainly in Semirechie.[33]

Local transportation, before the railroads, in the settled areas of Central Asia was carried on mainly by mules, donkeys, and carts (*ärawä*). Because the dirt roads were intersected frequently by irrigation ditches, cart wheels had to be large enough to cross such obstructions. The two-wheeled cart was put together without the aid of nails or metal and was pulled by a horse. The primitive nature of this vehicle made it unsuitable for transportation over any extended distance. The camel caravan provided transportation for long hauls. The advantages of the camel over the horse in arid countries has been known for centuries, and surprisingly great distances were covered by the slow-moving caravans through regions with semidesert and desert conditions.

However, even camels need regular supplies of water, and the course of many caravan routes was determined by the availability of water. Methods of obtaining water for the use of caravans and other travelers differed in many respects from those used to obtain water for irrigation, mainly because of the difference in the quantities required. Wherever possible a well was dug and water raised to the surface in a leather bag tied to a rope, generally pulled at the other end by a camel. Brick-lined cisterns (Tajik and Uzbek: *särdabä*) were built to collect rainfall. This kind of storage tank had a thick domed masonry roof over it to prevent evaporation and was located at the bottom of a hollow to collect rainwater running off the surrounding hills. Although it was an ingenious method of storing water over a considerable period, the water it collected often became badly polluted by animals or by dirt washed in with the rain. Because of this problem encountered in all types of wells, a well attendant (*quduqchi*) was employed to keep the wells clean at the caravan stops.

TRADE WITH INDIA AND RUSSIA

Before railroads changed much of Central Asian trade, Bukhara's excellent location made it an important link between India and

[33] Suvorov, p. 38.

Europe. During the period of the Russian protectorate, this fostered several problems involving Bukhara's role in Indian trade. In the last half of the nineteenth century Indian goods began to appear on the Bukharan market in increasing quantities, and it was not until the arrival of Russian merchants in southern Central Asia after 1865 that Russian goods began to arrive in Bukhara in any quantity to compete with those from India. But no appreciable advance was possible in Russian trade with Central Asia until the capture of Tashkent allowed greater Russian pressure to be applied directly on the Bukharan emirate.[34]

In order to curtail the importation of Indian goods into the Russian empire a customs barrier was set up on the Russian-Bukharan border, but even this did not prevent Indian goods from coming into the emirate and also from reaching Khiva and Samarkand. Finally, by 1894 the Russians were powerful enough to call for a customs union with Bukhara which involved the removal of the customs control on the Russian-Bukharan border, the closing of the Bukharan-Afghan frontier, and the consequent blocking of the direct entry of all Indian goods.

From this time on there was no problem of competition for Russian goods, which increased in quantity, in the Central Asian market. Books, and some Indian products, especially tea, managed to circumvent the closure of the Afghan frontier by coming in via Baku across the Caspian to Krasnovodsk, and thence to Bukhara and points east. Green tea also still reached the region from Eastern Turkistan. In 1903 about 50 percent, by value, of Bukharan exports to Russia consisted of cotton, while qarakol skins made up about another 30 percent. Skins of sheep, rams, and other animals accounted for about 5 percent, as did wool; silk supplied another 4 percent and carpets 0.5 percent of the total value of exports. About 50 percent, by value, of imports from Russia consisted of manufactured goods, the balance being mainly dry goods, ironmongery, porcelain, sugar, kerosene, soap, and dyes.[35]

Second to Bukhara as a trade center in southern Central Asia

[34] Kostenko, pp. 254–55.
[35] Logofet, I, 282–83, 284–85.

was Samarkand, but after the arrival of the Russians and the construction of the Orenburg-Tashkent Railroad in particular, Tashkent gradually overtook it in importance, eventually eclipsing Bukhara itself. Khokand, because of its location in the Farghana Valley, was not a meeting place for trade routes, and had less importance as a market town, except as a terminal point for caravans. Khiva, on the other hand, constituted an important focal point for caravan routes to the north and to the shores of the Caspian Sea (*see* Figure 12.3).

After the capture of Tashkent the main Central Asian caravans to Russia, beginning and ending at Khiva, Bukhara, and Khokand, continued in use until new means of transportation made them obsolete. Three caravans a year traversed the Bukhara-Orenburg route, two or three a year went to Troitsk, and an occasional caravan reached Petropavlovsk. The timing of caravan movements coincided with the migration of the Kazakhs and their flocks, because the Kazakhs conducted most of the caravans which crossed the plains. The first caravan from Bukhara to Orenburg would leave at the beginning of spring, when the Kazakh flocks started to move north, followed by two more at intervals of about a month. The caravans would depart Orenburg at the end of the fall, when the Kazakhs began their trek to the winter pastures. The fact that en route the Kazakhs had business to take care of other than merely looking after the caravan meant that the paths taken often varied and the arrival time of a caravan could never be accurately predicted.[36]

The sedentary agricultural economy of the oases complemented that of the nomadic herders, as was demonstrated in these combined caravan and flock movements showing the importance of trade relations between oasis and plain. This interaction was, in fact, more important than any of the earlier trade contacts with the Russians in developing the traditional economy of Central Asia. Their traders exchanged cotton and silk cloth, and such articles as tools, weapons, and domestic utensils manufactured in homes in return for the nomads' felt, cloth, and wool carpets. Milk and

[36] Kostenko, pp. 283–84.

dairy products played but a small role in this exchange, because the nomads consumed most of their own production. However, cattle for meat entered into the bartering to a considerable extent. This earlier interregional trade had led to the development of Bukhara and Khiva as important trade centers before the Russian merchants appeared on the scene.[37]

RIVER AND RAIL TRANSPORT

Before they built their railroads in Central Asia the Russians tried to use the river system for transport, the first serious attempt with steamboats beginning on the Sir Darya in 1853. Two ships were launched, but the draft of one was too deep and the other was not powerful enough to overcome the swift current. In 1862 two additional ships were obtained, but they were even less successful than the first pair. A fifth ship arrived in 1868, but like the others found the strong current and the changes in depth and direction of the many channels of the Sir Darya a great problem. The commissioning of a sixth vessel in 1870 was of little help;[38] therefore, the Sir Darya flotilla was officially abolished in 1883, although it continued sailing until 1888.

Navigation on the Amu Darya was more successful, in spite of the vagaries of its course and shoals. Bukharans and Khivans had long sailed the whole length of the river from the rapids on the Panj to the Aral Sea in small boats and skiffs (*qäyiqs*) carrying products like cotton, carpets, felt, and foodstuffs. By the late 1880s the Russians had five vessels operating on the Amu Darya for military rather than trade purposes, although some civilian freight was carried. The main function of the fleet was to maintain connections between the railroad at Charjuy and the military forts and settlements along the river. Two of these vessels were shallow-draft paddle-wheel steamers which had difficulty breasting the swift current. By 1895 there were four steamships on the Amu Darya, and eight other vessels, mostly sizable barges. At the beginning of

---

[37] A. N. Rakitnikov, "Nekotorye osobennosti istoricheskoi geografii zemledeliia i zhivotnovodstva v Srednei Azii," *Istoricheskaia geografiia, Voprosy geografii,* L (Moscow, 1960), 87–89.

[38] Kostenko, pp. 296–97; Schuyler, I, 56–60.

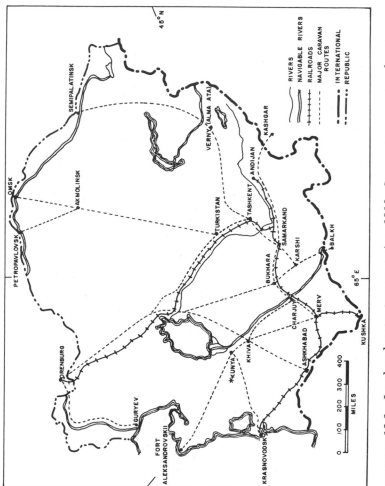

FIGURE 12.3 Land and water transportation, 1910. Some caravan routes shown were then losing importance because of rail competition.
* Russian form of Kohna Urganch.

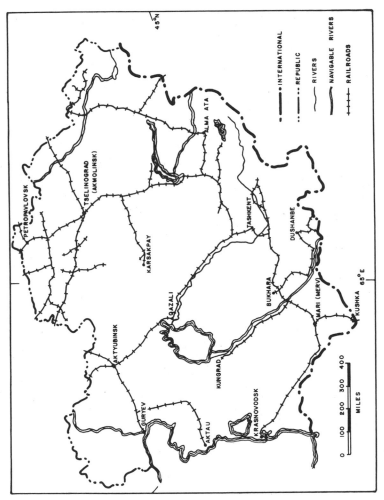

FIGURE 12.4   Land and water transportation, 1962.

World War I twenty-six of the Russian flotilla plied the river along with a small commercial fleet.[39] Although navigation grew considerably between 1887 and 1914, the river proved to be very unsatisfactory as a trade connection with the outside world. Its terminus, the land-locked Aral Sea, had no links with the Caspian Sea or Russia except via caravan.

The construction of the Orenburg-Tashkent Railroad in 1906, with its ties to the remainder of the area through the Central Asian railroad, removed the necessity of making further attempts to navigate the Sir Darya, and limited traffic on the Amu Darya to shipping services between the towns and settlements along the river.

Building the Trans-Caspian Railroad (to Samarkand by 1888) called for considerable engineering skill. It was a challenge to lay track in areas of shifting sands and to put a bridge across the Amu Darya at Charjuy with wood that had to be entirely brought in from Russia, mainly via the Volga and the Caspian. This railroad first began at Uzun Ada, a port which rapidly silted up, so that the line was extended over to the port of Krasnovodsk in 1894.

The road had to by-pass the city of Bukhara, because the citizens there regarded the train as an instrument of the devil which could not be allowed to enter their holy city. This decision materially contributed to the economic decline of Bukhara, because the ten-mile gap between the railroad and the city was not spanned by a line until 1907. In the meantime the Russian settlement of Novaia Bukhara (Kagan) grew up beside the railroad and immediately developed a small industry of its own at Bukhara's expense.

Furthermore, not until the Trans-Caspian Railroad was extended beyond Samarkand to Tashkent in 1898 and to Andijan in the Farghana Valley in 1899 did the major cotton-growing areas of Central Asia acquire rail communications. Because the primary purpose of the Trans-Caspian Railroad was to facilitate the military subjugation of the Turkmens, and not primarily to promote trade, the line proved unsatisfactory as a major artery for Russian–Central Asian commerce. Its route necessitated the transshipping of

[39] M. W. de Kovalevsky, *La Russie à la fin du 19e siècle* (Paris, Dupont et Guillaumin, 1900), p. 838; Suvorov, p. 89.

freight at Krasnovodsk and again either at Baku or the mouth of the Volga, adding both to the cost and the time in transit of all goods.

The Orenburg-Tashkent line, completed in 1906, was intended to provide a more economical and faster route between Russia and Central Asia, and it opened the area to even greater Russian influence, at the same time permitting the speedy delivery of ever greater quantities of cotton to Russian textile mills. The new railroad also facilitated the import of Russian grain into Central Asia, consequently releasing even more land for cotton growing.

In 1893 the low rate for shipping Russian wheat on the Trans-Caspian Railroad in effect caused wheat prices to fall in southern Central Asia and thus prodded the local population to expand areas sown to cotton. Because ever larger supplies of cheap wheat were needed to encourage yet more cotton growing, the construction of a railroad from Siberia to bring in supplies of cheap Siberian wheat was begun from both ends of the projected line in 1912 and 1913, but was abandoned during World War I. Work begun again on this line in 1927 was completed in 1930, when the line was named the Turkistan-Siberian Railroad or Turk-Sib.[40]

The impact of rail transport on the economy was thus considerable. There is a significant correlation between the construction of the railroads, the extension of the area sown to cotton, the export of cotton from Central Asia, cotton imports into Russia from abroad, the price of cotton on Central Asian, Moscow, and world markets, and the construction of industrial enterprises for the period 1880–1915.

A steady rise in the total area sown to cotton took place between 1880 and 1900, but there was no sign of a sudden swelling in acreage after the completion of the first stage of the Trans-Caspian Railroad in 1888. However, export of Central Asian cotton to Russia took a sudden jump in 1890 and made an even steeper climb between 1905 and 1915, after the completion of the Orenburg-Tashkent Railroad, and coincided with a period of rapid decline in the rate of cotton imported into Russia from abroad. Starting in

[40] R. A. Pierce, *Russian Central Asia, 1867–1917* (Berkeley and Los Angeles, University of California Press, 1960), pp. 167, 189.

1905 the total area sown to cotton also showed a sudden more rapid rate of increase.

But, a simple correlation between railroad construction and cotton production cannot be shown, because between 1900 and 1905, just after the railroad had reached the Farghana Valley and work had begun on the Orenburg-Tashkent line, world cotton prices slipped to their low point, and Central Asian and Moscow prices stood little higher. This period witnessed an actual decrease in the total sown area of cotton and a leveling off of exports to Russia from Central Asia. The big increase in the sown area and in exports noted after the completion of the Orenburg-Tashkent Railroad in 1906 also accompanied the sudden and rapid revival of world and Moscow prices, which soared to an all-time high in 1915. Hence it is dangerous to attempt too glib an explanation of the expansion of the cotton industry in terms of railroad construction. It is interesting in this connection to note, however, that the growth of industrial enterprises practically parallels that of railroad expansion, illustrating the contention that a major part of southern Central Asia's industry arose along the railroads.[41]

If a direct tie between the growth of the railroads and the increases in cotton production over the 1880–1915 period is not clear, there is no question that the direction of traffic changed dramatically after the completion of the Orenburg-Tashkent line. Statistics for trade through Krasnovodsk show that between 1900 and 1905 imports and exports increased in volume by a total of 158,000 tons (9,825,000 *pud*), while the increase in total trade for the period from 1906 to 1912 was only 26,500 tons (1,646,000 *pud*). This decrease in the rate of trade growth through Krasnovodsk is accounted for by the completion of the Orenburg-Tashkent line in 1906, which resulted in the dramatic rise of trade via Tashkent. Between 1906 and 1912 imports and exports through Tashkent increased by 459,-600 tons (28,239,000 *pud*), and in 1912 the Orenburg-Tashkent Railroad was hauling 214,000 tons (13,303,000 *pud*) more freight than the Transcaspian line.[42]

[41] Suvorov, p. 161, fig. 5.
[42] *Istoriia uzbekskoi SSR* (Tashkent, Izdatel'stvo Akademii Nauk Uzbekskoi SSR, 1956), vol. I, Book 2, p. 210.

There is no doubt that the greatest Russian impact on the traditional economy of Central Asia was in transportation. The replacement of the slow and inefficient camel caravan by the railroads opened Central Asia to the Russian merchant and enabled the Russian authorities to transform southern Central Asia into a cotton-growing colony which relied on Russian industry for virtually all manufactured goods. This one-sided development of the economy preserved the traditional agricultural activities, and explains why the arrival of the railroad resulted in only a limited development of industry, apart from the processing of agricultural products.

SOVIET CRISIS AND ECONOMIC PLANNING FOR THE SOUTH

Thus, on the eve of the 1917 revolution, the industry of southern Central Asia consisted almost exclusively of cotton processing, while production of low-grade coal and some oil virtually represented the entire mining industry. Upon Soviet seizure and nationalization of the cotton industry, the coal mines, oil wells, and steamship and railroad lines in 1918, what little industrial activity there was shrank even further. The decline in cotton sowing led to a slump in cotton ginning and oil pressing, and the production of coal and oil also dropped, although more gradually.

This industrial disintegration continued throughout the civil war, and by 1922 industry had collapsed completely. During the period of Basmachi activity many factories were destroyed by the warring factions. It is claimed that in Farghana oblast alone ninety-six (about 50 percent) of all the cotton-processing plants were destroyed, and large quantities of cotton fiber, thread, and seed were destroyed by burning. Of those cotton-processing plants left standing at the end of 1920, 12.7 percent had no equipment. Only 25 percent were fully equipped but needed repair. The number of workers employed at cotton ginning in Central Asia dropped from 6,000 in 1917 to 650 in 1920.[43]

Activity in the coal and oil industries followed a different pattern during the same period. The lack of any railroad connections between Russia and southern Central Asia until October, 1919,

[43] O. B. Dzhamalov, ed., *Istoriia narodnogo khoziaistvo Uzbekistana* (Tashkent, Izdatel'stvo Akademii Nauk Uzbekskoi SSR, 1962), I, 59, 63.

caused a serious fuel crisis which was met to a certain extent by the maintenance of coal production. In 1919 and 1920 the total production of coal was 173,800 tons (10.8 million *pud*) and 157,800 tons (9.8 million *pud*) as compared with 183,500 tons (11.4 million *pud*) in 1917. Petroleum production dropped, however, in 1920 to about half the level of 1917, while the use of wood as a fuel increased considerably.[44] This had a serious effect on the already depleted groves and orchards and increased problems of soil erosion. At the worst period of the fuel crisis cotton seed and dried fish were burned, even by the railroads. About the only branch of industry which did not suffer to any great extent was domestic handicraft manufacturing which was kept busy supplying articles of everyday use for the local population.

The period from 1922 to 1928 was devoted to restoring industry to the pre-1917 level. By 1928 cotton processing was back on its feet, and a start had been made on the introduction of new industries such as small clothing and footwear factories and two small oil refineries built in the Farghana Valley. Silk-spinning plants opened in Samarkand, Marghilan, and Bukhara, and metal-working facilities expanded in several cities. However, industrial structure and output did not change significantly during this period in comparison with the situation before the revolution.

Between 1928 and the outbreak of World War II the industrialization of southern Central Asia proceeded more rapidly. Such development was based to a great extent upon an increase in electric power production. In 1928 the power output in southern Central Asia totaled 46 million kilowatt-hours and by 1937 it had reached 390 million kilowatt-hours, mainly because of the construction of new thermal power stations in the major cities. The largest were located at Farghana, Tashkent, Quwasay, Chimkent, Alma Ata, Frunze, Ashkhabad, and in Uzbekistan's Kadyrinskii raion. The Boz Su and Varzab hydroelectric plants were built near Tashkent and Dushanbe respectively.

Between 1928 and the outbreak of the war a start was also made on the establishment of a cotton textile industry. In particular, the completion of the initial stage of a large textile mill in Tashkent in

[44] *Ibid.*, I, 66–67.

1935 gave the region its first large supplies of locally manufactured textiles. Under the second Five Year Plan industry was particularly stressed and several new enterprises begun. This development was not intended to make Western Turkistan a self-sufficient region, but primarily was meant to aid the development of the cotton-growing and processing industries.

In this program, for example, two fertilizer plants were constructed at Khokand and Novaia Bukhara, an oil extracting facility was established at Katta Qorghan, and several big mechanized cotton gins were erected at various locations, including Bukhara and Chust. A large factory for manufacturing agricultural machinery needed by the cotton industry and equipment for ginning was opened at Tashkent. This installation, known as the Tashsel'mash, remains the largest industrial complex in southern Central Asia today.

In 1940 an electrochemical works at Chirchiq began the production of nitrogen fertilizer for the cotton growers. Apart from industries serving the cotton industry, most of the other new enterprises turned out to be fruit-canning, silk-spinning, and leather-processing plants, this last giving impetus to the rise of a footwear industry of some importance. During this period of development Tashkent began to emerge as the major industrial center of the whole of Central Asia and the only city with a fully developed engineering industry.

The outbreak of World War II caused some important changes in industrial structure. The possibility that the region might become detached from Russia by the disruption of communications, the evacuation of plants and workers from the western parts of the Soviet Union, the loss of important industrial centers in the west, and the necessity for building up industrial bases well to the rear of the battle line, all called for a greater development and diversification of Central Asian industry.

STEEL AND HYDROELECTRIC POWER
IN SOUTHERN CENTRAL ASIA

In particular, some local production of steel was required. The answer to this need was met by the construction of a plant at

Bekabad (Begovat) to produce steel ingots and rolled steel from scrap metal. In 1946, the first year of operation, 28,000 metric tons of steel were produced. The construction of the Farhad hydroelectric station on the Sir Darya at Bekabad enables the mill to use electric furnaces. Apart from these, there are open-hearth furnaces and a steel-rolling mill. There are indications that some pig iron comes from Magnitogorsk in the Urals and coke and coal from Kemerovo in West Siberia and Karaganda in Kazakhstan. Apart from the high costs incurred in the transportation of these materials there have also been complaints about careless selection and sorting of scrap at the plant.[45] The Bekabad installation does not thus have a full metallurgical cycle, and it has been suggested that blast furnaces should be built to use coking coal from Kazakhstan, but the plant is poorly located for the cheap assembly of raw materials, and production is likely to remain limited.

A rise in output has, however, taken place over the last few years, and in 1963 Uzbekistan produced 342,700 metric tons of steel, compared with 251,000 metric tons in 1958. The smallness of these amounts can be appreciated when they are measured against the total production of crude steel in the Soviet Union in 1963 (80.2 million metric tons). Without the emergency created by the war it is unlikely that southern Central Asia would have developed any steel industry at all.

The war period also ushered in the construction of several other enterprises of economic significance such as the Farhad power station and several other hydroelectric schemes, including a series of stations on the Chirchiq River to supply the Tashkent and Chirchiq industries with power. All these stations together form the major electric power network of Uzbekistan, the second area of power production being based on the large thermalelectric plants of the Farghana Valley. In Tajikistan, a second power plant began to go up on the Varzab. Apart from the construction of power facilities, the war caused the introduction of industry to such cities as Frunze, where an agricultural machinery factory and a meat-packing plant were built; a large cotton mill and tractor parts con-

[45] "Begovat: Key to Central Asian Industrialization," *Central Asian Review*, II (1954), 217–21.

cern were constructed at Dushanbe, and several engineering establishments arose in Tashkent.

Since 1945 the prewar emphasis on industry as a servant of the cotton grower has continued. Three major factories at present produce cotton machinery and equipment, two in Tashkent and one in Chirchiq. A large plant in Tashkent is manufacturing excavators and other equipment for the construction and maintenance of irrigation canals, and others are building suction pumps and electric motors, also essential for irrigation. A factory in Chirchiq makes equipment for the chemical fertilizer industry, and the Tashtekstil'mash complex in Tashkent manufactures machinery for textile plants. The production of mineral fertilizers has been expanded, with superphosphate works located at Khokand, Samarkand, Jambil, and Charjuy, all using phosphate from southern Kazakhstan, and two plants at Chirchiq produce nitrogen fertilizer by the fixation method, utilizing local electric power. In 1963, Uzbekistan's fertilizer production totaled 1.4 million metric tons or about 7 percent of total Soviet production. The cotton-ginning industry, too, has been continuously expanded and new installations are being added every year.

To provide a power base for the expansion of industry, the operation of irrigation pumps and electrification of rural areas, the hydroelectric potential of the rivers of southern Central Asia is being exploited at an increasing rate every year. Many of the mountain rivers are highly suitable for the development of electric power.

This can be seen in the fact that about 85 percent of Uzbekistan's electric power comes from hydroelectric stations. In addition to the Farhad stations and the sixteen small plants on the Chirchiq, the Qayraq Qum station on the Sir Darya, the largest in southern Central Asia, has also been completed recently. Construction of a hydroelectric power station at the Charwak gorge will raise the total capacity of the Chirchiq stations from 400,000 to almost 1 million kilowatts. In Tajikistan a hydroelectric station supplying Dushanbe was opened in 1963 on the Vakhsh River, and work has begun on the construction of the Nurek power station and one of the highest dams in the world on the same river, which will have a

capacity of 2.8 million kilowatts. The power will be used for manufacturing aluminum from kaolin mined at Ahangaran. The Narin
River in Kirgizistan is also being utilized, and work has started on
the Toktogul plant, with a planned capacity of 1.2 million kilowatts, to supply both Frunze and the Farghana Valley. Further
downstream the Uch Qorghan station was completed in 1962.

Production of electric power in the four southern Central Asian
republics rose from 679 million kilowatt-hours in 1940 to 12.45 million in 1963, of which 7.95 million kilowatt-hours were generated in
Uzbekistan. The overriding importance of hydroelectric power development in southern Central Asia derives in part from the lack
of coal and other fuel.

Because of their location near the major centers of industry, the
lignite deposits of the Farghana Valley and Ahangaran, near Tashkent, have some economic importance for the production of electricity and gas, but are not useful for metallurgical purposes. Lignite deposits, many already exploited in czarist times, are also
mined at Lenger, south of Chimkent.

Bituminous coal is mined at Kok Yangak at the eastern end of
the Farghana Valley, and at Tash Komir on the Narin, both in
Kirgizistan, and at Shargun, on the Uzbek-Tajik border. In 1963
the four southern republics produced 8.8 million metric tons of
coal, of which 4.7 million came from Uzbekistan and 3.2 million
from Kirgizistan. Although this represented a rapid increase in production since the war, it still only amounted to 1.7 percent of total
Soviet production in the same year.

Oil production has shown a more spectacular rise than coal, especially in Turkmenistan and the Farghana Valley. Turkmen output
advanced from 587,000 metric tons in 1940 to 7.8 million in 1963,
and Uzbek oil production, of which about 85 percent comes from
the Farghana Valley, rose during the same years from 119,000
metric tons to 1.8 million. Total oil output by the southern Central
Asian republics thus increased from 760,000 tons to 9.5 million during the period, the latter figure accounting for about 4.6 percent of
total Soviet production. This is still, however, below the requirements of the region. The major reserves of the area are now, as in
czarist times, in the Cheleken and Nebit Dagh areas of Turk-

menistan, no new discoveries of any importance having been made in recent years. Production at Nebit Dagh had increased especially rapidly after the early 1930s, when new reserves were found at a depth greater than that at which czarist engineers had operated. However, the total Central Asian proved reserves do not amount to more than about 2 percent of total Soviet proved reserves. The oil refining capacity of the region is small and is limited to the Farghana Valley and Krasnovodsk.

An important addition to the power resources of Uzbekistan has been natural gas, the major deposits of which occur in the Bukhara region at Gazli about sixty miles northwest of the city and at Jarkak and Murabek to the southeast. The extent of these gas fields was first noted when they were surveyed in the 1950s. Construction of pipelines from there to Samarkand and the Farghana Valley was then begun, with a branch leading to Tashkent, Alma Ata, and Frunze. A separate pipeline completed in 1963 from Gazli leads to Cheliabinsk in the Urals. Thus, a large part of Uzbekistan's gas seems destined to leave the region. Apart from the natural gas produced in the oil operations at Nebit Dagh, some has also been found in scattered areas in the Turkmen republic.

Besides lacking adequate oil, gas, and coal for its own needs, southern Central Asia is deficient in other important minerals. The major operation in nonferrous metals is the mining and smelting of copper at Almaliq, south of Tashkent, and the important lead mining to the north of Chimkent, which has its own smelting plant, as well as some mining of lead and zinc around Kansay to the south in Tajikistan. Mercury and antimony, important for the manufacture of electric batteries and for the chemical industry, are also found nearby. The ferrous alloys tungsten and vanadium are found in scattered locations, and the production of molybdenum began at Almaliq in 1963.

Sulphur is found in central Turkmenistan, and mined at Sernyi Zavod and Darwaza, as well as at Gaurdak in the southeast corner. Sodium sulphate (mirabilite) quarried along the shores of the Kara Bogaz Kol has given rise to a chemical industry of some value to Turkmenistan economy, while the fertilizer requirements of the cotton industry has increased the importance of phosphorite deposits at Chulak Tau in southern Kazakhstan, from where supplies are sent to the superphosphate plants at Charjuy, Khokand, Samarkand, and Jambil. These deposits supply about 14 percent of Soviet phosphate fertilizer.

Uranium is the only mineral of strategic importance about which no detailed information is available outside the USSR. Extensive deposits are known to exist in the Farghana Valley and the mountain areas of Kirgizistan, but the grade is thought to be low. Central Asia is, however, probably the major source of supply within the borders of the Soviet Union.

Since 1917 Soviet administrators have advanced various plans for the integration of the four southern republics into a "Central Asian Economic Region," Kazakhstan being set apart for planning purposes. Soviet authorities have not been consistent with regard to the formation of economic regions, at one moment regarding the self-sufficiency of a region as the main criterion for planning, while on another occasion emphasizing the necessity for interregional trade and regional specialization. In actual fact the four republics are far from self-sufficient in the production of such key materials as iron, steel, coal, oil, and machinery, and the narrow specialization of the region in the production of cotton for the mills of Russia is obvious. The "Central Asian Economic Region" set up February, 1963, ended by decree of the USSR Supreme Soviet December, 1964.

KAZAKHSTAN'S RECONSTRUCTION AND DEVELOPMENT

Kazakhstan, by virtue of its size and the diversity of its mineral resources and industries, can make a better claim than the south to self-sufficiency, but even in this case the accent on the production of nonferrous metals for the Russian industrial regions is clearly noticeable. In the plains of northern Kazakhstan, the development of industry, as in the case of agriculture, has followed a pattern very different from affairs in the remainder of Central Asia during the Soviet period.

Industrial activity (mining), as was noted, began in the plains before it started in the settled areas, and mining has remained one of the major branches of Kazakh industry up to the present. From

1917 to 1921, the revolution and civil war created havoc with such industry as existed. At the beginning of the civil war the food-processing industry accounted for about 62 percent of total industrial output, and mining of nonferrous metals, along with the fuel industry, accounted for 12 percent and 5 percent respectively.[46] As in the southern regions, the disruption of communications with Russia lead to the cessation of trade, and the local population turned for everyday necessities to domestic industry and handicrafts. Apart from these, most industries ceased to produce at all. During the fighting between the Red and White armies in the area a great deal of damage was done to factories, mine installations, and the Emba oil fields. By 1920 extraction of oil in Kazakhstan had dropped 75 percent from the 1913 level, copper production had completely stopped, and the coal mining at Karaganda represented 20 percent of the prewar figure. Woolwashing, tanning, and flour milling were carried on at a very low rate. The situation was further worsened by a famine in northwestern Kazakhstan in 1921–1922.[47]

The first attempts at restoring the economy began with the region's basic industry, the processing of agricultural products. This involved reconstructing meat-packing plants, woolwashing facilities, tanneries, and flour mills. Revitalizing the Emba oil industry began at the same time, and by 1924 the wells at Dossor and by 1925 those at Makat were functioning again, bringing the 1927–1928 production at the Emba field up to 249,800 metric tons from 57,400 metric tons in 1920–1921 and from 117,600 metric tons in 1913.[48]

Detailed study of industrial development in Kazakhstan shows that effective restoration of nonferrous metals and coal industries required large amounts of capital and complicated equipment as well as effective transportation. Attempts to restore the Ridder polymetallic mines were not very successful at first. Because the ores proved too complex for technicians of that period to process properly, this ore problem held up the restoration of production at

[46] Based on figures in I. M. Brover and N. A. Erofeev, *Promyshlennost' Kazakhstana za 40 let* (Alma Ata, Gosizdat KazSSR, 1957), p. 8.
[47] Alampiev, p. 126.
[48] *Ibid.*, p. 134; Brover and Erofeev, p. 57.

the Ekibastuz works, the largest industrial enterprise in Kazakhstan. Lacking lead from the Ridder mines, the Ekibastuz lead plant closed down in 1925, along with the coal mines. It proved impossible to move coal from Ekibastuz to other parts of the country because of inadequate transport. There were also attempts at restoring the Spasskii copper plant, but the Uspenskii mine flooded and the Sari Su concentration plant burned down, causing the lowering of coal production at Karaganda.[49]

As late as 1928 food processing was still the major branch of Kazakh industry, with 57 percent of the total production in the republic. Mining of nonferrous metals dropped to 6 percent, but fuel production rose slightly to 6 percent of Kazakh industrial production. An increase in the output of textiles during this period raised their share of the total product of Kazakhstan to 10 percent. On the whole, however, the pattern differed but little from that of prewar industry. With the start of the first Five Year Plan, however, the structure of Kazakh industry began to undergo some changes. In 1928 the Karsakpay copper plant was put into operation at Jezkazgan, and the Ridder lead plant also started operations again in the same year. This boosted the share of nonferrous mining in the total industrial output of the republic to 12 percent in 1932, while the share of the foodstuffs industry fell to 44 percent.[50] Nevertheless, industry of all types played only an insignificant role in the Kazakh economy, even at this date. In 1932, industry's share of the gross output of both agriculture and industry together was only 39.5 percent.[51]

By the beginning of World War II the industrial structure of Kazakhstan had changed more markedly. During the 1930s Soviet planners had concentrated upon the development of mining to the exclusion of most other branches of industry, except those processing agricultural products. The Karaganda coal pits, which a shortage of transport had closed until 1930, were opened again, and production started rising from 30,000 metric tons of coal in 1930 to 3.9 million in 1937 and 6.3 million in 1940. A realization that the

[49] Alampiev, pp. 137–40.
[50] Based on figures given in Brover and Erofeev, p. 8.
[51] Alampiev, p. 233.

Ural-Kuznets iron-and-steel combine was not an economical operation in view of the long hauls required for coal encouraged the
management to mine Karaganda coking coal after 1933 for the
blast furnaces of Magnitogorsk. Oil production also increased at
the Emba field when new wells were opened in the southern part
of the field, and production rose from 269,000 metric tons in 1928–
1929 to 864,000 tons in 1941. Mining and processing of nonferrous
metals received considerable attention at Ridder, at Karsakpay, and
other mining centers. A new enterprise was started at Balkhash, on
the north shore of the lake, where copper had been found and
a smelter started production in 1938. A lead and zinc plant also
began producing an Ust-Kamenogorsk from 1939, when Kazakhstan
led in the USSR output of copper and provided most of the Soviet
zinc.

Other branches were not developed to any great extent at this
time, although the chemical industry was represented by a fertilizer
plant at Aktyubinsk, which was built in 1936 to process, strangely
enough, apatite brought all the way from the Kola peninsula in
northwestern European Russia. However, this plant was in a position to use supplies of phosphorite from southern Kazakhstan after
the discovery of the Chulak Tau deposits in 1936–1937. Potassium
salts and borate were also worked at Lake Inder on the lower Ural
River in western Kazakhstan. Little development of the metal-
working industry took place in the 1930s except for the establishment of machine shops at various mining enterprises and transportation centers.[52]

As in the case of the southern republics, in Kazakhstan too World
War II accelerated the development of industries necessary for
defense. Perhaps the most important development in the whole of
the Central Asian economy during the war was the establishment
of a steel complex near Karaganda at Temir Tau. This mill produced its first steel at the end of 1944, but like Bekabad it did not
have a full metallurgical cycle and operated on imported pig iron

[52] Information on Kazakh industrial development in the 1930s comes mainly
from Brover and Erofeev, and Alampiev, as well as from articles on Central
Asia in *Bol'shaia sovetskaia entsiklopediia* (Moscow, Gosudarstvennoe Nauchnoe Izdatel'stvo "Bol'shaia Sovetskaia Entsiklopediia").

and on scrap metal, its capacity stretching only to about 250,000 metric tons of steel. Later, it was to form the basis for important developments. A ferro alloys plant was built at Aktyubinsk, to exploit the chromium deposit discovered in the area in 1937 and believed to be one of the largest finds of this metal in the world.

A drive for finding and utilizing new mineral deposits was set in motion, because sources of metallic minerals in the western parts of European Russia and in the Ukraine were occupied by the German army. Molybdenum and tungsten mining began in the Balkhash copper area, and manganese and nickel were also located and mined in central Kazakhstan. At Tekeli in the Jungar Alatau a lead and zinc combine began operations, and work started at Ust-Kamenogorsk on lead and zinc plants which came into operation after the war. In all, Kazakhstan contributed about 67 percent of the molybdenum, 50 percent of the copper, and 80–90 percent of the lead produced in the Soviet Union during the war.[53]

The wartime loss of the Donbass helped to accelerate coal extraction at Karaganda, where a plant for manufacturing mining equipment evacuated from the Donbass and a mining institute from Moscow were reestablished.[54] About twenty new shafts were sunk at Karaganda during the war, and total coal production in Kazakhstan rose from 6,972,000 metric tons in 1940 to 12,015,000 metric tons in 1945. Oil production at the Emba fields increased from 697,000 metric tons in 1940 to 788,000 metric tons in 1945, and was processed in part at least by the cracking plant and refinery built in Guryev at the terminus of the pipeline from the oil fields.

Evacuation of industrial enterprises from western Russia increased the industrial potential of Kazakhstan. Several of these included factories for the manufacture of mining equipment, heavy machinery, and automatic presses (presumably to Karaganda, Alma Ata, and Chimkent respectively), the Podolsk sewing machine factory, a mill for rolling nonferrous metals, shops of engineering plants, textile mills, and others.[55] However, the size of some of these

[53] S. A. Neishtadt, *Ekonomicheskoe razvitie kazakhskoi SSR* (Alma Ata, Gosizdat KazSSR, 1960), p. 44.
[54] Brover and Erofeev, p. 43.
[55] Alampiev, p. 299.

plants is not known, and it is difficult to assess how far their arrival boosted industrial production.

The record of the construction of electric power stations in northern Kazakhstan before World War II was unspectacular. By 1940 most of the mining centers and the larger cities had their own thermal power stations, and a hydroelectric power station had been built on the Ulba River, a tributary of the Irtish, to supply power for Leninogorsk. During the war electric power production in Kazakhstan almost doubled as plants were brought into commission, notably at the new mining sites. However, the postwar period has witnessed the construction of major hydroelectric plants, such as the Ust-Kamenogorsk station on the Irtish, with a capacity of 322,000 kilowatts, which started operations in 1953, and the Bukhtarma station, also on the Irtish, which will have a total capacity of 455,000 kilowatts when completed. The dam for this power station has created a reservoir on the Irtish which extends up-river to Lake Zaisan. A third plant on the Irtish is under construction at Shulba, below Ust-Kamenogorsk. This power complex is intended to provide cheap electricity for the mining and ore-processing centers of the Altay region.

Since World War II the most important advance in Kazakh industry has been the further development of the iron and steel industry in the Karaganda area. Construction of a fully integrated plant began in 1956 on the railroad between Karaganda and Temir Tau, and two large blast furnaces for the production of pig iron have been built and more are planned. The eventual annual planned capacity of 3.5 million metric tons of steel would make the plant one of the largest in the Soviet Union. The mill will specialize in the production of sheet steel. Assembling the required raw materials is relatively easy, because local coal and iron ore from central and northern Kazakhstan are available. Steel coming from this plant is among the cheapest in the Soviet Union.

One of the problems facing the management continues to be the lack of water in the area. Large quantities are required for steps such as quenching coke, cooling blast furnaces, and making steam, and although it is possible to re-use and conserve water to a certain extent, as the Fontana plant in arid southern California does, yet at least 3 million gallons of water a day are required by the American plant. There has been talk of using underground water for these purposes in the Karaganda area, but the solution now being attempted entails digging a canal from the Irtish at Yermak to flow north of Ekibastuz and then south to Karaganda. Work began on this 320-mile-long canal in 1961. Apart from industrial purposes the canal will supply water for irrigation, especially around the industrial areas.

The expansion of the iron and steel industry has been accompanied by the development of iron-ore mining. In particular exploitation of rich iron ore deposits in the Kustanay region is being developed, and smaller deposits south of Karaganda, near Jezkazgan and north of the Aral Sea, are also receiving attention. Ore-enrichment plants have been built, and northern Kazakhstan ores are being sent to the Urals.

A second large ferroalloy plant to supplement the one at Aktyubinsk has been erected on the Irtish at Yermak, and a large thermal power station of 2.4 million-kilowatt capacity has gone up at Yermak to provide this plant and alumina and aluminum plants at nearby Pavlodar with power. To supply this enormous power plant, production of coal at Ekibastuz has been expanded by the opening up of new surface mines. The location of thick seams of coal in a concentrated area and near the surface make coal extraction cheaper at Ekibastuz than at Karaganda, where shaft mining to an average depth of 270 feet is necessary. The Pavlodar aluminum complex will use bauxite from Kustanay oblast.

Other developments in Kazakhstan's industry mainly consist of expanding machine-building centers for the mining and ore-processing industries and for agriculture. At Ust-Kamenogorsk and Kustanay, factories are under construction for the manufacture of mining equipment, and a large combine harvester plant has been constructed in Pavlodar, supplementing the smaller farm machinery plants at Tselinograd and Makinsk.

Production of many basic raw materials, fuels, and ferrous metals in Kazakhstan has risen rapidly in recent years. This can be seen from the figures in Table 12.1.

Rapid growth in production of iron ore and pig iron can be

TABLE 12.1

Raw Materials, Fuel, and Ferrous Metals in Kazakhstan, 1940–1963

	1940	1950	1960	1962	1963
Coal (metric tons)	6,972,000	17,364,000	32,375,000	37,140,000	38,356,000
Oil	697,000	1,059,000	1,610,000	1,645,000	1,581,000
Iron ore	—	—	5,770,000	10,383,000	12,500,000
Pig iron	—	—	274,100	1,303,000	1,376,000
Steel	—	131,000	304,800	392,400	425,500
Electric power (million kilowatt hours)	632	2,620	10,470	13,370	14,910

Source: Figures come from *Narodnoe khoziastvo SSSR v 1963 godu* (Moscow, Gosstatizdat, 1965) and various other editions between 1956 and 1963.

accounted for by the emphasis placed upon the development of the iron and steel industry in recent years. Steel production has not increased so quickly as pig iron, but the installation of more equipment at Karaganda should insure a greater output in the future. The Kazakh growth of electric power production between 1950 and 1960 took place at twice the rate of growth of electric power production in Uzbekistan for the same period. Oil production may be boosted in the future by recent discoveries of oil on the Mangishlak peninsula.

IMPROVED COMMUNICATIONS TIGHTEN
THE COLONIALIST ECONOMIC CONTROL

The pattern of industrial expansion in Central Asia during the Soviet period shows that the northern part of the region is being developed as a supplier of ferrous and nonferrous metals to the Soviet Union. Thus, the development of northern Kazakhstan has been exactly as one-sided as has been the development of the Central Asian cotton country. In fact, the whole of northern Kazakhstan has been transformed into an appendage of the metallurgical complex in West Siberia and the Urals. Its important links no longer tie it principally with southern Central Asia but with the north and west. The development of the railroad network in northern Kazakhstan has made doubly certain that the region will be fastened more securely to Russia, and ensures the rapid transportation of nonferrous metals, iron ore, pig iron, and steel to the industrial centers of Russia. In recent years, the main Soviet rocket and space science complex has been placed south of this same Kazakh area with headquarters at Baykonur 200 miles northeast of the Aral Sea. Russian atom bomb testing has also been carried on as recently as January, 1965, in the open spaces of Central Asia in the vicinity of Semipalatinsk.

The much-vaunted Turkistan-Siberian Railroad completed in 1930 was to make possible the more rapid delivery of grain to southern Central Asia and the freeing of more land for cotton growing.[56] This line did not live up to expectations, mainly because the Siberian economy failed to meet Central Asia's needs for grain and timber. Eventually, the Turksib line became the major route for shipping timber to Central Asia, but grain imports came mainly via the old Orenburg-Tashkent line, and more recently from the Virgin Lands by the Karaganda-Chu (Trans-Kazakhstan) line completed in 1953. This road was actually intended for the transportation of Karaganda coal to southern Central Asia to replace coal from the Kuzbass, but grain hauling has become one of its principal functions.[57]

The transportation maps (Figures 12.3 and 12.4) show a network of rail lines built in northern Kazakhstan to transport Virgin Lands wheat. Along with this has gone the construction of branch lines to the main mining areas, such as Jezkazgan and Karsakpay, to the Emba oilfields, to the new oilfields on the Mangishlak peninsula, and to the mines at Balkhash. An important line joins Karaganda via Tselinograd with Magnitogorsk to supply the iron-and-steel complex of Magnitogorsk with coal. In southern Central Asia several branch lines have been built from the old Trans-Caspian Railroad,

[56] R. N. Taaffe, *Rail Transportation and the Economic Development of Soviet Central Asia,* Department of Geography Research Paper No. 64 (University of Chicago, 1960), summarized in R. N. Taaffe, "Transportation and Regional Specialization: The Example of Soviet Central Asia," *Annals of the Association of American Geographers,* Vol. LII, No. 1 (March 1962), pp. 80–98. I. V. Nikol'skii, *Geografiia transporta SSSR* (Moscow, Gos. Izd-vo Geografickeskoi Literatury, 1960), excerpted and translated as "Railroad Freight Traffic of the U.S.S.R.," *Soviet Geography,* Vol. II, No. 6 (June, 1961), pp. 39–92, and as "The Geography of Transportation of Kazakhstan," *Soviet Geography,* Vol. II, No. 3 (March 1961), pp. 44–54.

[57] Taaffe, "Transportation and Regional Specialization: The Example of Soviet Central Asia," pp. 88–89.

FIGURE 12.5   The Merv railroad station c.1900. Camel caravans then
linked rail lines with points not served by trains.

one leading by a roundabout route to Dushanbe, another, completed in 1956, goes from Charjuy to Kungrad along the Amu
Darya in order to improve transportation facilities for the cotton-
growing areas of the lower Amu Darya. This means that both the
Amu and the Sir Darya are paralleled by railroads, and the necessity for using these difficult rivers for transportation has been to a
great extent obviated.

The development of highways is very poor. One of the few
thoroughfares follows the route of the old czarist post road from
Tashkent via Chimkent, Jambil, and Frunze to Alma Ata, with another road from Dushanbe east to Khorog curving south into
southern Tajikistan and supplying the only major transportation
route for the whole Pamir region.

During the Soviet period an important addition to the communications system of Kazakhstan and other parts of Central Asia has
been air transport. All of the major cities and several of the minor
ones have been connected by a network of air lanes, and the
capitals of the republics are tied to Moscow by air, jet aircraft being
used to a great extent on these long, major routes. The airport at

Tashkent forms the nodal point for many of the Central Asian routes as well as for links with the Middle East and India. Air transportation has proved invaluable in moving persons over the vast distances and difficult terrain, and journeys formerly requiring several days of travel by rail can now be completed in as many hours by air. Indications are, however, that freight transportation by air is still unimportant and that a greater volume of passenger transportation in terms of frequency of flights and routes covered remains to be developed.

Some considerable advances in the development of several branches of Central Asian industry during the last four decades of Russian control can be documented. But with 7 percent of the total Soviet population inside their borders, the republics of southern Central Asia do not share an equivalent proportion of Soviet industrial output. A figure for the whole economy is difficult to arrive at, but if manufacture of single items in the USSR is compared with that in Central Asia it is clear that the production of

FIGURE 12.6 Dushanbe's modern airport has connections with other Central Asian capitals by air. *Sovfoto*.

fertilizer takes first place, and the other goods and services lag behind. Central Asia produces over 7 percent of the fertilizer but it generates only 2.8 percent of total electric power, manufactures but 5 percent of all cotton cloth and 2.2 percent of all footwear produced in the Soviet Union. In spite of recurring talk about encouraging the self-sufficiency of the region, however, Central Asia remains firmly tied to the rest of the USSR also by its needs for most manufactured goods.

The area's advance has been similar in many ways to that of India under the British. A modern transportation system has been built and a beginning made with industrialization. But the people of Central Asia, unlike those of sovereign India, are as yet unable to reap the ultimate benefits of the economic development stimulated by the Russian colonial administrators. In the case of India, difficult as her problems may be, there is a promise of a growth ahead based on an independent political and economic system, with freedom to trade throughout the world. Central Asia's trade is limited to the Communist bloc, and her future economic development seems tied exclusively to the Russian portion of the USSR.

I. M. M.

13

The Changing Intellectual and Literary Community

In capitals made great by medieval princes a Central Asian who matured after mid-nineteenth century was born into a tradition still vital enough to provide him the opportunity for extending his interests widely and becoming, if he had the drive and curiosity, a scholar or a kind of latter-day renaissance man. In Bukhara, Khiva, and perhaps also newer cities like Ashkhabad and Semipalatinsk he engrossed himself in the magnificent old literature, the legendary history of the past, and the geography of Western Turkistan plus the remaining Muslim East. Outside the seminary he engaged in vigorous sports, practiced techniques of irrigating arid land or conducted foreign trade, and traveled abroad. The talented Central Asian composed and performed original music, wrote elegant poetry employing a fine calligraphy, disputed religious questions with learned theologians, and actively participated in the witty, intellectual circles found in every important center. This cultured man, the best and peculiar human product of a civilization once more regenerating itself in Central Asia shortly before Russia suddenly took over the area in the nineteenth century, occupied singlehanded the place of various later specialists created by the mechanization of life, work, and thought in the division of labor which ultimately exterminated his remarkable breed.

Providently, the European systems brought by the Russians had not replaced the older educational tradition before outstanding members of the new generations born under czarist occupation or protection were able to reach their prime and influence the course of modern intellectual development there. Almost any gifted individual celebrating a birth date as late as 1900 still enjoyed a chance of benefiting from the now much-underrated Muslim madrasah, which so regularly stimulated the development of intellectual leaders with broad interests and high abilities. The process by which bright boys from even very poor families managed to acquire a formidable education through the schooling characteristic of Central Asia's greatest center of enlightenment, Bukhara, and at the same time developed the penchant usual there for writing poetry in early adolescence, is evidenced in the record everywhere and also minutely described in reminiscences like *Yāddāshthā* (Memoirs) of the period from the 1880s to 1904 left by the Tajik-Uzbek writer Sadriddin Murad Khoja Zada Ayniy (1878–1954).[1]

A Tajik, Turkmen, or Uzbek child in the Bukharan area from his earliest schooling studied Arabic and Persian religious books. From these he turned to the great Persian poetry of Khoja Shamseddin Muhammad Hafiz (c.1325–1389), *Maslak-i muttaqin* (The Path of the Believers) by Sufi Allah Yar (d.1723), and the poetic philosophical writings of Mirza Abdulqadir Bidil (1644–c.1721), all this after memorizing *Alifbe* (The Alphabet) and while practicing penmanship. In classes where Turkmen or Uzbek youngsters outnumbered Tajiks, additional readings were assigned from the Turkic poetry of Muhammad Sulayman-oghli Fuzuliy (1498–1556), Mir Ali Shir Nawaiy (1441–1501), Khoja Nazar-oghli Gaib Nazar-i Chimianiy Huwayda (late eighteenth early nineteenth centuries), and Ishan Shah Baba Rahim Mashrab (1657–1711). Not only in Bukhara but throughout the Tashkent and Farghana area also, boys in the primary grades followed this curriculum almost precisely. Serious pupils consumed far more than the required religious readings and poetry. Like Ayniy himself, a surprising number of precocious boys who later became the recognized authors in Central Asia initially composed a few verses around the end of their primary school (*maktab*) years at the age of fourteen.[2] The education of a

---

[1] Sadriddin Aini, *Vospominaniia* (Moscow-Leningrad, Izdatel'stvo Akademii Nauk SSSR, 1960). Issued in Tajik as *Yāddāshthā:* Parts I and II (Stalinabad, 1949); Part III (Stalinabad, 1950); Part IV in *Sharq-i surh,* Nos. 1, 2, 4, 5 (1953); Nos. 6, 7, 8, 9 (1954).

[2] The programs of both maktab and madrasah are detailed in Khanikoff, *Bokhara: Its Amir and Its People* (London, Madden, 1845), pp. 274–94, and

girl, also a budding poet, along nearly identical lines in mid-nine-teenth century Khokand is described by Abdullah Qadiriy (Jolqun-bay) (1894–1939) in his second Uzbek novel *Mehrabdän chäyan* (Scorpion from the Pulpit), 1929.[3]

In Ayniy's time, after finishing the lower school the student capa-ble of more advanced education entered one of the Bukharan madrasahs or found a place at like institutions in Orenburg, Semi-palatinsk, Khiva, and other major cities. Around mid-nineteenth century the number of madrasahs in the Bukharan emirate had been estimated to be about 180 with some 15,000 students, and around 1,800 maktabs at the same time taught another 150,000 pupils.[4] The khanate of Khiva counted twenty-five madrasahs in the same period,[5] and toward the end of the century, as the Central Asian intellectual reawakening accelerated, the numbers of madrasahs again started to grow rapidly. The city of Bukhara alone boasted 103,[6] the 118 Khokand seminaries functioning in 1890 had never seen so many students, and the town of Tashkent claimed over 10 madrasahs. Samarkand oblast then also supported 50 such institu-tions, and Sir Darya oblast 21.[7]

To complete such madrasah training the student continued twelve or more years under the seminar and tutorial systems. A diligent, capable scholar emerged with the command of the Central Asian Turkic, as well as Persian and Arabic literary languages and a thorough grounding in the great writings of the poets, theologians, philosophers, historians, and geographers of the Muslim world, plus long experience with the pedagogical methods employed in the mak-tab and madrasah. In the main, the graduate hoped to become a teacher or professor, a secretary to merchants, nobility, or other men of affairs, manager of a philanthropic institution, a judge or law

---

N. P. Ostroumov, *Sarty: Etnograficheskie materialy* (3d ed.; Tashkent, Tipo-grafiia Gazety "Sredneaziatskaia Zhizn'," 1908), pp. 247–58.

[3] Abdullah Qadiriy, *Mehrabdän chäyan* (2d ed.; Tashkent, OzSSR Däwlät Bädiiy Ädäbiyat Näshriyati, 1959), pp. 21–22.

[4] Khanikoff, p. 294.

[5] G. I. Danilevskii, "Opisanie khivinskago khanstva," *Zapiski Imperatorskago Russkago Geograficheskago Obshchestva,* V (1851), 108–12.

[6] Annette M. B. Meakin, *In Russian Turkestan: A Garden of Asia and Its People* (London, Allen, 1903), p. 82.

[7] H. Carrère d'Encausse, "Tsarist Educational Policy in Turkestan, 1867–1917," *Central Asian Review,* No. 4 (1963), pp. 375–87.

FIGURE 13.1   Dormitory at Barak Khan, Central Asia's only active madrasah, in Tashkent. *Photo by Edward Allworth.*

FIGURE 13.2   Tashkent's worshipers, 1964. *Photo by Paula Rubel.*

FIGURE 13.3   Sketches (1922) by Central Asians contrast the new
schooling with the old.

clerk, or as a last resort a member of the clergy. Depending upon his personality, connections, and a certain amount of chance he found a suitable place, but whatever his profession, ultimately he was almost sure to be a leader of thought in the community. In this respect, even more unique than Sadriddin Ayniy's testimony regarding educational opportunities in the Bukharan emirate are his intimate recollections portraying the intellectual life there of the educated Muslims:

Among the students of the Bukharan madrasahs, Sharif Jan unquestionably belonged to the modest number who possessed beautiful penmanship, had mastered languages and grammar, and loved and understood poetry. He considered himself a patron of education. . . . Every week on Tuesday, Wednesday, and Thursday when the free evenings came, the house of Sharif Jan Mahdum turned into a gathering place of poets, devotees of literature, tellers of entertaining narratives, and wits.[8]

Muhammad Sharif Jan Mahdum (Sadr Ziya) (1865–1931), who is twice mentioned in this passage, became one of Ayniy's principal benefactors and teachers. Sharif Jan himself had been a pupil of the Tajik thinker, poet, professor, court astrologer, and diplomat Ahmad Mahdum Kalla (Dānish), who visited Russia in 1856, 1868, and 1870. Following Ahmad Mahdum's example Muhammad Sharif Jan Mahdum became a historian and prolific poet as well as a politician. His personal library was considered one of the richest in the city, and from the many fine manuscripts in his collection he compiled an anthology in 1910 of nineteenth-century Bukharan Tajik poetry called *Tizkār-ul ashʿār* (Remembrance of the Poems). He also wrote extensive memoirs, as yet unpublished, concerning political and cultural life in Bukhara during the late nineteenth century, and he served as a judge (*qazi*), and in other official posts up until 1917. His modesty and friendliness, as well as his ability to recognize talented young people and his willingness to use his personal influence and wealth to encourage development of their minds and skills were qualities especially praised by Sadriddin Ayniy. Tall and athletic, among Bukharan sportsmen Muhammad Sharif Jan Mahdum loved to converse about horses or fighting cocks and often

[8] Sadriddin Aini, pp. 383–384.

personally participated in the rough contest known as *buzkashi,
ulaq, kokbori tartu,* or *kök bori,* described so often in Central Asian
literature, in which horsemen compete with each other to seize a
decapitated goat carcass from the ground and deliver it to a specified goal.[9]

At the conversational evenings held in Muhammad Sharif Jan
Mahdum's home arguments ranged beyond literature and art to
politics and social questions. In those discussions the younger men
like Mirza Abdul Wahid Munzim (1877–1934), another of his pro-
tégés, and Ayniy heard criticisms against the rascals in public life
which counterbalanced somewhat the glowing evaluations made in
such conversations of outstandingly effective and honest figures
such as Mirza Hayit Sahbā, an accomplished poet who was executed
in 1918 at the age of seventy by the emir for welcoming the February, 1917, revolution. Mirza Hayit Sahbā had been an adviser for
years at the court of Emir Abd al-Ahad, who subsequently appointed him water supervisor (*mirab*) of the main city canal, and
then police chief (*mirshab*), key government positions which he
filled honorably, though others who held these posts usually en-
riched themselves through bribes.[10] Also prominent at the Bukharan
court had been Shamsiddin Mahdum Shāhin (1859–1894), a fine
poet who frequented Muhammad Sharif Jan Mahdum's gatherings
until his rise to political importance forced him to avoid them in
order to protect his position in court intrigues,[11] and Mirza Muhammad 'Abdal'azim Sami Bustani (1835–1907), the swarthy court secretary, historian, and poet who participated in Bukhara's campaigns
against the Russians, and who was also a close friend of Ahmad
Mahdum and Muhammad Sharif Jan Mahdum.[12]

Difficulties discouraging membership in court circles simultaneously with participation in outside intellectual society represented
by men like Muhammad Sharif Jan Mahdum suggest that the educated people of Bukhara were loosely divided into the adherents of
political and religious orthodoxy and those with contrastingly more

[9] *Ibid.,* pp. 415–21, 1037.
[10] *Ibid.,* pp. 399–400.
[11] *Ibid.,* p. 401.
[12] *Ibid.,* pp. 397–98.

liberal attitudes and compassionate behavior. Despite this separation, there is no reason to believe that the liberal-minded Muslims
were less devout than the orthodox. Nor did they possess a view
of life that was different, except in degree, from the men of the
emir's establishment.

At the same time, men of Muhammad Sharif Jan Mahdum's type
were not necessarily products of outside influence, for the ideas
trickling in from abroad via occasional copies of newspapers like
Terjuman from Bakhchesaray, *Habl ul-Matin* from India, and
Chehra nama from Egypt, began to come only around the 1890's
and had not had time to make a deep impact. Furthermore, thinking men like Ahmad Mahdum, with firsthand observations of Russia, were yet rare individuals in Central Asia. Together, then, educated citizens of all stripes in the Bukharan emirate were bearers of
the ideas largely conditioned by centuries of Muslim wisdom and
practice, and also of the limitations characterizing their society.
These men worked and wrote self-assuredly as partners in the old
way of life relatively untouched by the Russian control exerted only
indirectly upon Bukharan thought under the protectorate.

NEW IDEAS IN KHIVA AND TASHKENT

During the same period, in Khiva innovations were being introduced by its khan, Sayyid Muhammad Rahim Bahadur II (r.1865–
1910; see Figure 4.2), which may have qualified him to be known
as the most influential Central Asian "enlightener" of all for the
adult community and ultimately for the young people by virtue of
his position and his vital role as patron and preserver of the best
Khivan art of the time. Sayyid Muhammad Rahim Khan's long reign
saw at least three major contributions to the growth of ideas and the
arts in the khanate.

First in importance was his introduction of lithography and publishing into his realm in 1874. This not only made inexpensive local
books in their mother tongue available to some people there for the
first time, but increased the possibilities to preserve excellent writings heretofore often lost to posterity. Before that, published books
had been imported from Kazan, Teheran, Lahore, and other outside
cities, but Central Asians had issued none of their own.

Second, intensely interested in all art forms, the khan, only a year before he opened Central Asia's first local publishing house, commissioned Palwan Niyaz Muhammad Mirza Bashi Kamil Khwarazmiy (1825–1899), a talented Chaghatay poet and composer, skilled calligrapher and wood sculptor at his court, to devise a system for writing down the serious classical music of the area. Palwan Niyaz Khwarazmiy produced a system believed to be the first of its kind in all Central Asia (see chapter 15).

Third was his indisputable contribution as a patron of letters. At his court, besides the musicologist Palwan Niyaz Khwarazmiy, the khan employed the distinguished services of Muhammad Riza Erniyaz Bek-oghli Agahiy (1809–1874), eminent historian, courtier, poet, and translator, who demonstrated his ability also as a man of affairs in the important capacity of official water supervisor. The Khivan court historian succeeding Muhammad Riza Agahiy, Muhammad Yusufbek Bababek-oghli Bayaniy (1859–1923), keen-witted and gifted product of the maktab-madrasah system, also excelled in both music and literature. Art was joined to the advancement of learning in the madrasah the khan erected in 1871. He encouraged participation in the royal writers' circle and wrote his own poetry under the pen-name of "Firuz." His poems were eventually combined in a large anthology of Khivan verse along with works by many other local poets, and lithographed in 1909. He was interested in foreign, non-Islamic authors, such as Alexander Pushkin. He opened his library, one of the greatest in Central Asia, to scholars of his time, including the Russians. Also, the khan showed some tolerance for the European style of theater as well as the modern type of schooling advanced in the early twentieth century by innovators in Central Asia. Finally, the great official chronicles begun in the early nineteenth century to record Khiva's entire history in prose and verse were continued, by Sayyid Muhammad Rahim Khan's order, into the twentieth century.

The shifting fortunes of writers gathered around the courts of the Central Asian khanates had almost always depended upon the favor of highly placed officials or directly upon the will of the ruler, and when these patrons died or fell from grace, the largess of their successors often went to the artists and poets in the new men's retinues. Such a calamity struck the Bukharan historian and poet Mirza Bustani, who had served as secretary to the emirs Muzaffar al-Din (r.1860–1885) and Abd al-Ahad, but who lost this post and suffered real privation in his old age. Further testimony to the insecurity of the literati in that age is supplied by one of Mirza Bustani's own literary studies, an important anthology in which he included the ten most outstanding Bukharan poets from the second half of the nineteenth century. In sketching the biographies of each, Mirza Bustani noted in detail the misfortunes and persecutions they suffered in their relations with the emir and his courtiers.[13] Often a discouraged artist or poet was forced by this treatment to leave one location and seek out another where he could be comfortable in his profession.

During the czarist regime such mobility continued to be possible. For intellectual circles, the significance of the relocation of capitals within Central Asia became more critical in the twentieth century than it had been in the Middle Ages. In the fifteenth century the best-paid and most renowned artists and writers, for no very mysterious reasons, grouped themselves as closely as possible around powerful protectors and enjoyed the appreciative audiences most artists require. And they gained from one another, for the commingling of writers and thinkers contributed to their own excellence, especially to the communication between themselves and other leaders of society. This was true in medieval times and is true today.

But Soviet strictures against movement from place to place, added to the official nationalization imposed on particular areas, nearly eliminated any chance for the informal mixing of the writers. The concentration of Central Asia's active writers and intellectuals in the present republics' governmental centers, such as Alma Ata, Dushanbe, and Frunze, since the 1930s unchanged in location, has effected a distribution of these men and women which reflects the realities of nationality policies in the USSR today, but which bears no consistent connection with the patterns of the past. For, although Tashkent, for example, became the locus of supreme power in Central Asia after 1865, this metamorphosis exerted little effect upon

[13] L. M. Epifanova, "Predislovie," Mirza Abdal'azim Sami, *Ta'rikh-i salatin-i manghitiiya* (Moscow, Izdatel'stvo Vostochnoi Literatury, 1962), pp. 16–19.

the local literary-intellectual community of the area except that the Russian capture of Tashkent no doubt initially caused an exodus of some educated men and writers to Khiva, Bukhara, Khokand, or Samarkand, the real centers of civilization, where the Russians were not yet in control. But in any case, Muslim Tashkent had never been the artistic or cultural center for the people of Western Turkistan, and its occupation by Russian Christians temporarily disadvantaged the city even more for such a role. In the late nineteenth century Tashkent produced only a few second-rank Uzbek poets such as Qari Fazlullah Mir Jalal-oghli Almayi (1852–1891), and Nihaniy, whose ode on the death of Alexander III and to Nicholas II's accession reads in part:

> The heir of the Sovereign, light of his eye
> Ascended to his throne and a new epoch began:
> Be joyful, Turkistanians and citizens of Tashkent!
> Pray that God exalt his affairs!
> Pray thou, Nihaniy, about the thriving of this Sovereign.[14]

Also from Tashkent was Karimbek Sharifbek-oghli Kamiiy (1866–1923), after 1905 sympathetic to the Jadids, whose effusive rhyming praise of the Russians likewise caught the fancy of the czarist authorities in many poems like "Gimnaziya khususida" (Regarding the High School):

Binabär ilmning khasiyätidin *Bolubdur dawlat-i rusiya a"la.*	So, by virtue of science No doubt the Russian state became supreme. . . .
Hisab etgändä yuz rusiyä ichrä *Chiqar bir ami, ul häm ittifaqa.*	When they count a hundred in Russia One illiterate would come out, and he accidentally.
Wäle särtiyä khälqi ichrä yuzdin,	But in the Sart people out of a hundred
Chiqär bir mullä, ul häm undä- *munda.*[15]	One educated man would show up, and he poorly.

The primary characteristic distinguishing Tashkent, Pishpek (Frunze), or Nokis from the old intellectual capitals, augmented

[14] *Turkistan wilayatining gazeti*, No. 5 (1895), cited by Boris Tagieev-Rustam Bek, *Po Azii* (Moscow, Knigoizdatel'stvo "Pravda," c.1903), p. 42.

[15] *Ozbek ädäbiyati* (Tashkent, OzSSR Däwlät Bädiiy Ädäbiyat Näshriyati, 1960), Vol. IV, book 1, pp. 348–49.

by some younger cities like Orenburg along the northern fringe, was
the cosmopolitan internationalism of cities like Khiva, which served
Uzbeks, Turkmens, Kazakhs, and Karakalpaks; Bukhara, a main urban concentration for Tajiks, Turkmens, and Uzbeks; and Samarkand, which was a metropolis for both Tajiks and Uzbeks. The
towns of the Farghana Valley had their mixture of "Sart" and "Kipchak" populations, and Orenburg brought together Tatars, Bashkirs,
Kazakhs, and Kirgiz.

Coteries of intellectuals had been meeting to exchange ideas and
read poetry regularly for at least a thousand years before the Russians came to Tashkent, so it was hardly a novelty when informal
groups clustered around men like Muhammad Sharif Jan Mahdum
at Bukhara in the late nineteenth century. Unofficial gatherings no
doubt had originated when Central Asian men first learned to write
poetry, and subsequently the medieval royal circles of Ulugh-bek
(1394–1449) in Samarkand, Sultan Husayn Bayqara (r.1469–1506)
in Herat, Muhammad Shaybaniy Khan (1451–1510) in Samarkand,
and Zahiriddin Muhammad Babur (1483–1530) in Samarkand,
Kabul, and Delhi, supplied brilliant precedents for the custom carried on to the last at the court in modern Khiva. The Khokand
khanate was the first to crumble and dissolve under the Russian
flood, but the cities of Namangan, Andijan, Khokand, and Marghilan
nevertheless followed the old traditions of literary circles such as one
bringing together the poets Mawlana Hajji Muhiddin Muhammad
Riza Akhun-oghli Muhyiy (1835–1911), Muhammad Amin Mirza
Khoja-oghli Muqimiy (1850–1903), Zakir Jan Hal Muhammad-oghli
Furqat (1858–1909), Ubaydullah Salih-oghli Zawqiy (1853–1921),
and Mawlana Nasbat (late nineteenth century).

Tashkent became in time a magnet to intellectuals repressed by
the emir or harassed by conservative clergy in other centers. The
presence in Tashkent of the many Russians made the city a kind
of sanctuary for Central Asian reformers as life became more difficult
in Bukhara. Despite the support gained by Tashkent's local conservatives from the Russian colonial and military bureaucracy, this
sluggish mechanism at best moved inconsistently in domestic affairs,
so that the Muslim liberals found in the Russian-occupied city a
relatively safe ground upon which to develop the new literary and

intellectual activity which they initiated beginning with the twentieth century. In its character as a haven for the harassed or disgruntled poets and thinkers from outlying areas, Tashkent came to resemble the cities acting as centers for the population of Central Asia's northern tier (Uralsk, Orenburg, Omsk, Petropavlovsk, and Semipalatinsk), where the reformers of the plains came together.

As Tashkent became more and more important economically and grew in size, it also naturally achieved greater significance for men of affairs already attracted by the concentration of governmental authority. With the destruction of the Khokand khanate in 1876, Tashkent turned into the unchallenged seat of power in Central Asia outside Khiva and Bukhara, and when the Bolshevik and local insurgent forces overthrew the last khan and the emir in 1920, and the short-lived people's republics were abolished in 1924, even those two ancient centers finally lost all but local significance for contemporary intellectuals and writers. Simultaneously, the seat of government for the new Kirgiz (i.e., Kazakh) ASSR jumped from Orenburg to Aq Meshit, which was renamed Qizil Orda and remained the Kazakh capital until it moved permanently to Alma Ata in 1929. When the Turkistan ASSR, with its headquarters in Tashkent, was dissolved in 1924, the capital of the new Uzbek SSR was placed at Samarkand, and not until the Russian authorities shifted the Uzbek republic's government back to Tashkent in 1930 did that city start its final period of rapid growth, which has made it the metropolis of Central Asia. But even now Tashkent has not regained the importance as an intellectual and literary focus which it enjoyed as the capital of the vast Turkistan ASSR, when it formed the cosmopolitan center for all Central Asian nationalities except those Kazakhs who were oriented northward.

The earlier placid pursuit of excellence among the intellectuals of Bukhara and Khiva, made more comfortable if anything by vassalage to Russia (which removed most threats of internecine war), did not last forever even under these circumstances, but up until the turn of the century Khivans and Bukharans hardly underwent the experiences which shocked men's minds in occupied Semipalatinsk or Tashkent. There, enlightened local individuals were forced by daily affairs to realize how ill-equipped they were to

cope with increasing threats to their traditional way of life following their failure to stave off the Russian military challenge. Like
the Egyptians under British rule, Central Asian intellectuals after
mid-nineteenth century, from Turgay to Andijan, were torn by a
recognition of the need to acquire techniques and practical, modern
information from the Russians, while at the same time passionately
wishing to be rid of the Christian influence and alien political
domination which seemingly came hand-in-hand with these acquisitions.

Among those exposed to the radiation of European attitudes and
knowledge in the nineteenth century was the eminent Uzbek educa-
tor, poet, judge, and scholar from Katta Qorghan, Muhammad
Achildimurad Ne"matulla-oghli Miriy (d.1898), sometimes called
the "Father of the Reform Movement" in parts of Central Asia. His
great erudition in old Chaghatay literature and Muslim law perhaps
distinguished Miriy from men like Ibrahim (Ibray) Altynsarin, an
energetic Kazakh teacher and versifier from Kustanay oblast, trained
only at a Russian school for interpreters in Orenburg from 1850
to 1857, or Ibrahim (Ibray; Abay) Qunanbay-uli, born in the Chingis
mountains of Semipalatinsk oblast and educated briefly by mullahs
in his home village and later for three years in a Semipalatinsk
madrasah, after which he became a self-appointed schoolmaster, a
prolific translator, and a fine poet. But Muhammad Miriy, Ibrahim
Altynsarin, Abay Qunanbay-uli, and allied "enlighteners" shared the
ambition, if not the means, to make possible better use of Central
Asian human resources in intellectual pursuits. For this end, all
agreed that more children had to be educated, though general attempts to modify or expand the curriculum to broaden the program
offered in local Muslim schools had barely begun in their time.

The most important achievement of the nineteenth-century Central Asian "enlighteners," therefore, no doubt lay in their cultivation
of the idea that society as a whole would profit if the talents of
greater numbers of able people were utilized. Some "enlighteners"
operated out of an altruistic sense of compassion and love, demonstrated repeatedly in documents like Sadriddin Ayniy's memoirs,
to put to practice a desire (still notable today among some circles
in the Middle Eastern countries) to help fellow men gain intellectual

awakening. This attitude created a succeeding generation whose receptivity to fresh impressions and renewed notions of egalitarianism set in motion a revolution in Central Asia that began among certain intellectual circles. For them, educating promising youngsters became something more than a theoretical issue and evolved into what they saw as an economic and political necessity and eventually as a moral problem. The resultant excitement, spurred by the infiltration of what seemed like radical ideas from Turkey, Persia, the Crimea, and Tatarstan, plus the clumsy interference of Russian officials touching the methods of education, social and family relationships, religious and legal practices, and even the political rights of individuals, brought some members of the new intellectual generation to embark upon programs of social action almost exactly at the start of the new century.

Literary circles continued to be identical with intellectual society in the early twentieth century, because every educated man of wit and intelligence up through 1915, whatever his profession, devoted himself at least occasionally to writing poetry. But the split widened between the educated conservative (*qadimchi/qadimpäräst*), who remained unaware of or hostile to the new ways of life, and the Jadid, who pushed for changes beginning with purification of religious practices and going on to other seemingly drastic social and political renovations.

JADIDS IN THE CITIES AND PLAINS

The nineteenth-century "enlighteners" had thus created, in their own mould from among their younger followers, an energetic Jadid group. Its members included thoughtful, inventive leaders like Mufti Mahmud Khoja Behbudiy, a legal authority, politician, journalist, and playwright, a family man from Samarkand educated in Bukhara's madrasahs, who organized the first local Jadid ("New Method") school in the city of Samarkand in 1903 and later edited the controversial magazine *Ayina* (1913–1915).

Some Jadids from outside the old cities were equally effective and energetic in putting the new program across. Aqmet Baytursinuli, a Kazakh from Sartubek in the Turgay *uezd* north-northeast of the Aral Sea, received some tutoring from Tatar mullahs in his

FIGURE 13.4 Mir Jaqib Duwlat-uli (left), Kazakh reformer, clasps hand of close friend Ahmed Vali Ibrahim-oghli (Menger). Petropavlovsk, 1906. *Photo, Collection of Azamat Altay.*

village, and then finished the Russian-Kazakh school at the provincial town of Turgay, after which he went to Orenburg and completed the four-year Kazakh teachers' institute in 1895. He immediately began to teach in various Kazakh villages and larger towns like Aktyubinsk, Kustanay, and Karkaralinsk. Baytursin-uli's activity as a poet, later, editor at Troitsk of the newspaper *Qazaq* (1913–1918), and linguist, spread his influence through most principal Kazakh centers. A founder of the Kazakh nationalist party Alash Orda, a member of the All-Russian Constituent Assembly in 1917, active in the government of the new Kirgiz (i.e., Kazakh) ASSR starting about 1920, and commissar for Kazakh education in the later 1920's,

Baytursin-uli was a truly important political figure. Mir Jaqib Duwlat-uli emulated him in many activities.

Other outstanding Jadid intellectuals included men from every large Central Asian nationality. Munawwar Qari Abdurrashid Khan-oghli, an Uzbek from Tashkent, opened the first local "New Method" school there in 1901 and authored *Adib-i awwal* (First Teacher), a Jadid schoolbook, in the same year. Munawwar Qari published one of the first Uzbek newspapers, wrote a number of books and oc-casional poetry in Uzbek and Tajik, and worked in many capacities as a public servant, including, in the early 1920s, a term served as commissar for education of the Turkistan ASSR.

Like Mufti Behbudiy in Samarkand and Munawwar Qari in Tashkent, Mirza Abdul Wahid Munzim led the local Jadid move-ment in Bukhara, a very risky and difficult effort for which he suffered under the tyranny of the emir. Mirza Abdul Wahid Munzim and Sadriddin Ayniy, who had both lived there for a time in the home of their patron, Muhammad Sharif Jan Mahdum, compiled a primer and opened a "New Method" school around 1909 at Mirza Abdul Wahid Munzim's house in Bukhara, after a similar attempt in 1901 had failed. For this school Ayniy wrote and published *Tāhzīb-uṣ sibyān* (Improvement of the Children), 1909, a little reader made up of poetry in Tajik.[16]

Although these new directions in Central Asian education prom-ised to revolutionize the process of expanding a thinking, literate population, the "New Method" of the Jadids, flourishing fifty years after the taking of Tashkent, was not generally celebrated along with the Russian contributions. Special observances in 1915 on the anniversary of the conquest, inviting that praise from subjugated people which seems to be so sweet to the Russian ear, prompted local residents of the city who worked for the government or other-wise enjoyed czarist favor to render homage to St. Petersburg.[17]

In response to the scheduled half-century commemoration of the

---

[16] Sadriddin Aini, p. 520; Sadriddin Aini, *Pages from My Own Story: Memoirs* (Moscow, Foreign Languages Publishing House, 1958), pp. 75–76; Baymirza Hayit, *Turkestan im XX. Jahrhundert* (Darmstadt, C. W. Leske Verlag, 1956), pp. 39–40.

[17] L. N. Klimovich, *Islam v tsarskoi Rossii* (Moscow, Gosudarstvennoe Anti-religioznoe Izdatel'stvo, 1936), pp. 36–38.

taking of Tashkent, the Uzbek editor of the government bulletin *Turkistan wilayatining gazeti* printed his essay summing up what were considered to be the principal innovations, including new educational methods, resulting from Russian occupation:

A cultured (*kul'turnoe*) Russian administration, through its postal service, telegraph, and railroad, has united Central Asia with the world of knowledge and culture. Order and security are preserved; where earlier huge caravans could not pass, now solitary passersby may go. Turkistanian goods have received a ready market: fruit, wool, pelts, cotton, silk, and other goods are exported from Turkistan to the Russian interior at high prices; money has begun to flow from Russia to Turkistan like water.

The wealth of the inhabitants has increased tenfold or even more; the wages of the poor, and the return from plots have risen markedly. . . . To ride to distant cities, which once took six months on horseback or cart, now people travel by train in six days; by telegraph one can exchange conversation with them in six minutes. Inside the city one can ride where he wishes by streetcar or automobile cheaply and quickly. In all cities and uezds of Turkistan there are various factories. . . . Muslims also began to build factories and derive a great deal of benefit from them. Unheard of things like the phonograph, photography, motion pictures, and the gramophone have appeared. The former candlesticks are replaced by electric lights. . . .

The author, of course reminds his readers that without mastering education they are deprived of material benefit; educated traders and artisans drive out the Muslims . . . as still in Muslim times Muslim products were crowded out by the products of Russian factories. The low level of education of Muslims is shown by the fact that among them the most learned professors and teachers have no understanding of geography and don't know what happens beyond the fence around their yard. . . . As it is impossible to achieve the heavenly kingdom without knowledge of the faith, so it is impossible to achieve earthly bliss without temporal knowledge. Such parochial schools as we have are found among all cultured people, but in addition they have secular schools which we do not. True, a desire for education also increases among the Muslims—thirty years ago there was but one Russian-Muslim school in the city of Tashkent and there were practically no pupils in it. Now, there are eight Russian-native schools, and they don't suffice. . . . Among the population of Turkistan the best supporters of the Russian authorities are the traders, then the farmers, and finally the women.[18]

[18] V. V. Bartol'd, "Istoriia kul'turnoi zhizni Turkestana," *Sochineniia* (Moscow, Izdatel'stvo Vostochnoi Literatury, 1963), Vol. II, book 1, pp. 389–91.

Without question, installing telephones, telegraph, and transport systems in Central Asia, as well as circulating information bulletins and opening a small network of "Russian-native" schools to supplement Muslim education, somewhat increased the velocity of and added still more complexity to the intellectual life of the population, but it is particularly significant, as the Uzbek editor showed, that such actions failed to win for Russia the genuine support of most local leadership. In 1915, educated men like Mullah Alim Mahmud Hajji, author of the above fifty-year editorial, and a man known as a historian as well as one of Central Asia's first modern journalists, ignored an opportunity to applaud the rise of the indigenous Jadid schools in favor of extolling the czarist institutions for "natives," and in so doing inadvertently substantiated the existence of another dimension to the local intellectual society, one supplied by the Central Asian apologists for Russian rule. Mullah Alim's seeming willingness to fraternize with the enemy earned disdain for him and for persons like him from the anti-Russian leaders who comprised the largest part of the educated community.

But, probably more meaningful than these antipathies, to the development of thought in the area at any rate, was the greater diversity which the influence of the "enlighteners" and Jadids, incoming Western technology, and the like—gave to the limited variety already provided by the unique characteristics of each major center, from Semipalatinsk to Bukhara and Ashkhabad. Together with wider diversity, the competition for men's minds produced stronger incentives for interested groups to increase the general literacy and understanding throughout all of Central Asia, but the total achievement of the competing factions (conservative, Jadid, Tatar, and Russian) spread out over a gigantic area and by 1915 left a layer of educated persons so thin that it seemed to be impotent to generate the proportionately higher literacy from which a deeper intellectual stratum might have been developed.

LITERACY AND OCCUPATION

Only 6 percent of the 10 million Turkic and Iranian inhabitants supplemented by the 1,145,000 Russians and Ukrainians in Central Asia, excluding Khiva and Bukhara, could read and write in 1915.

In this 6 percent the *local* literate population then made up only about half of the total literate population, including the Slavs. In Ferganskaia oblast where just 0.6 percent of the population was Russian and Ukrainian in 1915 and 99.1 percent was identified as Turkic or Tajik, the literacy rate stood at 2.9 percent of all nationalities. Again, in Samarkandskaia oblast the same year, the 1,207,400 people included about 1.6 percent Slavs, and the percentage of those who could read and write came to 3.2 percent. Overall literacy in 1926, including Khiva and Bukhara but excluding Russians and Ukrainians, took in a mean of 3.5 percent of the population (see Table 13.2), which makes it likely that the numbers of local people who could read and write in 1915 in the other seven oblasts may not have been higher than those in the two singled out here. Conversely, whenever Russians and Ukrainians comprised relatively larger parts of the settlements, as in Akmolinskaia oblast, where they already made up 33.1 percent, and Uralskaia oblast, in which they registered 25.4 percent of the total, combined literacy figures for all people reached 10.4 percent and 12.3 percent, respectively, far the highest for any oblasts in Central Asia.

Furthermore, regardless of the great supremacy in numbers of Turkic and Iranian people over all others in the countryside, the local nationalities supplied only 50.1 percent of those inhabiting the nine metropolitan centers of the Russian-occupied Central Asian oblasts listed in Table 13.1: Omsk, Ashkhabad, Samarkand, Semipalatinsk, Vernyi, Tashkent, Kustanay, Uralsk, and Skobelev. In other cities, notably those of the Farghana Valley like Andijan, Khokand, Marghilan, and Namanagan, where very few Russians were located, the ratio of local residents to Slavs held extremely high, so that the urban indigenous population of Central Asia in 1897 given as 462,239,[19] may be put at 364,157 for the nine oblast centers plus an estimated 300,000 in other cities (see Tables 3.3 and 3.6). From the census taken in the Turkistan ASSR in 1920 it was discovered that the Uzbeks of Tashkent (152,500) were already

[19] *Statisticheskii ezhegodnik Rossii 1915 g.* (Petrograd, Izdanie Tsentral'nago Statisticheskago Komiteta; MVD, 1916), pp. 70–71; *Materialy Vserossiiskikh perepisei 1920 goda. Perepis' naseleniia v turkestanskoi respublike.* Part III: *Poselennye itogi Syr-Dar'inskoi oblasti* (Tashkent, Izdanie TsSU Turkrespubliki, 1923), pp. 126–27.

TABLE 13.1

Population and Literacy, 1915 *

Nationality groups

Oblast	Turkic	Tajik and others†	Russian and Ukrainian	Total	Number of literates	Percent literate
Akmolinskaia	995,946		511,891	1,546,500	160,836	10.4
Zakaspiiskaia	474,045	12,707	48,067	552,500	39,780	7.2
Samarkandskaia	856,047	328,413 (Tajik: 323,583)	19,318	1,207,400	38,637	3.2
Semipalatinskaia	786,535		87,490	874,900	51,619	5.9
Semirechenskaia	1,133,950	1,281	124,286	1,281,300	53,815	4.2
Syr-Darinskaia	1,945,056	12,157	60,783	2,026,100	81,044	4.0
Turgaiskaia	648,292		54,377	706,200	31,779	4.5
Uralskaia	660,973		225,958	889,600	109,421	12.3
Ferganskaia	1,989,523	160,550	13,018	2,169,600	62,918	2.9
Total	9,490,367	524,108 (Tajik: 506,434)	1,145,188	11,254,100	629,849	

* does not include Bukhara or Khiva.
† does not include Armenians, Caucasus mountain people, Finns, Germans, Jews, Lithuanians, Mongols, or Poles.

Source: *Statisticheskii ezhegodnik Rossii 1915 g.* (Petrograd, Izdanie Tsentral'nago Statisticheskago Komiteta M.V.D., 1916), pp. 56–57, 65, 98–99.

18 percent literate, many times more than the average for the area, and 27 percent of the Uzbek men in the city were literate. The cities, of course, could not claim all the literate and educated people nor the entire professional class of the area, but any developing intellectual currents were bound to have the greatest effect within the active centers concentrating such educated persons.

The method of earning a living in 1915, as at the end of the nineteenth century, provided only a vague indication of the extent of the educated and literate circles or the configuration of intellectual groups. In 1897, for example, 82.8 percent of the Central Asians, a higher proportion than in any other region of the Russian empire, worked in agriculture. Those few who were not farmers (including Slavs) were in light industry and mining, 6.5 percent; in trade, 3.4 percent; self-employed or in servant capacities, 3.1 percent; in transport and communications, 0.9 percent; in military service, 0.8 percent; in government administration, courts, and the independent professions (*svobodnaia professiia*), 0.7 percent; in clerical work, 0.4 percent; pensioners, 0.5 percent; or in miscellaneous, 0.9 percent.[20] Central Asian intellectuals were then usually to be found within those tiny clusters of the "independent professions" —the clergy, and to a certain extent, the merchant class.

Perhaps the only significant change between 1897 and 1915 inside the literate professional community was the shift of modest numbers from conservative to reformist schools of thought. Startling in their similarity to the old "enlighteners" as well as their Jadid elders were the Central Asian Jadids coming of age in the hectic decade after Japan defeated Russia in the war of 1904–1905.

Although the younger men resembled their forerunners in outlook, they were more militant in spirit and exhibited greater literary virtuosity in writing the new poetry. There was Mir Jaqib Duwlat-uli, a close associate of Baytursin-uli, who was in his own right a novelist, poet, journalist, and teacher. Born in Turgay uezd, Mir Jaqib Duwlat-uli had been educated by a village Tatar mullah and in both village and Turgay (town) Russian-Kazakh schools. There was Abdalrauf Fitrat, considered by Sadriddin Ayniy the most outstanding Bukharan student and scholar of the Jadid era, who wrote

[20] *Statisticheskii ezhegodnik Rossii 1915 g.*, p. 102.

his poems, tracts, dramas, and scholarly books in both Uzbek and Tajik, and knew Urdu, Arabic, and Russian as well. Educated in Bukhara and Istanbul, Fitrat was active in politics as a "Young Bukharan" and in 1920 became minister of culture briefly for the Bukharan People's Republic; he served as a tireless organizer of the nationalistic intellectuals in Tashkent from 1918 on. There was Qasim Tinistan-uulu (c.1900–1934), who, in national terms, was probably much more important to the Kirgiz than Fitrat was to the Uzbeks and Tajiks, for Tinistan-uulu stood more nearly alone at his time in the separate Kirgiz society as an accomplished poet, linguist, scholar, nationalist political leader, one-time commissar for Kirgiz education, and editor of both *Erkin too* (1924–   ), the first Kirgiz newspaper, and *Janga madaniyat jolunda* (1928–1931), the republic's most influential magazine of its time.

The Kirgiz and Turkmens, because of their dispersal and relatively small numbers, naturally possessed fewer intellectual centers than the populous Kazakhs and the Uzbek-Tajik concentration. Even where the population was greater, men of the caliber of Mir Jaqib Duwlat-uli or Abdalrauf Fitrat were not numerous, but a promising nucleus of intellectuals rivaling them in some of their attainments grew in nearly every city. Moreover, each succeeding year brought with it additional offspring of parents affected by the upsurge in Central Asian Muslim education which had begun in the 1890s. Thus, the most enlightened, inventive, and active generation of Central Asians to appear in modern times was probably that formed of men like Tinistan-uulu in Kirgizistan, Magjan Jumabay-uli (1896–c.1938) in Kazakhstan, Abdulhamid Sulayman Yunus Cholpan (1898–c.1938) and Mannan Ramiz (c.1900–c.1931) in Uzbekistan, Berdi Kerbabay-oghli (1894–   ) and Abdulhakim Qulmuhammad-oghli (c.1900–c.1937) in Turkmenistan, all of whom reached manhood just when the Russian revolutions of 1917 offered opportunities for what seemed like the widest expression of their united talents. From this generation emerged the fervent young nationalists and nationalistic Communists who dominated the literary, publishing, and educational institutions toward the end of the 1920s after the grip of their elders had slipped as a result of ferocious opposition from the Russian Communist Party.

Typical among local Communist intellectuals were Mannan Ramiz
and Abdulhakim Qulmuhammad-oghli. Ramiz, a poet, playwright,
several years editor of the influential Uzbek magazine *Maarif wä
oqutghuchi*, active in the literary society Qizil Qalam, and at one
time commissar of education for Uzbekistan, in adapting to the new
political situation had become a tough-minded ideologist for a
kind of special national Communism in Uzbekistan. His ideas were
judged so dangerous to Moscow goals that Ramiz was "liquidated"
even before the great purges of the late 1930s which annihilated
most of the nationalities' intellectuals. Comrade (*yoldash*) Qulmuhammad-oghli likewise busied himself with editing, publishing,
research, writing, organizing the Turkmenistan writers and other
educated men into a coherent body, and carrying on all these
activities more or less within the local Communist Party framework.

REGROUPING THE WRITER-INTELLECTUALS

Like the prerevolutionary societies Tarbiya-i atfal and Turan,
the first literary or educational associations to originate after 1917
generally set no national limits to membership. Thus, they acquired
a cosmopolitan profile matching the intellectual population of the
place where the circle functioned. The roster of the Chaghatay
Gurungi group, organized privately and led by Abdalrauf Fitrat at
Tashkent from 1918 to 1922, was naturally dominated by the Uzbeks,
but Tajiks, Tatars, and other Muslim nationalities were represented.
Fitrat himself was one of a number considered to be both an Uzbek
and a Tajik poet because he wrote in both languages.

As in so many other procedures throughout Central Asian society
affected by the political reorganization of 1924–1925, the educated
men, including the writers found themselves playing the game of
letters with new regulations. After 1925 the first principle which
those active in literary life had to obey more closely might be called
the rule of nationality. But, though each major nationality of Central Asia was now recognized through the existence of its official
republic, the local writers' associations which began to unite authors
and poets in each republic around 1926 still in most cases avoided
labels connected with the nationalities.

In the Kirgiz ASSR, Kirgiz and Russian writers segregated themselves into two literary organizations: Qzil Uchkun (Red Spark), which served the Kirgiz writers exclusively, and Kirgizskaia As-sotsiatsiia Proletarskikh Pisatelei (Kirgiz Association of Proletarian Writers)—KirAPP—which enrolled only Russians until the Party merged the two groups in August, 1930, under the Russian name, with a membership of some hundred writers. This politically important administrative act also linked the local writers with a parent group in Moscow and instituted for the first time an official circle for Kirgiz writers bearing the national designation.[21]

Organizations comparable in spirit and conception to the Kirgiz Qzil Uchkun, and joined mainly by "fellow travelers," according to critics, led a brief, chaotic existence in Uzbekistan's capital, Samarkand, where the Qizil Qalam (Red Pen) group formed the sole authorized literary circle of the republic between 1927 and 1930. In the Kazakh area, the writers' association Alqa (The Circle) brought together men from Qizil Orda (Aq Meshit) regardless of nationality,[22] although the mixing in the cities of the plains was less notable than at cosmopolitan centers like Samarkand and Khokand.

The Turkmens, like the Kazakhs, pioneered in establishing intellectual circles in their region uncomplicated by ancient city traditions. Nevertheless, the new literary society founded in Turkmenistan derived its leadership not from the novice proletarians being created by the Party, but received direction entirely from the small core of Jadid nationalists who had recently grown up in the republic. As one Turkmen author put it a few years later:

Until 1931 our literary movement was headed by national bourgeois writers like Qulmuhammad-oghli, Vopay-oghli, Kerbabay-oghli, Burunoghli, and others. . . . These writers set up their own organization in 1926–1927. It was the Turkmen Scientific Literary Society, into which they accepted only writers or national intelligentsia raised in the bourgeois spirit. . . . In their regulations and program they wrote and said openly that young writers or poets might enter this society only as corresponding members, that they could have no decisive voice, could

[21] I. Toichinov "Kirgizskaia literatura," *Literaturnaia entsiklopediia,* V (1931), pp. 211–12.
[22] Thomas G. Winner, *The Oral Art and Literature of the Kazakhs of Russian Central Asia* (Durham, Duke University Press, 1958), p. 189.

not be elected, etc. . . . . These bourgeois writers headed nearly all the literary and cultural institutions. Until recently they played the major role among us on the literary front.[23]

Under the pressures applied to all the semi-independent local literary and intellectual organization in Central Asia at this time, the Scientific Literary Society of the Turkmens disintegrated and left the field to a TurkAPP hastily put together in 1931.

Born as they were almost at the moment the new federative republics came into being in Central Asia, the first quasi-official writers' societies were at the same time nationalistic, which, in fact, they were expected to be in order to substantiate and materialize a new intellectual and literary culture separate in each case from the community of old Western Turkistan or Central Asia at large. The nationalism they expressed, however, resembled in spirit and aims the patriotism which had grown up throughout the new intellectual circles between 1900 and 1925, becoming "national" mainly with the contraction of borders which limited the numbers of people and expanse of terrain that poets and prose writers could properly identify themselves with. This carry-over of the old, Turkistanian mentality into the groups founded around the mid-1920s continued to obstruct the adoption of requisite Communist and proletarian attitudes among intellectuals and readers.

For that reason and others, in each case the local arm of the proletarian writers' association extending itself into Central Asia from Moscow in the 1920s had to capture enough power to push the more cosmopolitan and nationalistic "Red" societies out of existence by the beginning of the following decade. In this drive, KhwAPP (Khwarazmian), founded in 1924 at Khiva, seems to have been the first local proletarian writers' group organized in Central Asia. KarAPP (Karakalpak), KazAPP, and KirAPP appeared soon after, along with SAAPP (Central Asian), but UzAPP, TajAPP, and TurkAPP, which came into being as late as 1929 to 1931, were in fact the last APP's to be formed in the USSR, and their appearance finally made VOAPP (All-Union Society of Associations of Proletarian Writers), shortly before its fall, an all-Union organiza-

[23] Chariev, "Preniia," *Sovetskaia literatura na novom etape* (Moscow, Sovetskaia Literatura, 1933), pp. 122–23.

tion.[24] At least one city group, TAPP (Tashkent), attempted to combine both Russian and local members, but TAPP, whose history was extremely stormy, was basically a Russian society with Uzbek members relegated to a subordinate section.

The smallness of the struggling writers' groups is a hint of the modest number of those who could qualify as potential members, but the exact size of the local intelligentsia for each major Central Asian nationality really became known for the first time just a year after these nationalities were proclaimed official occupants of their specific sections of Central Asia. The census for 1926 revealed predictable patterns, showing that the nationalities having the largest cities also possessed the highest number of educated and professional persons, but the cities were also found invariably in the domains of the most numerous Central Asian nationalities (Kazakhs and Uzbeks). Literate Kazakhs, who congregated mainly at Russian headquarters like Orenburg, Akmolinsk, and Semipalatinsk, plus smaller towns in the plains such as Vernyi (Alma Ata), Troitsk, Qizil Orda, Turgay, and Uralsk, had outgrown literate Uzbeks, who inhabitated Central Asia's ancient capitals, in both absolute and relative figures by 1926, and in relative figures even in 1959, as Table 13.2 shows.

LITERACY AND THE PROFESSIONS, 1926

Yet, curiously enough, there were more Uzbeks than Kazakhs in any of the professions (law, medicine, the arts) other than higher education. Tables 13.3a and 13.3b show the distribution of the Central Asian intelligentsia by profession. The number of Uzbek professional men or women in all categories was three times the number of Kazakh men or women in the same fields. Furthermore, the Uzbek factory manager, teacher, or clergyman, for instance, in many cases resided and worked beyond the borders of his titular republic, usually in the Kirgiz ASSR and the Turkmen SSR, whereas Kazakh professionals only occasionally lived and worked permanently outside their own ASSR, and then it was likely to be in the Karakalpak Autonomous Oblast. This

[24] *Proletarskaia literatura SSSR na novom etape* (Moscow-Leningrad, Gosudarstvennoe Izdatel'stvo Khudozhestvennoi Literatury, 1931), p. 296.

TABLE 13.2

Literacy in Central Asia in the Soviet Period

National group	1926 census			1959 census		
	Population	Number of literate	Percent literate	Population	Number of literate	Percent literate*
Karakalpak	146,303	2,056	1.3	170,822	87,261	51.0
Kazakh	3,831,611	264,340	7.0	3,232,403	1,785,352	52.1
Kirgiz	762,391	34,560	4.5	962,001	504,376	52.4
Tajik	978,627	21,983	2.2	1,385,835	725,912	52.3
Turkmen	755,963	15,465	2.0	985,643	511,524	51.9
Uyghur	42,524	1,946	4.5	92,974	50,716	54.5
Uzbek	3,903,585	148,938	3.8	5,973,147	3,070,460	51.0
Total	10,421,004	489,288	(mean) 3.6	12,802,825	6,735,601	(mean) 52.1

* The 1959 Soviet census, which did not pretend to be a sampling, excluded from its published literacy tables all persons over 49 or under 9 years of age, thus limiting the "total" Central Asian population whose literacy or illiteracy was reported to not more than 52.4 percent of the Karakalpaks, 57 percent of the Kazakhs, 53.5 percent of the Kirgiz, 54.3 percent of the Tajiks, 54.4 percent of the Turkmens, 57 percent of the Uyghurs, and 52.4 percent of the Uzbeks. Therefore, the literates in each nationality shown in the census came to somewhat fewer than the numbers of persons falling within the 9-to-49 age bracket, according to literacy rates supplied in the sources. This elicits a figure for literate persons which is probably somewhat lower than it should be for these groups, because unquestionably there were still living, in 1959, literate persons of local nationality, including a number of important writers and intellectuals who had been born before 1910. A small though presumably not significant variant also could arise in this table because 9-year-olds,

for whom no separate census count is provided, are included in the Soviet calculations of literacy. At the same time, an overlap in the Soviet presentation of age and literacy groups results in the exclusion of 9-year-olds (who are statistically lumped with children aged 1 to 8) from the population of any Central Asian nationality for purposes of determining the percentage of persons actually falling outside the 9-to-49 age category.

Source: *1926 census.* "Kazakhskaia ASSR, Kirgizskaia ASSR," *Vsesoiuznaia perepis' naseleniia 1926 goda* (Moscow, Izdanie TsSU Soiuza SSR, 1926), VIII, 15–16, 200–1; "Turkmenskaia SSR," *ibid.,* XVI, 6–7; "Uzbekskaia SSR," *ibid.,* XV, 8–9. *1959 census.* "Kazakhskaia SSR," *Itogi vsesoiuznoi perepisi naseleniia 1959 goda* (Moscow, Tsentral'noe Statisticheskoe Upravlenie pri Sovete Ministrov SSSR, 1962), pp. 26, 60, 168–72; "Kirgizskaia SSR," *ibid.* (1963), pp. 19, 37, 132. "Tadzhikskaia SSR," *ibid.,* pp. 19, 37, 122; "Turkmenskaia SSR," *ibid.,* pp. 21, 38, 132; "Uzbekskaia SSR," *ibid.* (1962), pp. 21, 42, 144–46.

strong competitive position of the Uzbeks probably would have allowed them to dominate Central Asian groups if their movements had not been restricted by the Russian government after 1925 within Central Asia's new internal borders.

From these circumstances a direct correlation between literacy rates alone and the extent of the Central Asian intellectual or professional circles cannot be established. Some time after 1926, however, when white-collar workers in all jobs had become designated officially as members of the intelligentsia, statistical correspondence between literacy and the occupations became much closer than it had been earlier. Census reports for 1926 do not specify the literacy rate of the various professional groups listed in Tables 13.3a and 13.3b, although writers, editors, and some others obviously had to be able to read and write. Judging from other sources of information, however, there is reason to doubt that all musicians and clergymen, for example, were literate.

In 1926 the urban complement of the intelligentsia varied in size by profession, most musicians, for example, being located in cities. By contrast, the greater part of the Muslim clergy, which in the mid-1920s still supplied the most widespread single ideological force among the Central Asians, worked in the countryside where most of the ordinary people lived. Of the 5,898 mullahs, imams, ishans, and others in the religious calling, one-third claimed town residence in 1926. As in other fields, Uzbeks (3,339) dominated the influential Central Asian religious world, and Tajiks (1,952) made up most of the other clergymen. Again, very important for the development of the attitudes characterizing intellectuals and other educated men were the Muslim primary and secondary school teachers (2,056 Uzbeks, 970 Kazakhs), considerable numbers of whom lived and taught in the villages. Certain professions, such as the medical and university academic had been from the beginning of the Russian occupation almost the exclusive province of the new colonists.

The very small quantity of literary men counted in the census provides a misleading picture of their actual numbers unless it is remembered that poets rarely earned a livelihood in Central Asia penning verse. Logically, when asked by statisticians what

TABLE 13.3a

Distribution of the "Intelligentsia" by Profession (Institutionally [State] Employed), 1926

	Management	Law	Medicine	Higher education (excluding madrasah)	Primary and secondary education	Literature and journalism	Library and museum work	Theater	Music	Art	Total
In Karakalpakistan											*180*
Karakalpaks	10	5			17						32
Kazakhs	25	4			25						54
Uzbeks	8	1			5						14
Russians, Ukrainians	41	8	9		17					5	80
In Kazakhstan											*9,993*
Kazakhs	930	208	20	9	905	20	7	6	1		2,106
Russians, Ukrainians	2,681	336	416	28	4,106	29	109	85	83	14	7,887
In Kirgizistan											*1,649*
Kirgiz	235	18	1		215	5			2	3	479
Uzbeks	55	7			63						125
Russians, Ukrainians	486	43	70	1	396	5	11		9	24	1,045
In Turkmenistan											*2,057*
Turkmens	265	37			235	6	4			5	552
Uzbeks	51	6			31	1	1			1	91
Russians, Ukrainians	575	76	127	3	467	7	45			114	1,414
In Uzbekistan, Tajikistan											*13,510*
Uzbeks	2,093	218	14	7	1,831	67	10	29	50		4,319
Tajiks	485	45	4	1	409	20	4	1	4		973
Other indigenous	179	14	13	17	165	12	1				401
Russians, Ukrainians	3,066	395	944	278	2,417	148	168	175	226		7,817
Totals											
Central Asians	4,336	563	52	34	3,901	131	27	36	57	9	9,146
Russians, Ukrainians	6,849	858	1,566	310	7,403	189	333	260	318	157	18,243

Source: "Kazakhskaia ASSR i Kirgizskaia ASSR: otdel II, zaniatiia," *Vsesoiuznaia perepis' naseleniia 1926 goda* (Moscow, 1929), XXV, 70–72, 167–71, 243–51. "Turkmenskaia SSR: otdel II, zaniatiia," *ibid.*, XXXIII, 48–54. "Uzbekskaia SSR: zaniatiia," *ibid.*, XXXII, 76–83, 177–182. Izdanie TsSU Soiuza SSR.

TABLE 13.3b

Distribution of the "Intelligentsia" by Profession (Noninstitutionally [Privately] Employed), 1926

	Law	Medicine	Primary and secondary education	Literature and journalism	Theater	Music	Art	Clergy*	Other†	Total
In Karakalpakistan										377
Karakalpaks								27	142	169
Kazakhs								25	126	151
Uzbeks								25	26	51
Russians, Ukrainians								1	5	6
In Kazakhstan										6,076
Kazakhs	9	4	40		4	4		296	3,178	3,535
Russians, Ukrainians	46	33	97	4	58	70	24	23	2,186	2,541
In Kirgizistan										959
Kirgiz	1		2			3		45	507	558
Uzbeks			2			6		95	68	171
Russians, Ukrainians	11	1	9			17			192	230
In Turkmenistan										1,342
Turkmens			8			7		79	647	741
Uzbeks						3		32	53	88
Russians, Ukrainians	6	5	11		4	7	5	1	474	513
In Uzbekistan, Tajikistan										15,278
Uzbeks	20	28	124	2	36	244	10	3,187	4,425	8,076
Tajiks		3	38		2	32		1,952	703	2,730
Other indigenous		5	13		1	30		135	1,050	1,234
Russians, Ukrainians	41	61	128	6	55	99	37	95	2,716	3,238
Total										
Central Asians	30	40	227	2	43	329	10	5,898	10,925	17,504
Russians, Ukrainians	104	100	245	10	117	193	66	120	5,573	6,528

* non-Orthodox and Muslim   † includes Russian-Orthodox clergy and scholarship students   Source: same as Table 13.3a

he did for a living a writer would call himself a secretary, copyist, attorney, merchant, or designate another profession from which he derived his primary or perhaps his entire income.

LITERARY POLITICS AMONG THE SOVIET INTELLIGENTSIA

Authors' obscurity in the census did not protect them from being identified and pressured to conform to new demands. At the end of the 1920s nationalistically minded writers faced a choice, in cases where their published hostility to the regime had not taken them beyond a political safety point, of saving themselves from destruction by openly confessing their past intellectual and ideological "sins" and promising to toe the Party line thereafter. Self-criticism effective enough to save the sinner's life in most instances had to come forth no later than 1934—like these public recantations issued in Turkmenistan by Berdi Kerbabay-oghli and Garaja Burun-oghli:

All the questions touched upon in our works had been resolved from the standpoint of ideology hostile to the proletariat, from the standpoint of counterrevolutionary nationalism. . . . We entirely and absolutely realized the complete harmfulness and erroneousness of our nationalistic aim. . . . We shall not spare our strength or abilities in order to prove in action and in creative work that we have broken with the ideas of counterrevolutionary nationalism and have been ideologically rearmed.[25]

Kerbabay-oghli and a few others were reprieved, and surviving together with them were the immediate heirs to the last, openly nationalistic group of intellectual leaders to rise in Central Asia, the transitional figures like Musa Tashmuhammad-oghli Aybek (1905–) in Uzbekistan, Amandurdi Alamish-oghli (c.1908–) in Turkmenistan, Hamid Alimjan (1909–1944) in Uzbekistan, and their near coevals who started literary activity with writings strongly resembling those of the nationalists.

Alongside the transitional group then developed the proletarian poets who were nurtured by SAAPP (Central Asian Association of Proletarian Writers) in the late 1920s. These were

[25] O. Tash-Nazarov, "Doklad o literature turkmenskoi SSR," *Pervyi vsesoiuznyi s"ezd sovetskikh pisatelei, 1934* (Moscow, Gosizdat "Khudozhestvennaia Literatura," 1934), p. 139.

young people who revealed in their writings no links with the recent or distant past, but, though continuing the ageless custom of verse composition, seemed to be engrossed entirely in ideas expressed by the slogans and programs of the All-Union Communist Party concerned with industrialization and collectivization. This purposeful anti-intellectualism sponsored by the authorities probably not by coincidence produced almost no literary men or women who were outstanding as leaders in the whole community as had been the case in the previous generation. Nor did such narrow preoccupations develop public figures who could be considered first-class writers in their society.

Thus began what now looks to have been a calculated process of whittling down the stature of writers in general and splitting them off from the other intellectuals with the consequent reduction in their influence among their peers. It is significant, too, that through the 1930s and 1940s those who survived the terror and enjoyed the greatest success in combining literary prowess with even a relatively active public life proved to be the very men, like Aybek and Amandurdi Alamish-oghli, who had learned their earliest lessons in poetry and politics from the nationalists. Like the proletarian poets, however, none of these transitional authors attained the importance of their elders in the society at large. With the diminution of intellectual leadership from this source, public opinion became managed exclusively by Party propaganda units installed in all the literary and publishing outlets, and intellectual life as it had been known ended or was forced to go underground.

The decade of the 1920s therefore had become a ten-years' war against the hard core of local pro-Russian Communists made up mostly of near-illiterates or malcontents, like the Uzbek Hamza Hakim Zada Niyaziy (1889–1929), once a Jadid teacher, poet, and playwright, with the close support of Russian leaders on the spot determined to keep independent Central Asian intellectuals in check while grooming loyal and less imaginative replacements for them. Throughout the period and into the late 1930s the opinion leaders and other educated men remained divided into antagonistic groups for and against the new political system.

The principal alteration to the balance of forces in 1920 occurred with the waning of influence of the Muslim religious hierarchy through loss of status, funds, properties, and convenient communications channels, and the systematic isolation of nationalist leadership from both its bases of power in the state institutions and support from the political factions. Simultaneously, with the decline of the nationalists a new breed of public figure still concerned, like his predecessors, with the education of the young and shaping of the civilization, developed out of the proletarian movement in the cities. With the appearance of Soviet socialist governments and stronger Russian leadership throughout the area after 1925, the preparation of greatly broadened generations of educated people continued, but in a different ideological direction. From their ranks were to come the leadership of the intelligentsia, a circle no longer necessarily coincident with the pool of writers.

Related to this fundamental change in the intellectual stratum of society, a different conception about intellectual leadership came into play. The old understanding, expressed in the terms *aqïldï adam* (Kazakh), *äqilliq adäm* (Uyghur), *aqïllï kisi* (Karakalpak), *akïlduu kishi* or *estüü kishi* (Kirgiz), *insan-i aqil* (Tajik), and *aqil* (Uzbek), began to be blurred by a usage common in nineteenth-century Russia. There, the word intelligentsia had implied particular social concerns on the part of a certain class of educated men. Concrete form had been given to a similar kind of Central Asian figure among the Jadid intellectuals who insisted upon the social commitment of all enlightened individuals.

For a time after the 1917 revolutions, however, the term intelligentsia remained under a shadow cast by the opinion prevalent among the Bolsheviks that members of the intelligentsia present in the USSR in the 1920s, necessarily carry-overs from czarist days, were, as Sabit Muqan-uli (1900–   ), a Kazakh writer, termed them, in 1933, nothing but *jolbike* (fellow travelers).[26] The literary men from the first proletarian generation wrote into their poems and stories a renewed concern with the old intelligentsia. One of Ch. Ashirov's Turkmen poems, "Intelligent" (The Educated Man),

[26] Mukanov, "Preniia," *Sovetskaia literatura na novom etape* (Moscow, Sovetskaia Literatura, 1933), p. 75.

1933,[27] defined what he saw as the traits of such intelligentsia: a "thoughtless" attitude toward life and "old fashioned" views concerning the place of women in society.

Once this prejudice had been overcome, the new Soviet *intelligents* became characterized as any persons who worked at mental, not physical, tasks, whether in the factory, kindergarten, or university regardless of the quality or level of activity, and were now called *bilimpaz* (Kazakh), *fazil, ziyali* or *ahl-i ma'rifat* (Uzbek), *bilimli* (Turkmen), or *okugan adam* (Kirgiz). Nevertheless, the intelligentsia of Central Asia in the 1920s included all those who might have made up the group of intellectuals from the past with the exception of the educated clergy and businessmen, and the widening of the definition brought in exactly the proletarian in-intelligentsia who altered the previous understanding of the term.

Mobilizing this broader section of the population to serve specific purposes of the new regime inevitably introduced a conformity among the intelligentsia which perhaps paralled the community of thought met among the old Muslim intellectuals before the arrival of the Jadids but fell far short of encouraging that free, creative thinking displayed among the nineteen-century intellectual leaders and their followers. A mark of the generation growing up under the influence of Russian Communism in Central Asia became, therefore, so far as the intelligentsia was concerned, its ideological uniformity, with the state once again enforcing the official viewpoint. After the Russian Communists succeeded in stripping Central Asia of its main independent nationalistic intellectuals in the purges of 1937 and 1938, this obligatory conformity remained attached to the principles of Soviet Marxism as interpreted by Communist leaders in Moscow. Gone was the exhilarating diversity of ideologies and rival intellectual currents which colored Central Asian life up to the 1930s.

So that no vacuum in political and social thought would be created by the elimination of pan-Islamic expressions and the sudden removal of nationalistic ideological leadership, the organizers of the Communist Party in Central Asia had begun, soon

[27] *Türkmen sovet edebiyatining tarïkhï: Boyuncha ocherk* (Ashkhabad, Türkmenistan SSR Ilïmlar Akademiyasïnïng Neshiryatï, 1958), I, 134.

after the Bolshevik take-over, to indoctrinate the leaders in various professions such as teaching, publishing, and theater. Emphasis upon collective therapy for changing the minds of the intelligentsia increased soon after the partition of Central Asia in the mid-1920s when Party authorities drew representatives from various professions into combined sessions planned with the aim of unifying their thoughts and swinging them all behind the efforts of the Party.

Themes of the first Soviet congress of the intelligentsia of Kazakhstan (1924) and Uzbekistan (1926), for example, were in good part reflected in the slogans: "unite knowledge and labor," "end illiteracy," "the political proletariat is the basis for culture," "take the direct road to Communism," "unite Soviet teachers around the Party," and "fight the nationalists." Because the Communists had not then achieved complete control over the intelligentsia, the 1926 congress, obviously beset with political rivalries, was merely a dress rehearsal for the second Uzbek congress of intelligentsia held the following year. The 1927 congress excluded the nationalist opposition and concentrated upon problems in this order of priority: 1) Latinizing the alphabet; 2) emancipating the women; 3) promoting Red workers' and farmers' news reporting; 4) forwarding education and cultural "progress." [28]

From that time onward, the intelligentsia in the main cities of Central Asia found itself schooled constantly for responsibility which, in cases like the drive for literacy, resembled the old Jadid causes. Political and social indoctrination of the ordinary citizen has remained up to now its first task, and subsequent congresses of writers, of teachers, or of the entire intelligentsia never fail to emphasize it.

The tendency to regard Central Asia as a unit for purposes of organizational arrangements continued when the decrees striking down KazAPP, KirAPP, UzAPP, SAAPP, and the others simultaneously erected a new Central Asian literary edifice based ul-

[28] Ramiz, "Ziyalilar qurultayining gäldägi wäzifäläri," *Maarif wä oqutghuchi*, No. 6 (1927), pp. 3–4; Sh. Sulayman, "2-nchi shora ziyalilar qurultayi aldida," *Maarif wä oqutghuchi*, Nos. 9/10 (1927), p. 9; *Qazaq bilimpazdarining tonghish siyezi* (Orenburg, Kirgizskoe Gosudarstvenncc Izdatel'stvo, 1925).

timately upon Moscow but enclosed by the barriers of a literary department in the Communist Party's Central Asian Bureau. This bureaucratic mushroom was gobbled up soon after it sprouted but before being consumed in the eternal Party reorganizations, it dominated the measures taken to introduce a network of literary circles responding directly to Party control and linked only to the central management located in Moscow, without lateral ties or intermediary, all-Central Asian echelons. The Central Asian Bureau of the Party relayed the Russian announcement terminating the existence of the APPs and other societies in 1932, and at the same time ordered the publication of a new magazine devoted to the contemporary literature of all Central Asians. The editors of this publication were mainly Russian, but there was a board which drew together sympathetic representatives from Tajik, Turkmen, Uzbek, and comparable writers' groups.[29]

WRITERS' UNIONS PURGE AND REHABILITATE THEIR CIRCLES

Before the events launched by the 1932 declarations had run their course, the revamped literary associations, called in Russian, Soiuz Sovetskikh Pisatelei (Union of Soviet Writers), or Ozbekistan Sovet Yazuchilari Soyuzi (Uzbek), or Qazaq Sovet Jazushïlarï Odaghï (Kazakh), started to take shape. Throughout the area organizing committees rushed to set up new structures to replace discredited APPs. In Turkmenistan each of five major regions was required to form its own committee of writers with leaders supplied from the Ashkhabad center, where, in addition, the capital provided a special section for writers from smaller minorities in the republic. This new pattern of literary activity characterized the changing literary situation in other parts of Central Asia also. Bustle and organization for the time being everywhere supplanted the immobility into which writers had been frozen by the APP strife.

Thus, the 1932 decrees introduced a period, perhaps not yet

[29] "O perestroike literaturno-khudozhestvennykh organizatsii v Srednei Azii: Postanovlenie Sredazbiuro Ts. K. VKP(b)," *Pravda Vostoka*, May 26, 1932, p. 2; English text given in *Uzbek Literary Politics* (The Hague, Mouton, 1964), pp. 132–33 *n*.10.

ended, when the operational aspects of literary activity dominated the creative side of literature. Nothing could have emphasized this tendency more strongly than the florid orations made by writers at the First Congress of Soviet Writers in 1934. At that meeting, called to affirm the ideological direction of the new Union of Soviet writers, 41 Central Asians participated in sessions which heard much plain speaking about the supposed shortcomings of the past. A literary formula for the future was adopted, called "socialist realism," which promised—and now can be seen to have delivered—a kind of nonliterature from Soviet writers who succeeded in adhering to its prescriptions. Central Asians, no less than their Russian counterparts, lost under this dictum the freedom to regard literature as art, and had it not been for the fact that such an ambiguous and sweeping rule or decree is rarely carried out to the letter in the USSR, including Central Asia, where writers and others have become adept at circumventing bureaucratic controls, there should be very little else to talk about in connection with the developments after 1934.

The affairs of the Union of Soviet Writers, established in 1932 and confirmed by the Congress of 1934, have been managed by the Russian hierarchy which controls the powerful secretariat through the manipulation of the Russian members whose great numbers dominate meetings, and by elections in which ballots are never counted by republics, that is one vote for one republic, but by the "deciding voice" of each qualified participant at the meetings. The Russian delegation voting at the Second Congress of Soviet Writers, in 1954, for example, numbered 242 from Moscow and Leningrad alone, more than enough to swamp the remaining national delegations such as that from Central Asia if issues ever came to contest. But, so tight has been the rein upon the post-World War II congresses that open disagreement has never been expressed in the balloting, and unanimous decisions monotonously follow one another from each congress.

Particulars concerning the structure and functioning of the Union of Soviet Writers codified in its official regulations apply to Central Asian writers' unions as well as the USSR group at large. The first section of the regulations devotes itself to "The Aims of the

Union of Writers of the USSR," the second to "Members of the Union of Writers of the USSR, Their Duties and Rights," the third to "Organizational Structure of the Union of Writers of the USSR," and the fourth to "Legal Rights of the Union of Writers of the USSR." According to the wording of these rules, the initial section changes with the turns in the Party line. Section two provides that members may be accepted into the Union on the basis of works published which have original artistic or "scientific" (ideological) significance. Such members are expressly obligated "with all their creative and social actions to participate zealously in the building of Communism, to aid the creative growth of young literary men, and to participate in the work of the writers' organization, fulfilling the social commands of the elected organs of the Union, and upholding the honor and integrity of the Union of Writers." [30]

The supreme body of the Union in the USSR is the All-Union Congress of Writers, now required to convene once every four years according to section three of the regulations, though no such meeting has been held between 1959 and 1965, and the executive body of that Congress is the Board of the Union of Writers of the USSR, elected at the Congress and holding plenary sessions no less often than once a year. These plenums elect from themselves the permanent working body known as the Secretariat of the Board, which carries on the day-to-day activity of the Union. The Secretariat has the authority to enforce the decisions of the congresses and the Board. In Central Asia the republic congresses of writers must be called once every four years also, and they select boards whose plenums, like their all-Soviet counterpart, elect from themselves bodies, here called presidiums or bureaus, of the board. In any republic union, a division having no fewer than forty members may elect its own board for that division. The republic unions and local divisions organize additional literary subunits among the large administrative and cultural centers in which work is conducted with authors. Related literary circles are also established among the editorial staffs of newspapers and

[30] "Ustav soiuza pisatelei SSSR," *Tretii s"ezd pisatelei SSSR 18–23 maia, 1959 g.* (Moscow, Sovetskii Pisatel', 1959), p. 249.

publishing houses. Little or no independence is allowed to the republic board or lower echelons of the Union because resolutions and acts of the Moscow congresses as well as those of the central Board and Secretariat of the Board are binding for republic unions in Central Asia and elsewhere.

In practice, because the Kazakh, Uzbek, and similar local unions do not enroll large numbers, these circles remain exclusive in-groups whose control over nonmembers is great because of the economic influence affecting job placement or purchase of manu-scripts, and the power a union can exert in the press or publish-ing houses to disbar writers attacked in criticism or published ideological condemnation. From the viewpoint of the Soviet gov-ernment therefore, it is clear that the most important duty carried out by writers' unions is the policing of ideas among the literary men, who in turn shape the thinking of the remaining intelligen-tsia and the reading public.

In performing the function of controller the Union resorts to arguments which scarcely contain any element of what non-Com-munist writers would recognize as literary criticism, because it is mainly arbitrary ideological interpretation without reference to literary style or artistic verisimilitude. Character portrayal in the latest Kazakh novel, for example, will hardly be criticized for de-ficiencies in warmth, believability, artistry, or appropriateness in the given situation, but rather for its failure to take a Communist stance or represent a "socialist man," or to express the contem-porary Party view about China and peaceful coexistence.

In the strident polemics which passed for criticism during the proletarian era in Central Asian literature, extra-literary attacks upon prose or poetry were even more extreme than today, and the official dissolution of SAAPP in 1932, although it tempered that vindictiveness, did not end the tendency to indulge this habit. Castigating writers, dead or alive, for literary "sins" of the mo-ment had a great impact upon the intellectual community in Alma Ata, for example, when Abay Qunanbay-uli, now lionized as the greatest "progressive" poet of the nineteenth-century Kazakhs, was dismissed contemptuously from Kazakh literature as "semi-feu-dal," one of the Communist's thunderous critical epithets, or when

Mukhtar Auez-uli (Auezov) (1897–1961), whose Kazakh novels and plays today receive the highest praise, was characterized as a "counterrevolutionary" and "political enemy." [31]

This fantastic style of literary evaluation might have been laughed off as an irrelevancy had the Party not made it a nightmare come true when it harassed writers mercilessly, and ultimately, on the basis of formal denunciations extracted mainly from the writers' unions, still under the name of literary criticism, imprisoned and executed hundreds of intellectuals wholesale. Among them were outstanding writers like Jumabay-uli, Tinistan-uulu, Qulmuhammad-oghli, Fitrat, Cholpan, and most other nationalists mentioned here. The ritual of the purge occurred mainly at meetings of organizations like the writers' Union. Though people outside the writers' meetings were quite aware of the midnight arrests, only gradually did they understand the enormity of the catastrophe and the official explanation for it. Blame for this crime must be borne partly by an irresponsible, undemocratic writers' Union which in its witch hunt exercised power derived from arbitrary Communist Party and police control over Central Asian intellectual affairs.

The irony in the tragedy of the 1930s has been emphasized since 1956 by the often grudging rehabilitation of such victims, sometimes conducted self-righteously by the very sort of Uzbek, Kazakh, or other organization men in the Party who marked Central Asia's intellectual leaders of the 1920s and 1930s for death. Curiously, although the printed record of 1937–1938 frequently names the accusers and "critics" who denounced their fellows with what are now conceded to have been trumped-up charges, the present official decontamination of the formerly accused writers cites as the cause merely the "personality cult" surrounding Stalin, and the authorities have failed in every single instance to demand answers to the concrete questions: "Who killed Abdullah Qadiriy?" "Who murdered Aqmet Baytursin-uli?" "Who, in fact is responsible for each life lost?" and to bring the guilty to justice publicly.

Rehabilitations, almost invariably posthumous, have been care-

[31] *Kazakskii sbornik* (Moscow, Gosizdat Khudozhestvennoi Literatury, 1934), pp. 3–11.

fully selective, have been ostentatiously legalized with official, court-ordered amnesties, and in the main have been intended to return to political acceptability figures and works useful for patching up weak spots in official Communist intellectual and literary history. For this review, each republic has assigned a few writers to the task of reviving certain works banned since 1938 while reinterpreting, favorably, their authors' activities in that period. Foremost among the rehabilitators in Uzbekistan, for instance, has been the playwright, scholar, and critic Izzat Sultanov (1910–   ), who in 1956 not only provided the ideological rationale for reinstating the deceased Abdullah Qadiriy to honor in the first of the Uzbek rehabilitations, but subsequently supplied also the obstructions to returning other nationalists such as Abdalrauf Fitrat or Cholpan to full respectability. The careful, incomplete performance by Dr. Sultanov and his colleagues has left still unanswered all queries regarding culpability in the case of Qadiriy or other martyred nationalists.

This means that quietly walking the streets of Alma Ata, Ashkhabad, Dushanbe, Frunze, and Tashkent, mingling still in many cases with active literary and intellectual society, are living participants from that era of the purge who deserve prosecution for crimes against free thought and life itself in Central Asia. In such a sinister atmosphere, true intellectual exchange or genuine competition in social, educational, or artistic fields does not usually exist. Evidence corroborating this may be the fact that original Central Asian currents flowing in any of these fields have not been revealed through literary material published from the middle of the 1930s to the middle of the 1960s.

One important development, however, which can freshen the air in intellectual circles, has come from increased extra-literary activity in which Central Asian writers are obliged more and more to take part. The opportunity has improved for a literary community otherwise encircled by rigid boundaries and with internal travel curtailed to come again in closer contact with intellectuals from outside their world. The 41 Central Asian delegates to the First Congress of Soviet Writers in Moscow (1934) met 40 foreigners besides almost 600 Soviet writers, and those at the Second

FIGURE 13.5 Uzbek literati in conference (left to right): critic and playwright Izzat Sultanov; novelist and playwright Abdullah Qahhar; critic and scholar Wahid Zahidov. *TASS photo.*

Congress (1954), in an enlarged Central Asian contingent, met Soviet and foreign writers, most of them Communists of course, when they invaded the Soviet capital with a 68-member group. Besides the major nationality from each Central Asian republic, the Russians and Uyghurs living there also sent their representatives to the Congress. In 1959, Central Asia dispatched a delegation on a somewhat reduced scale (only 51 Central Asians made the journey as delegates) to meet with over 500 writers from the USSR and abroad.

Besides internal Soviet mixing, the Central Asian intelligentsia of today, hemmed in as it is with Communist restrictions, still has several outlets which may in time influence the thinking and expression of writers and other intellectuals. Now that the intolerable tension of the Stalin era is reduced visitors have come from the West and, particularly important for Central Asia, from independent Egypt, India, Indonesia, Iran and Pakistan. In addition, a handful of local writers, politicians, scholars, and others have begun to travel from Tashkent and like capitals to Paris, London, and even New York, as well as Colombo, New Dehli, Cairo, and Havana. This cannot fail to have some impact upon those who enjoy such contacts and upon colleagues and friends of travelers to whom the experiences are surely communicated. Similarly, some publications from outside the USSR appear in libraries at Tashkent, Alma Ata, or Frunze, and considerable tourist, cultural, and student exchange, correspondence between Central Asia and outsiders and the like, adds to the variety of ideas accessible to the local person. This will have an effect upon the great distinction between the intelligentsia of Central Asia today and that of Turkey or Iran, for example. Most Uzbeks or Tajiks for decades have lived in a kind of cocoon where they were unable to exercise their minds in dealing with the larger issues in their society, for the Party leadership managing them countenanced no such involvement or discussion. On the other hand, Turkish and Iranian intellectuals, whatever the limitations of their technology, have engaged in passionate debates, and if not always immune to government reprisal, the habit of challenging pronouncements, decisions from above, of questioning decrees affecting freedom of the press or the citizen's life or way he may think, have never completely died there since the Iranian and Turkish revolutions.

EDUCATION FOR THE 1960s

Another factor promising to change the minds of Central Asians is their much wider literacy. By the 1960s a very substantial number of Central Asians (6,735,601 in 1959 by contrast with 489,188 in 1926) had learned to read and write, raising the literate portion reported for the entire local population of Central Asia from a mean of 3.5 percent to a mean of 52.1 percent in thirty-three years, according to census data reported in Table 13.1.

But real difficulty still was met in raising the general literacy rate for Central Asia as can be seen in the fact that large numbers of local people continue to receive little or no education. This is documented in persistent Soviet reports such as a recent one showing that of 5,151 Kirgiz girls entering the first grade in Osh oblast in 1950–51, all but 421 had dropped out of school by the tenth grade in 1959–60.[32] Among the local nationalities in Central Asia, the Uyghurs now enjoy the highest percentage of literacy, and the Uzbeks lead Central Asians by far in absolute numbers of the literate, but in the ratio between literate persons and the total population the Uzbeks in comparison with most other nationalities have lately fallen to the bottom to join the Karakalpaks, of whom 51 percent are reported to read and write. This level has surpassed that achieved in certain countries of the Near and Middle East, but not all. Turkey's 9,100,000 literate group (age sixteen or older), much larger than Central Asia's, made up 35 percent of the population in 1950, Israel's was 95 percent and Lebanon's came to 50 percent,[33] and some growth may have occurred in those rates during the decade ensuing since the previous reports.

Along with expansion of literacy and education, the most noticeable of the changes concerning the professions engaged in by Central Asians in 1959 (Table 13.4) as compared with 1926 (Tables 13.3a and 13.3b) is the complete loss of a significant number of clergymen. None, in fact is reported separately in the latest census, though Tashkent today houses Barak Khan, the one remaining Muslim madrasah functioning in all Central Asia. It trains between 50 and 100 students at a time,[34] and there are some older mullahs still living in the countryside who were not counted. Almost as significant as the near disappearance of the religious

---

[32] Aitmyrza Chotonov, *O natsional'nykh traditsiiakh narodov Srednei Azii* (Frunze, Izdatel'stvo Akademii Nauk Kirgizskoi SSR, 1964), p. 64.

[33] *World Illiteracy at Mid-Century* (New York, UNESCO, 1957), pp. 39–43.

[34] A. Bennigsen "Central Asia Comes of Age: The Moslem Intelligentsia in the USSR," *Soviet Survey*, No. 28 (1959), p. 3.

TABLE 13.4

Distribution of the "Intelligentsia" by Profession, 1959

Occupation	Kazakh SSR	Kirgiz SSR	Tajik SSR	Turkmen SSR	Uzbek SSR Karakalpak ASSR	Total
Management in government, Party, and enterprises	53,745	10,539	7,989	8,446	32,467	113,186
Medicine	62,798	13,170	10,364	11,989	48,705	147,026
Education and research	120,829	29,186	28,149	20,534	106,850	305,548
Literature and press	4,215	1,111	1,021	722	2,583	9,652
writers, journalists, editors	(3,183)	(818)	(732)	(539)	(1,893)	(7,165)
Cultural enlightenment	17,393	3,515	2,515	3,012	10,733	37,168
Arts	5,544	1,569	1,576	1,210	6,486	16,385
actors, directors	(2,289)	(690)	(678)	(557)	(2,725)	(6,939)
composers, musicians	(1,084)	(326)	(309)	(277)	(1,604)	(3,600)
artists, sculptors	(1,777)	(410)	(418)	(228)	(1,777)	(4,610)
Law	3,351	812	679	631	2,366	7,839
Total	267,875	59,902	52,293	46,544	210,190	636,804

Source: "Kazakhskaia SSR," *Itogi vsesoiuznoi perepis' naseleniia 1959 goda* (Moscow, Tsentral'noe Statisticheskoe Upravlenie pri Sovete Ministrov SSSR, 1962), pp. 112–15; "Kirgizskaia SSR," *ibid.* (1963), pp. 77–80; "Tadzhikskaia SSR," *ibid.* (1963), pp. 75–78; "Turkmenskaia SSR," *ibid.* (1963), pp. 79–82; "Uzbekskaia SSR," *ibid.* (1962), pp. 86–89.

Note: Soviet census reports for 1959, unlike those for 1926, do not distinguish local nationalities from Russians, Ukrainians, Tatars, and other outsiders in these tabulations, so that no meaningful information concerning only the local "intelligentsia" can be presented from the reports available so far.

hierarchy has been the precipitous decline in numbers of persons in the independent professions (*svobodnaia professiia*), a fact signaling the demise of the free enterprise which in the mid-1920s persisted on a fairly large scale, as Table 13.3b demonstrates. Starting then, the intelligentsia in Central Asia as represented by professional groups listed in the tables, climbed in numbers from 51,421, of whom 26,650, over half the men and women, were local citizens and the minority were Russians and Ukrainians, to 636,804 of all nationalities throughout the area in 1959. By then each of the five "Union" republics in Central Asia seemed to be provided with a fair supply of professional people of whom a large share were Russian and Ukrainian. In Turkmenistan, for example, in which the relative size of the Slavic population today is lower than elsewhere in Central Asia, there is a correspondingly smaller number of writers and journalists (539) serving the republic, but although Turkmenistan has more Turkmens than Kirgizistan has Kirgiz, the Kirgiz republic claims 818 writers and journalists. Similarly, comparing Uzbekistan to Kazakhstan, with its smaller indigenous population and much lower number of literate Kazakhs, the Kazakh SSR, reversing the situation in 1926, now boasts substantially more writers and journalists, teachers, and research specialists, medical personnel, in fact more of each of the professions than registered by Uzbekistan except representatives in the stage and musical arts. These seeming paradoxes can only be explained by the presence of Russians in these professions living in the Kazakh and Kirgiz SSRs in numbers proportionately greater than in the Tajik, Turkmen, and Uzbek SSRs.

Such comparisons suggest that Russian and Ukrainian professionals in Central Asia might, through sheer numbers, absorb or displace their local counterparts, and there is no reason to doubt that in the past hundred years the Slavs have occupied many positions which could have gone to the Kazakhs or their countrymen in the south. But the educated inhabitants and immigrants have remained surprisingly aloof, causing them to miss much of the mutual enrichment possible between intellectuals of the nontechnical professions in both groups. As a result, the local intelligentsia remains far from integrated into the Russian system, despite continuing government pressure to move in that direction. The Central Asians clearly were equipped to lead the intellectual development of their area beyond the third decade of the twentieth century, if they had been permitted to do so, but the route they preferred would have diverged considerably from that finally set for them by the Russians.

E. A.

14 The Focus of Literature

Qibchaq, qirghiz buzilma!
Tashkanddi alsa bu kafir,
Saghan ham bir kun jaqindar . . .

Kipchaks, Kirgiz, don't give in!
If this unbeliever takes Tashkent,
One day he will also draw near you . . .

Mullah Hali Bay Mambet-uli[1]

Few places on earth have given literature the importance it has attained in Central Asia, where mighty and meek have for centuries composed, recited, listened to or read, and lived with the poetry which remained their constant companion. Placed at the center rather than on the fringes of life by both intellectuals and others, literature not only entered into every ceremony, it came out of the facets of daily existence and constituted the prime esthetic pleasure of man.

"Literature" and "poetry" had been synonymous in the Central Asia of the past, for creative written prose existed only as an oddity in the long artistic development of the area, and before the first decade of the twentieth century had failed to achieve a status which might have guaranteed its acceptance from educated readers or writers. People thought that any feeling which warranted literary expression and every story which could claim an audience was worthy of verse. So strong was this general conviction that many local witnesses to dramatic episodes such as Shimkent's (Chimkent)

[1] N. Veselovskii, ed., *Kirkizskii razskaz o russkikh zavoevaniiakh v turkestanskom krae* (St. Petersburg, Parovaia Skoropechatnia P. O. Iablonskago, 1894), Mullah Hali Bay Mambet-uli, "Orus lashkarining turkistanda tarikh-i 1269–1272 [sic] sanälardä qilghan futuhatlari," p. 90 (in Arabic script).

or Tashkent's fall a hundred years ago neglected to record their observations only because they lacked the skill to put such chronicles into what they saw as proper, that is poetic, form. The poetic tradition was pervasive, and the extraordinary burden of the great literary heritage pressed heavily upon anyone who seriously engaged in the writer's craft, prescribing his forms, meters, themes, and even a vocabulary which had long since become not only fashionable but obligatory.

In the search for beauty, lyric poets wrote of the seasons and the landscape, of feelings and perceptions, and in all this persistently devoted verses to their ideal of feminine grace. Inevitably among people like the Central Asians, looking especially to their poets for the formulation and communication of ideas, true literature has been accompanied by a great deal of writing which is concerned not so much with art as with a message. In this sense, Central Asian writers often deviated from the esthetic path when, besides creating beauty and with it, pleasure, they began, for example, to alter the images and roles of women like society itself, in a changing time, and so in literature embraced arguments beyond the bounds of pure art. Moreover, writers in modern times composed lines in order to instruct others, to celebrate their piety or ideological loyalties, to identify themselves as ethnic or national groups, and frequently to commemorate or influence the state of social and political affairs.

Years before the Russian armies approached Tashkent itself, militant Central Asian poets opposed this foreign invasion by exhorting their brave young men and the feuding Western Turkistanian leaders to emulate in battle the broad literary attack launched with song and verse upon the enemy. The first Central Asian literature to feel the Russian invasion was naturally the poetry composed by the nomads roaming the very outer limits of the plains. From the early nineteenth century, their grazing lands began falling increasingly behind the line of czarist forts pushing inward along the entire northern frontier. When war struck, the conflict inspired themes of resistance to the Russian invaders and sarcasm for ineffective local generals, but before long poetry expressed the terrible despair over the vanishing of that independent life enjoyed on the plains before this martial "Europeanization," overcame the area.

RESISTANCE LITERATURE

Nothing reveals that Central Asian dilemma or the minds of the men caught in it more clearly and powerfully than the language of the contemporary poets. Their unique contribution consisted in capturing the mood and thinking of the indigenous population while they documented the historic events of the conquest. The local poet understood very well that for tribal leaders in the plains facing a variety of threats at once, it was a matter of life or death to deal effectively with the enemy who would ultimately prove most dangerous.

Musa-bay, an epic singer (*jirau*) of Qazali (Kazalinsk) related how this trial was endured by one renowned Kazakh chieftain, Jan Qoja Nurmuhammad-uli (d.1860), who led a tribe ranging from southwest of the Aral seacoast and on the lower Sir Darya to the Qara Qum in more or less equal contest with its traditional antagonists, the "black Sarts" (*qara sart*)—the Uzbeks of Khiva, the Karakalpaks, and Turkmens. Jan Qoja promptly recognized the encroaching Russians as a hazard to his people even greater than the "black sarts," and in Musa-bay's poem "Janing qojä batirding tolghaui," (A verse Reflection on Jan Qoja Batir), the Kazakh hero is shown teaching his men why they must fight and how to regard this new opponent.

Qayiqdan ustab aldi eki oristi	He captured and held two Russians from a kayak;
Janing qojä jaw bolarda jasin aldi	Jan Qoja, being hostile [to Russians] brought the young men together,
Balasin musulmanning qasina aldi	He brought the sons of the Muslims to him;
Bul oris bizoning minan jaw bolar deb	Saying, "These Russians are our enemies,"
Ab kelib eki oristing basin aldi[2]	He took the two Russians and beheaded them.

While portraying Jan Qoja Nurmuhammad-uli's lesson to the assembly of young braves, this 170-line poem also conveys its story

[2] Musa Bay, "Janing qojä batirding tolghaui," in Veselovskii, p. 120 (in Arabic script).

of the gathering Russian forces and the baffling failure of Khiva and Bukhara to answer the Kazakh warrior's pleas for help in what was actually their own defense against Russia. In these verses Jan Qoja's last stand is made, ironically, against a rival Kazakh band after the Kazakh hero has been driven away from his home territory by Russian forces. This poem conveys the ultimate futility of Jan Qoja's efforts and his tragic and almost lonely death, symbolizing so well the hopelessness of resistance by courageous but isolated Central Asian leaders when their worst enemies, as always in civil war, turned out to be fellow countrymen indifferent to the alien menace. Not as poignant as this theme but equally strong in Musabay's poem is the scornful depiction of a local turncoat who guides Russian troops against a Kazakh desert stronghold. Such treachery provided one more explanation for the impotence of nomadic Central Asians against the first organized invasion of unbelievers in the nineteenth century.

The internecine conflicts characterizing most of the nineteenth century did not always prevent military cooperation between tribes or ethnic groups of the area. Tashkent's defense proved to be an instance when Central Asian armies combined assortments of Uzbeks, Tajiks, Kirgiz, and other troops who participated in the final, but unsuccessful, fight to hold Tashkent against the Russians.

The defenders were given a peculiarly appropriate literary and linguistic monument in the historical narrative poem by Mullah Hali Bay Mambet-uli (b.1856) "Orus lashkarining turkistanda ta'rikh-i 1269–1272 [*sic*] sanälardä qilghan futuhatlari" (Conquests made in the years A.D. 1852–1855 [*sic*] in Turkistan by the Russian Armies), 1885. In alternating verse and prose sections, the prose serving to recite events ensuing between poetic passages of this 108-page composition, Mambet-uli employs a language exhibiting features of both the Kipchak and "Turki" idioms of some late nineteenth-century Uzbeks. The last round for the local Tashkent garrison is described in lines with these linguistic traits as well as a few Russian elements:

The Tashkentians, overjoyed at the coming of Shir Ali [The Bukharan representative], played the karnay and surnay screaming the cry of the peacock; the cannon fired; in turn, the aforesaid Cherniaev put his troops in order, the karnay and surnay they played, screaming the cry of the peacock and shouting "hurrah, hurrah," the cannon, Chinese jazail, Western European gun, and black gun suddenly opened fire, they ran and mounted to the city but Mullah Salih Bek Akhun, seeing this occurrence, fought the unbelievers as the head of the entire Muslim army.[3]

The fighting poets were offset to a certain extent by some local versifiers who adopted a diplomatic stance toward the invaders, simultaneously ridiculing what they termed the cowardice of Central Asian military men and praising the conquerors from Russia. Odes to the victors were so much in evidence for a time that some Russian observers acquired the mistaken impression that such panegyrics, which had formed a special genre for centuries in Central Asian poetry, constituted in fact the bulk of the local literature.[4] Actually, throughout the century since the Russians took Tashkent, this sort of poem, artificial as its spirit may be, has been officially encouraged in local literature as a form of ritual admiration for czars, Party secretaries, or Russian "culture." That the complimentary verses written in 1865 deriding local armies were designed as much for Russian consumption as for Central Asian is quite possible, but one example of this war poetry at least, "Orusning kelgani" (The Coming of the Russians), 1891, would seem also to show a citizen's genuine resentment toward ineffectual defenders who had, until the crisis at Tashkent, insisted so emphatically upon their arbitrary right to rule:

Orus lashkar chekti deb	"The Russian raised troops"
Boldi awazä	Were the rumors
Tashkänd degan shahardä	At the city called Tashkent
Komdi darwazä	People strengthened the walls;
Bek fansadlar chiqib	Beks and officials went out
Qurdi khawazä	And built barriers;
Orushmasdin zor fadshä deb	Without fighting, saying "the mighty czar,"
Qachä bashladi. . . .	They began to flee.
Galawachob turmasdin	Golovachev, not stopping,
Bashlab urushti	They began fighting.
'Alim qul kelmadi deb	Saying, " 'Alim Qul didn't come,"
Beklar tutushti	The beks procrastinated.
'Amir-i lashkar 'askarin	[The Russian] started to destroy
Qira bashladi	The commander-in-chief's troops.

[3] Mullah Hali Bay Mambet-ulï, in Veselovskii, p. 99 (in Arabic script).
[4] "Sarty," *Entsiklopedicheskii slovar'*, vol. 28A (1900), p. 451.

Galawachob keldi	Golovachev came
Shahar chimkantgä	To Chimkent city;
Salat qoydi qarawul deb	Stationed soldiers "on watch" and
Barï bäkätgä	At all the pickets.
Sart beklari aytadur	The Sart beks say
Chiqmas mashitga	He won't go out to Mashit.
Qïrïq kun bolmay	Forty days had not passed when
Tashkandgä yetä bashladi	They began to approach Tashkent.
'Amir-i lashkar 'alim qul	The commander in chief, 'Alim Qul
Turub urushti	Stood and fought;
Qal'ä khalqi anga	The city people
Kob din bolushti	Aided him greatly, but
Oz 'askari 'alim qulni	'Alim Qul's own soldiers together
Atib komoshti	Shot and buried him.
Galawachob [sic] *tashkandga*	Golovachev began
Kirä bashladi.[5]	To enter Tashkent.

After Tashkent fell, notice of the Russian advance was served emphatically upon all parts of Central Asia, warning the emirate and khanates (Bukhara, Khiva, and Khokand) as well as the remaining nomads of the impending danger, but still the contending factions in the southern half of Central Asia failed to unite, and their poets like Gayib Berdï Miskin Qlïch (Mullah Qlïch) (1845–1905), an educated Turkmen who commemorated in verse the bloody Russian massacre of the Turkmen population at Gok Tepe, recorded the chronicle of military defeats and bitter subjugation in terms seldom significantly different from those heard in verses of their kinsmen conquered earlier in the area. One nuance peculiar to the cities with their stronger Muslim traditions was a special insistence that the Russian invasion was a religious war disgracing Islam:

Orus kelib sening yurtingni aldi	The Russian came and took your country;
Musulman yurtinä qozghalang saldi	He raised havoc in the Muslim's country;
Diningni alurghä emdi nä qaldi	Taking away your religion, now what remains?
Orusghä qaradi kuning khwarazm.[6]	Your fate depends upon the Russian, Khwarazm.

The Turkmen poet Kör Mullah (1874–1934) spoke along these same lines:

[5] "Orusning kelgani," in Veselovskii, pp. 112–14 (in Arabic script).
[6] "Khwarazm nama," in A. N. Samoilovich, "Dva otryvka iz 'Khorezm-name,' " *Zapiski Vostochnago otdieleniia Imperatorskago Russkago Arkheologicheskago Obshchestva,* XIX (1910), 079.

If this [Russian] nation remain long among us
It will separate our people little by little from the faith!
[Those Russians] as if resembling Jinnis, like swine,
Will separate our people little by little from the faith! . . . .
They will separate us from the elders, from the saints! . . . .
They will separate us from all the [other] Muslims! . . . .
They speak falsehoods, drink "vodka-wine"! . . . .
May God save [us] from these unbelievers, friends! [7]

LOCAL HISTORY AND VERSE REFLECT THE RUSSIAN CONQUEST

The sad saga of defeat in one sector after another of the Central
Asian battleground, like the legendary victories over mighty kings
of the past, was celebrated mainly in poems or chronicles which
were invariably composed by artists whose convictions about what
was beautiful and proper conditioned the record strongly. The form
employed by different writers of history varied mainly in their
arrangement of verse or prose passages of a work, in the proportion
of poetry to straight writing, and Chaghatay to Persian language
adopted, but no Central Asian historian worth the name ignored
verse completely in producing his narrative.

Poetic accounts often treated events occurring within a short
span of time, or, occasionally, writers exerted their talents in versi-
fying the events of whole epochs. Thus, Mullah Shamsi (Mullah
Shawki) wrote *Jang nama* (Book of Battle), 1852, concerning the
Kipchak uprising, or there was the Chaghatay *Shah nama* (Shah's
Book), 1875, relating the entire history of the Khokand khanate up
to Khudayar's enthronement, and another short work, in Persian,
which came from Mirza Muhammad 'Abdal'azim Sami Bustani.
His *Dakhma-i shākhān* (Sepulchre of Shahs) detailed the Mangit
emirs' views regarding Bukharan events of the time and their own
role in them.

As common, perhaps, as these long poems were prose chronologies
into which each author, almost certainly a poet himself, sprinkled
his own and borrowed verses. That is how this homely couplet
poking fun at the parochialism of local savants crept in at the end

---

[7] A. Samoilovich, "Turkmenskii poet-bosiak Kör-Molla, i ego piesnia o
russkikh," *Zhivaia starina*, XVI (1907), 224–25.

of Mullah Alim Mahmud Hajji's *Turkistan ta'rikhi* (History of Turkistan), 1915:

> To each worm which needs but a tiny space
> Heaven and earth become the same place.

Mullah Alim Hajji spread his scope more broadly than the narrow-minded scholars lampooned in this verse. In his 215-page Chaghatay-language work, he attempted, after completing the main treatment of Farghana's (Khokand's) history, to cover briefly the developments in Bukhara and Khiva as well.[8]

No later than the last half of the nineteenth century each of the Central Asian states began to employ the talents of men specializing in writing dynastic records up through the current potentates' reigns. Khiva has probably been best served in this respect by a succession of court secretaries who carried the story from early times through 1918. The Chaghatay-language chronicles prepared by Shir Muhammad Munis Khwarazmiy (1778–1829), *Firdaws al-iqbal* (Paradise of Felicity), and his followers, Muhammad Riza Erniyaz Bek-oghli Agahiy, *Shahid al-iqbal* (Witness of Felicity), and Muhammad Yusufbek Bababek-oghli Bayaniy, *Shajara-i khwarazmshahiy* (Genealogy of the Khwarazm Shahs), not only bracketed events in the modern era, but displayed many long poems and separate couplets which enhanced the literary flavor of the work or occasionally supplied further historical information and interpretation. Likewise, the Persian-language composition by Mullah Niyaz Muhammad bin Mullah 'Ashur Muhammad Khoqandiy, *Ta'rikh-i shahrokhi* (History of Shahrukh), tells the story of Khokand's triumphs and tribulations up to 1871, and in the course of the narration introduces some poems in Chaghatay as well as many in Persian.[9] Regarding Bukhara, among several interesting modern histories embellished with verses, two were composed by the same Mirza Bustani who wrote the *Dakhma-i shākhān* (Sepulchre of Shahs). The first of this pair of Bukharan histories was the 298-

---

[8] P. P. Ivanov, *Ocherki po istorii Srednei Azii* (Moscow, Izdatel'stvo Vostochnoi Literatury, 1958), p. 232.

[9] Mullah Niyaz Muhammad bin Mullah 'Ashur Muhammad Khoqandiy, *Ta'rikh-i shahrokhi* (Kazan, Nikola Pantusif, 1885).

leaf, official Persian-language *Tuhfa-i shāhi* (Royal Shah's Gift) (1902–1903), and the other, also in Persian, was an "unauthorized" 75–leaf *Ta'rikh-i salātīn-i manghītīya-i dar as-saltana-i bukhara-i sharif* (History of the Manghit Sultans Who Ruled in Holy Bukhara, the Capital) (1906–1907).[10] Like the historians of Khokand and Khiva, Mirza Bustani interspersed poems in his prose text, such as the following fragment about the Russian capture of Tashkent:

Chun gaburnāṭor be 'amr-e kārfarmāyān-e rus	When the *gubernator,* following his Russian masters' order,
Bahr-e faṭḥ-e shāsh bar owj-e tamannā zad kamand	For the conquest of the city of Shash [Tashkent] threw a lasso at the zenith of desire,
Biniyāzihā-ye ḥaqq ta'yid-e bāzuyash nemud	God's freedom from need supported his arm.
Bar morād-e khāṭer-e kh(v)od gasht ākher bahreh-mand	Ultimately, he succeeded in reaching his heart's desire.
Sāl-e tārīkhash be-porsidam, kherad goftā marā	I asked for the year of its [the conquest's] date, and reason said:
Az sar-e karb o balā tārikh-e faṭḥ-e tāshkand [11]	"From the evil of suffering and calamity, the date of the conquest of Tashkent"

The lineage of topical, battle poetry could be traced back directly to literature like the 9,000-line Chaghatay poem *Shaybaniy nama* (Book of Shaybaniy) by Muhammad Salih (1455–1506), detailing the famous Uzbek khan's campaigns, but the modern genre also owed a great deal to the oral heroic epics. The epic singer in at least one well-known case has in fact been responsible for preserving in oral form an entire versified history, the manuscripts for which have presumably been lost.

Composed originally by Berdi Murat Kargabay-uli Shair (Berdaq Baqsi) (1827–1900), the best-known older Karakalpak poet, *Shejire* (Genealogy), 1889, and lesser works join Khwarazm's legendary happenings to the author's interpretation of nineteenth-century events. This book-length poem, like Berdaq Baqsi's *Aqmaq patsha* (The Foolish Padishah), while exhibiting many of the hyperbolic and fantastic qualities of folk literature, was a late specimen of the

---

[10] L. M. Epifanova, "Predislovie," Mirza 'Abdal'azim Sami, *Ta'rikh-i salatin-i manghitiya* (Moscow, Izdatel'stvo Vostochnoi Literatury, 1962), p. 10.

[11] Mirza 'Abdal'azim Sami, *Ta'rikh-i salatin-i manghitiya,* (*Moscow, Izdatel'stvo Vostochnoi Literatury, 1962*), L 67a; trans. by Ehsan Yar-shater.

extended historic narrative in verse, and, if the long proletarian tractor-sagas of the 1930s are disregraded, may even be considered one of the last of its kind in Central Asian literature.

Like the Central Asian literary community united by the widely circulated manuscript poetry, the folk singers and their auditors shared throughout the area not only in the migratory themes characteristic of folk literature around the Middle East and Central Asia, but enjoyed and recounted exploits usually attributed to legendary supermen known especially by Kazakhs and Uzbeks, Turkmens, and neighboring Azerbaijanians. Famed epics such as *Gor-oghli* took their names, like the *Shaybaniy khan dastani* from particular heroes and were sung in differing versions throughout Central Asia. *Gor-oghli*, well known in Turkey as *Kor-oglu*, has been recorded as *Gorgulu* in Tajik, and partly under the title of one of its sections, "Rawshan Khan," in Uzbekistan, and as *Gor-oghli* on Turkmen territory where it presumably entered Central Asia from Azerbaijan, its country of origin. Also popular has been *Dede Qorqut*, another Azerbaijanian epic, a version of which circulated in Turkmenistan under the title *Qorqut Ata*. The most widespread epic tale peculiar mainly to Central Asia was probably *Alpamish* (*Alpamïs* or *Alpamïs batïr*), first recorded from Jiyemurat Bekmukhamed-uli in the 1880s, published in Karakalpak (1901), Kazakh (1899), and Uzbek (1922), and known also among Bashkir, Oyrot, and Tatar traditions.[12]

PATRIOTISM AND PESSIMISM

Whatever pan-Turkic or all-Central Asian unity might have been inspired by folk or literary epics, the patriotic mood of resistance existing in face of the Russian invasion had collapsed temporarily among local intellectuals after mid-nineteenth century, and another more somber attitude gained expression through the new literature of the period. In bitter poems which earned notice as a special genre, the Kazakh *zar zaman* and Kirgiz *akïr zaman* or *tar zaman* (bad time) literature reflected the unhappy state of mind and heart which gave such poetry its name and in turn labeled the

[12] I. T. Saghitov, *Qaraqalpaq khalqïnïng qahramanlïq eposï* (Nokis, Qaraqalpaq Mämleket Baspasï, 1963), pp. 181–291.

era. This dejection was paralleled in Turkmen circles by the *akhïr zamana* (fatal time) motif noticeable earlier in the poetry of Magtim Guli (Mahtum Quli) Azadi-oghli Fragi (1733–c.1782) as an outgrowth of the misery caused in the eighteenth century by raiding between warring tribes and the attacks of foreign armies,[13] and continued by poets in the second half of the nineteenth century when Russian punitive expeditions slaughtered tribes and devastated Turkmen villages. In the melancholy time after Russian hegemony had been established in the plains, Kazakh verses like "Opasïz jalghan" (Traitorous Slander) spoke of the calamity as a punishment for the country's sins. The author of that poem, Shortambay Qanay-uli (1808–1871), crystallized the despondent Kazakh spirit of the early occupation period and in doing so unwittingly provided a rallying point for future nationalists with his long poem entitled "Zar zaman" (A Bad Time). Speaking directly for the Kirgiz in a similarly pessimistic vein at that time was Aristanbek-uulu (1840–1882), whose poem "Tar zaman" (A Bad Time) enumerated the unhappy results of Russian colonization on the Kirgiz range and the impoverishment of local cattlemen through the Russian appropriation of grasslands:

Özü sarï közü kök,	The blonde, blue-eyed,
Orus chïghat dechü ele.	Russian will go out, it seems.
Uzun jöbtün barïsïn,	All the tall grass
Orub jïghat dechü ele.	Will go out and cut, it seems.
Qisqa chöbtün barïsïn	All the short grass
Qorub chïghat dechü ele. . . .	Will go out and defend, it seems. . . .
Öro töbö, tashkendi,	The Ura Tube and Tashkent
Ordosu menen jay qïldï	Citadels he captured
Qayratuu erdin barïsïn,	All who were the strong men
Shiber jol közdöy qayïldï. . . .	Were sent in the direction of Siberia. . . .
Bul oorustu qarasang:	If you but observe this Russian:
Chenchi salïb jerdi aldï,	He reconnoitred, the land he took
Beeden tuughan kerdi aldï	The dark grey, born from the mare, he took,
Qardï salïq baydï aldï.	Fat, wealthy men he took.
Qacha turghan jaydï aldï.[14]	Every hiding place he took.

---

[13] *Istoriia literatur narodov Srednei Azii i Kazakhstana* (Moscow, Izdatel'stvo Moskovskogo Universiteta, 1960), p. 237.

[14] Ajiyman, "Orusuya badïshalïghï qïirghïzdï jangï baghïndïrghan doordoghu qïrghïz ïrchïlarï. 1: Aristanbek," *Jangï madanïyat jolunda*, Nos. 2/3 (1929), pp. 44, 49.

But the hopeless anguish expressed in the plains scarcely touched the indifference with which the great southern cities watched Russian soldiers staking claims to huge expanses of Kazakh and Kirgiz territory. The mood in the settled areas, which changed to concern only as the enemy approached their suburbs, was transformed, after the cities succumbed, into a confused, shocked disbelief which only palely resembled the Kazakh and Kirgiz response. The different focus of the reaction to the occupation in north and south may be ascribable in good part to the fact that city poets and intellectuals in particular rarely held farming land, and with no livelihood from that source to lose to the Russians, felt hardly any direct threat to their Muslim way of life after the czarist armies had become peaceful garrison forces. Nevertheless, before long, men of letters not entirely apathetic to their fate came to the realization that all was not right with a civilization that so complacently accepted a foreign yoke.

In the Farghana Valley, Muhammad Amin Mirza Khoja-oghli Muqimiy had barely returned home after completing his higher education in Bukhara when the Khokand khanate, already tottering and frequented by many Russian traders, intelligence agents, and other travelers, fell into czarist hands. Muhammad Muqimiy's predominately lyric poetry of the 1880s and 1890s, therefore, often reflected the gloom of the times with expressions like "unhappiness" (*bäkhtsizlik*) and "helplessness" (*tale zäbunlik*) repeated throughout a poem. The verses spoke of "crows replacing nightingales" (*bulbullar ornini zaghlär*).[15] In his despondency Muhammad Muqimiy wrote to the poet Zakir Jan Hal Muhammad-oghli Furqat:

Dost boldim här kishighä,	I became a friend to every person
kordim ändin ming jäfa,	suffered from this a thousand torments,
Tapmädim, dunyani kezdim,	Gained nothing, wandered through the world,
munis-u ghämkharmän.[16]	I am a comforter and am afflicted.

Muqimiy's writing and that of Mawlana Muhyiy and Muhammadqul Muhammad Rasul-oghli Muhayyir (1850–1920), sounding culti-

[15] Muqimiy, *Äsärlär toplämi* (Tashkent, OzSSR Däwlät Bädiiy Ädäbiyati Näshriyati, 1960), Ghulam Karimov, "Muhammad Aminkhoja Muqimiy," I, 21.
[16] Muqimiy, "Jäwab-i sälam-i muqimiy bä furqätiy," in Muqimiy, II, 102.

vated and restrained when heard against the robust poetry of Kazakh or Kirgiz plainsmen, nevertheless set the tone of lyric, almost nostalgic attachment to the beautiful Farghana area, which later reappeared in much of the Uzbek nationalistic verse. Such poetry became a modern inspirational genre much like the product of the "bad time" school of poets in Kazakhstan.

The *Zar zaman* group which formed around Shortambay Qanay-uli included men such as Bazar and Murat-aqin (1843–1906), who, because of their forthright opposition to the Russians, are now described in Soviet history as backward, pan-Turkic feudalists. The same epithets are reserved for Z. Nuraliqan-uli, S. Shorman-uli, D. Imanqul-uli, and particularly for Aliqan Bokeyqan-uli.

Under the penname Qïr Balasï (Child of the Uplands) Bokeyqan-uli began in the late 1880s on the pages of the government's Kazakh-language bulletin, *Dala ualayatining gazeti*,[17] and elsewhere to appeal, in the spirit of the poetry by Shortambay Qanay-uli's circle, for a revival of local patriotism. From this grew stirrings of national awareness agitated by contact with Tatars and other outsiders who prompted, among the relatively small number of enlightened men, increasing dissatisfaction over domestic affairs. Coupling feelings of patriotism with the urge to reform and improve their country, the new Jadid social leaders, like almost all the literate of Central Asia, employed poetry to propagandize their ideas, so that the difference between the lines they composed and those of the traditional literary school was profound.

Often the Jadid was an anguished protestant—sufficient wrongs were perceivable at every hand to keep him in constant agitation. At the same time, the effective figures in the Jadid movement like Aqmet Baytursin-uli and Mufti Mahmud Khoja Behbudiy, though as different in background as nomad and urbanite could be, concentrated their strength behind enlightening the local populace by whatever constructive means came to hand. Despite the fact that Baytursin-uli and Behbudiy became better known for the practical leadership they gave to the Jadid movement than for their literary contributions, each made such a mark on the development of letters

---

[17] M. I. Fetisov, *Zarozhdenie kazakhskoi publitsistiki* (Alma Ata, Kazgosizdat Khudozhestvennoi Literatury, 1961), p. 344.

that the evolution to the new era in Central Asian literature can be fixed to some extent in relation to their activities and to the works of their friends and followers. The transformation from traditional to Jadid literature, therefore, took place in the period 1901–1911, coincident with the maturing of new men in literature together with the assimilation and application of political, social, and literary ideas from abroad.

Aqmet Baytursin-uli's poetic output scarcely overflowed one slim volume, *Masa* (The Mosquito) (c.1910), of translations and original verse plus his adaptations from a collection of fables by the Russian, Ivan A. Krylov (c.1769–1844), entitled in his Kazakh version *Qiriq misal* (Forty Fables) (c.1904). Beyond this, Baytursin-uli's major productivity lay in journalistic exposition of the Jadid philosophies, the publishing of textbooks for local language study, and establishment of a new, modified Kazakh alphabet. The tenor of his verse, however, provided his large following with a focus for its intensifying patriotic sentiments, and the persecutions which he suffered at the hands of the Russians and the Muslim conservatives only added to his popularity. Sitting in the Russian prison at Semipalatinsk in 1909, Baytursin-uli recalled the consequences of an attack on his father by a Russian punitive detachment in 1885 which shattered the family circle, dispersing its members to Siberia, Orenburg, and other widely scattered points. This disaster he wrote about in a lyric "Letter to Mother" (1909):

> My heart, torn at the age of thirteen,
> Bore an unhealing wound, an indelible mark[18]

His passionate outburst could hardly have contrasted more with the cool logic which Mufti Behbudiy, his contemporary and fellow Jadid, employed in the best-known literary monument he left behind. Although Behbudiy was regarded as a Samarkand poet, his most notable literary work continues to be the tragedy *Padarkush* (The Parricide), 1911, published 1913, one of two plays (the other as yet apparently unpublished) which he wrote. Where Behbudiy and Baytursin-uli resemble one another is in their activity around

---

[18] M. Dulatov, "Akhmed Baitursunovich Baitursunov: Biograficheskii ocherk," *Trudy Obshchestva Izucheniia Kirgizskogo Kraia*, III (1922), 18–19.

the periphery of the literary institutions—in publishing, literary politics, journalism, teaching, editing, language reform, and the like—to which each gave his principal energies and thus drew the supporters who later carried on the important Jadid work. In this atmosphere of reawakened consciousness after the pained swoon of the "bad time" were maturing the dedicated young leaders like Mir Jaqib Duwlat-uli, whose spirit corresponded to the attitude of rising Kirgiz thinkers and poets like Moldo Kilich Mamirkan-uulu (1867–1917), author of *Kissa-i zilzele* (The Earthquake), published 1911; Balik-ooz Abdulkasim Jutaka-uulu, author of "Confusion and Flight"; and Isak Shaybek-uulu, who wrote "The Dear People," 1916.

Duwlat-uli (see Figure 13.3) first published some of his poetry in the initial issue of the Kazakh newspaper *Serke*, which appeared briefly at St. Petersburg in 1906. Three years later came his inflammatory collection of poems, *Oyan qazaq!* (Wake Up, Kazakh!), 1909, which quickly ran through two editions and was then banned by the Russian director of press affairs while Duwlat-uli was on the staff of the magazine *Ay qap* in 1911. Despite this setback, the poet's second book of verse *Azamat* (The Heroes) came out in 1913 at Orenburg, where he then worked regularly with Baytursin-uli on the newspaper *Qazaq*. The fervid tone which caused Duwlat-uli's *Oyan qazaq!* to be confiscated sounds through his poem "Kazakh Lands":

Noble, influential men, pay attention to this! They say
"Strike while the iron is hot;" by not following this proverb,
You take responsibility on yourselves for the tears of future generations.
Oh, dear native land, you have gone entirely to the [Russian] settlers!
The sacred graves of our forefathers are now amidst village streets.
The tombstones over them will be used by the *muzhiks* for bathhouses,
The wooden fences [around them] will go for firewood.
Then, finding no signs of our old graves we shall pour out streams of
    tears.
The huge lakes and flowing springs, like the summer pastures and forests,
    are all alienated.
When I think about all this I go out of my mind and burn (as in a fire)
    from grief.
But we accepted citizenship without giving up our land,

We hoped to live under the shelter of justice.
If we now give up the last land, the cattle will have to be pastured on
    sand.
The simple people are stunned. . . .
Kazakhs, now where is the land on which you have lived since the
    Kazakh tribe was formed?
They drove you off and put the land under *khokhlatskie* [Little Russian]
    settlements. . . .
Only the salt lakes and waterless plain, useless for agriculture, are left
    to us.[19]

The fictional gloom evoked in poetry about the Russian conquest, and the serious mood of early novels and plays describing the plight of young women in Western Turkistan's society, was pierced momentarily by the joy expressed in some writing of the Jadid period concerning the benefits expected from the "new method" in education. Taking this positive approach to the subject was *The Happy Family*, a Tajik epistolery novelette in prose which its author, Sadriddin Ayniy, added to the second edition of his textbook for Jadid school children, *Tāhzīb-us sibyān* (Improvement of the Children), published in 1917. In this story the correspondence between an enlightened father, son, mother, brother, and sisters extols the benefits of literacy and education. Similarly, Hamza Hakim Zada Niyaziy's short *Yangi saadat: Milliy roman* (New Happiness: A National Novel), 1915, which, despite its title cannot qualify generically as anything more than a novelette, wholeheartedly espoused in spirit and theme the Jadid principle concerning education as the source of all gains for the "nation" and the individual. This prose work describes the good fortune awaiting a youth being supported in his academic efforts by a Jadid patron and persevering to acquire an education and achieve the new life together with an enlightened Central Asia. Despite their optimism, because of the strong Jadid character pervading The Happy Family and New Happiness, neither of these early works has apparently been reprinted since 1917, although the Soviet authorities currently hold both authors in high esteem.

[19] *al-Sharqiyyat: Vostochnyi sbornik v chest' A. N. Veselovskago*, Mer Iakub Dulatov, "Kirgizskie zemli" (Moscow, Trudy po Vostokoviedieniia Izdavaemye Lazarevskim Institutom Vostochnykh Iazykov), XLIII (1914), 234.

With the upheavals between 1917 and 1921 the unpleasant realization that the new "nation" was to be controlled from Moscow even more tightly than the old guberniia had been managed from St. Petersburg abruptly generated another era of disillusionment comparable to the "bad time" immediately after the conquest. The reason men of the 1920s became, if anything, even more pessimistic than their grandfathers had been, was that the 1917 revolutions, in raising high hopes that Central Asia would be free and that the aims of Jadid intellectual circles could be realized, had caused proportionately greater disappointments. Also, people were now politically more articulate and possessed newspapers and many other publications through which to share their anguish with literate individuals elsewhere in the area. Most significant of all, they had developed a kind of national awareness that had been almost completely muted sixty years earlier.

The clearest spokesmen for the collective gloom which set in around 1922 were the young lyric poets, who were the most nationalistic, and, as it turned out, the most utopian and the most politically naive in their dreams of an independent Central Asia. One whose hopes were badly disappointed was Magjan Jumabay-uli, who had published poems as early as 1912 in the magazine *Ay qap* and who in the 1920s had come to be regarded as "the most important contemporary Kazakh lyric poet." [20] After brief, postrevolutionary enthusiasm for an independent East, Jumabay-uli withdrew in his frustration over thwarted nationalistic aspirations into a moody discouragement which he recorded in whole books of verse like *Karkit* (The Camelskin Bag), *Bayan* (A Narrative), and *Ölim/Ajal* (Death), around the mid-1920s.[21] Nearly a coeval of this Kazakh nationalist, the Uzbek writer Abdulhamid Cholpan stirred the Communist regime's hostility and enraged the apprentices of proletarian literature in Central Asia when he published poetic laments against Russification or Sovietization such as *Buzulgan olkaga* (To a Ruined Land), 1923. Cholpan's contemporaries, like Kirgiz poet Qasim Tinistan-uulu, celebrated their national home-

[20] "Magzhan Dzhumabaev," *Malaia sovetskaia entsiklopediia* (1st ed.), II (1929), 848.

[21] G. Togzhanov, "Kazakskaia literatura," *Literaturnaia entsiklopediia*, V (1931), 20–21.

lands by singing affectionately of the beautiful lake, Issik Kol, or the stately Ala Tau mountains. In his major literary work, *Qasim irlarinin jiynaghi* (Qasim's Collection of Poems), 1925,[22] Tinistan-uulu also recalled obliquely the war cry *alash!* adapted in the Kazakh nationalist party name, Alash Orda, though he at first failed to recognize the changing times in his poem "*Alashqa*" (To the Alash), 1920.[23]

Like the depression of Kirgiz and others, the dejection of nationalistic Turkmen writing was characteristically attributed by Communist Party critics to the negative influence of the literary heritage:

the basic tone—the deep pessimism, the disenchantment which was particularly intensified in the art of the last prerevolutionary poets (Molla Murat, Molla Nepes, Molla Durdi, and others) in total forms the background for the works of Qulmuhammad-oghli . . . this is to be explained . . . for a nationalistic group of poets of the Soviet period . . . in forebodings of the final ruin of their own class.[24]

But the thoroughly modern poet, Abdulhakim Qulmuhammad-oghli, author of the Turkmen *Umit yalqimlari* (Flames of Hope), 1926,[25] and many other books, was also repeatedly singled out for attack like similar intellectual nationality leaders because of his despairing opposition to the Russian Communists which he expressed in indirect, allegorical terms:

Won't the black winter [Russian occupation] pass on after so many
    years?
Speak, weeping, beloved music! . . .
Beautiful, wholesome winds which raised to the heavens,
Tell me, when will my joyous spring [liberation] arrive? [26]

In a comparable vein went the Uzbek poem "Awunchaq" (Consolation) by Fitrat:

[22] Qasim Tinistan-uulu, *Qasim irlarinin jiynaghi* (Moscow, SSSR Qalqtarinin Bor Bor Basma Mahkamasi, 1925), pp. 19–20, 24–29.

[23] *Ibid.*, pp. 8–9.

[24] *Literatura Turkmenii* (Moscow, Gosudarstvennoe Izdatel'stvo Khudozhestvennoi Literatury, 1934), p. 7.

[25] Abdulhakim Qulmuhammadof, *Umit yalqimlari* (Ashkhabad, Turkmenistan Däwlät Näshriyati, 1926).

[26] O. Tash-Nazarov, "Doklad o literature turkmenskoi SSR," *Pervyi vsesoiuznyi s"ezd sovetskikh pisatelei, 1934* (Moscow, Gosizdat "Khudozhestvennaia Literatura," 1934), p. 137.

Tosub turghan aydinliqning yolini	Obstructing the path of the moonlight are
Shu qapqara, eski, titräk bulutlär	These jet black, trembling old clouds [Russians].
Kuchli bir yel korgäch turmas yirtilär.	When a strong wind comes, they will break up.
Omid kuni sening uchun häm tughar! [27]	It will bear you a day of hope!

The nationalists, many of whom were by this time Communists themselves, spoke in allegorical poetry as well as drama, but people could hardly mistake their meaning. As a result, Fitrat's Tajik play 'Vose's Uprising," Bagdadbekov's "Emir Alim Khan," and others were politically unacceptable to the Party. A Tajik charade, "Joking," for example, presents Komsomol members as cafe loungers roughly accosted by a ragged, stupid man dressed as a Russian in a filthy pair of overalls specially outfitted with huge extra pockets. He drunkenly serenades the Tajiks with this song:

> Give me, hand over,
> Everything you own,
> Fill up my pockets;
> Above all, give me cotton.[28]

Such daring, unmistakable gibes at the Russian policy of exploiting Tajikistan and other parts of Central Asia as cotton-producing colonies left a noble record of intellectual bravery as yet generally unrecognized from a period otherwise remembered for the passive acquiescence by Central Asians in their own disenfranchisement.

ODES TO STALIN

Practically, around 1930 the resistance through intellectual activity had earned most local literary and national leaders the ugly label *opasïz* (Kazakh), *eki jüzdüü* (Kirgiz), or *ikiyuzlamachi* (Uzbek), each signifying "a two-faced person," but carrying the political connotation, "a nationalist who hides his true hostility while opposing the Party." Name-calling at that point became a

[27] *Ozbek yash sha'irlari* (Tashkent, Turkistan Däwlät Näshriyati, 1922), p. 8.
[28] G. A. Lakhuti, "Doklad o literature tadzhikskoi SSR," *Pervyi vsesoiuznyi s"ezd sovetskikh pisatelei, 1934* (Moscow, Gosizdat "Khudozhestvennaia Literatura," 1934), p. 143.

serious part of literary warfare in Central Asia, for a number of the prominent "two-faced" intellectuals were quietly removed from the scene by the Russian secret police never to reappear again, thus offering a mild foretaste of events that transpired when "two-faced," changed to the epithet "enemy of the people," *qalq dusmeni* (Kazakh) and *kalk dushmani* (Kirgiz). This initial fright prompted some local leaders to attempt a reconciliation with the political authorities to stave off conflicts which they realized might have even more widespread repercussions.

Writers intensified efforts to feed Stalin's already psychopathic appetite for the adulation of his subject nationalities by turning out entire collections of slapdash verses glorifying him and Russia. No superlatives were too hyperbolic to express the "admiration" for the Soviet dictator enunciated by Central Asian folk artists and writers like Jambil Jabay-uli (1846–1945), Orimbay, Ghafur Ghulam (1903–   ), and many more. In a Kazakh poem, "Stalin," typical of this theme, Omirzaq-aqin sings that the Soviet dictator miraculously made the old "bad time" disappear:

Zamanda, zaman zamandï	In the time, the time of times [the best time]
Zar zamanda tappap em	I didn't find in the bad time,
Tengdik bir tabar amaldï	Find a way out to equality [in the bad time]
Osï künde, Stalin	In these days, Stalin
Ay tuqghïzïp ongïmnan, . . .	Made the moon rise from my right
Kün tuwghïzïp solïmnan. . . .	Made the sun rise from my left. . . .
Gawharim, künim, Stalin,	My jewel, my sun, Stalin,
Juparday iysing angqïghan.	Like musk your scent has spread around.
Aqïl oyding kenisin	Your mine of intellect and thought
Telegey tengiz chalqïghan.[29]	The limitless sea has encompassed.

Individual expressions of fealty like these were still not enough for the Communist leadership, and institutional or "collective" verse arranged in the form of messages to Stalin received official inspiration all over Central Asia. Drawing suggestively upon the phraseology of the old Chaghatay odes like "Hilaliya" (Crescent-Mooned One), dedicated by Mir Ali Shir Nawaiy to Sultan Husayn Bayqara in 1469, Joomart Bokombay-uulu (1910–1944), Ali Tokom-

---

[29] Omirzaq Aqin, "Stalin," *Stalin tuwrali jïr* (Alma Ata, Qazaghïstan Körkem Ädebiyet Baspasï, 1937), pp. 23–25.

bay-uulu (1904–   ), and Qasim Tinistan-uulu, with the assistance of
some Russian writers, put together a panegyrical Kirgiz epistle (*qat*)
on the Stalin theme:

> Eternally young is thy name,
> We write thy name with gold,
> And it rings as a hymn, Stalin,
> And shines in our eyes! . . .
> Thou lightest the entire East,
> The whole West thou lightest,
> Thou shinest on the two poles,
> And warmest the whole world,
> The never setting sun—Stalin!
> Thou art the constant moon, Stalin,
> Thou art our shining star, Stalin,
> Thou art our lovely dawn, Stalin. . . .
> Wisdom inexhaustible, Stalin,
> Courage unshakable, Stalin,
> Joy unquenchable, Stalin!
> Be immortal, great Stalin! [30]

Relatively modest in comparison with this full-scale Kirgiz republic loyalty oath had been a very early example of "epistle" entitled "The Epistle from Male and Female Workers of the Central
Asian Combine Named for Stalin to Comrade Stalin" (1935).[31]
Compositions like this flowed out of Uzbekistan, Tajikistan, and the
rest of Central Asia to Moscow. Now, finally repudiated by the
officialdom which formerly required their production, the Stalin
"epistles" remain huge monuments to the abuses perpetrated under
Soviet nationality policy in the 1930s, but in the 1960s continue to
be addressed to "Russia" and "the Party."

The Stalinist evil which permeated literature gave way finally to
natural pressures arising from the Soviet-Nazi conflict, during which
Central Asian poets eagerly returned to lyric adoration of their own
homeland and the glorious moments of the past. When World War
II ended Stalin again tightened the ideological screws which had

[30] *Pis'mo trudiashchikhsia Kirgizistana velikomu vozhdiu narodov, ottsu vsekh
trudiashchikhsia, tovarishchu Stalinu* (Moscow, Gosizdat "Khudozhestvennaia
Literatura," 1936), pp. 31–32.

[31] "Pis'mo rabochikh i rabotnits sredne-aziatskogo tekstil'nogo kombinata imeni
Stalina Tov. Stalinu," *Revoliutsiia i natsional'nosti*, No. 8 (1935), pp. 64–65.

been loosened somewhat during the emergency, and again put writers and intellectual leaders painfully on the defensive with attacks against what were called unpolitical poems, plays, and novels, most of which dealt with historical themes or spoke in loving terms about the countryside's beauty and human feelings engendered by personal losses in the war. Underscoring the return of tough thought control, the Communist Party in 1946 produced a resolution, some provisions of which hit particularly at the wartime literary developments in Central Asia.[32]

The Party also lectured poets and critics to upgrade the political emphasis of their work. An assault was again made upon the Central Asian heritage, this time directly against the folk tradition, above all hitting the principal oral epics like *Qoblandï Batir, Alpamish, Manas,* and *Goroghli,* which in most cases were only now appearing in Russian translation. Despite the raucous campaigns and the strident tone of journalism devoted to changing the writer's state of mind after the war, the momentary panic during 1946–1951 did not result in another widespread purge. Mercifully, despite collective poetic Kirgiz prayers (in their epistles) to the contrary, 1953 proved that Stalin was not immortal, and the post-Stalin decade in the century of Russian rule over Central Asia has seen a revival, which cannot yet be called a renascence, in local literature about human beings.

RISING MOON—THE IMAGE OF THE BELOVED

Variations on the theme of love and the charms of the beloved had already delighted readers and writers throughout Central Asia and the Near and Middle East for hundreds of years before 1865, yet the momentum of this old Chaghatay and Persian tradition continued on in the late nineteenth century among Karakalpaks, Kazakhs, Tajiks, Turkmens, and Uzbeks. In romantic melancholy their poetry still spoke of lovers' quarrels, sad separations, or passionate despondency represented by sighs, tears, laments, and repeated plaintive reproaches. Through the complex forms of tradi-

[32] *Decisions of the Central Committee C.P.S.U. (B) on Literature and Art (1946–1948)* (Moscow, Foreign Languages Publishing House, 1951), pp. 13–19.

tional Arabic metrical constructions (*aruz*), the mood was expressed by the highly stylized language which symbolized a beauty's brows, eye lashes, lips, hair, and other attributes, with the familiar saber, thorn, moon, and nightingale, the poplar or cypress, and tulip and rose.

One of Khokand's best-known late-Chaghatay lyricists, Muhammad Muqimiy, excelled in the use of this genre. Sometimes he wrote topical verse, but mainly carried on the old themes in these quatrains and many other poems:

Yuzni aydek nagäh taban äyläding,	Like the moon, you brightened the face unexpectedly,
Chun ayinä mäwhu häyran äyläding,	Like a mirror, you caused complete amazement.
Ashiqlärgä roziy hijran äyläding.	You caused the lovers the fate of separation.
Äghyarimgä wäsling ärzan äylä-ding. . . .	You eased my rivals' meeting you. . . .
Lalä käbi yäshnäb chiqsäng mästanä,	When you blossom out like a tulip, intoxicatingly,
Korgän adäm nächuk bolmäs dewanä,	How will the man who sees you not go mad?
Khalq ichidä qilib mundagh äfsanä,	Making among people such a legend,
Awaräyu pur besaman äylä-ding. . . .	You made and completely impoverished [this] wanderer.
Ey chehräsi qämärdin ham munäw-wär,	Oh, you whose face is even brighter than the moon
Läbing lä'lu tishing säfadä gäwhär.	Your lips are rubies, your teeth jewels in bliss.
Salib bashgä ketib ghawghayi mäh-shär,	When into a head you put the din of judgment day,
Päri yängligh ozni pinhan äylä-ding.[33]	Like a peri, you hid yourself.

Although a different sort of "heart's darling" might have been expected from the Kazakh plainsmen's written literature, in it the similarities to the idealized beauty of the town were remarkable evidence of the Chaghatay literary influence on the nomadic mind, as shown by Abay Qunanbay-uli (1884):

> White brow—silver whose rendering is fine
> Illumined by radiant eyes.
> As if a crescent traced from two eyebrows.
> The look of a young moon is given the beauty. . . .

[33] Muqimiy, *Äsärlär toplämi*, I, 217.

Faultless the curve of finely moulded shoulders.
From pomegranate breasts comes an intoxicant.
Perfect the fullness of these two fruit,
And alluringly resilient the willowy figure! [34]

Following the lead of the nineteenth-century poets who preserved the sensual figure of the medieval literary sweetheart, the
Central Asian historical novelists of this century continued in another medium (prose) and social system (Communist) to re-create
the beauty of the past. From *Otgän kunlär* (Days Gone By), 1922,
the first Uzbek novel, written by Abdullah Qadiriy (Jolqunbay),
the plot of which turns entirely upon a tragedy growing out of an
arranged, polygamous marriage, comes this familiar picture:

Her black braids had scattered in disarray across the down pillow;
under thick, curling lashes her coal black eyes were then fixed on one
spot as if scrutinizing something . . . the jet black, delicately fine bow
of her curved brows just then frowned as if startled by something . . .
her full moon-like flawless, white face then changed to a slight blush, as
if embarrassed by someone. . . . At that moment, turning back the
blanket and holding it with her white hands, she brushed the black mole
which had been seated to the right of her exquisite nose by the superbly
skillful hand of nature, took her head from the pillow and sat up. Under
the yellow colored satin gown her well-proportioned bosom was standing
slightly raised. . . . This angel seen in the form of a girl . . . was
Kumushbibi! [35]

For the Kazakh novel Abay Qunanbay-uli's poems must have inspired the representation of the slightly sun-tanned loved one found
in *Abay* (1942–1947) by Mukhtar Auez-uli, the central theme of
which again focuses upon the misery produced from arranged
marriages:

A silver *sholpy* [a belled hair ornament] tinkled in her braids and the
rosy tint of her cheeks emphasized the fairness of her skin. She was
smiling as she entered, a reserved and yet playful smile, revealing an
even row of teeth . . . [she had] the same rosy apple of a chin [as an
earlier beloved], light and delicate, the same black silky hair . . .
there was the same nose, slightly upturned in such a provocative and

[34] Abai Kunanbaev, *Izbrannoe* (Moscow, Gosizdat Khudozhestvennoi Literatury, 1945), p. 9.
[35] Abdullah Qadiriy, *Otgän kunlär* (Tashkent, OzSSR Däwlät Bädiiy Ädäbiyat
Näshriyati, 1958), p. 27.

charming way. The red of her lips, daintily outlined and somewhat child-ish, the dark eyebrows, long, and rising to the temples like the wings of a swallow. . . . She was like a rising young moon—ever new, yet ever the same.[36]

When picturing the idealized female beauty, both the late-Chaghatay poets and the new historical novelists startlingly reproduced images from medieval masterpieces of Central Asian writing such as Mir Ali Shir Nawaiy's *Färhad wä shirin* (Farhad and Shirin), 1484, in whose 5,600 rhymed couplets are extended passages such as these devoted to Shirin, the heroine:

Iki qashi hilali fitnä ängez,	The crescent moons of her two brows are the discord-sowers,
Yazilghan kop ul ay bashidä khunrez.	Great blood spilling [by saber-like brows] on this moon's rise has been inscribed.
. . . .	
Shäkärdek läb wäle yoq tuz käm ändä,	Lips like sugar, but no little salt on them,
Tuzikim qänd aläm aläm ändä. . . .	But salt that has no end of sweet lumps in it. . . .
Säwadi khali oghirliqqä manänd,	Her mole's blackness like theft,
Kelib kunduz kuni eltur uchun qänd. . . .	Comes in broad daylight to carry off the sweet lumps. . . .
Kumushdek räng näsrin fami aning.	Her tint like the silver-colored white jonquil
Kumushdin ghunchädek ändami aning.	Her figure like a bud made of silver.
Bolub här kirpiki bir nugi khamä,	Her every eyelash the point of a pen,
Qarartib qätl uchun yazmaqqä namä.[37]	Having blackened the warrant for death [of a man].

The elegant images filling Ali Shir Nawaiy's poetry stood worlds apart from the attributives employed by popular storytellers who also repeated fantastic, romantic narratives about Farhad and Shirin or Layli and Majnun which were loved throughout Central Asia and the Middle East. In those verses and tales, generally concerned with unrequited passion, was prepared the basis for the ensuing literary genre of sentimental tragedy adopted by the Jadids in the

---

[36] Mukhtar Auezov, *Abai* (Moscow, Foreign Languages Publishing House, n.d.), II, 44.

[37] Alisher Nawaiy, *Färhad wä shirin* (Tashkent, Ozbekistan SSR Däwlät Näshriyati, 1956), pp. 352–54.

FIGURE 14.1   Romantic love in art and literature. *Layli and Majnun,*
lithographed in Tashkent, 1910.

early 1900s for the didactic purpose of modernizing Central Asian family and social life.

Accustomed to portraying their own women in a stylized way, the Central Asians readily adapted the traditional vision to obscure

FIGURE 14.2 Kirgiz novelist Chingiz Aytmatov meets the press. *Sovfoto.*

reality in the persons of the newly arrived Russian girls who, in the cities at least, created a sensation by appearing freely in public unveiled. Sadriddin Ayniy reported in Tajik verse (1899) his surprised delight at observing a Russian circus performer called Nina:

Nāzukbuter ā dar sayrgāh dosh	The fragrant one, at the entertainment place last night
Dar sirk dīdam, gashtam madḥūsh.	I saw [her] in the circus and was amazed.
Yevropazāde, rūsīnazhāde *Nasrin bar u dosh, safi bana gosh.*	A child of Europe, of Russian descent With shoulders and bosom like white jonquils, and flawless cheeks.
Navbar nihāl e, dūhaft sāl e,	She is a young sapling of twice seven years
Nātvān tama' kard zo bos u āgush. . . .	This humble man did desire an embrace from her. . . .
Ārām-i jān e, jān-i jahān e,	She is peace for the soul, she is the soul of the universe,
Āzād sarv e sarv-e qabā posh.	She is a slender cypress, a cypress in raiment.
Nāme guzāri, tā yādgāri, *Bā nām-i ān shokh ayniy qadahnosh!* [38]	If you seek to leave a name, Oh Ayniy, drink a goblet to the name of that playful one!

Ayniy's Nina was no more astonishing to the local population than Mahmud Khoja Behbudiy's Liza, another Russian type who appeared in Central Asian literature before 1917, and it is curious to notice that in Behbudiy's play *Padarkush* (The Parricide), although this heroine is a Russian prostitute catering to the "natives" and therefore of low standing in the profession, her Uzbek admirers nonetheless attempt to speak of Liza in the old, fanciful language of Central Asian poetic amour:

Däwlat: *Joralar! Mayni ichtim endi yadimgha lizakhan tushdi. Ah liza jan!*	Friends, I drank the wine and now to my mind sweet Liza came. Oh Liza dear!
[Everyone]:*Ah lizajan way lizajan qaydasan!*	Oh Liza dear, ah Liza dear, wherever art thou?
Nar: *Zalim falak firaqiga kuydurdi meni; billahki kelmasa bomidi.*[39]	Tyrannical fate has made me suffer separation from her; In the name of Allah, it is impossible that she not come [to me].

Thoughtless satisfaction among contemporaries like Ayniy with these stereotypes of Central Asian literature prompted Jadid writer Abdalrauf Fitrat to satirize the "nightingale—rose" (*bulbul—gul*)

[38] Sadriddin Ayniy, "Nāzukbuter ā dar sayrgāh dosh . . ." *Ozbek ädäbiyati* (Tashkent, OzSSR Däwlät Bädiiy Ädäbiyat Näshriyati, 1960), Vol. IV, book 1, p. 406; trans. by Sakine Berengian.

[39] Mufti Mahmud Khoja Behbudiy, *Padarkush* (Samarkand, Tipolitografiia T-va B. Gazarov i K. Sliianov, 1913), p. 9.

school's creation of fantasy women and call for purposeful poetry in one of his prerevolutionary Tajik verses, *"Tāziyāne-yi ta'dib"* (The Scourge of Warning), 1914:

Jam'i be tāv-i zolf-i parichehre-gān asir,	Some [poets] are bound by the chains of the beloved's hair,
Yad-i negāh-i mast-i botān rā piyāleh-gir;	Some are drunk from the languid eyes of idol-like beauties;
Gah az neshāt-i sobhadam-i vasl dar ghariv,	Now they clamor for the joy of re-union's dawn,
Gah az balā-yi nim-shab-i hejr dar nafīr;	Now they wail at the pain of separa-tion's midnight;
Har qāmati ki dideh hameh sarvrā shabih	Some ever liken all figures to a cypress,
Har chehre-yi dideh, hameh māhrā nazir	Some ever liken all faces to the moon;
Ruy-i vatan ze nakhon-i ghaflat jarihe-dār	The face of Vatan [the homeland] is scratched by the fingernails of neg-ligence;
Ānhā be-yād-i ru-yi bātān kardeh jān nesār. . . ¦[40]	They bestow their lines on the face of the sweetheart!

THE UNLUCKY MAIDEN OF THE JADIDS

Perhaps as a consequence of Fitrat's sarcasm, the epitomized Chaghatay and Persian literary images, though they persisted even occasionally in writings as late as the second half of the twentieth century, did not bar the appearance of a different kind of modern fictional female. The home-grown daughter who suddenly appeared in the Central Asian prose first published beginning with the sec-ond decade of the 1900s was a more realistically portrayed girl in a recognizable environment presented now as the anguished victim of social customs which condemned her to misery in marriage. This new heroine of Jadid literature quite logically came to life first in genres—novel, drama, and short story—fresh for local writers.

Thus, the talented girl in Mir Jaqib Duwlat-uli's 94-page Kazakh novel, *Baqïtsïz jamal* (Unlucky Jamal), 1910,[41] a work called by the author "the first novel of Kazakh life," [42] makes a more natural fig-

---

[40] 'Abd al-ra'uf Fitrat-i Bukhariy, "Tāziyāne-yi ta'dib," *Ayina*, No. 13 (Janu-ary 18, 1914), p. 215; trans. by Sakine Berengian.

[41] First edition (1910), 8,000 copies; second edition (1914), 10,000 copies (Kazan, Izdatel'stvo i Tipografiia Br. Karimovykh).

[42] Dulatov, "Avtobiografiia," in *al-Sharqiyyat*, p. 232.

ure than her predecessors, although she herself is depicted somewhat in the old terms by an admirer:

A beautiful maiden . . . when she reaches seventeen is as priceless as
rare, precious stones. She is like the apple trees growing in paradise—
if he will but reach out his hand, what *jigit* [young brave] will refuse
to taste the fruit.[43]

Contrasting sharply with this idyllic vision sounds the lament from
all prospective Kazakh brides pictured by the luckless Jamal as
frightened song birds:

But the unfortunate girls spend their lives in a cage like nightingales.
People marry them to whoever will give the highest bride price, and
the unlucky ones with tears in their eyes leave their fathers' homes. And
the parents are not kind to them in this instance, no matter how much
they might love them.[44]

Under the circumstances it was not surprising that the theme of
the second Central Asian novel to be published, the Kazakh *Qalïng
mal* (Bride Price), 1913, by Spandiyar Kobe-uli (1878–1956), revolved also around the plight of Ghaysha, a young girl subject, like
unlucky Jamal, to the arbitrariness of existing marriage customs.
Touching the same theme were two other Kazakh works, sometimes
generously described as novels, by Sultanmaqmut Torayghir-uli
(1893–1920): *Qamar sulu* (Qamar the Beautiful), 1914, and *Kim
jazïqtï?* (Who's to Blame?), 1914/1915. The first, unfinished, was
written in prose heavily interlaced with poetry, and the second
entirely in verse.

Following after the old-time saber-browed beauties and Jadid
novelists' wretched Jamal and Ghaysha, came a procession of tearful Central Asian leading ladies who first appeared on the new
stage. There was sixteen-year-old Qadisha in the first published
Kazakh drama, *Nadandïq qŭrbandarï* (Victims of Ignorance), 1914,
by Kolbey Toghis-uli, brokenhearted over the loss of her exiled
lover, Aspandiyar, and her impending wedding to an older man
with three wives. There was beautiful young Jamila in *Bay ila
khizmatchi* (Master and Servant), 1918, an Uzbek melodrama by

---

[43] Dulatov, "Bakhtysyz Dzhemal," in *al-Sharqiyyat*, p. 238.
[44] *Ibid.*, p. 239.

Hamza Hakim Zada Niyaziy, who poisons herself after being torn from her beloved husband and remarried forcibly to a lustful intriguer. And there was lovely Kakey in one of the earliest Kirgiz plays, *Kaygïlu kakey* (Ill-fated Kakey), performed 1927, by Moldogazi Tokobay-uulu (1905–   ), who commits suicide when doomed to separation forever from her Omurkul by forced marriage to an older man. This last play, which subsequently underwent revision to arrange for a happy ending, appeared in Kirgiz theaters as late as 1951.[45]

Happy literary endings having become a matter of principle in the official "optimistic" mood of the Soviet period, these sorrowful scenes always made Communist critics uncomfortable, but they brought on no more unease than did the opposite emotional strains —the wild and sometimes painful humor of the folk satirists, the Jadid authors' illiterate brothers. Uniting the popular literature throughout great sections of Central Asia were at least a trio of witty rogues enlivening the extensive anecdotal repertoire of the subliterate population. None could outdo the impious, rascally behavior of the widely known *Käl* "scald head" (favus head), whose escapades with maidens, merchants, and mullahs provided storytellers of Central Asia with their most ribald tales and colorful, picaresque vagabond. Also infamous is Nasriddin Afandi, whose adventures never end in Uzbekistan and Turkmenistan, and who is known in Azerbaijan and Turkey as Nasriddin Khoja. Outrageous was Aldar Kosa, an older replication of the modern confidence man, a real "deceiver," as his name signifies. Both Kazakhs and Uzbeks know Aldar Kosa, who is not above adding to the confusion of local girls by stealing a bride, as this brief anecdote shows:

> Once Kosa said to Shigay Bay: "Dear Bay, lend me your *biz* [awl]. I want to leave and my boots have completely fallen apart."
> "Go ahead, ask my wife, she will you give you my *biz*," answered Bay, who went to the fields after his cattle.
> Kosa went up to the Bay's wife and said: "Baybishe, Shigay Bay ordered you to give me your daughter, Biz-Bekesh, in marriage.
> "What's happened, have you gone crazy?" screeched Bay's wife. "Now really would my husband marry Biz-Bekesh to you?"

[45] N. L'vov, *Kirgizskii teatr* (Moscow, Gosizdat *Iskusstvo*, 1953), p. 29.

Kosa then led her out of the yurt and in her presence shouted to Bay: "Bay, Bay, you promised me your *biz* but your wife won't give Biz to me."

At this Shigay Bay shouted from the field: "Give him, wife, give him *biz* so that he'll stop pestering!" What else could be done? The old woman had to give up her beautiful daughter. . . .

Kosa saddled his horse, seated Biz-Bekesh before him, touched the reins, and disappeared without leaving a trace.[46]

The heroine of folk literature was not always a pawn of fate or tricksters. In the old Karakalpak epic *Qïrq qïz* (Forty Maidens) the fairy-tale beauty of Gulaim is only one of the heroine's impressive attributes sung of in the 25,000-line oral poem by folk singer (*jrau*) Qurbanbay Tajibay-oli, although even this Central Asian Amazon, true to form, possesses the traditional charms enhanced in poetry with a few special similes and some unusual metaphors:

Tal shïbïqtay taulanghan,	Lissom as a young willow,
Qara-qaslï, qulang shashlï,	Black-browed and luxuriant tressed,
Jaudïr kozli, shirin sozli,	Sparkling eyed, sweet speeched
Juqa yerni qaymaqtay,	Delicate lips like cream,
Piste murïn, badam qabaq.	A pistachio nose, almond eyelids.
Hinji tisli, peri tusli,	Coral toothed, fairy faced,
Auzï sulu oymaqtay.[47]	Little mouth beautiful as a thimble.

Far more striking than Gulaim's appearance was her activity in the affairs of the town where she lived and especially her role in defense of the Khwarazmian area as a warrior and military leader of the forty maidens whom she trained to follow her in battle. On the field or in single combat, Gulaim directs the men in her world, tells them when to fight, what strategy to use, when to kiss and love, and whom to marry. Though fifteen-year-old Gulaim comes closer in her style of behavior to the independent prototype sketched in Communist literature toward the close of the 1920s, Central Asian women have seldom yet appeared in modern written literature in such romantic actions as this heroic Karakalpak girl.

Between the old folk tale or epic figure, the new woman of the Jadids, and the stern Communist female, appeared the transitional

---

[46] Leonid Sobolev, ed., *Pesni stepei: Antologiia kazakhskoi literatury* (Moscow, Gosudarstvennoe Izdatel'stvo "Khudozhestvennaia Literatura," 1940), p. 168.

[47] Nazhim Davkaraev, *Ocherki po istorii dorevoliutsionnoi karakalpakskoi literatury* (Tashkent, Izdatel'stvo Akademii Nauk Uzbekskoi SSR, 1959), p. 117.

personality of Halima, heroine of the first original Central Asian opera. In *Halima* (1919) by Ghulam Zafariy (1889–1944), an Uzbek from Tashkent,[48] this girl melodramatically became the pawn in a class struggle represented by the poor young man, Ne"mat, whom she loves, and the wealthy, older Artiqbay to whom she is betrothed. Halima's father, like Jamila's parent before her, insists upon the marriage of convenience and Halima kills herself.[49] *Halima* became extraordinarily popular throughout the 1920s and early 1930s and was performed hundreds of times all over Central Asia. "The music for *Halima* was chosen from widely known popular and classical melodies . . . selected to match the basic emotions appropriate for the various actors [roles] and becoming their leitmotifs."[50] A manuscript version of this opera was reconstructed from an Andijan presentation offered in 1926 and has been preserved.[51] The immense popularity and longevity of *Halima*, despite the fact that it was never published, gave tribute to the excellence of the music and the story, but showed above all the compelling nature of the opera's theme.

The appearance of those fictional young ladies of the folk, Chaghatay, or Jadid traditions, and the figures of speech chosen to depict them, differed somewhat from the new verse constructed after 1920 by nationalist poets, but even then, though portraying ordinary flesh-and-blood girls, the old vocabulary and sentiment remains strong in this emancipated Uzbek poetry:

Hay baghban qizi,	Oh gardener's daughter,
Kongil yulduzi,	Star of the heart,
Nega qaraydi,	Why did it darken,
Tali'ing yuzi?	The face of your luck?
Erkala quwnarding,	You were frolicking overjoyed,
Qushdek ucharding.	Like a bird you flew and flew.
Kapalak kabi,	As a butterfly,
Chechak qucharding. . . .	You embraced the flower. . . .

[48] B. Pestovskii, "Uzbekskii teatr. Noveishie uzbekskie dramaturgi," *Nauka i prosveshchenie,* No. 1 (Tashkent, August-September 1922), p. 36.

[49] T. Tursunov, *Formirovanie sotsialisticheskogo realizma v uzbekskoi dramaturgii* (Tashkent, Izdatel'stvo Akademii Nauk Uzbekskoi SSR, 1963), p. 58.

[50] G. Uvarova, *Uzbekskii dramaticheskii teatr* (Moscow, Gosizdat *Iskusstvo,* 1959), p. 59.

[51] Tursunov, p. 57.

Baghda bulbullar,	In the garden the nightingales,
Chamanda gullar,	In the flowerbed the roses,
Alqish soylardi,	The hyacinths, to you
Senga sunbollar.	Spoke their applause.
Dard quchaq achmish.	It seemed grief opened its arms.
Koz yashing sachmish	Your eyes' tear apparently fell,
Kulgan chaqlaring,	The times when you laughed,
Qaylargha qachmish.	Seemed to flee somewhere.
Nechun? Bir soyla!	Why? Say something!
Siniq nay, koyla.	Sing, broken flute.
Gozal kongilda,	In the lovely heart,
Qayghu—gham tola? [52]	Is sadness, woe, complete?

Communism's optimism had not yet dried the tears of these damsels dampening literature in the 1920s, because the story from real life constantly retold in poetry and prose after 1925 concerned girls whose days ended tragically in the conflict arising over the earlier Jadid drive, now taken up by the Party, to emancipate the female from seclusion and undemocratic Muslim marriage traditions. Amandurdi Alamish-oghli closed a pessimistic 2,800-line Turkmen poem on this theme entitled *Söndi* (Extinguished), 1928, with the dying lament of an unfortunate young woman caught in this struggle.[53] Intending to counteract the pessimistic tone of literature like Alamish-oghli's long poem, Agakhan Durdiy-oghli had written his short Turkmen story "Bagtli gïzlar" (Happy Girls), c.1927, and in a later, revised edition of *Söndi*, which appeared under the heroine's name, *Sona*, closing passages of the poem were altered radically to provide the happy ending desired by officials.[54]

PROLETARIAN AND SOVIET WOMEN

The true woman of the proletarian period, differing from all previous figures in Central Asian literature, remained psychologically as thin as her earlier sisters, but her behavior had reverted from the docile immobility of Chaghatay beauties and helplessness of

[52] Aybek, *Tuyghular* (Tashkent, Ozbekistan Däwlät Näshriyati, 1926), pp. 14–15.

[53] Tash-Nazarov, p. 138.

[54] G. Veselkov, *Ocherki turkmenskoi literatury* (Ashkhabad, Turkmengiz, 1945), pp. 90–91; *Türkmen sovet edebiyatïnïng tarïkhï: Boyuncha ocherk* (Ashkhabad, Türkmenistan SSR Ïlïmlar Akademiyasïnïng Neshriyatï, 1958), I, 40–42, 55–56.

Jadid heroines back to the assertive activity of the Karakalpak Gulaim. In keeping with one of the Communist Party slogans pressed upon writers and other intellectuals around the mid-1920s, much of the new literature called for the emancipation of women, and although one obvious purpose of the Soviet leadership in breaking down the old family system in this manner was to make large numbers of women available for cheap manual labor in factories and farms, the appeal met a strong response, among the literate at least, precisely because public opinion had been prepared so thoroughly by the writings of the early 1900s favoring the emancipation drive. Creation of a believable literary type of free woman, however, proved to be nearly as difficult as the actual campaign to remove her veil in some cities, and for some time, angular, schematic figures replaced the personages who had decorated early prose and drama.

Epitomizing the newly liberated Central Asian woman, Zeyneb, leading character in a Kirgiz play, *Tör agha zeyneb* (Chairman Zeyneb), 1929, by the Communist nationalist Sidiq Qarach-uulu (d.c.1938), is characterized in the cast listing merely as an "educated woman" (*oqughan ayal*) but her rise to power as chairman of a local soviet (*sel'sovet*) takes place in the company of Komsomol and Party members included among the *dramatis personae*. Unlike most previous Central Asian literary ladies, who had ranged from fourteen to seventeen years old, Zeyneb appears at twice that age. Furthermore, she is neither tearful nor beautiful according to the text of the three-act play. Here, emancipation consists, too, in the heroine's becoming a manager of business usually handled by men.[55] Zeyneb provides an example of the fictional women developing in Communist Central Asia through the period of several prewar Five Year plans. The standard plot complications in this literature arose from the refusal of a "backward" man, sometimes the heroine's husband or brother, to permit any public activities by women in the family.

Even continuing after 1945 a major theme in Central Asian liter-

[55] S. Qarach-uulu, *Tör agha zeyneb* (Frunze, Qïrghïzïstan Memleket Basmasï, 1929).

ature remained women's rise to supposed equality. Asqad Mukhtar (1920–   ) devoted a lengthy Uzbek novel, *Apa-singillar* (The Sisters), to it as late as 1955. In contrast to her recent Uzbek fictional rivals, Jamila, a country girl living at the edge of the Kirgiz mountains and Kazakh plains, in the recent novelette bearing her name, takes only a personal step in the emancipation movement. Chingiz Aytmatov's heroine receives an almost naturalistic literary treatment reminiscent of the characterization given to Aksin'ia in Mikhail Sholokhov's famous Russian novel *Tikhii Don* (The Quiet Don), and this Jamila of the late 1950s, like predecessors from earlier generations, has been married to a man, probably selected by her elders, with whom she is unhappy. Her dissatisfaction in this cold union leads her to elope to Kazakhstan with a lover and supplies the motivation for the entire action of the plot. The heroine herself is described in a detailed, realistic manner:

Jamila was good looking. Well-built, full bodied, with straight, wiry hair plaited into two tight, heavy braids, she deftly tied her white kerchief slightly slantwise, pulling it down on her forehead, and this suited her very well, setting off beautifully the dusky skin of her smooth face. When Jamila laughed, her blue-black almond-shaped eyes blazed with youthful zest, and when she suddenly started to sing the salty *ail* [village] songs an unmaidenly glint would appear in her beautiful eyes.[56]

The main line of development for Central Asia's most persistent modern literary theme—women and their roles in society, or more accurately, how men see women, for male authors produced all these examples—has thus undergone evolution from the lyrically elusive love objects of Chaghatay verse through the sad-faced, talented damsels in distress championed by Jadid writers, to mannish Party functionaries bossing men in the proletarian era, and now the free-spirited, beautiful felines, ferocious in work, play, and love, but without any thoughts in their healthy, handsome heads except those which can be expressed through popular songs. Lacking moral or philosophical discipline, the new literary personage has no more control over her destiny than those helpless, moon-

[56] Chingiz Aitmatov, *Povesti gor i stepei* (Moscow, Sovetskii Pisatel', 1963), p. 17.

faced ones of the nineteenth century. Literate she has become, like her Jadid grandmother, but not intellectual, a fault to be found likewise almost uniformly with the heroine's masculine counterparts in recent Central Asian literature.

E. A.

15

Musical Tradition and Innovation

Every population and every ethnic group seems to have its musical configuration. Songs of different, well-defined culture groups have certain characteristics which, although difficult to describe, are clearly felt to represent discrete cultural ethos. "Cultural" is used here in its anthropological sense, meaning nonbiological, socially transmitted traits in a society, including artistic, social, ideological, and religious patterns of behavior and techniques of mastering the environment. "Ethos" is used in the anthropological and not in the musicological sense. "In a single cultural system even under highly dynamic conditions there is a unifying groundwork of experience as represented by common premises, values, and goals which the interacting groups and individuals share." [1] This applies to music as well as to other parts of culture.

In the typology of music the investigator proceeds much like an archaeologist in looking for a motif or pattern and any unique diagnostic means of identifying the art of a distinct period and culture. While the archaeologist finds his clues in styles, forms, colors, or textures, the musicologist looks for indications such as tonal systems, melodic and rhythmic patterns, melody types, forms, performance practices, and instruments. Like the historian, the musicologist searches for inner correspondences, the history of problems of formation and change, and, similar to the cultural anthropologist, he deals with the style of music as a manifestation of the whole culture, the visible sign of unity, projecting the inner form of shared thoughts and feelings. What is important here is not the style of an individual or of a single art form, but forms and qualities shared

[1] Felix M. Keesing, *Cultural Anthropology* (New York, Rinehart, 1958), p. 386.

by all the music of a culture during a significant span of time in a definite culture area.

Musically speaking, a culture area is a region of musical characterization; it is often a geographical territory where musical cultures tend to be similar in significant aspects while they are different from musical cultures in adjacent areas. For instance, all musical cultures of the Middle Eastern culture area are similar to one another but different from the musical cultures in neighboring Negro Africa, Europe, India, or China. Conditioned by a similar way of living, the music expresses the thoughts, feelings, and aspirations, the value system and ideology of the people inhabiting the same culture area.

All culture areas have culture traits, usually irreducible units of learned behavior patterns, or a material product itself. Musical behavior patterns in the Middle East include performance practices like nasal, throaty, guttural voice production, microtonal melodic structures, and glottal trills. A material product could be exemplified by a musical instrument fashioned in a characteristic way and made of particular woods, gourds, and skins, often in agreement with ancient magical practices and beliefs, cosmological connotations, or venerated units of measurement which have nothing to do with acoustics or musical considerations. All individual traits are grouped into culture complexes which in turn make up a culture area.

Every culture area has a culture center where the most distinctive and typical music of that culture area develops and flourishes. The culminating point of a flourishing culture can be called a culture climax. Such culture climaxes in the Middle East were reached, for example, during the time of Harun al-Rashid, caliph in Baghdad (786–809); or, later when two famous musicians, Ishaq al-Mausili and the caliph's own relative, Ibrahim al-Mahdi, competed for primacy in Samarra during the time of Muhammad ibn Tarkhan abu Nasr al-Farabi (870–950) in Aleppo and Damascus, and during the development of the shashmaqam (six-mode composition; described under Modes) in Tashkent and Bukhara in the sixteenth century. The culture centers of the Middle East moved with a powerful ruler and his court to whatever location he chose for residence. At various times in history centers of musical culture were established in Basra, Kufa, Baghdad, Cairo, the Maghreb, al-Hira, Isfahan, Merv, Samarkand, Tashkent, Bukhara, and Istanbul. Yemen and the Hijaz (Mecca and Medina) were traditionally among the oldest (pre-Islamic) and most prestigious centers of music.

While the geographical location of a culture center shifted from place to place as musicians followed the court, the culture traits and culture complexes of the music remained essentially the same or altered little, since the same musicians and the schools they established continued to practice the art and to set the standards regardless of geography. Famous musicians were sent from court to court, slaves were sold from country to country and spread the styles and instruments of their homelands. Since the fifth century, musicians and instruments traveled all over the civilized world disseminating their music throughout the entire Middle Eastern culture area and beyond. The Persian king Bahram Gur (r.420–438) was sent to the Mesopotamian town of al-Hira to study Arabic music, and in about 600 Hassan ibn Thabnit saw at the Syrian court of the Ghassanids "ten singing girls, five of them Byzantines, singing the songs of their country . . . others from al-Hira . . . singing songs from their country, [and] Arab singers from Mecca and elsewhere." [2] In the *Thousand and One Nights* the princess called on her slave girl to bring instruments of music, and "the maid returned in the twinkling of an eye with a Damascus lute, a Persian harp, a Tartar pipe, and an Egyptian dulcimer." [3] All these different styles of songs and instruments fused and contributed to the overall type of music called today "Middle Eastern."

THE MIDDLE EASTERN CULTURE AREA

The Middle Eastern culture area, designated by different authorities "Muhammedan," [4] "Western Oriental," [5] "Islamic," [6] and "Mid-

---

[2] Aghani, XVI, 15; as quoted in H. G. Farmer, *A History of Arabian Music* (London, Luzac, 1929), p. 12.

[3] Curt Sachs, *The Rise of Music in the Ancient World, East and West* (New York, Norton, 1943), p. 278.

[4] Robert Lachmann, "Muhammedan Music," *Grove's Dictionary of Music and Musicians* (New York, Macmillan, 1948), III, 575.

[5] Sachs, p. 71.

[6] R. G. Kiesewetter, *Die Musik der Araber* (Leipzig, Breitkopf and Härtel, 1842), and others.

dle Eastern," [7] comprises roughly the North African coast, North Arabia, Turkey, Armenia, Azerbaijan, Iran, and the area of Central Asia of today. Some of the subareas which have developed a very distinct style of music, and now represent subcultures in Middle Eastern music are the Maghreb (Morocco, Tunisia, and Algeria), Arabia (Egypt, Palestine, Syria, and Iraq), Turkey, Iran, and Central Asia (Kazakh, Kirgiz, Turkmen, Tajik, and Uzbek SSRs).

The differences lie in varied microtonal structures, modality, emphasis on different instruments, and preference for certain musical forms over others. Thus, while both Arabic music and Turkish music divide their octave into 24 microtones, the Arabs use the tempered 24-tone scale. The Turks, however, use five different interval units for the same 24-tone scale. The Iranians, on the other hand, divide the octave into seventeen, twenty-two, or twenty-eight intervals, following al-Farabi and Qutb ed Din.[8] Terminology for modes differs from area to area. Although the major instrument of the Arabic countries is *al-'Ud* (the short-necked lute), it is the *tanbur* (long-necked lute) in Turkey and the *santur* (dulcimer) in Iran, while Central Asia prefers two- and three-stringed lutes, little used in the other areas mentioned. But if all subareas of the Middle East differ in particulars they agree in general on the following traits: microtones, maqamat (modes), homophony, improvisation, complex rhythm and meter, small ensembles, and kinds of instruments.

Except for recent times, musical notation has never found a following in the Middle East. Musicians there preferred to transmit their art by word of mouth through an oral tradition, sometimes called "earmarks," using a great many terms to indicate individual notes, modes, melodic structure, melody types, modulation, rhythmic structure and meter, often even tempo and mood. Therefore it does not seem quite justifiable to assert that the people of the Middle East did not have a musical notation at all; it should rather be said

[7] Henry G. Farmer, "Turkestani Music," *Grove's Dictionary of Music and Musicians* (New York, Macmillan, 1954), VIII, 610–12.

[8] Khatschi Khatschi, *Der Dastgah: Studien zur neuen persischen Musik* (Regensburg, Gustav Bosse Verlag, 1962), p. 54 and Table I. See also *La Musique Traditionnelle de l'Iran* (Teheran, Secrétariat d'État aux Beaux-Arts, 1963), pp. 5–25; and "Les Échelles Regulières du Cycle des Quintes," in *La Resonance dans les Échelles Musicales* (Paris, Editions du Centre Nationale de la Recherche Scientifique, 1963), p. 177.

that they did not care for notation committed to paper, parchment, papyrus, stone, or clay. It was oral notation, expressed through exact terminology.

Although Central Asian music earlier had always been handed down by word of mouth, it had enjoyed a rich and varied history documented in writing and proved by archaeological finds. In Uzbekistan, Tajikistan, and Turkmenistan, but no adjacent areas, very early writing and sculpture were discovered, including terracotta figurines of male and female musicians from the first millennium B.C., silver platters showing musicians and musical instruments from the third and second centuries B.C., a mural depicting a woman harpist from the third century A.D., and other art objects showing musical activity from the fifth to seventh centuries A.D. Some of these came to light around ancient Khuvaragur and others in Panjakent, near Samarkand.[9] Among the instruments depicted were longitudinal open flutes, panpipes, drums of different shapes and sizes, lutelike instruments, and harps called changs. A stone frieze dating from the first centuries A.D. unearthed not far from the city of Termez shows barrel-like and hourglass-shaped drums, platters, a double flute, a harp, and a rabab identical with the contemporary Tajik rubab, thus supplying evidence that musical culture was highly developed there during the time of the Bactrians, predecessors of the contemporary Tajiks.[10]

The great cities from Merv to Khiva in the west, through Bukhara and Samarkand, to Khokand in the east have been centers of culture from early days to modern times. The greatest of the Arab theorists of music, al-Farabi, was a Turk from Wasij, not far from Keder on the left bank of the Sir Darya, and his *Kitab al-musiqi al-kabir* (The Great Book of Music) is still a major classic to be studied by all students of Middle Eastern music. In the Muslim world, his greatness has been likened to that of Aristotle. Khwarazm was the home of Muhammad ibn Ahmad abu Abdallah al-Khwarizmi (tenth century) the author of *Mafatih al-ʿulum* (Keys of the Sciences). One of these keys unlocked the secrets of music theory. Abu Ali

[9] *Muzykalʾnaia kultura sovetskogo Uzbekistana* (Tashkent, Gosizdat UzSSR, 1955), pp. 11–12.
[10] Viktor Beliaev (Belaiev), *Ocherki po istorii muzyki narodov SSSR* (Moscow, Muzgiz, 1962), p. 193.

al-Husayn Ibn Sina, the Avicenna of the Middle Ages (980–1037), who wrote at least two treatises on music, was born in Bukhara. From the period of the Khwarazm shahs (thirteenth century) music and musicians flourished at the courts, and elsewhere it was around the throne of Miran Shah (d.1408) that music became a center of attraction. Samarkand, Timur's capital, had had the great music theorist 'Abd al-Qadir ibn Ghaibi (d.1435), while the minstrels of Shahrukh (r.1409–1447) at Herat were the envy of the Middle East. From Khokand came Fakhr al-Din al-Khokandi (circa fourteenth century) who wrote a glossary to the *Kitab al-adwar* (Book of Modes) by the eminent Safi al-Din 'Abd al-Mu'min (d.1294). Also from this area came *Bahjat al-ruh* (Garden of the Soul), written in the fifteenth century by 'Abd al-Mu'min ibn Safi al-Din, and even today the poets and musicians of Central Asia talk of Mir Ali Shir Nawaiy's fifteenth-century *Mahbub al-qulub* (Beloved of the Heart), which tells about the singers and players (*hafaza*). In addition there is Qasim ibn Dost Bukhari, who wrote *Risala dar 'ilm al-musiqi* (Treatisé on the Science of Music) for the emperor Jalal al-Din Akhbar (1542–1605). Besides these towering international figures there were local personalities of great stature, such as Najmuddun Kaubaki (d.1576), a famous Bukharan musician and poet.[11]

CENTRAL ASIAN CROSSROADS

Through these same lands came many instruments from the Far East such as the yatughan (a species of Chinese *cheng* with nineteen pipes) and the chubchiq (the Chinese *ch'ao-sheng*, a mouthorgan), which passed into Persia and Mesopotamia. Likewise, the Chinese took the *tan-pu-la* (the Turkic tanbur), *huo-pu-ssu* (the Turkic qubuz), *la-pu-pu* (the Turkic rubab), and other instruments from Western Turkistan.

The Central Asian chang is related to the Shanghai *yang-k'in* (foreign zither or dulcimer), both in turn being related to the Persian *santur*. The chang has the curved upper board of a Chinese instrument signifying "the sky," quite unlike the Persian *santur*, which does not curve. The chang's two bridges are perforated for the strings, which go over and under the bridges crossing each

[11] See H. G. Farmer, *The Sources of Arabian Music* (Leiden, Brill, 1965).

other, and the bridges are not movable, differing from those of the Persian *santur* (see Figure 15.3b). The term *yang-k'in* reveals that the instrument was brought to China from somewhere outside. Because a like instrument was known in the fourteenth century in Afghanistan,[12] it seems quite possible that the chang (*yang-k'in*) was brought to China from Central Asia. The sketch in Figure 15.3 is drawn from a photograph taken in Israel in 1951 of the chang being played by a Bukharan Jew who had brought the instrument from Uzbekistan and called it a "chank."

Central Asia thus was the crossroads for the exchange of instruments from East to West and from West to East, so that traces of both East and West are found in Central Asia itself. The Chinese influence manifests itself, for example, in the construction of certain wind instruments taking the Chinese norm of 276 mm (a Chinese water-foot, about eleven inches), as exemplified by the ghärawnay, a transverse reed-flute brought in via Kashgar.[13] Another influence from the East is evident in the strong pentatonic melos (sum total of melody or song) pervading some of the Kirgiz tunes. Pentatonic traces are also found in Kazakh music, but to a much lesser extent.

On the other hand, much of the Central Asian musical terminology is borrowed from Arabia and Iran. For instance, the names of some musical instruments, rabab, tanbur, naghara, qanun and designations of certain maqamat (modes) such as *bayat* and *hijaz* are Arabic. Other instruments like the dutar, setar, chartar, panjtar, shashtar, chang, nay, daira, and dool, plus the maqamat *rast*, *dugah*, and *segah* have Persian titles.

There is often a similarity of terminology in border areas of different cultures. The Central Asian karnay and dool, for example, have counterparts in the *karna* and *dhol* of India.[14] During the thirteenth-century invasion of Central Asia by Chingis Khan, many musicians from the area took refuge in India and Iran, carrying their art to foreign countries. But this is not the only explanation

[12] Farmer, "Turkestani Music," pp. 610–12. Curt Sachs, "Čank," *Reallexikon der Musikinstrumente* (Hildesheim, Georg Olms, 1962), p. 100.

[13] Viktor Beliaev, *Uzbekskie muzykal'nye instrumenty* (Moscow, Narkompros UzSSR, 1933).

[14] Curt Sachs, "Karna," and "Dhol," in *Reallexikon*, pp. 204, 109.

FIGURE 15.1   Display of musical instruments at 1890 exposition at Tashkent. Strings (left to right); temir-komuz (?); tanbur; tanbur; dutar; ghijjak; singer(?) mascot(?) rabab (cross between Kashgar and Tajik types?); ghijjak; dutar; tanbur; Kirgiz komuz.

FIGURE 15.2 Display of musical instruments at 1890 exposition at Tashkent. Winds and percussion (Standing, left to right): man's right hand, safail(?) kairoks(?) kairoks; left hand, crescent(?); kairoks; karnay; karnay; daira; daira; daira; kairoks (stone); kairoks (wood?); (Seated, left to right): naghara; naghara; naghara; surnay; surnay; surnay; surnay.

for such similarity of terminology and instruments. In border areas there is always a great deal of give and take, and just as people living at the border of two countries usually speak both languages, they also know and appreciate each other's music. Therefore, music on the Turkmen-Persian, Uzbek-Afghan, Tajik-Indian, and Kirgiz-Chinese borders has the benefit of dual cultures.

But foreign music generally does not seem to penetrate very far beyond the actual border area. For example, the south of Turkmenistan formed for many centuries part of Persia, the Margiana (the province of Merv), and a large number of Turkmens still live in contemporary Iran. Nevertheless, the music of Turkmenistan remains distinct from the music of Persia, having a very well-defined ethos with unusual features—fourths and fifths in parallel progression (see Table 15.8: Turkmen two-voiced *mukhammas* for dutar), but lacking dance music and percussion instruments, and other elements considered to belong to the most ancient traits of Central Asia. Persia, in contrast, has only homophonic music, has no fourths or fifths, uses percussive instruments a great deal, and has dance music. Music has been called the least changeable and the most traditional and tenacious aspect of any culture, and this belief seems to be borne out at least in the area of Turkmenistan.

In a musical sense, Kirgiz and Kazakh belong in one subculture, Uzbek and Tajik in another, and the Turkmens form a third, which seems to be intermediate. The Kirgiz and Kazakh ethnic relationship and material culture as well as their geographical location adjacent to China are the basis for their similar musical ethos. Uzbeks and Tajiks have lived at least since the sixteenth century in the same location near today's Afghanistan, India, and Pakistan, and share a common material culture and history which makes their close musical relationship not very surprising. The Turkmens developed a unique musical culture different in some important respects from both the Kirgiz-Kazakh and Uzbek-Tajik, but perhaps similar to a few aspects of Persian and Azerbaijanian music such as Shirvan *perde*. The maqamat *shirvan perde* (maqam or mode from the city of Shirvan), *zarin perde* (gentle maqam), and *lal perde* (mute maqam) may represent survivals of Persian influence.

TURKMENISTAN STANDS APART

No festive or processional music and no folk or popular music is indigenous to the Turkmens. Music there exists only as an elevated art practiced by a professional class of bakhshis (bestowers). They are not only singers, instrumentalists, poets, and composers, they are storytellers as well. The names of the prominent bakhshis are known everywhere, even in neighboring countries, a fact which attests to their importance in social and cultural life.[15]

The most striking feature of Turkmen music is its polyphony (two-voice melodic structure primarily in parallel fourths and fifths) in dutar- and tüydük-playing, for example. Nowhere in Central Asia is polyphony so important. This contrasts not only with the other music of Central Asia, but with the entire music of the Middle East, which is monophonic. Not even Iran, the Turkmens' closest neighbor, has music of this type.

Table 15.3 shows that Turkmenistan enjoys the five principal instruments of Central Asia, but that it has no percussion. Therefore it has no dance music—perhaps because the Turkmen does not approve of dance music and regards percussion instruments as an unnecessary temptation to dance.

Some feel that the Turkmen's two-voiced polyphony may have resulted directly from this absence of percussion instruments. But another, perhaps more valid, explanation, is that two-voiced polyphony may represent the earliest Central Asian musical stratum in existence, surviving in Turkmenistan because, although most of the Central Asian territory was overrun by conquerors and thus opened to influence and change, isolated, desert Turkmenistan was rather inaccessible and therefore could continue with its ancient musical culture without much interruption. These ancient features include: 1) the five basic types of instruments; 2) no percussion; 3) two-voiced polyphony; 4) small melodic range (fourth to sixth, for example C-F or C-A); 5) no instrumental ensembles except duets for singer and dutar, gijak and dutar, or two tüydüks playing the same melody; 6) no choirs; 7) no dance music; 8) no popular music; 9) no military band.

Except for Turkmenistan, Central Asia's music throughout shows the same monophonic configuration, types of instruments used, modal structure, complicated rhythms and meters, folksong types, epics, musical form (from the simplest among the Kirgiz to the most complex among the Uzbeks and Tajiks), small ensembles, and military bands.

Musical rhythm follows the verse structures and verse forms of *ghazal, murabba,* and *mukhammas.* The verse form most popular for folk tunes is *barmak* (syllabic), and the more elevated is called *aruz,* utilizing variations in vowel length. The Tajiks and Uzbeks are also fond of *rubai* or *charbait* (aaba) and *taranä* (aaaa) rhyme schemes. The Turkmens utilize the device of parallelism in their poetry.

Musical form includes simple one-, two-, and three-part melodies, rondoforms, long and complicated küys, and shashmaqams. The shashmaqam is the most sophisticated, original musical creation of Central Asia not found in other parts of the Middle East.

All Central Asian republics have the epos, a partly historical, partly legendary-mythical poem, recited to a melody (see Table 15.8). The most important Kirgiz epos is the versified *Manas.* Other famous works are *Oghuz-name* (Turkmen); *Shahname* (Tajik); *Farhad and Shirin* (Uzbek); *Gor-oghli* (Turkmen), *Gurguly* (Tajik), *Goroghli* (Uzbek); *Shahsenim and Garip* (Turkmen), *Shahsenem and Garib* (Uzbek); *Layli and Majnun* (Tajik and Uzbek); *Tahir and Zuhra* (Tajik and Uzbek).

TABLE 15.1

Structure and Range

	Kirgiz	*Kazakh*	*Turkmen*	*Tajik and Uzbek*
Melody structure	ascending descending	descending ascending-descending	recitative	descending ascending-descending
Range	mostly sixth	recitative, small; song, large	recitative, fourth to sixth	up to 2½ octaves in art music
Modal structure	majorlike minorlike pentatonic chromaticized	majorlike minorlike pentatonic (much less) chromaticized	pentachordal majorlike minorlike phrygian	majorlike minorlike chromaticized augmented seconds

[15] Farmer, pp. 610–12.

TABLE 15.2

Musical Form, Rhythm, and Meter

	Kirgiz	Kazakh	Turkmen	Tajik and Uzbek
Musical form	A	A AAAA	A	A
			AAAA + aa AAAB	AABA
		AABC + DEBC + ABCD		
	AB	AB	AaBb AB	ABABA ABABCB (*awj*)
	ABCB ABCD refrains	ABCB	ABAB + abc	ABCB
		refrains	ABCD	*lerma*
Rhythm (according to verse form)	5 + 3	4 + 3	7	7
	4 + 4 + 3	4 + 1 + 3	8	8
		4 + 1 + 3 + 1	11	4 + 5
		3 + 4 + 4; 4 + 3 + 4		11
		(4 + 3) + (4 + 2)		13
				15
				16
			parallelism	professional music
				syncopated rubai or charbait (aaba), taran (aaaa)
			barmak	ghazal
			aruz	murabba
			gazel	mukhammas
			murabba	
			mukhammas	
Meter	$\frac{2}{4}$, $\frac{5}{4}$, $\frac{6}{8}$, $\frac{3}{2}$, $\frac{7}{8}$; changing: $\frac{10}{8} + \frac{9}{8} + \frac{8}{8} + \frac{7}{8} + \frac{8}{8} + \frac{11}{8}$	similar to Kirgiz	$\frac{2}{4}$, $\frac{3}{4}$, $\frac{7}{8}$ and $\frac{2}{4} + \frac{3}{4} + \frac{2}{4} + \frac{3}{8} + \frac{5}{8}$	$\frac{2}{4}$, $\frac{4}{4}$, $\frac{6}{8}$; changing:; $\frac{4}{4} + \frac{3}{4} - \frac{2}{4} + \frac{3}{4} + \frac{5}{4} + \frac{3}{8} + \frac{5}{8} + \frac{3}{4}$

Each of the nationalities has a rich heritage of folk songs. Weddings, funerals, and annual festivals—spring, the New Year—are commemorated in song. There are magical songs to call for rain, medicinal songs, historical songs celebrating events of the past, and songs of social protest. Certain songs of the Kirgiz, Turkmens, and Kazakhs reflect their nomadic background and deal with sheep, horses, camels, and hunting, while those of the Tajiks, and Uzbeks tell of agricultural pursuits—sowing, threshing, harvesting—and craftsmanship—metalworking, silk processing, weaving.

PERFORMERS AND THEIR PRACTICES

There are numerous honorific names for the various musical performers, of which bakhshi, akin, and hafiz are the most widely used. Distinctions are made by the Kirgiz between jïrchïs, primarily singers with enormous repertoires, and akins, professional poets and musician-composers. While the first performer is primarily an interpreter of known music, the second one is a creative poet and composer who sings and plays his own compositions as well as music traditionally handed down. The Kirgiz perform *maktoo* (eulogies), *sanat* and *nasiyat* (didactic pieces), and *kordoo* (songs of social protest). The Kazakhs make the same distinction as the Kirgiz, calling the singer-interpreter änshi or ölengshi, and the poet-composer akin. The Turkmens have, in addition to their revered bakhshi, their instrumental players: dutarchï (dutar player), tüydükchi (tüydük player), and gïjakchï (gïjak player).

The Kirgiz *Manas* is performed by a special manaschï. Other Kirgiz epics are performed by the jïrchï. The Kazakhs call their performer of an epos a jïrshï, the Turkmens call him ozan, the Tajik gurgulugu, and the Uzbek sha'ir (poet and musician). The different terminology for musicians indicates importance and function.

The bakhshi of Turkmenistan, according to some, is heir to the ancient shamanist magician and plays a role, as important as his predecessor did, in the Turkmen culture of today. Although the word bakhshi once designated a scribe who wrote in the old Uyghur alphabet (see also chapter 2), ordinary people called a shaman "bakhshi," and this meaning has been preserved in *bakhsy* (magician) (not *bakhshi*) among the Kirgiz and Kazakh of today. When shamanism was replaced by Islam, and the shaman yielded his place to the mullah, the bakhshi retained only the old music and singing functions, and from then on bakhshi meant "folk singer." He played an enormous role in preserving and disseminating the oral literature. The institution of bakhshi is prehistorical.

One ancient feature of Central Asian music is the playing of flutes by pairs of players facing each other, a custom characteristic only of the early Oghuz as depicted in old representations.[16] Other unusual performance practices also exist, like the Yomud Turkmens' singing, which is frequently interrupted by sudden shouts, spasmodic inhaling with closure of the glottis, sighs, and long sustained notes in a vibrato reminiscent of strings in a low register. The special term applied to this voice projection is *alkïm ses* (singing in a "hoarse voice"). The singing is shrill and the range does not exceed a fourth or a fifth. Outcries and singing in a high register are found among the Kazakhs. In Merv, singing has been heard which did not sound human at all, but resembled some kind of primitive flute. The appoggiatura was taken with a quite unnatural position of the Adam's apple and the vocal cords.[17] Apparently only bakhshis with high tenor voices master this art, the technical term for which is *sekdirmek* (to make hop, skip). Other Turkmen vocal performance practices include *jolotmak* (low, inhuman singing on the syllable *gu*) and *khemlemek* (singing with the mouth closed). Tajik and Uzbek singing is throaty and nasal, characterized by high *tessitura*. The vocal line is melismatic, embellished, and microtonal.

Instrumental performance practices also fascinate the observer. In playing the dutar, the Turkmen musician uses glissando and *itremek* (vibrato) effects as well as *pitimlemek* (snapping the fingers on the soundboard). The Tajik and Uzbek tutiq and ghijjak are both played to produce trembling, wavering, whining sounds.

INSTRUMENTS

The indigenous musical instruments of Central Asia can be divided into stringed instruments, wind instruments, and percussion

---

[16] Viktor Uspensky and Viktor Beliaev, *Turkmenskaia muzyka* (Moscow, Muzykal'nyi Sektor, 1928), pp. 39–40.

[17] Unpublished letters from Uspensky, as reported by Ian Pekker in *V. A. Uspensky* (Moscow, Muzgiz, 1953).

instruments. Five basic instruments appear throughout: 1) the spike fiddle; 2) the long-necked lute; 3) the longitudinal flute; 4) the clarinet; and 5) the ancient and almost obsolete jaw's harp.

Table 15.3 lists the spike fiddle in two forms: the two-stringed fiddle, called qobïz in Kazakhstan, kïyak in Kirgizistan, qobiz in Uzbekistan; and the three-stringed fiddle called gïjak in Turkmenistan, ghïjjak in Tajikistan, and ghijjäk in Uzbekistan. The two-stringed spike fiddle is the older and more primitive form, the three-stringed is the more advanced form. Figure 15.1 and the sketch in Figure 15.3a show that the gijak is extremely small, with a little, round resonating body on a long, round neck. The neck protrudes through the body at the lower end, forming a foot similar to the spike of a European cello. Like a miniature cello, the diminutive instrument is held in a vertical position. The spike is made of metal and the body of gourd, coconut, or wood covered by animal skin which forms the soundboard. Its bow is made of horsehair, and older instruments have even horsehair strings. However, in more modern times, strings are fabricated from silk, and occasionally from gut or metal. The gijak strings are tuned in fourths (E^b—A^b—D^b)

Long-necked lutes like the Kazakh dombïra and the Turkmen, Tajik, and Uzbek dutar are two-stringed instruments with thirteen or more frets. The body of a dutar consists of ten to twelve thin, curved, wooden boards glued together. Its soundboard is a thin wooden piece, sometimes punctured with a few holes. Many instruments are beautifully decorated with inlaid bone. The tuning of the strings can be in unison, a fourth apart, a fifth apart, or an octave apart. Unison or octave tunings, however, are rare; tuning the dutar strings a fourth apart seems to be the oldest procedure.

Longitudinal flutes represented by the Kirgiz sïbïzgï, the Kazakh shoor (choor), the Turkmen tüydük, and the Uzbek quray are flutes blown from above. Clarinets include the Turkmen dilli tüydük, the Tajik qūshnay, and the Uzbek qoshnay plus the balaban, which were usually made of cane or reed, as suggested by the word *nay* (cane). Clarinets are tubes closed at the upper end. Near the upper end there is a small lateral opening or breath hole, which is covered by a vibrating tongue (reed). This end with the vibrating reed is held entirely within the player's mouth. Breathing, there-

TABLE 15.3

Musical Instruments

Instrument	Kirgizistan	Kazakhstan	Turkmenistan	Tajikistan	Uzbekistan
Strings[1]					
violinlike, bowed (nonfretted)	kïyak(2)	qobïz(2)	gïjak(3)	ghïjjak(3, 4)	qobïz(2) ghïjjak(3) violin(4)
lutelike (nonfretted)	komuz(3)	dombïra(2)	dutar(2)	dumbura(k)(2)	dombïra(2)
lutelike (fretted)				dutar(2)	dutar(2)
plectrum (nonfretted)				rubab[2]	rabab(4)[3] rabab(5)[4] rabab(3)[5]
plectrum (fretted)				tanbur(3)	tanbur(3) chartar(4) panjtar(5) shashtar(6)
plectrum or bowed (fretted)					setar(3)
zitherlike, plectrum					qanun
dulcimerlike, 2 sticks				chang	chang
Winds					
flutes (whistle)	choor	duduk	tüydük	nay tutiq	nay tutuq
flutes (longitudinal)		sïbïzghï		nay	quray
flutes (transverse)					nay sibizgha balaban
clarinets			dilli tüydük	qūshnay juftnay	qoshnay balaban
jaw's harps	temir komuz	shan qobïz	gopuz		chäng or chängawuz
oboes	surnay[6]	surnay[6]		surnay[6]	surnay[6]
bass trumpets	karnay[6]	karnay[6]		karnay[6]	karnay[6]

Percussion				
kettledrums	doolbash	dauïlpaz	nägharä[6]	nägharä[6]
drums	dool		tavlak[6]	dol[6]
snared frame drums			daira[6]	daira[6]
castanets			qäyraq	qäyraq
rattles			safail	safail
			zang	zang
other				harmonium

[1] Figures in parentheses indicate number of strings
[2] Pamir
[3] Dulan
[4] Indian
[5] Kashgar
[6] Military orchestra

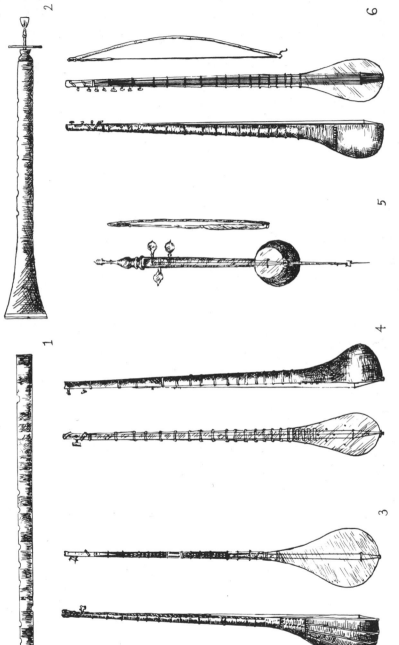

FIGURE 15.3a   Central Asian musical instruments. 1) nay, Uzbek flute; 2) surnay, Uzbek oboe; 3) dutar, two-stringed lute; 4) tanbur, three-stringed lute; 5) ghijjak, three-stringed violin with bow; 6) setar, three-stringed lute with additional sympathetic strings, and bow.

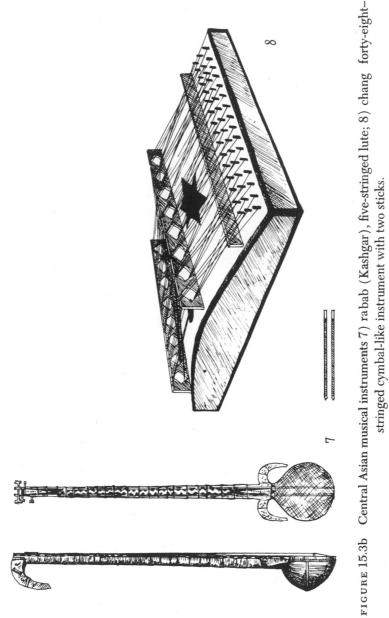

FIGURE 15.3b   Central Asian musical instruments 7) rabab (Kashgar), five-stringed lute; 8) chang forty-eight–stringed cymbal-like instrument with two sticks.

fore, has to be done through the nose alone (for tunings see Tables 15.4 and 15.5).

The jaw's harp (temir komuz, chängawuz), better known under its misnomer "Jew's harp," is a small iron frame in the shape of a horseshoe with an attached elastic strip of metal. When held between the teeth the strip is made to vibrate by a flip of the fingers. By shaping his mouth in different ways, a player may make different partials of the basic tone audible on the jaw's harp. An ancient instrument widely distributed all over the world, it is today generally regarded as a children's toy, but in many parts of Central Asia the jaw's harp is still played by women and young girls. The Turkmens play their gopuz, the Kirgiz their temir komuz, and the Kazakhs their shan qobïz both solo and accompanying their songs.

In addition to these five basic instruments there is a large variety of lutes such as the unfretted, Kirgiz three-stringed komuz, the Tajik two-stringed dombura(k), and the Uzbek two-stringed dombira, all played without the use of a plectrum. A number of rababs (lutes) are fretted or without frets, but they are all played with a plectrum. The unfretted Dulan rabab has four melody strings and ten sympathetic (resonating) strings, the Indian rabab employs five melody strings, and the Kashgar rabab three melody strings. All rababs, and the setar, chartar, panjtar and shashtar have sympathetic strings in addition to melody strings, differentiating them from the tanbur, which has no sympathetic strings. The setar, a fretted three-stringed lute with sympathetic strings, is sounded by a bow and held in the same vertical position as the spike fiddle.

The kalin and the chang are dulcimers played with two sticks or mallets like their counterparts, the Persian *santur,* the Hungarian *cimbalom,* and the German *Hackbrett.* The qanun, popular in many Middle Eastern countries, is a zitherlike instrument played with a plectrum. The Tajik nay and the Uzbek nay and sibizgha are transverse flutes. Like the Uzbek balaban they are played held sideways.

There are many varieties of drums, including the Kirgiz dool, the Tajik tavlak, and the Uzbek dol. The naghärä or nägharä are small Uzbek and Tajik kettledrums played in pairs (see Figure 15.2). The dauïlpaz (doolbash), a Kirgiz kettledrum, is often so small that, attached to a belt, it can be used for hunting calls. The Tajik and Uzbek qäyraq are castanets.

Of special interest is the daira, also known as the chilmanda, childirma, or dapp, a drum of large diameter consisting of a narrow wooden frame and covered with skin only on one side, the edge fitted with snares or metal rings (see Figure 15.2). It is the percussion instrument par excellence in Uzbekistan, where it not only accompanies dancing or ensemble-playing, but also is used as a solo instrument. The rhythmical formulas called *usul* are best expressed by the daira, for which there is an oral notation to represent the most complicated rhythms and meters.[18]

bum	center of drum	
bak (or tak)	rim of drum	
bakko (or tak tak)		
baka (or taka)		
ist	pause	

Two drum sequences in verbal notation:

1. usul thaqil

bum ist baka baka   bum ist baka baka   bakko bum ist
baka baka bum ist   bak ist bak ist   bum ist bum ist
bak ist bum ist   bak ist bak ist

2. ufar thaqil

bakko bakko bak bum bak ist bum bak baka bum bak ist bum ist

In modern musical notation:

1. usul thaqil

2. ufar thaqil

The Uzbeks have many famous masters of the daira with a special gift for rhythm. The variety and intricacy of the rhythmic combina-

[18] Beliaev, *Uzbekskie muzykal'nye instrumenty*, p. 8.

tions are so great that an audience can sit for hours listening to a solo daira without becoming bored.

Another instrument of special importance is the karnay, a bass trumpet of enormous length (see Figure 15.2). Its six-and-a-half to eight-foot length consists of three parts and a mouthpiece fitted into one another for playing and disassembled for transportation. This copper or brass karnay is the only instrument which plays a melodic pattern, a fanfare, independently of other instruments in the military band. This creates occasional polyphony, because the surnays (oboes) play a melody in unison over the accompaniment of one or more drums and kettledrums. Karnays play in pairs. One of their fanfare patterns is this:

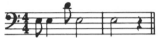

Instrumental ensembles of Central Asia were of two kinds: the "classical" (art-music in Central Asia performed by professional musicians) and the military. Such classical instrumental ensembles in Turkmenistan combined two tüydüks or one dutar and one gïjak, and in Uzbekistan and Tajikistan they consist of one nay, one tanbur, and one daira. For shashmaqam performances, gijak, tanbur, chang, daira, and other instruments were played together. Kirgizistan's and Kazakhstan's stringed and wind instruments were mainly played solo. The Kirgiz temir komuz was sounded in an unusual manner which combined playing a melody in the high register, producing flageolet sounds, and simultaneously making a buzzing sound in the low register, which some scholars think gave one of the earliest forms of polyphony. This form of playing is called khömey (in Tuvin) or özläü (in Bashkir). The Kirgiz choor and temir komuz and the Kazakh sïbïzghï and dombira were played together.

The military ensemble consisted of surnays, karnays, and drums or kettledrums, or both. Two or more surnays played the melody, punctuated by one naghara and/or one or two dairas, while the karnays executed a fanfare whenever the spirit moved the players to do so, without any set pattern.[19] The Bukharan emirate also em-

[19] Beliaev, *Ocherki po istorii muzyki narodov SSSR*, p. 27; *Uzbekskie muzykal'nye instrumenty*, p. 19.

ployed eight European horns and brass nays in its military band,[20] which played at all official occasions and festivals. The ensemble of instruments shown in Figure 15.2 has remained virtually unchanged in three hundred years.[21]

TUNING

The tunings of Central Asian musical instruments are given in Tables 15.4 and 15.5 in Ellis Cents. Ellis Cents designate the exact scientific unit for measuring musical intervals introduced by A. J. Ellis (1814–1890) which has been widely accepted in acoustics and ethnomusicology. The "Cent" is one-hundredth of the well-tempered semitone; thus the semitone equals 100 Cents, and the octave contains 1,200 Cents. The various tones of the chromatic scale are represented, as follows, by the multiples of 100:

0	100	200	300	400	500	600	700	800	900	1000	1100	1200
C	C#	D	D#	E	F	F#	G	G#	A	A#	B	C

This scale can be conveniently used as a basis for diagrams showing the exact position of the other intervals of the Central Asian scales, the Pythagorean chromatic scale, and the scale of the Azerbaijan tar.

Table 15.5 compares the instrumental scales of Central Asian instruments with the equal temperament of the Western world, which divides an octave into twelve equal intervals of 100 Ellis Cents each. If 100 Ellis Cents measure the smallest interval unit in Western music (for example, the semitone c to c# on the piano). Table 15.5 gives graphic proof that not a single Central Asian interval conforms to it. Intervals on the nay (tutiq), for instance, are 12, 19, 28, 39 and 47 percent larger than the interval of the Western equal temperament of 100 Ellis Cents, and the intervals of the dutar, the Indian rabab, the Kashgar rabab, and the setar are 10 percent smaller or 14 percent larger, and conform to the Pythagorean intervals of the Pythagorean chromatic scale.

Tuning of the tanbur, the major instrument for classical music

---

[20] *Ibid.*, p. 22.
[21] Compare the astonishing resemblance to the seventeenth-century painting "The Surrender of Kandahar," reproduced in A. H. Fox Strangways, *The Music of Hindostan* (Oxford, Clarendon Press, 1914), plate 6, facing p. 77.

WINDS

Nay, Tutyq

Sibizgha

Quray

Qoshnay

Surnay

STRINGS

Dutar

Rabab (Kashgar)

Rabab (Dulan)

Setar

Tanbur

TABLE 15.5

Intervals of Central Asian Musical Instruments Compared to Intervals of the Azerbaijan Tar and the Pythagorean Chromatic Scale

Instrument	Interval values (cents)
Equal temperament	100, 100, 100, 100, 100, 100, 100, 100, 100, 100, 100, 100
Winds	
nay, tutyq	112, 119, 128, 139, 147
nay, sibizgha	195, 145, 158, 174, 193, 218, 181
quray	152, 164, 182, 99, 105, 152, 86, 165, 267, 181
qoshnay	152, 164, 182, 204, 231, 231, 267
surnay	152, 164, 182, 204, 231, 231, 129, 138
Strings	
dutar	90, 114, 90, 114, 90, 204, 90, 114, 90, 114, 90
rabab (Dulan)	204, 112, 92, 90, 204, 204, 112, 92, 90, 90
rabab (Indian)	90, 114, 90, 214, 231
rabab (Kashgar)	90, 114, 90, 114, 498
tanbur	204, 139, 155, 155, 204, 139, 204, 155
setar	204, 204, 204, 204, 204, 204
Total intervals of above instruments	90, 112, 152, 195, 204, 231, 294, 316, 343, 359, 408, 498, 597, 645, 672, 702, 792, 814, 841, 854, 865, 906, 933, 996, 1019, 1045, 1062, 1083, 1110, 1200
Azerbaijan tar	90, 24, 90, 24, 66, 24, 90, 24, 90, 90, 90, 24, 90, 90, 24, 90, 90, 24, 90, 90, 114
Pythagorean chromatic scale	90, 114, 90, 114, 90, 114, 90, 90, 114, 90, 90, 114

TABLE 15.6

Microtones of Central Asian Musical Instruments Compared to Microtones of the Ancient Arabic Lute and Western Equal Temperament

(0–600 cents)

Equal temperament: 0 100 200 300 400 500 600

Strings: 90 92 99 112 114 139 155 — 128 129 138 139 147 152 158 — 105 119 145 — 164 181 182 193 195 — 204 218 231 — 267 294 316 343 — 408 498 588

Winds: 316 340 359 435 498 597

Ancient lute: 90 99 145 151 168 — 204 294 303 355 384 — 408 439 462 498 — 588 597

(600–1200 cents)

Equal temperament: 600 700 800 900 1000 1100 1200

Strings: 645 672 702 792 814 841 906 996 1045 1110

Winds: 643 649 666 702 792 801 853 854 865 882 906 933 937 960 996 1019 1062 1083 1086 1095

Ancient lute: 702 792 801 853 882 906 960 996 1086 1095 1141 1147 1164

in Tajikistan and Uzbekistan, deviates considerably from this, especially in the intervals of the third and the sixth (see Table 15.4) which are called "neutral" because they stand between the minor and major thirds and between the minor and major sixths. The minor third is 300 Ellis Cents and the major third is 400 Ellis Cents in equal temperament, but the Pythagorean minor third is 294 Ellis Cents and the major third 408 Ellis Cents. The third of the tanbur measures 343 Ellis Cents, and is thus intermediate for both "equal temperament" and the Pythagorean minor and major thirds. The minor sixth in "equal temperament" is 800 Ellis Cents, the major sixth 900 Ellis Cents, the Pythagorean minor sixth is 792 Ellis Cents, and the Pythagorean major sixth is 906 Ellis Cents, but the neutral sixth of the tanbur is 841 Ellis Cents, again between the minor and major sixths of "equal temperament" and the Pythagorean. For comparison with the indigenous Central Asian instrumental scales, see the scale of the Azerbaijan tar, which is played also in Uzbekistan; although having the semitone of 90 Ellis Cents (Table 15.5), this instrument in addition has minute intervals of 24 Ellis Cents and 66 Ellis Cents.

The tunings of Central Asian instruments are by no means uniform, and though unfretted stringed instruments may be adjusted to any tuning, fretted instruments present great difficulties, and so do wind instruments. It is important to notice that no wind instrument in Tables 15.5 and 15.6 is tuned like the stringed instruments, but some wind instruments such as the quray, qoshnay, and surnay have tunings similar to one another, as do the stringed instruments dutar, rabab, and setar. This disparity prevents strings and winds from playing together, although certain wind instruments and some stringed instruments taken separately might be adjusted to each other; however, the question of performing in ensembles did not arise persistently until the last forty years or so, because solo playing predominated. Such ensemble playing as there had been was limited to two or three instruments. The Turkmens played in parts either on two tüydüks or one dutar and one gïjak, and because the gïjak is unfretted there were no problems in adjusting intervals. The Tajiks and Uzbeks used the classical ensemble of nay, tanbur, and daira, in which only the nay and tanbur clashed, if at all, due to the fact that

they are solo instruments of equal importance. In the 1930s the nay
in Uzbekistan had already been adjusted to the tuning of the tanbur.
It was said that a nay player could always take his neutral intervals
higher or lower by blowing more or less exactly and in this way
produce instead of neutral intervals, major or minor ones. Because
neutral intervals were of such importance in Central Asian tuning,
there was an attempt to include them in a new musical notation.[22]

All intervals of strings and winds can be summarized theoretically
in order to show every existing possibility, regardless of limitations
in individual instruments, but no instrument ever plays them all, and
especially not in chromatic succession. Table 15.6 presents the
familiar musical intervals of the Western world as expressed in
equal temperament. There are only eleven equidistant semitones to
an octave, based on the 100 Ellis Cent unit. The table also shows
that there are twenty-three intervals to an octave in Central Asian
stringed instruments, by no means equidistant, and that there are
thirty-seven intervals that occur in an octave in wind instruments.
The tuning of the ancient lute as described in medieval writings is
also shown,[23] and all possibilities through two octaves are given.
Comparing the tuning of the lute (which shows thirty-four intervals
within an octave) with the Central Asian tunings of winds and
strings, it can be observed that almost any interval of the ancient
lute is paralleled by some Central Asian instrument either by the
winds or strings, and sometimes by both. Table 15.6 reveals how very
far removed Central Asian tuning of intervals is from the equal temperament of the Western world.

MODES

"Mode" is an ambiguous term designating in this book, in addition
to ecclesiastical modes, non-Western scale structures such as maqamat and ragas. In ancient Greece, ethos designated the ethical
character of the various modes (harmoniai), including Dorian,
manly and strong; Phrygian, ecstatic and passionate; Lydian, las-

[22] Viktor Beliaev, *Muzykal'nye instrumenty Uzbekistana*, pp. 32, 125.
[23] Alexander J. Ellis, "Über die Tonleitern verschiedener Völker," *Abhandlung
zur Vergleichenden Musikwissenschaft* (Munich, Drei Masken Verlag, 1922),
p. 18.

civious and feminine; and Mixolydian, mournful. The later ecclesiastical modes or church modes were similarly characterized.

When analyzing the modal structure of Central Asian music, contemporary Soviet Russian authorities divide the modes into those that are 1) majorlike; 2) minorlike; 3) chromaticized; and 4) pentatonic. Modes resembling major scales are called "majorlike," modes resembling minor scales are called "minorlike," and modes both major and minor with chromatic changes are called "chromaticized." To the majorlike modes belong the Ionian and Mixolydian, to the minorlike belong the Aeolian, Dorian, and Phrygian, and to the chromaticized belong the so-called mixed modes (see Table 15.7 for details).

Kirgiz and Kazakh music, as in everything else, has similar modality with a greater share of the pentatonic scale in Kirgiz modality perhaps because of closer proximity to the Chinese (Eastern Turkistan) border. Two different pentatonic scales can appear in one melody. Uzbek and Tajik modality is also similar, but Turkmen is different from both in the number of modes and their range (pentachord).

None of the modes conforms to "equal temperament," but they come closest, some think, to the Pythagorean chromatic scale, especially if played on the tanbur. From the above discussion of instrumental tunings, however, it is clear that the tunings of wind instruments in particular are very different from the Pythagorean tuning, and with them the modes will differ accordingly from instrument to instrument.

Limiting close examination to the tuning of the tanbur alone, it can be found that the Central Asian modal structure does not deviate from the modal structure of the Middle East in general. Comparing the modes of the Tajik-Uzbek subculture with, for example, the contemporary practice of Arabic music in Egypt, Palestine, Syria, and Iraq, it becomes evident that the Central Asian "Ionian," for example, is nothing other than the Arabic *rast*, "Dorian" is *bayati*, "Phrygian" is *segah*, "Mixolydian" is *nawa*, "Aeolian" is *ashiran husseni*, while "major with a flatted second" is *hijaz*, and "major with a flatted second and sixth" is *hijaz kar*.

These modes are called *maqamat* in Arabic and exist all over the

Middle East, often in many versions. A maqam is not only a tone row of specified intervals, but is much more than that. A maqam is a tone row subject to many rules, some of them limitations of range, direction, definite melodic and rhythmic patterns, and even tempo. *Rast*, for instance, is supposed to begin and end on its first note; it is obliged to be moderate and sober in expression, that is, it should have a minimum of trills and embellishments, and all performed at a moderate tempo. *Rast's* "son" *mahur*, however (there is often a "father-son" relationship between maqamat), should begin an octave above the first note and end on the first note; *mahur* should be fast and playful and may have trills and melismatic embellishments. The same relationship exists between *chargah* (the father) and *agam* (the son).

None of the maqamat can be transposed, since with transposition their character changes, and they are known by different terms. A maqam, therefore, is circumscribed and leaves much less room for free improvisation than ecclesiastic modes like Ionian, Dorian, and Phrygian, or Western major or minor scales which are distinguished only by their interval structure. The improvisation in a maqam can be likened to constructing a Greek temple, in which process the styles require specific proportions between columns, capitals, cornices, gables, and friezes. The architect has little latitude for variation, and his inventiveness is restricted to detail work and general harmony;[24] likewise, when a maqam is announced by the performer his audience knows what to expect and looks forward to familiar musical patterns rearranged, elaborated upon, and in the true sense "composed." In the West, not "free improvisation" but "a theme with variations" would be spoken of in this connection. In Iran, there is even a restriction upon modulation into different maqamat.

Contemporary Iranians prefer the term dastgah to maqam. The Turkmen (Iranian) perde is analogous to maqam, although today perde means only "fret" or "tone," but it is still within memory that perde meant also maqam. Baba Jan Ishan reported that his father, a famous gijak player, had known thirty-two different maqamat, but they have now been forgotten.[25]

[24] Curt Sachs, *Rise of Music*, pp. 172–173, as applied to Indian ragas.
[25] Uspensky and Beliaev, p. 57.

Table 15.7
Modes
Note: None of the intervals conform to equal temperament. These Greek names, applied by Russian musicologists to Central Asian modes, only approximately represent the Central Asian modes. The exact Arabic names are given in parentheses. To make comparison easy, all maqamat start from C. The Arabic *rast* and *hijaz kar* start normally on C and are thus the only ones not transposed.

Ionian *(with minor, or major third)*

Hijaz *(with a neutral or minor third)*

Lydian (Jarka)

Hijaz-kar

Motifs

Scale based on motifs   *pentatonic*

SHASHMAQAM—THE "CLASSICAL" MUSIC OF THE UZBEKS AND TAJIKS

The Uzbek and Tajik shasmaqam has preserved a great many original names of maqamat like *rast, segah, dugah, hussein (husayni), chargah, bäyat,* and *shähnaz,* which are still used in all Middle Eastern areas, and especially in the Arabian, Turkish, and Iranian subareas. The musical and linguistic relationship of the terminology, however, is denied by most Soviet students of Central Asian music, and only the form of the shashmaqam is discussed, without reference to the essence of the maqam as a melody type or "leitmotif" as Westerners understand it. The maqam in Tajikistan and Uzbekistan is a large form comprised of many parts. It consists

FIGURE 15.4   Buzruk and rast maqamat transcribed into Western notation by Uspensky.

of two main divisions; the instrumental *mushkulat* (literally, "difficulty"), and the vocal and instrumental *näsr* (literally, "prose," music and text).

The *mushkulat* has the following five basic parts for stringed and wind instruments, with the major role taken by the tanbur: 1) *tasnif* (melody), often called maqam; 2) *tarjeh* (literally, "repetition," in the rhythm of the preceding piece); 3) *gardun* (literally, "heavenly arch"); 4) *mukhammas;* 5) *thaqil* (in slow movement). All the parts of the *mushkulat* with the exception of *gardun* are in rondo form and consist of separate episodes (*khanä*) ending in the unchanging basic theme (*bozquy*). *Täsnif,* a rondo, is called *peshrav* (fellow-traveler, forerunner, leader) and consists of short motifs, each time starting a note higher on the tone row of the mode, and ending in the basic theme. The episodes and the basic theme vary in length in *mukhammas,* but *tarjeh* is similar in form to both *tasnif* and *mukhammas. Gardun* is characterized by a rhythmic formula (*usul*) of irregular and changing meter and is not in rondo form. The attack in the upper register with emotional culmination points, and the return to the lower register for calming down, is characteristic of the Tajik style. All parts of the maqam start in the low register introduction (*däramäd*), rise higher and higher until they reach the climax (*awj*), and then descend again to the low register. The instrumental *mushkulat* serves as an introduction to the vocal *näsr.*

The *näsr,* which has four long vocal parts, is made up of 1) *säräkhbar,* introduction or overture; 2) *tälqin,* a melody for voice; 3) *näsr,* another melody for voice; 4) *ufär,* finale in dance rhythm. Between these main parts of the *näsr, talans,* smaller instrumental pieces, are inserted. They prepare the way for the vocal solos by introducing the maqam (mode). The musical form as described always remains essentially the same, but the text of the maqam can change according to necessity or occasion.

The shashmaqam (six modes) is a cyclic form perfected in the sixteenth century by musicians of Bukhara, Khwarazm, Tashkent, and Farghana. The Bukharan cycle consists of the following six maqamat: *buzruk, rast, nawa, dugah, segah,* and *iraq.* The Khwarazm cycle consists of seven maqamat: *rast, buzruk, dugah, segah, nawa, iraq,* and *panjgah,* which has no vocal part and is therefore considered incomplete. The Farghana-Tashkent cycle is called charmaqam (four modes), and is less strict in style than the Bukharan, has more freedom of melody and rhythm, and, for example, introduces the Kashgar-style folk song of the city dweller. Each of the six-, seven-, or four-maqam compositions has the musical form just described, based on the modal structure of the individual maqam such as "great mode" (*buzruk* or *buzurg*), "true mode" (*rast*), "melodic mode" (*nawa*), "second mode" (*dugah*), "third mode" (*segah*), "from Iraq" (*iraq*). Every one of these maqamat modulates into side maqamat called *shubas* (branches) of the basic modes. *Shuba* is the equivalent of the *sho'ba,* used in Iran to designate branch maqamat (*dastgah*). There are more than twenty side maqamat in the shashmaqam, which make the extensive modulation from maqam to maqam possible.

The extent of the shashmaqam may be judged by the length of one of its parts, such as the *dugah*, which runs to 3,288 bars, not counting repetitions of single sections. The length and duration of the shashmaqam can be compared to a Western opera which lasts several hours. A shashmaqam performance may require two and a half hours, and the music committed to paper covers more than 250 pages. Since the shashmaqam, a classical art form, takes its inspiration from many sources, some Uzbek musicologists believe that the clearest and simplest parts of the maqam are derived from folk songs.[26] In addition to these great instrumental and vocal compositions, there are vocal suites of smaller size with instrumental accompaniment, consisting of the following parts: *sawt, tälqincha(i), kash, karcha, sakinama,* and *ufär.*

MUSICAL NOTATION

The music of Central Asia came down orally from father to son, from teacher to pupil. The rote learning process by repetition of musical phrases was slow, but it would be erroneous to assume that no memory devices of a complex nature were used. Each musical form, meter, mode, melodic pattern, or individual sound had a name. This all added up to hundreds of terms and patterns to be learned, and when mastered served as detailed, memorized instructions. No room was left for doubt about their execution, so that once a musician knew in what maqam and what metrical pattern (*usul*) a composition was to be played, he also knew automatically what melodic patterns to use and what modulations to employ. In the nineteenth century written notation was invented in Khiva using the eighteen frets of the tanbur as point of reference.

Muhammad Rahim, one of the Khivan khans, conceived the desire to have the melodies which are played on the tanbur, dutar, ghijjak, and other instruments written down on paper and put into a book. He ordered Palwan Niyaz to carry out this idea. . . . Uzbek notation was invented in

[26] M. Ashrafi and U. Kon, "Narodnoe muzykal'noe tvorchestvo," *Muzykal'naia kul'tura sovetskogo Uzbekistana* (Tashkent, Gosizdat, UzSSR, 1959), p. 50.

Khwarazm between the years 1873 and 1874. . . . This notation became famous under the name tanbur chiziqi (tanbur line).[27]

Palwan Niyaz Mirza Bashi, the inventor of Khwarazm notation, was born in Khiva and became one of the most eminent musicologists of his time. It is curious to note that Beliaev (Belaiev) attributed this notation, shortly after the Russian scholar Uspensky became aware of it, to the time of 'Ala ad-Din Muhammed Khwarazmshah (r.1200–1220),[28] but Beliaev recently agreed with the date of origin given here by Bakjan Rahman-oghlu.[29]

But although the system was devised by a Central Asian musician, and was therefore close to the mentality of Central Asian performers in general, it did not take hold widely. This can only be explained by the fact that no Middle Eastern musician likes written notation, believing that it represents at best a skeleton, a shadow of the music itself.

A musician does not need notation, because there is more to music than just its outline. The musician learns his music from his teacher to-

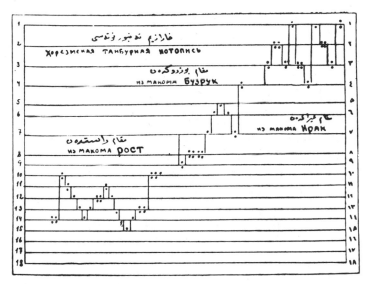

FIGURE 15.5   Khwarazm notation for the tanbur.

[27] Bakjan Rahman-oghlu, "Özbek notasï," *Älängä*, Nos. 3/4 (1928), p. 13.
[28] Uspensky and Beliaev, p. 9.
[29] Beliaev, *Ocherki po istorii muzyki narodov SSSR*, p. 27.

gether with the interpretation. And as for the layman? He would not
even begin to know what the music meant and how to interpret it even
if he knew notation. He would only distort it. No, a musician does not
need notation.[30]

Formerly, there must have been reasons other than artistic conviction for this antipathy to written notation, such as considerations of
social status and professional competition, or religious prohibitions
and fear of corruption by the uninitiated or the unbeliever.[31]

In the study of Central Asian musical culture, it is imperative to
establish definite levels of development in time and space, distinguishing between 1) baselines or archetypes, that is, traditional
characteristics of the "musical style" in the culture area; 2) diffused
traits or complexes borrowed through trade, migration, and the like
and not acquired through continuous and close culture contact as
are musical instruments and musical terminology; and 3) acculturation resulting from close and continuous contact of groups with
different cultures often resulting in similarities of varying degrees in
both interacting cultures. The first two have already been defined; a
discussion of the third follows.

ACCULTURATION

The varying degrees of similarities in acculturation may manifest
themselves in adaptation, acceptance, enculturation (for example,
through schooling when young), and assimilation. Musical adaptation, in acculturation, fits foreign traits and complexes into the
pattern of the indigenous culture. These traits and complexes remain, however, clearly discernible foreign elements, such as the
Middle Eastern modes, melodies, and rhythmic elements used by
Rimsky-Korsakov in an otherwise European symphonic style. Other
examples are the adaptation of a Russian-style melody to an Uzbek
text in contemporary Uzbekistan (see "Hay ischchilar," Table 15.8)
or a modification of a Russian melody in Kirgizistan (see "Katiusha,"
examples 1 and 2).

[30] Ravi Shankar, concerning notation for Indian music, in a personal communication to the author.
[31] Jules Rouanet, "La Musique Arabe," *Encyclopedie de la Musique et Dic-
tionnaire du Conservatoire* (Paris, Librarie Delagrave, 1922), I, 2678.

Musical acceptance involves the taking over of foreign traits and complexes without change, the indigenous music usually continuing to exist side by side with the new foreign music. Acceptance is manifested in Central Asia in the use of European instruments in European-style orchestras playing symphonies and other compositions composed in Europe or in the Western style, and opera houses presenting operas composed in the West or in Western style, while Russian, French, German, or Italian style conservatories teach European music curricula. While European music is being taught and played in Central Asia, indigenous music is also learned and performed. Both Western and local music exist side by side, and the situation is comparable to that in many other culture areas including Turkey, Israel, and Japan where Western music now has a dominant role in musical life.

During enculturation, foreign musical culture is acquired in schools and through hearing recordings and radio broadcasts. This is a process which if given time, could eventually result in a musical synthesis of East and West. Such a course would not cause the abandonment of the one and complete acceptance of the other; however, the prerequisite for this "cultural fusion" would be a compatibility of both cultures.

Assimilation is the replacement of the indigenous culture by a foreign culture, a final phase of acculturation if "cultural fusion" is impossible because of an incompatibility in culture traits. Assimilation results in "cultural loss" or "extinction" of the indigenous musical culture.

Acculturation under Russian rule in Central Asia during the past hundred years is best traced by examining Tashkent as a focal point, because that city was the most important Russian concentration in Central Asia. The Russian section of Tashkent included a considerable group of the military and bureaucratic intelligentsia which took an interest in urban musical life. Music lovers arranged concerts and operatic performances with local Russian talent, often for charitable purposes. Small chamber ensembles were also brought together, and in 1884 a music society was founded which boasted 500 members by the 1890s. Among those on the roster were over eighty singers,

TABLE 15.8 Music Examples

Kirgiz adaptation of the Russian song *Katiusha* (Vinogradov, 1952)

Russian song *Katiusha*

Hay ishchilar (Hey, Workers) by Hamza Hakim Zada Niyaziy. Turkic text
Andante   set to Western or westernized melody.

etc.

From *Gulsara wa Qadir* (excerpt from duet), by T. Sadiqov and R. Gliere
Allegretto

Piano

etc.

From Turkmen two-voiced *mukhammas* for dutar

Dutar

etc.

soloists, and choristers. A symphony orchestra of music-loving army officers was also created.

With the Trans-Caspian Railroad in operation, communication to Samarkand and, later, to Tashkent was greatly facilitated, so that many visiting artists as well as entire opera companies toured the Central Asian cities. In 1889, Tashkent heard the ensemble of Argenev Slaviansky, in 1891 the French operetta of Lassale, in 1894 the Tiflis opera company, and in 1895 and 1899 the Ukrainian ensemble of music and drama. Tashkent welcomed soloists like the fourteen-year-old pianist Kostia Dumchev (1895), and the Czech "king of flutists," Adolf Tershak, who had toured North and South America, Australia, China, and Japan. The Bukharan emir decorated Tershak with a Golden Star. At the beginning of the twentieth century Tashkent became one of the active musical centers of imperial Russia, and boasted of local musical creativity.

In the 1870s and 1880s kapellmeister August Eichhorn, director of the Russian military band, started to publish compositions for dance and "salon music," using Central Asian themes under the titles "A Tashkent Girl" (a polka), "In the Wide Turkistan Plains" (a waltz), "A Moonlit Night in the Ruins of Samarkand," and others. Eichhorn, originally a violinist at the Bol'shoi Theater in Moscow, was also very much interested in indigenous Central Asian melodies. One such tune popular in Bukhara and other cities was later used by Glinka for the "Persian March" in his opera *Ruslan and Ludmila*, which was otherwise written entirely in the style of French grand opera. This folk melody is called in the indigenous tradition "The March of Iskender Khan" (Alexander the Great). Eichhorn was also the first to harmonize Uzbek melodies and publish them.

Others who notated indigenous music were F. V. Lesek and G. I. Gisler, a physician in Tashkent, who wrote a cantata *The Song of Oleg*, which was performed in 1905, and other compositions. But the greatest Russian contribution to the music and musicology of Central Asia was made by V. A. Uspensky (1879–1949), who published a complete Bukharan shashmaqam in 1924. He was a highly qualified musician trained at the Conservatory of St. Petersburg, a distinguished composer, teacher, and musicologist.

The influence of Western music upon the indigenous population is suggested by the late Chaghatay poet Zakir Jan Hal Muhammadoghli Furqat in a poem regarding music and the piano entitled "Näghmä wä näghmägär wä äning äsbabi wä ul näghma ta'siri khususida" (About Music and the Musician and his Instrument, and about the Effect of this Music), 1891. Not only does he express unbounded admiration for Western music, he also issues the fervent prayer that his grandsons will acquire a knowledge of Western music and master it.[32]

Furqat's homage to Western music seems exaggerated and out of tune with what is generally true of Middle Eastern and Indian musicians who are, as a rule, indifferent to Western music and feel that it is too "monotonous" and "simple" to qualify as art, unless they have been trained in it. Their position is understandable if it is realized that Oriental musicians think in terms of melodic line, the dominant force in Middle Eastern music, and not in terms of harmony or polyphony, and vertical texture and structure, as Western musicians do. The more elaborate the embellishments, intervallic finesse, and complex rhythm of the melodic line, the more interesting and satisfying to the Oriental musician.

The years 1914 and 1915 saw the creation of songs of social protest and revolution, many in marchlike rhythms not previously popular in Central Asia. The poet and scholar Abdalrauf Fitrat, author of the study *Ozbek eski zaman musiqasi wä uning tarikhi* (Uzbek Classical Music and Its History), 1927, and the poet and song writer Hamza Hakim Zada Niyaziy wrote such songs as "Turkistan" and "Hay ishchilar," (Hey, Workers!), the second of these to a Western or westernized melody in 3/4 time, *not* usual in Central Asia (see Table 15.8). The emancipation of women was also advocated in song, and there were women who were well known as poets and musicians, like Mairy Shamsudinova (1896–1929) who pressed for the rights of Kazakh women and their equality with men. But women had been musicians even earlier in Turkmenistan, where the famed Kheley Bakhshi traveled all over

[32] Furqat, *Tanlangan asarlar* (Tashkent, Ozbekistan SSR Fanlar Akademiyasi Nashriyati, 1958), pp. 49–52.

Turkmenistan and earned her title by defeating men in stiff musical competition.[33]

When imperial Russia gave way to Soviet Russia the new governmen focused great attention on Central Asia. The area was considered as a show window to the East, a place of tremendous potential interest to its neighbors, China, Iran, and Afghanistan. Considerable efforts were made to enlarge educational facilities and develop music, the state of which was judged to be "backward." This lack of Russian-style development was now ascribed to the "cruel feudal system" and the "capitalist exploitation" of the past.

With great enthusiasm Soviet authorities proceeded to build opera houses, to create symphony orchestras, and to organize large choral ensembles where there had been none before. Musicians no longer customarily received instruction by word of mouth from a single teacher but were trained in conservatories. Nearly all teachers, composers, conductors, and performing artists were imported from European Russia. Within less than twenty years the major cities in the Central Asian republics were provided with music schools, opera and ballet theaters, symphony orchestra, and large choirs.

The Russian musicologist, Uspensky, for example, in the early 1920s taught the basic principles of Western music to students of the Bukharan Eastern Music School (*Sharq Musiqa Maktabi*). Among the subjects of instruction were musical theory, harmony, and orchestration. It was said that "These courses played an important part in the acquisition of polyphonic music by Uzbek young people." [34] This curriculum was gradually expanded until it duplicated the curricula of European conservatories.

In 1918 the National Conservatory of Music and the Russian Opera Theater and Choral Ensembles were established in Tashkent; two years later the Musico-Ethnographic Research Commission started its investigations under the auspices of the Leningrad Conservatory; in 1936 the Composers' Union and the Uzbek Philharmonic Orchestra, with an affiliated Folk Instrument Ensemble, were established. In 1935 the Higher School of Music began operation and was superseded in 1936 by the Tashkent State Conservatory. The reconstruc-

---

[33] Uspensky and Beliaev, p. 38.
[34] Pekker, p. 50.

tion of folk instruments with chromatic and tempered tuning was initiated under Petrosants.[35] Today, many of the composers are Kazakhs, Kirgiz, Tajiks, Turkmens, and Uzbeks, trained either in the conservatories of Moscow, Leningrad, and Kiev, or in Central Asian conservatories run by musicians trained in Western music, who replace the Russian composers of the past generation and officially advocate progress in music along the lines of Western music.

The first Westernized operas for Central Asia were written by the Russian composers Uspensky, S. Vasilenko, and Reinhold M. Gliere. (On the theme of the first original Central Asian opera, see Chapter 14.) The first Central Asian composers and conductors of the Soviet school were the Uzbeks Mukhtar Ashrafi and Talib Sadiq-oghli; others trained in Moscow were Mutal Burkhanov, Minas Leviev, Dani Zakirov, and Akbar. Some of the most famous Central Asian operas utilized local poetic, legendary, and epic materials in attempts to integrate Central Asian melos into a Western conservatively romantic style with soloists, choirs, and symphonic orchestras. A local musician like T. Jalilov collected folk material for the opera *Ortaqlar* (Comrades), which then was rewritten by the Russian Tsvetaev. Muhammadov wrote the music for Kamil Nu"manov Yashin's *Gulsara*, originally entitled *Ichkarida* (In the Women's Quarters), which was later rewritten by Gliere in a romantic style according to concepts of Western music (see Table 15.8). *Farhad and Shirin* was rewritten several times by Uspensky and G. Mushel after the opera had been strongly criticized for its "excessive" local coloration (which disqualified it as an opera); *Layli and Majnun* was written by Sadiq-oghli and Gliere; music for Yashin's *Boran* (The Blizzard) was composed by Ashrafi and Vasilenko as late as 1939.

RESISTANCE TO WESTERNIZATION

Judging by the criticism leveled against them in the Russian press, most Central Asian musicians put up considerable resistance to the

[35] See *Atlas muzykal'nykh instrumentov narodov SSSR, Nos 551–698* (Moscow, Gosudarstvennoe Muzykal'noe Izdatel'stvo, 1963).

innovations brought in via Russia from the West. Such Russian attacks concentrated upon the stubborn preference of Central Asians for traditional music and texts, monophony instead of polyphony and harmony, liking for a throaty manner of singing, and microtonal and heterophonic orchestra music. (Heterophony, which must be distinguished from European polyphony, is a simple type of polyphony involving the use of slightly modified versions of the same melody by two or more performers, for example, in the rendition of a singer and an instrumentalist who adds extra ornamentation to the singer's melody.)

The critics decried local fascination with the maqam musical culture and its glorification and accused Uzbeks and others of intentionally avoiding the composition of Western types of operas or performance of Western ballets. Moscow spokesmen charged local composers with using over 70 percent legendary and epic stories and less than 30 percent Soviet Kolkhoz and factory themes, of not forming professional choruses, and of employing in opera houses, broadcasting studios, or on recital stages, eight traditional Central Asian singers to every singer trained and performing in the Western style. Worst of all, claimed the Russian press, was the persistent contention that only the local people understood the indigenous music. As a result of such an "unsatisfactory" state of affairs in Uzbekistan, T. Muhamadov, chief of the Bureau of Arts, was removed from his job in 1951.

But 1961 still brought mention of "unjustifiable" resistance to the Russian style of musical Westernization. D. Kabalevsky, the composer, writes: "I cannot quite see that the usage of major and minor scales would distort Uzbek national music [or] that the music of East and West runs along parallel lines which never cross." [36] Kabalevsky cannot understand why musicians born into the Soviet age still prefer to be what he calls "half-literate melodists" when they have every opportunity to study Western composition in all its complexities. As late as 1964 it was instructive to see what resistance the Tajiks continued to put up against the encroachments of West-

---

[36] Z. Vartanian, "K dal'neishemu rastsvetu uzbekskoi muzyki," *Sovetskaia muzyka,* VI (1951), pp. 33–39. D. Kabalevsky, "O muzyke Srednei Azii i Kazakhstana: Na poroge rastsveta," *Sovetskaia muzyka,* VI, (1961), 89–90.

ern music when the Tajik composer, Y. Sabzanov, introduced a television program primarily devoted to Beethoven. The program soon had to be discontinued, the program director said, because there was no public interest whatsoever in it. At the same time, protests persist that the melodies of Tajikistan are being "distorted" by foreign influences.[37]

The reason for this "stubbornness" and musical "backwardness" probably lies deeper than mere unwillingness to go along with "modern" trends in Soviet music. The explanation most likely is that one of the major problems of acculturation in music remains the question of compatibility. Two cultures may, through past historical connection or as a result of parallel invention, have a considerable similarity. Or, two cultures may be so different that there are virtually no musical bridges between them, and an individual or a group trying to go over to the new culture has to abandon his own and start over from the beginning. "When two human groups which are in sustained contact have a number of characteristics in common in a particular aspect of culture, exchange of ideas therein will be much more frequent than if the characteristics of those aspects differ markedly from one another." [38]

Of all the differences that can be found between Central Asian and Western music, the most important are the tunings of instruments, with the resulting unequal temperaments, the lack of unison, harmony, and polyphony, and the absence of choirs, orchestras, and notation. Unless all instruments are tuned the same way they produce the most dissonant chords when playing together. This certainly may have been one reason why Central Asia did not have unison, choirs, orchestras, and notation. It is also the reason for practicing heterophony.

To overcome these obstacles to acculturation inherent in the musical traits of the Central Asian culture area, Western traits had to replace them. First, attention was given to changing the tuning. It was proposed in 1933 that a uniform tuning be based upon the system of the tanbur (see Tables 15.4 and 15.5), because it was felt that

---

[37] I. Vyzgo, "Dialektika iskusstva," *Sovetskaia muzyka*, I (1964), 9–16.
[38] Alan P. Merriam, "The Use of Music in the Study of a Problem of Acculturation," *American Anthropologist*, LVII (1955), 28.

tanbur tuning was close enough to Pythagorean tuning, provided neutral intervals were introduced. It was known that flutes with neutral intervals could play both major and minor intervals (in addition to neutral intervals) when over- or underblown, and some, therefore, thought that neutral intervals were a perfect solution to the tuning problem. Pythagorean tuning was close enough to equal temperament to be replaced by it eventually. The largest discrepancy between Pythagorean and equal temperament was 12 Ellis Cents:[39]

Pythagorean
0	90	204	294	408	498	588	702	792	906	996	1110	1200

equal temperament
0	100	200	300	400	500	600	700	800	900	1000	1100	1200
0	+10	−4	+6	+8	−2	+12	+2	−8	+6	−4	−10	0

A notation was also advocated which would include the neutral intervals, and there was even talk about the possibility of dividing the octave into twenty-four equal intervals in order to insure greater accuracy. According to Sufi Ezgi, Turkish musical notation, based on twenty-four unequal intervals of the octave, uses the following signs:

	Sharps	Flats
24 Cents	♯	♭
90 Cents	♯	♭
114 Cents	♯	♭
180 Cents	♯	

Arabic musical notation is based on twenty-four equal intervals of 50 Cents each (since Mikhail Mushaqa and Kamel ibn Kholay, 1888):

C 50 C+ 50 C# 50 D−ᵎ 50 D 50 D+ 50 D# 50 E− 50
E 50 E+ 50 F 50 F+ 50 F# 50 G− 50 G etc.

The plus sign stands for "50 Cents higher" and the minus sign for "50 Cents lower." But although both Turkey and the Arab culture area employ the 24-tone division of an octave, it does not ever seem

[39] Beliaev, *Uzbekskie muzykal'nye instrumenty*, p. 125.

to have been adopted in Central Asia. All Central Asian music is now notated in the Western notation of equal temperament.

With the major obstacles of tuning and notation surmounted, unison, harmony and polyphony, choirs and orchestras, could be introduced to Central Asia, but very soon it was found that the timbre of the traditional instruments did not suit the solo and ensemble purposes of the Soviet era. Strong objections were leveled against the quavering and plaintive tone production of the nay and tanbur. It was felt that this was a carry-over from "feudal times" when Central Asia produced a great deal of "plaintive," "sobbing" music. Though such sounds might have been justified for expression by a once suffering population, they were no longer considered appropriate for the optimistic new socialist world. The "vibrato" on the nay, which was achieved by an almost imperceptible shaking of the head while playing, was said to be rejected by Western flutists who refused to play with local musicians because of it. The same "plaintive," "sighing" and "throbbing" tone production was observed on stringed instruments. The dutar and the tanbur had already been rebuilt for more sonorous sound by the 1930s, and the chang was declared obsolete, with the hope that eventually it would be replaced by the piano. Although almost all other instruments had to be rebuilt to alter both sonority and tuning, the daira and the surnay were considered superior to Western instruments by some Russian musicologists, the daira because of its tradition of complex rhythmical and metrical formulas, and the surnay because of its exceptional tone quality, which was considered superior to the European oboe or English horn, and equal to the sonority of the European trumpet. Quavering and throaty voice production was also condemned as an unwelcome residue from the days of "subjugation."

Few people dared to remark openly that timbre of instruments, voice production, small ensembles, as well as tunings, modality, and musical forms of expression, were a matter of cultural preference and not "backwardness" at all, and existed to a similar degree in many musical culture areas around the Middle East at large and beyond. India, especially, is very proud and specific about performance practices, including šruti (microtones), ragas, and homophony. In defense of microtones an Indian specialist has said: "If the color blue is shown, the whole line will bear imprints of different blues, each almost imperceptibly paler or darker in hue than the one preceding it. There would be blue again with a slight suggestion of the green in it, or with a resemblance to the purple . . . well, we would say that all these blotches of color are the same in so far as they are blue, but they are different nevertheless in tint." [40]

In Central Asia there is still firm resistance to the "streamlining" of music occording to Western, Russian concepts, and a desire lingers to maintain and develop traditional musical traits and complexes in line with the configuration of Central Asian music and not replace them with borrowings from an incompatible musical culture.

J. S.

[40] Mani Sahukar, *The Appeal in Indian Music* (Bombay, Thacker, 1943).

16   Modernizing Architecture, Art, and Town Plans

The most startling architectural result of Russia's conquest of Central Asia was probably the genesis there as in Algeria after the French invasion of the "double city," as it is known in Russian parlance.[1] In creating the original part of this duality, the local population had produced an organically sprouting, somewhat haphazard, city, usually centered either about a palace or a major religious building. Dating from medieval times, the Registan in Samarkand provides an instance of perhaps the most famous central city square in Muslim architecture.

Muslim cities grew up about a citadel as did many cities of Europe in the Middle Ages, and older Central Asian cities served as models for later ones, so that a fundamental continuity preserved the main features of the ancient town even in the nineteenth-century urban concentration. In these traditional towns the central elevation, called *qäl'ä* or *kuhändiz*, in nineteenh-century Bukhara and Khiva was also sometimes named the *ärk* and in Khokand the *qorghan ordäsi* (citadel). This fortress was surrounded by the *shähristan*, or city proper. A third area, the *rabad*, was the suburbs, encircling the *shähristan*. The citadel usually included the ruler's palace, treasury, and prison, with thick, towered walls guarding the whole. The *shähristan*, in certain instances, was planned on a

[1] *"Dvoinoi gorod;"* see B. V. Veimarn, ed., *Arkhitektura respublik Srednei Azii* (Moscow, Gosudarsvennoe Izdatel'stvo Arkhitektury i Gradostroitel'stva, 1951). The best general, introductory bibliography to Muslim architecture in Central Asia is to be found in K. A. C. Creswell's *A Bibliography of the Architecture, Arts and Crafts of Islam* (Cairo, American University Press, 1961), pp. 304–12.

rectangular grid, as in Bukhara, Khiva, or Shahr-i Sabz, with its
major arteries intersecting the center. In other locations, such as
later Bukhara and Samarkand in Timur's time, the cities grew
radially, but sometimes simply followed the local topography in
complete dependence. In the *shāhristan* appeared closed bazaars,
larger mosques, tall minarets, caravansaries, ponds (*hawuz*), the
houses of those close to the khan, officials' and merchants' dwellings, and the richer madrasahs. A long evolution moved the center
of active city life from the original *shāhristans* to the suburbs, which
accommodated a new bazaar area, by the eleventh century,[2] thus
transforming the former suburb into the functional city proper.
Each part of this *shāhristan* and suburb fell into a definite ward
associated with the neighborhood mosque serving that segment of
the population living nearby. At the same time, the *shāhristan* and
later the suburb-turned-*shāhristan* was divided into precincts according to trades or crafts of the inhabitants, and each block contained its own pond. Nineteenth-century Tashkent, shortly before
the Russians came, enclosed within its walls the citadel, main
bazaar, and artisans' quarters, but a sprawling suburb lay virtually
unprotected outside (see Figure 1.3).

Modernizing this old-style Central Asian city according to czarist
ideas took place beginning in 1866 even before large numbers of
Russians began immigrating into Central Asia. Czarist garrisons
from the outset had attached themselves to several of the larger
southern Central Asian cities and, adding a second complete town to
the first, had given the whole a peculiar, split personality. Typical is
Tashkent (see Figures 5.1 and 8.1), where the old city's streets twist
and meander organically, the Russian addition attempting to penetrate its heart in a highly organized and completely regular shape.
Combining radial avenues with intersecting *ringstrasse*, the Russian
sector points like an arrow at the citadel of the old city. This dramatic architectural demonstration of Russian political aims simultaneously mirrors planning derived from nineteenth-century Russian ideas of rational, scientific town layout.[3] Some students of urban

    [2] V. V. Barthold, "A Short History of Turkestan," *Four Studies on the
History of Central Asia* (Leiden, Brill, 1956), I, 24.
    [3] V. A. Lavrov, *Gradostroitel'naia kul'tura Srednei Azii* (Moscow, Gosizdat
Arkhitektury i Gradostroitel'stva, 1950).

development have found particular significance in the placement and arrangement of certain classes of Russian institutions within the "double city:"

Raying outward from the citadel were the streets and boulevards of a new town, moving westward [west of the old city of Samarkand extends the Russian town] was it a coincidence that these boulevards terminated, north and south, in a barracks, [a prison], and a military hospital? [4]

TRADITIONAL AND BORROWED FORMS

Throughout Central Asia the major clusters of building in the Muslim tradition during the nineteenth century continued to develop most strongly in those areas relatively unaffected by the Russian influx: Bukhara, Khiva, and until 1876, Khokand. Palace and mosque buildings rose until 1917, and a number of monuments reveal remarkable tenacity in adhering to a conservative, ancient tradition. This old time style combined a potpourri of influences. In the seventh century, Rabi ibn al-Harith found Buddhist temples in Bukhara, and subsequent work under the Mongol and Turkic dynasties united Persian and Chinese workmanship. Thus, in Central Asia, the Oriental East met the Oriental West head-on, creating an exciting blend of architecture. The thirteenth-century invasion of Chingis Khan wiped out much of the previous Arab culture but left a new mark in the yurt, the round, hide tent adapted from the portable Mongol dwelling. [5]

Though great structures from Karakhanid times (eleventh and twelfth centuries) stand today notably in Uzgan and Bukhara, not until the reign of Timur in the fourteenth and early fifteenth centuries, did Central Asia come architecturally into its own. Mosques, minarets, and palaces, extraordinary mausoleums like the magnificent tomb of Timur himself, the Gur-i Emir with its gadrooned dome rising above glittering facades of ornamented tile, took form. Other outstanding examples are the Bibi Khanim mosque and the Shah-i Zinda complex, monuments considered by many to be comparable in quality and interest to any building in all Islam, including those at Cordova and Isfahan. Timur had brought in many

---

[4] Lewis Mumford, *The City in History* (New York, Harcourt, 1961), p. 390.
[5] Veimarn, p. 122.

builders from Persia and other lands, and it is to the masters of those circles, which produced the glories of Persia, India, Georgia, and Azerbaijan, that Central Asian architecture owes much of its inspiration.

The types of building done on a monumental scale were almost wholly religious, although bazaars, palaces, and private dwellings also share much in common with those of the Middle East and the Transcaucasus. Though certain forms may vary from city to city, throughout Central Asia the style remains quite consistent. In Samarkand, for example, pre-1865 structures embody compatible elements from different areas of Western and even Eastern Turkistan: houses were built in the Bukharan, Khivan, or Kashgar manner according to individual preference. The bases of Central Asian building are similar in their adherence to Muslim origins and forms down to the influx of the Russians. The majority of the late, monumental Muslim works built in Central Asia are in the area bounded by the Amu Darya and Sir Darya. Bukhara and Khiva remain among the most interesting in recent architectural history.

The glories of fifteenth- and sixteenth-century Central Asian arts generally dimmed and declined through the ensuing two centuries, and only at the beginning of the nineteenth century came the resurgence of artistic, architectural, and literary expression which continued actively even after 1865, especially at Khiva and Khokand, but which slowed down in occupied territory. Khiva's khan, Sayyid Muhammad Rahim Bahadur II (see Figure 4.2), in 1871 erected in his capital city, opposite the gate of the old citadel (*kohnäärk*), his monumental madrasah shortly before Russia subdued his domain, but even under the protectorate and at the end of his reign there arose, in 1910, the elegant, 182-foot minaret (Figure 16.1), the highest in Khiva, with a diameter of 22¾ feet at the base, to adorn the corner of the great Islam Hajji (Khoja Islam) madrasah put up in the same year by Islam Hajji (d.1913), the khan's progressive vizir. Both structures were designed and constructed by a Khivan craftsman and builder, Qurban Niyaz Khiwäqiy,[6] who ornamented the late monument to the old tradition

[6] *Istoriia uzbekskoi SSR* (Tashkent, Izdatel'stvo AN UzSSR, 1956), Vol. I, book 2, p. 361.

FIGURE 16.1   The Islam Khoja minaret (1910) in Khiva.

with bands of pink on blue ceramic tile in varied designs, none of which is repeated. Gently curving inward as it rises, the minaret is columnar and terminates in a circular play on the stalactitic cornice of domestic architecture. This denial of decorative repetition is comparable to the facade on the palace of the khan of Khokand (Figure 4.4). Though Islam Hajji's minaret appeared more delicate, it is reminiscent of the powerful, twelfth-century Kälan minaret in Bukhara, which stands 148 feet high and measures 29 feet in diameter at the base.

Also, during Sayyid Muhammad Rahim Bahadur Khan's long tenure (r.1865–1910), substantial additions or alterations were made to existing older structures. Among these efforts, the women's section (*häräm*), which occupied the entire north portion of Khiva's old citadel, was constructed later than elements making up the ensemble such as the audience room (*korinishkhanä*) and the summer mosque (*yazgi mäsjid*), and in 1910 the *häräm's* north wing was also considerably renovated with the use of fired brick.

Samarkand, too, had its special school of architecture in the nineteenth and early twentieth centuries providing a late resurgence of building and design. The modern Samarkand school of local architects and builders (*me'mar* and *chobkar*) alone produced at least thirty-four projects after 1865, sixteen of these in the twentieth century before the Soviet takeover. Mosques, madrasahs, and mansions, in that order, predominated, although new structures such as an ablutions facility (*täharatkhanä*), Jewish synagogue, mausoleum, public bath, and minarets also rose in the period. Moreover, the ancient practice of improving or enlarging aged architectural complexes persisted. Dozens of plasterers and carvers (*gänchkar* or *gilkar*) and wall decorators (*näqqash*) devoted their talents to beautifying buildings like the Yangi Masjid mosque erected at Dahbed in Samarkand oblast as late as 1909. Engaged in the construction of this particular religious center were at least three of the area's builders, Murad, Tura, and Turdy (1857–1921), as well as the wall decorator Nawruz.[7]

[7] W. A. Bulatova and I. I. Notkin, *Khiwaning arkhitektura yadgarlikläri* (Tashkent, Ozbekistan SSR Däwlät Näshriyati, 1963), pp. 30–31. P. Zakhidov, *Samarkandskaia shkola zodchikh. XIX-nachalo XX veka* (Tashkent, Izdatel'stvo "Nauka" Uzbekskoi SSR, 1965), pp. 143–60.

Elsewhere, creative energy in this field had also retained some momentum, and in Tashkent one of the largest Muslim structures erected in the late nineteenth century went up with czarist government support. Surprisingly, for Russian policy then strongly opposed the encouragement of Islam in southern Central Asia, this was a *jum'a mäsjidi* (Friday, or cathedral mosque), rebuilt in 1886 on the plan of the fifteenth-century Khoja Ahrar mosque there which had crumbled into ruin by the eighteenth century. The reconstruction became remarkable, in both forms and technique, for the obvious hand of the Russian engineers who introduced Gothic and Byzantine elements as they participated in rebuilding it.[8]

Though a great tremor of Russian building shook Central Asia under the czarist occupation, the fact that Muslim traditions predominated at least until alien Soviet innovations replaced them with newer Russian forms is amply illustrated by the persistence of standard Muslim architecture such as the tiny Kamal Qazi madrasah which rose at Khokand as late as 1913 (Figure 16.2). Lasting Muslim tradition is evident in its pointed arch and decorated Khokandian tile which ornament the facade, building up to an intricate panel carrying a verse from the Koran on the cornice. But another late building in Bukhara for example, the Bala Hawuz masjid, begun in 1712, was completed as late as 1914, and to its traditional facade finally were added bits of modernity such as fragments of mirrors and painted decorations which supplanted the old, glazed, ceramic decoration.[9]

The word *masjid*, or mosque, which applies to the principal structures of the Muslim world, means "place of the generation," and there are four general types. First, the columned mosque consists of an open court surrounded on four sides by colonnades. Second, on the huge cathedral mosques, of which the medieval Bibi Khanim in Samarkand and the Kälan mosque at Bukhara are outstanding examples, architects usually placed a cupola over the *mihrab*, the Muslim counterpart of the Christian pulpit. A third type of mosque displayed an arch the width of the building on the

[8] G. A. Pugachenkova and Lazar I. Rempel', *Vydaiushchiesia pamiatniki arkhitektury Uzbekistana* (Tashkent, Gosizdat Khudozhestvennoi Literatury UzSSR, 1958), pp. 150–51; *Istoriia uzbekskoi SSR*, Vol. I, book 2, p. 193.
[9] *Istoriia uzbekskoi SSR*, Vol. I, book 2, pp. 360–61.

FIGURE 16.2   Entrance to a twentieth-century madrasah building in
Khokand.

main facade which "opened" the building to the large crowds of
worshipers who gathered here on holy days. Fourth, the smaller,
local neighborhood mosque, common in southern Central Asia and
also found in Kazakh towns such as nineteenth-century Qarqaralinsk,
derived from domestic architecture.

In designing minarets, the tall, slender towers that provide an
elevated platform for men issuing a vocal call to Muslim prayer,
practice depended on local traditions. Though in Arabia minarets
are generally rectangular, in northern Iran they tend to be round
or conical, as do most minarets in Central Asia. The minaret was
used by Central Asian and other architects to enhance the grandeur of the overall composition of the mosque complex. Eight

minarets surround the mosque of Bibi Khanim, while most Central Asian mosques and madrasahs have but two to four, and, as has been seen in Khiva and Bukhara, sometimes only one.

Madrasahs are planned to enclose a court surrounded by a two-story arcade in which are located an auditorium and cells for the faculty and students. The madrasah presents blind outer walls to the streets on three sides, but the main facade usually carries a richly ornamental portal. Mausoleums are numerous and were maintained and repaired regularly. All are rather small, about thirty feet on a side, square or rectangular in outline, and in southern Central Asia always cupolaed.

SECULAR BUILDINGS

Though nineteenth-century religious structures are notable for their persistent adherence to these conservative traditions, the palaces built by Muslim leaders toward the end of the century, being secular structures, relate more closely to the building later attempted under Communism. Such were the suburban villas Shirabuddin, the Sitarä-i Makhi Khassä at Bukhara, and the palace of Khudayar Khan in Khokand, which exhibit a mixture of European taste along with ancient tradition. As a Westerner who saw the Bukharan palaces at the end of the nineteenth century wrote:

There is something sham or theatrical about these buildings. They resemble a cross between a circus or menagerie building and a palace. There is no real style about them, no dignified refinement. . . . They are, as a matter of fact, something like fairy palaces with a confusing multitude of glittering halls with balconies, niches, and recesses, with rooms for the harem to which lead narrow winding staircases and passages, difficult to discover, with arched prayer rooms, with reservoirs and fountains.[10]

Soviet critics of pre-1917 Bukharan and Khivan building agree with the observation concerning artifice in the late Central Asian decor, although for different reasons. "(In the) dwellings of the khans and emirs of Bukhara . . . a rich national tradition was re-

[10] O. Olufsen, *The Second Danish Pamir Expedition. Old and New Architecture in Khiva, Bokhara and Turkestan* (Copenhagen, Gyldendalske Boghandel Nordisk Forlag, 1904), pp. 10, 32.

placed by cheap tinsel and distorted forms of European architecture." [11]

Two forces seem to be at work in creating this late palace architecture. One is the direct influence of the Russians, and through them that of Europe proper. In fact, the local Muslims, fascinated by the novelty of their occupiers' strange utensils, tried to incorporate them into the decoration of their own buildings: "a certain art has been brought to bear upon a frieze of small stucco recesses along the whole top of the building in which are placed about a thousand Russian tea pots, all the same color, as decorative objects." [12]

Love of lavish decoration is the main characteristic of late nineteenth-century Central Asian architects. In the sumptuous palace erected in 1870 for the khan of Khokand (see Figure 4.4), the ornamental facade not once repeats itself in the decorated tile patterns spread all across it. Except for the bases of two towers flanking the entrance, each pattern is different, giving the entire wall a delightfully anarchistic play of patterns. The richly decorated palace exteriors were excelled by the ornamentation of their interiors (Figure 16.3). Here, in the Sitärä-i Makhi Khassä, a typical pre-Soviet interior in the Bukharan style displays a motif, characteristic in Bukhara—a bouquet of flowers in an urn. The design conforms to the Muslim ogee arch with its inverse curves near the apex, and works most effectively within that framework. There is also a tricky sophistication in operation making the Bukharan bouquet, though slightly exaggerated, exactly the reverse of the form used in the Bukharan column and capital. Inverted, the precise outline of that most characteristic of Bukharan structural forms shows clearly.

The old Central Asian tradition was most completely maintained in domestic architecture. Certain characteristics of Uzbek house construction, for example, go back to the time of Alexander the Great. Especially in house and mausoleum construction, the Central Asians have kept alive a tradition of building that dates from the beginnings and sources of Muslim architecture. Dwellings not only derive from a type known in pre-Muslim history, but the form

[11] Veimarn, p. 9.   [12] Olufsen, p. 33.

FIGURE 16.3 A room in the Bukharan palace Sitarä-i Makhi Khassä.

FIGURE 16.4   Large *äywan* (veranda) of a Khivan home.

of the court is also of ancient origin, and has been traced back to the hypostyle court of the Achaemenid Persians.[13]

The dwelling usually consists of an open room between two closed-in rooms on one side of a walled-in court (Figure 16.4). More affluent or prominent families enjoyed the luxury of owning two such houses opposite one another on the same court.

Accommodating to Central Asia's heat, the outstanding feature of the house was the *äywan* (*aivan*), veranda, from which our word "awning" most likely derives.[14] This open room covered with a

[13] E. E. Herzfeld, *Iran in the Ancient East* (London and New York, Oxford University Press, 1941), p. 97; Philip Rawson, "Islamic Architecture," *World Architecture: an Illustrated History* (New York, McGraw-Hill, 1963), p. 447.

[14] Old Persian *apadana* (audience hall); see Herzfeld, p. 94.

roof supported by wooden columns served as the center of the house. Often there were two, the higher *ulugh äywan*, the summer court, and the *ters äywan*, a winter court which stood opposite. In Khiva, the axes of the *äywans* were always strictly oriented north and south, the windows to the north being the main ones of the summer rooms and the winter quarters facing the south. The *äywan* is actually an outdoor living room, and the scarce wood was used in its construction. The supporting column, usually of peach or nut timber, was very richly carved and stood on a wooden or carved marble base (Figure 16.5). The elaborate column is a direct descendant from that of the early Persians and was employed by them for identical purposes.[15] One particular stylistic difference is notable: in Bukhara the column supporting the *äywan* has a star-shaped, polygonal capital which is close in form to the stalactite cornice, whereas that of Khiva teminates in the Persian-like carved bracket. Variations on these two capital types run throughout Soviet Central Asian buildings. The high, awning-like structure was meant to catch any chance breeze and direct it downward on the persons sitting below.

Other cities' dwellings, for example those in Khokand, differed from Khivan residences in that the house was supplied with a facade. The Khivan mosque resembles the house, emphasizing the high central *äywan*, and the mosques, particularly the smaller ones, were related to the dwelling especially by their decoration, as in the Dar Dar Qishlaq mosque (1892) at Zarafshan, Tajik SSR (Figure 16.6).

The Bukharan house, not surprisingly, stresses interior decoration, since the dwellings in the city proper of Bukhara were squeezed within the city's sixteenth-century walls and could not spread out. They are generally similar to houses in Khiva, but under urban pressure rose higher, acquiring in some cases little, second-story rooms called *balakhanä*, while in others, simple skeletal walls insured privacy. Vestibules are usually decorated with interior niches and ornamental stalactites. Inside the house, three walls are decorated, but the fourth is divided into shelves. From below, the stalactite cornices give the appearance of clustered stars. Upon

[15] Herzfeld, p. 33. Compare capitals in Herzfeld's illustration with Figure 16.5 in the present text.

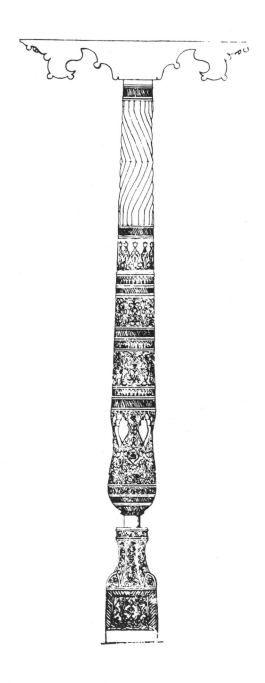

FIGURE 16.5   Carved wooden column from Khiva.

FIGURE 16.6 Decorated ceiling of the mosque at Dar Dar Qishlaq, Tajikistan.

the internal walls of the rooms are placed large hangings sewed
with striking, bold designs in strong reds, yellows, and greens (see
Figure 16.7. Decorated archways surround the windows.

In Farghana, the dwelling had two courts, a garden, vineyard,
and, occasionally, a pool. The house itself consisted of two rooms,
with a third, general room which could be converted into an *äywan*.
In Tashkent, the house generally included one large court, two
rooms, and the *äywan*, usually supported by a single column.

FIGURE 16.7   Decorative wall hanging of Tashkent, collection of A.
Oktay. *Photo by Edward Allworth.*

Samarkand was also rich in private dwellings. Here, many and
various influences were at work, but, in domestic architecture, the
prime achievement of pre-Soviet builders was, as in Bukhara, the
ingenious use of space within the confines of the old city. Multi-
story dwellings were common, and the upper *balakhanä* appeared

here as well. Not only were columns and bases of capitals of the *äywans* intricately carved, but the entire ceiling and walls of many of the rooms were carefully and richly worked, often with consummate skill (Figure 16.8). This pronounced preference for the decorative still predominating in Central Asian architecture around the end of the nineteenth century may have had genuine compatibility with current European fashions in decoration, but the problem has

FIGURE 16.8 Detail from decorative wall hanging of Chimkent, collection of Karl H. Menges.

hardly been touched upon in the literature except in brief, deprecatory remarks from Soviet scholars.[16]

SLAVIC REVIVAL AND ART NOUVEAU

The most popular European fad in turn-of-the-century Europe was *art nouveau*, which had followed, generally, medieval revivalism. This exotic, remarkable style, characterized by free-flowing tendril-like design and curved surface had penetrated into Russia from France and Austria and enjoyed immense popularity there, both in Moscow and St. Petersburg.

Since young Russian architects often found their first commissions in the provinces, contemporary stylistic innovations were carried along by them. The first to be exported to Central Asia was the Slavic Revival, or, as termed by less-exacting Russian scholars, the "pseudo-Russian style." This Russian variant of medieval revivalism

[16] Veimarn, p. 9.

was based upon the complexities of sixteenth-century brick work
such as that used in the mighty Vasili Blazhennyi Cathedral on Red
Square. The best known and most obvious nineteenth-century Russian examples, not of a quality which reflects the most finished of
Russian Slavic Revival architecture, are Sherwood's Historical Mu-

FIGURE 16.9   *Äywan* of an early twentieth-century mansion in Tashkent.

seum (1874–1883) on Red Square and Chichigov's Duma (1892),
now the Lenin Museum.

This Slavic Revival style ran concurrently in Russia with another revival, that of a classicism, which stemmed from baroque

FIGURE 16.10   Sketch for the Tashkent duma building, 1898.

and from mannerist buildings executed at St. Petersburg in the European spirit. The earliest instance of a ricochet of this style into Central Asia became the heavy, incongruous State Bank Building in Tashkent, designed by Vil'gelm S. Geintsel'man in 1875.[17]

Geintsel'man graduated from the Institute of Civil Engineering in St. Petersburg and worked in Turkistan guberniia from about 1875 on. He held a post as chief architect in the governor general's office up until the 1890s, and his approach in art was that of an inveterate eclectic at the end of the century.

Among Russian architects in Central Asia, more interesting, perhaps, was Aleksei Benua, who graduated from the St. Petersburg Academy of Art in 1865 with the degree of "Free Artist." From 1874 to the end of the 1890s, he worked in Tashkent as the architect of the Syr-Darinskaia oblast.[18] One of his contributions is the remarkable project for a building to house the State Duma of Tashkent, which he planned in 1898 with the help of Evgenii P. Dubrovin, who was city architect for Tashkent from 1897 to 1898 (Figure 16.10). Together, the pair of architects had built an exhibition pavilion at Tashkent in 1897.

The Duma project typifies the appearance of the Slavic Revival in Central Asia. Though the style had no immediate meaning for the indigenous population, the immigrating Russians found a wealth

[17] G. A. Pugachenkova, ed., *Arkhitekturnoe nasledie Uzbekistana* (Tashkent, Institut Iskusstvoznaniia Akademii Nauk UzSSR, 1960), p. 227, *n.*1, Fig. 2.
[18] *Ibid.*, p. 230.

of national pride and historical association in this kind of building. It sprang up where the Russians lived, while the Central Asians very likely looked upon it as a fanciful phenomenon, though a few wealthy Central Asians built large, glass-windowed brick mansions emulating such structures as the Tashkent State Bank Building. Arif Khoja Aziz Khoja-oghli and his uncle Said Azim Muhammad Bay, Tashkent merchants dealing with the Russians in the nineteenth century, built such residences. Arif Khoja's had both a Russian and a "Sart" part, the Russian wing roofed in iron, having an entrance from St. Petersburg street complete with doorbell; the large entry hall, reception room, and living room were all outfitted with overstuffed furniture and draperies.

Medieval revivalism was popular among Russian architects in the 1870s and 1880s, but probably much more surprising is the fact that it was attractive to the Muslim khans of Central Asia as well, although for them this represented a continuation of tradition rather than a revival of it. The emir of Bukhara, for example, collected ancient designs for door carvings and wall decorations, and adhered to the old tradition in planning buildings during the last period of the emirate.[19]

However, between the lines of Central Asian history appears the suggestion that the khans and emir at the turn of the century, as well as Muslim rulers elsewhere, were also susceptible to *art nouveau*. It seems quite unlikely that the wealthier members of the Muslim elite were unaware of the style's popularity, and such architectural journals as the Russian *Zodchii* and other illustrated magazines would have been readily available in Turkistan guberniia. In 1902, in fact, *Zodchii* ran an extensive, three-part series on the "Modern Style" (*stil' modern*), as *art nouveau* is termed in Russia. Architects like F. I. Lidval', who accepted the style completely, worked in Central Asia,[20] designing the Azovsko-Donskoi Bank in Tashkent, now the State Bank located on today's Kirov Street.

Moreover, there certainly was good reason why the sinuous line and exotic designs of *art nouveau* which may have had its own links with the East, would have appealed to Muslim aristocrats.

[19] Olufsen, plates xvi–xx and p. 31.
[20] Pugachenkova, p. 248.

Even such an eighteenth-century piece as the mihrab decoration of a mosque at Marghilan (Figure 16.11) shows how compatible were the freely intertwining tendrils of earlier Muslim design and the "tinsel and distorted forms" of current European fashion.[21] *Art nouveau*, which lent itself readily to integration with other national styles as well, combined with the Slavic Revival in Russia to produce a fertile mixture from which were born the Ballet Russe's decor, with Bakst's costumes and Goncharova's sets. The flexibility of *art nouveau* very likely, then, was partly responsible for the flurry of exotic ornament which ripples over the later palaces of Central

FIGURE 16.11   Interior wall decoration in a Marghilan mosque.

Asia, an outburst of enthusiastic decoration which was brought to an abrupt halt by the 1917 revolution.

RUSSIAN USE OF CENTRAL ASIAN STYLES

In a somewhat different mood stands one other late pre-Soviet structure noteworthy for a certain accommodation to local influence. This is the "Khiva" Theater in Tashkent, which had been preceded by an example of assimilated Russian and Central Asian architecture, a Russian orthodox church of 1868, which purportedly was merely decorated by local craftsmen.[22] Because of conservative

[21] Herzfeld, p. 94.
[22] G. N. Chabrov, "Russkie arkhitektory dorevoliutsionnogo Turkestana," in Pugachenkova, p. 227.

Muslim prejudice against profane amusement, the "Khiva" Theater was necessarily built primarily for the enjoyment of the Christian colony. What is remarkable is that the building represents the first all-out adoption of Central Asian forms by a Russian architect. The architect, Georgii M. Svarichevskii, who had graduated in 1895 from the Institute of Civil Engineering at St. Petersburg, arrived shortly afterward in Central Asia, where he developed plans for a railroad. From 1899 to 1905 he served as city architect of Tashkent, and, from 1906 to 1917, during which period the "Khiva" appeared, was the chief czarist architect for the entire Turkistan guberniia. The "Khiva" went up in 1910–1912 but burned in 1916, and was then rebuilt as the "Great Khiva," reportedly incorporating the "monumental forms of the Timurids." [23]

Svarichevskii described his first "Khiva" as follows:

The hall was worked out in Khivan taste. The cornice had 1,400 *shtyky* [bayonets] and as many Kazakh "checkers." About the walls were pictures of Khivan caravans (copies by Akhmatova of Vereshchagin's paintings). The curtain showed a parade on the great square of Khiva. In the foyer were tropical plants, monkeys, and parrots, and on the walls pictures of tropical flora.[24]

These paintings were actually copies from works by N. N. Karazina, not Vasilii V. Vereshchagin. The originals had been rendered for the Winter Palace at St. Petersburg in the 1890s.[25] To find mention of Vereshchagin here, however, is not surprising. In the Russian mind, the name of this late nineteenth-century artist is inseparably associated with the Central Asian battles in which he fought (as at Samarkand), and his multitude of sketches and detailed canvases of the 1860s and 1870s stressing the exotic and the local color of Samarkand.

Both sketches and canvases stimulated and reflected contemporary Russian interest in Central Asian civilization. The "Khiva" theater itself was a later manifestation of czarist Russian interest in the Oriental and picturesque. Svarichevskii, after completing the "Khiva," built the administrative center for the Tashkent Railroad

[23] *Ibid.*, p. 226.
[24] *Ibid.*, p. 246.
[25] *Ibid.*, pp. 246, 247n.10.

Authority and here turned back to a Russian classicism, a reversion which puts his theaters in proper perspective as pleasantly flamboyant freaks among the output of Russian architects in Central Asia, in no way indicating a genuine trend toward the incorporation of local forms into architecture as a whole by pre-Soviet Russian builders.

With the turmoil created by World War I and the Russian revolutions of 1917, large-scale building in Central Asia temporarily came to a standstill.[26] No extensive building or planning was undertaken until the mid-1920s. One early accomplishment of the new era was the Turkistan ASSR Pavilion built in Moscow for the All-Russian Agricultural and Industrial Exhibition of 1923, a major event in the development of Soviet architecture. The structure at the fair occupied a choice site near the entrance and was relatively large. The architect chosen for the commission was not a Central Asian, however, but Fedor O. Shekhtel', the builder of Iaroslavskii Station and the huge *art nouveau* apartment house above Nogin Square in Moscow, which has since been taken over by the Communist Party Central Committee as an official building. That Shekhtel' should have been chosen for the commission points not only to the virtual exclusion of local Central Asian architects from control of large Soviet projects, but back to the compatibility of *art nouveau* and Central Asian decoration. Shekhtel' was the outstanding practitioner of that style in Moscow, and his elegant use of Central Asian forms in the Turkistan ASSR Pavilion is a masterful combination of the two styles.[27]

CONSTRUCTIVISM AND SOCIALIST REALISM TRANSPLANTED

A major figure in Soviet architecture at this time was Aleksei V. Shchussev. In writing of the Agricultural and Industrial Exhibition he stressed current interest in a new architectural style called "Constructivism."[28] This peculiarly Russian phenomenon grew from a culmination of forces at work in Russia prior to the

[26] Maurice Perkins, *City Planning in Soviet Russia* (Chicago, 1953).
[27] K. N. Afanas'ev, ed., *Iz istorii sovetskoi arkhitektury 1917–1925 g.g.* (Moscow, Izdatel'stvo Akademii Nauk SSSR, 1963), pp. 175–78 and illustration No. 226.
[28] *Turkmenskaia pravda*, No. 190 (September 12, 1923).

1917 revolution which stemmed from the theories of the sculptor Vladimir Tatlin, and which were later modified in architecture by European-trained Moisei Ia. Ginzburg and the Vesnin brothers, Leonid, Viktor, and Aleksandr.

With a heavy emphasis upon function and rational planning, this style was characterized by an almost complete lack of decoration and, at its best, a fine integration of blocklike, geometric forms. The buildings often incorporated the ribbon window, derived from Le Corbusier, and were usually finished in stucco painted either neutral gray or yellow, or, if cement were employed, left unpainted.

Constructivism was seized upon by enthusiastic young architects who found in the style a solution to their problems of building for a socialist state. They applied it widely to early projects until forced to desist by a return to neo-classicism in the mid-1930s. It was only natural that the earliest Soviet buildings in Central Asia should be planned in the Constructivist style. One of the more extensive projects undertaken during the Constructivist period was the design of a government complex for Alma Ata by Ginzburg himself. This massive monument reflects Ginzburg's preference for certain aspects of Le Corbusier's style, although these are used intelligently and modified to fit the conditions required by socialist theory. As he described the building, "[It was done with] a simple, laconic means corresponding to the specific topography of Alma Ata as well as peculiarities [climate, etc.] of the Kazakh ASSR. This was one of my first experiments in the building of a new image for Soviet architecture." [29]

Because of later Soviet attacks on Constructivism and its official suppression in the 1930s, little is known of the extent of building in that style, although it was probably considerable, given the resources at hand and in light of such major works as Ginzburg's Alma Ata project. Building during this period tended to be mainly administrative or associated with industry. Common structures were those like G. Gerasimov's Telegraph Center for Alma Ata (Figure 16.12), school buildings, and workers' clubs. Local architectural work by Central Asians themselves had practically stopped between

[29] M. Ia. Ginzburg, "Tvorcheskii otchet," *Arkhitektura SSSR*, No. 5 (1935) p. 8.

1918 and about 1928 except for small-scale, individual building, but this hiatus ended when the first Five Year Plan saw the rise of Constructivism. Most of the building in this manner would have gone into cities which were expanding with the fast-paced urbanization resulting from the Soviets' heavy concentration on industrialization in this area. Entire new cities for Frunze, founded as Pishpek by the Khokand khanate in 1846, and Dushanbe (Stalinabad), a mere village up to 1929, were planned, but most projects sketched out for new cities during the Constructivist period failed to go into operation until the 1930s, and by then sharp changes in Soviet theories of planning and architecture brought about their revision. The modular

FIGURE 16.12 Alma Ata telegraph office building.

town plan for Przheval'sk in Kirgizistan is typical of most Soviet projects of the 1930s (Figure 16.12).

As in Tashkent and Samarkand, pre-Soviet Russian planners had no compunction about laying out rigidly functional and unimaginative grids or radial plans for new towns which pushed insistently against the old cities of Muslim Central Asia. In the later era, if anything, Soviet planners paid even less attention to the living habits of the local population, and for this reason have been criticized for their unimaginative town layouts, but in fairness the enormous scale and rush of events in the new undertakings should be taken into account. In Kazakhstan alone, ten entirely new urban centers were projected along with one hundred settlements "of the city type." Given the huge volume of work to be done, apparently there were simply not enough qualified planners to accomplish it, and a great deal seemingly had to be left to quickly trained, barely qualified draftsmen.

Basic requirements, from the Soviet point of view, were that the plan be regular, usually symmetrical, functional, and that the long, straight streets be lined with greenery. Astronomical numbers of

FIGURE 16.13   Perspective of a plan for Przheval'sk, Kirgizistan.

trees were transplanted to line the streets, but although they serve to provide shade and make the towns more pleasant to live in, the military regimentation of this vegetation into rows and regular spacing imparts a stultifying monotony to these inhumanly scaled, often meaninglessly wide, unvarying arteries which, to a Western or even Central Asian eye, disfigure so many Russian cities. With Russian designers doing the work, in this regard Central Asian cities have fared no better than those of the Soviet Union in general. The practice of shaping Soviet cities with a pretentious, neoclassic style was only exceeded by a return, in the 1930s, to a ponderous, anachronistic, and often vulgar revival of classicism in architecture. The result of inflicting this "style," which Soviet functionaries called Socialist Realist architecture, on Central Asia to supersede the Constructivist style, makes the work of the Constructivists stand out as a rational, well-organized movement, a true "new image for Soviet architecture." [30] Socialist Realist building in Central Asia has left some of the most appropriate monuments to nonart which Communist Party architects could have devised.

The Socialist Realist attitude in art and architecture persisted down to Stalin's death in 1953. World War II had caused another break in Central Asian building, but 1946 saw Socialist Realism come back with renewed vigor and resources. It culminated, in Moscow, in the unattractive, high-rise buildings of the late 1940s which still stand as the definitive symbol of Stalin's pernicious influence on Soviet arts.

In applying the Socialist Realist, neoclassic style to Central Asia in the 1930s, Soviet architects faced the same problem which they had found in the Caucasus: how to deal with a strong tradition of local forms. This tradition was nowhere stronger than in populous Uzbekistan. The solution seemed simple: to graft the more obvious elements of Central Asia's forms onto neoclassic building.

Using this method, one imaginative early project intended for Kirgizistan was designed by V. Veriuzhskii to be a museum in Pishpek (Frunze) (Figure 16.14). Since, except for tombs, the Kirgiz had developed little architecture of their own beyond the yurt, Veriuzhskii seized upon this form and expanded it in scale to a huge, carousel-like pavilion, completely encrusted with decoration deriving from Kirgiz embroidery patterns. For an entrance, he borrowed the Uzbek and Tajik *äywan*, supported here by four Khivan columns *in antis*, and framed by a somewhat doric portico. Because it does not subordinate local forms to the accepted Russian mode in building, this fanciful project constitutes an example of what Soviet critics today would call "the uncritical use of local forms." [31] Never built, the plan remains a charming curiosity and perhaps the only Russian

[30] *Ibid.*, p. 8.
[31] T. S. Basenov, "Arkhitektura kazakhskoi SSR," in Veimarn, p. 77.

FIGURE 16.14   Plan for a Kirgiz museum.

project to emerge from Central Asia which exhibits a courageous, creative adaptation of local forms.

Although lacking restraint in transplanting Russian architecture to Central Asia, the Russians soon expressed a true respect and admiration for the older monuments of Central Asian architecture. Russian funds had gone into the restoration of local monuments as early as 1870, when the Gur-i Emir's restoration, however unscientific and haphazard, was undertaken. Khivan restorations to a madrasah have been criticized by Western visitors for replacing missing glazed tiles (*kashi*) with plaster imitations.[32] Except for the awkward rebuilding seen in the case of the Khoja Ahrar mosque at Tashkent, in the 1880s, large-scale, organized restoration of Central Asian monuments began mainly after 1917, and has been as carefully and consistently pursued there as in Russia proper where, like Samarkand or Khiva, the religious significance of the monuments is ignored today and only their value as examples of the architect's and decorator's art provide a claim to Soviet attention.

[32] Olufsen, p. 15.

In repairing, studying, and using local forms, the task of the Russians was immensely simplified by the fact that the long craft tradition handed down from father to son for so many centuries was still very much alive in Central Asia after 1917. State funds were supplied to support the work of artisans in workshops and their services were used not only in restoration but in contemporary Soviet constructions.

DECORATIVE ART, ARCHITECTURE, AND IDEOLOGY

A major, typical monument demonstrating the handiwork of many local decorators as well as other forces at work in recent Central Asian architecture is the State Academic Theater named for Ali Shir Nawaiy in Tashkent. Artistic considerations aside, a rather sinister meaning for Central Asia under Russian rule can be read in the information that this huge building was completed in 1948 by the Russian architect Shchussev (d.1949), who received the Stalin Prize, First Class, for its design; who, when living, was regarded in the USSR as the major figure in Socialist Realist architecture; and who numbered among his enormous output the plans for the city of Stalingrad (Volgograd) and the infamous Liubianka NKVD building on Dzerzhinskii Square in Moscow, as well as the mausoleum of V. I. Lenin on Red Square. His approach to designing what may be the major new building in Tashkent shows clearly that fifty years of practice had not altered his heavy-handed eclecticism nor tempered his borrowings with the slightest touch of originality.

A zealous archaeologist, Shchussev had begun early as a Slavic Revivalist by plagiarizing the forms of ancient Russian architecture wholesale. He jammed these together in the Kazan station, begun before and finished after the Bolshevik uprising, a building which constitutes a three-dimensional catalog to the unaltered forms of architecture from medieval Pskov and Novgorod. Shchussev knew Central Asian architecture personally, for he had traveled to that part of the Russian empire before the 1917 revolutions, and there had drawn and studied the early monuments.

The Ali Shir Nawaiy Theater is frosted with details and ornament of Central Asian origin, although it has the same petrified symmetry (Figure 16.15) as Shchussev's earlier Hotel Moskva on Manezh

FIGURE 16.15   Ali Shir Nawaiy State Opera and Ballet Theater, Tashkent. *Photo by Edward Allworth.*

Square in Moscow. In plan, the theater building represents a normal, Soviet show house chopped up into vestibule, lobby, auditorium, stage and service areas (Figure 16.16). In the facade of the
theater are combined such dissonances as neoclassic orders sur-
charged with local elements; a stalactite cornice of Muslim origin is
plastered immediately over the neoclassic entablature, giving the
building the appearance of a "double exposure." Externally, the
Ali Shir Nawaiy Theater evokes the image of a small-town "First
National Bank" decked out in the frivolities of Hollywood's Moorish
"East." Its already cluttered facade was to have been adorned with

FIGURE 16.16   Floor plan of the Ali Shir Nawaiy Theater.

gigantic sculptures, rather than be borrowed from the Muslim tradition, and topped off with the modest towers it now carries.[33]

Originally conceived even larger than at present, the building was meant to seat 2,300 spectators. Though it is the main opera house serving a city of over one million, the scale was cut down to accommodate an audience of 1,500 in the final building, a fact lamented by some Soviet architect-critics of the theater.

The presence of such a monumental opera house in Tashkent seems, at first glance, to have arisen from the traditional Russian love of theater and ballet, but its presence here has further significance. Not only are drama, opera, and ballet important vehicles for directly disseminating Communist propaganda to the local population, and the theater itself a showplace for visiting Asians and Africans, but the theater building can serve antireligious purposes. For, even as early missionaries in converted Russia forwarded Christianity by making pagan dieties into Christian saints, the Soviet leaders employed familiar architectural forms to sanction the intrusion of the secular West and to make Communist atheism more palatable. Marrying forms in composites such as mosque-styled theaters and madrasah-like workers' clubs must have been intended to play a part in reducing the impact of westernization, giving to the unwary the impression that the Muslim civilization there was not disappearing, though it was changing by merger, thus preparing it, through a long antireligious campaign still going on, to break traditional ties with local forms of architecture connected with religion and identified by their religious nature.

In decorating these buildings, the Soviet Russian designer often exploited an old Muslim practice of ornamenting the walls of religious buildings with inscriptions from the Koran. Adapting this device, Socialist Realist artists applied to the walls of their secular structures slogans and quotations from the Marxian "Koran" and the words of the new ideology's prophets, Lenin and Stalin. Thus, with rather frightening simplicity, in architecture and art Central Asian tradition became an ideological weapon against itself in the continuing attempt to convert local people to atheism and socialism.

[33] G. B. Barkhin, *Arkhitektura teatra* (Moscow, Izdatel'stvo Akademii Arkhitektury, 1947), p. 135 and figs. 207, 208, and 209.

The decorating of the Ali Shir Nawaiy Theater illustrated the procedure of joining traditional Muslim forms to present-day anti-religious institutions. Each of the various lobbies grouped about the auditorium was named for a region and was given over to an artist from that area to decorate in a manner peculiar to the region. A Khiva Hall, a Samarkand Hall, and, among others and most interesting, the Bukhara Hall, carry such special characteristics (Figure 16.17).

Usta (master) Shirin Murad-oghli, a noted stucco (*gänch*) worker from Bukhara, decorated the Bukhara Hall. He had won fame as early as 1912–1914 for his White Hall in the Sitarä-i Makhi Khassä, a palace completed in 1917 for Bukharan Emir Sayyid Mir Muhammad Alim (1910–1920).[34] In addition to being a skilled stucco worker, Murad-oghli was also a master house designer and ornamenter who knew thoroughly such ancient theories as those of stalactite projection. As a result of his craft and his willingness to be employed by the Soviet authorities, the Uzbek SSR Academy of Sciences later made him a member, and he also received recognition in the form of a Stalin prize.

The Bukhara Hall in the Ali Shir Nawaiy Theater represents some manifestations of a true continuation in the Muslim tradition of interior design. Murad-oghli's efforts there provide a fine example of the elaborate Bukharan wall ornamentation. It is, in addition, left stark white, as was his hall in the emir's palace. Bukharan columns are used in the theater as dividers between the panels, and even the chandeliers present a variant on the crystalline Bukharan capital. Design of the panels follows that of the traditional Bukharan urn with bouquet (compare Figure 16.3).

In more modest structures devoted not to public affairs but to the homely pleasures of the main segment of the Central Asian populace, the farmers, most features of the past art have been attempted in quite recent times. A "rest house" built for Tajik kolkhozniks in 1948, for example (Figure 16.18), imitates the traditional tea house (*chaykhanä*) so popular and important in Central Asian life. This

---

[34] Veimarn, p. 38; Pugachenkova and Rempel', p. 64; B. N. Zasypkin, *Arkhitektura Srednei Azii* (Moscow, Izdatel'stvo Akademii Arkhitektury, 1948), p. 152.

FIGURE 16.17   Bukhara Hall in the Ali Shir Nawaiy Theater.

Tajik example reveals the flamboyant mixing of colored tiles of contrasting hues and patterns, the arched mezzanine sections, the intricately painted ceiling and upper wall spaces, and other features. Despite the desire to continue local art into the present, the execution of the intention falls short of the old standards in every respect.

Another recent building which embodies some Central Asian tra-

FIGURE 16.18   Room in a kolkhoz "rest home," Tajikistan. *Sovfoto.*

ditional forms is the "Rodina" cinema built in 1939 at Tashkent and
designed by A. Ṣidorov and N. Timofeev, both Russian architects.
The curious decision to apply to the motion-picture house a Russian
name for which a perfectly good Uzbek counterpart in current
usage, yurt, could have been chosen underscores the cosmopolitan
nature of Tashkent's population as well as the alien character of the
film and movie emporium. The theater building itself is a conglomeration of miscellaneous Uzbek architectural elements including a
main entrance developed as a colossal *äywan* with five, gross columns imitating the Bukharan style, which are apparently cast from
concrete, unlike true Bukharan columns delicately carved from local hardwood.

Thus, in the 1930s and 1940s Central Asian Muslim traditions
were still flourishing where the practice of decoration was concerned, but Central Asian craftsmen were rarely entrusted with
major building projects. For example, the round, open Uzbek pavilion for the Moscow Agricultural Fair of 1939 was built in an over-
decorated Uzbek form by S. Populanov, a Russian architect.

Apartment houses and administrative buildings built during the 1930s and 1940s differed very little from those erected in Russia proper in the same period. Having little ideological significance except for the aspects of enforced collectivity accompanied by lessened individual privacy, the majority of these secondary structures were turned out in a characterless, neoclassic Russian style. With entire new cities going up, the Russians had a magnificent opportunity

FIGURE 16.19   Apartment house in Krasnovodsk, Turkmenistan.

to employ the newest and most radical as well as the most rational building techniques and to develop an esthetically pleasing style. Yet, a typical Central Asian city dwelling block for Krasnovodsk (Figure 16.19) has been produced in the same banal style as standard Moscow structures such as Stamo's pedestrian No. 19/21 Chaikovsky Street, an apartment house which now serves as the American Embassy. Central Asian and Russian multiple-family dwellings

resemble one another right up to the imitation escorialesque obe-
lisks which punctuate the roof line. Despite the extraordinary vari-
ance in climate, way of life, and habitat of areas, the only fundamental difference between the two styles is that in Central Asia
apartment houses are limited to about three stories because of the
prevalence of earthquakes, one of which demolished Ashkhabad,
capital of Turkmenistan, as recently as October 6, 1948.

FIGURE 16.20   Tomb of Jambil Jabay-uli, Kazakhstan. *Sovfoto*.

Notwithstanding these contemporary Russian housing developments planted in Central Asia, recent visitors to cities there have
discovered that another wave of private, domestic construction initiated by local inhabitants is now hemming in the outskirts of urban
centers, promising to change the shape of the existing plans once
more, obscuring or swallowing up the sharp outlines of the geometri-
cal Russian quarters, and adding a present-day suburb of small
houses and gardens in the old, southern Central Asian fashion
around the dual town which continues to survive wherever any
great number of Russians and Ukrainians has colonized the area.

This new version of the old tendency has been particularly notable at Tashkent, but in Khiva (Khwarazm) today the relatively small number of Russians has not produced such a striking division in the city, and therefore has most likely failed to stimulate the suburban migration seen elsewhere. The profile of Tashkent, for this and other reasons, is becoming quite unlike its outlines of fifty years ago (compare Figure 8.1 and Figure 16.21).

Another legacy from pre-Muslim and Muslim style is the mausoleum. This relatively small, cupolaed building which repeatedly has been met all over Central Asia from at least the tenth century A.D. up to the present, can be seen in the mausoleum of Sovietized Kazakh folk bard Jambil Jabay-uli (1846–1945). The tomb erected outside Alma Ata by I. Belotserkovskii is a faithful, if clumsy, copy of an ancient tradition which goes back as far as the Sassanian fire temples of antiquity (Fig. 16.20).[35]

THE DECLINE OF PAINTING AND CALLIGRAPHY
AND THE RISE OF THE "GLASS BOX"

In addition to the generally disastrous effect which Socialist Realist architecture has had upon building in Central Asia, two further artistic genres suffered severely, as examples regularly show. U. Tansykbaev's 1927 "Portrait of an Uzbek" (Figure 16.22) seems to be an awkward, unprofessional attempt on the part of a new Central Asian artist to conform to Soviet principles of portraiture. The background displays a pathetic recollection of I. I. Shishkin, the nineteenth-century Russian landscapist, and the figure itself is a sad caricature of a skull-capped nationality "type," painted in the vaguely impressionistic pattern of the Socialist Realist manner. This modern Soviet painting is a feeble descendant of Russian art and a pale successor to the great tradition of Central Asian miniature painting.

Calligraphy, miniature painting, and the illumination of manuscripts continued in Central Asia under the czars, but lithography (see Figure 14.2), introduced to local use by the Khivan khan in the third quarter of the nineteenth century, and other innovations, to-

[35] M. M. Mendikulov, "Pamiatniki arkhitektury Kazakhstana s konisheskimi ili piramidal'nymi kupolami," in Veimarn, p. 229f.

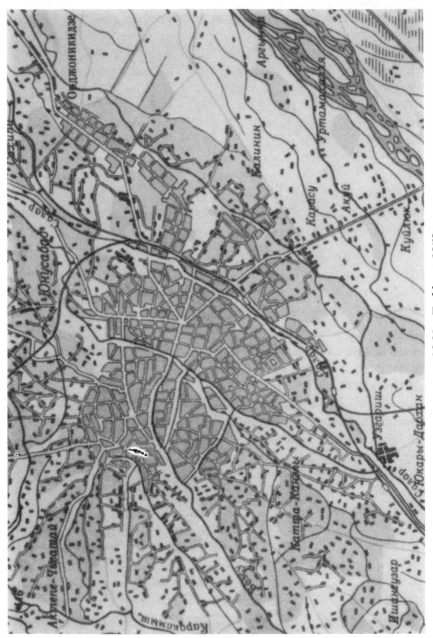

FIGURE 16.21   Tashkent, 1958.

FIGURE 16.22   Painting, "Portrait of an Uzbek."

FIGURE 16.23   Ornamental plate (1936) with head of Stalin.

gether with the gradual disappearance of wealthy patrons, suffocated these great arts. Even so, older nineteenth-century craftsmen like Ahmad Mahdum Kalla (Dānish) carried on this activity to the end of their lives. A young contemporary of Ahmad Mahdum at Bukhara has recalled that:

[Ahmad Mahdum] was a superb calligrapher and fine graphic artist. Income from this craft kept him well provided for. He not only rendered manuscript illumination and vignetted with great mastery, but was also a remarkable artist and made very lively sketches. All of Ahmad Mahdum's art was especially well applied in manuscripts of *Layli and Majnun, Yusuf and Zulayha,* and other lyric poems. I saw a copy of the manuscript of *Yusuf and Zulayha* done in Ahmad Mahdum's hand and even decorated with miniatures, illumination, and headings by him. The book was sold then for a value equal to the cost of over 10,000 pounds of wheat.[36]

In "modernizing" the older tradition of miniature painting the Socialist Realists mistreated it as much as they had twisted Central

[36] Sadriddin Aini, *Vospominaniia* (Moscow-Leningrad, Izdatel'stvo Akademii Nauk SSSR, 1960), pp. 405–6.

Asian architecture. The walls of many public buildings were plastered over and painted in a style which bears the superficial outlines of the art of the miniature, but, as in other such adaptations, is executed on such a gigantic scale as to contradict its source and render the whole pointless. The damage done to the decorative arts under Stalin and his successors may be epitomized by vulgarities such as plates decorated in 1936 and at other times with faces of Soviet leaders (Figure 16.23). In considering this thorough negation of art, no connection can be found to the fine, old ornamented pottery of Samarkand and Khwarazm (Khiva).

In architecture, with the era of Khrushchev and his successors, the neo-classic idiom has been abandoned by Soviet specialists, who look westward for a solution to their architectural dilemma. A new attitude is evidenced in buildings such as the International Post Office and the huge Palace of Congresses in Moscow. While the Palace is in some respects impressive, such structures seem to suggest that Soviet building has adopted the "Glass Box," embracing the materials and superficial appearance of the International Style but few of its principles.

Since all major influence in monumental building must now come to Khiva, Frunze, or Alma Ata from Russia, presumably this latest Moscow variety of construction will make its appearance in Central Asia before long. Russia, in becoming Central Asia's channel to the West, has affected not only the fate of local architecture and art but the developments which have occurred in literature, with its recent emphasis upon alien forms like the novel, novelette, and short story, or in music with the adoption, via Moscow and St. Petersburg conservatories, of the piano and French horn.

Beyond arts and letters, moreover, similar incursions into politics and economics, where Marxism, Communism, and planning try to replace Islam and free enterprise, and into society where the collective rides against the individual, have put the people in the grip of a great dialectic. Like the "Glass Box," there may be and have been innovations which do and did promise change and even advancement to the area. Probably more significant, many old values and features of their civilization continue, and Central Asians are reconciling some of the ancient with aspects of the modern on the way to a new life which, despite the aberrations of 100 years of colonial rule, may offer them once again the opportunity for truly independent expression in architecture and all other fields.

A. S.

17

The New
Central Asians

By 1967 many Central Asians had experienced the Soviet version
of Russian rule for close to half a century. The impact upon them
drastically altered many life patterns and most institutions. The
Soviet regime openly worked toward creating a uniform citizenry,
modeled on Russians, throughout the Asian parts of the USSR.
Great economic and political changes accompanied the social re-
modeling. Therefore, in the 1970s and 1980s it is appropriate to ask
how much of their sense of distinctiveness the indigenous people of
Central Asia have retained. Toward the end of the twentieth century, what attitudes characterized those feelings of Central Asianness?
Both the subjective expression of attitudes found in writings or
conversations and objective facts quantified in statistics eventually
should give some provocative answers to these queries.

Innovations in architecture and other arts had started to enliven
the Central Asian scene in the 1920s, but they lapsed into conformity before the late 1930s. In urban areas, artistic and intellectual
life remained a shambles for many years following the period of
devastating political repression that culminated in 1938. In an area
renowned for artistically defined space and horizontal, linear con-

In this chapter, "Central Asians" generalizes a corporate identity embracing many
ethnic subgroups of the region, including Dungans, Karakalpaks, Kazakhs, Kirgiz,
Tajiks, Turkmens, Uyghurs, Uzbeks and a few smaller entities. The term "subgroup"
refers to any one of these. "Sublanguage" designates one of their tongues. "Subregion"
refers to the autonomous Soviet socialist republic (ASSR), Soviet socialist republic (SSR),
oblast', *raion*, or other territory within the region where a subgroup lives somewhat
compactly.

struction, state builders now cemented over huge, sterile town squares. Official taste fringed them mainly with assertively vertical, cold new buildings and monuments usually erected in styles borrowed from outside. Even after that, monoliths of officially inspired clichés or ideological formulas obstructed moves toward advancing productive indigenous cultural and social activity. They mainly glorified the Communist Party of the Soviet Union (CPSU) and its policies or the ideology termed "Marxism-Leninism-Stalinism" by Soviet spokesmen throughout Central Asian cities, as in other parts of the USSR. That phase in regional history continued through the 1950s.

Notwithstanding stubborn official resistance to progress, an important trend became increasingly perceptible after the mid-1960s. During a period when political dissatisfaction repeatedly came to the surface in the region—in artistic, cultural, and vocational spheres—the separation widened between younger and older adults. Did it develop in time to relieve the new generation of the fear and passivity disabling their elders? Along with its positive effects, Soviet culture now introduced a cleavage between younger and older generations that put Central Asians at odds with themselves, making common cause difficult in the cultural sphere.

The term "participation" generally suggests individual social or political volition, sharing in joint action, perhaps engaging with others in large enterprises. But in a dictatorial state, such as the Soviet Union, the meaning of participation also encompasses passive following, token representation, uncreative repetition, and inequality. Public affairs give many examples. A very small percentage of Central Asians belonged to the Communist Party (CP), the region's sole party. Political exclusiveness not only affected governance, it severely limited satisfying participation in cultural life to those willing to recite the conservative prescriptions that prevailed. It has been seen that nonconformity to the ways or slogans of the party and government—particularly for literate Central Asian men and women—meant banishment, forced labor camps, and worse. On the other hand, to comply unthinkingly with official directives meant artistic disaster, cultural sterility.

Only the trauma of World War II and the involuntary departure of thė long-entrenched, reactionary, and aged communist leadership after the mid-1950s began to reverse some of these tendencies. Beginning in the 1960s, the generally unimaginative stage writing and other literature did find new material and ideas in one specific sphere. Writers now focused cautiously upon two fresh, related themes. Both of them concerned ethical and social damage suffered during the reign of terror launched earlier by the Stalinists in Moscow. More generally, bolder playwrights showed regret that candor and honesty had succumbed to power and lies. In the broadest terms, CPSU Secretary Nikita S. Khrushchev in 1956 first officially spoke out about the putrefaction in Soviet politics. He acknowledged that CP and government illegalities had already inflicted terrible wounds on arts, culture, and the intellectuals who created them. For a while after that announcement, an old rigidity continued to inhibit creative intellectuals. Nor did a children's crusade come forth immediately in patriarchal Central Asia to battle for truth. Instead, a few experienced authors carefully approached one aspect of the problem — the false denunciations that had marked the era, and their converse, the honesty so scarce within the secretive regime. Everyone knew that political leaders at all levels had suborned those fatal libels and slanders, sending hundreds of thousands to prison or destruction.

ARTISTIC AND CULTURAL CHALLENGES

Around the theme of such insidious defamations, Rahmatullah A. Uyghun (1905–) of Tashkent wrote a play in 1961 called, *Friends: Groundless Doubt (Dostlär. Orinsiz shubha).*[1] A few years later, Chinghiz Aitmatov (1928–) and Kaltay Muhammadjanov of Frunze and Alma Ata adapted one of Mr. Aitmatov's stories for the stage in another drama. It, too, scrutinized the consequences of Soviet authority's punitive nature. What interested these playwrights most were the ethical implications in society's readiness to condone official outrages. These writers condemned the crimes perpetrated against even minor nonconformists by politicians and their police forces operating above the law.

[1] Uyghun, *Äsärlär. Beshinchi tam. P'yesälär* (Tashkent: Ghäfur Ghulam namidägi Ädäbiyat wä Sän'ät Näshriyati, 1978), pp. 167–222.

While accomplishing that purpose, dramatists Aitmatov and Muhammadjanov along the way gave forceful testimony concerning another broad problem. By easily crossing ethnic subgroup boundaries within Central Asia in their art they relegated to secondary importance the ethnic and linguistic subgroup identity in the region's culture. Defying the previous untouchableness of such topics, Mr. Muhammadjanov, though coming from Kazakhstan, wrote about intellectual life in Kirgizistan. Native to Kirgizistan, Mr. Aitmatov in his recent fiction recreated a tiny community in the Kazakhstan prairies. Their two-act drama, *The Ascent of Mount Fuji*, originally composed in the Kazakh language as *Köktepaga shïghu* (*To the Blue Mountain*), came to international attention when it appeared on stage in their Russian translation as *Voskhozhdenie na Fudziiamu* in Moscow in 1973, through English in Washington, D.C. in 1975, and elsewhere at other times.[2] In Mr. Aitmatov's collected works (1982), a Kirgiz-language translation of the play carried the title *Fudziyamadagï kadïr tün.*[3]

Mr. Aitmatov's novels and stories acquired wider and wider audiences in the period. They have attracted readers internationally in large part because his fiction compellingly faces significant issues in Soviet society. His coauthored play, apparently the only stage work to his credit up to the early 1980s, distressed Central Asians who felt that a true patriot would not reveal the nasty sides of Soviet society and politics. Moreover, *The Ascent of Mount Fuji* looked directly at the many who, to save their skins, had quietly ignored a profound human obligation. The dramatist portrayed people who failed in the duty to try and save friends and others victimized by the regime through exaggerated or completely false, secret denunciations. This play, intensely interesting, unquestionably important to concerned intellectuals, found rather limited popularity by comparison with many of Mr. Aitmatov's novelettes or stories.

The drama, *Friends*, written earlier by Mr. Uyghun, had under-

[2] Chingiz Aitmatov and Kaltai Mukhamedzhanov, *The Ascent of Mount Fuji. A Play*, trans. Nicholas Bethell (New York: Farrar, Straus, and Giroux, 1975, in English and Russian).

[3] Chïnggïz Aytmatov, *3 tomdon turgan chïgarmalar* (Frunze: Kïrgïzstan, 1982), pp. 448–502.

gone an equally disconcerting but different experience. This probably occurred in spite of the author's senior status in the literary establishment and his great caution. The essence of the play attacked the bad habits of managers in a rotten system rather than the unethical behavior of individuals cowed by it. Men in the conspiratorial power structure, high and low, naturally disliked this sort of public literary foray into controlled candor; therefore, the drama apparently exerted a lasting but paradoxical impact. Instead of opening the doors to truth through forceful presentation, its performance provoked repression. Evidence of disapproval continued to emerge as late as the 1980s. A popular small-town staging in 1974 instantly brought orders to the theater from local CP officials to close the production. In addition, a standard directory to Central Asian writers that had included reference to the play in 1977 dropped mention of *Friends* from Mr. Uyghun's biography in the 1984 edition of the same compilation.[4]

Under less Soviet censorship, writers of the 1970s and 1980s enjoyed greater individual latitude than before in choosing new literary topics. Perhaps because of that, most Central Asian authors treated subjects that related to the region's distinctive identity; that is to say, subjects that came close to ideological controversy. Soviet Russian officialdom promoted urbanization and industrialization in largely rural Central Asia. Sensitivity to that intrusion from outside seemed to stimulate especially fiction writers from regions recently still nomadic. They praised the virtues of countryside and village. In a novel such as Sabit Dosjanov's *Road to the Mountain* (*Tau joli*) (1978), the author portrays a kind of ethical contest between town and country. He examines the primary loyalties of a young man and woman attracted to the city for advanced education. The natural, even poetic, beauty of the village depicted in this fiction wins the competition over Kazakhstan's capital, Alma Ata. The village holds the young couple or attracts them back to the virtues and satisfac-

---

[4] *Pisateli sovetskogo Uzbekistana. Bibliograficheskii spravochnik* (Tashkent: Izdatel'stvo Literatury i Iskusstva imeni Gafura Guliama, 1977), p. 196; *Pisateli sovetskogo Uzbekistana. Spravochnik* (Tashkent: Izdatel'stvo Literatury i Iskusstva imeni Gafura Guliama, 1984), pp. 373–74; Edward Allworth, "A Document about the Cultural Life of Soviet Uzbeks outside Their SSR," *Central Asian Survey* nos. 2/3 (November 1982), p. 121.

tions in Central Asian rural life.[5] Thus, by turning his back on the town, Mr. Dosjanov indirectly rejects the exhortations of Russian industrializers and urbanizers. This drove a point home about the ethnic nature of Central Asian urbanization. Slavs and other outsiders dominate the population as well as key administrative positions in Alma Ata and most other sizable cities of the region:

> Alma Ata in 1970: Central Asians 111,724; Russians and other Slavs 548,056.
> Ashkhabad the same year: Central Asians 101,243; Russians and other Slavs 120,459.
> Dushanbe: Central Asians 136,623; Russians and other Slavs 171,903.
> Frunze: Central Asians 72,707; Russians and other Slavs 313,601.
> Tashkent: Central Asians 543,504; Russians and other Slavs 611,224.
> All told, in the five union republic capitals in 1970: Central Asians 965,801; Russians and other Slavs 1,765,243.[6]

In long novels Mr. Dosjanov's contemporaries often relished the heroics of the real or mythical past of Central Asia. Historical fiction embellished the region's heritage by offering episodes from the lives of famous Central Asians without the same degree of ideological encumbrance so burdensome in Soviet history books. And, in ways inaccessible to Marxist historians, creative writers could dramatize the qualities of eminent medieval figures such as philosopher al-Farabiy (878–950), or Prince Zahiriddin Muhammad Babur (1483–1530) in thought and statecraft.[7]

Literature reflected other controversies between ideology and Central Asian humanity in the period. Two more works that came out in the early 1980s, Chinghiz Aitmatov's arresting *The Day Lasts More than a Hundred Years* (*I dol'she veka dlitsia den'*) (1981), and a short, passionate novel by Mamadali Mahmudov entitled *The Immortal Cliffs* (*Olmäs qayälär*) (1981), each raised clouds of dust in the still arid, Soviet Russian-style cultural landscape of the region.

---

[5] Sabit Dosanov, *Tau jolï* (Alma Ata: Jazushï Baspasï, 1978), cited by Timur Kocaoglu, "Nationality Identity in Soviet Central Asian Literature: Kazakh and Uzbek Prose Fiction of the Post-Stalin Period" (New York: unpublished Ph.D dissertation, Columbia University 1982), p. 110.

[6] *Itogi vsesoiuznoi perepisi naseleniia 1970 goda* (Moscow: Statistika, 1973), vol. 4, pp. 218, 233, 290, 299, 311.

[7] Timur Kocaoglu, "Nationality Identity . . .," pp. 100–101.

Мамадали Маҳмудов

РОМАН

Ю лдузли тоғи... У одамни ўйга толдирадиган даражада ба-
ланд. Унга ўлмас қоялар билан сирли даралар зийнат ҳам
виқор бериб турибди.

Бу тоғда Оққоядан ҳайбатли қоя йўқ. Унинг учида подшога кин-
дирилган тождай бир туп қатранғи қад кўтарган. Илоҳийлик тимсо-
лига айланган бу чайир дарахтни ака-ука Қўниш, Қўнор боболар экиш-
ган. Улар Урта Осиёни Чингизхон талаган замонда, узоқ Туркистондан
бу хилват ерларга келиб қолганлар.

Кейинчалик, нима сабабдандир, Қўнор бобо ўз бола-чақалари билан Қашқадарё томонларга кўчиб кетишган. Қўниш бобо эса ўғил-қиз-
лари, келин-куёвлари билан Оққоя тагига — Қадимбулоқ атрофига
омонатгина-омонатгина бошпана қурганлар. Негаки, улар яна ўз она
юртлари — Туркистонга қайтиш ниятида бўлганлар.

Бироқ, бир куни Қўниш бобонинг суюкли набираси — Гулюм
илон чақади. У уч-тўрт кун азоб чекиб вафот этади. Уни Оққоянинг
кун ботиш томонига, ёввойи бодомзор ичига дафн қиладилар. Шундан
кейин бу ерда Қўниш боболар ўтроқ бўлиб қолишади.

Қўниш боболар ва уларнинг иккинчи, учинчи авлодлари ҳам Қадимбулоқ атрофида яшаганлар. Тўртинчи авлод эса Қадимбулоқдан
етти чақирим пастга, Каттабоғсой соҳилларига кўчишган. Шу тахлит
Каттабоғ қишлоғи вужудга келган. Ундаги ҳар бир хўжалик баҳордан
то куз ўрталаригача боғ уйларида яшашади. Қишни эса Каттабоғ
ўтказишади. Фақат бир оила тўрт мавсум ҳам ҳеч ёққа жилмайди Б

FIGURE 17.1   Mamadali Mahmudov's controversial novel, *The Immortal Cliffs*, published in the journal *Shärq yulduzi* (October–November 1981), gives a Central Asian view of Central Asian history.

One passage in *The Day* depicts how conspiring Soviet officials in a regional center trumped up charges and denunciations about class enmity. They ruined the father of Kazangap, a leading fictional character. In addition to that illustration, the novelist shows town life altering the values of inmigrating country folk by draining them of customary generosity and nobility. One more major theme in the novel by Mr. Aitmatov concerned crucial beliefs that suffer when powerful outsiders ruthlessly obliterate people's sacred places and traditions to make way for alien military or technological expansion.

The Immortal Cliffs spoke similarly about the importance of tradition in Central Asian life and the dangers of expunging it. Mr. Mahmudov shows Russian penetration of the region as a violation of nature (see figure 17.1). His novel insistently expresses love for the homeland—a homeland distinct from Russia—that requires protection from Russia by every Central Asian. Therefore, the fiction excoriates those who collaborate with the invading Russians, calling the traitors "serpents" (*ilan*). Though the novel tells about events of the 1850s and 1860s, politicians as well as the officers in a Central Asian Union of Soviet Writers 120 years later evidently felt a contemporary bite from that reptilian allusion. They vociferously denounced Mahmudov for taking what they called an un-Marxist approach to Central Asian-Russian relations and history. Ideological critics felt especially squeamish about his portrayal of patriotic Central Asian resistance to Russia around the town of Jizzakh. During a session of the state-run Writers' Union of Uzbekistan, his elders particularly deplored what they considered Mr. Mahmudov's failure to delineate sharply the ethnic and social class traits of his characters. Cultural authorities apparently aimed no such public attack against *Friends: Groundless Doubt, The Ascent of Mount Fuji,* or *The Day Lasts More Than a Hundred Years.*[8]

That official selectivity probably resulted from the fact that three

[8] Chingiz Aitmatov, *I dol'she veka dlitsia den'. Roman.* (Frunze: Kyrgyzstan, 1981), pp. 30, 59, 66; Mämädäli Mähmudaw, "Olmäs qayälär," *Shärq yulduzi* nos. 10, 11 (October, November 1981), pp. 32–87, 60–124; ibid., no. 10, p. 70; ibid., no. 11, pp. 114–15; "Ozbekistan yazuwchilär sayuzi sekretäriyätidä," *Ozbekistan ädäbiyati wä sän'äti* no. 4 (January 22, 1982), p. 7; William Fierman, "Cultural Nationalism in Soviet Uzbekistan: A Case Study of *The Immortal Cliffs*," *Soviet Union/Union Soviétique* no. 1 (1985), pp. 1–41.

out of those four controversial works share one serious omission. Except for Mamadali Mahmudov's novel, none attempts to probe behind the manifestations of sociopolitical and cultural abuse deeply enough to place responsibility where it belongs for the injustices each depicts. Like an isolated community resigned to living downwind from a noxious paper mill where every adult in town finds employment, these otherwise courageous authors in various corners of the country tacitly agree not to mention an essential condition of life known to all. They avoid direct reference to the crucial role of Russia and the Russians in sustaining and directing the oppressive system and regime under which Central Asians of the USSR strive for a satisfyingly independent or autonomous spiritual and political existence.

Absolving Russia of responsibility for the condition of Central Asians under its rule, like most falsity, has led to many contradictions in Soviet thought and society. To begin with, ideological guidelines and censorship of publications and school curricula enforce unrealistic treatment of the relationships between Russians and non-Russians in Central Asia and elsewhere. Though Russians pervade the region, they are usually missing from adult literature or, if portrayed, play meaningless, stereotyped roles. In the earliest grades children receive from teachers and textbooks a sanitized version of the Russian role in Central Asian history and culture. In history children learn that the conquering Russian armies, whose advanced European weapons killed so many poorly armed warriors of the Central Asian prairies and towns in the nineteenth century, must be considered liberators of the inhabitants (from their own Central Asian governments). The discussion of undoctrinaire new writings, above, revealed that adults have received a similar lesson in the scandal that greeted Mamadali Mahmudov's novel, *The Immortal Cliffs*. Its description of resolute Central Asian opposition to Russian forces fell outside accepted Marxist guidelines. Schoolchildren of Tashkent, Dushanbe, and other parts of the region have discovered in their classroom textbooks a Russocentric version of Central Asian history and a peculiar combination of Russian authors.

The Russian portion of one local-language tenth-grade textbook compiled in Kirgizistan amounts to a token reminder. Out of a total of 391 pages, twenty are about or translated from Soviet novelist Mikhail A. Sholokhov. An Uyghur-language schoolbook produced in Alma Ata in 1968 for tenth graders likewise included Mr. Sholokhov as the sole Russian representative. In a comparable textbook used in Turkmenistan, earlier in the 1960s, works by Maksim Gorky and Vladimir V. Mayakovski supplied the forty-five pages translated from Russian.[9] Selections from those three Russian writers or Nikolay V. Gogol also consistently appeared in textbooks of Uzbekistan and other Central Asian subregions for sixth to ninth graders in the 1970s and 1980s.[10]

Crimean Tatars, exiled to Central Asia in May 1944, gained permission to compile schoolbooks for children in their own language years after they arrived there. The content in a one-volume textbook, *Native Literature (Tuvghan edebiyat*, 1983), published (ten thousand copies) in Tashkent for grades four to seven, displayed a familiar pattern. Besides Crimean Tatar and Central Asian authors, fourth graders read translations from nineteenth-century Russian poetry by Aleksandr S. Pushkin and an essay by the Marxist ideologist Vladimir D. Bonch-Bruevich (1873–1955). Fifth graders, too, read Pushkin. The next year, Maksim Gorky headed the list of selections. In the textbook, seventh graders encountered first a story by Anton P. Chekhov in translation, followed by works from a Central Asian and seven Crimean Tatar writers and poets. Another Crimean Tatar schoolbook, for the eighth grade, issued in 4,000 copies under the title *History of Literature (Edebiyat tarikhï*, 1982), showed similar organization. On the whole, writings by Crimean Tatar poets or authors occupied most of the pages in these textbooks.[11] Persistence in their small-to-medium amount of Rus-

[9] B. Kerimjanova, K. Imanaliev, Sh. Ümötaliev, *Kïrgïz sovet adabiyatï* (Frunze: Mektep Basmasï, 1977), p. 329–49; Gh. Sädwaqasaw, A. Kaydaraw, Sh. Kibiraw, *Uyghur sawet ädäbiyäti. Ottura mäktäpning X sinipi üchün därislik* (Alma Ata: Mektep Näshriyati, 1968), pp. 170–83; Nagim Ashirov, Kurbandurdï Kurbansakhatov, [Ata Kerimov], *Khäzirki zaman edebiyatï. Orta mekdebing X klasï üchin okuv kitabï* (Ashkhabad: Türkmenistan Dövlet Okuv-Pedagogik Neshriyatï, 1963), pp. 65–108.

[10] Gulsum Rähimawä, comp. *Wätän ädäbiyati. 6-sinf uchun därslik-khrestamätiyä* (Tashkent: Oqituwchi, 1983); Hämil Yaqubaw, Äskär Zunnunaw, Rähim Usmanaw, comps., *Wätän ädäbiyati. 7-sinf uchun därslik-khrestamätiyä* (Tashkent: Oqituwchi, 1981).

[11] Abdulla Balich, Yusuf Bolat, and Riza Fazïl, *Tuvghan edebiyat, IV-VII sïnïflar ichyun* (Tashkent Oqituwchi, 1983), pp. 246–48; Jafer B. Bekirov, *Edebiyat tarikhï. VIII sïnïf ichyun derslik-khrestomatiya* (Tashkent: Oqituwchi, 1982), p. 96.

sian content reminds publishers, teachers, pupils, and parents about the important Russian presence in their lives.

In a standard reader, sanctioned by the ministry of education of the Uzbekistan SSR, schoolbook editors expected fifth graders studying in the local Central Asian language, for example, to read thirty-three pages translated from various Russians, along with Central Asian authors. Wording in the title carried on the eighth printing of that textbook, *Literature of the Homeland* (*Wätan ädäbiyati*, 1982), gave no specific reference to the Central Asian region or any part of it. A decade earlier, in the first edition of that same anthology, Central Asian children in the fifth grade had found exactly the same Russian literary figures present in their books. They encountered nineteenth-century writers Ivan A. Krylov and Aleksandr S. Pushkin, as well as older Soviet Russian authors Lidiia Bat' (b. 1900), Sergei V. Mikhalkov (b. 1913), and Boris Polevoi (b. 1908).

Literary critics would hardly classify those three from the Soviet period as the best twentieth-century writers available in Russian. But ideological function took precedence over esthetics in this selection, for the education ministry recognized them as reliable programmatic authors. The book's Central Asian authors of the Soviet period included Musa Tashmuhammad-oghli Aybek (1905–68) and Uyghun (b. 1905), two well regarded poets, as well as several lesser writers. None of the many excellent younger Central Asian writers and poets of the contemporary decades received space in these books for children. Compilers and publishers anthologized stories and poems long in print, literature that had passed the test of ideological acceptance and time. These selections testified not only to the type and amount of compulsory Russian content but to the inflexibility of the educational system. By failing to bring the content of schoolbooks up to date for a decade or more, editors reduced the chances that children would soon become acquainted with and relate to their own new, innovative writers during that phase of schooling. This practice of exclusion constituted a serious avoidable loss to the youngsters' cultural self-knowledge. It also contributed to the conservatism so apparent in artistic and cultural expression.[12]

[12] Subutay Dalimaw, comp., *Wätän ädäbiyati. 5 sinf uchun khrestamätiyä* (Tashkent:

A new general literacy has inculcated in Central Asian children suitable reverence for reading and books. Besides some of their own literature, they receive a little introduction to Russian writings from translated passages in the textbooks already described. More significant exposure comes in the centrally prescribed curriculum, which requires that all Central Asian youngsters now receive extensive training in the Russian language. They learn to read Russian authors in the original from early grades. The announced pedagogical aim is to make the pupils bilingual in a Central Asian language and Russian; for Russian, according to ideologists, is "a second mother tongue" all over the USSR, including Central Asia.[13]

In city schools, the goal of a new bilingualism seems attainable. The program for teaching Russian to local children in city schools seems intensive enough to become reasonably effective. Nevertheless, the author of this chapter observed a few practical difficulties in achieving it. During a stop in a secondary school in Tashkent late in October 1983, a visitor heard the Slavic principal—identifying herself as a "Sibiriak" (Siberian)—make revealing comments concerning the use of languages in the institution. Of the ten grades, three among the lower levels had recently begun employing a Central Asian language for instruction. The others continued to function only in Russian. An escorted tour through certain schoolrooms confirmed that the children in classes employing a Central Asian language all came from Central Asian families. Older Russian-speaking pupils contacted in the corridors and schoolyard understood not a word in a spoken Central Asian language and appeared reluctant to study the region's languages.

Although some pupils learn European languages and English well, relatively few will live and converse in areas where those foreign languages prevail. Presuming that urban Central Asian schoolchildren will acquire fluent command of Russian and use it more or less continuously, how will this affect them and their

Oqituwchi Näshriyati, 1972), 296 pp.; Subutay Dalimaw, comp., *Wätän ädäbiyati. 5-sinf uchun därslik-khrestamätiyä* (Tashkent: Oqituwchi, 1982, 8th printing), 255 pp.

[13] Isabelle Kreindler, *The Changing Status of Russian in the Soviet Union* special issue, *International Journal of the Sociology of Language* no. 33 (The Hague 1982), pp. 21–24.

society? It would be a mistake to think that for most youngsters the schoolbook readings into Russian writings could supplant or diffuse to an important extent the child's basic affiliation with his parents' culture. Nevertheless, the persistent teaching of Russian literature and culture will make an alien civilization familiar and unfrightening. The importance of the small amounts of translated writing in textbooks for primary grades lies in their contribution to this gradual familiarization. Ultimately, if Central Asian children begin to accept Russian literature without resistance as part of their own heritage, they may as adults regard a Russian leader and his system as their own. That attitude will not necessarily obliterate the regional identity with which Central Asian children grow up. But it can mitigate the tension between the two cultures and favor the general Soviet Russian model offered from Moscow.

Country schools and pupils greatly outnumber city institutions and children in Central Asia. Out of town, the acculturation to Russian literature and history generally occurs more slowly and incompletely under the present circumstances and demographic patterns. Without a doubt, the future of Central Asian regional identity depends greatly upon the outlook of the large classes of pupils now proceeding through Central Asia's rural and urban schools. The schoolbooks have insistently emphasized an ideology that thinking people of the region often repudiate. The ethnic question remains the crucial one for Russian authorities and for Central Asians as well.

The practice of depriving younger cohorts of schooling in writings by their own new poets and prose writers became magnified in the 1960s for two reasons. The literary establishment favored assigning its own works for classroom study rather than those of most younger men and women; that was also when the rising Central Asian generations increased so greatly in the proportion of the region's people obtaining an education. Growth in the school classes persisted, but in parts of Central Asia—Tajikistan and Kazakhstan —the rate of graduation without delay from the first eight grades remained much below the union-wide average of 95.4 percent. As late as 1977 only 80 percent of the potential school-age contingent in Kazakhstan and Tajikistan actually went to school. That loss in enrollment occurred because many girls, probably Central Asians, did not enroll. In Uzbekistan, according to Soviet statistics, ninth and tenth graders numbered 231,250 in the school year 1966–67, but enrollments in those classes increased to 349,530 by 1970–71. In that later school year, 72 percent of those children attended country schools. The distribution of ethnic groups ensured that the preponderance of rural pupils were Central Asians rather than Russians and other outsiders. Boys and girls of all ethnic groups graduating from secondary (in Soviet terminology, "middle") schools of Uzbekistan in 1970 amounted to 140,000, up from 59,500 in 1966.[14]

Census reports for 1959 and 1970 showed large youthful cohorts among Central Asians. In those two censal years, 49 percent and 48 percent of all Central Asians, respectively, fell into groups aged 10–49 or 11–49 (Soviet statistical cohorts vary between censuses). The authorities claimed complete literacy for that part of the population. Well over 80 percent of the entire population of Central Asians in those two census years belonged in the cohorts aged 0–49. That trend would continue. Average family size in Central Asia at the time census-takers collected data in 1979 considerably exceeded that found in any other major region of the USSR. In each Central Asian family, children under the age of 18 numbered, on the average, 5.7, despite the large numbers of Russians there whose families presumably lowered that average. By comparison, the 1979 census reported an average of 4.1 children under 18 for each family throughout the USSR, including Central Asia. Without the Central Asian families, the USSR average dropped much lower. In the most populous administrative units of the Soviet Union, smaller family size prevailed. Russian Soviet Federated Socialist Republic (RSFSR) families averaged 3.8 children in that same age bracket, and in the Ukraine, 3.9 children.[15] Central Asia's very youthful, large majority,

[14] K. Nozhko, "Glavnoe—kachestvo i effektivnost'," *Narodnoe obrazovanie* no. 5 (1977), p. 11, also cited by Mervyn Matthews, *Education in the Soviet Union. Policies and Institutions Since Stalin* (London: George Allen & Unwin, 1982), p. 41; E. Q. Qadiraw, *Ozbekistan umumtä'lim mäktäblärining riwajlänish tärikhi (1917–1975)* (Tashkent: Oqituwchi Näshriyati, 1979), p. 388.

[15] *Itogi vsesoiuznoi perepisi naseleniia 1959 goda. SSSR (Svodnyi tom)* (Moscow: Gosstatizdat. TsSU SSSR, 1962), pp. 214–15, 221–22, 224; *Itogi vsesoiuznoi perepisi*

characterized by high literacy rates, inevitably concentrated attention upon many pertinent developments in the society, most urgently on schooling and reading materials for all ages in the region.

Data regarding those who continued in the school system beyond primary years confirmed that pattern decisively. Among Soviet Central Asians in 1959 an average of only 299 out of 1,000 people who were ten or more years of age had received at least partial secondary schooling or higher education. By the census year 1970, that average had increased to 401, and in 1979 to 592. Thus, nearly at the onset of the 1980s, a little more than half of such Central Asians, on the average, had by then received a minimum of some high school training or perhaps some higher education, as well.[16] This record showed progress but perhaps not the achievement that greater autonomy and other conditions might have allowed.

Although central authorities constantly harped on the obligatory themes of internationalism in cultural programs, their efforts to denationalize loyalties ran into the obstacle of localization. In the education of young teenagers, for example, the authorities tried to ensure that patriotic campaigns planned in Moscow exerted the intended effect in outlying regions. During the tenure of Leonid I. Brezhnev as CPSU General Secretary, 1964–1982, one expensive program aimed to inculcate union-wide patriotism and a counter-ethnic internationalism among schoolchildren. A new study that analyzed this effort has discovered that in spite of great insistence on uniformity throughout the USSR by directors of that drive, the program has necessarily accommodated to the local environment. Application of this indoctrination plan in parts of Central Asia somehow resulted in emphasizing substate group identity rather than generating the ideal patriotic, ethnically indifferent Soviet-wide man or woman.[17] Some hints regarding weaknesses in such

naseleniia 1970 goda (Moscow: Statistika, 1973), 4:361, 363–64. Edward Allworth, ed., *The Nationality Question in Soviet Central Asia* (New York: Praeger Publishers, 1973), p. 11; *Chislennost' i sostav naseleniia SSSR. Po dannym Vsesoiuznoi perepisi naseleniia 1979 goda* (Moscow: Finansy i Statistika, 1984), p. 354.

[16] A. A. Isupov; N. Z. Shvartser, eds., *Vsesoiuznaia perepis' naseleniia 1979 goda* (Moscow: Finansy i Statistika, 1984), p. 160. The author thanks Nicholas Smirensky for the reference to this source.

[17] Karen Collias, "Heroes and Patriots: The Ethnic Integration of Youth in the Soviet

programs come from official reports about patterns of innovative draft-dodging by young Central Asian males in several subregions of Tajikistan, for example. Numbers of draft-age men changed addresses, suddenly took up religious studies, registered under girls' names, presented false marriage certificates, or simply vanished from the area when it came time to report for service.[18]

The general revamping of vocational education that started in 1984 also exerted its special impact in Central Asia. The Moscow leadership found fault with applications of the new arrangements for vocational education in the region. Problems arose because women have special status there and relatively few entered such programs. The fact that Central Asians in the south give very high priority to cotton harvesting regularly caused wholesale absences of young people from the vocational training. Differences between USSR regions in the quality of such education expressed themselves in Central Asia, where the local programs evidently could not come up to the standard observed in the Soviet West.[19] Through these various kinds of localization, the Central Asian child and adolescent gained further self-awareness about the ethnic context in which he or she lived.

The effect of a rising educational standard, of course, extended through an increasingly large school population. It grew as Central Asian numbers, excluding outsiders, enlarged tremendously between 1959 and 1979. In all, they amounted in the 1959 and 1970 census reports respectively to 13.3 million and just over 20 million people. Figures for 1979 showed a further rise to 26.4 million, almost exactly doubling the numbers from 1959. Unlike many Soviet groups, Central Asians (26.26 million in 1979) largely remained concentrated within their own territory. In the same decades Russian settlement and natural increase within Central Asia lost a share of the total while they gained in absolute numbers. Russians numbered 6.24 million in the region in 1959. That amounted to more

Union During the Brezhnev Era, 1965–1982" (New York: unpublished Ph.D dissertation, Columbia University, May 1987), chapter 5.

[18] V. V. Petkel, "Deistvovat' na vsekh napravleniiakh Vystuplenie predsedatelia Komiteta gosudarstvennoi bezopasnosti Tadzhikskoi SSR V. V. Petkelia," *Kommunist Tadzhikistana* (December 30, 1987), p. 2.

[19] Gregory Gleason, "Educating for Underdevelopment: The Soviet Vocational Education System and its Central Asian Critics," *Central Asian Survey* no. 1 (1985), pp. 74–78.

than any Central Asian subgroup at that time and supplied 32 percent of the area's entire population. In 1970 the census counted 8.5 million Russians, 30 percent of all inhabitants in Central Asia. By 1979 Russians grew to 9.3 million, but fell to 26 percent of the regional total, because Central Asians increased even more rapidly.[20]

The pattern of indigenous concentration meant that the learning environment for most inhabitants embraced only the Central Asian homeland and the formal or informal educational factors present in it. Large numbers of Russians settled in the cities, rather than spreading themselves evenly throughout the area. Comparatively, this reduced the degree of direct contact between Russian speakers and indigenous farming families.

For such reasons, divergence between regional sublanguages, more than the intrusion of Russian as a second tongue, may represent a most divisive factor within the culture of Central Asia, under certain circumstances. Up until at least 1925 the literate men of the region converged intellectually in society, in religion, and in commerce by reading Turkic, Arabic, or Iranian writings in the universal Arabic script. People in the cosmopolitan, indigenous urban society employed one or more of the three, one in the mosque and seminary, the remaining language families for practical interaction. Beginning in the 1920s and continuing to the 1980s, the Russian authorities stigmatized Arabic in anti-Islamic propaganda and redefined the remaining means of communication into ethnically named sublanguages with rather distinct alphabets (see chapter 2). This procedure specifically channeled a Turkic or Iranian written and printed sublanguage to each subregion, whereas the spoken tongues remained highly intelligible between groups. Administra-

---

[20] *Itogi vsesoiuznoi perepisi naseleniia 1959 goda* (Moscow: Gosstatizdat. TsSU SSSR, 1962), pp. 184–86, 206, 208; *Itogi vsesoiuznoi perepisi naseleniia 1970 goda* (Moscow: Statistika, 1973), 4:20–21, 202, 222–23, 284, 295, 302, 306; *Naselenie SSSR. Po dannym vsesoiuznoi perepisi naseleniia 1979 goda.* (Moscow: Izdatel'stvo Politicheskoi Literatury, 1980), pp. 23–26; "Vsesoiuznaia perepis' naseleniia. Natsional'nyi sostav naseleniia SSSR," *Vestnik statistiki* no. 7 (1980), pp. 41–44; ibid., no. 8 (1980), pp. 64–70; ibid., no. 9 (1980), pp. 60–70; ibid., no. 10 (1980), pp. 70–73; ibid., no. 11 (1980), pp. 60–63; *Chislennost' i sostav naseleniia SSSR. Po dannym Vsesoiuznoi perepisi naseleniia 1979 goda* (Moscow: Finansy i Statistika, 1984), pp. 71–73, 110–23, 130–38. From these data, the following subgroups make up the category "Central Asians": Crimean Tatars, Dungans, Karakalpaks, Kazakhs, Kirgiz, Tajiks, Turkmens, Uyghurs and Uzbeks.

tive measures added to the segregation of these sublanguages by closing off distribution of publications between the partitioned areas. People of Alma Ata rarely saw local-language books or newspapers from Dushanbe, and those in Frunze or Osh lacked access to similar works printed on the presses of Ashkhabad. Bookstores in the USSR capital almost entirely ignored local-language Central Asian book production. Several visits to bookstores in Moscow between 1983 and 1988 revealed its shortage of representative books or periodicals in the Central Asian vernacular. And nowhere else did the USSR's authorities support a large bookstore that offered a comprehensive collection of publications in the various regional sublanguages. In addition, the numbers of different books issued in such languages hardly kept pace with the growth in literate population.

During the years 1958–1986 the annual average number of Central Asian language editions of books remained strangely stable, considering the great population increase that it accompanied.

The relative decline shown in numbers of editions issued in Central Asian languages during that twenty-eight-year period reduced the variety from which to choose but not necessarily the quantity of native-language materials. As an indicator, the number of copies of books and pamphlets available for each person in Central Asia may show a more important correlation to language use and retention. That would be especially true if the distribution system for books were very efficient, but it is not. Between 1983 and 1986 publishers produced an average of 1.83 copies for every Central Asian each year, including those too young or old to read. That figure comes from comparing the 1979 population census reports with the annual average number of book and booklet copies issued in Central Asian languages (table 17.1).

The number fell significantly short of the average 2.47 yearly copies per person issued in the period 1958–1961, calculated on the basis of table 17.1 and the 1959 census data cited earlier in this chapter. Fewer available books and brochures could mean that more people read less, notably in the countryside, where users lacked convenient access to sizable bookshops, libraries, and reading rooms. The downward trend evidently reflected a reversal in the more expansive government policy—followed during the era of very low

TABLE 17.1

Publishing in Central Asian Sublanguages, 1958–1986

	Yearly average editions	Yearly average copies
1958–1961	3,170.6	32,932,900
1968–1971	2,777.4	47,996,200
1983–1986	2,986.5	48,376,200

Sources: *Pechat' SSSR v 1983 godu. Statisticheskii sbornik* (Moscow: Finansy i Statistika, 1984), pp. 24–25; ibid. . . . *v 1984 godu* (1985), pp. 24–25; ibid. . . . *v 1985 godu* (1986), pp. 24–25; . . . *v 1986 godu* (1987), pp. 14–15; Edward Allworth, "Mainstay or Mirror of Identity—The Printed Word in Central Asia and Other Soviet Regions Today," *Canadian Slavonic Papers* nos. 2/3 (1975), tables 1 and 2, pp. 440–41, 444. Table 17.1 includes data for the following Central Asian sublanguages: Crimean Tatar, Dungan, Karakalpak, Kazakh, Kirgiz, Tajik, Turkmen, Uyghur, Uzbek.

literacy between the 1920s and 1950s—to provide an abundance of local-language books for everyone trying to read. The decision affecting recent decades might aim to encourage or compel Central Asians to begin consuming more and more books published in Russian, instead of their own sublanguages.

That reduction in numbers of volumes published for each Central Asian in his own language does not represent a commensurate native-language loss by the population since mid-century. In 1979, 98.8 percent of all Central Asians living within the region still claimed a Central Asian tongue as their identifying language.[21] Furthermore, lexically, the vocabulary of Central Asian language from the 1960s to the 1980s remained very self-oriented. Commentators have speculated that Russian would flood non-Russian languages with its vocabulary, assimilate them or replace them. Printed evidence does not point that way in Central Asia. A new study into the vocabulary of the Central Asian periodical press between 1966 and 1984 has shown that the proportion of international terms such as *revolyutsiia* or *sotsialist* (revolution and socialist) borrowed through Russian into the written Central Asian vocabulary has hardly changed in the recent decades. Sampling shows that purely Slavic words

[21] *Chislennost' i sostav naseleniia SSSR. Po dannym Vsesoiuznoi perepisi naseleniia 1979 goda* (Moscow: Finansy i Statistika, 1984), pp. 110–11, 116–17, 130–31, 132–33, 134–35.

comprise an extremely small part of the Central Asian lexicon, ranging from 0.2 of one percent to a high of 2 percent (in the most political texts) of the words used in the periodical press. Slavic loans to the Central Asian language by 1984 seemed to slip to percentages lower than those found in the years previously surveyed.

The growing Central Asian preference for Arabic words may have blocked some of that borrowing from Europe and Russia. The increase has exerted influence in another direction as well. Evidently it has to some degree crowded out both the former numbers and proportion of Farsi or Tajik words used in non-Iranian languages of Central Asia.[22]

But these internal shifts moving between normal word pools for a single tongue do not appear to weaken the bonds between user and his/her identifying language. They may strengthen the linkage by defending a perimeter of linguistic integrity to some extent. In that case they preserve the crucial function of reinforcing group identity with its own medium of communication. Journalists, creative writers, speechmakers, and other Central Asians whose words appear in print now seem intentionally to engage in altering their practical vocabulary. If they deliberately enrich it with words from Arabic, while they stave off Slavic or European borrowings, their action takes on a certain political coloring.

SOCIAL AND POLITICAL PARTICIPATION

The wrenching political turmoil engineered under Communist Party (CP) leadership, headed by Joseph V. Stalin between 1924 and 1953, left most people of the region disconnected from the dominant political machine. Several factors worked against Central Asia's parity in CP membership. Because it was a farming area, the precondition for genuine communist strivings—dogmatically believed to be an indigenous industrial workforce—at first scarcely existed there. Moreover, many potential urban candidates from non-Russian Central Asia declined to join because they judged class war, proletarian dictatorship, and state ownership to be inimical to

---

[22] Lesley-Anne Zullo, "The Status of the Lexicon of Modern Written Uzbek: An Investigation" (New York: unpublished M.A. thesis, Columbia University, 1988), pp. 101–3, table 1.

the region's life-style. Conversely, over decades, patterns of enrollment showed that party officials, for political reasons, preferred a strong core of non-Central Asians, especially Russians, in the regional party. That proved strikingly true in the less urbanized parts of the area. The CPs of the two southernmost administrative units in Russian Central Asia, the Tajikistan Soviet Socialist Republic (TajSSR) and Turkmenistan Soviet Socialist Republic (TurkSSR) offer clear examples of this. The TajSSR CP in 1938 listed 2,747 Central Asian members from various subgroups of the area out of a total of 4,715. The remaining 42 percent consisted mainly of Russians and some other outsiders. Central Asian CP members within the TurkSSR after the purges numbered 3,749 in early 1939. That gave them 43 percent of the membership. Russians and additional European outsiders constituted 50 percent of that CP branch. Those enrollment figures clashed strikingly with the demographic proportions of those groups living in the two SSRs. As late as 1933, Central Asians had made up 96 percent of the TajSSR population, and more than 82 percent of the TurkSSR's inhabitants. By 1979, because the numbers of outsiders rose steadily, the proportion of Central Asians in those constituent republics had decreased noticeably, but still amounted to 83 percent of the population in the TajSSR and 73 percent in the TurkSSR. Statistics from the two branches of the CP showed that Central Asians continued to lag behind their demographic share. In 1974 Central Asians comprised 66 percent of TajSSR CP members, Russians and others supplied 34 percent. In the TurkSSR in 1978, Central Asians held 68.4 percent of the memberships, Russians and others, almost 32 percent.[23] And the first set of figures pertains to a period decades before the time when

---

[23] *Kommunisticheskaia partiia Tadzhikistana v dokumentakh i tsifrakh (1924–1963)* (Dushanbe: Izdatel'stvo Irfon, 1965), p. 98; *Kommunisticheskaia partiia Turkmenistana v tsifrakh* (Ashkhabad: Izdatel'stvo Turkmenistan, 1967), p. 59; "Naselenie," *Bol'shaia sovetskaia entsiklopediia. Soiuz Sovetskikh Sotsialiticheskikh Respublik* (Moscow: Gosudarstvennyi Nauchnyi Institut Sovetskaia Entsiklopediia, 1947), p. 62; *Kommunisticheskaia partiia Tadzhikistana v tsifrakh za 50 let (1924–1974 gg.). Rost i regulirovanie sostava partiinoi organizatsii respubliki* (Dushanbe: Izdatel'stvo Irfon, 1977), p. 77; *Kommunisticheskaia partiia Turkmenistana v tsifrakh (statisticheskie svedeniia za 1974–1977 gg.* (Ashkhabad: Izdatel'stvo Turkmenistan, 1979), p. 24; *Chislennost' i sostav naseleniia SSSR. Po dannym Vsesoiuznoi perepisi naseleniia 1979 goda* (Moscow: Finansy i Statistika, 1984), pp. 132, 134.

youth strikingly characterized the Central Asian population. That circumstance revealed the very low ratio of CP members to indigenous adults in that branch of the party.

Such discrepancies have persisted. Officials can no longer explain them by blaming economic and political chaos or the stress of getting the CP established. Numbers mean something at the lower, broader levels of membership, for they reflect some employment and local influence. But participation in the upper layers of control and decision exerted the decisive effect. In that regard, Central Asians as a group again suffered disabilities disproportionate to their numbers and their political needs.[24]

The facts about CP membership within Central Asia pointed to statistical peculiarities in the local situation. But they only indirectly reflected the unequal position of Central Asians in union-wide party ranks. In 1927, when the entire region had come under direct Russian rule, Central Asians made up 3.5 percent of the USSR's CP membership, just half of their proportion then in the country's population.[25] Some sixty years later, their relative position in CPSU membership had altered by only one percentage point. In 1986 Central Asians constituted about 6 percent of the union-wide CPSU roster, as against an approximately 10-percent share in the Soviet population (1979), a share undoubtedly greater seven years later.[26]

Out of that impasse, something more crucial than quantity would emerge to affect the impact of sharing in decisionmaking as well as the status of Central Asian CP members. It would also raise fundamental questions about the role of indigenous leadership in the region. Because the CPSU centered itself in Moscow and insis-

[24] John H. Miller, "Cadres Policy in Nationality Areas—Recruitment of CPSU First and Second Secretaries in Non-Russian Republics of the USSR," *Soviet Studies* (January 1987), pp. 8–9, 26, 30; Michael Rywkin, "Power and Ethnicity; Regional and District Party Staffing in Uzbekistan (1983/84)," *Central Asian Survey* no. 1 (1985), pp. 3–40; Michael Rywkin, "Power and Ethnicity: Party Staffing in Uzbekistan (1941/46, 1957/58)," *Central Asian Survey* no. 1 (1985), pp. 41–73.

[25] *Sotsial'nyi i natsional'nyi sostav VKP(b)*, p. 117, cited by T. H. Rigby, *Communist Party Membership in the USSR* (Princeton, N.J.: Princeton University Press, 1968), p. 366.

[26] "KPSS v tsifrakh. Nekotorye dannye o razvitii partii v period mezhdu XXVI i XXVII s"ezdami KPSS," *Partiinaia zhizn'* no. 14 (June 1986), p. 24; *Chislennost' i sostav naseleniia SSSR . . .* (1984), p. 71.

FIGURE 17.2   Prominent Central Asian politicians Dinmuhamed A. Kunayev (back, 2d from left) and Sharaf R. Rashidov (back, 2d from right)—discredited in the mid-1980s—sit in USSR Politburo, behind Leonid I. Brezhnev, Nikolai V. Podgorny, and Andrei A. Gromyko (March 1971). (TASS from Sovfoto)

tently disclaimed ties to ethnic groups, for many years it failed to root itself deeply or extensively in Central Asian society. When Central Asians finally succeeded in orienting their branches of the Party toward regional purposes, their very initiative laid shaky groundwork that would destabilize the organization's localization.

Changes began with the anti-Stalinist drive in 1956 that exposed CP lawlessness. Ironically, the new possibilities started to take shape in 1964, especially after the politicians deposed General Secretary Khrushchev, the official who had launched Soviet de-Stalinization. During the tenure of Leonid I. Brezhnev as General Secretary of the CPSU, Central Asian leaders who had risen to key posts late in the 1950s and 1960s learned how to domesticate their branches of the supposedly internationalist CP.

The Moscow political center in March 1959 had appointed Sharaf R. Rashidov (b. 1917–d. Oct. 31, 1983) to the leading position in one Central Asian branch of the CPSU, naming him First Secretary of the Central Committee of the Communist Party of Uzbekistan (CC CPUz). Two years later he entered the CC CPSU in Moscow and, without relinquishing those positions, became an alternate member of the Soviet Union's Politburo, his highest political post (see figure 17.2). The Central Committee of the CPSU in late 1957 selected for membership in itself and as one of its secretaries another Central Asian, Nuritdin A. Muhitdinov, also born in 1917. The year after that appointment, the Moscow leadership brought him into the Politburo. There he had the distinction of becoming the youngest among the fifteen members, whose mean age had already reached 58.7 years in an aging cadre for that body.[27]

Party personnel directors evidently carefully calculated membership quotas for each region of the USSR according to unannounced formulas. They gave extra members to certain Slavic and Transcaucasus groups, but worked against proportionate representation for Central Asians within their administrative subunits. Nevertheless, under Sharaf R. Rashidov's leadership and that of comparable party chieftains around the Central Asian region, its branches of the CPSU began to gain a larger part of the overall membership. As Mr. Rashidov started his new job, 187,541 members stood on the rolls of the CPUz branch. Of them, Central Asians from the six main subgroups (Karakalpak, Kazakh, Kirgiz, Tajik, Turkmen, and Uzbek) constituted almost 60 percent of the membership. Russians, Ukrainians, Belorussians, Jews, and other outsiders made up more than 35 percent. Numbers had multiplied, but that proportion differed surprisingly little from the percentages reported for the year when the CPUz was established. In October 1924 Central Asians had numbered 8,291—56.7 percent of the regional membership; 6,253 Russians and other outsiders then made up 42.8 percent of the enrollees.[28] During the intervening years, Russian officials had manipulated ups and downs in the percentage of Central Asian membership. But absolute numbers became steadier after 1959.

---

[27] "Sekretari Tsentral'nogo Komiteta KPSS," *Izvestiya* (December 22, 1957), p. 1; Rein Taagepera and Robert Dale Chapman, "A Note on the Ageing of the Politburo," *Soviet Studies* no. 2 (April 1977), p. 300.

[28] *Pravda Vostoka* (March 14, 1959), p. 1; *Kommunisticheskaia partiia Uzbekistana v tsifrakh. (Sbornik statisticheskikh materialov 1924–1964 gg.)* (Tashkent: Uzbekistan, 1964), p. 14.

Between 1972 and 1978 Central Asian enrollments in the CPUz increased each year by approximately 3 to 4 percent annually, whereas the usual yearly growth in CP membership by Russians, Volga Tatars, Ukrainians, Jews, and Belorussians in the UzSSR subunit came to around 1 percent. Although the numbers of outsiders slowly continued to rise, their proportion on the whole sank each year from 1972 to 1978.[29]

Uzbekistan's political silhouette represented the situation in Central Asia to a degree, but other subregions varied, usually to the benefit of outsiders. In the Kirgizistan CP (CPKir), for example, the spread between outsiders and insiders remained much closer than the difference seen in CPUz during the 1970s and 1980s. In 1981 outsiders comprised 39.7 percent of the CPKir branch. Out of 126,402 enrolled, Slavs numbered 49,828 persons. Central Asians came only to slightly above 50 percent of the CPKir membership.[30]

By 1978 Sharaf R. Rashidov had remained continuously in his top CPUz position longer than any sitting CP first secretary in Central Asia, while indigenous CP enrollments greatly expanded. As a consequence, in 1978 Central Asians held nearly 70 percent of the memberships in the CPUz, outsiders, 27 percent. That was well up from 1976, when among 487,507 members in the CPUz, 67.7 percent were Central Asians. Party archives showed 28.3 percent Slavs and other outsiders in that year.[31] Proportions in the general membership reflected fairly closely the ethnic subdivision within Central Asia's political centers. Outsiders made up 26 percent of the 246 full and alternate members in the Central Committee CPUz in 1976.[32] The Central Asian majorities might have influenced policymaking if local leaders had resolutely disagreed with the Russians, but they avoided direct confrontation. Instead, in retrospect, it seems evident that the Central Asian CP leadership worked to counter-coopt—in the language of some, perhaps, to corrupt

[29] *Kommunisticheskaia partiia Uzbekistana v tsifrakh* . . . (1979), pp. 329–30.

[30] *Kommunist* (Kïrgïzstan) no. 3 (March 1982), pp. 29–42, cited in "USSR Report, Political and Sociological Affairs" JPRS, *Central Asian Press Surveys* (March 1982), p. 16.

[31] *Kommunisticheskaia partiia Uzbekistana v tsifrakh. (Sbornik statisticheskikh materialov 1924–1977)* (Tashkent: Uzbekistan, 1979), p. 352.

[32] "Ozbekistan Kammunistik Pärtiyäsining XIX s'ezdidä säylängän Ozbekistan KP Märkäziy Kamitetining ä'zaläri," *Sawet ozbekistani* (February 6, 1976), p. 1.

—the Russian party officials assigned to oversee CP affairs in the region.

Dinmuhamed A. Kunayev (1911–), Kazakhstan's foremost indigenous politician for decades, came to his office in 1960, lost it in late 1962, and returned to the rank of First Secretary, CC CPKaz in December 1964. Mr. Kunayev showed remarkable resourcefulness in creating loyal allies among Russian officials in Kazakhstan. Probably as a result of this, in April 1971 he also became the only Central Asian politician since Mr. Muhitdinov who ascended to full membership in the Politburo of the CC CPSU. An expansion in Central Asian participation throughout party and government hierarchies has been directly associated with his long stewardship in the CP of the large Kazakhstan Soviet Socialist Republic (KazSSR).[33]

The same year that Mr. Kunayev took his chair as First Secretary in the CC CPKaz, Jabar Rasulov (b. 1913), rose to a similar rank in the CP branch of the Tajikistan Soviet Socialist Republic (TajSSR). Mr. Rasulov likewise became a member of the CC CPSU in 1961. An identical pattern obtained in the Kirgizistan CP branch, where Yurdakun Usubaliev (b. 1919) became both First Secretary CC CPKir and a member of the CC CPSU in 1961. Those leaders all continued in place in 1978, along with the youngest of the five top indigenous politicians in Central Asia, Muhammednazar Gapurov (b. 1922). He went from the highest governmental post in TurkSSR —Chairman, Council of Ministers, TurkSSR—to First Secretary of the Turkmenistan branch of the CPSU in 1969. By 1978, the five First Secretaries had cumulatively served seventy-eight years between them as party chiefs in Central Asia. They set an unprecedented modern record for time in office since 1925, the year Central Asia had lost all remnants of its partial political autonomy.[34]

Since its earliest days, CPSU managers had contrived to limit a Central Asian impact on the regional and union-wide party organizations. Restrictive quotas and frequent purges kept out or removed

[33] Martha Brill Olcott, *The Kazakhs* (Stanford: Hoover Institution Press, 1987), pp. 243–44.
[34] Grey Hodnett and Val Ogareff, *Leaders of the Soviet Republics, 1955–1972. A Guide to Posts and Occupants* (Canberra: Department of Political Science, Research School of Social Sciences, Australian National University, 1973), sections devoted to Central Asian SSRs.

what the managers deemed excess local membership. Class discrimination against rural dwellers and urbanites outside the proletariat excluded from the organization most farmers and middle-class urbanites. Anti-intellectual attitudes toward educated individuals blocked other potential nonconformists from joining. Finally, statistics show that outsiders received disproportionate representation in the CPs of Central Asia and preempted claims to influential assignments in its structures. This last method denied appointment of Central Asians to certain key positions throughout the organizational apparatus. CPSU leaders ensured that Slavs and some additional non-Central Asians sat in a network of jobs that controlled decisions regarding important social or political matters in the region.

Actual and legal ethnic segregation provided the functional technique that kept all four limiting methods in effect. In Uzbekistan and the remaining subregions of Central Asia in 1985, and earlier, a parallel, separate, and unequal CP framework encompassed key positions. A Slavic or, infrequently, Transcaucasus CP bureaucrat oversaw each action. Thus, behind the Central Asian First Secretary CC CP of each branch stood a Slavic Second Secretary CC CP with authority to direct and countermand decisions. The normal arrangements additionally placed in the region's union republics a non-Central Asian Second Secretary for each of the many oblasts (thirteen in CPUz, counting the Karakalpak ASSR, for example). The same sort of Russian-dominated parallel CP bureaucracy prevailed in the governments (Councils of Ministers) of the union republics and the Communist Youth Organizations (Komsomol). Besides these supervisory positions, higher authorities placed only outsiders at the top in certain sensitive offices. They included those of the attorneys general, CP organizations, CP administrative agencies and Committees of State Security (KGB) throughout Central Asia.[35] Considering the pervasiveness and persistence of that parallel system, Central Asians seemed relegated to superficially prestigious token positions. The authorities assigned those jobs in order to

[35] Michael Rywkin, "Russian Party Apparatus in a Muslim Republic: The Case of Uzbekistan," *Journal, Institute of Muslim Minority Affairs* no. 2 (London, July 1987), pp. 266–67.

placate ethnic sensibilities without inconveniencing CP management from the outside. CP officials meant these arrangements to squelch complaints and smother Central Asian initiatives or wishes with a hierarchy of omnipresent advisors.

For those reasons, in the second half of the twentieth century, a Central Asian who became a party or government leader usually conformed to a set of unannounced traits: he, usually not she, spoke and wrote Russian fluently and actively promoted the universal employment of that foreign language in Central Asia; he obtained some higher education, if possible at an institute or university in Russia; he enunciated fulsome panegyrics to Russians and the CP orally and in writing on state occasions, frequently at other times as well; he strove to maintain for himself a noticeably general, ethnically neutral public exterior and avoided any overt expression of localism; he exercised tight control over Central Asians in his territory's political machinery.

That profile of the Central Asian leader in the late twentieth century made him a difficult choice for sincere public admiration. Much more important, if an effective group leader will draw and crystallize the fire of his followers' ethnic fervor, he must become the epitome of the group's ideals. The absence of this essential leadership quality removed the likelihood that these Central Asian politicians could offer the magnetism that might solidify their potential constituencies into a whole body. Thus, as a party boss or center of a clique, such a person might survive for long periods in an undemocratic political system. He could not offer the true group leadership that would bring whole populations into modern ethnic unity.

Old societies holding their home ground over the ages devise tested ways to survive pestilence, famine, invasion, and other disasters. Central Asians have endured temporary conquest from all directions by Arabs, Mongols, Indians, Persians, and now Russians. If the process lasted long, the leaders of the region and their people learned to live with the invader until they tamed him and he acculturated to them. The four earlier invaders largely returned to their places of origin, leaving remnants to assimilate into Central Asian society and culture. Some five decades along in the latest invasion, circumstances suddenly altered. The situation had previously taken the form of a sharp ideological conflict between Islam and Christianity, East and West. When the Sovietization of Russia dulled, but did not remove the Christian fervor, it caused twentieth-century Central Asians to face mainly an ethnic contest for supremacy under an atheistic ideology. Russians in Central Asia now appeared unassimilable because of the stark ethnic differences and sustained inmigration of outsiders. The dilemma compelled inventive Central Asia to discover a way other than the time-honored method of assimilating the invaders in order to get out of the colonial status that Russian occupation enforced.

Russia used the Soviet system to guard itself against the dangers of ethnic assimilation. Since the 1950s, the smothering of Central Asian decisionmaking in the political structures erected by the Russian parallel hierarchy purposely worked against rapprochement between insiders and outsiders. That happened, in part, because CP managers rotated overseers between positions fairly often. For instance, none of the main central positions in Uzbekistan's parallel hierarchy was held by the same outsider/Russian in 1980 and in 1985, and only Bukhara and Jizzakh oblasts out of the thirteen in the union republic retained in 1985 the man who had served as CP second secretary in 1980.[36]

If Central Asians wanted to shake the rigidity in the occupying official network, they would have to look for flexibility in human personalities, not in the structure itself. The CP doctrine of "selflessness" (material and political self-denial) for its officials and members played an unexpected role in this. Enforced frugality or modesty provided an opening to the region's political insiders for making outsiders in the hierarchy more amenable to Central Asian interests. Many political devices such as back scratching and log-rolling combined with outright influence peddling, payoffs, bribery, embezzlement, extortion, theft of government property, and the like to effect an alliance. They helped to draw the two hierarchies, the outsiders and insiders, together for mutual benefit. Not every official sinned so easily, but corruption became pervasive and insti-

[36] Rywkin, "Russian Party Apparatus," 1987, p. 266.

tutionalized, as it had been some seventy years earlier, when Count Pahlen's investigations found Russian malfeasance everywhere in Central Asia.[37]

This kind of unofficial "drawing together" between ethnic groups contrasted radically with the rapprochement (*sblizhenie*) envisaged by the CP sloganeers who had so long advocated "friendship between ethnic groups." The official version implied a polite relationship between peripheral nationalities and Russians in their heartland. This new "friendship" involved close local interactions between Russian and Central Asian political structures meant to remain apart. Pragmatic indigenous politicians determined that the establishment of such an informal community of interest between the Central Asians and their overseers could not remain merely a profitable end in itself. As the collaboration broadened, it fundamentally served wider purposes and produced an alternative ideology.

Experienced Central Asian CP officials aimed to go beyond the tokenism of the positions assigned to them by CP personnel managers. In order to make that step, they intended to accomplish the domestication of the CP in their region. Whether they anticipated it or not, that move would subvert the CP system of ethnic segregation in the CP structure that supported the parallel hierarchy of outsiders. They carefully set about this with a lengthy procedure that amounted to reverse cooptation—those excluded from power drawing the decisionmakers into a virtual alliance through patience, persuasion, and irresistible hospitality. This cautiously nurtured understanding between the two gave some hidden autonomy to Central Asian politicians in their homeland. The well-fed southern region gave outsiders an opportunity to live better than they could in the harsh doctrinal climate and economic restrictions prevalent in the western part of the Russian Socialist Federative Soviet Republic (RSFSR).

That informal autonomy allowed strong, extensive political machines to develop sub rosa in the Central Asian union republics. The adaptation of the CP structures to create these shadowy indige-

[37] [K. K. Pahlen], *Mission to Turkestan. Being the Memoirs of Count K. K. Pahlen, 1908–1909* (London: Oxford University Press, 1964), pp. 126–45.

nous combines for years gave insiders unusual latitude in some unofficial economic, political, and social actions throughout the region. These practices revived and strengthened an ideology of Central Asian self-awareness and self-interest that reached much of the educated population, a stratum already seen to be growing fast. The domestication of the regional CP and certainly the tacit collaboration between the two hierarchies in it could hardly have occurred without the widespread cooperation of CP outsiders in Central Asia. In general, urban people of either ethnic faction apparently knew about these arrangements and regularly sought the political patronage they offered. A distrust amounting to dislike of the outsiders omnipresent in city society encouraged Central Asian participation in this system directed by their own people.

The unofficial network permeated Central Asian life, influencing cultural activity, economic priorities, political appointments, housing decisions, and a multitude of related matters. Disruption of these durable arrangements would inescapably raise tensions in the party and the region. When it broke out, the scandal that seemed sure to ensue could not fail to have an ethnic coloring. Sure enough, extensive Soviet publicity since 1982 has dramatized what the USSR's media has called criminality and corruption among Central Asian officials. The exposés have ultimately led to wholesale political purges identified with the regime of CPSU General Secretary Mikhail S. Gorbachev in the 1980s. The housecleaning seems the most sweeping in Central Asia since those directed by Joseph V. Stalin in the 1930s.

The narrow official focus upon the simple matter of corruption so well known in all parts of the USSR missed more troublesome problems. It masked the significant feature of the unofficial second-level autonomy of Central Asia that had developed between approximately 1965 and 1983. The implications in the existence of such an alternative ideology and political arrangement could not have eluded CP politicians in Moscow. To denounce it clearly as a Central Asian phenomenon, a striving for self-fulfillment by indigenous populations of the area, would have raised ethnic grievances openly. That would injure the CP leadership's sense of dogmatic purity and public perception of its supposedly evenhanded nationality policies. Admitting the absence of class solidarity or the presence of ethnic dissension might have raised those problems in unmanageable ways.

Exactly that sort of protest has persistently marked the unending drive for ethnic justice of Crimean Tatars exiled to Central Asia since May 18, 1944. From Alma Ata, Frunze, Dushanbe, Samarkand, Tashkent, and other towns, they consistently demanded that the CPSU in Moscow return to them the civil, human, and political rights protected in the USSR and UzSSR constitutions as well as in published CP Programs. For open activity distributing information and demonstrating in Moscow, Leninabad, Tajikistan and Marghilan, Uzbekistan, for example, court officials sentenced Jeppar A. Akimov to spend three years in a labor camp. The record also charged him with complicity in publicly displaying black banners in the town of Bekabad, Uzbekistan on May 18, 1972 that read "18 May, the Day Crimean Tatars were Deported from the Homeland."[38] For at least three decades other Central Asian residents have witnessed the spectacle presented by this resolute group. Crimean Tatar demonstrations, petitioning, lobbying, and circulation of publicity and extensive *samizdat* (self-publishing) came to the attention of many non-Crimean Tatars. Russian officials and their proxies seemed especially concerned that Crimean Tatars would succeed in enlisting the active sympathy of the Central Asians among whom they lived so closely.

Occasionally, Central Asian politicians have followed the Russian lead in condemning Crimean Tatar actions and complaints against unfair nationality policies of the CPSU. In 1968 the secretary of the Party organization in the UzSSR Writers' Union, Sh. Sagdiyew (Sagdullayew) joined Secretary Voronkov, Presidium of the USSR Union of Writers, and others in a confidential denunciation. They directed a letter to the KGB that blamed a Crimean Tatar activist, Reshat Bayramov, and his associates, for circulating information about CP and government discrimination against the Crimean Ta-

---

[38] "Delo Akimova. Obvinitel'noe zakliuchenie," *Khronika zashchity prav v SSSR* vypusk 9 (May–June 1974), pp. 57–62; Edward Allworth, ed., *Tatars of the Crimea: Their Struggle for Survival* (Durham, N.C.: Duke University Press, Central Asia Book Series, 1988), pp. 3–8.

tars. Conformity with the Russian position in this conflict has not earned those Central Asians wide respect.[39]

As late as mid-1987, public efforts on the part of Crimean Tatars led to meetings of their representatives with Central Asian politicians. In one interview, CPUz First Secretary Usmanhojayew endeavored to learn directly about the protesters' demands.[40] The motive in that type of domestic diplomacy aims to quiet dissent, but it has not deflected the authorities' attacks upon Central Asian officials for what is referred to as "corruption." Especially since the death of Sharaf R. Rashidov in October 1983—some emigrants say official pressure drove him to suicide in Khwarazm—Soviet press reports have concentrated upon what they term venality among Central Asian leaders, finally including Mr. Rashidov himself.

If public assertions about such corruption are correct, they still comprise the less crucial part of a bigger story. From the regional standpoint the entire unresolved ethnic question in the USSR and, in this case, the Central Asian aspect of it remain incomparably more important than political graft. A few examples: Russian CP managers investigate and sensationally publicize the alleged graft of Abduwahit Karimaw (later executed by firing squad), from 1977–84 First Secretary of the Bukhara Oblast CP Committee, in Uzbekistan. Or, the press reports accusations against Mr. I. Qasimbetaw, minister of education, Nukus, Karakalpakistan. In the publicity, the journalists and their sources usually play down what must have been his collusion with the pervasive Russian infrastructure in the CP of the Karakalpak Autonomous Soviet Socialist Republic (KarASSR). Nor do these official announcements allude to the ethnic significance of the crisis.[41]

[39] *Shest' dnei. "Belaia kniga"* (New York: Fond Krym, 1980), pp. 80, 346.

[40] "Qrim Tatarlarining vekillerinen ameliy koryushyuv," *Lenin bayraghi* (August 4, 1987), p. 1; Edward Allworth, ed., *Tatars of the Crimea. Their Struggle for Survival* (Durham, N.C.: Duke University Press, Central Asia Book Series, 1988), p. 8.

[41] G. Ovcharenko, "Kobry nad zolotom. Dolguiu i trudnuiu bor'bu s organizovannoi prestupnost'iu v Uzbekistane vedet sledstvennaia gruppa Prokuratury SSSR," *Pravda* (January 23, 1988), p. 3; G. Awchärenka, "Altingä hirs qoygän gäzändälär. SSSR Prakuräturäsining tergaw gruppäsi Ozbekistandä uyushgän jinayätchilikkä qärshi uzaq wä mäshäqqätli kuräsh alib barmaqdä," *Sawet Ozbekistani* (January 24, 1988), p. 3; Viktor Loshak and Valery Dyomin, "Minister Spills Beans in Billion Rouble Scandal," *Moscow News* (July 1988), p. 2; "Top Soviet Uzbekistan Aide Dismissed for Incompetence," *New York Times* (August 4, 1985), p. 11.

In light of these arcane intrigues, can an ordinary citizen's involvement in any aspect of the USSR's closed political system qualify as active participation? Soviet politicians have not tolerated the development of nongovernmental organizations or institutions in Central Asia or elsewhere in the USSR. Among those authorized agencies and institutions of government allotted to each soviet socialist republic (SSR) and autonomous soviet socialist republic (ASSR) since 1938 has been a "supreme council (soviet)." Though sometimes called parliaments by foreigners, these bodies have no genuine legislative power and until the mid-1980s, at least, have engaged in few, if any, consequential open debates. Their work consists principally of listening to prepared reports and speeches. Their open sessions virtually never reach spontaneous decisions, but merely unanimously ratify directives relayed to them from the SSR or ASSR branch of the CP. Nevertheless, to create a show of public participation in government, the authorities stage elaborate balloting procedures and short formal convenings periodically for these impotent creatures of the system. A single, uncompetitive list of candidates nominated behind the scenes by CP chiefs regularly receives nearly 100 percent of the ballots cast, for most citizens of legal age obediently go to the polling places.

In spite of these great shortcomings, membership in a union republic's chamber of deputies seemingly gives desirable public recognition and conveys social status upon individual deputies. Their photographs and some biographical information appear in the local press and in special published directories, such as those cited below. Each deputy comes into contact with a number of his/her fellows as well as an assigned chief while serving on a special or standing commission within the supreme council. Deputies occasionally meet with people in their districts. Deputies may try to improve local amenities such as schools or forestation, but are not expected to work for any political goals.[42]

If objective, systematic sampling of opinion was possible in Central Asia, popular views about the value of such service would no doubt contrast considerably with educated attitudes toward it. Re-

[42] "Ozbekistan SSR Aliy Sawetining Daimiy Kamissiyäläri," *Sawet Ozbekistani* (July 3, 1975), p. 2.

gardless of the acceptance obtained from the unsophisticated, politically meaningless public activity in an ostensibly political body probably cannot qualify as affirmative participation of Central Asians in their governance. Besides questions about the substance or symbolism of such token participation, there are problems concerning the extent of it in Central Asia's large, rapidly growing population.

The deputies preselected by CP officials in 1971 for seats in the Kirgizistan SSR Supreme Council's eighth convocation at Frunze numbered 339. Of them, Central Asians comprised 219 (139 men and 80 women)—64.4 percent—a disproportionately high share of the total. The 1.7 million Central Asians in the KirSSR made up 58.2 percent of the population in the Kirgizistan SSR in 1970. Russians and other Slavs occupied 103 (66 men, 37 women) places. Information about a variant of this type of representation comes from Tashkent. For the Uzbekistan SSR's Supreme Council, officials in 1975 chose 470 deputies. Among them, 321 Central Asians (228 males, 93 females) made up 68.3 percent, 97 Russians and other Slavs (61 males, 36 females) filled 20.6 percent of the seats, with Armenians and Koreans taking most of the remainder.[43]

In the Kirgizistan subregion of Central Asia, 983,000 Slavs made up 33.5 percent of the people in 1970. The 30.3 percent of the seats they occupied seems a relatively low component of Slavs in a governmental body such as the Kirgizistan Supreme Council. The figures testify to the minor importance accorded by the CP to the supreme council of an SSR in Central Asian political affairs. On the other hand, because Central Asians comprised 80 percent of the population in the UzSSR in 1979, their quota—less than 70 percent of the places—noticeably underrepresented them in the supreme council of that union republic. A Central Asian form of political patronage practiced then probably explains that discrepancy. The UzSSR CP First Secretary, Sharaf R. Rashidov, very likely favored granting an unwarranted share of these token rewards to non-Central Asians in Uzbekistan in return for other considerations.

---

[43] Kïrgïz SSRinin segizinchi shaylangan jogorku sovetinin deputattarï ([Frunze]: Kïrgïzstan Basmasï, 1972), 343 pp.; *Ozbekistan SSR Aliy Sawetining deputätläri. Toqqizinchi chäqiriq* (Tashkent: Ozbekistan, 1976), 336 pp.; *Itogi vsesoiuznoi perepisi naseleniia 1970 goda. Natsional'nyi sostav* . . . (Moscow: Statistika, 1973), pp. 202, 284.

Theoretically, the Supreme Councils in Kirgizistan, Uzbekistan, and elsewhere, possessed great potential, but, like their counterparts in the other union republics and autonomous SSRs, these bodies exercised no power under the existing system.[44] That fact emphasizes an earlier point about participation in politics and society.

Powerless leadership, normally a contradiction in terms, poses a great problem for Central Asian group identity. Soviet Russian politicians at the Moscow center from Vladimir I. Lenin and the Russianized Joseph V. Stalin to Mikhail S. Gorbachev have persistently undermined the peripheral local leadership. Their motive, to neutralize possible ethnic initiatives and preserve their own hegemony, are clear. The long-term results of their effort reveal themselves less surely. But the evidence amassed in this study seems to project ambiguity in Central Asian cultural, political, and social integrity under these circumstances.

RELIGIOUS VERSUS ETHNIC GROUP IDENTITY

At the same time, that Russian dominance, carrying a residue of institutionalized Christianity, exerts a very strong reverse unifying force in Central Asian life. All Central Asians understand the distinction between them and the Russians, both in a nominal religious sense and in political terms. Ethnicity normally overrides religion as a cultural or social force in the region today, but in this configuration the larger, ethnic cleavage between Russians/Slavs and Turkic/Iranian Central Asians coincides with religious divisions on the two sides. Historically, Islam claimed more universal and fervent adherence in the south than in the north of the region. That gradation divided settled ethnic subgroups from nomadic and seminomadic people. In the 1980s, such divisions signified little. A tendency by some outsiders, including Soviet Russians, to see threats to the state from what they term a resurgent Islam in Central Asia probably have exaggerated the potential of religious revival as a disruptive social or political thrust in the region. The region has undergone greater change through modern education and development than most other neighboring countries. The fashion in the

---

[44] *Chislennost' i sostav naseleniia SSSR* . . . (1984), p. 110.

West of generally categorizing Central Asians as Muslims, therefore, distorts the reality and confuses issues of primary identity and loyalty.

As a consequence of the Russian presence and hegemony, regional or subregional identity continue to function there reactively. If the omnipresent Russian politicians and bureaucrats appointed to jobs in the region were greatly to diminish in number, Central Asians would face a drastic necessity to revise their attitudes about themselves and their primary ethnic allegiance. Many developments at different levels of society would have an impact upon their ultimate choice of group identity. The continued existence of a viable Central Asia has great importance culturally and politically for all surrounding territory. In turn, the messages from Central Asia's technically modernizing civilization reach to most parts of the less-developed world. Before the region can play its appropriate role in international affairs it must settle the questions of identity and autonomy restricting it domestically.

The collaborative unofficial structures erected in Central Asia by its durable indigenous CP chiefs starting generally in the 1960s apparently had all been razed no later than the mid-1980s. Under Mr. Gorbachev, the most formidable of them underwent destruction so thorough that no one can with certainty expect a renewal soon in that informal system of subregional leadership developed to counterbalance the Russian-centered CP. While Soviet investigative prosecutors continued to probe the connections that had made Sharaf R. Rashidov's alternative empire so effective in Uzbekistan, another investigation focused upon the network elaborated in Kazakhstan.

Dinmuhamed A. Kunayev, the First Secretary of the CP, Kazakhstan SSR, saw his political edifice fall around him while he remained in office. From Moscow, the Politburo discharged him from his post as First Secretary in December 1986 and from membership in the Politburo in January 1987. Published statements specified political and economic corruption in the union republic as the reason for dismissing Mr. Kunayev from these responsibilities.

Soviet newspapers reported a more plausible, dangerous charge than corruption against the seventy-five-year old political leader.

They accused him of "tribalism" and "tribal protectionism" in Kazakhstan. That indictment makes plain that the Russian authorities worried about any stimulus to the vitality of Kazakhstan's Central Asianness far more than over the misappropriation of state funds or property. As they did earlier in Uzbekistan and Karakalpakistan, Moscow's prosecutors followed leads ostensibly opened through the discovery of political graft. More likely, they did this in order to root out reviving ethnic growth.

An American graduate student present in Alma Ata during summer 1986 as well as spring 1987 learned from young Kazakhs that their personal economic concerns may have played a role in the outburst that greeted news of the CPKaz official's dismissal. The most active portion of the crowds involved in the protest seemed largely to have been made up of students from the State University of Kazakhstan located in Alma Ata, according to the American visitor. The presence of a Central Asian in the important position of CP First Secretary had symbolized future opportunity to the young people. General insecurity growing out of fear that suitable employment would now elude them under another official prompted their sudden outcry against the action taken by the Russians at the top of the USSR's political system.

The disruptions occurred in Alma Ata December 17–18, 1986, after news circulated that Mr. Gorbachev and his Russian associates in the Politburo had discharged Mr. Kunayev from his position as head of the CPKaz, replacing him with a Russian. Officials also blamed Mr. Kunayev for this public disorder. In connection with the Alma Ata events, ideologists also singled out and denounced the phenomenon of nationalism, regarded negatively by Russian and similar Marxists. Some Russian as well as Central Asian observers and participants regarded the demonstrations in Alma Ata in large part as expressions of ethnic friction and discontent on both sides.[45]

But economic concerns underlay public anxiety over such politi-

---

[45] "The Events in Kazakhstan—An Eyewitness Report," *Central Asian Survey* no. 3 (1987), pp. 73–75, translated from *Arkhiv Samizdata* AC5913 (April 10, 1987); personal observations by William McCabe in Alma Ata during spring and summer 1986, and spring 1987; "Soviet Press Reaction to Alma Ata Riots," *The Central Asian Newsletter* no. 2 (June 1987), pp. 3–7.

cal incidents. The great influx of outsiders into Kazakhstan, especially to the northern oblasts and towns of the union republic,
preempted much of the skilled employment, leaving Central Asians
to take less remunerative and desirable work. Even so, a trend
toward filling industrial jobs with Central Asians could be seen
more clearly in Kazakhstan than in the southern parts of the region.
That occurred because the sparsely populated north felt little population pressure. Notwithstanding the huge expanse and rich natural
resources present in the Kazakhstan SSR, about two-thirds of Central Asian industrial production comes from the south, largely the
Tashkent region and the Farghana Valley, and to some extent from
the Bukhara-Samarkand parts of the Zarafshan River valley in
Uzbekistan. In agriculture, where most Central Asians worked,
cotton reigned as king in the south and wheat growing plus cattle
raising in the north. Central Asians could take small comfort from
the 188,000 hectare growth in area sown to cotton between 1970
and 1976. That 7.7 percent increase, like most of the output of 89.7
billion cubic meters of natural gas from Central Asia in 1975,
supplied the factories and enterprises of central Russia and the
Soviet West rather than enriching the local economy. Over two-
thirds of the natural gas extracted in Uzbekistan goes north of
Central Asia by pipeline to industrial centers in the Ural hills and
the area that Soviet economists call European Russia.[46]

The planning and administration of the Central Asian economy
lies in the hands of the bureaucracy of ministries staffed and located
in Moscow. Their union-wide priorities relegate regional interests to
second place. The result is a kind of internal colonial arrangement
in which raw materials proceed from Central Asia to the USSR
center for exploitation. The authorities transport most of Central
Asia's main agricultural and industrial production—such as cotton,
beef and hides, oil and gas—to other users. Economic development only loosely connected with the people of the region fails to
reinforce or engender a sense of group identity. Central Asians

[46] Ian M. Matley, "Central Asia and Kazakhstan," in *Economics of Soviet Regions*, eds.
I. S. Koropeckyj and Gertrude E. Schroeder (New York: Praeger Special Studies, 1981),
pp. 447–48, 427, 420, 425, 433; *The Industry of Soviet Uzbekistan* (Tashkent: Uzbek
Society for Friendship and Cultural Relations with Foreign Countries, 1977), pp. 11–12.

cannot escape a knowledge of this reality, and it must contribute to a sense of powerlessness.

Two crucial economic issues captured the imagination of Central Asians in the 1980s—the region's desperate thirst for more water and dismay over increasingly severe damage to the area's environment from industrial and agricultural development. Both relate especially to the USSR's central planning, which often overlooked ecological consequences of its decisions and orders to the outlying regions. Central Asians saw these difficulties demonstrated in a pair of related problems. From the early 1970s to 1980s, Russian planners, with encouragement from certain Central Asian leaders—such as Sharaf R. Rashidov—studied a project that would draw some water from the north-flowing Irtysh and Ob rivers near Tobolsk and send it 2,550 kilometers (1,300 miles) southward across the Sir Darya and into the Amu Darya River and Aral Sea of southern Central Asia after irrigating large acreages in the Turgay lowlands of northern Central Asia. They appeared to abandon that grand plan by December 1983, without public announcement or full explanation. Nonetheless, arid Central Asia persisted in calling for transferring a portion of the Siberian river water. A few Asian ministers in the USSR government, such as Polad A. Polad-Zade, First Deputy Minister of Melioration and Water Economy of the USSR, termed it essential for the southern regions.[47] In Moscow, the debate revolved around possible harm to the northern ecology through depleting water resources and around financing the expensive project that would largely benefit areas outside the Russian Soviet Federative Socialist Republic. In Tashkent and elsewhere around Central Asia, the urgent need for water to sustain the fast-growing population and the economic expansion required to support it took first place in public discussions. Behind that lay a strong regional sense that Moscow's decisionmakers once again seemed to discriminate against non-Russian Central Asia. In 1985 and later the local press insis-

---

[47] V. Zakhar'ko, "Severnaia voda dlia iuga," *Izvestiya* (June 22, 1984), p. 2. Theodore Shabad kindly drew the author's attention to this and other references concerning the project to pump Siberian river water down to Central Asia; Ziyawuddin Äkrämaw and Asam Räfikaw, "Aral mädäd soräydi," *Shärq yulduzi* no. 6 (1986), pp. 166–77. Peter Sinnott first drew this article to the author's attention.

tently argued in favor of spending the money and effort to strengthen Central Asia's ecological and economic base by providing more water from the only place offering a great surplus—Russian Siberia.[48] When official enthusiasm for that effort waned, Central Asians focused attention upon the related plight of the Aral Sea. Huge demands from irrigation canals upriver along both the Sir Darya and Amu Darya diverted so much water that the Aral Sea level fell drastically, the sea visibly shrank in size, and salinization intensified. During an Aeroflot flight in November 1983 passing over the eastern reaches of the sea, the author of this chapter observed several huge dead ponds of its waters by then completely detached from the main body of the sea, and thus from resupply, cut off by dessication that raised extensive sandbars above the surface of the water. In addition to influencing climatic conditions negatively in that area, the loss and pollution of the sea's water destroyed its important fisheries and surrounding agriculture in a broad area.

The ruination of the Aral Sea has become an issue that Central Asia's writers and other intellectuals have grasped with great feeling and have eagerly joined economists, scientists, and managers in trying to rectify. Such a concrete problem has given the region's indigenous population a rare public sense of solidarity toward reluctant Moscow that partly offsets the disintegrative impact of remaining so many decades outside the decisionmaking process.

Beyond the political wreckage created by dramatic clashes in Alma Ata, around the Aral Sea affair, and through basic disconnection from economic responsibility, some quiet processes continue in Central Asia. They should have great influence in the future. Devotion to the indigenous languages, celebration of family and group traditions, guidance given abundantly by literary intellectuals, and other things, all steadily contribute to continuing the self-awareness of Central Asians. Despite ethnic inadequacies in educational programs the schooling given large numbers of local children will have

[48] "Tärjimäi halning bashlänishi," *Sawet Ozbekistani* (January 10, 1985), p. 2; "Ab' däryasidän Ämudäryagächä chozilädigän bolghusi 'Sibir'—Ortä Asiya'," (photographs with caption), *Ozbekistan ädäbiyati wä sän'äti* no. 2 (1985), p. 2; Ä. Mämantaw, "Sibir' däryaläri suwining bir qismi Ortä Asiyagä aqädi. Ulkän qurilish täräddudi," *Sawet Ozbekistani* (August 6, 1985), p. 1.

an impact. Literature and education of the late twentieth century will necessitate a reinterpretation in cultural identity, a reexamination of the meaning of Central Asianness. Regular, obligatory schooling has produced in Central Asians a self-confidence and preoccupation with competence in managing their own affairs that had been muted in earlier decades. Persistent experience in dealing effectively with administrative problems will most likely increase the attractions to Central Asians of greater group responsibility within the Soviet framework and system.

In the era of Mikhail S. Gorbachev the CPSU in Moscow probably will not yet permit Central Asians to establish institutions of their own. Owing to that likelihood, they must find another outlet for their group needs and expression. Central Asians can and have made some Soviet institutions their own, such as learned institutes, departments of instruction, and cultural centers. Their group self-esteem demands that they extend this into more organizations and agencies. They appear capable of accomplishing still more in this sphere.

Many small things demonstrate these positive attitudes about the vitality of a self-reliant Central Asia and its subregions. The maintenance of the local language stock and conscious rejection of excess borrowings from Russian give one hint. The careful upbringing of the younger and older children in the schools supply another. Kindergartens fill with selected children all over Central Asia. A visit to preschool classes given in a most pleasant, well-equipped establishment in Tashkent in 1983 made one fact obvious to the author of this chapter. Those Central Asian children, most of them seemingly the offspring of the elite, were starting a journey that would lead many of them to important responsibilities in Central Asia. Their Central Asian headmistress and teachers offered professional models of achievement. They also provided a focus of ethnic identity. Although the four- and five-year olds wore Russian-style hair ribbons or shirts, they spoke their own tongue and showed the assurance of the confident (see figure 17.3).

Central Asians openly categorize those kindergartens and pre-schoolers as their most precious resource in the effort to sustain regional identity. Like other schools, they must train pupils in

FIGURE 17.3   School principal, Masturakhan Musaeva, and teachers in Baghchä 426 elite kindergarten, with Central Asian girls wearing Russian hair bows. Tashkent, Ts.-1 Kuibyshev raion (November 1983).

Russian language and history.[49] Nevertheless, Marxist ideologists have recently criticized such schools for emphasizing indigenous language and literature from the very beginning of the curriculum. Many educators, party and government officials, and construction workers celebrated the opening of a new Central Asian kindergarten in Alma Ata in December 1986. An indigenous poet also supported the idea of opening more such kindergartens in Alma Ata and elsewhere. He wrote: "It is one of the main duties of every Kazakh, every Kazakh family, everyone who regards himself as a

[49] Bill (William) Fierman, "Comment [about the status of Russian-language training in Central Asia]: The View from Uzbekistan," *The Changing Status of Russian in the Soviet Union*, special edition of *International Journal of the Sociology of Language* edited by Isabelle Kreindler no. 33 (1982), pp. 74–75.

FIGURE 17.4   Schoolchildren waiting for a bus in Alma Ata (1987).
(Photo by William McCabe.)

Kazakh, and the entire population, to be proud of their native
language, to be concerned for its purity and to promote its development. . . . The strength of a people lies in the strength of their
language."[50]

These new Central Asians will be well prepared for life in the
ambivalent Soviet society. They are emerging unfrightened through
a fierce adult dialectic between the convictions of people like the
poet from Kazakhstan and the Russian-oriented ideological urge of
the leadership. Their Central Asia will surely differ significantly
from the one known between 1865 and the 1980s (see figure 17.4).

Russian rule introduced two major changes in the area from the
beginning of the occupation. The reclusive, isolated social existence
led by Central Asians in towns could no longer continue. Russia's
conquest not only excited the curiosity of Europeans and Americans about the region. It brought in many travelers, merchants,

---

[50] *Leninshil zhas* (October 3, 1985), *Vecherniaia Alma-Ata* (December 10, 1986), and
Sotsialistik Kazakhstan (December 16, 1986), cited in *The Central Asian Newsletter* no.
2 (June 1987), pp. 8–9.

students and scholars, and, ultimately, tourists. From those visits, as much as from the important manuscripts obtained in the capitals, outsiders gained impressions and understanding about Central Asian life and culture. At the same time, Central Asians revived their once lively interest in the outside world. The convenience of using Russian—a recognized world language—in addition to the native tongue also helped put this population in touch with foreign lands. In practical terms, that contact on various levels and through different modes of communication has advanced very little. Central Asians may not travel abroad without permission granted only in Moscow. Foreigners may not visit the region informally. Private persons have limited access to people of the territory.

Nevertheless, that opening to places beyond the homeland inescapably introduces modern technology and associated life patterns into the towns of the region. Expansion of Russian institutions and practices such as museums, libraries, and universal, required schooling, prepared the population for further change. Russian channels transmitted and transmit information about Europe, America, Africa, and other parts of Asia to people in the USSR. Ideologically interpreted news comes to Central Asian ears daily from Russia. An unfree press conveys many mistaken ideas to listeners, but in the presence of competitive sources of information it, too, awakens the interest of people earlier largely denied any news at all.

What have these changes meant to Central Asians and what will result from them? The evidence shows that indigenous people of the area retain a strong sense of self. Attachment to language, culture, arts, place, and custom remains vigorous. Technical modernization seemingly leaves these ties undisturbed, their strength perhaps enhanced. In light of this, what about the connections with Russian culture and Soviet Russian institutions? They seem formal, accepted by habit or necessity, but relatively unintegrated into the group identity of Central Asians. As the generations expand and grow older, more educated, and professionally skilled, other drives will probably augment the present emphasis upon cultural expression. Renewed ambition for a greater political say, for participation in economic and administrative decisions, will likely develop out of the competence and experience built in the previous cohorts of

Central Asians. To a notable extent, the twelve decades of Russian rule may have altered the ways people in the region work, behave and think, but not the basic values and beliefs that pervade the society and create its attitudes. As a result, Central Asia remains a distinct, vital region that has created its own reputation, recognized name, and a history with meaning for informed persons everywhere.

E. A.

18

The Hunger for Modern Leadership

Central Asians endured decades of debilitating famine in empowerment between 1938 and 1991.[1] Deprived of their true leaders, they hungered for inspirational guidance. Craving significant group identity with an epitome of their own great civilization, they barely subsisted on meagre allowances of nonentities. Marxist cultural ideologists, Communist Party politicians, and Soviet government officials imposed by Moscow drove, rather than led, Central Asian society. Their hegemony blighted the normal cycle of creating and replacing indigenous leaders. They purposely malnourished the spirit of community long blending the region's population. Those deprivations condemned people of the area to an indefinite period of elementary self-rediscovery and a difficult adjustment to rapidly changing conditions.

Even so, strong-minded executives and cultural leaders occasionally rose above the general mediocrity that the Soviet system fostered in Central Asia. But whenever such figures achieved too much popularity and influence within their own nationality or administrative unit, their species faced starvation. [See Chapters 9 and 13 about the purges under Joseph V. Stalin, and Chapter 17 concerning the actions of Communist Party of the Soviet Union (CPSU) chiefs who selectively disgraced

[1] For published chronologies of recent events in Central Asia, see the following sources: "Birlik, Major Landmarks," Special Issue. Press-centre of the Popular Movement "Birlik" of Uzbekistan (Tashkent, n.p., 1990), pp. 1–5; Ian Bremmer; Ray Taras, eds., "Appendix A. Chronology of ethnic unrest in the USSR, 1895–1991," Nation and Politics in the Soviet Successor States (Cambridge, Cambridge University Press, 1993), pp. 529–49; "News and Comments," Central Asia Monitor, Nos. 5 (1993), 6 (1993), and earlier issues; "Birlik's Birth," Turkistan Today, no. 1 (October 1, 1989), pp. 2–4; "Weekly Review," RFE/RL Research Report, 1992 and earlier issues; RFE/RL News Briefs. 1993–; Russia and Eurasia. Facts and Figures Annual. (Gulf Breeze, Academic International Press, vol. 18 1993).

Dinmuhamed A. Kunayev (1911–93), Sharaf R. Rashidov (1917–83), and other prominent Central Asian men and women such as Yadgar S. Nasriddinova (1920–).]

A public assault upon a leading cultural or political figure threatened more than the career and life of an executive. It harmed the well-being of the community and its group identity. Appropriate leaders formed perhaps the most essential leg upon which to balance the self-awareness of a twentieth-century nationality. Unsteady executives only intensified the ambivalence undermining Central Asia's collective feelings.

The further crucial issue of regional unity confronted Central Asia: For survival and strength in dealings both with Russia and China as well as certain combative neighbors to the south—Iran and Afghanistan—should the former Soviet Central Asian region's half-dozen main nationalities not try to merge into one great unit? Or, would continuance of the individual monoethnic republics of Soviet origin, with their evident weaknesses, serve people better? The right response to these queries depended as much as anything upon the quality of the territory's leaders. What sort of improvement could the region expect from leaders trained as followers, or, at best, regarded merely as mediators between outside authority and subjects like themselves? To what extent did persisting Russian dominance affect the ideas and behavior of Central Asia's new leaders? The difficulty in finding leadership that could answer these basic questions and satisfy the needs of the people of Central Asia seemed sure to play a significant part in developments after Kazakhs, Kirgiz, Tajiks, Turkmens, and Uzbeks declared independence.

SIGNS OF IMMINENT CHANGE

Partially symptomatic of the release from tight Soviet control in the second half of the 1980s, large-scale violence flared up in two places 1,650 kilometers (1,000 miles) apart, rocking the eastern Farghana Valley of Uzbekistan and far western Kazakhstan. As described by foreign reporters and the controlled Soviet press, bloody ethnic conflict erupted in Farghana on the weekend of June 3–4, 1989, and continued for several days. Violence spread to the towns of Kokand, Kuvasai, Marghilan, and Namangan. Those accounts described a spectacle unimaginable to anyone convinced that Islamic solidarity lay in Central Asia's immediate future. They saw assaults by different Turkic and nominally Muslim groups upon each others' lives and property. Meskhetian Turks and some Crimean Tatars, both relatively small groups exiled without cause to the region in 1944 by the Soviet regime, suddenly underwent attack by numerous bands of young Uzbeks. Dozens upon dozens of Meskhetian Turks and Uzbeks died. Looters robbed and burned hundreds of homes, automobiles, and buildings, including offices of the Communist Party of Uzbekistan (CPUZ).[2] In the end, the populace held the leadership responsible.

"The overwhelming belief of people here [in Tashkent] is that the many officials and local leaders . . . are orchestrating the unrest to show authorities and local residents alike that they still control the republic," said a Western reporter covering the story in Uzbekistan.[3] That view accords with other, unverifiable reports that blamed the secret police (KGB—Committee for State Security) for provoking the clashes. People reasoned that local leaders and secret police together intended to set nationalities against one another. That kind of action, as in the past, would benefit the incumbent politicians, especially Russians. It might do so by weakening a potential alliance among Muslim coreligionists and members of Turkic-language subfamilies. However, this catastrophe in ethnic relations immediately prompted an outflow of non-Uzbeks from the Uzbekistan SSR.

Another sign of the coming change: Soon after those events in the Farghana Valley, journalists reported an armed rampage by young people in Kazakhstan that caused severe damage and some deaths. The trouble broke out on June 16, 1989, in the Kazakhstan oil town of Novyi Uzen'. From there it spread to Fort Shevchenko, Kul'sary, Mangishlak, and Yeraliev, all near the Caspian Sea. Authorities attributed the rioting to poor living standards and resentment over special amenities allowed migrant workers, presumably Transcaucasians and Slavs.[4]

RESENTMENT TOWARD OUTSIDERS

This exposed a problem much deeper than the backlash released by a slackening of taut Soviet control over the area. To some extent, these violent attacks may have expressed resentment against poor living con-

[2] Francis X. Clines, "57 Reported Dead in Uzbek Violence. Assault on Minority Group in Southern Republic is Likened to a Pogrom," *New York Times* (7 June 1989), p. A11.

[3] Esther B. Fein, "In a Soviet Asian Republic, Cause of the Strife is Elusive," *New York Times* (14 June 1989), p. A12.

[4] Esther B. Fein, "Soviets Report an Armed Rampage in Kazakhstan," *New York Times* (20 June 1989), p. A11; Esther B. Fein, "Rioting Youths Reportedly Attack the Police in Soviet Kazakhstan," *New York Times* (26 June 1989), p. A10.

ditions and other inequities. Also, they could have reflected tensions engendered by the imperfect ethnic divisions introduced earlier in the Soviet administrative demarcation.

But the broader pattern shows something more insidious. Together with frequent smaller incidents, those dramatic outbursts in Farghana and Novyi Uzen' represented a mindless lashing out against all kinds of outsiders.

They concentrated especially upon non-Central Asians occupying Central Asian soil, populating its universities, institutes, and other cultural centers, and filling the best residential housing and respectable employment. The riots revealed a deep frustration focused not only on the millions of Slavs, European Jews, and similar migrants from the Soviet West (see Table 18.3). As noticed, the rage vented itself also upon Crimean Tatars, Meskhetian Turks, Volga Tatars, Uyghurs, and related Eastern minorities alien to the groups in Western Turkistan (that is, in Russian Central Asia, including Kazakhstan). Some educated Kazakhs, for example, characterized Uyghur migrants from the Peoples' Republic of China (PRC), now settled in Kazakhstan, as inferior people, as shady businessmen, as wealthy exploiters, and in other negative terms.

Not only that, members of Central Asia's indigenous nationalities also regarded each other as aliens when one lived within the Soviet-drawn borders of the other group. The killings and arson in and around Osh, Kirgizstan, early in the following year, discussed below, demonstrated the consequences of this contrived alienation in intergroup relations. Such rancor stemmed partly from revulsion at the hypocritical slogans of the CPSU relating to the ostensible "Friendship among Ethnic Groups." Many ordinary Central Asians felt that CPSU authorities favored Armenians, Slavs, Volga Tatars, and certain other nationalities widely dispersed around the USSR.

Central Asians without doubt longed for new, exemplary chief executives and peerless cultural chairmen and -women. Some looked for models from the Middle Ages, such as the Kirgiz epic hero Manas or the Timurid, Amir Timur. On the second anniversary of Uzbekistan's declaration of independence, August 31, 1993 (though the anniversary date officially falls on September 1),[5] the Republic dedicated another

---

[5] Äbdullä Äʻzämaw, comp. *Mustäqil Ozbekistan. Tärikh silsiläläridä. Mälʻumatnamä* (Tashkent, Qamuslär Bash Tähririyäti, 1992), inside front cover.

monument in Tashkent. A large equestrian statue portrayed the medieval tyrant, who claimed a genealogy that traced back to the Chinggisid Mongols, not to early Uzbeks. The inscription displays an aphorism, mixing might and right, attributed to Amir Timur: "Power Exists in Justice" or, "Power Is Indeed [Derived from] Justice" (*Kuch ädalätdädir*).[6]

In regard to the person of the leader, another use of bias expressed itself repeatedly during the years from 1989 to 1993. When Tajiks actively distrusted their leader, Rahmon Nabiyev, some called him an Uzbek (he came from Khojand, Leninabad Province, heavily populated by Uzbeks). Dissidents in Uzbekistan suffering under the repression of Islam A. Karimov consider him a Tajik (President Karimov comes from Samarkand, a strongly Tajik City in Uzbekistan). During the presidential election of 1991 in Uzbekistan, the politicians around candidate Islam A. Karimov spread a rumor meant to demean his main opponent, Muhammad Solih, an Uzbek native of Khwarazm (far from Tashkent), by calling him an Uyghur or Iranian.[7] To raise suspicion about the candidate's ethnic identity, officials omitted all reference to Mr. Solih's nationality from his election biography, but included a sentence in Mr. Karimov's accompanying sketch, saying: "by nationality, he is Uzbek."[8]

PACIFIC STEPS BY POTENTIAL LEADERS

From 1986 on, the Soviet "openness" (*glasnost'*) that further enlarged the circle of rehabilitations, reintroduced into the record many important early cultural and political figures. At different times, Soviet ideologists had slighted or deliberately ignored Hazrat Ahmad Yassawiy, Sultan Husayn Bayqara, Muhammad Shaybaniy Khan, Ablay Khan, Kenesari Qasim-uli, and dozens like them, in the approved encyclopedias,

---

[6] Hämid Ziyayew, "Istiqlal uchun birläshäylik," *Ozbekistan ädäbiyati wä sän'äti* (22 November 1991), p. 5; representations of the heroic figure in the Kirgiz epic, *Manas* as well as the tomb revered as his burial place, appeared on the new paper money issued by Kirgizstan in 1992–93; "Bäkht quyashing sonmäsin, Wätan! Ozbekistan Respublikäsi Prezidenti Islam Kärimawning Sahibqiran Amir Temur häykälining achilishgä bäghish-längän täntänädä sozlägän nutqi," *Turkistan. Yashlär ijtimaiy-siyasiy gäzetäsi* (1 September 1993), pp. 1–3.

[7] Bess Brown, "Whither Tajikistan," *RFE/RL Research Report*, Vol. IF, No. 24 (12 June 92), p. 4; *Sredniaia Aziia. Spravochnye materialy. Istoriia, politika, ekonomika.* Moscow: Institut Gumanitarno-Politicheskikh Issledovanii. Seriia "Spravochnye Izdaniia," (1992), p. 16.

[8] "Biografiia Mukhammada Solikha (S. Madaminova)" and "Biografiia I. A. Karimova," *Pravda Vostoka* (30 November 1991), p. 1.

histories, textbooks, and academic studies prepared according to the Marxist-Leninist-Stalinist canon. Now, a rush of new publications and commentaries gave both students and adults a bigger taste of Central Asia's splendid heritage.

Yet another kind of significant indicator signaled trouble for the USSR. Since 1965, the whole country had suffered from inadequate leadership at the very top. After the mid-1980s, the central government of the USSR and the CPSU, only half-heartedly trying to keep up with the times, at first ignored the existence of the tremendous array of Soviet nationality problems. Repeating the old formula, claiming that they had resolved the nationality question, CPSU chiefs hardly alluded to it in their meetings in Moscow in early 1987. The growing tensions forced them, by summer, 1989, belatedly to promulgate what they termed a comprehensive new nationality policy.

The "Platform" document began with the acknowledgment that nationality affairs in the USSR required urgent attention: "The nationality question in the Soviet Union has acquired exceptional acuteness in recent times."[9] This action amounted to an admission, for the first time since the death of Joseph V. Stalin in 1953, that the Soviet government sensed the risk present in its failure to resolve the nationality question equitably. Nevertheless, in his speeches referring to that question, Mikhail S. Gorbachev, First Secretary of the Central Committee of the CPSU, continued to insist that no nationality could choose to secede; therefore, the USSR, imitating the Czarist Empire before it, unknowingly declared itself indivisible shortly before events demonstrated exactly the reverse.[10]

THE SEARCH FOR ALTERNATIVE LEADERSHIP

In Uzbekistan, the Birlik Khälq Häräkäti (Unity Popular Movement —referred to hereafter as the Birlik Popular Movement or Birlik Party) had first appeared in November 1988, led by a scientist, Dr. Abdurahim Pulatov (see Figure 18.1).[11] It then claimed at least 15,000 members

[9] "Natsional'naia politika Partii v sovremennykh usloviakh (platformma KPSS)," *Pravda* (17 August 1989), pp. 1–2.

[10] Francis X. Clines (from Moscow), "Gorbachev Offers Fractious Nationalists Both Olive Branch and Stick," *New York Times* (20 September 1989), p. A8.

[11] Formally, they named it The Popular Unity Movement for Defense of Nature and of the Material and Spiritual Riches of Uzbekistan—Ozbekistan Täbiyati, Maddiy wä Mä'näwiy Bayliqlärini Muhafäzä Etish Birlik Khälq Häräkäti.

FIGURE 18.1   Dr. Abdurahim Pulatov, Chair, Birlik Popular
Movement, Uzbekistan, at Columbia University, June 8,
1992. Photo by Ibrahim Yüksel.

and carried on vigorous public actions during 1989–92. The Birlik Party
protested against Communist Party of Uzbekistan (CPUz) harassment
of the movement, held mass meetings and demonstrations, and began
issuing a newsletter, *Birlik*, in 1989 (see Figure 18.3a), then edited by
Fähriddin Khudayqulaw.[12]

The Birlik Party's "General Draft Program" of spring 1989 emphasized cultural reform. Among other things, it demanded adoption of
Uzbek as the sole national language of the Uzbekistan Soviet Socialist
Republic (UzSSR), as well as institution of real justice and achievement
of genuine equality for women in the Republic.[13]

---

[12] See *Birlik. Märkäziy kengash argäni*, Nos. 15 and 16 (May 1990); "Birlikning tughu-
lushi," *Bugünkü Türkistan* (ed. in Uzbek and English by Dr. Timur Kocaoglu, Munich,
Germany), no. 1 (Oct. 1, 1989), pp. 1–3.

[13] *Ozbekistan SSR Täbiäti, Maddiy wä Mä'näwiy Bayliklärini Muhafäzä Etish Birlik
Khälq Häräkäti Umumiy Pragrämining Layihäsi.* Affirmed May 26, 1989, at the Tashkent
Quriltay (Congress) of the Birlik Movement. 9-page typewritten copy, pp. 4, 8–9. Thanks
to Paul Goble for this document.

Active discussions of the national language question as an aspect of sovereign right took place throughout 1988–89. They aroused concern over the fate of the languages in each republic spoken by many citizens from other nationalities. Some cultural leaders spoke out vehemently in favor of requiring the eponymous language of each republic for education and for people in government service.[14] Wording in the law establishing a state language in Uzbekistan reflected that attitude. Its Article 4 required all leaders of government and of official agencies to command and use the state language. Ultimately, those debates led to formal declarations of the state languages. For example, the Supreme Council of the Uzbekistan SSR adopted Uzbek as the official language of the still-dependent republic on October 21, 1989.[15]

The language issue also emerged prominently elsewhere in Central Asia. Kazakhstan's National Democratic Party Azat, for instance, made the status of its native language the number one issue in its statement of principles.[16] Other republics also moved to establish national languages. Constitutional requirements for high officials in Kazakhstan, Kirgizstan, and Turkmenistan, as well as Uzbekistan, likewise include in each case mastery and public use of the eponymous language.[17]

Sixteen months after the emergence of the Birlik Popular Movement in Uzbekistan, another reformist organization arose there, the Erk Demakrätik Pärtiyäsi (Liberty Democratic Party, hereafter, Erk Democratic Party). On April 11, 1990, Muhammad Solih (b.20 Dec. 1949) (see Figure 18.2) poet and activist, along with another prominent poet, Erkin Wahidov (b.28 Dec. 1936), established the competing organization. The Erk Democratic Party, ostensibly oriented toward the more educated portion of society, to some extent divided Uzbekistan's forces seeking reform and opposing the communists.[18]

---

[14] Mirzä Kenjäbayew, "Til erki—el erki," *Ozbekistan ädäbiyati wä sän'äti* (24 Feb. 1989), p. 2.

[15] Adil Yaqubaw, "Khälq dilidägi gäp," *Ozbekistan ädäbiyati wä sän'äti* (7 April 1989), p. 1. At that time, the novelist Adil Yaqubaw held the position of First Secretary of the Board of the Writers' Union of the Uzbekistan SSR; *Ozbekistan Sawet Satsiälistik Respublikäsining Qanuni. Ozbekistan SSRning däwlät tili häqidä* (Tashkent, "Ozbekistan," 1989), pp. 5–16.

[16] "Qazaqstanning ûlttïq-demokratiyalïq partiyasïnïng baghdarlamasï," *Azat*, Nos. 11–12 (15 qïrküyek 1993), p. 1.

[17] Edward Allworth, "The Cultural Identity of Central Asian Leaders: The Problem of Affinity with Followers," *Central Asia Monitor*, No. 6 (1993), p. 30.

[18] Sabir Mirwäliyew, *Ozbek ädibläri (ikhchäm ädäbiy partretlär)* (Tashkent, Ozbekistan Respublikäsi Fänlär Äkädemiyäsi "FÄN" Näshriyati, 1993), pp. 93, 161–63, 217–18. The entry in this writers' directory for Sharaf R. Rashidaw details his CPUZ and other

FIGURE 18.2   Muhammad Solih (left), Chair "Erk" Democratic
Party, Uzbekistan, at Columbia University, June 8, 1992.
Photo by Ibrahim Yüksel.

The new organization's bulletin, *"Erk,"* published Party Chairman
Solih's speech made to the First Congress of the Erk Democratic Party
on April 30, 1990. He declared that "one of the first duties that the "Erk"
Party puts before itself, in fact, is [to achieve] the independence of
the republic [of Uzbekistan]."[19] A branch of the "Erk" Party separately
published its own bulletin in Tashkent.[20]

At the same time, in Kazakhstan, three of the approximately twenty
political-social and cultural movements active there made some impression upon public opinion. People especially gained awareness of the
Alash Party, the "Azat" Partiyasï (Freedom Party or Azat Party), and
the Zheltoqsan Komiteti (December Committee, sometimes referred
to as the December Party). The latter first set out to correct a specific

---

political activity. Entries for Mr. Solih and Mr. Wahidaw include no mention of their
leadership and activities in the Birlik and Erk Parties or in the elections for President,
giving an example of old-style state censorship in newly independent Central Asia.
    [19] Muhämmäd Salih, "'Erk' Pärtiyäsining Pärtiyäsining birinchi qurultayidägi nutq,"
'Erk' (Erk Demakrätik Pärtiyäsining Näshri), No. 3 (May 1990), p. 2.
    [20] *Hurriyät*, edited by Dilaram Ishaqawa, No. 2 (September 1991), No. 3 (Novem-
ber 1991).

FIGURE 18.3a   Uzbek-language newspapers of Birlik Popular Movement
and "Erk" Democratic Party, 1989–92.

injustice. It attempted persistently to defend and to obtain the release
from prison of individuals charged with breaking laws by demonstrating
against the Communist Party of Kazakhstan (cpкaz) and the Government of Kazakhstan in December 1986. Those events occurred upon
the removal, by Moscow communists, of the cpкaz First Secretary,
Dinmuhamed A. Kunayev, a Kazakh, from his post (see Chapter 17).

Continuing that effort, the Zheltoqsan Committee later also aimed
more broadly, opposing the prevailing communist bureaucracy and calling for a coalition government that would crowd communists out of
the center of power. In mid-1992, the Zheltoqsan Committee's leader,
Khasen Kärimzhanulï Qozha-Akhmet (in Russian, Kozhakhmetov) (see
Figure 18.4), organized large public demonstrations by his opposition
group against the republic government. He insisted that officials bring
more balance (that is, more Kazakhs) into the parliament and govern-

ғ ı ɢ ᴜ ʀ ᴇ 18.3b   Samples of Kazakhstan's unofficial press, in Kazakh and Russian, 1990–93: *Zheltoqsan, Azat,* and *Khäq.*

ment agencies, still dominated by Russians and communists.[21] Zheltoq-san spokesmen and press sharply criticized the policies of Kazakhstan's president.

Kazakhstan's National-Democratic Party Azat held its Constituent Assembly September 4, 1991. It aimed originally to establish an independent Republic of Kazakhstan. Later, it defined its several aims as "real democratization of Kazakh society," by working against "the dominance of former CPKaz appointees," in favor of "reforming the election system," and to accomplish "the complete decolonization of Kazakhstan." Azat issued a newspaper entitled *Azat, Täuelsîz sayasi gazet (Azat,* an

---

[21] Khasen Kärimzhanulï Qozha-Akhmet, "Büyrekten siraq shïgharmaylïq," *Zheltoqsan,* No. 3 (1992), p. 1; "Thousands Rally in Kazakhstan to Urge Communists to Quit Posts," *New York Times* (18 June 1992), p. A16.

Independent Political Newspaper) (see Figure 18.3b). The Azat Party
first chose M. Esenaliev, S. Shapagatov, and others as leaders. In 1993,
Dr. Kamal Ormantay served as Party chairman, with the Zheltoqsan
Committee's Khasen Qozha-Akhmet holding the office of First Vice-
President. The Azat and Zheltoqsan movements had effectively joined
forces.

The new Alash Party of Kazakhstan, founded in April 1990 and
headed by Aron Atabek (Nutushev), in November 1991 started issuing a Russian-language tabloid bearing an Arabic name, *Khäq* (Truth)
written in both Cyrillic and Arabic script. The periodical described
itself as an "Islamic Political Newspaper" (see Figure 18.3b). The formal
"Program of the Party of National Freedom, 'Alash'," listed five main
aims: (1) achievement of a genuinely independent national state; (2) promotion of the idea of Turkic unity and Muslim solidarity; (3) national
rebirth of Kazakhstan as a historical nucleus of a future unified Turkic-
Islamic state of Great Turkistan; (4) improvement of the standard of
living of Kazakhs and all backward people living in Turko-Islamic lands;
(5) rejection of neocolonial expansion both from Russia and other world
powers.[22] (To compare these goals with those of the original Alash Orda
Party during 1917–22, see Chapters 8 and 9.)

The Alash Party and its paper, in addition, carried on a strong polemic
against the government of Kazakhstan and specifically against President
Nursultan A. Nazarbayev. Unaccustomed to free speech and open
political rivalry, Kazakhstan, Uzbekistan, and other jurisdictions
adopted ordinances that forbad criticism of the chief executives. In
this, the republics imitated the vaguely worded Soviet law prohibiting
dissent by terming it slander against the Soviet state.

The *Khäq* press printed excerpts from the anti-Nazarbayev political
exposé by Karishal Asanov, *Thoughts about the Fate of the People or
A Word Regarding the Phantom of "Sovereignty"*. Violently reacting to
publication of that material, government authorities threw Mr. Asanov
in prison on August 19, 1992, closed down the newspaper, and trashed
the home offices of editor Aron Atabek, forcing him to flee to Azerbaijan
for political asylum. Representatives from the New York City office of
Helsinki Watch and other human rights organizations protested in person and in writing to the chief prosecutor of the Kazakhstan Republic

---

[22] "Programma Partii natsional'noi svobody 'Alash'," *Häq*, No. 2 (1992), p. 2.

FIGURE 18.4 Khasen Qozha-Akhmet, Chair, Zheltoqsan Committee of Kazakhstan (from *Zheltoqsan* newspaper, no. 3 (1992), p. 1.

against this denial of free speech and fair trial.[23] Attention focused specifically upon the infamous Article 170-3, part 2, of the Kazakhstan Republic's Criminal Code.[24]

In Kirgizstan, popular discontent erupted especially among the young unemployed and the landless poor. Protests shook the complacent communist leadership and paved the way for substantial change. In June 1989, in and around Bishkek (before 1926, Pishpek; from 1926–91, Frunze), many young people began confiscating plots of land from the state. Squatters by the thousands claimed building sites for private cabins on the outskirts of town and began erecting their own small

[23] Karishal Asanov, "Ne ver' ulybke prezidenta (Iz knigi K. Asanova, Dumy o sud'be narodnoi ili Slovo o prizrake 'Suvereniteta')," *Häq*, No. 3 (1992), pp. 1–2 (to be continued); Karishal Gabduldanovich Asanov, "General'nomu Sekratariu OON Gospodinu Butrosu Galiiu!," *Azat*, Nos. 11–12 (15 Qïrküyek 1993), pp. 1–2; Karishal Asanov, "Ia ne nameren byt' osuzhdennym za deianie drugikh," *Azat*, Nos. 11–12 (15 Qïrküyek 1993), pp. 3–7.

[24] Karishal Aslanov, "Ia ne nameren byt' osuzhdennym za deianiia drugikh," *Azat. Täuelsîz sayasi qazet*, Nos. 11–12 (15 Qïrküyek 1993), p. 6.

homes after waiting years for allocations of government housing that Communist Party officials never delivered.

That movement soon organized itself and elected a Council and a president, journalist Jumagazy Usupov (b.1953), educated in Leningrad State University. He had joined the radical "Ashar" (Mutual Aid) Movement of Kirgizstan in 1989 and became chairman of its governing board in autumn the same year. Later on, its members reelected him for another term. Besides "Ashar," many other organizations functioned actively in the life of Kirgizstan, rather peacefully, for the most part.[25]

CENTRAL ASIAN CIVIL WARS

Educated reformers in Tajikistan, bolstered by the physical vigor and faith of Muslim believers, pressed hard on the communist monolith controlling the existing political machine. A spiritual leader in the new situation, Qozi Akbar Turajonzoda Hajji, for a time offered Tajiks a different option for leadership in the ideological and political turmoil (see Figure 18.6). As a result, the Qozi soon bore the communists' epithet for opponents: "enemy of the people." But still in 1989, reconstruction in that republic permitted scholars and other intellectuals the chance to draw together a coalition of persons eager for reform. The *Rastokhez* (Resurrection) group strove peacefully for cultural changes, including adoption of Tajik as the official language, replacement of the Cyrillic alphabet with the Persian script, revival of the Islamic culture, and the like. To these, before long, *Rastokhez* added both economic and political aims.[26]

Their unexpectedly ardent pursuit of freedom shook all Central Asia's political incumbents and drew the startled attention of the outside world. Early in 1990, hundreds and thousands of ordinary people came from village, town, and countryside to the capital, Dushanbe, to demonstrate their faith and hope for a new, noncommunist society and government. After frequent rumblings, on February 12th, 1990, rioters sacked Communist Party of Tajikistan (CPTaj) headquarters and set it on

[25] *Sredniaia Aziia. Spravochnye materialy. Istoriia, Politika, Ekonomika* (1992), pp. 49–50; Francis X. Clines, "Frunze Journal. Off the List, into a Lean-to: A Hammer Beckons," *New York Times* (18 November 1989), p. 4.

[26] Shahrbanou Tadjbakhsh, *The Bloody Path of Change: the Case of Post-Soviet Tajikistan*. New York: Harriman Institute Forum, No. 11 (July 1993), pp. 2–3.

fire. On February 13th, an essentially peaceful outdoor protest began to turn violent.[27]

Spokesmen attributed the immediate cause of the many killings and woundings to the information, spread rapidly by word of mouth, that Soviet authorities may have resettled some Armenians from Azerbaijan in Tajikistan and provided them with units of the very scarce government housing in Dushanbe. A similar notion unsettled many Kirgiz in their republic. In the first ten days of August 1989, trouble between Turkmens and Armenians had also broken out in Ashgabat in the bazaar, where many Armenians ran cooperative shops.[28]

In Tajikistan, thousands of Tajiks reacted to the news about the Armenian arrival in their country by swarming onto the squares and streets. Protesters halted public transportation, looted stores, wrecked offices, and chased many non-Tajiks from the scene. It took about a week for this chaos to drive Tajikistan's Communist Party and government leaders from office. They included the CPTaj First Secretary, Qahhar M. Mahkamov, Republic Prime Minister Izatullo K. Khayayev, and chairman of the Tajikistan Supreme Council, Gaibnazar P. Pallayev.[29]

Resentment over a severe shortage of apartments, combined with the hatred of outsiders, had widened its focus beyond the transplanted Armenians and the few thousands of them longtime residents of Tajikistan. Now, it openly encompassed also Russians and Ukrainians.

Slavs formed 36 percent of Dushanbe's population of 601,501 in 1989, according to census reports. But, the drastic upheaval in the Republic immediately affected this proportion. The City of Dushanbe experienced rapid immigration of Tajik refugees from the provinces and outmigration of Russians and Bukharan and European Jews fleeing the civil war. As a consequence, by the end of 1993 the number of Tajiks grew to an estimated 80 percent of the city's beleaguered population, according to a well-informed Tajik.[30] Throughout Soviet Central Asia

[27] Esther B. Fein, "Upheaval in the East: Boiling Over with Hatred. At Least 37 Die in Central Asia Turmoil," *New York Times* (14 February 1990), p. A12.

[28] *Sredniaia Aziia. Spravochnye materialy. Istoriia, politika, ekonomika* (1992), p. 88.

[29] Craig B. Whitney, "Upheaval in the East: The Soviet Unraveling. Amid Turmoil, Leaders Resign in Tadzhikistan," *New York Times* (16 February 1990), p. A8.

[30] *Natsional'nyi sostav naseleniia SSSR.* Moscow: Finansy i Statistika, 1990, page 126 of page proof; discussion of the author of this chapter with Dr. Pulat Pulatov, Rector, Tajikistan Technological University, Dushanbe and Khojand, January 25, 1994, in New York City.

TABLE 18.1

Central Asian Nationalities in Central Asia, 1989*

Ethnic Group	KazSSR	KirSSR	TajSSR	TurkmSSR	UzSSR	Total (mil.)
Kazak	6,534,616	37,318	11,376	87,802	808,227	7.5
Kirgiz	14,112	2,229,663	63,823	634	174,907	2.5
Tajik	25,514	33,518	3,172,420	3,149	933,560	4.2
Turkmen	3,846	899	20,487	2,536,606	121,578	2.7
Uzbek	332,017	550,096	1,197,841	317,333	14,142,475	16.5
Karakalpak	1,387	142	163	3,062	411,878	.42
Uyghur	185,301	36,779	566	1,308	35,762	.26
Dungan	30,165	36,928	22	—	1,353	.068
Bukharan Jewish	795	346	4,879	72	28,369	.034
Total	7,127,753	2,925,689	4,471,586	2,949,966	16,658,109	34.1

Sources: Vestnik Statistiki, no. 10, 1990, pp. 69–71; no. 11, 1990, pp. 77–78; ibid., no. 12, 1990, pp. 70–72; ibid., no. 4, 1991, pp. 76–78; ibid., no. 5, 1991, pp. 74–77; ibid., no. 6, 1991, pp. 72–74. Notice the rounding of totals given in the Total column at right, above.

*Generally, Central Asians reside within their own region, but in 1989, according to these Soviet census reports, 656,479 Kazakhs lived entirely outside Central Asia, mainly just north of Kazakhstan in the Russian SFSR. That figure, too, has probably changed as a consequence of the steady emigration of outsiders from Kazakhstan and of a movement underway in the Kazakhstan Republic to call home its Kazakh countrymen from abroad, especially those relatively large numbers present in the PRC and in the Russian Republic.

many different economic, ethnic, and other demographic forces quickly began to alter the population distribution numbers then so recently recorded.[31]

Violence again marred the peace of Uzbekistan, this time between two of Central Asia's nominal Muslim nationalities. On January 1, 1989, a fight started in the public farm market between Afghan students from the college of the Ministry of Internal Affairs and local Tashkent residents. Before it ended, three persons lost their lives, 23 received serious injuries. When militia members returned the young Afghans to their dormitories, the students wrecked the buildings, stormed into the street burning automobiles and destroying property. Reports attributed the outbreak to tension between Uzbeks and Afghans over the war between the USSR and Afghanistan, then just ended. Also, observers spoke of the refusal of Afghan students to abide by local customs in Uzbekistan.

As neighboring Uzbekistan's officials had feared, the ethnic tensions in Tajikistan proved contagious. Official radio broadcasts briefly reported that clashes between what they termed "Muslims" and Armenians broke out on February 16, 1990, in Samarkand City, where Tajiks figure in substantial numbers among the inhabitants.[32] Though the conflict in Tajikistan initially pitted Tajiks against each other, in time it would attract outside intervention from several directions, and the local fight could not remain confined.

Central Asia experienced yet another instance of ethnic strife stemming from the distortions caused by earlier Soviet nationality policies. In 1924–25, when Soviet administrators drew the lines demarking the nationality units of Central Asia, the borders of the Kirgizstan Autonomous Oblast' did not take in the old town of Osh, and the lands around it, just southeast of Andijan. But in the administrative-territorial reorganizations of 1936, their cartography placed large settlements and farming communities of Uzbeks within Kirgizstan's jurisdiction. This

[31] "Tajik Government to Take Action as Emigration of Russians Continues," *Summary of World Broadcasts, British Broadcasting Corporation,* from ITAR-TASS News Agency, Moscow World Service, April 15, 1993, part 1, p. SU/16 68/B; Chauncy D. Harris, "Ethnic Tensions in Areas of the Russian Diaspora," *Post-Soviet Geography,* No. 4 (April 1993), pp. 237–38.

[32] "Upheaval in the East: Unsnarling the Soviet Tangle. Soviet Union. Riots in Soviet Central Asia Spread to Another Republic," *New York Times* (17 February 1990), p. 9.

reallotment of lands immediately created a potential for interethnic rivalry.

Trouble broke out in that setting around June 3, 1990. Five days later, fighting continued to rage, with thousands of Uzbeks from Uzbekistan attempting to cross the border into Kirgizstan and join the combatants. Killing, burning, or plundering occurred in at least 30 villages near Osh, resulting in hundreds of dead and wounded, the burning of hundreds of homes, and the arrests of over 500 people.[33]

Rioters demonstrated the inadequacy of the country's leadership. During the clashes around Osh, protesters in Frunze (now, Bishkek), Kirgizstan's capital, demanded the ouster of the republic's political chiefs. A Kirgiz eyewitness to much of the disturbance at Osh subsequently related to the author of this chapter that Absamat Masaliev, the First Secretary of the CPKir, fearful for his safety, refused to emerge from his quarters and take command of the situation during the crisis between Kirgiz and Uzbeks. As a result, reported the observer, the top CP official in the republic completely sacrificed any authority he might have used to pacify the rioters. That loss of credibility soon paved the way for the ousting of the man from his post and destroying the influence of the Kirgizstan branch of the CPSU.[34]

When that occurred, the Democratic Movement "Kirgizstan" (Demokraticheskoe Dvizhenie "Kïrgizstan"—DDK), organized informally in May 1990, played a decisive role. The DDK, which had taken a constructive position during the crisis at Osh, gained much greater authority. As a result, when the Supreme Council of Kirgizstan selected a president for the Republic on October 25, 1990, it passed over the communist candidate, Absamat Masaliev, and chose instead Dr. Askar Akayev, a compromise figure. Within a year, they reelected Dr. Akayev to his high position.[35]

---

[33] G. Shipit'ko, "Konflikt ne utikhaet. Piatyi den' prodolzhaetsia mezhnatsional'nyi konflikt v Kirgizii, nesmotria na vvedenie chrezvychainogo polozheniia v oshskoi oblasti i v g. Frunze," *Izvestiia* (8 June 1990), p. 2; "Soviets Intervene in Ethnic Violence. Troops and Police Act to Halt the Riots in Kirghizia—Death Toll Put at 107," *New York Times* (11 June 1990), p. A12.

[34] A conversation between the author of this chapter and Mr. Kabay Karabekov, Director of the Press Office for the President of Kirgizstan, on June 28, 1993, in Columbia University, New York City. Mr. Karabekov noted that at the time of that clash between the Kirgiz and Uzbeks, he worked as a reporter for the Moscow newspaper, *Komsomolskaia pravda*, which sent him to Osh to cover the events there for the press.

[35] *Sredniaia Aziia. Spravochnye Materialy. Istoriia, politika, ekonomika* (1992), p. 42.

AWKWARD CONVERSION TO SELF-RULE

For convinced authoritarian heads of state, at the head of the list of serious problems—in cultural importance—came the urge among a population, reportedly quite literate, for greater human rights, for latitude in expression, and freedom in all respects.

Next, loomed the inescapable degree of Central Asia's persisting dependence upon outside countries, especially Russia, in spite of formal independence declared by each Central Asian republic. This relative lack of self-reliance showed itself acutely at home in the fields of economy and technology, in scientific training, and in security against banditry and other debilitating crime, such as the illegal narcotics trade.

Third, appeared the exposure to international competition, rivalry, deception, manipulation or pressure as well as military intervention. Now, Russian regimes—Czarist and Soviet—no longer screened Central Asia's capitals from external menace. In a peculiar contradiction, Moscow did continue to police the outer frontiers of the former empire with its notorious border guards and military units. Other neighboring states that posed problems included especially turbulent Afghanistan, with its unceasing civil conflict. Also, independence directly exposed Kazakhstan, Kirgizstan, and Tajikistan, at the eastern frontier, to an authoritarian, aggressive Chinese government intolerant of its own Central Asians; and to the militantly Shiite religious regime in Iran hostile to Sunni Turkic nations (constituting seven-eighths of all Central Asians. See Table 18.1). Some Central Asians with long memories still feared that resurgence of a Russian imperial drive could turn into the greatest threat from this direction.

Finally, the acute shortage of time increased the pressure felt from all the other factors affecting the attempts to govern. The hands on the domestic clock showed the lateness of the hour to meet ordinary people's desperate needs. Failure in this obligation would see the new countries degenerate further into the backwardness of nearby lands. Among the most urgent requirements stood the protection of the environment, which involved provision of pure and plentiful water supplies, balancing nutrition with inexpensive food supplies, providing much better health care, adequate housing, productive employment, and other essentials.

In these matters all leaders faced severe challenges. Central Asia in 1989 suffered from "the highest [rate of] infant mortality, maternal mortality and deaths from infections, respiratory and diarrheal diseases" in the territory of the USSR.[36] Within Central Asia, Turkmenistan and Tajikistan showed by far the greatest percentage of infant deaths per 1,000 live births in 1989. In general, the proportion of rural morbidity and mortality substantially exceeded that found in urban environments. Because more than 60 percent of Central Asians then lived outside the cities—substantially more than 60 percent lived in Tajikistan's country-side—the region's high death rate to some degree reflected its rural/urban population imbalance. Among farming and small village families in Uzbekistan, nearly four million people suffered from hepatitis. The average longevity of 59 years in the rural population of Uzbekistan fell far below that registered in the Soviet West and even farther under the European level.[37]

Man-made conditions devastated the physical well-being and morale of the population in several republics, once again, especially among the nonurban dwellers. Local journalists and eyewitnesses began openly reporting about the immediate and long-term effects of two great disasters directly traceable to faulty Soviet planning and maladministration. (Chapter 17 described the killing of the Aral Sea and its surrounding civilization.)

The second mass destruction authorized by high authority and managed locally, proved as damaging as the first in its willful poisoning of productive fields, deprivation of huge acreages from a beloved homeland, and fatal sickening of generations of farmers and villagers. The atomic explosions executed in eastern Kazakhstan at the Semey range took a great toll in human life. Residents in what Soviet authorities called "The Semey Polygon" describe the consequences of the Soviet government's indifference to the impact of radiation from atom bomb blasts on unprotected humans and, through deep contamination, its threats to all still living and born in the area. One witness spoke of the impossibility of finding fertile ground in the region. He writes that throat cancer remains especially noticeable in Ayryq, Arqalyq, Abay,

---

[36] Nina R. Schwalbe, *Factors Affecting Infant Mortality in Central Asia. An Analysis of Proximate and Indirect Determinants across Republics of the Former Soviet Union* (New York, unpublished Certificate Essay of the Harriman Institute, Columbia University, 1993), p. 9.

[37] Muhämmäd Salih, *Aydinlik säri* (Tashkent, n.p., 1993), p. 30; Nina Schwalbe, Table 1.1 and p. 10.

and Qaratau state farms. Blood diseases, cancerous lesions, tumors, and leukocytosis prevail among the very young. Many children come into the world without arms or tongues, and are born mentally deficient.[38]

In May 1990, the author of this chapter attended a session of the conference organized by the international anti-nuclear testing organization, Semey-Nevada (outside Kazakhstan, often called Nevada-Semey), held in Almatï, Kazakhstan. There, testimony and data added substantially to the evidence about damage inflicted on human subjects by radiation at Semey. Political authorities permitted the military to explode nuclear devices at ten sites throughout Central Asia, most of them in Kazakhstan, including two in the Aral Sea itself.[39] A medical specialist reported at the time of the Semey-Nevada conference in spring 1990 that in the Abay farm village, for example, 75–80 percent of the inhabitants suffered from dystrophy, hyperpigmentation, or other pathologies caused by exposure to radioactivity.[40]

Besides facing the acute problems of public health, leaders confronted a somnolent economy in the region. Except for Turkmenistan, which has benefited from its rich natural gas and petroleum deposits and its new independence from the Soviet Union, most of Central Asia suffers from economic distress. Economists say that this partly results from the selective placement and inadequacy of Soviet capital investment in the region during the period leading up to independence. In Kazakhstan, Kirgïzstan, Tajikistan, and Turkmenistan, industrial investment in 1987 went into fuel extraction, electric power, and nonferrous, precious, and strategic metals. Investment in these very industries benefited Central Asians themselves little, because those sectors of the economy employed mostly Slavs, and the management shipped these resources out to the Soviet West. At the same time, data gave an ominous forecast for the region's economy, recording that in the

---

[38] Kärim Sawghabayev, *Qazaq Ädebiyeti* (9 August 1991), p. 3, trans. by Paul D. Buell from Kazakh and published in English under the heading "I Saw the Horror with My Own Eyes," in *Ala-Tau* (Spring 1992), vol. I, No. 1, pp. 7–8; Gregory J. Celestan, "The Bitter Legacy of Semey (Semipalatinsk)," *Kazakh and Kirghiz Studies Bulletin* (Autumn/ Winter 1993), vol. 1, No. 2, pp. 20–22.

[39] "As World Narrows, Russian Army Seeks a New Mission," *New York Times* (29 November 1993), p. A10. Sketch map of the former USSR in "News of the Week" section, showing nuclear test sites.

[40] Bakhiya Atshabarov, "Shïngghïrghan shïndïq osïnday," *Khalïq kengesi* (newspaper of the Kazakh ssr Supreme Council) (14–21 Mamïr 1990), p. 6.

late 1980s a smaller percentage of working Central Asians labored in industry than had done so approximately 20 years earlier.[41]

The collapse of trade between the Republic of Kazakhstan and the Russian Republic caused a tremendous decline in Kazakh economic output during 1992–93. Nevertheless, 60 percent of Kazakhstan's exports continued to go to Russia and in return 50 percent of Kazakhstan's imports came from the Russian Republic in 1993.[42] With nearly all parts of the former Soviet Union in an economic slump, a renewal of the old economic ties, advocated by Dr. S. S. Satubaldin, Vice-President, Kazakhstan Institute of Management, Economics and Strategic Research, in the short run probably could not improve the economic health of Central Asia very much.

All observers termed Tajikistan's economy a wreck during the years of civil war. Kirgizstan's diplomats candidly referred to their land as a poor country in need of development and assistance. Uzbekistan, largely agrarian like the others, depends on ever-decreasing flows of water for irrigation from rivers controlled by up-stream neighbors. Arable acreage shrinks and the government maintains without reform the out-of-date arrangement of state orders and subsidies in an agriculture dominated by cotton growing and insufficient food production.[43]

Of the 6.8 million people employed in Uzbekistan in 1993, 50 percent worked in service and office capacities, 16.3 percent labored in industry, and 32 percent toiled on the farms for about one-tenth the monthly income received by the urban employee. Farmers lacked even that seasonal compensation three or four months a year. Inflation in Central Asia continued to grow alarmingly for the low-wage earners of the region, as high as 200 percent a month in Uzbekistan, by some accounts. The exchange rate for the Kazakh *tanga* declined from 2T:1$ in September 1993 to 4.5T:1$ in January 1994. According to reports

---

[41] Leslie Dienes, "Economic Prospects for Soviet Asia in the 1990s," *Notes from the Harriman Institute Seminar on Soviet Republics and Regional Issues* (New York, W. Averell Harriman Institute for Advanced Study of the Soviet Union and Program on Nationality and Siberian Studies, Columbia University), Vol. 1, No. 6 (24 March 1989), p. 2.

[42] Stephen E. Hanson, "Russia and Kazakhstan in Search of National Identity: Preliminary Reflections on 'The New Russia in Asia' Conference Meetings in Moscow and Almatï, 1993," *Kazakh & Kirghiz Studies Bulletin*, Vol. 1, No. 2 (Autumn/Winter 1993), p. 13.

[43] Don Van Atta, "The Current State of Agrarian Reform in Uzbekistan," *Post-Soviet Geography*, No. 9 (November 1993), pp. 600–601.

from Tashkent, Uzbekistan in late 1993 sank further into economic depression, in part brought on by the introduction in 1993 of Uzbekistan's separate currency (*som*) in place of the Russian rouble.[44]

In spite of the enormity of such concerns, for the most part the transitional leadership gave priority to the task of sustaining itself in power and position. In Turkmenistan and Uzbekistan, media revealed that each regime also busied itself with glorifying the head of state. These presidents' likenesses and names constantly appeared everywhere. Saparmïrat A. Niyazov affixed his image upon numbers of places, institutions, and streets and upon new currency in Turkmenistan. President Niyazov also awarded himself the first Magtïmgulï State Prize for Interethnic Relations, established in Turkmenistan in 1992.[45]

In response to the opportunities offered by independence, the new heads of government, generally conventional men, set off along four different paths of self-determination (see Figure 18.5):

1. Balancing an unusual freedom of speech and careful self-reliance with considerable formal deference to Russia and the persisting Soviet-era structures (Kazakhstan, Kirgizstan);
2. Convulsively contesting internal ideological ideas of reform vs. adherence to intolerant communist dictatorship (Tajikistan);
3. Reestablishing pre-*glasnost*' censorship and control modeled closely on practices of the communist regime, while assertively disengaging from the ex-USSR states (Turkmenistan);
4. Continuing or reviving the Stalinist authoritarian mentality and police-state methods to suppress dissent in the name of law and order (Uzbekistan). Such divergence mirrored the defining heterogeneity of Central Asia's population and of its different styles of leadership.

Central Asians now greatly desired new leaders, but they knew from long experience that the severe difficulty of finding a chief who shared their basic values left the followers with scant hope of improving the old system quickly. An American anthropologist tells of hearing some unusual remarks made to a youthful audience by a former top official and

---

[44] Nadira Artykova, "Uzbekistan Crisis Worsens as New Currency Flounders," *Inter Press Service Feature* (21 January 1994), p. 1; Muhämmäd Salih, *Aydinlik säri*, p. 30; comments to the author of this chapter by Mr. Serikkhan Zh. Zhakupov, Chairman, Committee on Foreign Relations and Interparliamentary Ties, Kazakhstan Republic, in New York, January 25, 1994.

[45] *Il oglï. Türkmen dövletining ilkinji Prezidenti, Magtïmgulï adïndakï Khalkara bayragïnïng birinji laureatï Saparmïrat Atayevich Nïyazov* (Ashgabat, "Türkmenistan" RNCHB, 1992).

FIGURE 18.5   Five Central Asian presidents meeting in Ashgabat,
Turkmenistan, December 1991 (l. to r.): Askar Akayev, Kirgizstan;
Nursultan Nazarbayev, Kazakhstan; Saparmïrat Niyazov, Turkmenistan;
Islam A. Karimov, Uzbekistan; Rahmon Nabiyev, Tajikistan.
Wide World Photo, Inc./Associated Press.

broadcast on radio Tashkent in July 1992. That Central Asian speaker
called openly for fresh indigenous moral leadership in the region in
order to stave off disaster.[46] The judgment by the ex-politician concerning the fundamental source of cultural, social, and political health for
his region holds great significance for the uneasy societies of the area
in the 1990s. Two of the region's leaders, the presidents of Kirgizstan
and Kazakhstan, late in 1993 once more conveyed an understanding of
their people's need for such idealism as the core of any new ideology.[47]

[46] M. Nazif Shahrani, "Islam and the Political Culture of 'Scientific Atheism' in Post-
Soviet Central Asia: Future Predicaments," unpublished paper presented in November,
1993 to an academic conference in College Park, Maryland, pp. 20–21. Professor Shahrani
quotes Nuritdin A. Muhitdinov, who had held high office both in Moscow and Tashkent.
About Mr. Muhitdinov, see also Edward Allworth, *Uzbek Literary Politics* (The Hague,
Mouton & Co., 1964), p. 103, n. 13.

[47] [President Askar Akayev], "Obrashchenie Presidenta Kyrgyzskoi Respubliki k Zho-
gorku Kengeshu," separate text of a speech, ca. November 15, 1993, p. 17; President Nursultan Nazarbaev, "Ideinaia konsolidatsiia obshchestva—kak uslovie progressa Kazakhstana," *Kazakhstanskaia pravda*, separate offprint of the text (October 1993), pp. 15–16.

Centuries earlier, medieval Central Asian thinkers had emphasized a conception of ideal rather than practical leadership. Those works often listed the traits they defined as the essence, not so much of leaderly goodness as of prerequisites to the throne or saddle of amir, khan, or sultan. None of those well-meant guides to perfection in a ruler attempted to define measures of effectiveness, as such.

The tenure of an idealistic amir or khan, when sovereign, could not guarantee a healthy, happy domain, despite the hopes implied in princely guidebooks. The biography of one of the most virtuous and pious rulers of modern history offers a pointed example. Amir Haydar Tore (r. 1800–26) of Bukhara, a learned man, failed miserably in extending the highly effective government of his illustrious father (Amir Ma'sum). Despite Haydar Tore's righteousness, during his rule the majority of Bukhara's Uzbek tribal leaders opposed him. Chroniclers described his reign as one long period of chaos.[48]

THE EFFECTIVE LEADER

Under those circumstances, the profile of an effective, though not necessarily an ideal, leader of the early 1990s in Central Asia looked approximately like the profile given in Table 18.2.

Observers might measure the effectiveness of a leader in such troubled times by examining some widely recognized indicators of social ills—poor public health, a troubling extent of banditry and other crime, extensive poverty, disturbing numbers and quality of emigrants and refugees leaving the country, frequent incidence of riot and public unrest, bribery, low productivity among employees and civil servants, and the like.

The world also judges leaders according to additional, external standards: an ability to carry on good relations in parity with significant foreign states offers one test. In practical terms, traditionally, both foreigners and citizens of the region regarded retention of or extent of domain as a yardstick for measuring the leader's effectiveness. Much earlier, a state's frontiers frequently shrank or enlarged, depending upon the leader's aggressiveness and the balance of military forces in

[48] Ahmad Donish, *Risolai Ahmadi Donish "Ta'rikhi saltanati manghitiya. Traktat Akhmada Donisha "Istoriia Mangitskoi dinastii,"* trans. to Russian by I. A. Najafova (Dushanbe, Izdatel'stvo "Donish," 1967), p. 36.

TABLE 18.2

Traits of an Effective Leader*

1. Decisive, certain	(8)
2. Magnetic, unifying	(5)
3. Strong in character and body	(9)
4. Experienced, practical	(7)
5. Communicative, persuasive	(4)
6. Identified with the homeland	(10)
7. Intelligent, inventive	(2)
8. Patient, tolerant	(6)
9. Honest, candid	(1)
10. Well-read, well-traveled, curious	(3)

---

*This list, prepared by the author, shows attributes in order of highest priority—numbers enclosed in parentheses tentatively suggest a ranking order for traits of a perfect leader in an ideal era.

the area. In the period 1989–92, uncertainties about the relative extent of domain as a gauge of leadership arose once again.

The twentieth-century state system showed much more acute sensitivity than earlier Central Asian ages to the recognition and precision of certain external borders. Though no government in the region announced a formal annexation of neighboring lands between 1989 and 1993, Tajikistan's pervious frontiers seemed to invite incursions from volatile Afghanistan in the south as well as intervention around the northern territory of Khojand, virtually surrounded by foreign lands. There, in 1989, Uzbeks made up more than half the number of Tajiks in the (Leninabad) oblast'. That territory had, until 1927, formed a part of the Uzbekistan Soviet Socialist Republic (UzSSR). Also, with the collapse of the USSR in 1991, the glaring imperfection in Soviet attempts of the 1920s to separate nationalities from one another by drawing borderlines between them now set the stage for an emotional rise in irredentism. Tajikistan and Uzbekistan each gave a home to more than a million other Central Asians on its soil.[49]

In Kazakhstan, some Kazakhs felt growing concern about the possible secession by a large expanse of their independent Republic located adjacent to the Russian Federation. In 1989, according to the census reports, Slavs (Belorussians, Poles, Russians, and Ukrainians together)

---

[49] *Natsional'nyi sostav naseleniia SSSR*, p. 128 of page proof.

averaged over 60 percent of the population in the oblasts of Karaganda, Kokshetau, Kustanai, North-Kazakhstan, Pavlodar, and Tselinograd (see Table 18.3). In addition, in the oblast' of East Kazakhstan, farther east along the border with the PRC, census takers found that Slavs made up almost 68 percent of the inhabitants. Further reducing Kazakhs in these areas to minority status, 555,000 Germans also concentrated especially in Karaganda, Kokshetau, Kustanai, Pavlodar, and Tselinograd oblasts.[50]

For the moment, people yearned not so urgently for justice, the medieval ideal, as for protection from criminals, including some police and military forces, and relief from severe economic distress.[51] This meant that priorities, not values, had changed. Earlier, people desired the old sort of equity for everyone, outsiders and Central Asians alike, in treatment by their governors, even if expressed harshly. Now, more and more people expected to exercise openly, without reprisal, a new option to make personal decisions. That implied flexibility about belief, and about the key personal human rights—freedom of assembly, occupation, speech, travel, and the like.

By the end of 1993, what sorts of leadership had the residents of the republics experienced? The event immediately responsible for putting an end to Moscow's direct rule in Central Asia and the breakup of the USSR, August 18–19, 1991, gave some answers. A group of conservative anti-reformists staged a coup d'état against the regime of USSR President Mikhail S. Gorbachev. During the few days before it failed, that coup exposed the stance toward reform of various incumbents at the top of Central Asian republics.

In the UzSSR, for example, on August 20, 1991, *Pravda Vostoku*, the bulletin of the CPUz, headed by First Secretary Islam A. Karimov, welcomed the coup by printing the Declaration and Resolutions, issued in Moscow, of a new "State Committee for the Extraordinary Situation in the USSR." Those proclamations called for acceptance of the decrees issued August 18, 1991, in the name of that Committee by G. I. Ianaev, V. Pavlov, O. Baklanov, and A. Luk'ianov.[52] *Pravda Vostoka*

---

[50] *Ibid.*, pp. 98–109 of page proof.

[51] Edward A. Allworth, *The Modern Uzbeks: From the Fourteenth Century to the Present. A Cultural History* (1990), pp. 4–14.

[52] "Postanovlenie No. 1 Gosudarstvennogo Komiteta po chrezvychainomu polozheniiu v SSSR," *Pravda Vostoka* (20 August 1991), pp. 1–2.

TABLE 18.3

Distribution of Slavs, Germans, and Kazakhs in Kazakhstan 1989

All Groups Province tot.	Russians	Ukrainians	Belorussians	Germans	Kazakhs
732,653 Aktiubinsk	173,281	74,547	—	31,628	407,222
1,121,395 Almaty City	663,251	45,598	7,459	20,117	252,072
977,373 Almaty Oblast'	294,236	18,496	—	61,277	406,823
1,038,667 Dzhambul	275,424	33,903	—	70,150	507,302
493,601 Dzhezkazgan	172,272	29,467	6,795	24,179	227,402
931,267 East Kazakhstan	613,846	16,186	—	22,768	253,706
748,951 Gur'ev	170,474	13,908	2,763	2,537	504,041
1,347,636 Karaganda	703,588	107,098	30,971	143,525	231,782
662,125 Kokshetau	261,797	55,575	17,228	81,985	191,275

Province					
Kustanay 1,222,705	534,715	177,986	35,356	110,397	279,459
Kzyl Orda 644,979	86,042	11,497	—	—	511,976
North Kazakhstan 599,969	372,263	38,059	7,104	39,293	111,631
Pavlodar 942,313	427,658	86,651	12,293	95,342	268,512
Semipalatinsk 834,417	300,533	19,503	—	44,113	432,763
Shimkent 1,818,328	278,473	33,033	—	44,526	1,012,265
Taldy-Kurgan 716,076	235,338	12,186	—	35,329	360,453
Tselinograd 1,002,793	447,844	94,455	28,683	123,694	224,809
Ural 629,494	216,514	28,092	5,112	4,550	351,123
Total	6,227,549	896,240	153,764	955,410	6,534,616

Source: *Natsional'nyi sostav naseleniia SSSR*. Moscow: Finansy i Statistika, 1990, pp. 98–109. Kokshetau Province also gave a home to 25,400 (Slavic) Poles. In addition, Almaty City housed 16,073 Koreans, Gur'ev Province had 3,816 Koreans, Dzhambul Province, 13,360, Karaganda Province 11,541, Kzyl Orda Province 12,182, Taldy Kurgan Province 13,581 and Shimkent Province 11,430; all told, census reports show 81,983 Koreans distributed in Kazakhstan without large concentrations.

on August 21, 1991, followed up with the Declaration from a combined session of the Presidium of the Supreme Soviet UzSSR and the Ministerial Office under the President of the UzSSR, with leaders of Karakalpakistan, of the ten oblasts, and of Tashkent city. Their Declaration recognized the heads of the State Committee in Moscow as "the Soviet leaders" and, rejecting the authority of President Gorbachev and his programs, formally accepted its Resolution instituting an "extraordinary situation" on the territory of Uzbekistan and other parts of the USSR.

In a separate statement, Uzbekistan's President Karimov called for "discipline and order" among the people of the UzSSR. He also pointedly commented that ". . . our history . . . shows that leadership which yields discipline and order can never recover them and becomes powerless. . . ." Showing characteristic Uzbek caution about the unfolding events, on August 21, President Karimov also signed an "Ukaz," asserting that decisions made by leaders of the coup in Moscow that contravened existing USSR and UzSSR laws and constitutions would not go into effect in Uzbekistan.[53]

Alone in Central Asia, the chief executives of Kazakhstan and Kirgizstan withstood the orders of the conspirators in Moscow's coup attempt. The top communists of Tajikistan, Turkmenistan, and Uzbekistan initially obeyed the directions coming from Moscow in opposition to the reforms of President Gorbachev. The coup failed its highly-placed Central Asian supporters.

On August 24, 1991, Mikhail S. Gorbachev, General Secretary, CPSU, resigned as head of the Party and called for the dissolution of the CPSU and distribution of its property, including that located in Central Asia, to the Councils of People's Deputies. Within four months, various of the Soviet Socialist Republics had declared themselves independent, leading to the dissolution of the Soviet state. On December 25, 1991, Mr. Gorbachev also resigned his post as president of the USSR. He confirmed the demise of the Soviet Union by signing over his authority

---

[53] "Zaiavlenie sovmestnogo zasedaniia Prezidiuma Verkhovnogo Soveta Uzbekskoi SSR i Kabineta Ministrov pri Prezidente UzSSR s uchastiem rukovoditelei Karakalpakistana, oblastei i g. Tashkenta," *Pravda Vostoka* (21 August 1991), p. 1; "Obrashchenie Prezidenta Uzbekskoi Sovetskoi Sotsialisticheskoi Respubliki, pervogo Sekretaria Tsentral'nogo Komiteta Kompartii Uzbekistana I. A. Karimova k naseleniiu respubliki," *Pravda Vostoka* (21 August 1991), p. 1; "Ukaz Prezidenta Uzbekskoi Sovetskoi Sotsialisticheskoi Respubliki," *Pravda Vostoka* (22 August 1991), p. 1.

to the head of the new Commonwealth of Independent States, Boris Yeltsin, President-elect of Russia.[54]

The membership of that insubstantial Commonwealth included the now independent republics of Kazakhstan, Kirgizstan, Tajikistan, Turkmenistan, and Uzbekistan. The formal termination of the USSR on December 8, 1991, occurred after the installation of chief executive officers had taken place throughout the Central Asian region. The array closely resembled its communist predecessor. Central Asians could feel some dismay in the circumstance that the end of the Soviet era, like its beginning on November 7, 1917, came about almost entirely without their direct participation.

Undercurrents of dissatisfaction swept through Central Asia constantly. On January 16, 1992, the newly independent government of the Ozbekistan Respublikäsi (Republic of Uzbekistan) suddenly encountered severe student unrest in one of its main higher educational centers, Tashkent State University. Official responses from Tashkent blamed unidentified instigators for stirring up the students in order "to discredit their own republic in the eyes of the world community. . . ." Those supposed provocateurs, said spokesmen for the Government of Uzbekistan, "unhappy about the policy of national reconciliation that we are implementing and the determined efforts of the leadership of the republic to consolidate society on the way to genuine independence, would dearly like to produce dissension . . . and occupy places in the structures of power. . . ."[55]

Uzbekistan's "Erk" Party came out openly in support of the students against this government repression. The organization's newspaper published photographs and interviews with students of the "Students' Town" and reported interviews with witnesses. They refuted the government's explanations for official violence.[56]

When the militia and secret police pushed into the university's grounds and buildings, they routed students violently from their dor-

---

[54] "Gorbachev Statement on Party," *New York Times* (25 August 1991), p. 14; Serge Schmemann, "The Soviet State, Born of a Dream, Dies," *New York Times* (26 December 1991), pp. A1, A14.

[55] TASS (20 January 1992), Foreign Broadcast Information Service (FBIS) (21 January 1992), pp. 87–88, cited in Erika Dailey, *Human Rights in Uzbekistan*. ed. Jeri Laber. New York: Helsinki Watch, A Division of Human Rights Watch, 1993, pp. 2–3.

[56] "Täläbälär shähärchäsi. Qanli päyshänbä," and "'Erk' Demakrätik Pärtiyäsining Bäyanati," *"Erk" Demakrätik Pärtiyäsi Gäzeti*, No. 2 (1992), pp. 1–2.

mitories and classrooms with clubs and other weapons. Dispatches from the City of Tashkent reported the deaths of two students and injuries to dozens of others. As told to an American reporter by witnesses a few days later, officials immediately closed the university, banished all its students to their hometowns and villages and stopped their university education indefinitely.[57] News services in Moscow at the time attributed the immediate cause of this outbreak to food shortages and sudden inflation in prices.

On the first night, rioters and police fought, overturned cars, smashed windows and doors, and threw rocks, according to observers. On the second day, thousands gathered again in the student quarter, but troops and Interior Ministry police cordoned off the area. In the name of stability and of an imagined affront to his authority, the Republic's leader opted to apply force rather than allow the country's disaffected young intellectuals the chance to reason with the government. In this way, Uzbekistan, like other authoritarian sectors of Central Asia, again squandered a chance to encourage a rising generation of new leaders.

THE PRICE OF STABILITY

Central Asia had lived on the brink of drastic, unforseen change in 1989. Though the region continued a quasi-Soviet existence for a while longer, nearly every aspect of public life in urban areas resonated with premonition. Intellectuals and politicians of the region, more than social scientists elsewhere, appeared to sense the Soviet empire's final deterioration. In Central Asia, an abundance of signs had presaged it.

In all five of the republics, the leadership on many occasions during this short period of relative independence (commencing at least two years before the formal breakup of the Soviet Union) frequently demonstrated its ineffectiveness in serving the people of the republics. Inefficiency might have signaled the preeminence of humane values motivating the leaders, but it did not. The practical men failed in many instances because they lost track of the ideals of the people they tried to govern. And, they mistook effectiveness for the totality of leadership. Except in Kirgizstan, where the communists disgraced themselves publicly, giving astute non-Party and some Party politicians the chance to

[57] "Uzbek Students Riot over Price Rises," *New York Times* (18 January 1992), p. 4; Information from Mr. Arthur Bonner, who traveled throughout Central Asia between September 1991 and March 1992.

follow the people's mood closely. And briefly in Tajikistan, where a genuine popular upheaval had, only for a short time, thrown the authoritarian communists out of power. Generally, the same Communist Party executives managed to stay atop the political apparatus in each republic other than Kirgizstan after 1991. That position evidenced neither their full sovereignty nor the complete independence of their domains from foreign interference.

In the economic and political spheres, old links with Russian centers continued to exert great influence in Central Asia. The region necessarily continued some dependence upon the Soviet, then Russian, systems of transport, pipelines, communications, finance, raw-materials shipment and processing, manufacturing, provision of foodstuffs, supplying medical services and medicines, managing large enterprises, maintaining internal and military security, and many other functions.

Besides all these intricate ties, equally important remained the impact and conditioning of the Soviet Russian culture. Especially among the politicians, attitudes and ideas came largely from the discredited Soviet ideology and practice, modeled on a Russian version of statehood and government. Visitors to Central Asia commonly observe that in offices throughout the region the very same persons or types of persons as before 1989 sit at most of the desks and affect decisions controlling the lives of intellectuals and other individuals in the cities of the republics. Remarks from Kazakhs, Tajiks, Uzbeks, and their countrymen confirm the observation. Under the circumstances, in the authoritarian states very little can change under independence, with or without social stability.

More than one kind of stability existed in Central Asia during the period 1989–93. Rational stability resulted from the considered judgment of citizens convinced, from experience and by temperament, that violent revolt endangered more than it gained and that their leaders might guide them to a decent life. Enforced stability really amounted to suppressed anger, an emotion likely to escape control. In public statements, President Karimov, of Uzbekistan, often emphasizes the conception and word "stability" (*bärqäralik*).[58] His government has repeatedly demonstrated and voiced a predilection for enforced stability,

[58] I. Kärimaw, *Ozbekistan keläjägi buyuk däwlät. Ozbekistan Respublikäsi Aliy Kenqäshi on birinchi sessiyäsidä sozlängän nutq. 1992 yil 8 wä 10 dekäbr'* (Tashkent, "Ozbekistan," 1992), p. 19.

FIGURE 18.6   Tajikistan's prominent religious leader. Qozi Akbar
Turajonzoda Hajji, May 10, 1992, in Dushanbe. Photo by
Shahrbanou Tadjbakhsh.

for control instead of flexibility. In February 1993, he acknowledged
that preference when he commented to a reporter from *Komsomolskaia
pravda,* in Moscow, that "there are signs of authoritarianism in my
actions."[59]

Presidents Akayev and Nazarbayev attempted to maintain stability
through the use of persuasian and reason with their constituencies in
Kirgizstan and Kazakhstan, respectively. Evidently their policies and
actions achieved sufficient effect, though neither one enjoyed the harsh
criticism he sometimes received from his open press. Despite such dissent, President Nazarbayev commented that "stability, understood as
a result of the process of coordinating various points of view, is [im-
portant] but not an alternative to justice."[60] His thoughtful concept of
stability in his part of Central Asia suggests an equilibrium achieved
through reconciliation and compromise, rather than a social-political
steadiness or rigidity maintained by executive inflexibility. The refer-

[59] V. Fronin (interview with President Islam A. Karimov), *Komsomolskaia pravda*
(12 February 1993), p. 2; reported in routine unclassified Department of State for European Affairs Information bulletin (February 1993) UZ 01, SOEC (01), p. 1.
[60] Presidential communication from Nursultan A. Nazarbayev to the author of this
chapter, January 3, 1994.

ence to "justice" as an absolute value contrasts significantly with the concept of relative justice readily observed in the area during communist days and continuing in some republics of the region in the post-Soviet period.

Unlike those two easternmost republics—Kazakhstan and Kirgizstan—in the ex-USSR, Turkmenistan and Tajikistan stood at opposite poles on the spectrum of stability. Without altering the system, President Niyazov maintained enforced stability at the price of any vestige of freedom for the well-subsidized citizenry of Turkmenistan. Tajikistan's old-line communists fought the reformists to the end of the period, destroying every opportunity for peaceful accommodation that might lead to rational stability. Chairman of the Supreme Council of Tajikistan, Parliamentary Speaker Imamali Rahmanov (b.ca. 1952) of Tajikistan (the country had abolished the presidency) spoke of punishing political, and especially religious opponents. He denounced by name Qozi Akbar Turajonzoda Hajji, Mohammad Sharif Hemmatzoda, Davlat Usmon, Shadmon Yusuf, Mullah Abdullah and Mullah Abadulgafor, rather than of reconciling his people (see Figure 18.6). He said "history will never pardon the guilty . . . and [they] should receive their punishment. . . . The people very well know who these so-called leaders of the nation are: and the curse of the people will be with them forever."[61]

The pattern of discord that spread across the republics brought the insight that in post-Soviet governance, effectiveness cannot long succeed without the guidance of idealism in Central Asia. Divorced from the balance of moral leadership, preoccupation with effectiveness soon revealed its sterility and degenerated here into a drive for authoritarian efficiency. Paradoxically, even in the short term, efficiency proved utterly wasteful when measured in terms of public confidence and morale. Much of Central Asia continued to await its new leaders.

E. A.

---

[61] "Rahmonov's New Year Message of Hope," Source: Tajik Radio, Dushanbe 18:43 gmt 31 December 1992. The British Broadcasting Corporation, January 5, 1993, p. SU/ 1578/B/1.

Selected Bibliography of Works in English

Researchers and observers completed much valuable scholarship and reporting about Central Asia after the editor prepared the second edition of this book in 1988–89. The present bibliography incorporates with the earlier list a selection of the many useful publications issued since 1987 in the English language. In addition, some new work constantly appears in unpublished form and deserves scrutiny. Research often requires several years to reach readers through university presses. Also, publishers avoid issuing many dissertations, because of their very specialized nature. Rather than waiting for the long process of publication to run its course, the editor introduces here the authors and names of many pertinent Ph.D. dissertations and masters' degree theses. The students' own academic advisers normally provide them with careful critiques of these writings. Because the situation in Central Asia changes so rapidly in this period of transition from Soviet hegemony, journals and newsletters offer the most up-to-date sources of current information. That list has greatly expanded in this edition of the book.

SPECIALIZED JOURNALS, DIGESTS, AND OTHER SERIALS

Ala Tau. International Association for the Promotion of Kazakh Studies (Seattle), 1992–1993.

Bulletin of the Association for the Advancement of Central Asian Research (New Britain), 1988–.

Central and Inner Asian Studies (New York City), 1987–.

Central Asia and the Caucasus in World Affairs (Hastings), 1992–.

Central Asia Brief (formerly, *Soviet Muslims Brief*) (Leicester), 1992–.

Central Asia File (London), 1987–.

Central Asia Monitor (Fair Haven, Vermont), 1992–.

Central Asia Today (Moscow), 1993–.

Central Asian and Caucasus Chronicle. See *Central Asian Newsletter*.

Central Asian Collectanea (Washington, D.C.), 1958–.

Central Asian Newsletter (London), 1986–1989 (later title *Central Asian and Caucasus Chronicle*), 1989–1990.

Central Asian Review (London), 1953–1968. (Indexed).
Central Asian Survey (Oxford), 1982–.
Central Asiatic Journal (Wiesbaden), 1955–.
Daily Report, Central Eurasia (Washington, D. C., The Service, FBIS).
Inner Asia Report (Bloomington; originally published in Cambridge, Mass.),
    first issue from Indiana: No. 12 (1993)–.
Journal of Area Study. Central Asia (Peshawar), 1978–.
Journal of Central Asia (Islamabad), 1978–.
Kazakh & Kirghiz Studies Bulletin. Newsletter of the Kazakh & Kirghiz
    Studies Group, University of Washington, Seattle, Washington. 1993–.

ENCYCLOPEDIAS, BIBLIOGRAPHIES, AND OTHER REFERENCE WORKS

Akiner, Shirin, comp. *Islamic Peoples of the Soviet Union.* London: Kegan
    Paul International, 2d ed. 1986.
Becka, Jiri, ed. *Dictionary of Oriental Literatures*, vol. 3, "West Asia and
    North Africa." New York: Basic Books, 1977.
Bainbridge, Margaret, ed. *The Turkic Peoples of the World.* London: Kegan,
    Paul International, 1993.
Bennigsen, Alexandre, and S. Enders Wimbush, comps. *Muslims of the Soviet
    Empire: A Guide.* Bloomington: Indiana University Press, 1986.
Bibliography of Central Asian Studies in Japan, 1879–1987. Tokyo: The
    Centre for East Asian Cultural Studies, c/o The Toyo Bunko, 1988, 2 vols.
Bosworth, C. E. *The Islamic Dynasties. A Chronological and Genealogical
    Handbook.* Edinburgh: Edinburgh University Press, 1980.
"Central Asia" an extensive section organized by republics, and Bibliogra-
    phy, in *Encyclopaedia Britannica* (Micropaedia), vol. 15, 1992, and subse-
    quent eds.
"Central Asia" an extensive section organized by subjects, and Bibliographies,
    in *Encyclopaedia Iranica*, vol. 5, 1990.
Frye, E. N. *Tajikistan 1994.* Benson, Vermont: Chalidze Publications, 1994.
Goldman, Bernard. *The Ancient Arts of Western and Central Asia. A Guide
    to the Literature.* Ames: Iowa State University Press, 1991.
Hofman, H. F., comp. *Turkish Literature. A Bio-Bibliographical Survey.
    Section III, Moslim Central Asian Turkish Literature.* Utrecht: Library of
    the University of Utrecht, 1969, 6 vols., bound in 2 books.
Konn, Tania, ed., *Soviet Studies Guide.* London: Bowker-Saur, 1992.
Pearson, J. D., comp. *Index Islamicus.* Cambridge, England, 1958–.
Philologiae Turcicae Fundamenta. Wiesbaden: Franz Staener Verlag, 1965,
    vol. 2 (articles in English, German, etc.).
Russia and Eurasia. Facts and Figures Annual. Gulf Breeze, Florida: Aca-
    demic International Press, 1993, vol. 18.
Wixman, Ronald. *The Peoples of the USSR. An Ethnographic Handbook.*
    Armonk, N.Y.: M. E. Sharpe, 1984.

BOOKS, DISSERTATIONS, AND M.A. THESES

Adshead, Samuel Adrian M. *Central Asia in World History*. London: Macmillan, 1993.

Against the Desert. Stories by Writers of Soviet Turkmenia. Moscow: Progress Publishers, n.d.

Aitmatov, Chingiz. *The Day Lasts More than a Hundred Years*. Trans. John French. Bloomington: Indiana University Press, 1983.

———. *Tales of the Mountains and Steppes*. Moscow: Progress Publishers, 1977.

———. *The White Ship*. Trans. Mirra Ginsburg. New York: Crown Publishers, 1972.

———. *The Place of the Skull*. London: Faber, 1989.

Akiner, Shirin. *Central Asia: New Arc of Crisis?* London: Royal United Services Institute for Defence Studies, 1993.

Akiner, Shirin, ed. *Political and Economic Trends in Central Asia*. London: British Academic Press, Imprint of I. B. Taurus and Co., Ltd., 1994.

Allworth, Edward. *The Modern Uzbeks. From the Fourteenth Century to the Present. A Cultural History*. Stanford: Hoover Institution Press, 1990, repr. 1992.

Allworth, Edward, ed. *Central Asia, 120 Years of Russian Rule*. Durham: Duke University Press, Central Asia Book Series, 1989.

———. *The Nationality Question in Soviet Central Asia*. New York: Praeger Publishers, 1973.

———. *Tatars of the Crimea. Their Struggle for Survival*. Durham, N.C.: Duke University Press, Central Asia Book Series, 1988.

Aminova, Rakhima Kh. *The October Revolution and Women's Liberation in Uzbekistan*. Moscow: "Nauka," 1977.

The Archeology of Central Asia. Russian edition edited by Boris A. Litvinsky; English edition edited by Richard N. Frye. Trans. Fred Hiebert. *Bulletin of the Asia Institute*, 1994, vol. 7.

The Art of Central Asia. Leningrad: Aurora Art Publishers, 1988.

At the Foot of the Blue Mountains: Stories by Tajik Authors. Moscow: Raduga Publishers, 1984.

Atkin, Muriel. *The Subtlest Battle: Islam in Soviet Tajikistan*. Philadelphia: Foreign Policy Research Institute, 1989.

Bacon, Elizabeth E. *Central Asians under Russian Rule: A Study in Culture Change*. Ithaca: Cornell University Press, 1980, 2d ed.

Baldauf, Ingeborg. *'Kraevedenie' and Uzbek National Consciousness*. Bloomington: Indiana University Research Institute for Inner Asian Studies, Papers on Inner Asia, no. 20, 1992.

Balzer, Marjorie Mandelstam, ed. *Shamanism: Soviet Studies of Traditional Religion in Siberia and Central Asia*. Armonk, N.Y.: M. E. Sharpe, 1990.

Becka, Jiri. *Sadriddin Ayni: Father of Modern Tajik Culture*. Naples: Instituto Universitario Orientale, Seminaro di Studi Asiatici, Series Minor 5, 1980.

Becker, Seymour. *Russia's Protectorates in Central Asia: Bukhara and Khiva, 1865–1924.* Cambridge, Mass.: Harvard University Press, 1968.

Belenitsky, Aleksandr. *Central Asia.* Trans. James Hogarth. Cleveland and New York: World Publishing Company, 1968.

Bennigsen, Alexandre and S. Enders Wimbush. *Mystics and Commissars.* Berkeley: University of California Press, 1987.

Bergholtz, Fred W. *The Partition of the Steppe: the Struggle of the Russians, Manchus and the Zunghar Mongols for Empire in Central Asia, 1619–1758; a Study in Power Politics.* New York: Peter Lang. American University Studies, 1993.

Bodrogligeti, Andras J. E. *Khalis' Story of Ibrahim: A Central Asian Islamic Work in Late Chagatay Turkic.* Leiden: E. J. Brill, 1974.

Bonner, Arthur. *Among the Afghans.* Durham, N.C.: Duke University Press, Central Asia Book Series, 1987.

Bremmer, Ian and Ray Taras, eds. *Nations and Politics in the Soviet Successor States.* Cambridge: Cambridge University Press, 1993.

Brown, Bess and John Tedstorm. *Privatization in Kazakhstan and Kyrgyzstan: An Update on the Economic Reform.* Munich: RFE/RL Research Institute, 1992.

Carrère d'Encausse, Hélène. *Reform and Revolution in Central Asia.* London: Tauris; Berkeley: University of California Press, 1988 [translation from the author's *Réforme et révolution chez les musulmans de l'empire russe. Bukhara 1867–1924* (1966)].

————. *The End of the Soviet Empire: the Triumph of the Nations.* New York: Basic Books, 1993.

Chadwick, Nora K. and Victor Zhirmunsky. *Oral Epics of Central Asia.* Cambridge: Cambridge University Press, 1969.

Collias, Karen. *Heroes and Patriots: The Ethnic Integration of Youth in the Soviet Union During the Brezhnev Era, 1965–1982.* New York: unpublished Ph.D. dissertation, Columbia University, 1987.

Conolly, Violet. *Beyond the Urals: Economic Development in Soviet Asia.* London: Oxford University Press, 1967.

Country Profile. Georgia, Armenia, Azerbaijan, Central Asian Republics. London: The Unit, n.d.

Critchlow, James. *Nationalism in Uzbekistan. A Soviet Republic's Road to Sovereignty.* Boulder: Westview Press, 1991.

Dailey, Erika. *Human Rights in Uzbekistan.* New York: Helsinki Watch, 1993.

————. *Schooling the Central Asian Spirit: The Evolution of the Madrasa under Russian Rule.* New York: unpublished M.A. thesis, Columbia University, 1990.

Deweese, Devin A. *The Kashf al-huda' of Kamal ad-Din Husayn Khorezmi: A Fifteenth-Century Sufi Commentary on the 'Qasidat al-burda' in Khorezmian.* Bloomington: unpublished Ph.D. dissertation, Indiana University, 1985.

Dienes, Leslie. *Soviet Asia: Economic Development and National Policy Choices*. Boulder: Westview Press, 1987.

Economic Integration: OECD Economies, Dynamic Asian Economies, and Central and Eastern European Countries. Paris: Organization for Economic Co-operation and Development, 1993.

Eickelman, Dale, ed. *Russia's Muslim Frontiers: New Directions in Cross-Cultural Analysis*. Bloomington: Indiana University Press, 1993.

Engelmann, Kurt E. *The Introduction of Market Forces and Structural Changes in Command Economies: A Linear Programming Analysis of Irrigated Agriculture in Uzbekistan*. Seattle: unpublished Ph.D. dissertation, University of Washington, 1993.

Feldman, Walter Robert. *The Uzbek Oral Epic: Documentation of Late Nineteenth-Century and Early Twentieth-Century Bards*. New York: unpublished Ph.D. dissertation, Columbia University, 1980.

Fierman, William. *Language Planning and National Development. The Uzbek Experience*. Berlin: Mouton de Gruyter, 1991.

Fierman, William, ed. *Soviet Central Asia, the Failed Transformation*. Boulder: Westview Press, 1991.

Frank, Andre Gunder. *The Centrality of Central Asia*. Amsterdam: VU University Press. Comparative Asian Studies 8, 1992.

Frye, Richard N. *The History of Ancient Iran*. Munich: Beck Verlag, 1984.

——. See *The Archeology of Central Asia*.

Fuller, Graham E. *Central Asia: the New Geopolitics*. Santa Monica, Calif.: Rand Corporation, 1992.

Gleason, Gregory W. *Between Moscow and Tashkent: The Politics of the Uzbek Cotton Production Complex*. Davis, California: unpublished Ph.D. dissertation, University of California, Davis, 1984.

Golombek, Lisa and Maria Subtelny, eds. *Timurid Art and Culture: Iran and Central Asia in the Fifteenth Century*. Leiden: E. J. Brill, 1992.

Gottlieb, Gidon. *Nation against State: a New Approach to Ethnic Conflicts and the Decline of Sovereignty*. New York: Council on Foreign Relations, 1993.

Gross, Jo-Ann. *Khoja Ahrar: A Study of the Perceptions of Religious Power and Prestige in the Late Timurid Period*. New York: unpublished Ph.D. dissertation, New York University, 1983.

Gross, Jo-Ann, ed., *Muslims in Central Asia. Expressions of Identity and Change*. Durham: Duke University Press, Central Asia Book Series, 1992.

Hanson, Paul L. *Sovereignty and Service Relationships in the Timurid Corporate Dynasty under Babur: the Continuing Legacy of the Chingis Khanid Political System*. Chicago: unpublished Ph.D. dissertation, University of Chicago, 1985.

Hayit, Baymirza. *Islam and Turkestan under Russian Rule*. Istanbul: Can Matbaa, 1987.

Herdeg, Klaus. *Formal Structure in Islamic Architecture of Iran and Turkistan*. New York: Rizzoli International Publications, 1990.

Hiebert, Frederick Talmage. *Bronze Age Oasis Settlements of Central Asia.* Cambridge, Mass.: unpublished Ph.D. dissertation, Harvard University, 1992.

History of Civilizations of Central Asia. Paris: UNESCO, 1992.

Hostler, Charles W. *The Turks of Central Asia.* Westport, Conn.: Praeger Publishers, 1993, 2d ed.

Ibrahim, Diloram. *Islamatization of Central Asia: A Case Study of Uzbekistan.* Leicester: The Islamic Foundation, 1993.

Ibrahimov, Isabella M. *The Identity of the Bukharan Jews: Their Culture at the End of the Nineteenth and Beginning of the Twentieth Century.* New York: unpublished M.A. thesis, Columbia University, 1988.

Iqbal Khan, M. *Muslims of Central Asia and Russia: A Brief Introduction.* Leicester: The Islamic Foundation, 1993.

Jarring, Gunnar. *A Tall Tale from Central Asia.* Lund: CWK Gleerup, 1973.

Kamberi, Dolkun. *The Significance of Medieval Uyghur Drama and Related Cultural Phenomena; from 'Matrisimit' to 'Qutadghu Bilik', ca. 767–1069 A.D.* New York: unpublished Ph.D. dissertation, Columbia University, 1994.

Kangas, Roger David. *Faizulla Khodzhaev: National Communism in Bukhara and Soviet Uzbekistan, 1896–1938.* Bloomington, Indiana: unpublished Ph.D. dissertation, Indiana University, 1992.

Kanlidere, Ahmet. *Reform within Islam: The 'Tajdid' (Renewal) Movement among the Kazan Tatars (1850–1917).* New York: unpublished Ph.D. dissertation, Columbia University, 1994.

Kappeler, Andreas, Gerhard Simon, Georg Brunner, and Edward Allworth, eds. *Muslim Communities Reemerge: Historical Perspectives on Nationality, Politics and Opposition in the Former Soviet Union and Yugoslavia.* Durham: Duke University Press, Central Asia Book Series, 1994.

Karimov, Islom. *Building the Future. Uzbekistan—Its Own Model for Transition to a Market Economy.* Tashkent: "Uzbekiston" Publishers, 1993.

Karimov, I. A. *Uzbekistan: The Road of Independence and Progress.* Tashkent: "Uzbekiston," 1992.

Kazakhstan: Economic Review. n.p.: International Monetary Fund, 1993.

Kim, Ho-dong. *The Muslim Rebellion and the Kashghar Emirate in Chinese Central Asia, 1864–1877.* Cambridge, Mass.: unpublished Ph.D. dissertation, Harvard University, 1986.

Knobloch, Edgar. *Beyond the Oxus. Archeology, Art and Architecture of Central Asia.* London: Ernest Benn, Ltd., Totowa, N.J.: Rowman and Littlefield, 1972.

Kocaoglu, Timur. *Nationality Identity in Soviet Central Asian Literature: Kazakh and Uzbek Prose Fiction of the Post-Stalin Period.* New York: unpublished Ph.D. dissertation, Columbia University, 1982.

Komaroff, Linda. *The Timurid Phase in Iranian Metalwork: Formulation and Realization of a Style.* New York: unpublished Ph.D. dissertation, New York University, 1984.

Krader, Lawrence. *Peoples of Central Asia*. Bloomington: Indiana University Publications, 1971, 3d ed.

Kramov, I., ed. *The Voice of the Steppe: Modern Kazakh Short Stories* Moscow: Progress Publishers, 1981.

Kreindler, Isabelle Teitz. *Educational Policies toward the Eastern Nationalities in Tsarist Russia: A Study of Il'minskii's System*. New York: unpublished Ph.D. dissertation, Columbia University, 1969.

Kunanbayev, Abay. *Selected Poems*. Moscow: Progress Publishers, n.d.

Lentz, Thomas W., Jr. *Painting at Herat under Baysunghur ibn Shahrukh*. Cambridge, Mass.: unpublished Ph.D. dissertation, Harvard University, 1985.

Levin, Theodore C. *The Music and Tradition of the Bukharan "Shashmaqom" in Uzbekistan*. Princeton, N.J.: unpublished Ph.D. dissertation, Princeton University, 1984.

Lewis, Robert A., ed. *Geographic Perspectives on Soviet Central Asia*. New York: Routledge, 1992.

Litvinsky, Boris A. See *The Archeology of Central Asia*.

Lubin, Nancy. *Labour and Nationality in Central Asia: An Uneasy Compromise*. London: Macmillan, 1984.

McCabe, William A. *The Durability of Chaghatay. Past Finite Verb Forms in the Late Prose History Ta'rikh-i Turkistan, by Mulla 'Alim Makhdum Haji*. New York: unpublished M.A. thesis, Columbia University, 1992.

McChesney, Robert D. *Waqf in Central Asia: Four Hundred Years in the History of a Muslim Shrine, 1480–1889*. Princeton: Princeton University Press, 1991.

Malcomson, Scott. *Borderlands. Nation and Empire*. Boston: Faber and Faber, 1994.

Mandelbaum, Michael, ed. *Central Asia and the World*. New York: Council on Foreign Relations Press, 1994.

Manz, Beatrice Forbes. *The Rise and Rule of Tamerlane*. Cambridge: Cambridge University Press, 1992.

Manz, Beatrice Forbes, ed. *Central Asia in Historical Perspective*. Boulder: Westview Press: The John M. Olin Critical Issues Series, 1994.

Maslow, Jonathan. *Sacred Horses. The Memoirs of a Turkmen Cowboy*. New York: Random House, 1994.

Massell, Gregory. *The Surrogate Proletariat: Moslem Women and Revolutionary Strategies in Soviet Central Asia, 1919–1929*. Princeton: Princeton University Press, 1974.

Masson, V. M. and V. I. Sarianidi. *Central Asia: Turkmenia before the Achaemenids*. Trans. by Ruth Tringham. New York: Praeger Publishers, 1972.

Medlin, William K., William M. Cave, and Finley Carpenter. *Education and Development in Central Asia: A Case Study on Social Change in Uzbekistan*. Leiden: E. J. Brill, 1971.

Meffert, Peter R. *The Population and Rural Economy of the Kazakh Soviet*

Socialist Republic. Stanford: unpublished Ph.D. dissertation, Stanford University, 1987.

Micklin, Philip P. *The Water Management Crisis in Soviet Central Asia.* Pittsburgh: University of Pittsburgh Center for Russian and East European Studies, 1991.

Mozur, Joseph P., Jr. *Chingiz Aitmatov and the Poetics of Moral Prose.* Chapel Hill: unpublished Ph.D. dissertation, University of North Carolina, 1983.

Naby, Eden. *Transitional Central Asian Literature: Tajik and Uzbek Prose Fiction from 1909 to 1932.* New York: unpublished Ph.D. dissertation, Columbia University, 1975.

Naumkin, Vitaly, ed. *State, Religion and Society in Central Asia: A Post-Soviet Critique.* Reading: Ithaca Press, 1993.

Nazarbayev, Nursultan A. *A Strategy for the Development of Kazakhstan as a Sovereign State.* Washington, D.C.: The Ministry of Foreign Affairs of the Republic of Kazakhstan; The Embassy of the Republic of Kazakhstan in the U.S.A., 1994.

Nazarov, Bakhtiyar A.; Denis Sinor, eds. *Essays on Uzbek History, Culture, and Language.* Bloomington: Indiana University Research Institute for Inner Asian Studies, 1993.

Nettleton, Susanna S. *Flourishing of the Khanate of Qoqan, 1800–1820: A Turkic-Iranian Cultural Partnership.* New York: unpublished M.A. thesis, Columbia University, 1981.

Nourmoukhammedov, Nagim-Bek. *The Mausoleum of Hodja Ahmed Yasevi.* Almaty: "öner" Baspasï, 1980.

Nove, Alec and J. A. Newth. *The Soviet Middle East: A Communist Model for Development?* New York: Praeger Publishers, 1967.

Olcott, Martha Brill. *The Kazakhs.* Stanford: Hoover Institution Press, 1987.

Paksoy, Hasan B., ed. *Central Asian Monuments.* Istanbul: Isis Press, 1992.

Poliakov, Sergei. *Everyday Islam in Central Asia.* Armonk, N.Y.: M. E. Sharpe, 1992.

Pulatov, Timur. *The Life Story of a Naughty Boy from Bukhara.* Trans. Dudley Hagen. Moscow: Raduga Publishers, 1983.

Rakowska-Harmstone, Teresa. *Russia and Nationalism in Central Asia: The Case of Tadzhikistan.* Baltimore: Johns Hopkins University Press, 1970.

Reichl, Karl. *Turkic Oral Epic Poetry.* New York: Garland Publishing, 1992.

Rezun, Miron. *Intrigue and War in Southwest Asia: the Struggle for Supremacy from Central Asia to Iraq.* New York: Praeger Publishers, 1992.

Rudelson, Justin Jon. *Bones in the Sand: The Struggle to Create Uiqhur Nationalist Ideologies in Xinjianq, China.* Cambridge, Mass.: unpublished Ph.D. dissertation, Harvard University, 1991.

Rumer, Boris. *Soviet Central Asia—"A Tragic Experiment."* Boston: Unwin Hyman, 1989.

Rypka, Jan. *History of Iranian Literature.* Dordrecht, Holland: D. Reidl Publishing Company, 1968.

Rywkin, Michael. *Moscow's Muslim Challenge: Soviet Central Asia*. Armonk, N.Y.: M. E. Sharpe, 1990, 2d ed.

Salihoglu, Hülya Emine. *The Main Themes and Imagery in Aybek's Lyric Poems*. New York: unpublished M.A. thesis, Columbia University, 1971.

Saray, Mehmet. *The Turkmens in the Age of Imperialism: A Study of the Turkmen People and Their Incorporation into the Russian Empire*. Ankara: Turkish Historical Society Printing House, 1989.

Schoeberlein-Engel, John Samuel. *Identity in Central Asia: Construction and Continuation in Conceptions of "Uzbek," "Tajik," "Muslim," "Samarqandi," and Other Groups*. Cambridge, Mass.: unpublished Ph.D. dissertation, Harvard University, 1993.

Seaman, Gary, ed. *Rulers from the Steppe: State Formation on the Eurasian Periphery*. Los Angeles: Ethnographics Press, 1990.

Selnick, Irwin S. *The Ethnic and Political Determinants of Elite Recruitment in the Soviet National Republics: The Uzbek Soviet Elite, 1952–1981*. New York: unpublished Ph.D. dissertation, Columbia University, 1984.

Shashenkov, Maxim. *Security Issues of the Ex-Soviet Central Asian Republics*. London: Brassey's for the Centre for Defence Studies, University of London, King's College, 1992.

Shirazi-Mahajan, Faegheh. *Costume and Textile Designs of the Il-Khanid, Timurid and Safavid Dynasties in Iran from the Thirteenth to the Seventeenth Century*. Columbus: unpublished Ph.D. dissertation, The Ohio State University, 1985.

Sinnott, Peter. *Urban Settlement in Soviet Central Asia: The Evolution of the Spatial Pattern and Structure, 1920–1989*. New York: unpublished Ph.D. dissertation, 1994.

Soper, John David. *Loan Syntax in Turkic and Iranian: The Verb Systems of Tajik, Uzbek, and Qashqay*. Los Angeles: unpublished Ph.D. dissertation, University of California at Los Angeles, 1987.

Söylemez, Orhan. *Preserving Kazak Cultural Identity after 1980*. New York: unpublished Ph.D. dissertation, Columbia University, 1994.

Soviet Literature. Special Issue "Literature and Arts of Soviet Tajikistan" no. 5 (1981).

Strong, John, ed. *Canadian Slavonic Papers*. Special Issue: "Russia and Soviet Central Asia." Nos. 2/3 (1975).

Suh, Sang-Guk. *Reflections of Buddhist Philosophy in Cingiz Ajtmatov's Literary Works*. Madison: unpublished Ph.D. dissertation, University of Wisconsin, Madison, 1992.

Tadjbakhsh, Shahrbanou. *Women's Poetry in Tajikistan: The Dynamics of a Changing Voice*. New York: unpublished M.A. thesis, Columbia University, 1991.

——— . *The Bloody Path of Change: The Case of Post-Soviet Tajikistan*. New York: The Harriman Institute Forum, vol. 6, no. 11, July 1993.

——— . *Inventing the a-Soviet Woman of the Muslim East: Nativization in*

Tajikistan, 1989–1992. New York: unpublished Ph.D. dissertation, Columbia University, 1994.

Teague, Ken. *Metalcrafts of Central Asia.* Princes Resborogh, Aylesbury, Bucks: Shire Publications, 1990.

Vaidyanath, R. *The Formation of the Soviet Central Asian Republics: A Study in Soviet Nationalities Policy, 1917–1936.* New Delhi: People's Publishing House, 1967.

Van Damme, Mark; Hendrik Boeschoten, eds. *Utrecht Papers on Central Asia: Proceedings of the First European Seminar on Central Asian Studies, Held at Utrecht, 16–18 December 1985.* Utrecht, Netherlands: Utrecht Turkological Series, No. 2, 1987.

Von Mende, Erling, ed. *Turkestan als historischer Faktor und politische Idee.* Cologne: Studienverlag, 1988. Includes articles in English.

Weinberger, James W. *The Rise of Muslim Cities in Sogdia, 700–1220.* Berkeley: unpublished Ph.D. dissertation, University of California, Berkeley, 1984.

Wilkins, Frances. *Uzbekistan.* New York: Chelsea House Publishers, 1988. For young people.

Zhou, Xijuan. *Cultural Interaction between Uyghurs, Chinese and Sogdians in the 8th to 13th Centuries.* New York: unpublished Ph.D. dissertation, Columbia University, 1994.

Zimmer, Terese S. *The Politics of Regional Development in the USSR: A Case Study of Uzbekistan.* Baltimore: unpublished Ph.D. dissertation, Johns Hopkins University, 1983.

Glossary

Ābikārī. Irrigated, 125.

Adat. Local customary law, 277

Ädir. Hilly area or a mountain slope, 124–25

Agam. Music: a modal form, 465

Ahl-i ma'rifat. An educated person; an intellectual, 383

Aivan, see *Äywan*

Akhïr zamana. A fatal time; fatal-time motif in poetry, 407

Akïlduu kishi. An intellectual, 382

Akin. A poet-composer, 447

Akïr zaman. A bad time; "Bad Time" (literature), 406

Alkïm ses. Singing in a hoarse voice, 448

Allahsizlar. Atheists, 257

Almä. An apple, 126

Al-'ud. A short-necked lute, 437

Amach. A small iron-tipped plowshare, 276

Ämlak. Land owned by a khan or emir. State land, 277

Ämlakdar. A tax collector, 278

Änhat. Main canal, 267

Änshi. A singer-interpreter, 447

Aqil. An intellectual, 382

Aqïldi adam. An intellectual, 382

Aqïlli kisi. An intellectual, 382

Äqilliq adäm. An intellectual, 382

Aqsaqal. A village elder, 154, 280

Aq tämäki. Smoking tobacco, 127

Äräwä. A two-wheeled cart, 321

Argamak. Breed of horses, 129

Ariq. A canal, 267

Ärk. The citadel in a traditional town, 485

Ärpä, Barley, 125

Aruz. Form of traditional Arab metrical construction, 418–19, 445

As. The Ossets; Alanic tribes, 85

Ashiran husseni. Music: an Aeolian mode, 464

At. A horse, 128

Awj. Music: the climax in an instrumental piece, 469

Ayïr tüye. Two-humped Bactrian camel, 129

Äywan. Architecture: a veranda, 496–97, 500, 502, 511, 518

Bähar. The spring season, 124

Bäharikarlik. A form of dry farming, 124

Bakhshi. Professional class of story tellers and musical artists, 444–48

Bäkhtsizlik. Unhappiness, 408

Baksy. A magician, 447–48

Balaban. A clarinet, 449; a drum, 454

Balakhanä. Architecture: little second-story rooms, 497, 500

Band. A large dam, 270

Bäng. Hashish, 127

Bärkhan. Mobile, crescent-shaped sand dunes, 121

Barmak. A syllabic verse form, 445

Basqaq. Tax farmers employed by the government, 21

Bay. A wealthy man, 302

Bayat, bayati. A musical mode, 440, 464

Bedä. Alfalfa, 126

Bek. Governor of a city or region of the khanates, 278

Bilimli. An educated man; an intellectual, 383

Bilimpaz. An educated man; an intellectual, 383

Bogara. Russian: a form of dry farming, 124

Bokey Jüz. Kazakh Inner Horde, 50

Boza. An alchoholic drink made from millet, 126

Bozquy. Music: the unchanging basic theme in an instrumental piece, 468

Bughday. Wheat, 125

Bulaq. Agriculture: a spring

Bulbullär ornini zaghlär. A motif in Central Asian poetry meaning "crows replacing nightingales," 408

Buzkashi. A contest of horsemen, 355

Buzruk (or *Buzurg*). Music: a great mode, 496

Centner (Russian: *tsentner*). A measurement of weight (50 kilograms), 289

Chälmä. Fuel, 123

Chang. A dulcimer, 439, 454

Chängawuz. A jaw's harp, 454

Ch'ao-sheng. A Chinese mouth organ, 439

Charäkar. Sharecropper, 279

Charbait. A rhyme scheme, 445

Chargah. Music: a modal form, 465

Chärkh. A primitive spinning wheel, 310, 312

Chartar. A stringed instrument, 440

Chaykhanä. A traditional tea house, 516

Chek. A portion of land divided according to the ownership of ox teams, 280

Cheng. Chinese: a musical instrument with nineteen pipes, 439

Chernozem. Russian: black soil, 122

Chighir. A waterwheel, 270

Chighiriq. Rough wooden rollers used in processing cotton, 309

Chigit. Cottonseed, 127, 310

Childirma. A drum, 455

Chilmanda. A drum, 455

Chobkar. A builder, 490

Chol. Waterless plain or desert, 124

Choor, *see* Shoor

Chubchiq. A Chinese mouth organ, 439

Cimbalom. A Hungarian dulcimer, 454

Dägh. Mountain, 76

Daira. A drum, 440, 455-56

Dapp. A drum, 455

Däramäd. Music: an introduction in the low register in an instrumental piece, 469

Darugha. Tax farmer employed by the government, 21

Da-shy. In China, Tajik; *see* Tazi

Dastgah. Music: a branch of a basic mode, 469–70

Dauïlpaz. A small kettledrum, 454

Desiatin. Measurement of land

Dhola. A drum; *see* Dool

Dil. Tongue, 76

Dilli tüydük. A clarinet, 449

Doignorirovalïs. Russian: wilfully blind, 169

Dokandästgah. A simple loom, 310

Dol. A drum, 454

Dombïra. A two-stringed, long-necked lute, 449, 454

Dombura (k). A two-stringed lute, 454

Dool. A drum, 454

Doolbash, *see* Dauïlpaz

Dugah. Music: a "second mode," 440, 469, 470

Dumbä. A fat-tailed sheep, 129

Dutar. A long-necked lute, 440, 449, 456

Dutarchï. A dutar player, 447

Echki. A goat, 129

Eki jüzdüü (Kirgiz). A two-faced person, with the political connotation "a nationalist who hides his true hostility while opposing the Party," 415

Eshäk. A donkey, 129–30

Estüü kishi. An intellectual, 382

Falbin. Fortune teller, 167

Fazil. An educated man; an intellectual, 383

Gänch. Stucco, 516

Gänchkar. Architecture: plasterer and carver, 490

Gardun. Music: in an instrumental piece, literally, "heavenly arch," 468

Gärmsil. A type of foehn, 121

Ghazal. A lyric verse structure, 445

Ghäzat. Holy war, 6

Ghazawat. Holy war, 142

Gïjak, Ghïjjäk, Ghijjäk. A three-stringed fiddle, 449
Gïjakchï. A gijak player, 447
Giläm. A carpet with nap, 314
Gilkar. Architecture: plasterer and carver, 490
Gopuz. A jaw's harp, 454
Gramota. Russian: an official message, 39
Gurgulugu. Performer of an epos, 447

Hackbrett. A German dulcimer, 454
Hafaza. Singers and players, 439
Hälwa. Oil made from sesame pressings, 127
Häräm. Women's quarters, 490
Häsär. Labor system involving masses of unpaid labor, 273
Hawuz. A pond, 126
Hijaz. A musical mode; a major with a flatted second, 440, 465
Hijaz kar. A musical mode; a major with a flatted second and sixth, 465
Huo-pu-ssu. Music: a qubuz, 439

Iasi. Old Russian: the Ossets, 85
Ikiyuzlamachi (Uzbek); see Eki jüz-düü
Insan-i aqil. An intellectual, 382
Intelligenty. Russian: People who work at mental, not physical, tasks, 383
Ipäk. Silk, 312
Ipäk qurti. Silkworms, 312
Iraq. Music: a mode from Iraq, 469
Ish Jüz. Kazakh Inner Horde. See also Bokey Jüz, 74
Itremek. Music: to make vibration effects on instruments, 448
Ittifaq ul-muslimin. Muslim Union, 191

Jailoolar. Summer pastures: mountain meadows above the tree line, 125
Jigit. A young brave, 426
Jihad. Holy war, 6
Jilqï. A horse, 128
Jirau. An epic singer, 399
Jirchï (Jïrshï). An epic performer, 447
Jokhari. Sorghum, 125
Jolbike. A fellow traveler, 382
Jolotmak. To sing in a low inhuman voice on the syllable gu, 448

Jrau. A folk singer, 428
Jum'a mäsjidi. Friday or cathedral mosque, 491
Jŭt. A thaw followed by refreezing, 129
Jüz. Kazakh "horde," 47

Kafir. Infidel, 139
Kaïr. A form of farming naturally flooded areas, 267
Käl. A "scald head"; hero of picaresque folk tales, 427
Kalin. A dulcimer, 454
Kalk dushmani. An enemy of the people, 416
Karanda. Land from which the revenues are devoted to communal needs, 279
Kariz. Underground reservoir, 271
Karnay. A long bass trumpet, 440, 456
Kashi. Art: glazed tiles, 512
Kendir. Hemp, 127
Ketman. A kind of hoe or spade, 276
Khälät. Local robe, 310
Khanä. Music: an episode in an instrumental piece, 468
Khemlemek. To sing with the mouth closed; to hum, 448
Khiraj. Tithe, tax, 278
Khirman. A collection point for goods or crops, 292
Khömey. Music: a form of polyphonic playing, 456
Khudasizlar. Atheists, 257
Kishmish. Small seedless grapes, 127
Kishshi Jüz. Kazakh Little Horde, 48
Kïyak. A two-stringed fiddle, 449
Kiyik ot. Antelope grass, 125
Kohnäärk. Khiva: old citadel, 488
Kök bori. A contest of horsemen, 354–55
Kokbori tartu. A contest of horsemen, 355
Kökmüz. A thaw followed by refreezing, 129
Koknar. Poppy, 127
Kok tämäki. Chewing tobacco, 127
Komuz. A lute, 454
Kordoo. Song of social protest, 447
Korinishkhanä. Audience room, 490
Kuhändiz. Bukhara and Khiva: the central elevation in a traditional town, 485

Kul'turnoe, Russian: cultured, 366
Kumiss. Fermented mares' milk, 128
Kunjut. Sesame, 127
Kurdiuk. Russian: fat-tailed sheep, 129

Lälmikarlik. A form of dry farming, 124
Lal perde. A mute musical mode, 443
La-pu-pu. A stringed instrument, 439
Latinlashdirish. Latinization of the Central Asian alphabet, 81
Layqa. Agriculture: fertile silt, 116

Mahur. Music: a modal form, 465
Makhorka. Russian tobacco, 128
Mäkkä jokhari. Maize, 126
Maktab. A primary school, 350
Maktoo. Eulogy, 447
Manaschï. A manas (an epos) performer, 447
Maqamat. Musical modes, 437–84
Maqta. Cotton, 127
Masjid. A mosque, 491
Mā-warā-'n-nahr. Arabic: Transoxania; Outer Iran, 87
Mayjuwaz. A small oil-pressing workshop, 312
Me'mar. An architect, 490
Mewäzar bagh. Orchard, 126
Mirab. A water controller, 280, 355
Mirshab. A police chief, 355
Molä. A wooden harrow, 276
Mukhammas. A two-voiced musical composition; a part of a *shashmaqam;* also a verse structure, 443, 445, 468
Mulk. Property; land, 278
Mulk-i hurr. Lands paying no tax, 278
Mulk-i khiraj. Lands paying tax of from one-seventh to one-half of the harvest, 278
Mulk ushri. Lands paying one-tenth of the harvest to the state, 278
Murabba. A verse structure, 445
Murid. Disciple, 167
Musalla. Nonalcoholic drink made from grapes, 127
Mushkulat. Music: instrumental piece, 468

Nägharä, Nagharä. A small kettledrum, 440–54

Näqqash. Architecture: a wall decorator, 490
Nar. A dromedary, 129
Nas. Powdered chewing tobacco mixed with ash and lime, 128
Näshä. Hashish, 127
Nasiyat. A didactic poem, 447
Näsr. Music: a combination of music and text, 468–69
Nasway. Powdered chewing tobacco mixed with ash and lime, 128
Nawa. Music: a Mixolydian mode, 464, 469
Nay. A transverse flute, or cane, 449, 454, 456

Obusurmanilsia. Russian: converted to Islam, 5
Okugan adam. An educated man; an intellectual, 383
Ölengshi. A singer-interpreter, 447
Opasïz (Kazakh); *see* Eki jüzdüü
Oqughan ayal. An educated woman, 431
Oraq. A sickle, 276
Orik. An apricot, 126
Orta Jüz. Kazakh Middle Horde, 6
Otdiel. Russian: a military zone; a division, 147
Ozan. Performer of an epos, 447
Özläii. Music: a form of polyphonic playing, 456

Päkhtä. Cotton, 127
Päkhtä mayi. Cottonseed oil, 127
Pälas. A carpet without nap, 314
Pamik. Cotton, 127
Panjtar. Music: a stringed instrument, 440
Perde. a musical mode, 443, 465
Peshrav. Music: a rondo in an instrumental piece, 468–69
Pilaw. Pilaf, 126
Pillä. Cocoons of silkworms, 312
Pillächi. A human brooder for silkworm eggs, 312
Pilläkäsh. Silk winder, 312
Pitimlemek. To snap one's fingers on an instrument's soundboard, 448
Prikaz. Russian: a jurisdiction, 11
Pud. Russian: a measurement of weight (16.38 kilograms), 276

Qadimichi Qadimpäräst. A conservative, 363

Qäl'ä. Bukhara and Khiva: the central elevation in a traditional town, 485

Qalq dusmeni. An enemy of the people, 416

Qanat. In western Iran, a series of underground ducts, reservoirs, 271

Qanun. A zitherlike musical instrument, 440, 454

Qaraqol. Karakul, 124

Qara Sart. The "black sarts"; *see* Sart, 399

Qat. An epistle, 417

Qawun. A melon, 126

Qäyiq. A skiff, 324

Qäyraq. A castanet, 455

Qazaqi qoy. Fat-tailed sheep, 129

Qazi. A judge, 354

Qazi Kalan. The chief justice of Muslim courts, 137, 197

Qimiz. Kumiss, 128

Qipchaq. Folk etymology: "Bolshevik," 238

Qishlaq. A village, 154

Qobiz. A two-stringed spike fiddle, 449

Qonqaq. Millet, 126

Qorghan ordäsi. Khokand: the citadel in a traditional town, 485

Qosh. A pair of oxen, 276

Qoshnay. A clarinet, 449

Qoy. Sheep, 128

Quduqchi. Attendant at a well, 321

Qulaq. An approximate measure of water, 280

Qumtepä. Mobile, crescent-shaped sand dunes, 121

Quray. A longitudinal flute, 449

Qurugh, Quruq. Dry, 75

Qushbegi. Prime minister of the khanate or emirate, 14, 197–98

Qūshnay. A clarinet, 449

Quyruq. Fat-tailed sheep, 129

Rabab. A lute, 440, 454

Rabad. A suburb, 485

Rast. Music: an Ionian mode, 440, 465–69

Riwayät. A ruling (religious court), 194

Rubai. A rhyme scheme and verse form, 445

Säbzi. A carrot, 126

Säksawul. The saksaul tree, 121

Sällä. A turban, 310

Säräkhbar. Music: the introduction or overture in a vocal piece, 469

Sanat. A didactic poem, 447

Santur. Iran: a dulcimer, 437, 439–40, 454

Särdabä. A brick-lined cistern, 321

Sart. The sedentary city person of Central Asia, 73, 104

Say. A stream, 267

Segah. Music: a Phrygian mode, 440, 464, 469

Sekdirmek. In singing to make a hop, skip, 448

Sel'sovet. Russian: a local soviet, 431

Serozem. Russian: grey soil, 122–24

Setar. A fretted three-stringed lute, 440, 454

Shäftali. A peach, 126

Shähristan. The city proper in a traditional town, 485–86

Sha'ir. A poet and musician; performer of an epos, 447

Shali. Rice, 126

Shan qobïz. A jaw's harp, 454

Shariat. Muslim law, 160, 259

Shashmaqam. Classical musical composition, 435, 468–70

Shashtar. A musical instrument, 440

Shinni. Syrup made from grapes, 127

Shirvan perde. Music: a Shirvan mode, 443, 465

Sho'ba. Iran: music: a branch of a basic mode, 469–70

Sholpy. A belled hair-ornament, 420

Shoor. A longitudinal flute, 449, 456

Shor. Type of soil formation between marsh and *solonets,* 123

Shorkhaq. Salt marsh, 123

Shor tupraq. Salt marsh, 123

Shuba. Music: a branch of a basic mode, 469–70

Shudgar. Fallow land plowed every spring and autumn, 277

Sibizgha. A transverse flute, 454

Sibïzgï. A longitudinal flute, 449, 456

Smerdy. Russian: free peasants as opposed to serfs, 30

Solonchak. Russian: a salt marsh, 123
Solonets. Russian: type of soil in an intermediate stage of salinization, 123
Stanitsa. Russian: a Cossack frontier post, 282
Surnay. An oboe, 456
Suw. Water, 267
Suw bashi. The mouth of a canal, 270
Suwli. Irrigated, 125
Svobodnaia professiia. Russian: an independent profession, 395

Tagh. A mountain; mainly referring to higher slopes of the mountains, 125
Taharatkhanä. Architecture: an ablutions facility, 490
Täkä. A goat, 129
Takyr. Type of soil formation between salt marsh and *solonets*, 123
Talan. Music: a small instrumental piece inserted into a vocal piece, 469
Tale zäbunlik. Helplessness, 408
Talqin. Music: a melody for voice, 469
Tänab. A piece of property slightly larger than one acre—fifty tanab equal about thirty-seven acres, 278
Tanbur. Turkey: a long-necked lute, 437, 456
Tan-pu-la. A long-necked lute.
Taranä. A rhyme scheme, 445
Täriq. Millet, 126
Tarjeh. Music: repetition in an instrumental piece, 468–69
Tärwuz. A watermelon, 126
Tar zaman. A bad time; "Bad Time" (literature), 406
Ta-shih. In China, Tajik; *see* Tazi
Tasnif. Music: a rondo, an episode in an instrumental piece, 468–69
Tavlak. A drum, 454
Tazi, Tajik. Earlier, all people of Muslim faith, 65
Temir komuz. A jaw's harp, 454, 456
Ters äywan. Architecture: a winter court, 497
Thaqil. Music: a part in the slow movement of an instrumental piece, 455, 468
Tim-i gilam. A carpet bazaar, 314

Tiramähï. Agriculture: autumnal, 125
Tüydük. Music: a longitudinal flute, 444, 447, 456
Tüydükchi. A tuyduk player, 449
Tut darakhti. A mulberry tree, 127
T'ut-guät. Chinese: the Türküt, 87
Tverdaia pshenitsa. Russian: Durum wheat, 128

Uchastok. Russian territorial division, 153
Uezd. Russian territorial division, 153
Ufär. Music: a finale in dance rhythm in a vocal piece, 469
Ulaq. A contest of horsemen, 355
Ulugh äywan. Architecture: a summer court, 497
Ulu Jüz. Kazakh Great Horde, 48
Ulus. Tribal areas; confederation, 32
Urus-i bidin. The Russian infidel, 6
Ushr. Tithe, tax, 278
Ustä. A master craftsman, 267
Usul. A rhythmical formula, 455
Uzum. A grape, 127

Volost. Russian: administrative unit made up of several villages, 154

Wahälär. A type of populated oasis of southern Central Asia, 125
Waqf. Local philanthropies; also a form of land tenure, 156, 259, 279

Yangalif. New (Latin) alphabet, 81
Yang-k'in. Chinese term indicating something brought in from outside China, 440
Yatughan. A musical instrument with nineteen pipes; *see* Cheng, 439
Yäylawlär. Summer pastures; mountain meadows above the tree line, 125
Yazgi mäsjid. Summer mosque, 490
Yeshkï. A goat, 129
Yoldash. A comrade. Used as a Communist form of address, 372
Yonghichqä. Alfalfa, 126

Zarin perde. A gentle musical mode, 443
Zar zaman. A bad time; "Bad time" (literature), 406, 407, 409
Zayk. Unworked fallow land, 277
Ziyali. An intellectual, 383

Index

Abay, 420

Abay Qunanbay-uli, *see* Qunanbay-uli, Ibrahim

Abd al-Ahad, Emir, 166, 194, 355, 358

'Abd al-Qadir ibn Ghaibi, 439

Abdulaziz, 169

Abdul Hamid Afandi, 252

Abdullah Khan, 3, 38–40

Abdul Malik Khan, 142

Abdurrahman Awtobashi, 146

Abdurrahman Bek, 19

Abidiy, Ismail, 189

Ablay Kahn, 11, 48, 577

About Music and the Musician . . . , *see* "Näghmä wä näghmägär . . ."

Abramov, A. K., General, 135, 140, 143

Abu Ali al-Husayn Ibn Sina, 438–39

Abul Ghazi, 4

Abulkhayr Khan, 48–49

Abulmambet Khan, 48

Abu Sa'id Khan, 38

Adam Biy, 40–41

Adib-i awwal, 365

Adnash, 40

Afghanistan, 27, 62, 65, 82, 90, 92, 116, 147, 149, 181, 201, 212, 230, 237, 248, 255, 263, 322, 589; Russian invasion of, xvii; *see also* Languages; Music

Agahiy, Muhammad Riza Erniyaz Bek-oghli, 357, 404

Agriculture: farm machinery, 108, 306; processing of products, 108, 319–24; crops and produce, 110, 121–22, 125–28, 274–77, 282–85, 287–88, 292, 299, 306, 308; agrarian reform, 250, 255; collectivization, 289–90; *see also* Cotton; Livestock

Ahmad Mahdum Kalla, 173–74, 354–56, 524

Ahmed-oghli, Shah, 220

Aitak-oghli, Nederbi, 264

Aitmatov, Chinghiz, 529–30, 532; *see also* Aytmatov

Ait-oghli, Muhammad Sharif, 33

Akayev, Dr. Askar, 590, 596

Akbar, 479

Akchora-oghlu, Yussuf, 208

Akhmatova, 506

Akimov, Jeppar A., 558

Akmolinsk, *see* Tselinograd

Akmolinskaia oblast, 368–69

Aktyubinsk, 107–8, 233, 285, 340–41, 363

'Ala ad-Din Muhammed Khwarazm-shah, 471

Alamish-oghli, Amandurdi, 380–81, 430

Alash Orda, 222–23, 227, 236–41,

Alash Orda (*continued*)
249, 259–60; party, 364, 414
Alash Party of Kazakhstan, 581,
583–84
"*Alashqa,*" 414
Ala Tau, *see* Alexander range
Alay, 62–63, 83
Alay-Pamir, 70
Aldar Kosa, 427
Alexander II, 163, 170, 173
Alexander III, 359
Alexander range, 63, 414
al-Hira, 436
Alifbe (The Alphabet), 350
Alike division, 11
Alikhanov, Colonel, 148
Alimjan, Hamid, 380
Alim Khan, Emir, 6, 197–98, 250–52,
415
Alim Mahmud Hajji, Mullah, 366–
67, 403–4
Alim Qul, General Mullah, 7, 18–19,
132, 134, 401, 402
Aliqan Bokeyqan-uli, *see* Bokeyqan-
uli, Aliqan
Ali Riza Bek, 252
al-Khursavi, Abu Nasr, 172
Allabergen-oghli, Veli Allah, 187
Allah Quli, Khan, 36–37
Alma Ata, 98, 101, 126–27, 180, 266,
316, 331, 336, 341, 346, 358, 361,
368, 375, 388, 390, 392, 508, 521,
525, 531, 532, 544, 558, 567; State
University in, 564; schools in,
569–70
Almayi, Qari Fazullah Mir Jalal-
oghli, 359
Alpamish, 406, 418
Alphabet, The, see *Alifbe*
Alphabets, *see* Writing systems
Altayic languages, 90–91
Altay mountains, 60–65, 73, 87, 108,
113

Altynsarin, Ibrahim (Ibray), 175, 177,
362
Amangeldi Iman-uli, 211–12, 238–39
Amu Darya, 45, 60, 62, 67, 82, 115–
19, 122, 125, 149, 153, 155, 256,
267, 270, 272, 297, 324, 327, 346,
488; canals, 297, 566–67
Andijan, 98, 102, 146–47, 164, 167–
71, 177, 179, 210, 320, 327, 360,
362, 368
Anjuman-i arwah, 204
Anusha Khan, 35–36
Apa-singillar, 432
Aq Bulaq, 7, 18
Aqmaq patsha, 405
Aq Meshit, 14–18, 361; *see also* Qizil
Orda
Arab Muhammad I, Khan, 8, 41
Arabs, 67, 87–88, 438; *see also* Lan-
guages; Music; Scripts
Aral region, 82, 84, 87
Aral Sea, 20, 57, 112, 116–17, 119,
123, 133, 284, 324, 327, 343, 345;
depletion, 566–67
Architecture: of cities, 485; regional,
485–88, 490–94, 496–97, 500,
503–6, 510–18, 521; traditional and
borrowed forms, 487–93; secular
buildings, 493–501; Russian and
Western influence, 494, 501–2;
Slavic revival and *art nouveau,*
501–5, 513; Russian use of Central
Asian styles, 505–7; constructivism
and socialist realism transplanted,
507–13; and decorative art and ideology, 513–26; "Glass Box," 525;
see also Mosques; Theaters
Arif Khoja Aziz Khoja-oghli, 504
Aristanbek-uulu, 407
Armenians, said favored by CP authorities, 576; riots against, 587,
589
Art, decorative, 513–21; decline of

painting and calligraphy, 521–26
Ascent of Mount Fuji, The (To the Blue Mountain), see *Köktepaga shïghu* and *Fudziyamadagï kadïr tün*
Asfandiyar Khan, 24
Ashar Mutual Aid Movement of Kirgizstan, 586
Ashirov, Ch., 382
Ashkhabad, 98, 114, 148, 180, 217, 228, 231, 271–72, 297–98, 317, 331, 349, 367, 385, 390, 520, 532, 544; oblast, 368
Ashrafi, Mukhtar, 479
Ashur Ali Zahiriy, see Zahiriy, Ashur Ali
'Ashur Muhammad Khoqandiy, Mullah Niyaz Muhammad bin Mullah, 404
Asiya, 190
Astanqulbiy, 197
Astrakhan, 3, 10, 22–25, 27, 29, 31, 85
Ata Jan, 145
Atabek (Nutushev), Aron, chief, Kazakhstan's Alash Party, 584
Auez-uli, Mukhtar (Auezov), 389, 420
Aulie Ata, 18, 167
Avicenna, see Ibn Sina, Abu Ali al-Husayn
Awgan Mirza, 41
"Awunchaq," 414
Aybek, Musa Tashmuhammad-oghli, 380–81, 429–30
Ayina, 201, 203
Ayniy, Sadriddin Murad Khoja Zada, 173, 196, 350–51, 354–55, 362, 365, 370, 412, 423
Ay qap, 201, 411, 413
Aytmatov, Chingiz, 423, 432
Azamat, 411
Azat National Democratic Party of

Kazakhstan, 581–83; assembly of, 583; press of, 583
Azerbaijan, 406, 437, 443
Azeri, 72, 186, 218, 406
Azeri Turkish, 74

Bababek, 143
Baba Jan Ishan, 465
Babur, Zahiriddin Muhammad, Emperor, 60, 82, 360
Bad Time, A, see "Zar zaman" and "Tar zaman"
Bagdadbekov, 415
"Bagtlï gïzlar," 430
Bahjat al-ruh, 439
Bahram Gur, 436
Bahr-i Tajik, 297
Bakhchisaray, 177
Bakst, Leon Nikolaevich, 505
Baku, 183, 231, 249, 317, 322, 328
Balgh (Balkh), 23, 36–37
Balkhash, Lake, 78, 118–19, 340
Bands, 270, 273–74
Baqïtsïz jamal, 425–26
Barak Khan, 393
Baranov brothers, 138
Bartol'd, Vasiliy V., i
Basiner, Th., 47
Basmachis, 228, 230, 232, 235, 241–42, 249, 250–53, 263, 285, 287; Soviet, 251
Basra, 436
Bat', Lidiia, 537
Batir Basi, 15–16
Batu Khan, 8, 21
Bayan, 413
Bayaniy, Muhammad Yusufbek Bababek-oghli, 357, 404
Bay ila khizmatchi, 426
Baykonur, 345
Bayramov, Reshat, 558
Baysum, 252
Baytursin-uli, Aqmet, 175–76, 201,

Baytursin-uli, Aqmet (*continued*)
216, 222, 236–39, 363–65, 389,
409–11
Bayut, 296
Bayyanat-i seyyah-i hindi, 205
Bazar, 409
Begjan, Mullah, 208, 242
Behbudiy, Mufti Mahmud Khoja, 97,
191, 193, 201–2, 213, 217, 363–65,
409–10, 424
Bekabad (Begovat), 273, 296, 333,
558
Bekmukhamed-uli, Jiyemurat, 406
Bekovich-Cherkassky, Alexander, 9,
13
Beliaev, Viktor, 471
Belotserkovskii, I., 521
Beloved of the Heart, see *Mahbub
al-qulub*
Beneveni, Florio, 5, 25
Benua, Aleksei, 503
Berdi Murat Kargabay-uli Shair
(Berdaq Baqsi), 405
Berke Khan, 21
Besh Kazliq, 44
Bidil, Mirza Abdulqadir, 350
Birlik Popular Movement (Party) of
Uzbekistan, founded, 578; draft
program of, 579–580; leaders of,
579; press of, 579, 582
Birzhevye viedomosti, 141
Bishkek (earlier, Pishpek; Frunze),
squatters movement around, 585
Black Sea, 3, 73, 85, 90
Blizzard, The, see *Boran*
Bokey Nuraliqan-uli, 50
Bokeyqan-uli, Aliqan, 175, 187, 201,
216, 222, 236–39, 409
Bolsheviks, 182, 214, 221, 224–26,
229, 232, 233, 237–38, 248, 250,
264, 361, 382, 513
Bonch-Bruevich, Vladimir D., 536
Book of Battle, see *Jang nama*
Book of Modes, see *Kitab al-adwar*

Book of Shaybaniy, see *Shaybaniy
nama*
Bookstores, 544
Boran, 479
Brezhnev, Leonid I., 541, 549
Bride Price, see *Qaling mal*
Budennyi, Simon, 252
Bukhara, 2, 4, 6, 10, 20–21, 23–27,
29–30, 32, 34, 36, 40–42, 45, 62,
69, 131, 134–35, 138, 143, 178,
192, 194–95, 197, 204–5, 225, 241,
244–45, 251–52, 256, 272, 312,
314, 316–19, 321–24, 349–50, 367,
400, 402, 404; and Moscow, 5,
139–43, 149, 153, 157, 159, 165,
197; under USSR, 92–94, 98, 101–
2, 105; Emir of, 132, 134, 139–42,
143, 145, 227, 246, 270; Bukhara-i
Sharif (Holy Bukhara), 138, 145,
196, 198; madrasahs of, 172, 363;
and Islamic reform, 173, 194;
Young Bukharans, 196, 246–48,
251; independence movement in,
228–36, 251; Peoples' Republic,
243–50, 254–55, 262; unification
with Russia, 254–55; politicians,
559
Bukhara-i sharif, 200–201
Bukharin, N. I., 263
Bukhgol'ts, Colonel Ivan, 9
Bulgar, 20–22, 29, 38
Burkhanov, Mutal, 479
Burnash-oghli, 194
Burun-oghli, Garaja, 373, 380
Bustani, Mirza Muhammad 'Abdal-
'azim Sami, 355, 358, 403–5
Buzulgan olkaga, 413

Calligraphy, 349, 521; *see also* Scripts
Camels, *see* Livestock
Camelskin Bag, The, see *Karkit*
Canals, 267, 270–73, 280–81, 294–
99, 343, 566–67

Caspian Sea, 7, 9, 13, 20, 22, 45, 60, 62, 64, 73, 85, 112, 116–19, 143, 284, 297, 317, 322–23, 327
Catherine II, 52; ukase, 3–4, 25
Cattle, *see* Livestock
Caucasus, 62–63, 67, 85, 120, 131, 143, 147–48, 181, 217, 274, 511
Censorship, 531, 535
Central Asianness, xv, 527, 564, 567–68, 571–72
Central Asians defined, 527
Chaghatay, 62, 66, 69, 208, 262, 403–4, 418–19, 421, 425, 429; texts, 78, 362; Gurungi group, 372
Chaghatay Khan, 72, 82
Charjuy, 105, 245, 270, 297, 319, 324, 327, 334, 337, 346
Chehra nama, 356
Chekhov, Anton P., 536
Cheleken Peninsula, 117, 335
Cherniaev, M. G., 18–19, 132–35, 138–41, 155, 163, 400–401
Chernyshevskii, N. G., 173, 175
Chimkent, 18, 73, 98, 101, 131, 266, 296, 307, 316, 331, 341, 346, 397
China, 36, 66, 84–89, 149, 211, 219
Chingis Khan, 21, 84, 89, 267, 440, 487
Chirchiq, 332–34
Chirchiq River, 101, 116, 134, 267, 276, 294, 295, 318, 333–34
Chokay-oghlu, Mustafa, 217, 220, 226–28
Cholera riots, 164–67
Cholpan, Abdulhamid Sulayman Yunus, 371, 389–90, 413
Chu River, 113, 117, 122, 295; canal, 297
Chu Valley, 63, 110, 298–99
Chuvash, 72, 84
City life: inferior to village life, 531–32
Climate, 119–24
Coal, *see* Minerals

Codex Cumanicus, 77
Collectivization, *see* Land
Coming of the Russians, The, *see* "Orusning kelgani"
Communications, 344–48, 367
Communist Party: Russian, 232–34, 253, 257, 371, 385, 418, 431, 507; Central Asian branches of, 243, 246, 255, 260, 263–64, 528, 575, 578, 586–87; All-Union, 381; underrepresentation in, 546–49, 551; Central Asian leaders in, 549–60; conformity in, 554
Comrades, see *Ortaqlar*
Conferences: Lausanne, 207; of Central Asian Muslims, 217–21, 225
"Confusion and Flight," 411
Congresses: Muslim, 186–87, 217–22; Pan-Kirgiz, 222–23; All-Russian, of Soviets, 225, 227, 241; Baku, 235, 248; Pan-Khwarazam, 243–44; Pan-Bukharan, 246; of southern Central Asian Republics, 254; *see also* Writers' associations
Conquest of Central Asia, 7–19, 131–50, 403, 406–8; survival techniques after, 554
Consolation, see "Awunchaq"
Constituent Assembly, 214, 239
Constitutional Democratic Party, 187, 191, 216
Cossacks (Russian), 105, 239, 283; Orenburg, 236; Ural, 315
Cotton, 29, 126–27, 131, 263, 274–76, 284–94, 308–10, 312, 319–21, 328–31, 333, 334, 336, 344; American, 275, 310; cloth, 348; shipments to Russia, 28–29, 565
Crescent Mooned One, see "Hilaliya"
Crimea, 4, 22, 65, 363
Crimean Tatars, 536, 558, 575–76
Crimean War, 131, 141
Cyrillic alphabet, 79, 81–82

Dairy products, 128, 323–24
Dakhma-i shākhān, 403
Dala ualayatining gazeti, 409
Danilevskii, Colonel G. I., 45
Dānish, *see* Ahmad Mahdum Kalla
Dar-ul Islam, 168, 206
Darwis Khan Tore, 164
Davletchin, General, 216
Day Lasts More Than a Hundred
    Years, The, see *I dol'she veka
    dlitsia den'*
Days Gone By, see *Otgän kunlär*
"Dear People, The," 411
December Committee (Party), *see*
    Zheltoqsan Komiteti
Dede Qorqut, 406
Democratic Movement "Kirgizstan"
    (DDK), 590
"Diplóma gegramménon Skythikoīs
    grámmasin," 77
Diplomatic relations, 37–53
Donduk, Cherin, 9
Dosjanov, Sabit, 531–32
Dosmaghambet-uli, Jihanshah, 236
Dosmaghambet-uli, Qalel, 222
Dossor, 315, 338
Dostek Bek Bahadur, 43
Dostlär. Orinsiz shubha, 529–31,
    534
Drama, opera, and theater, 371–72,
    378–79, 389, 395, 415, 418, 424,
    426–29, 431, 476, 479
Dubrovin, Evgenii P., 503
Dukchi Ishan, *see* Muhammad Ali
    (Madali) Dukchi Ishan
Dukhovskii, S. M., 157, 170–71
Duma, 186–87, 191, 193, 215–17
Dumchev, Kostia, 476
Dungans, 127, 211, 219
Dunsterville, General L. C., 231
Dushanbe, 95, 98, 125, 331, 334,
    346, 358, 390, 509, 532, 535, 544,
    558
Dutov, Ataman, 225–27, 236–37

Duwlat-uli, Mir Jaqib, 175, 201, 204,
    222, 364, 370–71, 411, 425

Earthquakes, 115, 271, 520
Earthquakes, The, see *Kissa-i zilzele*
Ebdul Muzafar Devlet Saadet Ishim
    Muhammad, Khan, 47–48
Ecology, concerns intellectuals, 567
Economy, problems of in C.A., 593–
    95
Educated Man, The, *see* "Intelligent"
Education, 194–98, 349–51, 354,
    356–64, 366, 370, 372–75, 392–96;
    Central Asian schoolbooks, 535–
    37; schoolbooks lack new litera-
    ture, 537, 539; truancy, 539–40;
    enrollments, 540–41
Educational associations, 372–75
Eichorn, August, 476
Ekibastuz, 315, 339, 343
Ellis Cents, 457, 462–63, 482
Elpatiev, 215
"Emir Alim Khan," 415
Emir of Bukhara, 133–34
Employment: outsiders preempt
    jobs, 565
England, 16, 36, 131, 133, 149–50;
    see also Great Britain
Enver Pasha, 250–52, 255
"Epistle from Male and Female
    Workers . . . ," 417
Erk Democratic Party, first Congress
    of, 581; founding of, 580; officers
    of, 580; press of, 581–82; supports
    student protest, 603–04
Erkin too, 371
Extinguished, see *Sondi*

Fakhr al-Din al-Khokandi, 439
Family size, 540
Farabi, Muhammad ibn Tarkhan abu
    Nasr al-, 435, 437–38
Farghana, 62, 95, 101–3, 105, 110,
    112–13, 116, 124–25, 134, 139,

147, 155, 157, 164, 168, 211–
12, 217, 219, 225, 243, 251, 256,
267, 279, 282, 290, 294, 297, 299,
316–19, 323, 327, 329, 331, 333,
335–36, 360, 368, 404; oblast, 272,
275, 320
Farhad and Shirin (opera), 479
Farhad and Shirin (epos), 445
Färhad wä shirin, 421
Fedot'ev, Ivan, 42
Ferganskaia oblast, 368–69
Firdaws al-iqbal, 404
"Firuz," *see* Sayyid Muhammad
Rahim Bahadur II
Five Year plans, 289–91, 294, 301,
303, 332, 339, 509
Fitrat, Abdalrauf, 198, 204; revival-
ism of, 204–6, 248, 255, 370–72,
389–90, 415, 424–25, 477
Flames of Hope, see *Umit yalqimlari*
Foolish Padishah, The, see *Aqmaq
patsha*
Forage plants, *see* Agriculture
Fort Novo-Alexandrovsk, 13–14
Fort Raim, 15
Forty Fables, see *Qiriq misal*
Forty Maidens, see *Qïrq Qïz*
Friends: Groundless Doubt, see
Dostlär. Orinsiz shubha
"Friendship among ethnic groups,"
556
Frolov, 231
Frontiers, republican, concern over,
598–99
Frunze, M. V., 233–34, 242, 245,
248
Frunze, *see* Bishkek
Fudziyamadagï kadïr tün, 530
Furqat, Zakir Jan Hal Muhammad-
oghli, 360, 408, 477
Fuzuliy, Muhammad Sulayman-
oghli, 350

Galkin, General Alexander S., 210

Gapurov, Muhammednazar, 552
Gaspirali, Ismail Bey, 177–78, 194
Geintsel'man, Vil'gelm S., 503
Genealogy, see *Shejire*
Genealogy of the Khwarazm Shahs,
see *Shajara-i khwarazmshahiy*
Generation gap, 528
Gerasimov, G., 508
Gerfalcons, 20, 36, 42
Ghäzat (Ghazawat), see Islam, Holy
War
Ghulam, Ghafur, 416
Giers, F. K., 151–52; Commission,
155
"Gimnaziya khususida," 359
Ginzburg, Moisei Ia., 508
Gisler, G. I., 476
Gladyshev, Dmitri, 49
Glasnost' (Openness) in C.A., 577
"Glass Box" architecture, 525
Glière, Reinhold M., 479
Godunov, Boris, 40
Gogol, Nikolay V., 536
Gok Tepe, 147–48, 402
Golden Horde, *see* Mongols
Golitsyn, Prince Boris A., 43
Goloshchokin, F. I., 260
Golovachev, General N. N., 147,
154–55, 401–2
Gorbachev, Mikhail S., 578, 599,
602; undermines local institutions
and leaders, 562–64, 568
Gorchakov, Prince A. M., 133–34,
147
Gorky, see Nizhegorod
Gorky, Maxim, 536
Gor-oghli (Gorgulu), 406, 418, 445
Goroghli (Uzbek epos), 445
Government: participation in, 560;
Supreme Council elections and
service, 560–62
Grains, *see* Agriculture
Great Book of Music, The, see *Kitab
al-musiqi al-kabir*

Great Britain, 230–31, 315
Grigoriev, V. V., 47
Grodekov, General N. I., 159–60,
165
Gromyko, Andrei A., 549
Guberniias, 152, 162; structures of,
153–57
Guide to Salvation, see Rahbar-i
najat
Guliaev, Ia., 25, 49
Gulsara, 479
Gurguly (Tajik epos), 445
Gur-i Emir, 487, 512
Guryev, 10–11, 307, 315

Habd-ul watan, 201
Habl ul-matin, 356
Hafiz, Khoja Shamseddin Muham-
mad, 350
Hajji Fariq, 36
Hajji Rafik, 196
Halima, 429
Hamza, see Niyaziy, Hamza Hakim
Zada
Happy Family, The, 412
Happy Girls, see "Bagtli gïzlar"
Haqq Nazar, 39
Hassan ibn Thabnit, 436
Hassan-oghli, 243
Hassan-zada, 264
Haydar Tore, Bukharan Amir, op-
posed by tribes, 597
"Hay ishchilar," 477
Heiden, Count Fedor L., 141
Heroes, The, see Azamat
Hey, Workers! see "Hay ishchilar"
"Hilaliya," 416
History of Shahrukh, see Ta'rikh-i
shahrokhi
History of the Manghit Sultans . . . ,
see Ta'rikh-i salātin-i manghïtīya-
i . . .
History of Turkistan, see Turkistan
ta'rikhi

History: Russocentric, 535–36
"Hordes" (Kazakh), 6, 48, 51
Hungry Steppe, 14, 113, 140
Husayn Bayqara, Sultan, see Sultan
Husayn Bayqara
Hydroelectric power, 332–37, 342,
344, 348

Ibn Battuta, 21
Ibn Sina, Abu Ali al-Husayn, 438–39
Ibrahim al-Mahdi, 435
Ibrahim (Ibray) Altynsarin, 175, 362
Ibrahim Bek, Mullah Muhammad,
251
Ichkarida, 479
I dol'she veka dlitsia den', 532, 534
Ignat'ev, Major Nikolai P., 45, 149
Ill-fated Kakey, see Kaygïlu kakey
Il'minskii, V. I., 175
Imam Quli Kahn, 40
Imanqul-uli, D., 409
Immortal Cliffs, The, see Olmäs
qayälär
Improvement of the Children, see
Tāhzib-us sibyān
India, 23, 42, 82, 91, 201, 321–24,
347–48, 356, 392, 488
Indo-European languages, 65, 76, 90
Inqilab quyashi, 244
Instruments, see Music
Intellectuals: early centers of, 35,
349–63; Soviet, 372–85, 392–96
"Intelligent," 382
Internal colonialism: production for
Russia, 565
"In the Wide Turkistan Plains," 476
In the Women's Quarters, see Ichka-
rida
Iran, 64, 66, 82, 86, 87, 89, 90, 271,
392, 437, 440, 443
Iranian languages, 65–68
Iron, see Minerals
Ironmongery, 322
Irrigation, 254, 267, 270–72, 274–76,

278–80, 282, 286–88, 294–99, 349;
see also Water
Irshad, 189
Irtysh River, 9, 64, 84–85, 118, 128,
342, 343
Iset Kutebar-uli, 17
Isfahan, 436, 487
Ishaq Agha Shah Niyaz, 43–44
Ishaq al-Mausili, 435
Ishaq Hasan Oghlu, *see* Polat Khan
Ishim dalasi, 201
Ishkashimi, 67–68
Islam, 1, 2, 4–6, 73, 88, 138–39,
159–63, 167, 170, 172–73, 177,
188, 191, 205–6, 246, 402; Holy
War, 6, 142, 146, 167; as unifying
force, 257
Ismail Khan Tore, 167
Issik Kol, 52, 69, 110, 113, 119, 133,
212, 414
Istanbul, 3, 192, 198, 207, 252, 371,
436
Itil, 20
Ittifaq ul-muslimin, 187, 191, 220
Ivan III, 38
Ivan IV, 23, 31, 38
Ivanov, General, 237

Jadids, 172, 191–97, 199–202, 204,
227, 229, 232–33, 242, 249, 409;
Communist, 248, 262; in educa-
tion and intellectual life, 363–67,
373, 381; literature, 409–13, 421,
425–30
Jalilov, T., 479
Jambil, 98, 266, 307, 334, 337, 346
Jambil Jabay-uli, 416, 521
Janga madaniyat jolunda, 371
Jangeldin, Alibii, 212, 238–39
Jang nama (Mullah Shamsi), 403
"Janing qojä batirding tolghaui," 399
Jan Qoja Nurmuhammad-uli, 17,
399–400
Jarkak, 336

Jenkinson, Anthony, 23, 31, 38, 40
Jeti Su, 78, 93–94, 105, 110, 118,
152, 155, 157, 211, 213, 217, 219,
222, 237, 266, 276, 281–82, 319,
321
Jizzakh, 140, 142, 210, 216, 237, 296,
534
"Joking," 415
Jolbaris Khan, 48
Jolqunbay, *see* Qadiriy, Abdullah
Jorabay, Mullah, 177
Jorabek, 142–43
Jumabay-uli, Magjan, 371, 389, 412
Junaïd Khan, Muhammad Qurban,
210, 242, 250

KGB (Committee for State Security),
558, 575
Kabalevsky, D., 480
Kabul, 360
Kafirnihan Valley, 62, 117, 166
Kagan, 101, 105, 196, 229, 319, 327,
332
Kaganovich, M. V., 235
Kaip Khan, 49
Kalkaman-uli, 11
Kämalan gate, 1, 46, 158
Kamiiy, Karimbek Sharifbek-oghli,
359
Kamyl, Qari, 213
Kara Bogaz Kol, 317, 336
Karaganda, 107, 183, 314–15, 338–45
Karaganda-Chu railroad, 345
Karakalpakistan, 47, 94, 559, 564
Karakalpaks, 48, 104, 106, 281, 360,
399, 405, 418, 428, 431; ASSR,
257, 295, 375
Karakul, *see* Qarakol
Karatay-oghli, Vakhitjan Besali, 187
Karazina, N. N., 506
Karimberdi-oghli, Muhammad
Yaqub, 165
Karimaw, Abduwahit, 559

Karimov, Islam (Islom) A., CPUz
1st Secretary, acknowledges his
authoritarianism, 606; demeans
opponent, 577; enforces "stability,"
605–6; supports coup against
USSR President, 602; Uzbekistan's
President, 596
Karki, 105, 270, 319
Karkit, 413
Karnachev (Karpachev), Ivan Semeno-
vich, 11
Karsakpay, 315, 339–40, 345
Kashgar, 15, 63, 440, 488
Kashgar Darya, 63
Kashghariy, 75
Kasimov, *see* Kenisari Qasim-uli,
Sultan
Katta Qorghan, 142, 362
Kaubaki, Najmuddun, 439
Kaufman, General K. P. von, 141–
43, 145–46, 154–56, 159, 161–63,
165, 167, 170–71
Kaygïlu kakey, 427
"Kazakh Lands," 411–12
Kazakhs, 4, 10, 14–15, 17, 26, 28,
31, 33, 38–39, 45, 48–51, 55–56,
104, 110, 126, 128–30, 163, 202,
212–13, 235–41, 281–83, 360,
377, 400, 406–7, 409, 414, 418,
425, 588, 600–1; "Hordes" of, 6,
44–48, 50–51, 74, 175, 186, 236;
resistance to Russia, 11; uprisings
in 1870s, 143; plain, 152–53, 159,
161, 177, 187, 211, 221, 264–66,
432; Russian intervention in culture, 174–75; press, 200–204; and
February revolution, 221–23; and
professions, 375
Kazakhstan, 28, 47, 60, 70, 72–73,
78, 81–82, 84, 88, 94, 131, 256–57,
261, 266, 282, 299–301, 303–4,
315–16, 336, 344, 371, 449; political status, 64, 96, 97, 103, 106–9,
111–13, 115, 117–19, 121–23, 128,

239, 241, 257, 508; agriculture of,
266–67, 296; virgin lands, 304–
8; Krais, 307; reconstruction and
development in, 337–44; rocket
and space science complex in, 345;
writers in, 530, 569–70; truancy
in, 539; politics in, 552, 563–64
Kazakov, A. A., 221
Kazan, 4, 20, 24, 31, 84, 186, 196,
218
Kenisari Qasim-uli, Sultan, 11, 13–
14, 17, 51, 56, 160, 577
Kerbabay-oghli, Berdi, 371, 373–74,
380
Kerenski, F. M., 171, 220–21
Keys of the Sciences, see *Mafatih
al-ʿulum*
Khalil-oghli, Tashpulat Abdul, 187
Khan Tengri, 63
Kheley, Bakhshi, 477–78
Khiva, 1, 3, 5–6, 8, 10, 13–14, 16–
17, 20, 24–27, 29–30, 32, 33–38,
40–45, 47–49, 55, 57–58, 60, 62,
125, 147, 194, 250, 272, 278, 290,
322–24, 349, 360, 399–400, 402,
404–5, 438, 559; under Russia, 57,
92–94, 143–47, 153, 157; Young
Khivans, 242–43
Khiwäqiy, *see* Qurban Niyaz Khiwäqiy
Khoja, Ubaydullah, 217
Khoja Islam, *see* Islam Hajji
Khojand, 142, 210, 316
Khoja-oghli (Khojaev), Faizullah,
199, 229, 245, 255, 262–64
Khoja-oghli, Tursun, 232–33
Khoja-oghli, Usman, 196, 198, 201,
213, 248, 252
Khokand, 4, 6, 10, 14, 16, 20, 27, 44,
47, 131, 134–35, 201, 219, 225–26,
312, 317–20, 323, 332, 334, 337,
368, 402, 419, 438–39, 574; contest
with Russia, 7, 15, 17–19, 132–35,
141, 143–47, 163–64, 169; under

Russia, 98, 101–3; destruction of, 227–28, 250
Khokhlov, Ivan D., 41–42
Khoja Muhammad, Mullah Oraz, 242
Khrushchev, Nikita, 304–6, 529, 549
Khudayar Khan, 141, 145–46; palace of, 144, 493
Khurshid, 189–92
Khuyilju Valley, 63
Khvorostov, 182
Khwarazm, *see* Khiva
Khwarazm (Khivan) Peoples' Republic, 242–44, 254–55
Khwarazmiy, *see* Palwan Niyaz Muhammad Mirza Bashi Kamil Khwarazmiy
Kiev, 1–2, 30, 38, 479
Kilevein, E., 47
Kim jazïqti?, 426
Kirgizistan: intellectual life in, 530; politics in, 551–52, 561
Kipchak languages, 72–74, 77
Kirgiz, 10, 14, 52, 55, 67, 76, 83, 88–89, 104, 129, 161, 208, 211–12, 220, 222, 238, 241, 243, 256, 261, 281, 300, 371, 400, 409, 414, 432
Kirgizistan (Kirgiziia), 65, 94–95, 109, 111, 113, 117, 119, 125, 130, 266, 295, 300, 335, 371, 456; political status, 96–97, 106, 108, 110, 257, 361, 364, 372, 375; kindergartens, 568–70
Kirov Canal, 295–96
Kissa-i zilzele, 411
Kitab al-adwar, 439
Kitab al-musiqi al-kabir, 438
Kobe-uli, Spandiyar, 426
Kobozev, P. A., 232, 234
Köktepaga shïghu, 530
Kolchak, Admiral, 236–38
Kolesov, 225–30
Kolpakovskii, General, 155
Komintern, 235, 249
Komsomol, 243–44

Kopet Dagh, 62, 115, 125, 267, 271
Kör Mullah, 402–3
Koreans, in Kazakhstan, 601
Kornilov, General, 218
Kor-oglu, see *Gor-oghli*
Korovnichenko, General, 221
Koshshegul-uli, Shahmardan, 186–87
Krasnovodsk, 9, 101, 118–19, 143, 147, 322, 327–29, 519
Krylov, Ivan A., 410, 537
Kryzhanovskii, General N. A., 134–38, 140, 153
Kuchum Khan, 3, 39
Kuibyshev, V. V., 233, 242
Kulakov, Petr Nikolaevich, 11
Kulman-uli, Mullah, 187
Kun, Bela, 235
Kunayev, Dinmuhamed A., 549, 552, 574, 582; downfall of, 563–65
Kungrad, 346
Kuropatkin, Colonel A. N., 148, 157, 210, 212, 215
Kustanay, 107, 364; oblast, 108, 306–7, 343, 362, 368

Lagan Canal, 294
Land: uses of, 112–15; tenure, 277–81; Soviet farm policy, 284–89; collectivization, 289–94
Languages, 60; Turkic, 62–65, 66, 70, 72–77; Iranian and minority, 65–69, 70; outside influences, 69–72; Arabic, 543; Iranian, 543; Turkic, 543; in group identity, 545, 569–70; official C.A. state: Uzbekistan, 579–580; Kazakhstan, 580; Kirgizstan, 580; Turkmenistan, 580; see also Russian language
Lapin, Mullah Shir Ali, 216, 224–25, 300–301
Latinization of alphabets, 79–82
Lausanne Conference, 207
Layli and Majnun (opera), 421, 479
Layli and Majnun (epos), 445

Lazarev, General, 147, 211
Leaders defined, 554
Lenger, 335
Lenin, V. I., 221, 234–35, 238, 513, 515, 562
Leninabad, 116, 316, 558; *see also* Khojand
Leningrad, 479
Leninogorsk, 108, 315, 338–40, 342
Lerkh, P. I., 47
Lesek, F. V., 476
"Letter to Mother," 410
Leviev, Minas, 479
Liapovskii, 215
Lidval', F. I., 504
Literacy, 369–72, 375–80, 392–93, 538, 540–41
Literature: regional, 359–61, 398; resistance, 399–403; "Bad Time," 407; prose, 412, 420; al-Farabiy and Zahiriddin Muhammad Babur in new historical fiction, 532; *see also* Drama; Poetry; Writers' associations
Livestock, 122, 128–30, 282, 284, 299–304, 314, 321–22, 324
Lykoshin, N. S., 219

Maarif wä oqutghuchi, 372
Madali, *see* Dukchi Ishan, Muhammad Ali
Madrasahs, 172, 193, 350–51, 357, 363, 393; architecture, 490–91
Madridov, General, 212
Mafatih al-'ulum, 438
Maghreb, 436–37
Magnitogorsk, 333, 340, 345
Magtim Guli Azadi-oghli Fragi, 407
Mahbub al-qulub, 439
Mahdum, Sharif Jan, 354–56, 360, 365
Mahkame-i Shariat, 220
Mahkamov, Qahhar M., 587
Mahmud, Abidjan, 213, 217

Mahmud Hajji, Mullah Alim, 367, 404
Mahmudov, Mamadali, 532–35
Mahtumbay, 41
Mahtum Quli, *see* Magtim Guli Azadi-oghli Fragi
Main Turkmen Canal, 118, 297
Maksimovich, Lieut. Col. Aleksei, 11
Malleson, General W., 231
Malov, Andrei Y., 1
Mambet-uli, Mullah Hali Bay, 397, 400
Manas, 418, 445, 447
Manchuria, 83, 87, 90–91
Mangishlak peninsula, 26, 29, 115, 147, 153, 345
Mansur-oghli, Mirza Muhitdin, 196, 199
Maral Beshi, 63
"March of Iskender Khan, The," 476
Marghilan, 146–47, 164, 168–69, 210, 360, 368, 505, 558, 574
Mari, 97, 125, 148–49, 267, 270, 274, 314, 436, 438, 443, 448
Marjani, Shihabeddin al-, 172
Maqsud-oghli, Sadri, 216
Maqsum, Nasratullah, 263
Maqsum-oghli, Muhitdin, 251
Masa, 410
Masaliev, Absamat, 590
Mashrab, Ishan Shah Baba Rahim, 350
Masjid, *see* Aq Meshit
Maslak-i muttaqin (Sufi Allah Yar), 350
Master and Servant, see *Bay ila khizmatchi*
Ma'sum, Amir, effective ruler of Bukhara, 597; *see also* Shah Murad
Mawaraunnahr, 21, 87–88
Mayakovski, Vladimir V., 536
Meat, 128; packing, 108, 315–16
Mecca, 3, 436
Medina, 436

Meeting of the Spirits, The, see
Anjuman-i arwah
Mehrabdän chäyan (Abdullah Qadi-
riy), 351
Melons, *see* Agriculture
Mensheviks, 182, 221
Merv, *see* Mari
Meskhetian Turks, attacks on, 574–
75, 576
Migrations, Turkic and Iranian,
82–91
Mikhalkov, Sergei V., 537
Military inroads, *see* Conquest
Military service: draft dodging, 542
Miliutin, D. A., 135, 138, 140–41
Mindash-uli, 238
Minerals, 25, 29–31, 107–8, 307,
314, 317–19, 322, 336–37, 340–41;
coal and iron, 107, 315–16, 319,
330–31, 335, 339–40, 342, 344–45;
see also Oil; Steel
Mingriav, Major, 11
Miniature painting, 524–25
Minjani, *see* Munjani
Miran Shah, 439
Mir'at-i ibrat, 204
Miriy, Muhammad Achildimurad
Nematulla-oghli, 362
Mirror of a Precept, see *Mir'at-i
ibrat*
Mirzachol Sahra, 113, 273–74, 294–
96
Mirza Nasrullah, 197
Mirzoyan, C. I., 260
Moldogazi Tokobay-uulu, 427
Moldo Kilich Mamirkan-uulu, 411
Mongolia, 87, 90–91
Mongols, 2, 89; Golden Horde, 8,
21–22, 35
"Moonlight Night in the Ruins of
Samarkand, A," 476
Morkovin brothers, 182
Morozov, M. V., 182
Moscow, 35–36, 38, 40, 43, 217, 251,

261, 318, 373, 383, 385, 388, 390,
417, 479–80, 502, 511
Mosques (architecture), 487–91, 493,
497, 512
Mosquito, The, see *Masa*
Muhamadov, T., 480
Muhamedjan-oghli, Salihjan, 187
Muhammad Ali (Madali), 168–69
Muhammad Baba, Mullah Nur, 243
Muhammad ibn Ahmad abu Abdallah
al-Khwarizmi, 438
Muhammadjanov, Kaltay, 529–30
Muhammadov, 479
Muhammad Rahim Bahadur II, 145
Muhammad Silah, 405
Muhammed Amin Bek, 146
Muhayyir, Muhammadqul Muham-
mad Rasul-oghli, 408
Muhitdin-oghli, Mirza Abdulqadir,
251
Muhitdinov, Nuritdin, 550, 552
Muhyiy, Mawlana Hajji Muhiddin
Muhammad Riza Akhun-oghli,
360, 408
Mullah Ir Nazar Bek Maqsud-oghli, 4
Mullah Shawki, *see* Shamsi, Mullah
Munawwar Qari Abdurrashid Khan-
oghli, 177, 189–92, 195, 201–2,
213, 365
Munis Khwarazmiy, Shir Muham-
mad, 404
Munjani (Mungi), 68
Munzim, Mirza Abdul Wahid, 355,
365
Muqan-uli, Sabit, 382
Muqimiy, Muhammad Amin Mirza
Khoja-oghli, 360, 408, 419
Murabek, 336
Murad, 490
Murat-aqin, 409
Murghab, 68, 117, 125, 267, 270,
273–74, 297, 319
Musa-bay, 399–400
Mushel, G., 479

Music, 35–36; modes, 435, 437, 443, 463–65, 468–70; regional, 435–40, 443, 445, 449, 456, 468–70, 472–73, 476–79, 481; instruments, 448–63; notation of, 470–72, 481–83, acculturation, 472–79; Western, 473; resistance to Westernization of, 479–84

Muslims, 4, 111, 135, 159–60, 162–63, 170–71, 178–79, 181, 184–86, 188–92, 205, 212, 226, 234–35, 248, 253, 265, 349, 410, 607; relations with Russia, 1–5, 165, 167; Shiite, 3, 196–97, 256; Sunnit, 3, 32, 196; Sufi orders, 163, 168; religious revival, 172; agitated by immigrants and exiles, 175–81; Ecclesiastical Administration, 188; and reform, 191–94; conservative, 195; councils and conferences of Central Asia, 216, 219–20, 225, 233; Bureau, 233, 235; and Enver Pasha, 252; unification attempts, 256

Mustapha Kemal, 252

Muzaffar al-Din, 132, 134, 358

Nabiyev, Rahmon, TajCP 1st Secretary, 596; distrusted, 577

Nadandïq qürbandarï, 426

Nadir Muhammad, Khan, 32

Nadir Shah, 48, 318

"Nägh mä wä nägh nägär . . . ," 477

Najmuddun Kaubaki, *see* Kaubaki Najmuddun

Nalivkin, V. P., 159, 163, 165, 170, 189, 216, 221

Namangan, 98, 147, 164, 168, 210, 317–18, 320, 360, 368, 574

Namaz Premkulov, 186

Naqshbandi brotherhood, 167–69

Narbutabek-oghli, 220, 248

Narcotics, 127, 283

Narrative, A, see *Bayan*

Nasbat, Mawlana, 360

Nasir Khan Tore, 217

Nasriddin Afandi (Khoja), 427

Nasriddin Bek, 146

National Center, 217–21

Nationalism and nationality problems, 172–88, 193, 214, 218–20, 224, 238–39, 241–44, 249, 251, 256, 265, 371, 380, 416–17; localization, 539, 541; segregation, 553; corruption, 555–56, 559; ethnic cleavage, 562; subverting local leadership, 562; "tribalism," 564; economic discrimination, 566–67; children deemed a national resource, 568

Natural gas piped to Russia, 565

Nawaiy, Mir Ali Shir, 350, 416, 421, 429

Nazarbayev, Nursultan A., Kazakhstan's President, 596; calls for justice with stability, 606; polemic against, 584

Nebit Dagh, 317, 335–36

Nessel'rod, Count Karl V., 4, 57–58

New Bukhara, 200; *see also* Kagan

New Economic Policy, 253, 301

New Happiness, see *Yangi saadat*

New Uyghur, *see* Languages

Nicholas I, 56

Nicholas II, 359

Nihaniy, 359

Nikiforov, Captain, 36–37

Niyazov, Saparmïrat, A., 595, 596, 607

Niyaz Bek, 134–35

Niyaziy, Hamza Hakim Zada, 317, 381, 412, 426–27, 477

Nizhegorod, 22, 30–31, 190

Nizhni Novgorod, *see* Nizhegorod

Nokis, 125, 359

Novel, the, 389, 412, 420, 423, 425–26, 432

Novyi Uzen', Kazakhstan, 575–76

Nurali Khan, 49
Nuraliqan-uli, Z., 409
Nurberdikhan-oghli, Mahdum Quli
  Khan, 187

Ob River, 64, 118
Oghuz, 74, 76, 82, 448
Oghuz-name, 445
Oil, 315, 317–19, 330–31, 335, 338,
  340, 344
Olmäs qayälär, 532–35
Omirzaq-aqin, 416
Om River, 9
Omsk, 9, 47, 51, 236, 361; oblast,
  368
"Opasïz jalghan," 407
Opera, *see* Drama
Orenburg, 9–12, 25, 27, 29, 108,
  133–34, 143, 152–53, 162, 201,
  222–23, 226–27, 236–37, 239,
  285, 318, 360–61, 375, 410; Border
  Commission, 55–56; loss of, 230;
  Cossacks, 236–37
Orenburg-Tashkent Railroad, 102,
  237, 310, 317, 320, 323, 327–29,
  345
Organizations: unions, 183, 207, 219,
  236, 244; Muslim, 187, 191, 219;
  societies, 198; committees, 207,
  252; *see also* Alash Orda; Writers'
  associations
Orkhon, 73 78, 82–83
Ormantay, Dr. Kamal, 584
Or River, 9, 48
Orsk, *see* Orenburg
Ortaqlar, 479
"Orus lashkarining turkistanda . . . ,"
  400
"Orusning kelgani," 401
Osh, 164, 168, 544, 589–90; oblast,
  393
Ostroumov, N. P., 165, 178
Otgän kunlär, 420
Ottoman Porte, 4

Oxus, *see* Amu Darya
Oyan qazaq! 411
Oyrot, 65, 73, 406
Ozbek eski zaman musiqasi . . . , 477

Padarkush, 410, 424
Pahlivan Niyaz, 213, 242, 244
Palwan Niyaz Mirza Bashi Kamil
  Khwarazmiy, 357, 470–71
Pamirs, 63, 67–68, 83, 113, 115, 117,
  120, 149; languages, 66–68
Pan-Islamism, 174, 218, 235
Panj, 67–68, 116, 122, 324
Pan-Turkism, 174, 195, 200, 218, 406
Paradise of Felicity, see *Firdaws
  al-iqbal*
Parricide, The, see *Padarkush*
Pashino, Petr I., 173
Path of the Believers, The (Sufi Allah
  Yar), 350
Patriotism, official, 541
Paul I, 50
Pavlodar, 107–8, 306–7, 343
Pavlovich, M., 235
Pazukhin, Boris, 35–36
Pazukhin, Semen, 35–36
Pereiaslavl'-Riazansk, 31
Perovsk, *see* Qizil Orda
Perovskii, General V. A., 13, 16
Persia, 16, 23, 27, 47, 62, 78, 86,
  148, 204, 212, 230, 318, 418, 425,
  443, 488; *see also* Languages
Pestkovskii, S., 238
Peter I, 5, 9, 25, 31–32, 43, 119, 318
Peters, Yakob, 235
Petrograd, 215, 221
Petropavlovsk, 6, 10–11, 107–8, 183,
  201, 360, 364
Pishpek, 18, 95, 98, 101, 105, 124,
  211, 331, 333, 335–36, 346, 359,
  390, 392, 509, 511, 525, 532, 544,
  558
Podgorny, Nikolai V., 549
Poetry, 350, 354, 357, 359, 360, 363,

Poetry (*continued*)
365, 377, 397–98, 401, 403–12,
415–20
Polad-Zade, Polad A., 566
Polat Khan, 146–47
Polat-oghli, 220
Polevoi, Boris, 537
Politburo, 563
Political network, unofficial, 556–58
Polovetsians, 7
Poltoratskii, 226
Populanov, S., 518
Population, 92–95, 588, 598–99,
600–1; urbanization, 95–103;
changes in national composi-
tion, 103–12; cities, 532; youthful
cohorts, 540; censuses of 1959,
1970, 1979, 541–42; Central Asian
and Russian growth, 542–43
Port Petrovsk, 143
"Portrait of an Uzbek," 521, 523
Preobrazhenskii, Pavel I., 215
Professions, 375–80, 394
Provisional Government (Russian),
214–16, 218–22, 224, 228–29
Przheval'sk, 211, 510
Public health, problems: radiation
poisoning in Kazakhstan, 592–93;
infant mortality in Tajikistan and
Turkmenistan, 591–92
Publishing: editions and copies of
local-language books, 544–55;
samizdat, 558
Pugachev, Emel'ian, 10–11, 49
Pulat-oghli, 220
Pulatov, Dr. Abdurahim, 579
Purges: of politicians, 235, 243–44,
249–50, 254, 260–65; of writers,
372, 385–92, 388–90, 552; of the
literate, 528; collaborators in,
called "snakes," 534
Pushkin, Aleksandr S., 536–37
Putintsev, Colonel S. R., 165

Qadiriy, Abdullah, 351, 389–90, 420

Qairaq Qum reservoir, 297, 334
Qaling mal, 426
Qamar sulu, 426
Qarach-uuly, Sidiq, 431
Qara Darya, 267
Qara Kirgiz, 257; *see also* Kirgiz
Qarakol, 124, 128, 322
Qara Qum, 62, 113–14, 242, 399;
canal, 117, 271, 295, 297
Qarayim, 70
Qari, Munawwar, *see* Munawwar
Qari Abdurrashid Khan-oghli
Qari Fazullah Mir Jalil-oghli Almayí,
see Almayi, Qari Fazullah Mir
Jalal-oghli
Qari-oghli, Abdul Vakhit, 187
Qarqali Mountains, *see* Besh Kazliq
Qarqaralinsk, 11, 492
Qashqa Darya, 117, 125
Qasimbetaw, I., 559
Qasim ibn Dost Bukhari, 439
Qasim irlarinin jiynaghi, 414
Qasimov city and khanate, 31, 54
Qasim-uli, Sultan, *see* Kenisari
Qasim-uli, Sultan
Qazaq, 201, 364, 411
Qazaqstan, 201
Qazi Kalan, 137, 197
Qiriq misal, 410
Qïrq Qïz, 428
Qizil Arvat, 147, 180, 184, 231, 320
Qizil Khwarazm, 244
Qizil Orda, 273, 296, 307, 361, 373,
375; *see also* Aq Meshit
Qizil Qalam, 372–75
Qizil Qum, 113–15, 140, 273
Qoblandi Batir, 418
Qorqut Ata, see *Dede Qorqut*
Qozha-Akhmet, Khasen Kärimzha-
nuli, Chief, Zheltoqsan Komiteti,
582–83, 584–85
Qozi Akbar Turajonzoda Hajji, *see*
Turajonzoda, Qozi
Qublay Khan, 83
Quiet Don, The, see *Tikhii Don*

Qulmuhammad-oghli, Abdulhakim, 371–73, 389, 414
Qunanbay-uli, Ibrahim (Ibray, Abay), 175, 362, 388–89, 419–20
Qurbanbay Tajibay-oli, 428
Qurban Niyaz Khiwäqiy, 488
Qutadhghu Bilig, 78
Qutb ed Din, 437
Qutluq Adam, 40

Rabi ibn al-Harith, 487
Radek, Karl, 235
Radlov, Vasiliy V., i
Rahbar-i najat, 205–6
Rahimbay-zada, 263–64
Rahim Quli Khan, 45
Rahmanov, Imamali, 607
Raim, 14
Ramiz, Mannan, 371–72
Rashidov, Sharaf R., 549–551, 559, 563, 566, 574
Rasulov, Jabar, 552
Rastokhez group, 586
Red Army, 231, 245, 249–51, 254, 338
Regarding the High School, *see* "Gimnaziya khususida"
Religion, *see* Muslims
Religious identity: Islam and Christianity, 555, 562
Remembrance of the Poems, see *Tizkär-ul ash'ār*
Resul Zadeh, Mehmet Emin, 218
Revolution of 1905, 184–88, 189
Revolution of 1917, 213–17, 224, 236, 330
Risala dar 'ilm al-musiqi, 439
Riskul-uulu, Turar, 232–33, 235, 248, 261–62
Road to the Mountain, see *Tau joli*
Romanovskii, Colonel D. I., 138, 140
Romanovskii Canal, 273, 295
Rosenbach, General N. O., 155, 163
Royal Shah's Gift, see *Tuhfa-i shāhi*
Rudzutak, Ia. E., 255

Rukavkin, Danila, 25
Rushan, 68, 149
Ruslan and Ludmilla, 476
Russia, 135, 400–401; political activities of, 53–59, 132, 151–53, 155, 156, 162, 181–84; and Union of Nations, 207; and Central Asian revolt, 208; *see also* Architecture; Conquest; Music; Muslims; Soviet Union; Trade
Russian language: in Central Asian life, 538, 543, 571
Russian Orthodox Church, 32, 379; and apostasy, 5
Russians, 104, 106, 108–10, 160–61, 163, 175–76, 179–81, 211, 226, 260, 367–68; invaders, 534; literature of, in textbooks, 535–37, 539; opposition to, 535, 556–58, 564; responsibility for backwardness, 535; dominate Communist Party, 547–49, 553; Slavs against Turkic/ Iranian Central Asians, 562
Russian Soviet Federated Socialist Republic (RSFSR), 540
Rykov, A. I., 263
Ryskulov, *see* Riskul-uulu, Turar

Saatbay, Muhammad, 19
Sabir-oghli, Mullah Niyaz, 194
Sabzanov, Y., 481
Sada-i Farghana, 201
Sada-i Turkistan, 201
Sadiq-oghli, Talib, 479
Sadriddin Murad Khoja Zada Ayniy, *see* Ayniy, Sadriddin Murad Khoja Zada
Sadr Ziya, *see* Mahdum, Sharif Jan
Safarov, Georgi, 235
Safi al-Din, 'Abd al-Mu'min, 439
Safonov, 243–44
Sagdiyew (Sagdullayew), Sh., 558
Sahbā, Mirza Hayit, 355
Said Ali Sultan, 49

Said Azimbay Muhammadbay-oghli, 190, 504
St. Petersburg, 4, 48–49, 133, 155, 476, 501, 503–6
Sakmara River, 10
Saksaul tree, 121, 124, 284
Salih Bek Akhun, Mullah, 401
Salt marshes, 123
Samarkand, 62, 68, 98, 101–2, 110, 115, 134, 142, 157, 168, 177–78, 180, 182, 213, 225, 256, 272, 282, 295, 299, 319–20, 322–23, 327, 334, 336–37, 359, 361, 485, 589; Crimean Tatars in, 558
Samarkand, 182
Samarkandskaia oblast, 368–69
Samarqand, 201
Samarra, 435
Samsonov, General A. V., 197
Saray, 21–22
Sariqamish, Lake, 117
Sari Su River, 14, 122, 315, 339
Sarjan Qasim-uli, Sultan, 11–13
Sartubek, 363
Sayha, 205
Sayyid Abdullah, Khan, 242
Sayyid Khan, Sultan, 136
Sayyid Muhammad Rahim Bahadur II, 136, 145, 356–57, 470, 488, 490
Schools, *see* Education; Madrasahs
Scorpion from the Pulpit, see *Mehrabdän chäyan*
Scourge of Warning, The, see *Tāziyāne-yi ta'dib*
Scripts, 77–81
Secret societies, 198–200
Semeke Khan, 48
Semipalatinsk, 9, 47, 107–8, 152, 155, 157, 161, 176, 187, 237, 239, 345, 349, 351, 361–62, 367, 375, 410; oblast, 368, 369
Semirechie, *see* Jeti Su
Sepulchre of Shahs, see *Dakhma-i shākhān*

Seralin, Muhamedjan, 201
Serke, 411
Shahid al-iqbal, 404
Shah-i Zinda complex, 487
Shah Murad, 270
Shah nama, 403
Shahname, 445
Shahr-i Sabz, 97, 486
Shah's Book, see *Shah nama*
Shahsenem and Garib (Uzbek epos), 445
Shahsenim and Garip (Turkmen epos), 445
Shajara-i khwarazmshahiy, 404
Shamil, Imam, 131
Shamsi, Mullah, 403
Shamsiddin Mahdum Shāhin, 355
Shamsudinova, Mairy, 477
Shankar, Ravi, 472n
Sharaf-oghli, Mir, 243
Shariat, 220, 259, 277; *see also* Islam
Sharif Jan Mahdum, *see* Mahdum, Sharif Jan
Shaybaniy Khan, Muhammad, 360, 405–6, 577
Shaybaniy khan dastani, 406
Shaybaniy nama, 405
Shaybek-uulu, Isak, 411
Shaykh-ul Islam, 220
Shchepkin, Nikolai N., 215–16
Shchussev, Aleksei V., 507, 513
Sheep, *see* Livestock
Shejire, 405
Shektel', Fedor O., 507
Shendrikov, Ilia, 182
Shihabeddin al-Marjani, *see* Marjani, Shihabeddin al-
Shir Ali Lapin, *see* Lapin, Mullah Shir Ali
Shir Muhammad Munis Khwarazmiy, *see* Munis Khwarazmiy, Shir Muhammad
Shohrat, 189–91
Sholokhov, Mikhail, 432, 536
Shora, Temir Khan, 259

Shora-i Islam, *see* Muslims
Shorman-uli, S., 409
Shortambay Qanay-uli, 407, 409
Shotemar, 263–64
Shout, The, see *Sayha*
Siberia, 24, 73, 89, 113, 120, 151,
155, 226, 237, 239, 303–4, 328,
344, 410; rivers: Irtysh and Ob,
566
Sidik-uulu, Abdulkerim, 261
Sidorov, A., 518
Silk, *see* Textiles
Siraj-ul akbar, 201
Sirat-i mustaqim, 201
Sirdar, Colonel Oraz, 217, 228, 231
Sir Darya, 17, 22, 29, 51, 60, 62–64,
82, 94, 105, 115–17, 122, 133, 135,
137, 152, 155, 157, 210, 225, 256,
270, 272–73, 281–82, 295–97, 299,
319–20, 324, 327, 333–34, 346,
399, 488, 566–67
Sisters, The, see *Apa-singillar*
Sitarä-i Makhi Khassä, 493–94
Skobelev, General M. D., 101, 147–
48
Skobelev, 317; oblast, 368
Slave trade, 30–35
Slaviansky, Argenev, 476
Social Democrats, 182–84, 188, 224
Socialist Revolutionaries, 182, 188,
219, 221
Soghdian, 66–67, 85–86, 89
Soghdian-Uyghur script, 78–79
Solih, Muhammad, 577, 580, 581
Söndi, 430
Song of Oleg, The, 476
Soviet Union, 60, 65, 69, 95–97, 110,
241–43, 265, 271; Komintern, 235,
249; Komsomol, 243–44; clashes
with Bukhara, 248–49; and Enver
Pasha, 251–52; pacification and
integration of Central Asia with,
252–54, 256; agricultural policy,
284–89; collectivization, 289–94;
tightening of economic control,

344–48; literary politics among
intelligentsia, 380–85
Spasskii Zavod, 314–15, 339
Stalin, Josef, 65, 226, 255, 259, 261,
415–18, 515, 525; his reign of
terror, 529; political turmoil under,
546, 562
"Stalin," 416
Stalingrad, *see* Dushanbe
Stalingrad, *see* Volgograd
Starenskoi, Ataman Nechai, 8, 151
Steel, 332–37, 341–42, 344
Stepanov, Vel'iamin, 39
Steppe Guberniia, 13, 266, 282
Stoletov, Colonel N. G., 143
Stolypin, P. A., 197
Stremonkhov, Petr N., 132, 135, 141
Strikes, 183
Struve, K. V., 47, 173
Struve, Peter B., 175
Sufi Allah Yar, 350
Sugar and sugar beets, 110, 126, 322
Sultan Galiev, 255
Sultan Husayn Bayqara, 360, 416,
577
Sultan Murad, Juma Niyaz, 242–43
Sultanov, Izzat, 390–91
Surkhan Darya, 117, 294
Svarichevskii, Georgii M., 506
Sviiazhsk, 31
Sydykovshchina, 261
Syr Darinskaia oblast, 369, 503

Tahir, 49
Tahir and Zuhra (epos), 445
Tāhzīb-us sibyān, 365, 412
Tajibay-oli, *see* Qurbañbay Tajibay-
oli
Tajikistan, 62, 72, 94, 110–12, 256–
57, 266, 295, 297, 300, 333, 346,
415, 417–18, 456, 539, 542, 547,
552, 558
Tajik Sea, *see* Bahr-i Tajik
Tajik SSR, 65, 94, 96–97, 106, 109,

Tajik SSR (*continued*)
  263, 497, 511; "mountain Tajiks,"
  67; press, 200–204
Tales of a Hindu Traveler, see
  Bayyanat-i seyyah-i hindi
Tamerlane, *see* Timur
Tanishbay-uli, Muhamedjan, 187,
  213, 216–17, 222, 226–27
Tansykbaev, U., 521
Taraqqiy, 189, 192
Tarbiya-i atfal, 372
Ta'rikh-i salatin-i manghītīya-i . . . ,
  405
Ta'rikh-i shahrokhi, 404
"Tar zaman," 407
Tarzi, Mahmud, 201
Tashkent, 6, 7, 20, 26, 33, 44, 47,
  52, 54, 62, 102, 113, 125, 135, 178,
  180, 182–84, 196, 201, 216, 218,
  221, 223, 226–27, 230–31, 233–
  34, 267, 276, 295, 318–20, 322–23,
  329, 331, 334, 336, 346, 359, 392,
  400, 429, 532, 535, 558, 566; Muslim, 1–2, 168; Kämalan gate, 1;
  fall of, to Russians, 7, 18–19, 59,
  401–2, 405; Qushbegi of, 6, 14;
  town plan of, 46, 158, 209; under
  Russians, 95, 132–39, 141, 145–
  46, 151, 157; under USSR, 98,
  101–2, 105, 110; cholera riots, 164–
  67; schools, 177; demonstration
  of 1917, 220; Osipov coup d'état,
  232; airport at, 347; oblast, 368;
  musical organizations in, 478
"Tashkent Girl, A," 476
Tashpulat Abdul Khalil-oghli, *see*
  Khalil-oghli, Tashpulat Abdul
Tatars, 25, 32, 42, 65, 104, 106, 109,
  161–62, 174–78, 181, 186–87, 189,
  193, 201, 217, 222–23, 360, 372,
  406, 576; language of, 74, 177,
  201; schools, 177, 194–95, 198;
  newspapers, 189, 192
Tatarstan, 363
Tatlin, Vladimir, 508

Tau joli, 531–32
Taxes, 145, 278–79
"Tāziyāne-yi ta'dib," 425
Tejen, 117, 125, 267, 270, 297
Tekke Turkmens, 147, 212
Terjuman, 178, 189, 356
Termez, 101, 105, 319
Tershak, Adolf, 476
Tevekkel, 39
Textiles, 128, 161; silk and wool, 108,
  128, 309, 312, 314, 316, 320, 322;
  see also Cotton
Theaters (architecture), 476, 505–6,
  513–18
Tien Shan, 52, 62–64, 78, 83, 89,
  113, 115, 117, 120
Timofeev, N., 518
Timur, 8, 22, 72, 82, 439, 487
Tinistan-uulu, Qasim, 371, 389, 413,
  417
Tin'tiak, Major, 11
Tizkār-ul ash'ār, 354
To a Ruined Land, see *Buzulgan
  olkaga*
Tobolsk, 9, 29, 31
Togan, *see* Validov, A. Z.
Toghis-uli, Kolbey, 426
Tokmak, 7, 18, 177
Tokombay-uulu, Ali, 416–17
Tör agha zeyneb, 431
Torayghir-uli, Sultanmaqut, 426
Tortkul, 117, 242
To the Alash, see "*Alashqa*"
Trade, 19–30, 321–24
Traitorous Slander, *see* "Opasïz
  jalghan"
Transcaspia, 93, 147–48, 157, 179,
  212, 225, 232, 256, 266, 282, 312,
  319, 321–32
Trans-Caspian Railroad, 102, 310,
  317, 320, 327–38, 345, 476
Transcaucasus, 488
Trans-Kazakhstan Railroad, *see* Kara-
  ganda Chu
Transoxiana, *see* Mawaraunnahr

Transportation, 324–30, 367; water, 116–19; rail, 344–46; air, 346–47
Travels of Ibrahim Bek, 204
Treatise on . . . Music, see *Risala dar . . . musiqi*
Tribes and peoples, 7, 20, 26, 32, 62–64, 66–68, 72, 104, 106, 113, 115, 117, 120, 127, 148–49, 211, 219, 223, 234, 237, 256, 360, 406, 506; *see also* Migrations; Tatars
Troitsk, 10–11, 27, 29, 201, 318, 364, 375
Tsalikhov, 217
Tselinnyi Krai, 108–9, 111, 307
Tselinograd, 107–8, 153, 155, 157, 161, 176, 187, 237, 239, 306–7, 343, 345–46, 375
Tub Qaraganbay, 9
Tuhfa-i shāhi, 405
Tujjar, 189–90, 192
Turan, 200–201
Turajonzoda Hajji, Qozi Akbar, Tajik religious leader, 586, 602, 606–7
Turgaiskaia oblast, 369
Turgay, 14, 113, 153, 157, 161, 176, 187, 211, 222, 237, 362–64, 370, 375
Turkestanskaia tuzemnaia gazeta, 192
Turkey, 6, 16, 36, 47, 80, 168, 196–98, 200, 205, 208, 230, 255, 363, 427; Young Turk revolution, 178
Turkic languages, 62–66, 69–78, 83–84, 88, 189, 200, 248, 351, 368
Turkistan, 60, 90, 143, 145, 208, 282; guberniia of, 29, 94, 152–53, 157, 159, 161–62, 179, 181, 185, 187–88, 191–98, 201–2, 210, 212–13, 215, 222–23, 229, 256, 266, 272, 281–82, 299, 312, 316, 320; Eastern, 63, 65–67, 73, 78–79, 81, 86, 88–90, 127, 318, 322; Western, 66–67, 69, 82, 86–88, 90, 119, 131, 133, 141, 262, 271, 318, 332, 349, 359, 374, 398, 412; under USSR,

92–94, 101, 103, 105, 111; political organizations, 183, 188, 215–18; SSR, 216; ASSR, 221, 224–26, 232–33, 242–43, 245, 248–49, 254–56, 285, 361, 365, 368
"Turkistan," 477
Turkistan-Siberian Railroad, 288, 328, 345
Turkistan ta'rikhi, 404
Turkistan wilayatining gazeti, 366
Turkmenistan (Turkmeniia), 47, 53, 63, 94–95, 109–10, 120, 125, 256, 264, 266, 295, 371, 380, 427, 547, 552; desert, 123; invasion of, 147–50; independence movement in, 228–36; Supreme Soviet of, 264
Turkmenistan-Iranian border, 121
Turkmens, 10, 26, 53, 55, 104, 129, 143, 212, 242–43, 271, 279, 281, 312, 350, 360, 399, 402, 406, 418; Mangishlak, 52, SSR, 96–97, 106, 109, 298, 375; Yomud, 147, 448; Tekke, 147; Mari, 148; industrialization and, 309
Turks, 66–67, 83–84, 104
Turtul-uli, 11

Ubaydulla Salih-oghli Zawqiy, *see* Zawqiy, Ubaydulla Salih-oghli
Uch Qorghan, 147, 316
Ufa-Tobolsk-Siberia line, 10
Ukraine, 299, 307, 341, 540
Ukrainians, 104, 106, 108–9, 160–61, 175, 211, 260, 367–69
Ulema Jamiyati, 218–19, 224–25
Ul'fet, 189
Ulugh-bek, 360
Umit yalqimlari, 414
United States, 112, 121, 291–92, 342–43
Unlucky Jamal, see *Baqïtsïz jamal*
Ural-Altayic languages, 90–91
Ural Mountains, 82, 113, 226, 236–37, 336, 343–44

Ural River, 8, 10, 29, 48, 50, 74, 87, 115, 315, 340
Uralsk, 10, 107–8, 153, 157, 187, 236, 307, 361, 375
Ural'skaia oblast, 283, 368–69
Ura Tube, 134, 140, 142
Urban-rural rivalry: idealized villages, 531–32; schooling exhibits, 539; ethnic distribution of, 543; in politics, 553
Urganch, 8, 20–23, 62, 117, 125
Uriangkhay, *see* Tannu Tuva
Ush Jüz, 223, 238
Usmankhojayew, 559
Uspenskii, 221, 226, 314, 339
Uspensky, V. A., 471, 478–79
Ust-Kamenogorsk, 9, 107–8, 340, 342–43
Usubaliev, Yurdakun, 552
Uyghun, Rahmatullah A., 529, 537
Uyghurs, 66, 73–76, 82, 88–89, 127, 576; language, 73–76, 82; script, 78–79; under USSR, 106
Uzbekistan, 62, 65, 72, 81, 94–97, 102, 109–10, 112, 124–25, 256, 262–63, 299–300, 336, 371–72, 380, 417–18, 427, 449, 455–56, 480, 551, 558, 563, 576–77, 581, 603–4; Supreme Council of, 561–62
Uzbek Classical Music . . . , see *Ozbek eski zaman musiqasi . . .*
Uzbeks, 22, 104, 121, 125, 129, 177, 210–11, 235, 242–43, 263, 309, 350, 360, 377, 399, 400, 405, 406, 409, 429, 432, 443, 445; under USSR, 106, 109, 361; newspapers, 189, 200–204
Uzboi, 62, 117–18, 297

Vakhitjan Besali Karatay-oghli, *see* Karatay-oghli, Vakhitjan Besali
Vakysh, 117, 122, 166
Validov, A. Z., 234, 237

Valiqan-uli, Shoqan Shingis-uli (Valikhanov), 175
Vaqit, 196
Varzab, 331, 333
Vasilenko, S., 479
Vegetables, *see* Agriculture
Veli Allah Allabergen-oghli, *see* Allabergen-oghli, Veli Allah
Vereshchagin, Vasilii V., 506
Verigin, Major General Aleksander I., 56
Veriuzhskii, V., 511
Vernyi (Verny), *see* Alma Ata
Vesnin, Aleksandr, 508
Vesnin, Leonid, 508
Vesnin, Viktor, 508
Viat'kin, Vasiliy L., 189
Victims of Ignorance, see *Nadandïq qŭrbandari*
Virgin Lands, 108, 345
Vladimir, 2
Vocabulary: changes in, 545–46
Volga River, 20, 22, 27, 50, 64, 74, 83–85, 87, 118, 162, 171, 174, 327–28
Volga-Kama region, 83
Voronkov, 558
Vorontsov-Dashkov, Count Ilarion I., 141
"Vose's Uprising," 415
Vrevskii, Baron A. V., 157, 165, 169–70

Wahidov, Erkin, 580
Wake Up, Kazakh! see *Oyan Qazaq!*
Wali, Muhammad, 16
Washington, D.C.: play performed in, 530
Water, 118–19, 277–81; rivers dry up, 566–67; Siberian river project, 566; *see also* Hydroelectric power; Irrigation
Wells, 321
White Guard, 236, 338

Who's to Blame? see *Kim jazïqti?*
Witness of Felicity, see *Shahid aliqbal*
Women, 312–13, 418–33, 477, 579; girls avoid school, 540
Woods, 121–22, 124, 284, 327
Wool, *see* Textiles
World War I, 108, 109–200, 207–8, 213, 284, 315, 327–28, 507
World War II, 65, 95, 97, 107, 110–11, 260, 290, 295, 299, 303–4, 332, 339, 342, 417–18, 511, 528
Writers' associations, 372–80, 384–92; Writers' Union of Uzbekistan, 534
Writing systems, 77–82, 543

Yadigar Mahlar Mugly Alim-oghli, 33
Yaik River, *see* Ural River
Yaitski Gorodok, *see* Uralsk
Yamantay Bokey-uli, Sultan, 11
Yangi saadat: Milliy roman, 412
Yaqub Bek, 15
Yashin, Kamil Nu"manov, 479
Yelsin, Boris, 603
Yermak, 343
Yomud Turkmens, 147, 212

Young Bukharans, 196, 246–49, 251
Young Khivans, 242–43
Young Turk revolution, 178, 252
Yulduz, 189
Yussuf Zade, Mirza Jelal, 200

Zafariy, Ghulam, 429
Zahiriddin Muhammad Babur, *see* Babur, Zahiriddin Muhammad
Zahiriy, Ashur Ali, 201
Zakir Jan Hal Muhammad-oghli Furqat, *see* Furqat, Zakir Jan Hal Muhammad-oghli
Zakirov, Dani, 479
Zarafshan, 62, 67, 115, 117, 125, 142, 153, 155, 267, 275, 497; river, 142, 277, 294, 297
"Zar zaman," 406–7
Zawqiy, Ubaydullah Salih-oghli, 360
Zermarchos' mission, 77
Zheltoqsan Komiteti of Kazakhstan, 581–82
Zhuan Zhuan, 84
Zinoviev, G. E., 235
Zirbulaq, 142
Zïryanovsk, 108

The Contributors
(in 1993)

Edward A. Allworth is Professor Emeritus of Turco-Soviet Studies, Columbia University, and a member of the executive committees of the Harriman Institute and the Center for the Study of Central Asia, Columbia University. Recent publications include *The Modern Uzbeks, from the Fourteenth Century to the Present: A Cultural History* (1990); "The Cultural Identity of Central Asian Leaders: The Problem of Affinity with Followers," *Central Asia Monitor* (1993); and coeditor of the English version of *Muslim Communities Reemerge: Historical Perspectives on Nationality, Politics and Opposition in the Former Soviet Union and Yugoslavia* (1994).

Hélène Carrère d'Encausse is Professor of Political Science in the Institut d'Etudes Politiques de Paris (Université de Paris). Like other authors of this book, she has traveled and carried on research in Central Asia. Her latest works include *Ni Paix ni Guerre* (1986 in French; 1988 in English); *Islam and the Russian Empire: Reform and Revolution in Central Asia* trans. from French (1988); and *The End of the Soviet Empire: the Triumph of the Nations* (1993).

Ian Murray Matley (1921–93) was Emeritus Professor of Geography, Michigan State University. His many contributions to the field include coauthoring with Arthur Adams and William McCagg *Atlas of Russian and East European History* (1967); "The Murghab Oasis: The Modernization of an Ancient Irrigation System," *Canadian Slavonic Papers* (Summer–Fall 1975); and "Central Asia and Kazakhstan," in *Economics of Soviet Regions*, eds. I. S. Koropeckij and Gertrude E. Schroeder (1981).

Karl H. Menges is Visiting Lecturer, University of Vienna, and was Professor of Altaic Philology, Columbia University, 1940–76. Recent publications include *Turkic Languages and Peoples: An Introduction to Turkic Studies* (1968); "Korean and Altaic. A Preliminary Sketch," *Central Asiatic Journal* (1985); and *Drei Schamanengesenge der Ewenki-Tungusen Nord-Sibiriens. Aufgezeichnet von Konstantin Mixajlovic Rickov in den Jahren 1905/1909* (1993).

Johanna Spector is Professor Emeritus, Jewish Theological Seminary of America, New York. Among numerous recent publications are "USSR II, Azerbaijan 2, Folkmusic," *New Grove Dictionary of Music and Musicians* (1978); "Azerbaijan, musical instruments," *New Grove Dictionary of Musical Instruments* (1984); and a 16mm color documentary film, "About the Jews of Yemen, a Vanishing Culture" (1986).

Arthur R. Sprague (1931–68) was Assistant Professor, Waynesburg College (1964–67). M.A. in art history 1967, Columbia University. Before his early death, he had published "Chernikhov and Constructivism," in *Survey, A Journal of Soviet and East European Studies*. He also supplied the translation, commentary, and material for the introduction to *Sotsgorod: The Problem of Building Socialist Cities*, by N. A. Miliutin (original Russian edition 1930; American ed. in English in 1974) prepared for publication by his advisor, Professor George R. Collins, and by William Alex.

Acknowledgments

The editor thanks Karl H. Menges, Azamat Altay, and Paula Rubel for providing three excellent illustrations used in the book, and acknowledges real debts to Janet Allworth, Muriel Dimin, and Carlene Richardson, who typed and retyped the difficult manuscript. Sketches of musical instruments were drawn by Asae Ukiya, the jacket design is by Douglas Lynch, and the fine translations of chapters four to ten from French were made by David Morgan. Sincere thanks for good advice graciously given at crucial stages in the project go to many persons, including especially Azamat Altay, Robert Austerlitz, Alexandre Bennigsen, George R. Collins, Alexander Dallin, Douglas M. Dunlop, Richard Ettinghausen, Morton Fried, Charles Issawi, Machmud Maksud-Bek, Kenneth Medlin, Natalia Menges, and Willard Rhodes.

Original maps have been edited by Ian Murray Matley, and the cartography provided by Betty Bellaire. Sources for the maps: Figure 1.1 (prepared by Edward Allworth): *Ozbekistan SSR tarikhi* (Tashkent, Ozbekistan SSR Fanlar Akademiyasi, 1957), vol. I, part 2, pp. 102–3, and Mikhail A. Terent'ev, *Istoriia zavoevaniia Srednei Azii* (St. Petersburg, Tipo-Litografiia V. V. Komarova, 1906), vol. I; Figure 1.3: Terent'ev, vol. IV, plate 5; Figures 2.1 and 2.2 (prepared by Karl H. Menges); Figures 3.1 and 3.2 (prepared by Ian Murray Matley): *Aziatskaia Rossiia, Atlas* (St. Petersburg, Pereselencheskoe Upravlenie Glavnago Upravlieniia Zemleustroistva i Zemledieliia, 1914), plate 26, and V. P. Semenov Tian-Shanskii, ed., *Rossiia: Polnoe geograficheskoe opisanie* (St. Petersburg, A. F. Devrien, 1913), XIX (Turkestanskii krai), 348, 352, and V. V. Zaorskaia and K. A. Aleksandr, *Promyshlenniia zavedeniia turkestanskago kraia* (Petrograd, M. Z. Otdiel Zemel'nykh Uluchshenii, 1915), and *Atlas SSSR* (Moscow, 1962), pp. 98–99, and P. G. Pod"iachikh, *Naselenie SSSR* (Moscow, Gosudarstvennoe Izdatel'stvo Politicheskoi Literatury, 1961), and other census reports; Figure 5.1: N. P. Ostroumov, *Sarty: Etnograficheskie materialy* (2d ed.; Tashkent, Izdanie Knizhnago Magazina "Bukinist," 1896), p. vii; Figure 8.1: *Aziatskaia Rossiia, Atlas,* plate 60; Figure 9.1 (prepared by Edward Allworth): *Ozbekistan SSR tarikhi,* II (1958), 222–23, and *Istoriia kazakhskoi SSR* (Alma Ata, Izdatel'stvo Akademii Nauk Kazakhskoi SSR, 1959), II, 232; Figure 10.1 (prepared by Ian Murray Matley): Figures 11.1 and 11.2 (prepared by Ian Murray Matley): *Aziatskaia Rossiia, Atlas,* plates 41, 56, and Zaorskaia and Aleksandr, cartograms 1–4, and P. Alampiev, *Where Economic Inequality is No More* (Moscow, Foreign Languages Publishing House, 1959), pp. 112–21, and *Atlas SSSR* (1962); Figures 12.3 and 12.4 (prepared by Ian Murray Matley): *Aziatskaia Rossiia,* I, 509–10, and D. N. Logofet, *Bukharskoe khanstvo pod russkim protektoratom* (St. Petersburg, V. Berezovskii, 1911), I, 190–201, and *Atlas SSSR* (1962), pp. 100–1; Figure 16.21: *Atlas Mira* (Moscow, Voennoe Izdatel'stvo Ministerstva Oborony Soiuza SSR, 1958), p. 244.